encyclopedia of international sports studies

The *Encyclopedia of International Sports Studies* provides comprehensive international coverage of all aspects of the science, medicine and social science of sport.

The encyclopedia is alphabetically organised and consists of the following:

- Principal entries of *c.* 3000 words covering disciplinary areas, e.g. 'sports economics', 'sports history';
- Large informational entries of *c.* 1200 words on broad topics, e.g. 'resistance training', 'diagnosis of sports injuries';
- Medium informational entries of *c.* 600 words on more specific topics, e.g. 'cross training', 'projectile motion';
- Small entries of *c.* 300 words comprising entries on narrower topics and small overviews directing the reader onwards, e.g. 'motivation, overview', 'muscle tension–length relationship'.

The aim of the editors has been to produce a work which will be of use to a wide variety of users: students, teachers, researchers, and professionals (coaches, development officers, physiotherapists, etc.). Entries are accessibly written and both 'facts-fronted' and critical. Entries carry cross-references and lists of further reading. There is a full index.

The *Encylopedia of International Sports Studies* is the basic all-in-one reference work for all those with an interest in sports science and medicine, and the social and cultural study of sport.

Roger Bartlett is Associate Professor in the School of Physical Education, University of Otago, New Zealand.

Chris Gratton is Professor and Director, Sport Industry Research Centre, Sheffield Hallam University, United Kingdom.

Christer G. Rolf is Professor of Sports Medicine, Consultant Orthopaedic Surgeon and Executive Director, Sheffield Centre of Sports Medicine, University of Sheffield, United Kingdom.

encyclopedia of international sports studies

edited by
roger bartlett
chris gratton
christer rolf

volume 1

A–E

LONDON AND NEW YORK

First published 2006
by Routledge
2 Park Square, Milton Park, Abingdon, Oxon OX14 4RN

Simultaneously published in the USA and Canada
by Routledge
270 Madison Ave, New York, NY 10016, USA

Routledge is an imprint of the Taylor and Francis Group

© 2006 Routledge

Typeset in Bembo and Helvetica by Taylor & Francis Books
Printed and bound in Great Britain by MPG Books Ltd, Bodmin

British Library Cataloguing in Publication Data
A catalogue record for this book is available from the British Library

Library of Congress Cataloging in Publication Data
A catalog record for this book has been requested

ISBN10: 0-415-27713-2   ISBN13: 9-78-0-415-27713-6   (set)

ISBN10: 0-415-97875-0   ISBN13: 9-78-0-415-97875-0   (volume 1)
ISBN10: 0-415-97876-9   ISBN13: 9-78-0-415-97876-7   (volume 2)
ISBN10: 0-415-97877-7   ISBN13: 9-78-0-415-97877-4   (volume 3)

T&F informa

Taylor & Francis Group is the Academic Division of T&F Informa plc.

contents

volume 1

volume 2

volume 3

illustrations

figures

tables

introduction

Encyclopedias with a sport theme not a novel idea, surely? Well, hardly, as there are many publications containing the words sport and encyclopedia in their titles. Most of these focus on sports, rather than the study of sport. The American College of Sports Medicine was involved in *The Encyclopedia of Sport Sciences and Medicine*, published by Macmillan as early as 1971. This book is out of print, but others have taken its place. Many of our readers will be familiar with the International Olympic Committee's series *The Encyclopedia of Sports Medicine*, each volume of which focuses on a given topic for example, volume 9 was on 'Biomechanics in Sports' and consists of around two dozen chapters written by various experts. Although a useful repository of knowledge, these volumes are essentially a series of books each on a broad topic, rather than an encyclopedia, as exemplified, for example, by the *Encyclopedia Britannica*. There are several encyclopedias covering the academic study of sport and exercise that do fit the normal structure of an encyclopedia. However, no English language encyclopedia has previously tried to bring together all of the various academic disciplines involved in the study of sport.

Although the academic study of sport is relatively recent, such university courses now exist in many, if not all, of the countries of the world. These courses, at first, were by and large in Physical Education,

Sport Studies, Sport Science or Sport Medicine (later Sports Engineering) or related titles. Later, many courses added 'Exercise' to their title to reflect a growing awareness of the health benefits of exercise. Even more recently, courses have been launched that have a wider perspective, allowing students to combine, for example, the study of the medical and scientific aspects of sport, or sports technology and science, or the social and life science aspects of sport.

Our purpose in compiling this *Encyclopedia of International Sports Studies* is to provide a comprehensive and useful reference work covering all aspects of the science, social science, and medicine of sport, through which different users can find their own paths. In doing so, we have assembled around 1,000 entries, drawing on established and current scholarship, from over 150 contributors in a wide range of disciplines from a dozen or so countries, who bring an unparalleled breadth of expertise to this project an international encyclopedia indeed.

This encyclopedia is unique, at least in the English language, in bringing together entries that cover Sports Medicine, Sport Science, the Social Science of Sport, and Sports Engineering and Technology. The structure, and the list of further reading that follows most entries, is designed to be of optimum use to a range of potential users. Because of the ubiquity of sport and exercise and the major roles they play in the lives of many people, the material in this book has current and ongoing relevance to events happening in competitive and recreational sport and in exercising for health.

The encyclopedia is alphabetically organised and consists of: principal entries of about 3,000 words explaining disciplines, such as sports biomechanics and sport and exercise psychology; large informational entries of about 1,200 words on broad topics, such as the origins of sport and lower back injury; medium-length informational entries of around 600 words on more specific topics, such as the anterior draw test and fanzines; and small entries of around 300 words, which are either general entries outlining the scope of broad areas, such as sport science, or small informational entries of either specific or short overview topics, such as motivation an overview, and the muscle tension-length relationship a specific topic.

Special features of the encyclopedia are its comprehensive coverage of sport 'knowledge', the 'facts-fronted' and critical focus of entries, the further reading sections, its avoidance of unnecessary jargon, the readability of the entries, and cross-referencing between entries.

Our target audience includes researchers in, and teachers of, sport science, sport medicine, and the social science of sport who seek a distillation of research that has taken place outside their particular topics of specialisation. A second group of potential readers includes students engaged in the study of the science, medicine, or social science of sport covering a broad spread of courses from sport technology to leisure studies. Entries have been written to be accessible to first-year UK undergraduates or their equivalents elsewhere but are targeted mainly at second to third year undergraduates. A third group encompasses sports professionals wishing to access sport-related knowledge, from coaches through sport development officers to physiotherapists, and educated lay readers with an interest in the science, medicine, and social science of sport. Any tertiary education course in, or including, sports medicine, sport science, exercise science, the social science of sport, kinesiology, physical education, human movement science, or human movement studies will benefit from the knowledge contained in these three volumes.

We would like to acknowledge the support of the publishers, Taylor and Francis, particularly when we did not always meet our deadlines, and all of our consultant editors and contributors for generally getting entries in on time and for tolerating our pestering them when they did not. We do appreciate that even in a three-volume work approaching a million words, some topics even sub-disciplines may not have been covered to the satisfaction of all our readers, somewhat inevitably. However, we believe that most, if not all, readers will find much useful information herein.

Roger Bartlett
Chris Gratton
Christer Rolf

consultant editors

contributors

Bruce Abernathy
University of Queensland

Cara Aitchison
University of the West of England

Rick Albrecht
Grand Valley State University

S. Talia Alenabi
Chinese University of Hong Kong

Mansoor Al-Tauqi
Sultan Qaboos University, Oman

Mahfoud Amara
Loughborough University

J. Greg Anson
University of Otago

Duarte Araújo
Technical University of Lisbon

Shawn M. Arent
Arizona State University

Michael S. Bahrke

Allison Bailey
Spaulding Rehabilitation Hospital

Shannon M. Baird
University of Iowa

Alan Bairner
Loughborough University

Susan J. Bandy
University of Aarhus, Denmark

Roger Bartlett
University of Otago

Di Bass
Loughborough University

Sian L. Beilock
Michigan State University

Yvonne Blomkamp
University of Cape Town

Hans Bonde
University of Copenhagen

Andrew Bosch
UCT/HRC Research Unit for Exercise Science and Sports Medicine, South Africa

Larry D. Bowers
United States Anti-Doping Agency

Andreas Breidbach
UCLA Olympic Laboratory

Susan Brownell
University of Missouri-St Louis

Louise M. Burke
Australian Institute of Sport

Christine Burton
University of Technology Sydney

Chris Button
University of Otago

Matt Carré
University of Sheffield

Julie Casper

Simon Chadwick
University of London

Melissa A. Chase
Miami University

Dikaia Chatziefstathiou
Loughborough University

Priscilla M. Clarkson
University of Massachusetts

Fred Coaltesr
University of Stirling

Mike Collins
Loughborough University

Robert Cooper
Northern General Hospital, Sheffield UK

Debbie J. Crews
Arizona State University

John L. Crompton
Texas A&M University

Sean Cumming
University of Washington

David Curtis
University of Sheffield

Keith Davids
University of Otago

David Denyer
Cranfield University

Michael R. Deschenes
College of William and Mary

Sharon J. Dixon
University of Exeter

Shideh Doroudi

Liz Engel
University of Copenhagen

Martha E. Ewing
Michigan State University

Kari Fasting
The Norwegian University

Deborah L. Feltz
Michigan State University

John C. Franco

Walter R. Frontera
Harvard University

Lori A. Gano-Overway
Bridgewater University

Gerald R. Gems
North Central College

Alan St Clair Gibson
University of Cape Town

Diane L. Gill
University of North Carolina, Greensboro

Allan Goldfarb
University of North Carolina, Greensboro

Simon Goodwill
University of Sheffield

Chris Gratton
Sheffield Hallam University

Andrew Gray
University of Cape Town

Gary Green
University of California, Los Angeles

Jennifer Green
Spaulding Framingham Outpatient Center

Allen Guttmann
Amherst College

Steve Haake
University of Sheffield

Keith Hanna
Fluent Europe Ltd

Munehiko Harada
Osaka University of Health and Sport Sciences

Ken Hardman
University College Worcester

Caroline K. Hatton
USA

Heather A. Hausenblas
University of Florida

Bruce Hayllar
Universityof Technology Sydney

R.A. Hedstrom
Michigan State University

Ben Heller
University of Sheffield

Ian P. Henry
Loughborough University

Richard Hildebrand

David Hindley
Nottingham Trent University

Victor W.T. Ho

Andreas Höfer
German Olympic Institute

Barrie Houlihan
Loughborough University

Chiachen Hsu

Mike Hughes
University of Wales Institute, Cardiff

Kindal A. Hunt
Texas A&M University

Michael A. Hunt
Texas A&M University

Imran Ilyas
Sheffield Centre of Sports Medicine

Charise L. Ivy
Harvard Medical School

Grant Jarvie
University of Stirling

John M. Jenkins
University of Newcastle, Australia

Mike Jenkins
University of Birmingham, UK

Leah A. Jensen
Spaulding Framingham Outpatient Center

Christina Johnson
University of Iowa

Mi-Sook Kim
San Fancisco State University

Anthony P. Kontos
University of New Orleans

Vikki Krane
Bowling Green State University

Shia Ping Kung
Sheffiled Hallam University

Mike Lambert
University of Cape Town

Vicky Lambert
University of Cape Town

Dan Landers
Arizona State University

Larry Lauer
University of North Carolina, Greensboro

Dawn Lewis
Michigan State university

Cathy Lirgg
University of Arkansas

Marc Lochbaum
Texas Tech University

T. Michelle Magyar
University of California at Los Angeles

Leapetswe Malete
University of Botswana

Nikolaos G. Malliaropoulos

Bert R. Mandelbaum

J.S.B. Mather
University of Nottingham

Jessica L. Maxwell
Spaulding Framingham Outpatient Center

Ian Maynard
Sheffield Hallam University

Sharon McCarthy
Sheffield Centre of Sports Medicine

M.P. Miles
Montana State University

Nigel Mills
University of Birmingham, UK

Clare E. Milner
University of Delaware

Kai Ming Chan
Chinese University of Hong Kong

Motohide Miyahara
University of Otago

Eva V. Monsma
University of South Carolina

Stuart Moyle
University of Otago

Erich Müller
University of Salzburg

Aron Murphy
University of Newcastle, Australia

Thomas H. Murray
The Hastings Center

Roland Naul and Uwe Wick
University of Essen

Timothy Needham
Spaulding Framingham Outpatient Center

Tim Noakes
University of Cape Town

Jani Macari Pallis
Cislunar Aerospace, Inc.

Emanuel T. Papacostas
Sheffield Centre of Sports Medicine

Athanasios Papaioannou
Democritus University of Thrace

Stylianos Papalexandris

Craig A. Payment
Michigan State University

Heather J. Peters
University of Arizona

Gertrud Pfister
University of Copenhagen

Jan Piek
Curtin University of Technology

Gunter A. Pilz
University of Hanover

Jeffrey A. Potteiger
Miami University, Ohio

Emma Rich
Loughborough University

Christer Rolf
Sheffield Centre of Sports Medicine

Laura Ryan
Spaulding Framingham Outpatient Center

Angela H. Ryan
Spaulding Rehabilitation Hospital

John M. Saxton
Sheffield Hallam University

Robert W. Schutz
University of British Columbia

Jessica Schutzbank
Harvard Medical School

Martin Schwellnus
University of Cape Town

Peter V. Scoles
Temple University School of Medicine

S.E. Short
University of North Dakota

Andy Smith
University College of York St. John

Angela D. Smith
University of Pennsylvania

Ann Snyder
University of Wisconsin

Harry Solberg
Trondheim Business School, Norway

Giselher Spitzer
Sport historian

Dawn E. Stephens
University of Iowa

Jennifer E. Sturm
Michigan State University

Philip Sullivan
Brock University

Terry Sutherland
Spaulding Framingham Outpatient Center

Peter Taylor
University of Pennsylvania

Tracy Taylor
University of Technology Sydney

Thierry Terret
Université Claude Bernard-Lyon 1

Ioannis Terzidis

Erin Tomasik
USA

Kristine Toohey
University of Technology Sydney, Australia

Frank Uryasz
National Center for Drug Free Sport

Tiffanye M. Vargas-Tonsing
Michigan State University

A.J. Veal
University of Technology, Sydney

Robin S. Vealey
Miami University, Ohio

Mark Watsford

Stephen Wearing
University of Technology, Sydney

Robert Weinberg
Miami University, Ohio

Kurt Weis
Technical University Munich

Andrea S. Wickerham
National Center for Drug Free Sport

Mareike Wieth
Michigan State University

Jean M. Williams

Rodney C. Wilson
Michigan State University

Charles E. Yesalis

Jeffrey J. Zachwieja
Gatorade Sports Science Institute

list of entries

A

ACCELEROMETRY

Accelerometers measure the acceleration of the object on which they are mounted. They consist, in effect, of a mass mounted on a cantilever beam or spring, which is attached to the accelerometer housing. As the housing accelerates, the mass lags behind because of its inertia, and the beam is deformed. That deformation is then converted to an electrical signal, which depends on the acceleration. Accelerometers that incorporate piezoresistive strain gauges are gravity-sensitive; their output is the vector sum of the acceleration being measured and that of gravity. To correct for gravity, information is needed about the orientation of any body segment to which such accelerometers are attached. Piezoelectric devices are unaffected by gravity but are insensitive to slow movements, which can limit their use; they are, on the other hand, more robust than piezoresistive devices.

For simple linear motion, a single accelerometer may be sufficient. Triaxial accelerometers, consisting of three pre-mounted and mutually perpendicular accelerometers, are needed to record the three components of the linear acceleration vector. These have been used, for example, in the assessment of sports protective equipment, such as cricket helmets. When mounted on a body segment, the measured acceleration depends on the position of the accelerometers on the segment. The accel-eration measured arises from both the linear and the angular motion (rotation) of the segment. The absolute accelerations of a single rigid body segment having six degrees of freedom can be determined by the use of six suitably orientated accelerometers. If the initial conditions and the orientations of the accelerometers are known, then the accel-erations can be integrated to obtain velo-cities and displacements. The integration produces noise-free values, providing that the acceleration signal was not contaminated by errors, unlike differentiation of the dis-placement signal in inverse dynamics, which increases the random error present.

Accelerometers provide a continuous and direct measure of acceleration with high frequency response characteristics. Typical figures are 0–1,000 Hz for piezoresistive and 0–5,000 Hz for piezoelectric devices. They are usually pre-calibrated and are high-precision instruments giving very accurate measures. The accelerations recorded from such devices are considerably more accurate than those that can be obtained from dou-ble differentiation of displacement signals from video analysis or on-line motion ana-lysis. However, for the results to be valid in studying human movements in sport, proper mounting and fixation procedures must be used. Ideally, the devices should be directly mounted to bone, although this is neither possible nor ethical for most analyses of sports movements. Errors can arise from skin-mounted accelerometers because of relative movement between the accelerometer and soft tissues. Some drift of the signal from piezoelectric accelerometers may also occur with time.

Although most accelerometers used in sports biomechanics are lightweight, cabling and fixation may affect performance. Discomfort to the sports performer may also arise from the attachment of the device. Accelerometers provide better estimates of net joint reaction forces, when combined with motion analysis data, than does the use of doubly differentiated displacement data and inverse dynamics alone. Accelerometers are relatively expensive, though valuable, research tools. They have been used to measure human accelerations in sports as diverse as running, skiing, and gymnastics. Accelerometry is, however, probably the most difficult of all of the measuring techniques used in sports biomechanics to use appropriately.

See also: inverse dynamics; linear motion; on-line motion analysis; sports protective equipment; video analysis

Further reading

Nigg, B.M. and Herzog, W. (1999) *Biomechanics of the Musculo-Skeletal System*, Chichester: John Wiley.

ROGER BARTLETT

ACHILLES TENDON INJURY

This entry focuses on current concepts and controversies regarding chronic Achilles tendon injuries and acute ruptures.

Achilles tendon injuries could affect the tendon insertion, the free tendon, the proximal tendon-muscle transition or the paratenon. The terminology is sometimes confusing in the literature. Tendinitis is an acute inflammatory reaction in the tendon causing localized pain and swelling. Tendinosis is used to describe an asymptomatic or symptomatic tendon disorder also causing localized swelling of the tendon often over a period of time. In up to 30 per cent of cases symptoms are not solely related to sports or excessive loading. Rheumatological, immunological, infectious as well as drug adverse effects may also be causative. There is a lack of controlled studies on operative and non-operative treatments on chronic tendon injuries. Treatment concepts in general consist of non-operative rehabilitation with calf muscle training, control of inflammation and correction of various biomechanical factors which give good results in the majority of cases. Different types of topical treatments have always been of interest among athletes, but the scientific evidence for use of these is doubtful. Topically applied gels can penetrate through the skin, via the lipid subcutaneous layer into the tendon, and are stored in high concentrations in the tendon itself after application. Thus, the skin barrier is not sufficient to keep such molecules out. The clinical implication of these findings is not fully established, but this treatment should probably be indicated only for acute inflammatory tendon conditions. In one of the few studies on chronic Achilles tendon, anti-inflammatory treatment had a poor effect. Since chronic tendinosis is not an inflammation, it is not surprising that one has not been able to show any reliable clinical effect of anti-inflammatory preparations. Cortisone injection around the Achilles tendon is a common but controversial treatment on chronic Achilles tendon disorders. During the late 1950s came the first report on Achilles rupture in association with a cortisone injection. Thirty per cent of 215 outpatients and 60 per cent of 298 operated patients with chronic Achilles tendons had received one or more cortisone injections in one study. Corresponding data in earlier published data on operated patients are around 50–75 per cent. Some authors have even associated cortisone injections with extensive tendinosis and partial ruptures. Cortisone-induced changes in the tendon's vicinity, such as pigment changes and atrophy of the skin and subcutis, are probably more common than tendon ruptures. Two groups of patients with chronic Achilles tendon pain were studied to assess the frequency of cortisone-related complications: 298 consecutive patients who were operated in Malmö during 1972–1990; and 215 consecutive cases were evaluated as outpatients during 1988–1989. In the operated group, partial ruptures occurred in 23 per cent of the cases. The risk of getting a partial rupture was doubled after preoperative cortisone injection. In the outpatient group, an annual incidence of total Achilles rupture was found to be 2.4 per cent and 0.2 per cent for patients with and without earlier cortisone injections, respectively, which can be compared to an incidence of 0.016 per cent for Malmö's general population.

Two operation methods have been described in the literature for insertional problems: resection of the posteriosuperior angle of the calcaneus, and wedge-osteotomy of the calcaneus. Some studies have described good clinical results while others have presented poor results with these operations. Surgical excision has, however, an excellent effect on chronic paratendinitis as shown by Kvist and Kvist, who studied 201 cases with a median symptom duration of 7.5 months before the operation: 90 per cent were elite athletes with a median age of twenty-seven years. Ljungqvist operated twenty-four cases with partial ruptures, and all these cases became symptom free, twelve cases after more than six months. Nelen et al. studied fifty cases of chronic tendinopathy who were operated with resection of macroscopic unhealthy tissue and half of the cases with a turn down flap. They found good results in 73 per cent of these cases who were not operated with reinforcement, and in 87 per cent of cases who were operated with enforcement, at follow up more than two years after the operation. Rolf and Movin reported that pain decreased in 90 per cent of the cases, while 79 per cent had returned to a higher level of activity eighteen months after the operation. The majority of these cases were operated with excision of the macroscopically unhealthy tissue without any reinforcement.

Postoperative treatment is individualized, depending on the patient's needs and the intraoperative findings. Below-knee cast or orthothics can preferably be used for wound healing. Full weight bearing is allowed, with limited dorsal flexion, directly after the operation in most cases. Controlled studies of rehabilitation alternatives are lacking. Clinical follow-up studies often report an improvement after the operation in form of decrease in symptoms and increased activity level. This can lead to the conclusion that all patients are helped by the operation, but results can very well depend on which evaluation criteria are chosen. If one compares the subjective criteria that Curvin and Stanish postulated with other classifications, the results can vary greatly. In view of this, a consensus is needed on criteria for evaluation of treatment so that studies can be comparable. Complications of surgery are relatively common, from 2 to 10 per cent.

Achilles tendon rupture was first described in the 1600s by Ambroise Par. In recently published reports, the incidence of acute Achilles tendon rupture is 10/100,000 inhabitants per year. The incidence has increased 3–5 times in the last 30–40 years. The male dominance is large, from 2:1 to 20:1 in different studies. The mean age of the patients is 35–40 years. Sports activity is the triggering factor in 75 per cent of cases. Different methods of bandaging and immobilization have been used as treatment. Towards the end of the nineteenth century, the first operation was performed. Queneu and Stoianovitch reviewed the literature in 1929, and in the light of the often unsatisfactory results of non-operation at that time, they recommended surgical treatment. Until 1972, acute Achilles tendon ruptures were therefore operated on to a large extent. A

3

number of studies were published where the operation methods were described, etiology investigated and the operated persons evaluated by follow up. After Lea *et al.* 1972 showed favorable results with immobilization with casting without operation, this treatment was now recommended. In the last few years surgery and early mobilization has been recommended again after good experiences and recent studies showing lower morbidity and earlier return to sports.

The diagnosis is easily assessed and the history is typical. The patient says that he felt as though something snapped in the calf, sometimes associated with a burning pain. He/she is not able to continue with the ongoing activity but does not always seek medical attention directly as it may initially be considered as an ankle sprain. If the diagnosis is uncertain after the medical examination, ultrasound investigation can be done. There is, however, a risk that ultrasound investigation in the acute phase overestimates the continuity in the tendon and thus underestimates the extension of the injury. With a typical history and clinical findings, the rupture is usually total. With an end-to-end suture, the tendon ends are adapted, followed by adaptation of the tendon ends round the perimeter and closing of the paratenon. The operation can favourably be done under local anesthesia without tourniquet in the outpatient clinic. After surgery, the active rehabilitation phase is usually around six months. An early return to work and sporting activity is important. Early mobilization gives better functional results in most cases, especially regarding muscle strength and endurance. Naturally these considerations and plans have to be made on an individual basis.

See also: tendinitis; tendinosis; tendon injury

Further reading

Kannus, P. and Josza, L. (1997) *Human Tendons,* Human Kinetics publishers, ISBN 0-87322-484-1.

Rolf, C. (1998) 'Achilles Tendon Injuries. An Overview', in *Controversies in Orthopedic Sports Medicine,* Williams and Wilkins Publishers, 8: 501–8, ISBN 962-356-025-7.

CHRISTER ROLF

ACROMIOCLAVICULAR JOINT DISLOCATION

This entry focuses on the definition and management of injuries to the joint between the clavicle and the acromion, which is part of the scapula in the shoulder.

Injuries to the AC joint are both acute and chronic overuse types of injury. The most common injury mechanism is a direct impact injury from falling forwards or to the side, landing directly on the shoulder. This type of accident can be seen in cyclists and skiers who fall at high speed. In contact sports like ice hockey, rugby, wrestling or judo such situations can also arise from direct tackling situations. These injuries, which also can cause other associated injuries, most often cause a dislocation of the joint with ligament ruptures. Fractures in the AC joint are rare. The joint injury and associated ligament injury is usually graded from I–VI, with a higher figure corresponding to a more serious injury.

Grade I is a partial rupture of the AC ligament without any visible dislocation. Clinically this is characterized by localized tenderness on palpation over the AC joint. Plain radiographs are normal. This injury heals almost always without any special treatment, even if there are reports showing residual symptoms in up to 36 per cent of cases.

Grade II is a sub-luxation with a complete rupture of the AC-joint ligaments but with a preserved coraco-clavicular ligament. A dislocation deformation is seen exteriorly and the radiographs show a cranial sub-luxation of the clavicle. Even this injury often heals without treatment, and secondary osteoarthritis is only seen rarely and develops within a year if at all. Initially no treatment is needed, but with residual symptoms surgery with lateral clavicle resection can be necessary.

Grade III is a dislocation of the AC-joint with complete ruptures of both the AC-joint ligaments and the coraco-clavicular ligaments. This is apparent when the shoulder is examined and radiologically verified, differentiating from a lateral clavicle fracture. Most of these injuries become better with non-operative treatment. Residual symptoms of local pain or instability of the lateral clavicle can be surgically treated. Some prefer lateral clavicle resection or in combination with a stabilization procedure.

Grade IV is a posterior dislocation where the clavicle penetrates the lateral mid-portion of the trapezius muscle. This dislocation can be explained by an avulsion of the anterior deltoid muscle from the lateral end of the clavicle. This type of injury is usually indicated for surgical treatment with re-fixation of the deltoid muscle by suture in addition to stabilization of the clavicle. Individual considerations have to be made from case to case.

Grade V is a dislocation with an excessive cranial dislocation. Even this dislocation is explained by avulsion of the anterior deltoid muscle from the lateral clavicle end. Surgery is recommended.

Grade VI is an inferior dislocation with sub-coracoid penetration of the clavicle end. This injury is usually treated with surgery with open reduction and repair.

Athletes who lift weights sometimes complain of pain around the AC-joint, among sports laymen often referred to as 'weightlifter's shoulder'. Typically bench press training in the end range lower position strains the AC-joint structures. By modifying the technique for bench press, such problems can be avoided before a chronic pain condition is established. Symptomatic treatment of later developing AC-joint osteoarthritis could be intra-articular steroid injection, and if the symptoms remain, surgery with lateral clavicle

resection, which today can be done with keyhole techniques. Arthroscopic lateral clavicle resection (ALC) was introduced by a surgeon called Gartsman. He showed that the same volume of bone was excised when one operated by open surgery and by arthroscopy. This has since inspired many other surgeons to test this technique and it is used extensively today. Rehabilitation is shorter with this technique, and many weightlifters can start training a few days after operation. In the long term, 90–95 per cent of patients are satisfied with this operation.

See also: shoulder injury; sports specific injury; type of injury

Further reading

Hawkins, R. and Saunders, W.B. (1996) *Shoulder Injuries in the Athlete. Surgical Repair and Rehabilitation*, ISBN 0-443-08947-7.

CHRISTER ROLF

ACTH (ADRENOCORTICOTROPHIC HORMONE)

ACTH is a peptide hormone that is secreted by the anterior pituitary in response to hypothalamic corticotrophin-releasing hormone (CRH). The target organ for ACTH is the adrenal cortex and an increase in corticosteroid production through stimulation of adenyl cyclase and eventually cholesterol esterase. It may also somewhat increase the synthesis of pregnenolone which can theoretically increase other steroids. Owing to the ban and testing for **glucocorticosteroids**, athletes have turned to ACTH to potentially reach the same effect.

Several studies have examined the natural variations of ACTH during exercise. It has been demonstrated that both ACTH and serum cortisol levels increase significantly with intense exercise of at least 60 per cent of VO_2 max. Much of this augmentation is related to a reduction in glucose levels during exercise because glucose-infusion studies have demonstrated an attenuated rise in ACTH. Inder and colleagues examined the exact mechanism for exercise-induced increases in ACTH in a series of elegant studies. They found that secretion of both CRH and arginine vasopressin (AVP) contributes to the rise in ACTH seen during exercise. Furthermore, high-intensity short-term exercise favors AVP release (associated with changes in osmolality) and exercise of prolonged duration favors CRH. Athletes have attempted to augment the natural secretion of ACTH with exogenous ACTH. There are no controlled studies of ACTH administration in athletes, nor any anecdotal reports of a positive effect on performance.

ACTH has a variety of therapeutic uses, such as nonsuppurative thyroidits, oncologic hypercalcemia, exacerbations of multiple sclerosis, as an adjunct to the treatment of tuberculous meningitis, as well as many glucocorticoid responsive diseases. It is also used in the diagnosis of diseases of the hypothalamic-pituitary-adrenal axis. As one of the **peptide hormones**, ACTH must be administered parenterally and can result in all of the adverse effects of **glucocorticosteroids**. In addition, ACTH can increase intracranial pressure, pseudotumor cerebri, and cause ACTH antibodies that produce ACTH and pituitary resistance. Finally, commercial ACTH is made from porcine proteins and may trigger severe allergic symptoms in those susceptible individuals.

ACTH remains banned by most sport organizations, and can be measured by serum immunoassay; however, there is no effective testing for its use. Despite its lack of proven efficacy, athletes who want to use glucocorticosteroids will likely attempt to circumvent the rules by using ACTH.

Reference

Inder, W.J., Hellemans, J., Swanney, M.P., Prickett, T.C.R. and Donald, R.A. (1998) 'Prolonged Exercise Increases Peripheral Plasma ACTH, CRH and AVP in Male Athletes', *Journal of Applied physiology* 85, 3: 835–41.

GARY GREEN

ACUPUNCTURE

Acupuncture has been used successfully as a therapeutic modality for thousands of years, primarily in the eastern hemisphere. In the West, acupuncture has been used more as a third or fourth line treatment for chronic problems. A scientific explanation of the efficacy of acupuncture is most well understood in the context of pain. Consequently, the use of acupuncture for treating pain associated with musculoskeletal and sports-related injuries has become more prevalent.

Acupuncture involves the insertion of tiny needles into the skin and muscle, sometimes stimulating the needles with electricity, heat or manual manipulation. The sites of needle insertion are not random, but rather are specific locations felt to correspond to invisible channels in the human body (meridians) that tap into the flow of the body's energy. According to Eastern philosophy, acupuncture is felt to work by maintaining the flow of this vital energy, or *qi*, in the human body. Doing so keeps the body in balance by helping it to heal damaged parts.

There are several different styles of acupuncture, the Chinese style being the most prevalent. Many of the eastern styles overlap and the acupuncture insertion points are similar. However, slightly different points may be used for different ailments, and the technique of needle manipulation may be different. There is also a newer medical style of acupuncture corresponding to our knowledge of neuroanatomy.

It is only since the 1970s that a scientific explanation for acupuncture's role in healing and pain relief has been proposed. The physiology of how we perceive pain is composed of a complex series of events that includes communication along several nerve pathways throughout the entire body. The insertion of acupuncture needles has been shown to influence this communication system, particularly the part that initiates pain inhibition. Specifically, acupuncture needles are known to activate our naturally occurring opioids, endorphins.

Acupuncture alone would not be sufficient to treat serious sports-related injuries, such as fractures. However, for certain acute or chronic problems that can accompany or interfere with sports, such as tendonitis, arthritis and myofascial (muscle and tendon) pain, acupuncture is a very safe and potentially beneficial modality for relief and to facilitate healing. The insertion of the needles is associated with little or no pain. Treatment length and frequency varies with the diagnosis and the style of acupuncture. In general, the frequency is a few times a week in the acute phase of an injury, with a slow taper in treatment frequency over several weeks. Occasional maintenance acupuncture may be beneficial to prevent an exacerbation of the condition. Although acupuncture can be the sole treatment for a musculoskeletal injury, it is generally used in conjunction with other treatments, such as **rehabilitation exercises**, heat and cold therapy, and even medications.

In the 1998 Winter Olympics, the Austrian skier Hermann Maier suffered traumatic myofascial pain following a severe fall during a downhill event. He underwent acupuncture treatment and subsequently won the gold medal in the men's super giant slalom three days later.

Although studies focusing on the use of acupuncture specifically for sports-related injuries are not nearly as abundant as those for chronic pain, there is success in the pain literature in using acupuncture for diagnoses such as myofascial pain, tendonitis, lumbar strain and cervical strain. Since these are the most common diagnoses in sports-related injury, the use of acu-

puncture in this population is a reasonable alternative.

Further reading

Audette, J.F. and Ryan, A.H. (2004) 'The Role of Acupuncture in Pain Management', *State of the Art Reviews in Physical Medicine and Rehabilitation* 15(4): 749–72.

Hsu, D.T. (1996) 'Acupuncture: A Review', *Regional Anesthesia* 21(4): 361–70.

ANGELA H. RYAN

ACUTE REHABILITATION

Rehabilitation is defined as the restoration of normal form and function (see **rehabilitation – basic principles**). By convention the rehabilitation process is divided into three phases, including: (1) acute phase (hours to a few days post injury or surgery); (2) recovery or sub-acute (days to a few weeks); and (3) functional or long-term (weeks to months). In the case of many chronic and overuse injuries, it is not easy to define with accuracy the start and duration of the acute phase and, in fact, the rehabilitation may begin in the recovery phase of the injury.

Acute rehabilitation refers to the rehabilitation plan that is implemented immediately after an acute injury or surgical procedure. In the context of sports injuries, the goals of the acute phase of rehabilitation are to: (1) alleviate pain and discomfort; (2) control inflammation; (3) minimize tissue damage; (4) enhance the environment surrounding the damaged tissue and the healing process; and (5) prevent further injury by protecting the affected area. With the early implementation of an exercise program the goals could also include the limitation of the loss of joint flexibility, the retardation of muscle weakness and atrophy, the preservation of endurance, and the early return to training and/or competition.

The acute phase is usually characterized by the presence of an inflammatory response.

This response is part of the natural defenses of the human body. Typical of the inflammatory phase is the presence of redness, swelling, increased temperature, pain, and loss of function. The most frequently used therapeutic intervention in this early stage is a combination of rest, ice, compression, and elevation (see **rest, ice, compression, and elevation (RICE)**). This combination is very effective and enhances the healing and recovery post-injury. Rest protects from additional tissue damage but must be used judiciously because it is known to have negative consequences on many organs and systems of the human body. Many tissues including skeletal muscle, bone, tendons, and ligaments atrophy when not used regularly. Furthermore, rest and inactivity, although beneficial in the early stages post-injury, may also affect cardiovascular function and psychological and emotional status. These observations have led to the development of the concept of relative rest. In other words, the injured area is rested (many times to a limited extent) while other non-injured areas continue to be exercised using various alternative methods. For example, swimming can be recommended as a way of maintaining cardiovascular or aerobic capacity in a volleyball player with an acute ankle sprain. It is worth noticing that protected mobilization of a joint, using a brace that restricts range of motion partially but allows some movement, leads to better outcomes (i.e. faster recovery of range of motion) than complete immobilization using a plaster cast. With regards to the use of rest in acute rehabilitation, it can be concluded that rehabilitation programs are based on the basic principle that injured tissues must be mobilized as soon as possible.

The ice has several effects (see **cold usage in rehabilitation**) including a reduction in swelling and pain, muscle relaxation, and diminished tissue damage. It should be applied using a wet towel to protect the skin. The duration of the ice application could range between 10 and 40 min and depends on the amount of subcutaneous fat at the site of the injury; athletes with thicker skinfolds require longer ice applications. Compression refers to the use of bandaging to reduce swelling. For example an elastic bandage could be applied with the pressure diminishing from distal to proximal (closer to the heart). Finally, elevation of the injured limb above the level of the heart uses the force of gravity to enhance the resolution of edema surrounding the injured tissues.

To control the symptoms during this phase, a physician may prescribe medications such as analgesics to control pain or non-steroidal anti-inflammatory drugs. The latter have both, analgesic and anti-inflammatory actions. Some examples of medications used include acetaminophen (paracetamol), ibuprofen, aspirin, indomethacin, and rofecoxib. Pain relief after severe injuries or surgery may require the use of stronger pain killers such as narcotic analgesics. The use of any of these medications must be monitored carefully because of potential side effects. Also, recent scientific evidence suggests that some of these medications may interfere with the biological process of tissue healing so important in the acute phase. Although the evidence is not conclusive, physicians must be cautious with the use of these drugs in the acute phase. Moreover, some medications are banned by the doping regulations of the International Olympic Committee and national and international sports federations. Physicians, coaches, and athletes must be knowledgeable about these rules to avoid drug-related suspensions. Pain control may also be achieved with the use of physical modalities such as ice (mentioned previously) and transcutaneous electrical nerve stimulation (TENS). TENS can sometimes be combined with the application of ice.

From a sports performance point of view, one of the most dangerous consequences of any injury is its deleterious effect on the basic physiological and functional capacities of the athlete. During the acute phase, injured athletes lose joint range of motion or flexibility, muscle strength, local muscular endurance, and cardiovascular endurance or aerobic capacity. This is the result of a combination of factors including the injury itself, the immobilization that may be required as part of the therapeutic process, and the effects of deconditioning since the athlete must stop his/her training or competition schedule.

In an attempt to limit or prevent these negative consequences, an exercise regimen can be implemented early as part of the acute rehabilitation program. This exercise program could include various types of exercise. Passive exercise, which does not require voluntary activation of muscles, can be initiated using a device or the assistance of a physiotherapist. Passive exercises are indicated when maintaining range of motion is important. Some rehabilitation protocols post-surgery include this type of exercise with the use of a special device to move the joint. When pain relief permits, isometric (static) exercises can then be initiated. These, by definition, do not result in joint movement and are very useful when the injury or post-surgical rehabilitation protocol restricts joint range of motion. Isometric exercises should include four or five voluntary activations with maximal voluntary effort at various joint angles every day. Sometimes, electrical stimulation can be superimposed on muscle that is voluntarily activated to maximize the recruitment of motor units. This may be needed because swelling and pain are known to inhibit voluntary muscle activation via reflex pathways. The use of electrical stimulation early in the rehabilitation process has been shown to be an effective way of preventing some of the muscle losses that accompanied immobilization.

At the end of the acute phase, the rehabilitation enters the second or recovery phase. The total duration of the acute phase is not always easy to define, but it is usually over in hours or days. This transition may be gradual and require the slow introduction of the various rehabilitation interventions that characterize phase 2 (see **recovery phase of rehabilitation**).

Further reading

DeLisa, J.A. (ed.) (1998) *Rehabilitation Medicine: Principles and Practice*, Philadelphia: Lippincott.
Frontera, W.R. (ed.) (2002) *Rehabilitation of Sports Injuries: Scientific Basis*, Oxford: Blackwell Science.

WALTER R. FRONTERA

ACUTE RENAL FAILURE

Acute renal failure is a most serious renal complication that may occur after exercise. The incidence of acute renal failure after physical exercise is not known. It is likely to be very variable, specifically with regard to (i) different types of exercise, (ii) intensities and duration of exercise, (iii) environmental conditions, (iv) state of hydration of the participants, and (v) the use of medication during exercise.

Acute renal failure in the setting of exercise is precipitated by a number of possible factors including dehydration, hyperpyrexia, myoglobinuria, haemoglobinuria, and the use of nephrotoxic medications during exercise. These factors usually cause acute renal failure during exercise in combination.

In severe dehydration, the renal blood flow is reduced, resulting in renal ischaemia that can cause acute tubular necrosis. Strenuous exercise, which is performed in hot, humid environmental conditions, can cause hyperpyrexia, which can damage a variety of organ systems. In particular it can cause skeletal muscle damage directly or indirectly by decreasing blood flow to muscles. Skeletal muscle damage (rhabdomyolysis) is associated with the release of nephrotoxic substances, in particular myoglobin.

Hyperpyrexia can also be associated with intravascular haemolysis and resultant haemoglobinaemia. The effects of these two pigments (myoglobin and haemoglobin) on the kidney require further discussion. Skeletal muscle damage (rhabdomyolysis) is associated with the release of myoglobin, which is a globin chain containing a haem pigment. In acidic media such as during metabolic acidosis, and during bicarbonate absorption in the proximal tubule, globin dissociates from this ferrihaemate compound. This ferrihaemate compound is directly nephrotoxic by interfering with renal tubular transport mechanisms.

Other factors that may cause renal failure during rhabdomyolysis are: (i) fibrin deposition in the glomeruli, (ii) intravascular volume depletion secondary to muscle damage, and (iii) release of purines resulting in a surge of uric acid production.

Clinical experience suggests that rhabdomyolysis leads to myoglobinuric renal failure only when other factors such as intravascular volume depletion, haemoconcentration, renal vasoconstriction or exposure to other nephrotoxins are present.

In general, haemoglobin has less dramatic effects on the kidney, and clinical experience indicates that haemoglobinuria compromises renal function only in the presence of other factors such as volume depletion, acidosis or hypotension.

The use of non-steroidal anti-inflammatory drugs (NSAIDS) by athletes, particularly during ultra-distance events, should be strongly discouraged because they may lead to acute renal failure. The mechanisms by which NSAIDS interfere with normal renal function are to inhibit the synthesis of prostaglandins that are important renal vasodilators. In the presence of high renin levels (such as during exercise) they can cause interstitial nephritis.

Clinical guidelines for management and prevention of acute renal failure during exercise

Athletes must be made aware of the measures to decrease the risk of developing acute renal failure after exercise. The general guidelines are:

- Drink enough fluid during exercise, particularly in hot, humid environmental conditions
- Acclimatize to hot, humid environmental conditions if possible
- Do not use any form of medication during exercise unless advised by your doctor
- Do not use any pain killers or anti-inflammatory drugs at least forty-eight hours before prolonged strenuous exercise
- Do not ignore blood in the urine after exercise
- Make sure that you drink enough fluid in the first few hours after exercise
- Seek medical advice urgently if you have not passed any urine twelve hours after exercise

If the athlete has not passed urine in the first twelve hours post exercise, it is important to encourage increased fluid intake, particularly if there is evidence of intravascular volume depletion. Intravenous fluids may be indicated if this depletion is severe.

If the athlete presenting has not passed urine twelve hours or longer after the exercise, further investigation is required. This may include:

- hospitalization for investigation and observation
- urine examination (microscopy and electrolytes)
- blood tests including serum urea and electrolytes
- renal function tests (creatinine clearance)
- renal ultrasound

See also: dehydration; eccentric exercises; muscle injury; non-steroidal anti-inflammatory drugs

Further reading

Poortmans, J.R. (1984) 'Exercise and Renal Function', *Sports Medicine* 1: 125–53.

MARTIN SCHWELLNUS

ADAPTED PHYSICAL ACTIVITY

Children who exhibit atypical motor development and people with disabilities often need adaptation for equipment, rules, and instruction to participate successfully in physical education, sports, exercise, dance, aquatics, leisure, and recreation. Adapted physical activity not only refers to the activity itself, but also to the academic knowledge and practical skills that promote participation, health, safety, athletic performance, fair competition, and personal satisfaction from a lifespan perspective. As far as the practical aspect is concerned, adapted physical activity may be otherwise termed special physical education, therapeutic exercise, disability sports, or leisure and recreation for the disabled. The difference between these terms and adapted physical activity is that adapted physical activity is also an academic discipline backed up with an international professional organisation and university education.

Academic studies of adapted physical activity encompass all disciplines of sports studies, such as philosophy, history, measurement and evaluation, sociology, psychology, pedagogy, motor control and learning, physiology, and biomechanics. In addition, it is essential to learn about different disabilities, advocacy, laws, and acts that protect the rights of people with disabilities for equal opportunity and access to an active lifestyle. The theoretical knowledge, research methods, and practical skills gained in any basic courses of sports studies can be applied to the context of disability. Adapted physical activity may be taught as an independent academic subject and as part of, or combined with, courses such as motor learning, motor development, and sports medicine.

There are several organisations that support the education, research, and practice of adapted physical activity. The International Federation for Adapted Physical Activity (IFAPA) is an umbrella organisation that coordinates regional branches, links with other closely related organisations, such as the International Paralympic Committee, and holds biannual International Symposia of Adapted Physical Activity. Research findings are disseminated in the official journal of the IFAPA, *Adapted Physical Activity Quarterly*. Other journals, such as Paleastra and Sport'n Spokes, serve as forums for the practical side of adapted physical activity. Students who want to pursue a post-graduate degree in adapted physical activity have an opportunity to study in the programme of the European Masters Degree in Adapted Physical Activity. During the first year, the students in the programme study the theory and practice of adapted physical activity in the English language in Leuven, Belgium. Then the students conduct research projects for their master's thesis in hosting universities throughout the world. In the USA the quality of physical education instruction is ensured for students with disabilities by setting the Adapted Physical Education National Standards. The fifteen standards consist of human development, motor behaviour, exercise science, measurement and evaluation, history and philosophy, unique attributes of learners, curriculum theory and development, assessment, instructional design and planning, teaching, consultation and staff development, student and programme evaluation, continuing education, ethics, and communication. The knowledge of the standards is annually tested by a national certification examination held all over the US. All these organisations have a common goal to advance the theory and practice of adapted physical activity through research, education, and practice.

See also: motor development – atypical

Further reading

Reid, G. and Stanish, H. (2003) 'Professional and Disciplinary Status of Adapted Physical Activity', *Adapted Physical Activity Quarterly* 20: 213–29.

MOTOHIDE MIYAHARA

ADENOSINE TRIPHOSPHATE IN HIGH-INTENSITY EXERCISE

Adenosine triphosphate (ATP) is the universal energy source and needs to be rapidly replaced in cells. The amount of ATP stored within any cell can last only a few seconds. Obviously, the higher the rate of ATP utilization, the faster the decrease in the stored ATP within the cell, unless it is resynthesized. Therefore activities that require a high rate of ATP utilization will typically degrade ATP more rapidly and require faster rates of resynthesis, or else the activity will be unable to continue at the same rate. High-intensity exercise usually can only last a short time, although ATP resynthesis occurs from anaerobic processes. The time one can maintain high-intensity exercise varies from individual to individual and may be influenced by muscle fibre type (see **muscle fibre types**), training status, and nutritional status. However, even with adequate stores, these activities can only last about 60 s. Since high-intensity exercise lasts a short time, such exercise is primarily anaerobic and will, therefore, activate anaerobic pathways to help resynthesize ATP. High-intensity activities are classified not only by the time over which the activity is performed, but also by the relative intensity of effort. These activities are typically at, or near, maximal capacities for the given activity. For example, in a lifting – resistance – activity, the workload will be near the maximal lifting capacity for one repetition (1 RM). In a sprint activity, the workload would be at least 90 per cent maximal sprint rate. Clearly, these activities are dependent on the stored high-energy phosphagens, ATP and phosphocreatine (PC). It has been estimated that human muscle has approximately 24 mmol ATP and 76 mmol PC per kg dry muscle from biopsy samples. It has also been estimated that the maximum rate of ATP utilization has been as high as 25–30 $mmol\,kg^{-1}\,s^{-1}$. If this were the case, the activity might last 1–2 s at these extremely high rates. Power rates on a cycle ergometer that lasted 3 s have been reported to utilize ATP at 7 $mmol\,kg^{-1}\,s^{-1}$. Clearly, as the time is increased the power rates decline rapidly.

Activities that last less than 10 s and require a great deal of energy will utilize the anaerobic metabolic pathways, such as the ATP-PC system and anaerobic glycolysis. Activities that last less than 5 s, such as short sprints, utilize the ATP-PC system for almost all the ATP needed for the work. Maximal resistance exercises that last only a few seconds could also be included in this category, as well as high-intensity lifts with only a few repetitions. The muscular contraction that is required to maintain the movement or the force rapidly utilizes ATP. Normally, the greater the load on the muscle the greater the amount of muscle recruited and, therefore, the more muscle mass activated to utilise ATP. Another way to increase force is to recruit the existing muscle more often. Therefore, if the muscle could be stimulated more rapidly, as for example a faster cycling cadence, there would be greater muscle ATP utilization per unit time. To replenish this ATP rapidly, the ATP-PC system is primarily recruited. The high-energy phosphagens, both ATP and PC, are utilized but can only maintain the rate of ATP hydrolysis for a limited time. It is believed this is, in part, a reason why power rate declines with continuous high-intensity muscle contractions. The ability to regenerate the ATP that is needed for the muscle contraction can only keep up with the utilisation rate for a limited time, partly because of the limited amount of stored high-energy phosphagens within the cell. Repeated interval training could also fit into this category of high-intensity activity. Repeated exercise bouts of less than 5 s can result in a decline in the amount of PC within the muscle. Therefore, if recovery time is not adequate, the rate of power decline may be faster since the amounts of PC are not adequate to maintain the rate of ATP hydrolysis.

If the activity lasts longer than 5 s there will be a transition towards some glycogen utilization and anaerobic glycolysis to meet the energy demands. The anaerobic resynthesis of ATP through glycolysis and glycogenolysis will contribute a greater percentage of the ATP resynthesized as the time of exercise increases. However, because these anaerobic processes have more steps, the rate of ATP resynthesis is not as rapid. Therefore, utilisation would overcome the ATP resynthesis rate, and the ability to maintain muscle force may be compromised. This can lead to a decline in force production. In addition, the by-product of anaerobic glycolysis – lactate – will build up within the muscle. This build up of lactate will result in a decline in the hydrogen ion concentration (pH) in the cell. The decrease in pH has a negative impact on muscle force production, within the muscle myofilaments as well as the calcium-handling or binding aspects. In addition, the decrease in pH will have an inhibitory influence on phosphofructokinase (PFK), the rate-limiting enzyme in glycolysis. This will prevent the pH from decreasing too far. The transition from utilising purely the ATP-PC system to activation of anaerobic glycogenolysis-glycolysis is a gradual shift. Two of the activators for these pathways are the increase in adenosine monophosphate (AMP) brought about by the adenylate kinase reaction and the increase in adenosine diphosphate (ADP). These two factors help to increase the key regulatory enzymes, phosphorylase for glycogenolysis and PFK for glycolysis.

Activities that last slightly longer than 10 but less than 60 s are also considered intense exercise, but are more reliant on anaerobic glycolysis and glycogenolysis to help supply the ATP needed for the activity. Clearly, as the time of the activity is increased, the rate of ATP hydrolysis declines. As the time approaches 45 s in duration, aerobic energetic pathways start to contribute to some of the ATP resynthesis. As the activity approaches 2 min duration, the intensity of effort has to decline and the contribution from aerobic pathways increases. As such, the rate of resynthesis for these activities is slower than that for the high-intensity exercise that last less time. A very small amount of oxygen is stored within muscle, which can assist in this transition. However, many studies have reported a decline in both ATP and PC concentration in response to high-intensity exercise within muscle. Additionally, repeated bouts of high-intensity exercise can result in a dramatic decrease in PC within the muscle, if inadequate recovery time is not given. Finally, small decreases in glycogen concentration within the muscle have been reported after high-intensity exercise.

Further reading

Hultman, E. and Sjoholm, H. (1983) 'Substrate Availability', in H.G. Knuttgen, J.A. Vogel and J. Poortmans (eds) *Biochemistry of Exercise*, 13: 63–75, Champaign IL: Human Kinetics.

ALLAN GOLDFARB

ADENOSINE TRIPHOSPHATE/ PHOSPHOCREATINE – ERGOGENIC AIDS

The most rapidly available energy source for exercise is provided by the liberation of phosphates from adenosine triphosphate (ATP) and its regeneration by donation of phosphates from phosphocreatine (PCr) stores within the muscle cell. This energy system operates for 2–10 s of high-intensity exercise – for example, a single sprint – but is also important in the performance of repeated high-intensity bouts. The capacity of this energy system is limited by the ability to resynthesize PCr stores between bouts, and perhaps by the loss of ATP and the diphosphate and monophosphate forms (AMP and ADP) when these cannot be regenerated at sufficiently high rates. Ergogenic aids that are proposed for this energy system include supplemental forms of ribose and creatine.

Ribose supplementation

Ribose is a pentose sugar that can be converted into various compounds in the body, including ATP, AMP, and ADP. It is found in the diet, but purified forms have also recently been produced. High-intensity exercise causes a reduction in muscle ATP, possibly because the rate of salvaging and synthesis falls behind the massive rates of degradation of ATP, ADP, and AMP during exercise. It has been suggested that oral intake of ribose might increase the rate of salvaging and synthesis of these muscle compounds, allowing quicker recovery of the total muscle content. Sports supplements, typically providing 3–5 g doses of ribose, have been produced with claims of 'dramatically reducing recovery times'. Several early studies of ribose supplementation in athletes undertaking repeated bouts of high-intensity exercise appeared in conference abstract form, with reports of benefits to performance. However, further studies that have been published in full in the peer-reviewed literature have failed to show that ribose supplementation, even at 10–20 g per day, alters the loss or recovery of ATP resulting from high intensity exercise, or changes muscle force or power characteristics during maximal testing. More work is needed to explore this substance, but the ultimate outcome might be challenged by the practicality and expense of consuming oral ribose, which sells for around $US50 per 100 g.

Creatine loading

The normal creatine content of the muscle cell is maintained by dietary intake of creatine – about 1 g per day from meat sources, as well as synthesis within the body from amino acids. A landmark paper by Harris *et al.* (1992) reported that the muscle content of creatine and PCr could be increased by 125–150 per cent by consuming creatine monohydrate powder in doses higher than the daily creatine turnover of 1–2 g. Rapid 'loading' of the muscle is achieved by a daily creatine supplementation protocol of 20 g (4×5 g doses) for five days, while the same muscle threshold can be achieved more slowly by consuming 2–3 g per day for four weeks. Creatine uptake into muscle is enhanced by consuming it in conjunction with a substantial amount of carbohydrate ($\sim$100 g) and in the absence of a 'maintenance' intake of oral creatine (2–3 g per day), muscle creatine content will gradually fall to normal after 6–8 weeks. Since the publication of the initial paper, creatine has grabbed the attention of both athletes and sports scientists, resulting in it becoming a widely selling supplement as well as the subject of over one hundred studies of the effect of its loading in muscle on exercise performance. Our current knowledge of creatine loading and exercise is now summarised:

- Creatine supplementation does not appear to benefit the performance of a single bout, or the first of a bout of sprints, because the contribution of PCr to such exercise is not limiting, and any likely benefit is too small to be consistently detected.
- The main benefit of creatine supplementation is to increase the rate of PCr resynthesis during the recovery between bouts of high-intensity exercise, producing higher PCr concentrations at the start of the next exercise bout. Creatine supplementation can

enhance the performance of repeated 6–30 s bouts of maximal exercise, interspersed with short recovery intervals of 20 s–5 min, by reducing the fall in force or power production that would otherwise occur. This outcome has been relatively easy to demonstrate in laboratory protocols, particularly involving weight-supported activities such as cycling.

- Theoretically, acute creatine supplementation might benefit a single competitive event involving repeated high-intensity intervals with brief recovery periods – for example team games and racquet sports. Similarly, chronic creatine supplementation may enhance training performance and long-term adaptation to exercise programmes based on repeated high-intensity exercise – for example, training for team and racquet sports, as well as interval training and resistance training, for example for swimmers and sprinters. However, in many cases these benefits remain theoretical since few studies have been undertaken with elite athletes or as 'field studies'.
- Since acute creatine loading is associated with a body mass gain of about 0.6 kg, believed to be water retention in the muscle, performance enhancements will only occur in weight-bearing, for example running, and weight-sensitive sports, such as lightweight rowing, if gains in muscular output compensate for increases in body mass.
- Evidence that creatine supplementation is of benefit to aerobic endurance exercise is absent.
- Whether the long-term gains in muscle mass reported in studies of resistance training are caused by direct stimulation of increased muscle protein synthesis by creatine, an enhanced ability to undertake resistance training, or a combination of both factors remains to be determined.
- There appears to be some variability in the response to creatine supplementation, with some individuals – perhaps those with naturally high muscle creatine content – failing to respond sufficiently to creatine loading to achieve a performance change.

The enthusiasm with which athletes have embraced creatine causes concern over the potential for side-effects or harmful outcomes, particularly with long-term use of large creatine doses. There have been anecdotal reports of gastrointestinal upset, headaches and muscle cramping or strains. However, the currently available literature has not found evidence of an increased prevalence or risk of these problems among creatine users. But it should be noted that studies of long-term use, particularly self-medication with doses far in excess of the recommended creatine usage protocols, have not been conducted. Although it is commonly suggested that creatine supplementation may cause renal problems, the few case reports have occurred in patients with pre-existing renal dysfunction. Until long-term and large population studies can be undertaken, some expert bodies, such as the American College of Sports Medicine (2000), have chosen a cautious view on the benefits and side-effects of creatine supplementation.

See also: aerobic glycolysis – ergogenic aids; anaerobic glycolysis – ergogenic aids; ergogenics; lipolysis – ergogenic aids

References

American College of Sports Medicine (2000) 'Position Statement: The Physiological and Health Consequences of Oral Creatine Supplementation', *Medicine and Science in Sports and Exercise* 32: 706–17.

Harris, R.C., Soderlund, K. and Hultman, E. (1992) 'Elevation Of Creatine in Resting and

Exercise Muscle of Normal Subjects by Creatine Supplementation', *Clinical Sciences* 83: 367–74.

Further reading

Juhn, M.S. and Tarnopolsky, M. (1998a) 'Oral Creatine Supplementation and Athletic Performance: A Critical Review', *Clinical Journal of Sport Medicine* 8: 286–97.

——(1998b) 'Potential Side-effects of Oral Creatine Supplementation: A Critical Review', *Clinical Journal of Sport Medicine* 8: 298–304.

Op' T Eijnde, B., Van Leemputte, B., Brouns, F., Van Der Vusse, G.J., Larbarque, V., Ramaekers, M., van Schuylenberg, R., Verbessem, P., Wijnen, H. and Hespel, P. (2001) 'No Effects of Oral Ribose Supplementation on Repeated Maximal Exercise and De Novo ATP Resynthesis', *Journal of Applied Physiology* 91: 2275–81.

LOUISE M. BURKE

ADENOSINE TRIPHOSPHATE-PHOSPHOCREATINE SYSTEM

Adenosine triphosphate (ATP) is considered the critical energy molecule in biological systems because it enables transfer of energy yielding and energy utilising processes. ATP in conjunction with phosphocreatine (PC), which has a higher free energy of release during hydrolysis stored within its bond compared to ATP, are considered high-energy phosphagens. It is now well established that ATP can be broken down in the process known as hydrolysis – splitting via water H_2O – to yield adenosine diphosphate (ADP) plus inorganic phosphate (P_i) plus free energy (G): $ATP + H_2O \rightarrow ADP + P_i + G$.

In this equation there is an enzyme that would speed up this process known as adenosine triphosphatase (ATPase). Hydrolysis of ATP would yield a molecule of ADP, inorganic phosphate and free energy which is approximately $7.3 \, kcal \, mol^{-1}$. Thus, $G°$ is the standard free energy and is dependent on the metabolite concentration, temperature, and hydrogen ion concentration (pH) of the system. The actual free energy for ATP in working muscle has been calculated to be closer to $11 \, kcal \, mol^{-1}$ because of the effect of pH and temperature. It should be noted that G is negative for spontaneous reactions in which energy is liberated. It should also be understood that there is an additive nature of free energy change in a set of coupled reactions. Thus, in the above reaction the free energy for equilibrium lies far to the right. If this reaction is coupled to the following reaction: $ATP + glucose \rightarrow ADP + glucose + P_i$, then the energy liberated can be determined by adding the free energy from both reactions and would drive the second reaction to the right.

Adenosine triphosphate is positioned near the middle or intermediate position of the standard free energy of hydrolysis of physiological phosphate compounds (see Table 1). As a result of its position, ATP can transfer its terminal phosphate group energy to lesser energy rich molecules. This would be important in the formation, for example, above for glucose to become glucose-6 phosphate in the glycolysis pathway. In addition, ATP can be formed from phosphocreatine because its free energy is greater than that of ATP. Therefore, phosphocreatine can help to restore the amount of ATP in the cell for a limited time in the presence of its enzyme creatine kinase to resynthesise ADP to ATP. This reaction is noted as: $ADP + PC \leftrightarrow ATP + creatine$. This reaction is reversible and depends on

Table 1. Standard free energy $(G°)$ of some phosphorylated compounds

Compound	$G°$ $(kcal \, mol^{-1})$
Phosphoenolpyruvate	−14.80
Phosphocreatine	−10.30
ATP	−7.30
Glucose 1-phosphate	−5.00
Fructose 6-phosphate	−3.80
Glucose 6- phosphate	−3.30

the amounts of the reactants. When there is little need for energy usage then the ATP can help synthesize PC. In contrast, when there is energy demand, PC will help to resynthesise ADP to ATP for a limited time. This is because there is a limited concentration of ATP and PC stored within cells.

Further reading

Lehninger, A.L. (1973) 'Bioenergetics', in A.L. Lehninger, *Biochemistry, Second Edition*, 387–416, New York: Worth.

McGilvery, R.W. (1983) *Biochemistry: A Functional Approach, Third Edition*, 356–69, Philadelphia PA: W.B. Saunders.

ALLAN GOLDFARB

ADIPOSE LIPID SUPPLY

Adipose is a tissue made up of cells referred to as adipocytes, adipose cells, or, more commonly, fat cells. Adipose tissue is found in various places throughout the body, but most prominently at subcutaneous and deep visceral locations. Subcutaneous adipose stores are those found below the skin and can vary tremendously from person to person. Deep visceral adipose stores are found surrounding many of the vital organs and serve a protective shock-absorbing function. Adipose has traditionally been thought of primarily as a storage site for triglycerides. However, adipose cells have receptors for and respond to various hormones and signal molecules, and they produce biologically functional molecules, such as the hormone oestrogen and the cytokine interleukin-6. These molecules may act as signals to other parts of the body, often providing information about the energy status of the body. Thus, an emerging area of research relates to the interactive nature of adipose tissue with other systems of the body.

Adipose is a dynamic tissue allowing for entry and exit of fatty acids, synthesis, storage and breakdown of triglycerides, and synthesis of fatty acids from glucose and other substrates. After a meal has been consumed, adipocytes are activated by the hormone insulin to take up glucose and fatty acids. The glucose is used to generate a phosphorylated glycerol molecule that can be used as the backbone for triglyceride synthesis. Adipocytes are capable of synthesizing fatty acids from glucose when it is available in substantial excess, although the liver is probably more important for fatty acid synthesis. Fatty acids taken up by adipocytes typically are esterified to glycerol for storage as triglycerides. The triacylglycerol fatty acid cycle involves repeated lipolysis and esterification of fatty acids. New fatty acids may enter the cycle, while fatty acids liberated from triglycerides can either leave the cell or be re-esterified. Transport of fatty acids away from adipocytes by the transport protein albumin is the key step determining the fate of non-esterified fatty acids in adipocytes.

Triglycerides are the storage form of fatty acids, and adipose tissue is the primary storage site for triglycerides. Fatty acids are more efficient for energy storage than carbohydrates because they are more energy dense and because, unlike glucose that is stored as glycogen along with two to three grams of water for each gram of glycogen, fatty acids can be stored anhydrous – without water. Fatty acids hold 38 kJ, or 9 kcal, of energy per gram compared to no more than 8 kJ (2 kcal) of energy for each gram of glycogen and its associated water.

Fatty acids are the primary fuel for individuals at rest, and they contribute a substantial proportion of energy for oxidation during exercise at low to moderate intensities. The energy in storage is the sum of the energy that can be liberated from the three fatty acid and the one glycerol molecules of each triglyceride. This is less than if fatty acids alone were the storage form. An 80 kg man with 15 per cent of his body mass (12 kg) as adipose has 404,000 kJ of energy stored as triglycerides. A 60 kg woman with 25 per cent of her body mass (15 kg) as adipose has 505,000 kJ of energy stored as triglycerides. By comparison, the 80 kg man is likely to have approximately 8,000 kJ of energy stored in the form of glycogen. With respect to energy for exercise, 12 kg of triglycerides provides enough fuel for an 80 kg man to walk for approximately 250 h. By contrast, 8000 kJ of glycogen will provide enough fuel for an 80 kg man to walk for approximately 5 h.

See also: lipolysis; lipolytic response to exercise; lipolytic response to training; regulation theory.

Further reading

Jeukendrup, A.E., Saris, W.H.M. and Wagenmakers, A.J.M. (1998) 'Fat Metabolism During Exercise: A Review. Part I: Fatty Acid Mobilization and Muscle Metabolism', *International Journal of Sports Medicine* 19: 232–44.

M.P. MILES

ADULTS – GLOBAL SCENE OF HEALTH PROMOTION

Statistics have shown that more than 60 per cent of adults do not engage in adequate amounts of physical activity which are beneficial to their health. Therefore, there is a global initiative to promote the importance of physical activity in every country around the world. The problem of physical inactivity is more prevalent among individuals from low socio-economic groups, older adults, and the disabled. The rate of obesity is increasing among middle-aged adults, which is the result of insufficient participation in sports during leisure time. In contrast, adults spend a great amount of time in sedentary behaviors such as watching television, computer usage, and excessive use of transport. The problem of sendentariness is a great concern globally, primarily in the well-developed countries.

Changes in dietary patterns towards a reduced fruit and vegetable intake and a higher fat and sugar intake also contribute to the health concern in adults. This change in diet is a result of industrialization and economic development, as well as increased food market globalization. Adherence to regular physical activity substantially reduces the risk of coronary heart disease, stroke, colon cancer, diabetes, osteoporosis, and hypertension, as well as obesity. Therefore, practising a healthy, active living style would be the best way for adults to prevent the development of age-related chronic diseases.

One of the major concerns that both male and female adults may experience during their middle age is the development of osteoporosis and related musculoskeletal disorders. Although genetics is the predominant factor controlling the increased risk of developing osteoporosis, factors such as physical activity and nutrition also have a significant impact on determining an individual's overall bone health. Two major events occur during life with regard to bones. First, attainment of peak bone mass, which occurs during early adulthood: this period is when individuals obtain their maximum bone mass. The second major event involves the gradual loss of bone that occurs following the attainment of peak bone mass. As adults grow older, the rate of loss in bones increases, thus increasing the risk of osteoporotic fractures in areas such as the spine, neck and knees. With regards to nutritional intake in adults, they require a sufficient amount of calcium intake to promote bone health. Sources of calcium include dairy products such as milk, cheese, yogurt, tofu, etc. The recommended daily intake (RDA) for calcium in adults is approximately 1,000 mg, but the majority of the people in the population could not reach this level (Maffulli *et al.* 2001).

Another major problem in adults is the concern with obesity. Obesity is the result of a high intake of fat and the lack of regular physical activity that helps burn off the fat. Fat can be either saturated or unsaturated. Saturated fats are composed of low-density lipoprotein (LDL), which is considered to be bad cholesterol. These fats cause the formation of plaques in arteries, and the accumulation of those plaques would lead to the development of atherosclerosis. In contrast, coronary heart disease and hypertension are closely related to a high fat intake. Obesity may also be a contributing cause of non insulin-dependent diabetes mellitus (type-two diabetes mellitus).

As people age they are reluctant to undertake physical activity regularly since they are not encouraged to do so. Through extensive research and studies, there is now abundant scientific evidence to show that physical activity and exercise may reduce the risk of chronic disease and delay the decline that occurs with ageing. Strengthening exercises are exceptionally crucial for adults, since these exercises can increase the strength of muscles and bones, and also improve balance, coordination and mobility for those adults. Regular exercise and a balanced nutritious diet may lead to improved quality of life in adults. Health organizations worldwide should continue their initiatives in promoting health in society in order to allow people to live an enjoyable and healthy life.

Reference

Maffulli, N., Chan, K.M., Macdonald, R., Malina, R.M. and Parker, A.W. (eds) (2001) *Sports Medicine for Specific Ages and Abilities*, London: Harcourt Publishers Limited.

VICTOR W.T. HO

ADVENTURE SPORTS

Adventure sports are that group of recreation activities which involve physical challenge and risk taking in an outdoor natural environment. Canoeing, rock-climbing, mountaineering, abseiling (rapelling), white water rafting and wilderness trekking are examples of these activities.

The connotations of the word 'adventure' are central to these sports. Adventure implies some form of undertaking involving risk where the outcome from participation is uncertain. As a corollary, adventure is arguably an experience of degrees – the greater the risk, the greater the adventure.

An individual testing themselves against the elements is an underlying theme of adventure sports. However, in reality this testing is increasingly undertaken in contrived or relatively controlled environments, as adventure sports have become commodified by educational institutions, commercial providers and voluntary or private organisations. In each case these providers create adventure experiences for a range of purposes and outcomes.

Many schools use adventure-based programmes for the purposes of building self-esteem, leadership and teamwork. Outward Bound, the quintessential adventure education provider, built its programme and reputation on this framework. Conceived in the early 1940s, Outward Bound conducted one-month-long adventure programmes using vigorous physical training coupled with small boat and land-based expeditions to build resilience into their participants. From this period, the ideas of Outward Bound spread worldwide and the use of adventure sports in the context of learning was established.

Adventure sports have also been used for a variety of therapeutic interventions. These activities have been used with groups as diverse as young offenders, people with disabilities, and educational underachievers. Over the past twenty years adventure sports have also been used by the corporate sector. Programmes using a range of activities have been developed which focus on management skills such as developing team cohesion and effectiveness and improving cooperation and trust.

The commodification of adventure sports is also evident in the growth of companies marketing adventure sport packages. Weekends involving multiple activities such as rock climbing, abseiling, and canoeing are widespread. Likewise, skills workshops that teach specialised techniques in particular activities are common. Adventure guiding has emerged as a profession and trained guides lead trips from 'soft adventures', where the perceived risks and physical demands are low, to more demanding high-risk adventures such as expeditions to Mount Everest.

The fact that adventure sports have continued to grow in popularity in both formal and informal settings suggests that they are meeting some fundamental human needs. Evidence suggests that successful participation can lead to enhanced levels of self-concept. With little in the way of extrinsic rewards to motivate, it seems that individuals are seeking opportunities for enjoyment and pleasure through challenging their personal boundaries. For some this may be experienced as '**flow**' (Csikszentmihalyi 1975), or a peak experience (Maslow 1970). For others participation in autotelic activities (activities done for their own sake and with few, if any, conventional rewards) may lead to internal rewards such as optimal levels of arousal through the management of anxiety, and heightened feelings of personal competence gained through successful completion of an experience.

References

Csikszentmihalyi, M. (1975) *Beyond Boredom and Anxiety*, San Francisco: Jossey Bass.
Maslow, A. (1970) *Motivation and Personality*, 2nd edn, New York: Harper and Row.

Further reading

Priest, S. and Gass, M. (1997) *Effective Leadership In Adventure Programming*, Champaign Il: Human Kinetics.

Swarbrooke, J. (2003) *Adventure Tourism: the New Frontier*, Oxford: Butterworth-Heinemann.

BRUCE HAYLLAR

AEROBIC GLYCOLYSIS

The tricarboxylic acid (TCA) cycle is the primary driver for aerobic glycolysis. A well-accepted hypothesis is that the rate of TCA cycling increases in proportion to the energy demand of muscle. The TCA cycle is a series of eight biochemical reactions that are enzymatically controlled and that yield carbon dioxide (CO_2) and hydrogen atoms (see Figure 1). The CO_2 is eliminated by expiration while hydrogen atoms are carried to the electron transport chain by the reduced coenzymes nicotinamide adenine dinucleotide (NADH) and flavine adenine dinucleotide ($FADH_2$). Production of reducing equivalents is the primary function of the TCA cycle.

The biochemical use of oxygen for aerobic glycolysis occurs in the electron transport chain. Electrons from NADH and $FADH_2$ are used to produce water and generate the free energy needed to synthesize adenosine triphosphate (ATP) from free adenosine diphosphate (ADP) and inorganic phosphate, a process known as oxidative phosphorylation. Electrons are transported in one direction down the electron transport chain, with each electron acceptor having a progressively higher affinity for electrons. Molecular oxygen is the highest affinity and final electron acceptor ensuring unidirectional transport and subsequent genesis of ATP. Proteins of the electron transport chain reside in the inner mitochondrial membrane, while intermediates and enzymes of the TCA cycle are located in the inner mitochondrial matrix.

Carbohydrates are a primary fuel for the TCA cycle. Glucose from the blood or that derived from the breakdown of muscle glycogen is metabolized to pyruvate in the glycolytic pathway (see anaerobic glycolysis).

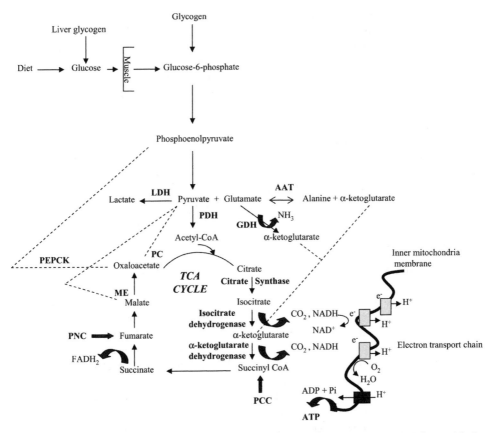

Figure 1. The TCA cycle: AAT, alanine aminotransferase; PDH, pyruvate dehydrogenase; LDH, lactate dehydrogenase; PNC, purine nucleotide cycle; GDH, glutamate dehydrogenase; PCC, Propinonyl CoA carboxylase; ME, malic enzyme; PC, pyruvate carboxylase; PEPCK, phosphoenolpyruvate carboxykinase.

Pyruvate is transported into the mitochondria and converted to acetyl coenzyme A (acetyl-CoA), which combines with oxaloacetate to form citrate. During the course of seven subsequent reactions, oxaloacetate is regenerated, reducing equivalents are produced and two carbons originating from acetyl-CoA are lost as CO_2. Acetyl-CoA can also be formed from β-oxidation of fatty acids and from certain amino acids. Therefore, the TCA cycle plays a central role in nutrient catabolism for cellular energy. The complete oxidation of 1 mole of glucose yields 38–39 moles of ATP.

See also: carbohydrate metabolism; lipid metabolism; protein metabolism; resynthesis of adenosine triphosphate in aerobic metabolism

Further reading

Gleeson, M. (2000) 'Biochemistry of Exercise', in R.J. Maughan (ed.) *Nutrition in Sport*, 17–38, Oxford: Blackwell Science.

JEFFREY J. ZACHWIEJA

AEROBIC GLYCOLYSIS – ERGOGENIC AIDS

The oxidation of carbohydrate by the muscle provides an energy source for prolonged submaximal exercise. The relative proportions of energy derived from aerobic

21

metabolism of muscle carbohydrate and fat stores depend on factors such as the duration and intensity of the exercise, and the athlete's training and nutritional status, for example the intake of nutrients before and during the exercise. The main limitation of this energy system is the relatively small size of the muscle's carbohydrate stores – muscle glycogen and glucose taken up from the plasma. Ergogenic strategies to enhance this fuel system are based on enhancing the availability of the muscle's carbohydrate stores.

Carbohydrate loading

The term 'carbohydrate loading' describes practices that aim to maximize or super-compensate muscle glycogen content before a competitive event that would otherwise deplete this important fuel store. Carbohydrate loading protocols, which can elevate muscle glycogen stores up to twice normal resting values, were first described by Scandinavian sports scientists in the late 1960s after investigations using muscle biopsy techniques to study muscle fuel use. These researchers found that muscle glycogen content could be manipulated by diet and exercise strategies – specifically, several days of low carbohydrate intake depleted muscle glycogen stores and reduced endurance compared with a normal carbohydrate diet. However, the subsequent intake of a high carbohydrate diet over several days caused a super-compensation of glycogen stores and prolonged cycling time to exhaustion. These pioneering studies produced the 'classical' model of carbohydrate loading, involving a 3–4 day 'depletion' phase of hard training and low carbohydrate intake, followed by a 3–4 day 'loading' phase of high carbohydrate eating and exercise taper.

Studies undertaken in the 1980s using well trained individuals produced a 'modified' version of this protocol. Sherman et al. (1981) showed that well trained runners

were able to super-compensate muscle glycogen stores with three days of taper and high carbohydrate intake, regardless of whether this strategy was preceded by a depletion phase. For well trained athletes, at least, carbohydrate loading can be seen simply as an extended period of 'fuelling up' before a prolonged event. This modified protocol provides a more practical strategy for competition preparation, avoiding the fatigue and complexity of extreme diet and training requirements associated with the previous depletion phase. The most recent studies suggest that optimal refuelling can be achieved within 36–48 h of the last exercise session with a combination of taper and high carbohydrate intake at 7–12 g per kg body mass per day.

Theoretically, carbohydrate loading can enhance the performance of exercise or sporting events that would otherwise be limited by muscle glycogen depletion. An increase in pre-event glycogen stores can prolong the duration over which moderate intensity exercise can be undertaken before fatiguing. It may also enhance the performance of a set amount of work, such as a set distance, by preventing the decline in pace or work output that would otherwise occur as glycogen stores decline towards the end of a task. A review of carbohydrate loading literature concluded that super-compensation of glycogen stores is beneficial for the performance of exercise of greater than 90 min duration, extending the duration of steady state exercise by about 20 per cent, and improving performance over a set distance or workload by 2–3 per cent (Hawley et al. 1997). Such an intervention should provide a substantial improvement in most simple endurance events, such as marathons, prolonged cycling and triathlon races, and cross-country skiing events. However, many athletes undertake prolonged events of a less predictable nature – for example, tennis matches or football games that extend for at least 80–90 min of playing time. Although it is intuitive that performance would be enhanced by super-compensation of muscle glycogen stores, it is extremely difficult to undertake studies that measure the outcomes of complex and variable sports such as these. Decisions about the benefits of carbohydrate loading may be specific not only to the sport, but to the individual athlete, depending on the requirements of their position or style of play.

Carbohydrate supplementation during exercise

When carbohydrate is consumed during exercise to enhance or maintain carbohydrate availability, there is a clear enhancement of endurance or exercise capacity. It is more difficult to measure the effect on sports performance, especially in the field or when the activity involves complex decision-making and motor skills. Nevertheless, studies have shown that carbohydrate intake during exercise enhances the performance of prolonged cycling and cycling, as well as the intermittent high-intensity running found in team sports. Other investigations have shown that carbohydrate ingestion during team and racquet games can benefit mental and physical skills by reducing the impairment usually associated with fatigue. There are a growing number of studies reporting benefits of carbohydrate intake during high-intensity exercise lasting about one hour. These findings are puzzling, since muscle carbohydrate stores are not considered to be limiting in events of this duration. Even where benefits are not found, carbohydrate intake during exercise does not cause an impairment of exercise performance.

There are various mechanisms to explain the benefits of the consumption of carbohydrate during exercise, including the prevention or correction of hypoglycaemia that occurs during very long events. Although the oxidation of ingested carbohydrate was first thought to 'spare' the utilization of muscle glycogen, most studies show that the role of carbohydrate feeding during prolonged exercise is to maintain high plasma glucose concentrations and provide an additional fuel source for the muscle once its glycogen stores become depleted. In the case of shorter bouts of high-intensity exercise, it is possible that carbohydrate intake provides further benefits to the brain and central nervous system that may affect pace judgment.

The current sports nutrition guidelines for exercise lasting longer than 60–90 min encourage athletes to consume a source of carbohydrate during the event to provide an available glucose supply of at least 30–$60 \, g \, h^{-1}$. A range of carbohydrates, for example glucose, sucrose, and glucose polymers, appears to provide a suitable fuel supply, reaching a maximal rate of oxidation of around $1 \, g \, min^{-1}$ after about 60 min of exercise. Although only small amounts of exogenous carbohydrate ($\sim 20 \, g$) are utilised during the first hour of exercise, athletes should begin their intake of carbohydrate from the start of exercise or at least well before the onset of feelings of fatigue. Special products that have been developed to allow athletes to consume carbohydrate during exercise include sports drinks – carbohydrate-electrolyte fluids providing 4–8 g of carbohydrate per 100 ml – and sports gels – concentrated carbohydrate solutions providing about 25 g of carbohydrate per sachet. Although sports drinks provide a convenient way to address both carbohydrate and fluid replacement during exercise, and are probably the most commonly used sports supplement, the culture and conditions of many sports allow a range of carbohydrate-containing foods and drinks to be consumed to meet fuel needs during the event.

See also: adenosine triphosphate/phosphocreatine – ergogenic aids; anaerobic glycolysis – ergogenic aids; lipolysis – ergogenic aids

References

Hawley, J.A., Schabort, E.J., Noakes, T.D. and Dennis, S.C. (1997) 'Carbohydrate Loading and Exercise Performance: An Update', *Sports Medicine* 24: 73–81.

Sherman, W.M., Costill, D.L., Fink, W.J. and Miller, J.M. (1981) 'Effect of Exercise-diet Manipulation on Muscle Glycogen and Its Subsequent Utilisation During Performance', *International Journal of Sports Medicine* 2: 114–18.

Further reading

Hargreaves, M. (1999) 'Metabolic Responses to Carbohydrate Ingestion: Effects on Exercise Performance', in D.R. Lamb and R. Murray (eds) *Perspectives in Exercise Science and Sports Medicine*, 93–124, Carmel IN: Cooper.

LOUISE M. BURKE

AEROBIC GLYCOLYSIS – REGULATION AND HORMONAL CONTROL

Oxygen is not directly involved in the tricarboxylic acid (TCA) cycle but, at the most basic level, the TCA cycle cannot continue without oxygen. As long as there is adequate oxygen and substrate, the oxidised coenzymes nicotinamide adenine dinucleotide (NAD) and flavine adenine dinucleotide (FAD$^+$) will be regenerated continuously. Reduction of NAD and FAD$^+$ to their reduced forms, NADH and FADH$_2$, allows TCA metabolism to proceed. Various control mechanisms for TCA cycle activity and oxidative phosphorylation are considered below.

The sum concentration of adenosine triphosphate, diphosphate, and monophosphate (ATP, ADP, and AMP) is often referred to as the total adenine nucleotide pool. The extent to which this pool is phosphorylated is representative of the energy charge of a cell, a powerful signal for control of energy metabolism. For example, a decline in cellular ATP with a concomitant rise in ADP will reduce the energy charge of the cell, a signal that will

stimulate reactions directly involved in oxidative ATP resynthesis. Adenosine triphosphate, ADP, and AMP can also act as allosteric activators or inhibitors of enzymatic reactions involved in aerobic glycolysis.

In the mitochondria pyruvate is converted to acetyl coenzyme A (acetyl-CoA) by a multienzyme complex known as pyruvate dehydrogenase (PDH). This is the first irreversible step in the oxidation of carbohydrates for ATP resynthesis. The PDH complex is regulated by a phosphorylation-dephosphorylation scheme; PDH kinase phosphorylates the enzyme, keeping it in a low activity state (PDH*b*) while PDH phosphatase removes phosphate, putting the enzyme in a more active form (PDH*a*). Thus, the relative activities of PDH kinase and PDH phosphatase determine the overall activity of the PDH complex. At rest there are several allosteric regulators of kinase and phosphatase activity. Sufficient ATP, acetyl-CoA, and NADH favour kinase activity. More important are the ratios of ATP to ADP, acetyl-CoA to CoA, and NADH to NAD. High ratios favour a greater relative distribution of PDH*b* through kinase activation. Low intramuscular concentrations of pyruvate also help to keep the enzyme in the less active *b* form. Indeed, availability of substrate – pyruvate and NAD – is needed for flux through the PDH complex, while a decreased concentration of products – Acetyl-CoA and NADH-may also stimulate flux. However, substrate and product control of PDH flux plays only a minor role.

The first reaction of the TCA cycle adds acetyl-CoA to oxaloacetate, producing citrate. This reaction is regulated by the enzyme citrate synthase. Citrate synthase is inhibited by ATP, so when the muscle cell is sufficiently energised, citrate formation is down-regulated. Other important enzymatic control sites within the TCA cycle are isocitrate dehydrogenase (citrate → isocitrate) and α-ketoglutarate dehydrogenase (α-ketoglutarate → succinyl-CoA). ATP and NADH inhibit these enzymes so, again, when the energy charge of the cell is adequate, low activity of the TCA cycle enzymes keeps flux at a minimum. Conversely, ADP is an activator of these enzymes and represents one mechanism by which TCA cycle flux is up-regulated. In some ways, points of regulation beyond the citrate synthase reaction act as a backup such that, if citrate is formed under conditions of low energy demand, other points of regulation keep TCA cycle flux at an appropriate level. Citrate can leave the mitochondria and act as a regulator of glycolysis thorough inhibition of phosphofructokinase. In this way, the TCA cycle can adjust the flow of pyruvate through the PDH complex to match better the substrate supply and demand. This mechanism is useful for fine-tuning energy needs of resting muscle.

The concentration of TCA intermediates is another control mechanism for flux. In addition to the citrate synthase reaction, other so-called anaplerotic reactions permit carbon entry into the cycle, several of them involving amino acids. One observed way to expand the TCA pool is through the near-equilibrium reaction catalyzed by alanine aminotransferase: pyruvate + glutamate ↔ α-ketoglutarate + alanine. Other potentially important reactions include those of the purine nucleotide cycle and those catalyzed by glutamate dehydrogenase, propinonyl CoA carboxylase, malic enzyme, and pyruvate carboxylase and phosphoenolpyruvate carboxykinase, which yield α-ketoglutarate, succinyl CoA, malate and oxaloacetate, respectively.

Oxidative phosphorylation is dependent on the flow of electrons along the electron transport chain, regulation of the movement of hydrogen ions (H^+) down an established proton gradient, and harnessing the free energy generated for phosphorylation of ADP to ATP. Indeed, this is a process that can be regulated, as evidenced by various poisons and uncoupling agents that prevent ATP synthesis by oxidative phosphorylation. For example, carbon monoxide prevents molecular oxygen from acting as an electron acceptor, and uncoupling agents such as 2,4-dinitrophenol can prevent the formation of a proton gradient across the inner and outer mitochondrial membrane, which upsets the hydrogen ion concentration (pH) gradient needed for ATP production by oxidative phosphorylation. Thus, proteins residing in the inner mitochondrial membrane for the purpose of electron transport and oxidative phosphorylation all represent potential points of control. Intracellular concentrations of ADP, NADH, and inorganic phosphate (Pi) and the ATP: ADP ratio are believed to have the greatest influence on the rate of oxidative phosphorylation.

Interplay of various hormones can also help regulate aerobic energy metabolism. Insulin, glucagon and the catecholamines epinephrine and norepinephrine are particularly important in this regard. Insulin's primary biological action is to increase glucose uptake from the blood. Increased glucose uptake promotes glycogen synthesis, particularly in muscle and the liver, but it will also stimulate carbohydrate oxidation through a substrate stimulus on TCA cycle flux. In addition, elevations of insulin after meals may activate PDH phosphatase converting the PDH complex into its more active PDHa form. However, periods of carbohydrate deprivation – and low insulin – lead to increased PDH kinase activity, which transpires into lower PDH activity and TCA cycle flux. Insulin is known to promote increased blood flow for delivery of nutrients, such as glucose, to insulin sensitive tissues. This represents another way in which insulin may stimulate carbohydrate flux for aerobic energy metabolism. The effects of insulin are not restricted to carbohydrate metabolism, as it can also promote amino acid transport into tissues such as muscle, inhibit lipolysis, and promote fatty acid synthesis. Indirectly, these actions of insulin can alter the aerobic metabolism of carbohydrates.

Glucagon is secreted by the alpha cells of the pancreas and serves to elevate blood glucose by increasing the rate of glycogenolysis in the liver. Glucagon can also increase the rate of gluconeogenesis from non-carbohydrate precursors, such as amino acids. These actions are particularly important for maintaining blood glucose concentrations during periods of carbohydrate deprivation or fasting and serve to keep a baseline of aerobic energy metabolism from carbohydrate under such conditions.

Epinephrine and norepinephrine are released from the adrenal medulla. Norepinephrine is also released from sympathetic nerve endings and this constitutes most of the norepinephrine found circulating in blood. Epinephrine plays a major role in substrate availability by promoting glycogenolysis in liver and muscle and by increasing lipolysis. Norepinephrine impacts aerobic energy metabolism primarily by nutrient delivery through its ability to regulate blood vessel diameter and stimulate heart rate and contractility.

See also: adenosine triphosphate-phosphocreatine system; resynthesis of adenosine triphosphate

Further reading

Baron, A.D., Steinberg, H.O., Chaker, H., Leaming, R., Johnson, A. and Brechtel, G. (1995) 'Insulin-mediated Skeletal Muscle Vasodilation Contributes to both Insulin Sensitivity and Responsiveness in Lean Humans', *Journal of Clinical Investigation* 96: 786–92.

Ludwig, B., Bender, E., Arnold, S., Huttemann, M., Lee, I. and Kadenbach B. (2001) 'Cytochrome C oxidase and the Regulation of Oxidative Phosphorylation', *Chemistry and Biochemistry* 2: 392–403.

Peters, S.J., St Amand, T.A., Howlett, R.A., Heigenhauser, G.J.F. and Spriet, L.L. (1998) 'Human Skeletal Muscle Pyruvate Dehydrogenase Kinase Activity Increases Following a Low Carbohydrate Diet', *American Journal of Physiology* 276: E980–E986.

JEFFREY J. ZACHWIEJA

AEROBIC GLYCOLYSIS – RESPONSE TO EXERCISE

Adenosine triphosphate (ATP) turnover increases at the onset of exercise. After the fall of phosphocreatine (PCr), adenosine diphosphate (ADP) concentrations increase and this, coupled with little or no change in ATP concentration, results in a decline of the ATP:ADP ratio. Reduced ATP:ADP activates glycolysis, pyruvate dehydrogenase (PDH) activity, enzymes of the tricarboxylic acid (TCA) cycle and oxidative phosphorylation. The net result is an increase in the oxidation of carbohydrates and an elevation in oxygen consumption.

Oxygen is required for the TCA cycle to proceed; when energy demand within muscle is increased, such as during dynamic exercise, oxygen delivery to, and utilization by the muscle must increase. One goal of this entry is to point out potential sites of regulation and metabolic factors that relate to the lag in oxygen consumption in the transition from rest to exercise. It has also been noted that an exercise power output of about one-third maximal is the highest that can be sustained for a prolonged period. Furthermore, the highest sustainable power output during exercise must eventually decline, the more prolonged the bout becomes. A second goal is to describe mechanisms, which affect the ability of aerobic glycolysis to maintain ATP supply for high sustainable rates of metabolic work.

The activity of PDH is central to increased carbohydrate oxidation during exercise and its activation is roughly proportional to power output. Glycolysis is stimulated with the onset of exercise and the resulting increase in pyruvate provides substrate, so the PDH reaction can endure increased flux. An increase in pyruvate availability also inhibits PDH kinase, and this will aid in the overall activation of the PDH complex. However, this substrate-level control is not the most powerful signal for PDH activation and flux during exercise. Intracellular calcium concentrations increase to initiate the muscular contractions characteristic of exercise. Calcium activates PDH phosphatase, which will dephosphorylate the PDH catalytic subunit, rendering the enzyme complex more active. Some have viewed this as a 'feed forward' mechanism to increase carbohydrate flux and oxidation rapidly during exercise. The ATP:ADP ratio declines with exercise and this will also contribute to PDH activation, through a lowering of PDH kinase activity. Thus, a rise in intracellular calcium grossly activates PDH flux during exercise. Pyruvate concentration and the ATP:ADP ratio fine-tune PDH to match more closely carbohydrate oxidation with the need for ATP in contracting skeletal muscle.

There is little doubt that the TCA pool expands with the onset of exercise and declines towards baseline as exercise continues to fatigue. The debatable issues are whether the TCA pool expansion is necessary for a high rate of flux to support aerobic glycolysis and whether a decline in the concentration of TCA intermediates initiates the onset of fatigue. It has been estimated that TCA flux can increase by up to a hundredfold during strenuous exercise in humans. However, by comparison, the relative increase in the TCA intermediate pool size is quite modest, only about four-fold. So, it appears that concentrations of pathway intermediates are stabilised within a fairly narrow range relative to metabolic rate. One way this could be achieved is through activation of 'non-equilibrium' TCA-cycle enzymes, such as citrate synthase, isocitrate dehydrogenase, and α-ketoglutarate dehydrogenase. In particular, the last two of these enzymes are thought to be stimulated

by exercise-induced increases in calcium and free ADP as well as by a decrease in the NADH:NAD ratio. Two recent studies have shed light on the potential metabolic significance of expansion and relative contraction of the TCA intermediate pool during exercise (Gibala et al. 2002a,b). Exercise under conditions of low muscle glycogen resulted in an accelerated rate of PCr degradation relative to control. Despite reduced aerobic energy provision – greater PCr degradation – expansion of the TCA intermediate pool was exaggerated during exercise with low muscle glycogen. Thus, it appears possible to disassociate the extent of TCA intermediate pool expansion from oxidative energy provision during rest-to-exercise transition. Likewise, thigh muscle oxygen uptake and PCr concentration during prolonged leg kicking exercise at 70 per cent of maximum effort were relatively stable; during the same time, the TCA intermediate pool size declined by about 50 per cent from its peak, which was achieved 10 min into exercise. Taken together, these studies indicate that TCA intermediate pool expansion may not be an important regulatory mechanism for tight control of TCA flux. Rather, TCA pool expansion may be a function of the rightward shift of the alanine aminotransferase reaction. For example, when pyruvate availability exceeds its rate of oxidation through the PDH complex, pyruvate and alanine combine to form glutamate and α-ketoglutarate, which is rapidly converted to other intermediates in the second half of the TCA cycle. In particular, increases in succinate, fumarate, and particularly malate, account for a good portion of the total TCA pool expansion with the onset of exercise. That intramuscular concentrations of glutamate decline and alanine is released from skeletal muscle at the onset of exercise further supports the role of the alanine aminotransferase reaction in TCA intermediate pool expansion.

As noted previously, an imbalance between glycolytic flux and PDH activity can lead to an increase in TCA intermediates through the alanine aminotransferase reaction. In much the same way, lactate will accumulate in skeletal muscle when pyruvate formation overwhelms the capacity for its oxidation. With this in mind, Brooks *et al.* (1999) challenged the classical model of pyruvate being the only oxidizable carbohydrate substrate, by proposing the existence of a lactate shuttle which would allow for direct oxidation of lactate in the mitochondria. Although the merits of this model will continue to be debated, the impact of anaerobic glycolysis on aerobic energy provision cannot be ignored. In fact, it has been estimated that anaerobic glycolysis contributes up to 20 per cent of the energy need during steady state submaximal exercise. In particular, the protons (H^+) released from lactic acid, forming lactate at physiological hydrogen ion concentrations (pH), may inhibit the rise in signals that activate oxidative phosphorylation and, thereby, limit the maximum sustainable work output through a restriction in ATP supply.

An elevation in ADP concentration during sustained exercise activates oxidative phosphorylation to help match ATP supply to demand. However, the extent to which ADP can increase is dependent on cellular pH. A decline in pH – an increase in H^+ – reduces ADP concentration. So, sustained exercise at a high power output is more difficult to maintain because the elevation in H^+ concentration restrains oxidative phosphorylation through limiting the rise in ADP concentration. At lower sustainable workloads, a greater harmony exits between glycolysis and oxidative phosphorylation. In this case, muscle pH is fairly normal and the muscle is able to generate an ADP concentration that activates oxidative phosphorylation to a sufficient extent. It is also known that a significant decline in the PCr concentration can offset the H^+ effect on ADP activation of oxidative phosphorylation. Walsh *et al.* (2001) have recently

shown that a lowering of the PCr:Cr ratio effectively raises the sensitivity of oxidative phosphorylation to the prevailing ADP concentration. This, and several of the arguments above, all testify to the importance of intramuscular factors in the regulation of aerobic glycolysis during rest-to-exercise transition, as well as the during sustained metabolic work of prolonged exercise.

See also: anaerobic glycolysis – response to exercise; biochemistry of exercise; muscle contraction – types of

References

Brooks, G.A., Dubouchaud, H., Brown, M., Sicurello, J.P. and Butz, C.E. (1999) 'Role of Mitochondrial Lactate Dehydrogenase and Lactate Oxidation in the Intracellular Lactate Shuttle', *Proceedings of the National Academy of Sciences* 96: 1129–34.

Gibala, M.J., Gonzalez-Alonso, J. and Saltin, B. (2002a) 'Dissociation Between Muscle Tricarboxylic Acid Cycle Pool Size and Aerobic Energy Provision During Prolonged Exercise in Humans', *Journal of Physiology* 545: 705–13.

Gibala, M.J., Peirce, N., Constantin-Teodosiu, D. and Greenhaff, P.L. (2002b) 'Exercise with Low Muscle Glycogen Augments TCA Cycle Anaplerosis but Impairs Oxidative Energy Provision in Humans', *Journal of Physiology* 540: 1079–86.

Walsh, B., Tonkonogi, M., Soderlund, K., Hultman, E., Saks, V. and Sahlin, K. (2001) 'The Role of Phosphorylcreatine and Creatine in the Regulation of Mitochondrial Respiration in Human Skeletal Muscle', *Journal of Physiology* 537: 971–8.

Further reading

Conley, K.E., Kemper, W.F. and Crowther, G.J. (2001) 'Limits to Sustainable Muscle Performance: Interaction Between Glycolysis and Oxidative Phosphorylation', *The Journal of Experimental Biology* 204: 3189–94.

Grassi, B. (2001) 'Regulation of Oxygen Consumption at Exercise Onset: Is It Really Controversial?', *Exercise and Sports Science Reviews* 29: 134–8.

Hughson, R.L., Tschakovsky, M.E. and Houston, M.E. (2001) 'Regulation of Oxygen Consumption at the Onset of Exercise', *Exercise and Sports Science Reviews* 29: 129–33.

JEFFREY J. ZACHWIEJA

AEROBIC GLYCOLYSIS – RESPONSE TO TRAINING

Adaptations to endurance exercise training include increases in oxygen delivery to contracting muscle and a greater capillary density around individual muscle fibres. The activity of the tricarboxylic acid TCA cycle and other oxidative enzymes, including those in the β-oxidation pathway, are increased after training. Substrate utilization during exercise shifts to a greater reliance on fat as an energy source; in particular there appears to be a greater use of intramuscular triglycerides. As a result, for a given absolute workload there is less muscle glycogen utilization and reduced lactic acid production. These physiological and biochemical adaptations result in a vastly improved endurance performance after exercise training.

Much of the enhanced functioning of aerobic glycolysis after endurance training and, in particular, increased maximal oxygen uptake, can be attributed to an increase in both the size and number of **mitochondria** in skeletal muscle. There is evidence for the existence of a mitochondrial reticulum, probably formed by fusion of mitochondrial organelles. This interconnected continuum of mitochondria extends throughout the muscle fibre and is more complex after training. Different populations of skeletal muscle mitochondria have been identified. Intermyofibrillar mitochondria are located between myofibrils and have a high respiratory capacity. Sub-sarcolemmal mitochondria are located beneath the sarcolemma of the muscle fibre and their volume is altered more dramatically by chronic endurance exercise. Such quantitative expansion of pre-existing mitochondria in response to exercise training has been termed 'mitochondrial biogenesis'.

Mitochondria are composed of outer and inner membranes, an intermembrane space, and an inner soluble matrix. The outer membrane contains transport proteins. The inner membrane contains proteins that comprise the electron transport chain. The soluble matrix contains enzymes for the TCA cycle and β-oxidation pathway, as well as mitochondrial deoxyribonucleic acid (DNA). Mitochondrial biogenesis involves the expression of genes arising from both the mitochondrial and nuclear genomes. Only thirteen proteins are derived from the mitochondrial genome, all of which are components of the respiratory chain complex. Nuclear encoded mitochondrial proteins are translated in the cytosol and then imported into the mitochondria. Synthesis of a functional mitochondrial organelle requires the production of membrane lipid components to 'house' functional proteins of the electron transport chain. Thus, lipid synthesis is an essential first step, so that newly synthesized proteins can be embedded within the growing phospholipid bilayers of mitochondria.

Exercise-induced mitochondrial biogenesis occurs in three sequential phases. The early phase, after 1–3 days of training, is characterised by expression of proteins, encoded by the nuclear genome, which have no direct role in ATP production. Examples are proteins that function in pathways of haem synthesis or membrane phospholipid synthesis, or proteins involved in chaperoning newly synthesized metabolic pathway enzymes in to or within the mitochondria. During the middle phase, after 5–7 days of training, proteins from the mitochondrial and nuclear genomes are induced and together they form the basis of functional mitochondria. These proteins, which comprise the TCA cycle, β-oxidation pathway, and the multi-subunit protein assemblies in the electron transport chain, have been used as biomarkers for mitochondrial content in skeletal muscle. The late phase, after about six weeks of training, involves replication of mitochondrial DNA. This event probably coincides with expansion of mitochondrial mass, and functions to maintain a consistent rate of mitochondrial DNA transcription. Despite characterization of exercise-induced changes in representative proteins from each of these three phases, there is much to be learned about the molecular events leading up to this adaptive response.

Despite the well-documented increase in mitochondrial mass after endurance training, it is prudent to ask whether the activity of skeletal muscle mitochondria, expressed relative to mitochondrial mass, is increased after exercise training and whether this contributes to functional benefit. Typically, the increase in mitochondrial oxygen consumption in response to endurance training is matched by a similar increase in citrate synthase activity, both on a percentage basis. In addition, Tonkonogi and Sahlin (1997) have shown that ADP stimulation of mitochondrial oxygen consumption relative to citrate synthase activity was similar in muscle samples obtained from trained and untrained participants. Taken together, it seems that an increase in mitochondrial oxygen consumption after training is related to an expansion of the mitochondrial mass and not to an increase in specific activity.

With more mitochondria, the amount of oxygen and ADP per mitochondrion is less after training than before. Therefore, the amount of ADP required to activate a given rate of ATP formation will be less, so, overall, there is an increased ADP sensitivity of muscle oxidative phosphorylation. However, it is also instructive to consider what happens at the level of each individual mitochondrion. Recent research shows that, after training, ADP sensitivity at the individual mitochondrion reacts in the opposite direction to that of the whole mitochondria population. That is to say,

there was a training-induced decrease in ADP sensitivity. In contrast, there was more of a stimulatory effect of creatine on respiratory function and this counteracted the decrease in ADP sensitivity (Walsh et al. 2001). This points to the complexity of mitochondrial control of oxygen consumption and energy production and how mitochondrial biogenesis can impact various control mechanisms within the respiratory process. Looking to the future, scientists will be charged with developing a better understanding not only of the molecular signals and events that lead to exercise-induced mitochondrial biogenesis, but also, and perhaps more importantly, of how a greater mitochondrial mass affects functioning of the individual mitochondrion organelle.

See also: exercise and training response of cellular structures; gene expression responses to training; training effects of oxygen dependent exercise

References

Tonkonogi, M. and Sahlin, K. (1997) 'Rate Of Oxidative Phosphorylation in Isolated Mitochondria from Human Skeletal Muscle: Effect of Training Status', *Acta Physiologica Scandinavia* 161: 345–53.

Walsh, B., Tonkonogi, M. and Sahlin, K. (2001) 'Effect of Endurance Training on Oxidative and Antioxidative Function in Human Permeabilised Muscle Fibres', *Pflugers Archives* 442: 420–5.

Further reading

Essig, D.A. (1996) 'Contractile Activity-induced Mitochondrial Biogenesis in Skeletal Muscle', in J.O. Holloszy (ed.) *Exercise and Sports Science Reviews*, 289–319, Baltimore: Williams and Wilkins.

Hood, D.A., Takahashi, M., Connor, M.K. and Freyssenet, D. (2000) 'Assembly of the Cellular Powerhouse: Current Issues in Mitochondrial Biogenesis', *Exercise and Sports Sciences Reviews* 28: 68–73.

JEFFREY J. ZACHWIEJA

AERODYNAMICS OF SAILS

Aerodynamics is the study of the forces that act on an object, as air or another gas moves against and around that entity. An understanding and knowledge of these forces is important in the design and performance of aeroplanes, yachts, and cars, as well as buildings and bridges.

The presence and correct balance of aerodynamic forces on a single sail or series of sails generates the power which can move the boat's hull – the frame or body – through the water. Although many of the same aerodynamic mechanisms, such as various forms of drag forces (see **drag forces – pressure, skin friction, and wave drag**), created on fixed wing aircraft also are generated in sailing, significant differences exist. Sails are deformable, without a fixed static shape. Yachts operate over a wide range of wind velocities and on a multitude of courses relative to the wind compared to the constant cruise speed of an aircraft. In addition to crew skill, the yacht's performance is dependent on the aerodynamics of the sails, the hydrodynamics of the boat's hull (see **hydrodynamics of boat hulls**), appendages – such as keels, and the interaction between the sails and the hull.

Sails have evolved in design and materials. While no individual is credited with its invention, the sail has followed a natural progression in the evolution of powering motion on water: floating, rowing, sailing, and motor power. An etching on a piece of 5,000-year-old Egyptian pottery depicts a drawing of a sail. The early sail appears to be no more than a square patch of material fastened to a stick near the front of the boat.

Modifications to sails continued throughout the Egyptian dynasties. By 2,400 BC the sail had become oblong and rose on a tall mast, which allowed it to catch the breezes between the many cliffs along the Nile. Although refinements continued, the sail's shape remained the same

for nearly 4,000 years. Although it could be angled to achieve maximum thrust, the square sail's biggest aerodynamic drawback was that it received air only from the rear. The boat was pushed by the wind.

Sailing was revolutionized in the ninth century AD by the lateen or triangular sail, believed to have been developed by Arab seamen. Hung fore and aft – front and back – of the mast, a long pole rising from the boat's deck, and easily shifted, the lateen sail received wind on either side. Effectively the boat was pulled as well as pushed. The inventors of the triangular sail recognized that their design greatly improved boat speed and responsiveness, but did not understand the aerodynamic principles behind this innovation.

The leading edge of a sail is called the luff and is positioned at the front, or fore, of the boat. The trailing edge at the back, or aft, is called the leech. An imaginary horizontal line from luff to leech is called the chord. The curvature in a sail is called the draft. The perpendicular measurement from the chord to the point of maximum draft is called the chord depth. The side of the sail that the air fills to create a concave curve is called the windward side. The side that is blown outward to create a convex shape is called the leeward side.

A boat is moved in a windward direction by using forces that are created on each side of the sail. This total force is a combination of a positive pushing force on the windward side and a negative pulling force on the leeward side, both acting in the same direction. Consider the case of wind that blows directly at the leading edge of the sail. If the sail is not angled or curved, but configured like a straight sheet, then the air, in principle, would separate equally on both sides of the sail. However, if the sail is angled to the wind, the sail fills and the aerodynamic forces develop.

This angle into the wind, called the angle of attack, must lie in a specific range. If the angle remains too close to the direction of the wind the front of the sail 'luffs' or flaps. If it is angled too widely, the airflow along the curve of the sail detaches and rejoins the surrounding air. This separation creates a stall zone of whirling air that causes a decrease in speed and an increase in pressure. Since a sail's curvature will always cause the aft end of the sail to be at a greater angle to the wind than the leading edge, the air at the leech is unable to follow the curve and turns its direction to that of the surrounding free air. Ideally, separation should not start until the airflow reaches the leech. However as a sail's angle of attack widens, this point of separation gradually moves forward and leaves the remaining portion of the sail in a stall zone.

In addition to an appropriate angle of attack, which allows air to pass smoothly onto it, the sail must have the correct curvature so the air remains attached all the way aft. Air separation can occur from too much curvature as well as from too wide an angle of attack. Each point of the sail has different pressures upon it. The strongest force exists at chord depth, where the curve of the sail is the deepest. Forces weaken as air moves to the rear and separates and the direction of forces change. At every point in the sail the force is perpendicular to the sail's surface. The strong forces in the forward part of the sail are directed forwards. In the middle of the sail, the force changes to a sideways, or heeling, direction. In the rear part of the sail, the force grows still weaker as wind speed decreases, and creates forces in the backward or drag direction.

Since the forward forces are also the strongest, the total force acting upon the sail is in a slightly forward, but mostly sideways, direction. Increasing the power of a sail to gain more forward drive also results in a much greater increase in the heeling force. Subsequently to move forward into the wind when the greatest force is to the side, the angle of attack of the sail to the wind, and the boat's resistance against water, must be utilised.

The direction of the total force is nearly perpendicular to the sail's chord. When a sail's chord is parallel to the boat's centreline, the main force is almost completely to the side. However, if the sail is angled slightly so that the sail force is in a slightly more forward direction, the boat itself moves forward at once. The centreline, or keel, of the boat reacts against the water similarly to that of the sail against the wind. The keel produces a force that opposes the heeling force of the sail and keeps the boat from simply moving in the direction of the sail force. Although total sail force is always to the side when sailing into the wind, a proper angle of attack will move the boat forward.

See also: boundary layer separation; hydrodynamics of boat hulls

Further reading

Bethwaite, F. (1993) *High Performance Sailing*, Camden ME: International Marine.
Marchaj, C.A. (2000) *Aero-Hydrodynamics of Sailing, Third Edition*, St Michaels MD: Tiller.
Townsend, M.S. (1984) *Mathematics of Sports*, Chichester: Ellis Horwood.
Walker, S.H. (1985) *A Manual of Sail Trim*, New York: W.W. Norton.
Whidden, T. and Levitt, M. (1990) *The Art and Science of Sails*, New York: St Martin's Press.

JANI MACARI PALLIS

AESTHETICS

The term aesthetic is derived from the Greek *aisthētikos*, which means sensitive, and *aisthanesthai,* which means to perceive. In the modern sense, aesthetics is the branch of philosophy that, with ethics and politics, comprises the more general category of axiology, which pertains to value. Ethics concerns morality, politics concerns the common good, and aesthetics concerns beauty. In general, aesthetics deals with art, its creative sources, its forms, and its effects.

According to Osterhoudt, aesthetics is prescriptive or normative in nature – as opposed to descriptive – and is concerned with the general principles of ideal form, beauty, and the beautiful, most particularly in the arts. More specifically, it is concerned with the form, content, and subject matter of the arts; the criteria of aesthetic judgment; the role of representation, contemplation, emotion, technique, and expression in the arts; the aesthetic experience and process; and the role of the artist and performer in the arts.

For centuries, the relationship between sport and art has been a reciprocal or symbiotic one. Sport has served as a subject for the arts (the literary and plastic arts in particular) and was initially and beautifully represented in such works as the poetry of Pindar and the sculpture and vase paintings of the classical age of Greece. In turn, art has compensated for the fleeting, ephemeral nature of sport, giving it enduring 'life' for centuries, as artists have recognised that sporting art is capable of evoking meaningful aesthetic experiences.

The central question in the philosophic literature that pertains to sport and aesthetics, however, concerns the status of sport as art and the terms in which sport constitutes an aesthetic experience. Some of the questions that have emerged in this literature include: What is aesthetic quality? What is an aesthetic experience; is it the same as an art form? Does sport, as a result of its commonalities with art, qualify as either an art form or an aesthetic experience? What is beauty? What are the relationships between sport, art, and aesthetics?

As Osterhoudt suggests, there are four main positions taken in this debate. The first of these maintains that sport is both aesthetic and artistic. In much of this literature, sport is often linked to play as a form of cultural expression that is nonproductive and 'unnecessary' and therefore fits the criteria of art. According to this view, sport is characterised as a movement and performing art, likened to dance, equal to other traditional forms of art such as literature and sculpture, and considered both artistic and aesthetic. According to the second position, sport does not meet all of the criteria of art but nonetheless can be considered a qualified form of artistic activity; sport is quasi-artistic and aesthetic. The position is based on ideas concerning the similarities and the dissimilarities between art and sport, and sport is seen as capable of or as having the potential for artistic achievement. Third, some views hold that sport has the potential for compelling aesthetic elements and is therefore aesthetic, but is not artistic. According to this view, the dissimilarities between sport and art are more compelling than the similarities. Sport does not meet the strict conditions of art. The fourth view suggests that sport is neither artistic nor aesthetic in any significant way.

Critics of this literature have suggested that this inquiry into the relationships between sport, art, and aesthetics is an attempt to exalt sport to the place of art. Others maintain that such inquiry is necessary for our understandings of the basic nature and significance of sport and to understanding the role, context, and intentions of the participants and the sport spectators.

References

Gerber, E. W. (ed.) (1972) *Sport and the Body: A Philosophical* Symposium, Philadelphia: Lea and Febiger.

Morgan, W.J. and Meier, K.V. (eds) (1995) *Philosophic Inquiry in Sport*, Champaign IL: Human Kinetics.

Osterhoudt, R.G. (1991) *The Philosophy of Sport: An Overview*, Champaign IL: Stipes Publishing Company.

Thomas, C.E. (1983) *Sport in a Philosophic Context*, Philadelphia: Lea and Febiger.

Further reading

Best, D. (1974) *Expression in Movement and the Arts: A Philosophical Inquiry*, London: Lepus Books.

Lowe, B. (1977) *The Beauty of Sport: A Cross-disciplinary Inquiry*, Englewood Cliffs NJ: Prentice-Hall.

SUSAN J. BANDY

AGE AND AGEING

Age is based on biological processes but it is also a social construction. On their way through life people pass through different phases which are defined by society and are connected with certain expectations as well as rights and obligations. 'Normal biographies', as defined by society, provide scripts for the appropriation and shaping of individual biographies. In this process, ageing signifies in general terms the physical and psychical changes during the course of time and is a differentiated process influenced by numerous biological and social factors.

Age and participation in sport

The links between age and participation in sport are closely intertwined. In each phase of life sport plays a specific role, and competitive sports have developed a differentiated system of age categories and classes designed to ensure equality of opportunity.

Although age unquestionably has a decisive influence on sporting performance, the age at which best performances are attained varies greatly according to the individual as well as to the kind of sport played. In the 1936 Olympics, for example, Marjorie Gestring won a gold medal in women's diving at the age of thirteen, while boxer George Foreman was forty-five years old when he won his last world championship title. In spite of this variation there are typical patterns discernible in individual sports with regard to the age at which best performances are reached.

Whereas the participation of **children** and adolescents in sport receives much attention, the sport of older people and the elderly has not so far been a focus of either public or academic interest. However, although sport was a privilege of youth until the last third of the previous century, increasing numbers of older people are now discovering and taking up sporting activities.

Ageing – present situation and tendencies

Ageing goes hand-in-hand with a decrease in health and fitness while the incidence of chronic diseases grows. The causes of the ageing process are not fully known. Nevertheless, in industrialised countries the state of health of the majority of the population between 65 and 80 is satisfactory. Even if almost everyone over seventy has one or more chronic diseases, most people do not subjectively feel ill. They can cope with their problems and adapt to the circumstances. However, the number of people with a problematic decline of physical fitness and health increases above the age of eighty.

Demographic data show that the proportion of older people in the populations of Western industrial countries is on the increase and today already amounts to more than 20 per cent. This is largely attributable to the rising expectation of life in these countries. In Germany, for example, girls born today have an average life expectancy of 86.5 years while for boys the figure is just below 80 years. Thus, the higher the age is, the greater the proportion of women to be found in the age cohorts.

Sufficient social welfare and improvement in the average health status are accompanied by changes in the self-awareness, definitions and life-styles of older people – making necessary a re-definition of age. Today, we must distinguish between the age groups 55–65, 65–80 and the over eighties. The 55–80 age group, at least, seeks to take advantage of numerous new opportunities. The 'young seniors', 55–65 years old, are trendsetters, increasingly being discovered by the media and the advertising industry. At the same time, the number of very old people (over eighty years) is increasing, among other things, because of improved healthcare.

In Western industrialised societies old age mostly has negative connotations. Stereotypes refer to competences (or lack of them, concerning their physical, mental and intellectual faculties); personalities (no longer strong, charismatic, interesting); and behaviour ('inadequate' activities). In contrast, studies show that older people are mostly quite satisfied with their lives. Furthermore, ageing brings with it opportunities and challenges. Retirement, for example, means reduced financial resources and social status but it also means reduced stress and increased leisure. Older people seem to develop a positive self-awareness and learn to adapt their wishes and dreams to the present situation. But ageing also means having to cope with changes and losses, e.g. the loss of competences as well as the loss of partners and friends.

Despite these positive tendencies, older people run the risk of becoming depressive, and with increasing age also the danger of mental and intellectual disorders increases.

Ageing and physical activities

Physical activities have a positive influence on ageing at both the individual and social levels. At the social level the participation of seniors in physical activities can contribute to a positive image of ageing and to combating stereotypes and myths. At the individual level, sport helps to preserve the body's functions and increase health and well-being. The WHO campaign 'Active Ageing' aims at physical, psychological and social well-being. With increasing age, physical performance (strength, speed, reaction, condition, endurance, flexibility) decreases. Physical activity can slow down this process and maintain performance and the functioning of the body. Other benefits

of sport can be the reduction of stress and anxiety as well as creating a positive self-awareness and building empowerment. In addition, sport can improve social networks, social resources and social support. However, the benefits of sport depend to a large extent on the type, intensity and duration of physical exercise, as well as on the conditions under which it takes place.

Although most women and men over fifty-five years of age agree that sport is important, all available statistical data show unanimously that only a small percentage of the population older than fifty-five years is physically active. The percentage of seniors who take part in physical activities varies from country to country; in Germany it is approximately 10 per cent. In Scandinavian countries participation in sport among seniors is much higher; in Southern Europe much lower; in Italy, for example, the figure for the over sixty-five age group is 1 per cent. With increasing age the number of people who are physically active decreases. This remains true today, even though there are now far more older people who take part in sporting activities than 20 or 50 years ago – a tendency which has been caused, among other things, by the emergence of age cohorts whose members developed a close commitment to sport during their childhood and youth.

This increase in the numbers of physically active seniors has also been caused by changes in the world of sport, especially the spread of 'sport for all'. In particular, older women have been attracted to new 'alternative' physical activities which promise health and well-being. Popular physical activities among seniors are hiking, swimming and gymnastics (women), which are not too strenuous and do not demand a high degree of skill.

Physically active seniors name the same reasons for taking up sport as young people who do sport, namely fun and health. When seeking the causes of older people's abstinence from sport, one must distinguish between different sport biographies as well as between different groups. People who have never been interested in sport frequently name: lack of interest, other hobbies, poor health, no time, too exhausting, risk of accident and age. Some of them would only take up sport if this was recommended by a doctor; many would not take up sport under any condition.

Those seniors who would like to do some sort of physical activity often mention specific barriers which prevent them from putting their intentions into practice, like the difficulty of access to sports facilities, social anxieties, lack of financial resources, lack of social support or lack of information. Irrespective of the type of sport or the provider, measures for winning over seniors to physical activities must begin right at these very barriers.

The policy aims of sport for and with seniors should be to win over individuals who are not physically active. This means, first, that the barriers which hinder older people from participating in sport have to be identified and removed; and second, that, once they are active, their commitment must be strengthened in order to prevent them from giving up their activities.

Types of sport

When recommending types of sport or when selecting the contents of courses, one must distinguish between the various needs and the objectives of older people. Many seniors will continue to practise the sport they have always played, or perhaps change to a related sporting activity. However, there are also courses specially designed for older people, often focusing on gymnastics, which cater for newcomers. Specially designed courses for senior citizens must be full of variety and not oriented towards biological age but rather towards the specific expectations and needs of the 'clientele'. For sport does not fulfil *per se* all the hopes put in it, as the many providers

would have us believe; it is, rather, the choice, range and intensity of the physical exercises that determine which goals can be achieved. If physical activities are aimed at counteracting 'processes of decline' in middle and old age, focus should be placed on stamina, strength, agility and coordination. Sports which are well suited to improving stamina are swimming, cycling, hiking and jogging. Weight training is also increasingly considered useful for older people.

Besides 'sport for all' activities, courses are also provided in the prevention and rehabilitation of various disorders such as back pain and osteoporosis. The exercises in these courses must be thoroughly consistent with the aims of the therapy, and it is essential to involve specialists in the process, whose tasks are to carry out diagnoses, give advice and develop programmes.

Sport for seniors should follow certain principles, i.e. it should make demands of an appropriate nature on the physical, mental and cognitive faculties of the participants; it should enable new physical, psychological and social experiences; it should create self-determination and 'empowerment'; and it should provide fun and excitement.

Sport may also be a challenge for older people, and a way of comparing their performance with others. In most sports there are now competitions for seniors, and the world-title competitions for 'masters' have become an established feature in the international sports arena.

Unquestionably, competitive sport is attractive only to a few seniors. But even the few competitive sportsmen and women among the older generation can still serve as models and as living examples of the fact that seniors are not yet 'ready for the scrap heap'.

Further reading

Collins, M. (2003) *Sport and Social Exclusion*, London/New York: Routledge.

Cousins, Sandra O'Brian (1998) *Exercise, Aging and Health*, Philadelphia: Taylor and Francis.

Denk, H. (ed.) (1996) *Alterssport* [Seniors' Sport], Schorndorf: Hofmann.

Gannon, L. (1999) *Women and Aging*, London/ New York: Routledge.

Kolb, M. (1999) *Bewegtes Altern* [Ageing in Movement], Schorndorf : Hofmann.

Mechling, H. (ed.) (1996) *Training im Alterssport* [Training in Seniors' Sport], Schorndorf: Hofmann.

GERTRUD PFISTER

AGENTS

Agents (sports agents, athlete agents, athlete representatives) are individuals or firms that represent professional athletes in a variety of manners: contract negotiation; financial planning and advice; endorsement solicitation and negotiation; legal consultation and representation in criminal or civil matters; medical or physical training consultation; public relations and image consultation; post-playing career counseling; personal counseling; and by providing a variety of personal services (household management, paying bills, arranging transportation, etc.).

One of the first known agents, Charles C. Pyle, gained notoriety for signing and negotiating contracts for such athletes as Jim Thorpe (American football) and Suzanne Lenglen (tennis) during the 1920s. The use of agents began to increase during the 1960s and 1970s, when competing leagues (the American Basketball Association (ABA) in basketball, the American Football Association (AFL) in American football, the World Championship Tennis (WCT) in tennis); strengthening unions; and several important court decisions (*Mackey v. National Football League*, for one) all combined to give professional athletes both the legal right and the bargaining power to successfully negotiate more advantageous contracts.

Agents may work individually or as members of sports management firms. IMG, founded by golfer Mark McCormack in 1960, is the largest such firm, representing such clients as Tiger Woods (golf), Pete Sampras (tennis), Derek Jeter (baseball); Vince Carter (basketball); and Jeff Gordon (auto racing), as well as many other athletes (active and retired), coaches, broadcasters, organizations, and entertainment industry individuals. Other prominent large firms include SFX Sports, Assante, and Octagon. During the 1990s, many prominent individual agents or smaller agencies have been purchased or have consolidated with these and other firms.

Athlete agents have also come under fire during the 1980s and 1990s for a variety of illegal and unscrupulous activities, such as providing cash, presents (cars, clothing, etc.), jobs, drugs, and even prostitutes to potential clients and their family and friends. Such illegal incentives cause athletes to lose their amateur or collegiate status and also often result in legal and financial sanctions for the college institutions where they attend. Other such activities include stealing clients from other agents, loan sharking, money laundering, and financial mismanagement of athletes' money. Lawsuits between agents and athletes have become commonplace.

Many states in the United States have passed laws that attempt to regulate agents' sometimes unsavory activities. In addition, the National Conference of Commissioners on Uniform State Law (NCCUSL) passed the Uniform Athlete Agents Act (UAAA) in 2000, which, if passed by all fifty state legislatures, would standardize state regulations on agents throughout the United States (similar to the Uniform Commercial Code or Uniform Probate Code). The NCAA (National Collegiate Athletic Association) and the players' associations for the NHL National Hockey League (NHL), National Basketball Association (NBA), and Major League Baseball (MLB) also have enacted rules that attempt to regulate agents.

Reference

Shropshire, K. and Davis, T. (2003) *The Business of Sports Agents*, Philadelphia PA: University of Pennsylvania Press.

Further reading

Ruxin, R. (1983) *An Athlete's Guide to Agents*, Bloomington IN: Indiana University Press.

MICHAEL A. HUNT

AGGRESSION

Aggression poses a current problem in sport as well as for society in general. Although aggressive acts in daily life are addressed though the legal and penal systems, in sport aggression is often rewarded and is many times seen as illustrative of the true sporting spirit. Although much research has focused on aggression in sport, major conclusions from these findings have been limited owing to differences in defining aggression, ways of measuring aggression – operational definitions, and theoretical frameworks.

Definitions of aggression

A substantial problem in research on aggression in sport lies in defining the construct. Adding to the confusion is the lack of distinction between, and the often-interchangeable use of, the terms aggression, violence, hostility, and assertiveness. Aggression has been defined as behavior with the goal of harming or injuring another individual. This behavior can include both physical and non-physical behavior, such as psychological intimidation. However, the intent to cause harm or injury must be present. Aggression can also be further distinguished by the goal of the aggressor. Hostile, or reactive, aggression refers to the aggressive response toward another person, who has angered or provoked the individual. The goal of hostile aggression is to cause harm or injury to a specific individual and is usually connected with anger. Instrumental aggression serves as means to a particular goal, such as winning, in which injury to the opponent is involved. This type of injury is impersonal and designed to limit the effectiveness of the opponent. When such goal-oriented activity does not involve injury – and injury is not intended – the term proactive assertion has been used. Often, assertive behavior that results in accidental injury is misclassified as instrumental aggression. Therefore, aggression must be behavior that is chosen with the intent of causing injury and must be non-accidental.

Operational definitions

To measure aggression, we must provide an operational definition. One of the greatest measurement difficulties is in addressing the intentional aspect of aggression. Often the judgment as to the player's intentions is left to officials to determine. Thus, some researchers use aggressive rule violations as the operational definition. Such violations include penalized actions that occur during the course of the game that are intended to inflict harm and are in violation of the rules of the game. However, intention cannot be measured when using rule violations to measure aggression. Other researchers have used interview techniques to ask the participant directly for her or his underlying intentions before certain behaviors. Paper and pencil inventories have also been used to assess sport participants' views of the legitimacy of injurious acts and rule-violating behavior, the likelihood of their aggressive actions in relation to assertive or submissive actions and their self-reported likelihood to aggress in a game, and their attitudes to such aggression. Other operational definitions have used the rating of aggressiveness of participants by their coaches or peers. All of these operational definitions have faults. Although some methods assess intention, these assessments either concern a hypothetical action or occur after the action has been taken. In either case, participants may misstate, deliberately or not, their actual intention because of the potential for socially desirable responses.

Theoretical frameworks

Four major theoretical frameworks are used in the study of aggression: instinctual, frustration-aggression, social learning, and moral reasoning. These theories are used to understand causes of aggression so as to be able to explain, predict, and direct or modify aggressive behavior.

Instinctual theories

Instinctual, or biological, theories of aggression assume that aggressive behavior is a natural, or innate, response in all individuals and has evolved to its present state through a struggle for survival. According to this theoretical position, aggression naturally builds up in humans and necessitates release. This release, or catharsis, can be sought through unacceptable – for example, criminal – behavior, or acceptable channels, such as sport. This viewpoint has been labeled the catharsis hypothesis. This theoretical stance has its opponents. However, research on twins at the Minnesota Center for Twin and Adoption Research and the University of Southern California has shown that aggressive tendencies may have a strong genetic component.

Frustration-aggression hypothesis

In its original state, this hypothesis stated that any thwarting of goal-directed behavior would result in frustration, with the inevitable outcome being an aggressive response. This hypothesis was modified to include non-aggressive responses to frustration, and by the addition of two conditions – the opportunity for aggressive action and the presence of suitable cues,

such as anger. Although anecdotal evidence in support of this hypothesis is readily available, empirical research is unclear.

Social learning theory

The social learning position views aggression as a learned response pattern, influenced by reinforcement and modeling. In particular, the observer learns how successful the model was in using aggressive behavior in achieving her or his goal. The observer also learns whether the model's aggressive behavior was rewarded or punished. Therefore, the observer has learned both the aggressive action and under what circumstances the action might be penalized or praised. Often, athletes are encouraged to display aggressive behavior toward opponents in pursuit of their sporting goals. Reward for this behavior can be significant, such as salary bonuses, renewed contracts, praise and recognition from teammates, coaches, fans, and the media; punishment is either minimal or inconsequential. This theory states that players learn, through a process of socialization, specific skills involved in aggression and that aggressive behavior is often expected, desired, and, often, considered legitimate in certain sport contexts. Much of the research in to aggression in sport has been based upon social learning theory and has included sport participants, spectators, and television audiences. Although considerable empirical support has been found for this theoretical approach, much of the research has operationally defined aggression as an overt, observable act, overlooking the basic concept of intention to cause harm. The meaning and intention behind a specific action is never transparent and necessitates interpretation by the observer.

Moral reasoning theory

Since the mid-1980s, researchers have used a moral reasoning framework for examining

39

aggression in sport. This theory is a structural-developmental approach that examines the reasoning, or meaning, associated with aggressive behavior. The value of this theoretical perspective is its focus on identifying the intent of the player. Rather than focusing on overt behavior, structural-developmental theorists study ways in which the individual defines a certain context and her or his choices in that context. Research on moral reasoning theory considers how athletes' aggressive actions and goals are mediated by how they interpret the context and their moral reasoning.

Key findings

A few key findings have emerged from research on aggression in sport. In general, male athletes tend to behave more aggressively than female athletes. Also, greater perceived approval by significant others, such as coaches and parents, and peers – team-mates – has been related to athletes' self-described likelihood to aggress against an opponent. Standard of competition, participation in contact or collision sports, and length of participation in organized sport, have all been found to be positively related to athletes' perceptions of legitimacy of injurious actions in sport. Overall, based on current research, it appears that factors representing the context or environment are the most useful in predicting aggression in sport.

See also: morality

DAWN E. STEPHENS

AGGRESSION AND MORALITY

Aggressive action is often preceded by a moral decision. Two aspects of morality considered to impact intentions to engage in aggression and aggressive behaviour are moral reasoning and game reasoning. Athletes who score higher on moral reasoning in sport are less likely to perceive an aggressive act as legitimate and to engage in physical and non-physical aggressive tendencies. Additionally, athletes with lower moral reasoning are perceived as acting more aggressively by their coaches. Bredemeier and Shields (1986) suggested that athletes might also determine the legitimacy of an aggressive act by using game reasoning. That is, within the athletic environment athletes negotiate a moral balance that maintains the structure and rules of the game and allows for legitimate acts of aggression that occur in the process of accomplishing the ultimate goal of the game. Therefore, game reasoning may facilitate a moral balance but may not necessarily be universally right or adopted outside the realm of the sporting context. In a qualitative examination of aggression and morality, those authors found that athletes used this game reasoning to justify aggressive acts towards another in the sporting context. Aggression was legitimate if it was for strategic gain or part of the written or unwritten rules of the game. However, aggression used for the sole purpose of seriously harming an opponent was considered illegitimate. Therefore, there was a sense that, if the result of the aggressive act transcended sport, it was not appropriate. Although all athletes may not attach moral meaning to aggressive acts, moral reasoning and game reasoning are important to consider.

See also: aggression; morality

Reference

Bredemeier, B.J. and Shields, D.L. (1986) 'Athletic Aggression: An Issue of Contextual Morality', *Sociology of Sport Journal* 3: 15–28.

Further reading

Shields, D.L.L. and Bredemeier, B.J.L. (1995) *Character Development and Physical Activity*, Champaign IL: Human Kinetics.

LORI A. GANO-OVERWAY

ALCOHOL – DOPING AND NUTRITION

Alcohol consumption and sports are closely linked, and it is no surprise that alcohol is the most abused drug by athletes. Athletic participation does not confer protection from the acute and chronic effects of alcohol and athletes experience the same health, legal, and social problems as non-athletes. Classified pharmacologically as a depressant, alcohol use precedes recorded history and there is evidence that ancient man brewed alcohol. Historically, alcohol was considered to increase performance and brandy was given to marathoners in the early twentieth century. The majority of athletes today, however, consume alcohol as a recreational drug.

Although the mechanism of action for alcohol is no different for athletes, usage patterns are unique to sports. Studies have demonstrated that athletes are more likely to suffer adverse alcohol consequences, 'binge' drink (more than five drinks per session), and consume more alcohol per week even when controlling for body-size. Far from reducing risk, studies show that being a self-identified team leader in a male sport increases one's risk of alcohol-related events. The risk of binge drinking goes beyond the health effects and is associated with a large number of social ills, including motor vehicle accidents, violent behavior, unintended sexual activity, etc.

The overall health risks of alcohol are well know, however alcohol may have unique effects on exercise. As a depressant alcohol has sedative effects at low doses but higher doses obviously can result in decreased reaction time, hand-eye coordination, accuracy and many other psychomotor tasks. All of these would be expected to reduce athletic performance, and studies have demonstrated an inverse relationship between blood-alcohol level and running times. Furthermore, there is a dose-dependent toxicity to striated muscle associated with chronic alcohol use. Owing to its toxicity to both skeletal and cardiac muscle, alcohol would be expected to negatively influence exercise ability.

From a nutritional standpoint, alcohol has significant negative effects on performance. Alcoholic beverages are considered 'empty calories', both because they lack nutrients and are often substituted for healthier foods. In addition, the diuretic effect of alcohol can lead to dehydration, which further erodes performance. Finally, alcohol has central effects on thermoregulation, and combined with dehydration can predispose to heat illness.

Despite the fact that the dangers of alcohol are well known, it is generally neither banned nor tested for by sports organizations. The exception is for sports involving shooting, such as rifle, pistol and archery, where the International Olympic Committee and National Collegiate Athletic Association specifically ban its use, largely due to the sedative effects leading to performance-enhancement. Interestingly, international volleyball prohibits alcohol for umpires and referees during competition. Lacking a formal ban, most sports organizations do have policies covering athletes who demonstrate alcoholism or adverse effects associated with its use. Although the definition of alcoholism is difficult, it is usually defined as someone who continues to drink despite repeated negative consequences. Most sports organizations have employee assistance professionals to help deal with these issues; however, alcohol problems may first become evident to coaches, teammates, athletic trainers, or physicians. It is imperative for all personnel to be trained in the early recognition of the common signs and symptoms of alcohol problems.

References

Green, G.A. (2003) 'Recreational Drug Use in Athletes', in: DeLee and Drez (eds) *Orthopaedic Sports Medicine: Principles and Practice*, 2nd edn, 483–92, Philadelphia PA: Saunders.

GARY GREEN

41

ALCOHOL – SOCIAL SCIENCE

At first glance alcohol and sport seem to have little in common. In the early days of modern sport, it is true, people believed that alcohol could increase sporting performance – and it was not without reason that the first Olympic marathon winner reportedly drank a glass of wine on his way along the course. Nevertheless, it is a proven fact today that drinking alcohol impairs performance since, among other things, it has an adverse effect on the nervous system, motor abilities and endurance.

A closer look, however, reveals many different and multifaceted links between sport and alcohol in different epochs and cultures.

The association of sport (in a broad sense) with pleasure – eating and drinking and music and dance but also boisterousness, laughter and mockery – was, for example, an important feature of 'sporting activities' in the Middle Ages and early modern times. This is true of the knights' jousting tournaments, and the riflemen's contests of the bourgeoisie, as well as the peasants' diversions. Spontaneity, fun and alcohol were important at a time when it was scarcely possible to plan for the future.

Alcohol, mostly beer, flowed also in abundance at the festivals of the German *Turnen*. On many occasions, they held ceremonial drinking sessions where, similar to the drinking rituals of students (*Kommerse*), strict rules were followed. At the end of the nineteenth century, as soon as sports clubs and teams were founded, a pub was chosen as a meeting place and centre for congenial get-togethers.

Today discussions of alcohol and sport focus mainly on the question of the extent to which sporting activities protect against the taking of drugs or, conversely, whether they encourage and further it. Several empirical studies were not able to prove that sport had a preventive effect; on the contrary, they showed evidence that sporting activities led to a higher consumption of alcohol. This seems to apply in particular to young men. These findings are explained by the social function of alcohol, which plays an important role in certain sport cultures, especially team sports.

Sport, club and clubhouses, meetings and celebrations are unimaginable without alcohol, and social networking is based to no small degree on enjoying a drink together. This may also apply to numerous other gatherings, but sport and sports clubs provide an especially informal and relaxed atmosphere with a high threshold of tolerance as far as drinking alcohol is concerned.

Studies have revealed that only a minority of football-club members do not drink alcohol in their club, and that the majority of young men categorise themselves as heavy drinkers. In order to encourage clubs to adopt a responsible policy with regard to drinking among members, projects have been established on drug prevention in sports clubs, for example in Australia and Switzerland. It must also be taken into consideration, however, that the extent and the form of alcohol consumption differ greatly according to the sporting context, especially the type of sport played.

Further, alcohol consumption can play an even greater role among spectators than it does among players. This is particularly the case among sports fans for whom drinking beer is part of a ritual and a trigger of deviant behaviour as well as often being a cause of violence.

The alliance between sport and alcohol is both strengthened and diffused by sponsoring and advertising. In many countries the alcohol industry provides funding for teams and sports meetings, and sport plays an important role in advertising for alcoholic drinks. Beer and baseball, for instance, are inextricably linked in the commercials for Speight's, a New Zealand brewer: beer and baseball together make men out of boys, and their masculinity is put to the test in both drinking and sport. In Germany the famous coach and former world class soccer player Franz Beckenbauer appears in commercials for the Erdinger brewery. The message is that alcohol and sport, especially men's sport, belong together – and that sport is more fun combined with the drinking of alcohol.

Further reading

Burke, L.M. and Maughan, R.J. (2000) 'Alcohol in Sport', in R. J. Maughan, *The Encyclopedia of Sports Medicine*, Vol. VII (pp. 405–16), Oxford: Blackwell.

Schweizerische Fachstelle für Alkohol-und andere Drogenprobleme (2001) *Schützt Sport vor Drogen (SFA-Studie)?* [Can Sport be a Protection against Drugs?] http://www.cannabislegal.de/studien/sfasport.htm

Snow, P. and Munro, G. (2000) 'Alcohol Consumption in Amateur Australian Football Clubs: Evidence From a Rural Region', *Health Promotion Journal of Australia* 10, 3: 237–43.

Stainbeck, J. (1998) *Alcohol and Sport*, Champaign IL.: Human Kinetics.

GERTRUD PFISTER

ALLERGIES AND INFECTIONS OF THE SKIN

An allergic reaction is an immunological response that occurs as a result of exposure to a physical or chemical stimulus. Exposure to the stimulus results in the release of vasoactive substances from activated cells (mast cells, basophils, mononuclear cells) or from enzymatic pathways (complement system). Vasoactive substances include histamine, bradykinin, prostaglandins, leucotrienes, complement C3a, C4a and C5a. These substances are responsible for vasodilation and bronchospasm, which present clinically as skin rashes and wheezing respectively.

In certain susceptible individuals, physical exercise can act as the stimulus for an allergic reaction. These reactions are known as exercise-associated allergies. A wide variety of exercise-associated allergies have been described. In this section, the clinical manifestations and management of the more common exercise-associated skin allergies will be discussed briefly.

Allergies

Urticaria

Urticaria is an allergic reaction characterized by an itchy red patchy (usually 10–15 mm in diameter) skin rash that develops 2–30 min after the onset of exercise. It usually starts in the upper thorax and neck and may spread to other areas of the body. Various types of urticaria are described.

Cholinergic urticaria are much smaller (1–3 mm in diameter) than so-called classical urticaria. They also occur in response to other physical stimuli such as anxiety, heat and sweating. Cholinergic urticaria are treated with H1 histamine antagonists, in particular hydroxyzine or cyproheptadine. A gradually increasing exercise program can induce tolerance to the condition.

Cold urticaria occur in response to exposure to cold and can affect athletes participating outside on cold winter days, or swimmers in cold water. Massive mediator release can result in hypotension and collapse but this is rare. Cold urticaria is best treated with avoidance of exposure to cold. The symptoms can be treated with anti-histamines.

Localized heat urticaria is rare, occurs in response to local heat application, and is difficult to treat. Anti-histamines and cortisone have not been very successful.

Solar urticaria and aquagenic urticaria are rare conditions caused by exposure to light and water respectively. In both cases, the treatment involves blocking the light or water by applying sunblocks and inert skin oils respectively. Pharmacological treatment with antihistamines is also indicated.

Dermatographism

Dermatographism is an allergic reaction characterized by linear wheals which occur

1–3 min after stroking the skin. It has been described in football players wearing protective gear. Treatment with anti-histamines is successful in most cases.

Angioedema (delayed pressure urticaria)

This syndrome is characterized by swelling or urticaria, which occurs 4–6 hours after the application of pressure to the skin (footwear, tight clothing). It has been postulated that diet may play a role in this condition. Treatment is to avoid skin pressure while drugs such as H1 antagonists, as well as non-steroidal anti-inflammatory drugs, can be used to control symptoms.

Infections of the skin in the athlete

A variety of skin and mucous membrane infections can be transmitted through direct skin contact. These can be viral, bacterial or fungal infections, and are common in athletes engaging in contact sports (see Table 2).

Viral infections related to skin contact

Herpes simplex virus is the most common viral infection that is related directly to skin contact in athletes. It has been termed 'Herpes gladiatorum' in wrestlers, and 'scrumpox' in rugby players. In players with this infection, contact sports should be avoided until no vesicles are visible. Anti-viral treatment may shorten the course of the infection, and should be started in the prodromal or erythematous phase of the infection.

Viral warts are common in athletes who have friction sites where callus develops. These include gymnasts, pole-vaulters, and runners. To distinguish them from ordinary callus, scraping of the lesion will reveal punctate bleeding in a viral wart, and just deeper skin layers in a callus with no infection. Sports can continue, but treatment consisting of topical agents, liquid nitrogen or laser ablation should be performed.

Bacterial infections related to skin contact

Skin infections can related to contact can be a superficial skin infection (impetigo), affect the hair follicles (folliculitis) or affect deeper skin layers (carbunculosis and furunculosis). Occasionally, systemic spread of the infection can occur. Most bacterial skin infections are caused by Staphylococcus aureus, which is highly contagious. Athletes with this infection should not play contact sports until the lesions are healed. Systemic antibiotics are the main form of treatment.

Fungal infections related to skin contact

Superficial fungal infections of the skin are very common in athletes. Regular screening and treatment with topical anti-fungal agents is necessary. Attention to personal skin hygiene is important (wearing dry absorbent socks and clothing), and exposure to contaminated areas such as shower floors should be limited by wearing shower sandals.

See also: sun damage

Reference

Adams, B.B. (2002) 'Dermatologic Disorders of the Athlete', *Sports Med.* 32: 309–21.

MARTIN SCHWELLNUS

ALLOSTERIC MODIFIERS OF HAEMOGLOBIN

The ability to alter the affinity of haemoglobin for oxygen has the potential to powerfully influence endurance capacity. This is a subject that has fascinated exercise physiologists and athletes alike. There is now experimental evidence of a drug that can alter that relationship, and it is likely that other drugs will follow and this will

Table 2. Infections related to skin contact between sports participants

Type of infection	Organism/s	Site of infection	Clinical presentation	Treatment
Viral	• Herpes simplex virus (HSV) Type I	• Skin • Conjunctiva • Cornea	• Skin: • Clustered vesicles with pink base which crust and heal in a few days • Conjunctivitis • Keratitis	• No contact sports until lesions form scabs and are dry • Anti-viral antibiotics (acyclovir, famciclovir or valacyclovir)
	• Papilloma virus	• Skin	• Cutaneous warts	• Topical salicylic acid • Liquid nitrogen • Laser ablation
Bacterial	• Staphylococcus aureus • Streptococcus pyogenes	• Skin (impetigo) • Hair follicles (folliculitis) • Furunculosis • Carbunculosis	• Erythema • Papules • Pustules	• General skin hygiene • Adequate chlorination of pools • Regular cleaning of skin with dry dressing • Oral antibiotics • Drainage of abscess if present • Return to contact sport only once crust or scab has formed
Fungal	• Trichophyton (tonsurans, rubrum, mentagrophytes) • Microsporum canis (Tinea capitis)	• Tinea pedis (skin of feet between toes) • Tinea capitis (scalp) • Tinea corporis (skin of body) • Tinea cruris (groin)	• Dry scaly pink plaques on skin with central clearing • Occasional erythematous papules	• Keeping skin dry • Preventing contact • Topical anti-fungal agents (ointments, solution, shampoos) • Oral anti fungal agents in resistant cases
	• Trichophyton mentagrophytes • Candida albicans	• Nails (onychomycosis)	• Thickened white nails • Paronychia • Cellulitis	• Oral anti fungal agents • Contact sports usually allowed as evidence is not clear linking this infection to contact sports

appeal to athletes. The first drug in the class of allosteric modifiers of hemoglobin is 2-[4-[[3,5-dimethylanilino)carbonyl]methyl]-phenoxyl]-2-methylpropionic acid, also known as RSR13.

Oxygen is bound to haemoglobin through diffusion in the lungs and then is unloaded at the tissues. The oxygen–dissociation curve is one of the hallmarks of exercise physiology, and a drug that can foster the unloading of oxygen at the lowered oxygen tissue levels would be favorable to exercise. RSR13 acts by modifying the hemoglobin to unload oxygen at low oxygen tensions, thereby shifting the curve to the right. Studies have examined the therapeutic potential of RSR13 to modify diseases associated with low oxygen levels, such as hypoxia and ischemia. If increased oxygen could be delivered to ischemic tissue, it might be possible to attenuate the damage that occurs from prolonged hypoxia, e.g. cerebrovascular events or myocardial infarctions. In addition, RSR13 has been demonstrated to improve oxygenation in some tumors, making them more sensitive to radiotherapy. RSR13 is being actively studied as an adjunct to radiation therapy of brain metastases.

Although there are no human studies, dog models have demonstrated an increased VO_2 max using RSR13 in skeletal muscle. The first mention of RSR13 in athletics was in a press report from a European cycling race in 2001. Although allosteric modifiers of hemoglobin were not specifically banned by at that time by the IOC, the potential for abuse convinced a drug testing lab to develop a method for the detection of RSR13 in urine. Using gas chromatography/electron impact ionization mass spectrometry, Breidbach and Catlin were able to confirm a method for the detection of this compound. Following that discovery, the IOC quickly developed a category of prohibited methods called 'Enhanced Oxygen Transfer', of which RSR13 is specifically named. These are defined as products that enhance the uptake, transport or delivery of oxygen. Clearly, the latter applies to RSR13.

Although RSR13 has the potential to improve human endurance and is banned by the IOC, there are several reasons why it is unlikely to be used in an effective way. Studies have demonstrated that a dose of 75–100 mg kg^{-1} is needed to produce a 5 mm Hg rightward shift in the oxygen-dissociation curve when given with supplemental oxygen. Owing to the fact that RSR13 has a half-life of 4–5 hours and that maximum efficacy occurs at the end of a 30–60 min infusion, RSR13 must be given in close proximity to an event. Furthermore, RSR13 is toxic to peripheral veins and requires infusion through a central vein, e.g. subclavian vein. It is difficult to imagine an athlete being connected to oxygen and a central vein infusion and then rushing directly to an endurance event. Finally, human oncology studies have revealed significant adverse reactions that include headache, nausea, vomiting and renal impairment.

Although RSR13 may not be practical for use by athletes, it is reasonable to assume that additional drugs will soon be developed with similar properties that are less cumbersome. RSR13 is an example that an understanding of exercise physiology can predict what types of substances will be sought for performance enhancement.

Reference

Breidbach, A. and Catlin, D.H. (2001) 'RSR13, a Potential Athletic Performance Enhancement Agent: Detection in Urine by Gas Chromatography/Mass Spectrometry', *Rapid Communications in Mass Spectrometry* 15: 2379–82.

GARY GREEN

ALPINE SPORTS

Alpine sports is a term which includes many different kinds of sporting activity ranging from 'sport for all' to top-level competitive sports, each kind putting different physical and mental demands on the participants as well as requiring different motor skills. Equally manifold are the motives of mountaineers, which may vary from the thrill of taking risks to experiencing '**flow**' or to being close to nature.

Until early modern times Europe's mountains were part of untamed nature, home to spirits and gods which men only disturbed at their peril. However, in the eighteenth century, in the wake of the Enlightenment, a thirst for knowledge and exploration began to spread which gave no immunity to the mountains.

The beginning of mountaineering – and also its first milestone – was the 'conquest' of Mont Blanc in 1786 by Michel-Gabriel Paccard, a doctor, and Jacques Balmat, a crystal seeker, who thus won the prize money offered by the Geneva physicist and geologist, Horace Bénédict de Saussure. Further summits were subsequently reached, although at lengthy intervals: first of all the Großglockner (1800), then the Zugspitze (1820), followed by the Großvenediger (1841). Then, in the 1850s, starting in England, the cradle of modern sport, a mountaineering 'craze' suddenly broke out, turning the mountains into a sporting challenge. Within a few years, from 1859 to 1865, most of the Alpine summits had been 'conquered'. The climax, which also marked the end of this phase, was the 'race' for the Matterhorn, lasting several years and finally won by the English mountaineer Edward Whymper in 1865. But Whymper had to pay dearly for his victory, four of his companions falling to their deaths during the descent.

Distinctive features of this phase of mountaineering, called 'conquest alpinism', were the dominance of the English (who in the words of Leslie Stephen (1871) used the Alps as the 'playground of Europe'), the appeal of the highest peaks, being the first to reach the summit as a sporting goal, a preference for the easiest routes, the use of local guides and the organisation of mountain climbing as expeditions.

The enthusiasm for mountaineering in this phase is also to be interpreted as a reaction to processes of modernisation taking place in the second half of the nineteenth century – processes which, finding their expression in urbanisation and **industrialization**, were seen by many as a threat.

At the end of the nineteenth century mountain hiking became a popular sport, not least because the railways now provided a convenient means of transport, alpine clubs were being founded and huts were being built in the mountains for shelter.

After the highest summits had been conquered, mountaineers turned their attention to lower peaks as well as more difficult mountain faces and ascents. 'Detail climbing' was the magic formula which paved the way for innumerable 'firsts'. This trend led to a continuous increase in the demands put not only on mountaineering equipment but also on the strength and stamina of the climbers, thus progressively subjecting alpinism to the principles of modern sport. Descriptions of tours began to list the time needed and the conditions of the ascent, enabling 'insiders' to compare achievements and mark themselves off from others.

Mountaineering, however, continued to be more than a sport. For alpinists like A.F. Mummery, a typical representative of mountain climbing without a guide, mountaineering was like playing with life and death – a game that he lost, incidentally, on the Nanga Parbat in 1895. For them it was a matter of personal achievement and the demonstration of their skills. Battling with danger was the key term around which everything revolved – intimidating and fascinating at the same time.

In spite of a clear tendency towards 'sportification', mountain climbing differed from other sports not only on account of its dependence on nature and the question of the technical resources required but also, generally, because of the difficulty in operationalising the achievement of climbers. The ethos of rock climbers, for example, prohibited 'artificial means of support' like rock pitons – the myth of two equal opponents, man and mountain, and the glorification of the risks taken could only be upheld in free climbing.

The First World War led to great social upheavals and cultural transformations in Europe, accompanied by rapid processes of modernisation. Mountain climbers frequently responded to these changes by fleeing to the supposedly intact world of the mountains. The constantly rising difficulties which the climbers exposed themselves to now made safety equipment indispensable. Thus, various technologies were developed for the use of the rope and pitons were employed at first for securing the climbers and later as a means of moving forward. These new technologies produced a fundamental change in the character and the image of rock climbing: from a dangerous, life-threatening battle with the mountain to a resourceful sport with sophisticated technology to overcome difficulties.

In the interwar period the mountains were all climbed, most of the routes had been accomplished and the masses 'invaded' the now well-trodden paths to the peaks. Those who wished to distinguish themselves from the rank and file by seeking new challenges and extending the borders of what is humanly possible had now to find new difficulties, i.e. solo ascents, winter climbs and the climbing of faces until then considered 'insurmountable', for example.

In the 1930s the last of the hitherto unconquered summits were climbed: in 1931 the north face of the Matterhorn and in 1938 the north face of the Eiger, which had claimed so many lives that it was debated in newspapers whether attempts to climb it should be banned.

Through imagined heroism and a fanatical obsession to achieve the impossible, mountain climbers remained aloof from mountain hikers and, establishing themselves as an elite, signified the survival of the fittest in a social-Darwinist sense (Amstädter 1996).

By the end of the nineteenth century the 'playground' of the Alps had already become too small for alpinists wishing to expand their scope. The 1920s thus saw a globalisation of mountaineering, helped by the fact that the discovery and exploration of the world by the great European powers was already very advanced. The new challenges were the 'eight thousanders' of the Himalayas, which from the 1930s onwards were 'besieged', above all by British and German expeditions using considerable resources of manpower, funding and logistics. The Nanga Parbat especially, the Germans' 'mountain of fate', claimed numerous lives (Märtin 2002).

The period following the Second World War was the heyday of 'superdirettissimas', the direct route to the summit, no matter how many pitons and rope ladders were needed. The mountain was turned into a sports ground, the mountain face into a piece of apparatus.

It was not until the 1970s that a decisive change occurred in alpinism with the rising popularity of free climbing. In free climbing only natural holds are used to scale rocks, the rope merely serving as a safety factor. A special form of free climbing is the free solo, in which the climber does without the safety of the rope completely. The following features of free climbing influenced the further development of this sport: training in difficult sequences of movements at low heights (bouldering); training in the required physical abilities such as holding power; training in agility; use of new safety equipment such as skyhooks and 'friends'; use of magnesia in order to increase the friction of grips; improved equipment such as special boots with high friction; and the securing of routes from above. To these may be added fashionable clothing, which is both tight-fitting and colourful.

Free climbing met with great opposition at first, not least because the relative safety of the routes had been seen as a leap forward from traditional climbing. However, the process of 'sportification' was unstoppable.

As in free climbing, artificial means of support are taboo in sport climbing, although dangers are eliminated through the use of pegs drilled into the rock face. Sport climbing is not considered to be a 'battle with the mountain' but a sport. What is demanded in sport climbing is no longer fearlessness, a fighting spirit and toughness, but suppleness, agility and elegance; and this gives women the chance of playing a more important role than in other forms of climbing.

Climbing contests became established first of all in Italy and France, but their popularity quickly spread to other countries. In 1987 the Union Internationale des Associations d' Alpinisme set up a commission to draw up guidelines for climbing competitions, and different disciplines were developed with different focuses such as speed and difficulty of the course.

The development of alpinism has always been accompanied by an ever greater differentiation, and today one distinguishes between numerous different forms of alpine sports ranging from mountain hiking to alpine ice scaling and to large-scale mountaineering expeditions. While climbing has undergone a process of 'sportification', mountaineering has become commercialised. Today one can book a 51-day expedition to Nanga Parbat with a travel agency. However much this commercialisation may be deplored by 'genuine' mountaineers like Reinhold Messner, it has demystified mountain climbing and freed it from the myths of heroism and sacrifice.

References

Amstädter, R. (1996) *Der Alpinismus. Kultur –Organisation – Politik* [Alpinism. Culture –Organisation – Politics] Vienna: WUV-Universitätsverlag.

Märtin, R.-P. (2002) *Nanga Parbat. Wahrheit und Wahn des Alpinismus* [Nanga Parbat. Reality and Delusion of Alpinism] Berlin: Berlin Verlag.

Further reading

Anker, D. (2000) *Eiger. Die vertikale Arena* [Eiger. The vertical arena] Zürich: AS-Verlag.

Keenlyside, F. (1976) *Peaks and Pioneers: The Story of Mountaineering*, London: Elek.

GERTRUD PFISTER

ALUMNI DONATIONS

As college athletic programs in the US have struggled to keep up with increasing costs and mandated growth in women's sports, they have become increasingly active in raising money from external support groups. One of the fastest growing areas of athletic department revenues is supporters' donations. A survey of the financial status of college athletics conducted by the NCAA reported that contributions from boosters and alumni accounted for 17 per cent of the annual revenues of Division IA programs, an average of $3.5 million per program. The importance of this source of revenue has increased appreciably over time. When the NCAA conducted its first financial assessment in 1965, funds raised from alumni and boosters accounted for an average of only 5 per cent of an athletic department's budget.

The growth and potential of this funding source is most apparent when the most successful collegiate sport fund-raising programs are considered. For example, in 2001, over $25 million in annual, capital and endowment gifts was raised by the athletic department at Ohio State, while the Fresno State University Athletic Department received slightly over 43 per cent or $7 million of its annual operating revenues from solicited monetary donations.

As the importance of fund raising has become more apparent, a growing number of athletics departments have established formal fund-raising programs. It is common to find, particularly within the largest athletics programs, an associate or assistant athletic director designated as the director of athletic development or fund raising. Typically, this staff member's responsibilities include developing a fund-raising program, cultivating potential donors and serving as the liaison to the department's athletic support group. Most athletic departments have adopted the term *development* rather than fund raising to describe these activities to try and avoid the negative connotations associated with asking for money.

Most athletic development officers solicit two primary types of gifts: (a) annual; and (b) major. *Annual* gifts are generally donations solicited from a broad base of alumni and boosters. Typically, they are smaller gifts, ranging from $100 to $10,000. Annual gifts are normally used to defray current operating expenses, such as the cost of grants-in-aid, travel, and recruitment. *Major* gifts are generated from a relatively small group of donors. Generally they are one-time donations of significant monetary value often directed at capital projects, such as a new arena. Another type of major gift that is growing in popularity is the endowment (i.e. a gift that is invested to generate income, which is available for spending in perpetuity). Also included in the major gift category are planned or deferred donations. These gifts are not outright gifts in that their benefits are deferred through legal instruments like wills and insurance policies until the death of the donor. Donors make the financial commitment during their lifetimes, but the benefits do not accrue to the athletic program until some future time, often after a donor's death.

Many athletic departments have established 'point systems' for assigning football and basketball tickets to donors as an incentive program. Usually, these unpublished systems award points on the basis of the amount of annual giving, number of consecutive years of contributing, and number of consecutive years of purchasing season tickets. The more points accumulated by the donor, the more preferred the seating location. Generally, the greatest number of points is awarded for gifts of the greatest magnitude, with each of the other categories receiving equal weight. A popular scheme is to use a three-step approach to calculating points based on length of membership, cumulative giving and the amount of the current gift. Under this system, a member receives one point for (say) every $250 of cumulative lifetime giving, and anything between 1 and 50 points, depending on the magnitude of the current gift amount.

A growing number of a sport support groups are utilizing a 'team' approach to organizing their annual fund-raising campaigns. The origin of the idea has been attributed to the Louisiana State University Athletic Department. Analogous to the athletic teams they support, under the team concept boosters are placed on teams that compete against one another to see who can raise the most money. In many cases an elaborate organizational structure is established, complete with league commissioners, team names, captains, league standings, and a sophisticated reward system.

The first year the Texas A&M-Kingsville athletic support group applied the concept, it increased its annual contribution to the athletic program tenfold, from $20,000 to $200,000. Ten five-person teams 'squared off' to compete for a number of incentive awards.

No criterion exists for precisely defining what constitutes a major gift. It is generally described as a substantial, one-time contribution. Depending on circumstances, a major gift could be anywhere from $5,000 to $50 million or more. With major gifts, the emphasis is on targeting a limited number of prospects who have the potential of making significant contributions, rather than attracting many small gifts. Fund raisers have found that a very few donors account for the largest portion of funds raised. This consistent pattern has led to the adoption of a formal principle known as Rule of Thirds, which says one third of a campaign goal is likely to come from the top ten donors, the next third from the next 100 donors, and the remaining third from all others.

The key to success in attracting major gifts is establishing a well organized system for identifying, cultivating, and soliciting the relatively few prospects who would be both capable and willing to make extraordinary contributions to the athletic department. Recently, database programs, such as BENEFACTOR, have been developed to help charitable organizations identify and cultivate donors.

JOHN L. CROMPTON

AMATEURISM

Whereas in antiquity the amateur ideal was of no significance, the ideas, associations and values related to amateurism have played an important role in sport discourse ever since the nineteenth century. The French term 'amateur' has the literal meaning of 'lover' and, applied to sport, it is used to designate people who play a sport 'for the love of it', without gaining or having ever gained any material benefit from it. By contrast, professional sportsmen and women (see **professionalism**) are paid for their sporting 'work'. Each epoch and each sport has had its specific definitions and rules, stipulating precisely under which conditions, for example, expenses could be paid. The ideas, associations and values related to amateurism, such as achievement from intrinsic motives or fair play, conformed with ideals of the middle classes and ascribed to sport an educational mission.

The amateur ideal and the drawing of borders between amateur and professional sports evolved from the eighteenth century onwards, and were linked to the development of modern sport. In the beginning 'gentlemen' of the upper classes had been competing among themselves while enjoying their leisure pastimes such as riding and hunting; however, when they now played some of the newly established sports, which included cricket, football, rowing and 'pedestrianism', they encountered members of other social classes, some of whom played sport to earn money. In order to preserve the exclusive nature of sport and in order not to have to compete with workers and tradesmen who were possibly their superiors in terms of physical strength and athletic abilities, sports clubs and associations issued regulations on amateur status – the British Amateur Rowing Federation, for example, excluding from membership not only professional athletes but anyone who did manual labour. In rowing, the striving for distinction of the 'leisure class' was especially intensive since, here, the aim was to exclude not only professional sportsmen but also watermen, who earned their living by rowing. This drawing of borders between amateurs and professionals can be attributed in part to the social divisions and class distinctions that were to be found in many countries, including Great Britain. Moreover, because of the growing popularity of sport among the working class and the accompanying rise of professionalism, for example in **football**, the **values** of sport appeared to be under threat. For the middle and upper classes in Britain 'gentlemen', 'amateur' and 'fair play' were one and the same.

In 1894, when Baron de Coubertin was preparing to present to the public his plan of holding Olympic Games, he chose the problem of amateurism and the necessity of drawing up international rules as a topic with which to gain attention. He was vindicated by the success of the congress in

51

1894, the issue of amateurism attracting a great many people interested in sport, including celebrities, to Paris.

From the very start the question of amateurism played an important role in the Olympic Games. It was thought that young men should appear in the Olympic arena not for the sake of money but out of their love of sport. This was Coubertin's vision, and a seemingly indispensable element of Olympism. Within the Olympic movement the regulations on amateurism were strictly enforced, as shown, for example, by the case of Jim Thorpe, an American and one of the best athletes of those times, who had to give back his gold medals for the pentathlon and decathlon because he had played semi-professional baseball two years prior to the 1912 Games.

The higher the standards of athletic performance became over the years, the greater, too, the problem of amateurism. Since the increasing time and energy devoted to training necessitated a full-time commitment to sport – which, in turn, jeopardised the athletes' chances of employment and thus their welfare provision in later life. Competitive sport was threatening to become socially exclusive and accessible only to members of wealthy families. In addition, the amateur status of athletes was being increasingly undermined by people evading the rules, for example by means of illegal transfers of money.

Nevertheless, Avery Brundage, president of the IOC from 1952 to 1972, defended the principle of amateurism; he feared that allowing professional athletes to take part would lead to a commercialisation of the Games, thus putting the lofty ideals of Olympism in danger.

The way this problem was solved differed from country to country. In socialist countries, 'state amateurs' trained at the expense of the state. They were given leave to train by the firms to which they had been assigned, and successful athletes received numerous privileges and benefits ranging from trips abroad to flats and cars. In the USA athletes were funded by means of college and university scholarships. In West Germany athletes were given financial backing by German Sport Aid (*Deutsche Sporthilfe*), founded in 1967, although at first the payments were understood as reimbursements for expenses rather than sponsoring.

In 1971 the IOC liberalised the rules governing amateur status and in 1981, at the eleventh Olympic Congress in Baden-Baden, Germany, these rules were largely rescinded: athletes were not to be put at a financial disadvantage because of their activities in sport. However, professional sportsmen and sportswomen were still not eligible to take part in the Olympic Games. It was not until 1991 that the IOC finally took leave of the amateur ideal, although with one significant provision: athletes, it was decreed, were not allowed to receive any financial reward for their participation in the Games, nor were they allowed to advertise during the Games. Both rules still exist, but – as can be seen from the Olympic reporting of the mass media – only on paper.

Amateurism was always more than a rule of eligibility; it was associated with ideals and aspirations and partly, too, with the hope of finding in sport a world of its own which had been spared many of the tendencies in society that were judged critically, such as consumerism and commercialisation. Sport was looked upon as the 'world's most pleasurable triviality', free from the cost-benefit calculations of the labour market and free from political intervention and pressures. From this perspective the amateur was regarded as an ideal and ethically superior; the professional athlete, by contrast, seemed to betray the values of sport – or sell them at the highest price. In spite of the criticism of the so-called 'own world theory', voiced, among others, by Marxists and also by the 'Frankfurt School', the concept of 'pure sport' remained an ideology with numerous supporters.

Stripping amateurism of its ideology gives us a clear view of the fact that paying athletes does not rule out the notion that they love their sport and represent amateur ideals. It must also be borne in mind that relatively few top athletes today (above all those in a number of 'media sports') are able to earn an above-average income, so that the majority of athletes are still amateurs in a broad sense.

Further reading

Allison, L. (2001) *Amateurism in Sport: An Analysis and a Defence*, London: Frank Cass.
Kretchmar, S. (ed.) (1993) 'Special Feature. History and Philosophy of Amateurism', *Quest* 45, 4.

GERTRUD PFISTER

AMBUSH MARKETING

Ambush marketing is a relatively new phenomenon that emerged first in the 1990s in the area of sports sponsorship of major sports events. Kolah (2003) defines ambush marketing as the actions of companies who seek to associate themselves with a sponsored event without paying the requisite fee. The 'ambush' consists of giving the impression to consumers that the ambush company or brand is actually a sponsor or is somehow affiliated with the event.

In contrast Bean's (1995) definition of ambush marketing, suggests that it is not so much the motive of the ambush marketeer to associate the company with the event as to target a competitor that is an official sponsor of the events. He defines ambush marketing as the direct efforts of one company to weaken or affect a competitor's official association with a sports organisation acquired through the payment of sponsorship fees. Through advertising and promotional campaigns, the ambushing company tries to confuse consumers and to misrepresent the official sponsorship of the event.

McAuley and Sutton (1999) argued that the increasing prevalence of ambush marketing reduced the growth in the value of sponsorship in the late 1990s as companies such as Coca-Cola and IBM renegotiated or ended sponsorship contracts because ambush marketing had reduced the value of the sponsorship benefits to them. They see ambush marketing as a serious threat to the funding of sports organisations through sponsorship revenue.

They identify five major different types of ambush marketing:

1. *Contests or sweepstakes:* this refers to companies organising a contest around the outcome of a game, or has a competition where prizes are tickets to the game;
2. *Broadcast sponsorship:* this refers to a company sponsoring a broadcast of an event or game, which will normally cost much less than sponsoring the event itself;
3. *Television commercials:* a company can place commercials during breaks in the broadcast of an event which in terms of content can relate the company's name by inference to the event;
4. *Sponsorship of a team or athlete:* individual athletes or whole teams taking part in the event may be sponsored by a particular company, although the company contributes nothing to the event organisers;
5. *Promotional advertising/marketing collateral:* this form of ambush marketing relates to flyers and give-aways distributed at the event, posters on billboards close to event venues, or specific marketing events staged in close proximity to the major sporting event.

Many companies use several of these tactics at a specific event. At the 1998 football World Cup, Nike was not an official sponsor but did have an endorsement contract with the favourites, Brazil. Nike bought advertising slots world-wide in the breaks in the games and featured the Brazilian team in the adverts. Nike also built a football village near Paris, and the Brazilian team was featured as a major attraction of the village. The campaign was backed by a major poster campaign. Nike achieved a slightly higher awareness rating for the World Cup than Adidas, its main rival and official sponsor of the event.

Ambush marketing fits in with Nike's image of an anti-establishment, innovative, aggressive company. Its adverts and endorsements have often concentrated on the non-conformist athlete, whether in behavioural terms, such as John McEnroe, or in dress/appearance, such as Andre Agassi. To be an official sponsor to some extent is in conflict with this image. By spending as much in ambush marketing as the official sponsors do in their sponsorship contract and then achieving greater awareness is consistent with Nike's image of winning by unconventional routes.

However, there is a clear danger in the growth of ambush marketing to those involved in staging major sports events. Although the ambush marketeers spend huge sums of money around the staging of an event (estimated at £20 million for Nike in the 1998 football World Cup), none of this money is revenue to the event organisers. Although broadcast sponsorship and athlete/team sponsorship do count as sports sponsorship, the other three types of ambush marketing would count as more generic advertising expenditure, and therefore the more companies engage in these type of activities, the less the total value of sports sponsorship.

References

Bean, L. (1995) 'Ambush Marketing: Sports Sponsorship Confusion and the Lanham Act', *Boston University Law Review* 75: 1099.

Kolah, A. (2003) *Maximising The Value of Sponsorship*, SportBusiness Group Limited.

McAuley, A. and Sutton, W.A. (1999) 'In Search of a New Defender: The Threat of Ambush Marketing in the Global Sport Arena', *Sports Marketing and Sponsorship* 1, 1: 64–86.

CHRIS GRATTON

AMERICANIZATION

Americanization is global homogenization under the hegemony of North American popular culture, particularly the United States. Academic debate has centered on the degree to which modern globalization has been synchronous with Americanization. Media outlets have been criticized for furthering Americanization as a social force by transmitting Americanized art, cinema, music, education, and sport in particular. Critics have also problematized two perceived outcomes of Americanization: the exportation of cultural hegemony and commercialization of sport worldwide.

Academic debate has evaluated the degree to which globalization has been synonymous with Americanization. Americanization has been identified as 'McDonaldization', 'CocaColonization', and 'Disneyfication'. Each term refers to the one-way diffusion of consumer products, cultural values, political policies, and popular culture from the United States to communities worldwide.

One view contends that US foreign policy has been intent on opening the world to US-based transnational corporations, preventing the rise of any society that might become a successful alternative to the United States and extending its political and economic hegemony over the globe to 'create a world order in America's image' (Blum 2002). To achieve this end, propaganda and violence have been applied world-wide. Accordingly, glittering sports stars and US-based 'World Championships' (*sic*) are part of this propaganda.

The second view contends that Americanization is only one option in a larger globalization movement stemming from the Information Age. Instead of Americanization as globalization, Fisher and Ponniah (2003) identified other distinctly non-American globalization movements, including the World Social Forum that advocates the reinvention of society such that economic production, political governance, and the organization of media is plural, diverse, and affirms regional experience. Other arguments against globalization as Americanization are the resistance of local cultures to the cultural imperialism of North American sport, the transference of non-North American sports to the United States, and the recent collapse of high-profile US-based transnational corporations.

Whether world citizens have options to accept other than Americanization, critics claim that the media has championed world Americanization. Hot button events in sports have triggered the media to articulate cultural events as crises of national identity. For example, the media transformation of North American professional baseball star Joe DiMaggio from an ethnic sport hero to a mainstream cultural icon was identified as an early symptom of Americanization. The 1988 marriage of Canadian hockey star Wayne Gretzky and US actress Janet Jones (and subsequent trade from Edmonton to Los Angeles) was identified in media reports as residue of Americanization and a threat to Canadian ideals. Racism within the United Kingdom's National Basketball League has been linked to the social dynamics of Americanization, as has the widespread adoption of North American sports idols by New Zealand youth. Thus, Americanization of sports has been added to film entertainment and musical style as another category for the exportation of Americanized culture.

One perceived outcome of Americanization is cultural hegemony. Cultural hegemony has been defined as the destruction of meaningful choice of social opportunities, knowledge, and expression. This is widely believed to be negative because cultural hegemony contradicts the principles of democracy and social justice for all people on which many societies are founded. Examples of the US cultural hegemony include Major League Baseball's (MLB) domination of Dominican baseball structure and sports reporting; the inclusion of North American sports rather than Filipino sports in a Manila carnival that celebrated traditional Filipino lifestyles; the United States' invasion of Japanese sport; and the preference for the Maccabi Tel Aviv – the team dominated by US players – in Israeli basketball. Even communist soldiers of Cambodia's Khmer Rouge have been susceptible to the cultural hegemony of US sport; photographs of soldiers participating in a US-style beach volleyball match were circulated world-wide in 1999.

Americanization has also been blamed for the world-wide commercialization of sport. In the 1990s, the commercialization of sport increased dramatically when, in many Australasian and European countries, traditionally amateur sports were transformed to professional sports. Also during the 1990s, multinational corporations based in the United States, United Kingdom, New Zealand, Japan and Australia increased sport-related contributions to highlight their companies' good corporate citizenship. Moreover, the National Basketball Association (NBA) and National Football League (NFL) have both staged contests in London, Mexico City, Tokyo, and Berlin. The World League of American Football (now NFL Europe) was initially underwritten by an American beer corporation. The export of American-based, commercially sponsored sport has been criticized for undercutting existing national leagues (e.g. in Israel, Hong Kong, and the Philippines) and for providing alternative (and seemingly less attractive) culture and pop culture icons for international youth.

References

Blum, W. (2002) *Rogue State: A Guide to the World's Only Superpower*, London: Zed Books.

Fisher, W.F. and Ponniah, T. (eds) (2003) *Another World is Possible: Popular Alternatives to Globalization at the World Social Forum*, Black Point, Nova Scotia: Fernwood Publishing.

Further reading

Houlihan, B. (1994) 'Homogenization, Americanization, and Creolization of Sport: Varieties of Globalization', *Sociology of Sport Journal* 11, 4: 356–75.

Xia, G. (2003) 'Review Essay: Globalization at Odds with Americanization', *Current Sociology* 51, 6: 709–18.

KINDAL A. HUNT
MICHAEL A. HUNT

AMPLIFICATION AND SIGNAL CONDITIONING

Although some sensors produce large signals that allow straightforward computer interfacing, many produce small signals that may be contaminated with noise. For example, the electrical signal obtained by surface electromyography (EMG) from a small muscle may be a few tens of microvolts – ten millionths of a volt – while interference from mains wiring at 50 or 60 Hz may be several volts, leaving a signal that is lost in 10,000 times the amount of noise. The process of making a signal suitable for input to an analogue-to-digital converter (ADC) is termed signal conditioning; it may consist of amplification – increasing the amplitude of a signal – or filtering – removing contaminating noise. Both amplification and filtering rely heavily on the use of operational amplifiers.

Operational amplifiers

Operational amplifiers are integrated circuits containing many transistors along with capacitors and resistors. They form amplifiers with almost ideal characteristics, having very high gains – the ratio of output voltage to input voltage – of 100,000 or higher, and close to infinite input impedance, such that very little current flows into their inputs. They are usually used with negative feedback, which reduces their gain in exchange for improved linearity and predictability. Because of their ease of use and flexibility, they are used as building blocks in many different types of amplifier circuit; some of the most useful are discussed now.

Types of amplifier

- *Voltage amplifier:* the output voltage is an amplified version of the input voltage. The amplification is termed the gain of the amplifier; it can be less than unity – an attenuator, negative – an inverting amplifier, or positive – a non-inverting amplifier.
- *Current amplifier:* some sensors produce large output voltages, but have such high output impedances that they cannot generate sufficient current to drive an ADC. An operational amplifier circuit with unity voltage gain faithfully follows the input voltage but allows much higher output current owing to its low output impedance. This process is sometimes termed impedance conversion.
- *Summing amplifier:* an inverting amplifier can input several voltages through resistors, the output is the sum of each input voltage scaled by the inverse value of each resistor.
- *Differential amplifier:* this circuit produces an output that is proportional to the difference between its two inputs. The differential amplifier has many uses in signal conditioning, for example, to amplify the output from strain gauges in a full-bridge configuration (see **force and other**

sensors). A particular form of differential amplifier constructed from three individual operational amplifiers is called an instrumentation amplifier. It has the characteristics of very high input impedances at both inputs and a high common-mode rejection ratio (CMRR), which is the ratio of the gain of the difference between the input signals to the gain of the mean input signal. The CMRR is a figure of merit for instrumentation amplifiers, and can be 10,000 or higher. Instrumentation amplifiers are used to extract signals from noise, such as in the EMG example given earlier.

- *Comparator:* if a differential amplifier with very large gain has a fixed – threshold – voltage applied to its inverting terminal and a variable input voltage applied to its non-inverting terminal, the output will be low when the input is below threshold and high when it is above threshold. Thus, a continuous input is transformed to a discretised output. Comparators can be arranged to have hysteresis to prevent multiple switching near to the threshold.

- *Charge amplifier:* this amplifier configuration is particularly useful for amplifying the output from piezo-electric sensors. The input terminal is kept very close to zero volts, which reduces the leakage of charge from the sensor and improves the low-frequency response.

Operational-amplifier filters

Filtering is the process of separating the desired part of a signal from the unwanted part by exploiting their different frequency characteristics. Low-pass filters pass only frequencies below the cut-off frequency, attenuating frequencies above it. A particular use for low-pass filters is anti-alias filtering before sampling by an ADC. High-pass filters attenuate frequencies below the cut-off frequency and pass frequencies above it. Band-pass filters attenuate both low and high frequencies, passing only mid-band frequencies. Band-stop filters attenuate mid-band frequencies and pass low and high frequencies; a very narrow band-stop filter designed to eliminate a particular frequency, such as mains frequency, is termed a notch filter. Simple filters can be constructed from combinations of resistors and capacitors; however, they tend to have a slow transition, or roll-off, from pass-band to stop-band. They form a 'single pole' filter – the maximum rate they roll-off is to halve the signal they allow through with each doubling of frequency. Improved roll-off can be achieved by using operational amplifiers as 'active filters'. Each operational amplifier acts as a double-pole filter, so roll-off is twice as fast as for passive filters. For sharper cut-offs, active filters stages can be combined giving two poles for each stage. Various filter implementations can be produced such as Butterworth, Chebyshev, Bessel, and elliptical filters – see the texts in the 'Further reading' section later for more details.

General amplification issues

Although there are many different configurations for operational amplifier circuits, some general issues are common to all.

- *Saturation:* the high and low voltage supplies to an operational amplifier are called the 'supply rails'. Most operational amplifiers cannot respond to input voltages close to their supply rails and cannot drive their outputs near to the supply rails. This leads to saturation, or reduced output, if the inputs or outputs approach the rails. Saturation can be a difficult problem to detect, particularly if there is a chain of several amplifiers; saturation

57

and signal distortion may occur in one of the amplifiers in the chain, while the output signal remains within the final operational amp's specified range. To guard against saturation the outputs of each operational amplifier should be individually checked and gains reduced if necessary. If signals close to the rails are likely to be encountered then operational amplifiers with 'rail-to-rail' inputs or outputs should be used.

- *Frequency response:* the 'open loop' gain of all operational amplifiers reduces with increasing frequency. Some operational amplifiers may not have sufficient gain to accurately amplify high-frequency signals. The 'gain-bandwidth product' – the gain multiplied by the frequency – will indicate if an operational amplifier is suitable for a particular frequency range. A related parameter is slew-rate, which is the fastest rate the output voltage of an operational amplifier can change; this may limit fidelity for large, rapidly changing signals. Frequency response and slew-rate are usually worse for lower-power operational amplifiers, so higher power-consumption must sometimes be 'traded-off' for improved frequency response.
- *Input impedance:* the input impedance of most operational amplifiers is high, usually a few million ohms. However, some sensors (such as piezo crystals) have very high output impedances and require larger amplifier input impedances to avoid distortion. In this case, field-effect transistor input operational amplifiers having input impedances of $10^{12}\Omega$ should be used.

There are very many different models of operational amplifier available. Selection of the most appropriate device depends on

factors such as power consumption, power-supply voltage range, input and output voltage range, frequency response, noise performance, input impedance, and output impedance, and will depend on the circuit design chosen and how stringent are the requirements. A detailed discussion of operational amplifiers and their many uses is beyond the scope of this entry; the interested reader is directed to the texts in 'Further reading' and manufacturers' data sheets for specific devices.

See also: computer interfacing; electronics; noise removal

Further reading

Horowitz, P. and Hill, W. (1989) *The Art of Electronics*, Cambridge: Cambridge University Press.

Lancaster, D. (1996) *Active-filter Cookbook*, London: Butterworth-Heinemann.

BEN HELLER

ANABOLIC AGENTS

Anabolic agents are a class of compounds that encompass **anabolic-androgenic steroids** (AAS) and partitioning agents, such as clenbuterol. AAS have been proven to increase lean muscle mass, i.e. anabolism, and are a classic ergogenic drug and include testosterone or its synthetic derivatives. AAS, when taken in supraphysiologic doses and combined with a high-protein diet and weight training, demonstrate increases in strength and muscle mass. Although AAS do increase lean body mass, they have not been proven to be effective in improving actual athletic performance. However, this has not deterred athletes from using them.

Owing to the fact that some AAS are naturally produced in humans, AAS can be classified as either exogenous or endogenous. Exogenous AAS refer to substances that are not naturally produced in humans. There are at least thirty known AAS in this group that range from androstadienone to trenbolone. Because these are exogenous compounds, the presence of any level on drug testing is usually presumptive of a positive test.

Endogenous AAS are substances that can potentially be produced by the body and examples include **nutritional supplements** such as androstenediol, androstenedione and dehydroepiandrosterone (DHEA), as well as testosterone and dihydrotestosterone (DHT). **Anabolic-androgenic steroid testing** for these endogenous compounds is complicated by the fact that these can occur naturally and makes interpretation difficult. **Nandrolone** is a special case in that low levels of 19-norandrosterone can occur naturally, and levels of $2\,ng\,ml^{-1}$ and $5\,ng\,ml^{-1}$, respectively for men and women are established as cut-off levels.

Clenbuterol is included under anabolic agents and is a **beta-2 receptor agonist** that is considered a partitioning agent. Most of the data on clenbuterol is derived from livestock and lab animal studies. Livestock research demonstrated that animals fed clenbuterol increased their muscle mass while decreasing fat composition. Furthermore, denervated rat hindlimbs exhibited attenuation in muscle loss following treatment with clenbuterol and decreased bone loss. The mechanism responsible for this is likely the ability of catecholamines to reduce amino acid loss from muscle. This is probably mediated through beta-receptors. One human study did give clenbuterol to patients undergoing a meniscectomy and found that the clenbuterol subjects regained strength more quickly. Although studies in athletes do not exist, it is expected that clenbuterol would have to be given orally in high doses, rather than inhaled, in order to have repartitioning effects. The major limiting factor in that case would be the significant beta-2 effects that include tachycardia, anxiety, muscle tremor and peripheral vasodilatation. There is also some evidence that cardiac function may decline

with chronic administration of clenbuterol. Clenbuterol is banned by the IOC and most sports organizations, and readily detectable in urine.

The last drug listed as an anabolic agent is zeranol, a non-steroidal estrogen analog. As with clenbuterol, zeronal has been used as an anabolic compound in livestock. There are no studies of zeronal and exercise in either animals or humans. What has been established is that zeronal is a mycotoxin and can cause significant hepatotoxicity. Rat studies reveal extensive hepatic injury, but those effects are blocked by the co-administration of tamoxifen. Zeronal can be detected through urine testing for anabolic agents.

Anabolic agents are among the most desired effects by athletes attempting to increase strength. The fact that many of these have only been used in veterinary settings is unlikely to deter their use, despite potential adverse effects. It is probable that additional AAS will emerge, along with newer compounds purporting to increase strength.

Reference

Olympic Movement Anti-Doping Code, Prohibited Classes of Substances and Prohibited Methods (2003) http://www.wada-ama.org/docs/web/research_science/prohibited_substances/Prohibited%20Classes%20of%20Substances%20and%20Prohibited%20Methods%202003.pdf

GARY GREEN

ANABOLIC-ANDROGENIC STEROID TESTING

Anabolic-androgenic steroids (AAS) represent an area of great concern in sports due to their ability to enhance strength and influence the integrity of athletics. As such, testing for AAS has been an integral part of doping control since the 1970s. The introduction of gas chromatography-mass spectrometry (GC-MS) in doping control in the 1980s heralded a new era and was illustrated by the walk-out of several United States weightlifters in the 1983 Pan American Games to avoid testing positive. Improved testing for AAS, along with out-of-competition testing, has helped deter the use of these ergogenic aids.

GC-MS testing involves separating the components of a mixture based on chromatographic retention time and fragmenting each component to its characteristic ions. The retention time and fragmentation pattern is then matched against those of reference standards. The assay process involves enzymatic hydrolysis and solid phase extraction from the urine in order to prepare the steroids for the analysis. The extract is then derivatized using a trimethylsilyl ether forming reagent before being analyzed by GC-MS. Derivatization protects the more polar groups and increases the molecular weight. This has the effect of assisting the fragmentation process and augmenting the amenability to GC-MS. A GC-MS can be operated in either the full scan or the more sensitive ion monitoring (SIM) mode. Typically, steroid screening tests are conducted in the SIM mode. If a banned drug is detected, a confirmation test must be employed for definitive identification. The more specific full scan mode is utilized for confirmation when the concentration of an AAS is high.

There are two types of AAS that are identified by drug testing: exogenous (xenobiotic) or endogenous compounds. In the early 1990s about two thirds of the positive steroid tests reported by IOC labs were for xenobiotic compounds. Identification is achieved by matching the relative retention times and mass spectra of the parent drug and/or metabolites with those of known reference standards. The finding of metabolites confirms that the AAS in question had been in fact ingested by the individual. The introduction of high resolution mass spectrometry (HRMS) in doping control has extended the period of detectability of exogenous AAS due to the instrument's greater sensitivity. It is not unusual for **nandrolone** decanoate to be detectable for up to a full year after an intramuscular injection.

The recent finding of norbolethone illustrates the ability of GC-MS to detect xenobiotic AAS. Norbolethone is an AAS that was synthesized in 1966, but not marketed and had never been reported in athletic drug testing. In 2002, Catlin et al. discovered unusual compounds in the urine of an athlete; the mass spectra and chromatographic retention times matched those of norbolethone and a likely metabolite. In 2003 a new chemical entity called tetrahydragestrinone (THG) was uncovered through the efforts of law enforcement, anti-doping agencies and an Olympic laboratory as part of a sophisticated scheme to develop an undetectable AAS. These cases illustrate both the means that athletes employ to use AAS and avoid testing, as well as the ability of current technology to detect new AAS.

As testing for xenobiotic AAS improved, athletes predictably utilized endogenous compounds, e.g. testosterone, as an ergogenic aid. Testosterone is problematic because pharmaceutical and endogenous testosterone both have identical patterns on mass spectrometry and are therefore indistinguishable. Since 1982, the accepted approach has been to monitor the testosterone/epitestosterone ratio (T/E) which normally exists in approximately a 1:1 ratio. The use of testosterone or compounds that increase testosterone (i.e. DHEA, androstenedione, androstendiol, etc.) will raise urinary testosterone proportionally much more than epitestosterone. A level greater than 6:1 is considered an indication of testosterone use. In order to prevent athletes from taking epitestosterone with testosterone to maintain a normal T/E, epitestosterone is quantified and concentrations above 200 nanograms/mL result in a positive test.

The T/E ratio has limitations, however, in that there are a small percentage of individuals who are naturally in the 6–10:1 range, despite not using testosterone or related compounds. Several options exist in these individuals to determine whether or not they are misusing testosterone. The most common method is to perform serial, unannounced drug tests and compare the results. T/E is normally very consistent and a marked drop in T/E would be suggestive of previous use. This test has the disadvantage of requiring a great deal of time and expense and still can be subverted by an athlete carefully monitoring his or her T/E. A more invasive procedure is the ketoconazole challenge in which the drug ketoconazole is orally administered and the T/E measured. Normal males will react with testosterone suppression and a reduced T/E in response to ketoconazole, whereas T/E increases in the face of exogenous testosterone administration. In fact this test is rarely employed. The best solution is likely to be **carbon isotope ratio testing**, which should be able to resolve these cases efficiently and offers a solution for endogenous AAS. Carbon isotope testing can differentiate exogenous epitestosterone from that which is naturally occurring.

AAS have been a part of athletics for the past fifty years, and testing for these compounds has helped deter their use. Significant challenges still exist, especially with respect to designer AAS, prohormone supplements and endogenous compounds. Further, since AAS confer little advantage at the time of competition, unannounced, out-of-competition testing is essential to reduce use at the time that athletes are most likely to utilize these drugs.

References

Catlin, D.H., Ahrens, B. and Kucherova, Y. (2002) 'Detection of Norbolethone, an Anabolic Steroid Never Marketed, in Athletes' Urine', *Rapid Communications in Mass Spectrometry* 16: 1273–5.

Catlin, D.H., Hatton, C.K. and Starcevic, S.H. (1997) 'Issues in Detecting Abuse of Xenobiotic Anabolic Steroids and Testosterone by Analysis of Athlete's Urine', *Clinical Chemistry* 43, 7: 1280–8.

Saugy, M., Cardis, C., Robinson, N. and Schweizer, C. (2000) 'Test Methods: Anabolics', *Bailliere's Clinical Endocrinology and Metabolism* 14, 1: 111–33.

GARY GREEN

ANABOLIC-ANDROGENIC STEROIDS

Anabolic-androgenic steroids (AAS) are a classic ergogenic drug in that they are not used for recreational purposes and have almost no therapeutic indications in athletes. In sport they are used almost exclusively to gain a competitive advantage. Although often referred to as 'steroids' or 'anabolic steroids', they should properly be referred to as 'anabolic-androgenic steroids' because they are testosterone or testosterone-like synthetic drugs that result in both anabolic (increased protein synthesis) and androgenic (development of male secondary sexual characteristics) effects. However, AAS have effects that are considered neither anabolic nor androgenic and account for some of their adverse consequences. Although athletes use AAS for their anabolic results, all AAS have varying amount of androgenicity that are responsible for most of their adverse reactions. *In vitro* it is possible to demonstrate AAS that are pure anabolic, but in practice all AAS have both anabolic and androgenic properties.

The history of AAS in sport is somewhat murky. There are oft repeated (but undocumented) reports of German soldiers being given testosterone in World War II and of AAS making their way to Russian athletes in the 1950s. It does appear that by the 1960s, field athletes, body builders and American football players were well into using AAS. Due to the secretive nature and penalties for its use, the prevalence of AAS in sports has been difficult to ascertain. Survey questionnaires of bodybuilders rate the prevalence approximately 50 per cent, while NCAA surveys of American collegians typically report 1–2 per cent use across all male and female sports. Drug testing underestimates use because testing is often of the announced variety and conducted at competition.

The history of AAS also reflects the progress of **drug testing.** Athletes used synthetic AAS until gas chromatography-mass spectrometry was introduced to **anabolic-androgenic steroid testing** and proved adept at their detection. This led to athletes using shorter-acting AAS and testosterone formulations, although the development of the testosterone/epitestosterone ratio somewhat curtailed the use of the latter. In recent years athletes have synthesized previously unknown AAS, such as norbolethone and tetrahyragestrinone, in order to circumvent testing. Norbolethone was an AAS that was discovered in the 1960s but never marketed, was detected in the urine of an athlete in 2002, and demonstrates the lengths to which that athletes will go to use AAS.

Although athletes have used high doses of AAS for many years, scientific studies did not document their efficacy until Bhasin's landmark publication in 1996 using 600 mg of testosterone. The mechanism of action of AAS has been the subject of some controversy, but it appears that many of the effects are mediated through an androgen receptor. At the cellular level, cytoplasmic proteins transport AAS to the nucleus and activate RNA polymerase that produces messenger RNA and ultimately protein synthesis. It is clear that AAS increase muscle fiber diameter and activate satellite cells. Biopsies have demonstrated structural changes in the myosin heavy-chain isoforms that further supports direct effects on contractile protein formation. It is likely that these are all mediated through the androgen receptors.

In addition to these mechanisms, there are additional AAS effects that may contribute to efficacy in athletes. Many have attributed AAS strength gains to increases in aggressiveness that promotes intensity in both training and competition. Although there are androgen receptors in brain tissue, their activity and role are unclear. It has also been suggested that AAS have anti-catabolic functions that attenuate the actions of cortisol through glucocorticoid receptor saturation (see **glucocorticosteroids**) by AAS.

There are legitimate therapeutic uses for AAS, with the majority of prescriptions being written for hypogonadal states. The 1990 United States Anabolic Steroids Control Act classified AAS as a Schedule III drug and limited the therapeutic indications. The predominant therapeutic AAS for hypogonadism is testosterone, which is available as intramuscular, dermal patch and gel, and buccal preparations. It is not absorbed orally. Additionally indications for AAS are HIV-associated wasting states, refractory anemias, hereditary angioedema, growth delay, osteoporosis and certain breast carcinomas. Some AAS, such as methyl-19-nortestosterone, have been studied as a potential male contraceptive.

Use of AAS can affect a multitude of bodily systems; however, adverse event reports must be interpreted with caution because they are mainly drawn from patients taking physiologic replacement doses of AAS. These studies do not begin to approximate the doses used by athletes, which may be 10–40 times the therapeutic dose and in multiple combinations. One of the most consistent findings with AAS is in the cardiovascular system, where a dramatic drop in HDL-cholesterol is observed, even with the relatively weak prohormone nutritional supplements like androstenedione. In addition, AAS cause increases in total cholesterol, LDL-cholesterol and blood pressure, making them atherogenic. Indeed, there have been case reports of myocardial infarctions and cerebrovascular events in young bodybuilders using large doses of AAS.

The liver is the part of the gastrointestinal system most affected by AAS, especially oral 17-alpha-alkylated AAS that undergo hepatic first-pass metabolism. Transaminitis is observed frequently, in addition to more severe hepatic dysfunction. AAS can also result in peliosis hepatits and hepatocellular carcinoma. The secret records of the state-sponsored German Democratic Republic doping program revealed three deaths attributable to liver failure.

There are many reports of psychological effects with AAS, but these may reflect underlying psychological problems. However, it can be safely concluded that AAS can exacerbate pre-existing psychiatric diseases such as bi-polar disorders and schizophrenia. AAS users have also been shown to abuse other drugs and the interaction may result in significant disorders. A study of depressed men demonstrated that the combination of AAS and imipramine resulted in an acute paranoid state in 80 per cent of the subjects. Finally, it has been suggested that an addiction can develop to AAS. While it is unclear whether this meets the criteria for a true addicted state, clinically it can be very difficult for AAS users to discontinue use.

Effects on the reproductive system depend on the sex of the user and the types of AAS used. In general, AAS act as weak androgens in males and cause oligorspermia, azoospermia, reduced testicular size and gynecomastia. It is also common for AAS users to develop acne and striae. The return of the normal gonadal function depends on the drug and duration of use. Although full recovery is the rule in males, 5–7 months may be required in the case of long-acting injectable AAS. Females experience the virilizing effects of AAS, including male-pattern alopecia, clitoromegaly, deepening of the voice and hirsutism. Menstrual irregularities inevitably occur, and recovery from many of these effects is very slow, if at all.

There are also many other miscellaneous effects from the use of AAS that may be idiosyncratic. There are reports of constitutional growth interruption in youths, suppression of humeral immunity, and unusual tendon ruptures, such as the iliopsoas. AAS use also carries the risk of contamination of black-market sources and blood-borne infections, i.e. hepatitis B, C and HIV, from shared needles.

Allegations of AAS use in sport have been present for at least forty years, and seem to be ingrained in athletics. Clinicians need to recognize their powerful incentive and be aware of clinical signs of use. Unfortunately, physicians have not always acted ethically with respect to AAS use. The doping program of the German Democratic Republic could not have been accomplished without physician input, and a 2001 US survey of intercollegiate athletes found that 21 per cent of AAS users obtained them from a physician. This is an alarming statistic and one that requires professional vigilance.

References

Bhasin, S., Storer, T.W., Berman, N. et al. (1996) 'The Effects of Supraphysiologic Doses of Testosterone on Muscle Size and Strength in Normal Men', New England Journal of Medicine 335: 1–7.

Catlin, D.H. (2002) 'Use and Abuse of Anabolic Steroids', in J. Leslie, J. deGroot and Larry Jameson (eds) Endocrinology: Fourth Edition, 3: 2243–56, Philadelphia PA: W. B. Saunders.

Green, G.A. and Puffer, J.C. (2002) 'Drugs and Doping in Athletes', in Mellion, M.B., Walsh, W.M., Madden, C., Putukian, M. and Shelton, G.L. (eds) The Team Physician's Handbook, 3rd edn, 180–98, Philadelphia PA: Hanley and Belfus.

GARY GREEN

ANAEROBIC GLYCOLYSIS

Glycolysis is the breakdown of carbohydrates, either glycogen stored in the muscle or glucose delivered in the blood, to produce energy. The process of glycolysis involves multiple enzyme-catalyzed reactions. The enzymes for glycolysis are located in the cytoplasm of the cells. The process of glycolysis may proceed in one of two ways, anaerobic or aerobic. During anaerobic glycolysis, the carbohydrate is converted to pyruvic acid and then to lactic acid. During **aerobic glycolysis**, the carbohydrate is converted to pyruvic acid, which then enters the mitochondria for further oxidation in aerobic metabolism. Recently anaerobic glycolysis and aerobic glycolysis were termed fast and slow glycolysis, respectively. This is because the process of glycolysis itself does not depend on oxygen, making the terms 'anaerobic' and 'aerobic' impractical for use.

Fast glycolysis occurs during periods of diminished oxygen availability in the muscle cells. Lactic acid is often formed during fast glycolysis. Muscular fatigue experienced during exercise is often associated with high concentrations of lactic acid in the working tissues. As lactic acid accumulates, there is a corresponding increase in intracellular hydrogen ion concentration (pH). This is believed to inhibit the reactions of glycolysis and interfere directly with muscle excitation-contraction coupling, possibly by inhibiting calcium ion binding to the troponin protein or by interfering with cross-bridge formation between actin and myosin. Additionally, the decrease in the intracellular pH may inhibit the enzymatic activity of the cell's energy systems. The cumulative effect is a decrease in available energy and contractile force within the muscle during exercise.

Fast glycolysis produces a net two molecules of adenosine triphosphate (ATP) per molecule of glucose and a net three molecules of ATP per molecule of glycogen. Fast glycolysis is stimulated during intense muscular contractions by adenosine diphosphate (ADP), inorganic phosphate, ammonia, and a slight decrease in pH, and it is strongly stimulated by adenosine monophosphate (AMP). Fast glycolysis is inhibited by the markedly lowered pH that may be observed during periods of inadequate oxygen supply or high-intensity muscle contractions, and increased concentrations of ATP, creatine phosphate, citrate, and free fatty acids.

See also: anaerobic glycolysis – regulation and hormonal control

Further reading

Greenhaff, P.L., Nevill, M.E., Soderland, K., Bodin, K., Boobis, L.H., Williams, C. and Hultman, E. (1994) 'The Metabolic Responses of Human Type I and II Muscle Fibres During Maximal Treadmill Sprinting', *Journal of Physiology* 478: 149–55.

Spriet, L.L. (1995) 'Anaerobic Metabolism During High-intensity Exercise', in M. Hargreaves (ed.) *Exercise Metabolism*, 1–39, Champaign IL: Human Kinetics.

JEFFREY A. POTTEIGER

ANAEROBIC GLYCOLYSIS – ERGOGENIC AIDS

The liberation of phosphates from adenosine triphosphate (ATP) provides the ultimate source of fuel for exercise, but for exercise to continue beyond a few seconds, ATP must be quickly regenerated by the utilisation of other muscle energy sources. The breakdown of muscle glycogen to pyruvate and then lactate, in the absence of oxygen, provides a relatively rapid source of energy for the regeneration of ATP molecules. This energy system is quickly turned on after seconds of high-intensity exercise and makes an important contribution to higher-intensity bursts of activity that characterise team and racquet sports or occur within prolonged moderate-intensity events – for example, sprinting to the line at the end of an endurance race, breaking away from 'the pack', or climbing up a hill. However, it is most often associated with being the 'limiting' fuel system in the performance of high-intensity events lasting 2–8 min – for example, a 2,000 m rowing event, a 1,500 m track run, or a 400 m swimming race. The depletion of muscle glycogen stores provides a theoretical limitation to this energy system, and athletes who start events reliant on anaerobic glycolysis with low glycogen stores will have a reduced capacity to perform. However, the most important limitation to this energy system usually results from the build-up of hydrogen ions (H^+) as a by-product of such metabolism. This causes a change to the hydrogen ion concentration (pH) of the muscle cell environment, and is believed to impair cell function through mechanisms such as interference with the activity of key enzymes. Therefore, the most effective ergogenic aids for enhancing the capacity of the anaerobic glycolytic system are those that can 'buffer' pH or neutralise the effects of the excessive build up of hydrogen ions within the intracellular environment. This is the rationale for bicarbonate and citrate loading.

Bicarbonate and citrate loading

Athletes have undertaken 'soda loading' or 'bicarbonate loading' for over seventy years, although this ergogenic practice is banned in horse and greyhound racing. The general protocol is to consume 0.3 g of sodium bicarbonate per kilogram of body mass, around 1–2 hours before exercise. This is commonly available in the form of the household product 'bicarbonate of soda' and equates to 4–5 teaspoons of bicarbonate powder for a typical athlete. Sodium citrate is another common buffering agent, and citrate loading is typically achieved by ingesting doses of 0.3–0.5 g per kg body mass. The effect of consuming bicarbonate or citrate is to temporarily increase the pH of the blood, thus enhancing its buffering capacity. This is then thought to increase the diffusion of hydrogen ions from the muscle cell into the plasma along a concentration gradient, helping to stabilise the intracellular environment. Bicarbonate and citrate loading are not considered to pose

any major health risk to humans, although some individuals suffer gastrointestinal distress such as cramping or diarrhoea. Consuming the sodium bicarbonate or citrate dose with plenty of water, for example a litre or more, may help to prevent hyperosmotic diarrhoea. In the 24–48 h after loading, the body eventually excretes excess bicarbonate and citrate to return the plasma to its normal pH.

There have been many studies of the effect of bicarbonate and citrate loading on athletic or exercise performance in humans. These have involved different doses of bicarbonate or citrate, different types of participants ranging from untrained individuals to highly trained athletes, and different exercise protocols ranging from single efforts of 30 s to 5–7 min of near maximal intensity to repeated intervals of 1 min with short rest times in between. A meta-analysis which allowed the results of many of studies to be pooled (Matson and Tran 1993) concluded that the ingestion of sodium bicarbonate has a moderately positive effect on exercise performance, with a weighted effect size of 0.44 – meaning that the performance of the bicarbonate trial was, on average, 0.44 standard deviations better than the placebo trial. Overall, only a weak relationship was reported between the increased blood alkalinity – increase in pH and bicarbonate – attained in the bicarbonate trial and the benefit to performance or exercise capacity. However, ergogenic effects were related to the extent of metabolic acidosis achieved during the exercise, suggesting a threshold for the pH gradient achieved within cell membrane, arising from the combination of the accumulation of intracellular H^+ and the extracellular alkalosis.

Significant variability in the results between and within studies suggests individual responses to bicarbonate and citrate ingestion, and that the effect on performance is more complex than the simple mechanisms suggested previously. It has been suggested that elite athletes or individuals who have undertaken specific anaerobic training might show less response to bicarbonate or citrate loading than untrained or recreationally active individuals, because they are endowed with better intrinsic buffering capacity. It is also hypothesised that the performance of prolonged high-intensity exercise might be impaired if bicarbonate or citrate supplementation leads to increased rates of glycogen utilisation and earlier depletion of this important fuel. However, the few studies that have examined bicarbonate or citrate loading using sports-specific protocols and well-trained individuals fail to support these theories. Some, but not all, studies using well trained athletes have found performance improvements after bicarbonate or citrate loading before brief, 1–10 min, or prolonged, 30–60 min, events involving high-intensity exercise.

The use of bicarbonate and citrate loading in real-life competition may be complicated by the fact that many of the events in which it could theoretically enhance performance involve heats and finals – and therefore more than one performance by the athlete over 1–2 days. Whether multiple loading strategies are still effective, require the same dose, or increase the likelihood of side-effects has yet to be adequately explored. Until further research can clarify the range of exercise activities that might benefit from bicarbonate or citrate loading, individual athletes are advised to experiment in training and minor competitions to judge their own case.

See also: adenosine triphosphate/phosphocreatine – ergogenic aids; aerobic glycolysis – ergogenic aids; lipolysis – ergogenic aids

References

Matson, L.G. and Tran, Z.T. (1993) 'Effects of Sodium Bicarbonate Ingestion on Anaerobic Performance: A Meta-Analytic Review', *International Journal of Sports Nutrition* 3: 2–28.

Further reading

Heigenhauser, G.F.J. and Jones, N.J. (1991) 'Bicarbonate Loading', in D.R. Lamb and M.H. Williams (eds) *Perspectives in Exercise Science and Sports Medicine, Volume 4: Ergogenics*, 183–212, Carmel IN: Cooper.

McNaughton, L.R. (2000) 'Bicarbonate and Citrate', in R.J. Maughan (ed.) *Nutrition in Sport*, 379–92, Oxford: Blackwell Science.

LOUISE M. BURKE

ANAEROBIC GLYCOLYSIS – REGULATION AND HORMONAL CONTROL

Anaerobic glycolysis provides the greatest source of adenosine triphosphate (ATP) during high-intensity physical activity. As much as 80 per cent of the total ATP production during high-intensity exercise may be derived from anaerobic glycolysis. During high intensity activity, anaerobic glycolysis is quickly activated and provides ATP at a rate that is considerably greater than aerobic metabolism. Research into the control and regulation of anaerobic glycolysis has focused on the enzymes glycogen phosphorylase and phosphofructokinase, substrate availability, and the influence of various hormones.

The enzyme glycogen phosphorylase catalyzes a non-equilibrium reaction that regulates the breakdown of muscle glycogen. The enzyme interconverts between less active and more active forms that cleave glycosyl units from muscle glycogen. During rest and low physical activity, glycogen phosphorylase exists primarily in the inactive *b* form. The activity of the *b* form can be increased by the compounds adenosine monophosphate (AMP) and inosine monophosphate (IMP) or inhibited by the compounds ATP and glucose 6-phosphate. In response to muscle contraction or stimulation by epinephrine, the inactive *b* form is phosphorylated by phosphorylase kinase to produce the active phosphorylase *a* form. In response to the hormone insulin, the enzyme glycogen phosphatase removes a phosphate from the active *a* form. During exercise and increased physical activity, the activity of glycogen phosphorylase is increased. The increase in cytosolic calcium during the process of excitation-contraction coupling activates phosphorylase kinase and, thereby, stimulates the conversion of phosphorylase *b* – inactive – to *a* – active. Additional activation is achieved when calcium binds to troponin C, which also serves to activate phosphorylase kinase. The increased phosphorylase *a* activity is transient and can be rapidly reversed, despite continued muscle contraction. Muscle glycogen breakdown and anaerobic glycolysis can continue during high-intensity exercise despite the reversal of phosphorylase activity. This may be caused by either an increased phosphorylase *b* activity or an adequate residual phosphorylase *a* activity. Increases in the intramuscular concentrations of ADP, AMP, IMP, and inorganic phosphate, which occur during moderate-to high-intensity exercise and physical activity, are strong stimulators of phosphorylase *b*, and an increased activity of phosphorylase *b* may be sufficient for continued stimulation of muscle glycogenolysis.

Phosphofructokinase is generally considered the rate-limiting enzyme in the metabolic pathway of anaerobic glycolysis. This enzyme catalyzes the conversion of fructose 6-phosphate to fructose 1,6-bisphosphate in a non-equilibrium reaction. The most prominent mechanism for allosteric control of phosphofructokinase is through an ATP-induced inhibition; ATP binds to a catalytic site of the enzyme with high affinity and is one of the substrates of the enzyme. When the muscle is at rest and ATP concentrations are high, ATP also binds to a low-affinity allosteric site that is responsible for inhibition of phosphofructokinase; ATP binding at the allosteric site makes it more difficult for the substrate fructose 6-phosphate to bind at its catalytic site. Most modulators of phosphofructokinase

appear to function by altering ATP-binding affinity at the allosteric site. Hydrogen ions, which are an inhibitor of phosphofructokinase, enhance ATP binding at the allosteric site. Other inhibitors include citrate, 2-phosphoglycerate, 3-phosphoglycerate, phosphoenolypyruvate, and magnesium. Possible positive modulators include free AMP and ADP, inorganic phosphate, ammonia, and fructose 1,6-bisphosphate. During high-intensity physical activity, the concentrations of fructose 6-phosphate, ADP, AMP, inorganic phosphate, and fructose 1,6-bisphosphate are high. As high-intensity physical activity is continued, the concentration of ATP in the cell begins to decrease while IMP and ammonia concentrations increase. As the hydrogen ion concentration increases in the muscle fibres there should be an expected increase in the ATP-induced inhibition. Anaerobic glycolysis continues, however, as the combination of decreasing ATP concentration, increased fructose 6-phosphate concentration, and increasing concentrations of ADP, AMP, inorganic phosphate, ammonia, and fructose 1,6-bisphosphate serve to stimulate phosphofructokinase.

Blood glucose and muscle glycogen are the substrates for anaerobic glycolysis. An increase in blood glucose concentration results in an increase in blood insulin concentration. The combined effect is to stimulate glucose uptake into the cells of the body. In skeletal muscle, the primary glucose transport protein is glucose transport protein-4. Once glucose enters the muscle cell an irreversible phosphorylation reaction occurs and this effectively traps the glucose in the sarcoplasm as glucose 6-phosphate. Hexokinase catalyzes this non-equilibrium reaction. The rate of glucose uptake can be regulated by hexokinase, and this reaction can control the rate of glucose flux through anaerobic glycolysis. Hexokinase activity is increased by high concentrations of glucose and inhibited by elevated concentrations of ATP and glucose 6-phosphate. A decreased blood glucose concentration can either increase the reliance on muscle glycogen as a fuel source for anaerobic glycolysis or result in a decrease in the rate of anaerobic glycolysis. Glucose uptake increases in proportion to the intensity of muscle contraction. At low-to moderate-intensity exercise the increased glucose uptake is followed by an increase in glucose utilization. At higher intensities of exercise there is an increase in the muscle glucose concentration, which is suggestive of an inhibition of glucose phosphorylation and glucose utilization. Muscle glycogen is the other substrate for anaerobic glycolysis. Evidence exists that the muscle glycogen concentration can influence glycogen phosphorylase activity and, thereby, can affect the rate of anaerobic glycolysis in contracting skeletal muscle. As glycogen binds to glycogen phosphorylase, it increases the activity of the enzyme. Many research studies, but not all, indicate that the rate of muscle glycogen breakdown is directly related to the pre-exercise muscle glycogen concentration. Increases in pre-exercise muscle glycogen typically result in enhanced muscle glycogen utilization during subsequent exercise.

The hormone epinephrine plays an important role in the regulation of anaerobic glycolysis. Epinephrine increases the activity of phosphorylase through cyclic AMP mediated activation of phosphorylase kinase and, subsequently, an increase in phosphorylase *a* activity. These enzymatic changes result in an increase in muscle glycogen breakdown. The effects of epinephrine on muscle glycogenolysis are believed to be mediated by beta-adrenergic receptors. Insulin can also affect the rate of anaerobic glycolysis by increasing glucose uptake in the muscle cell. The effects of increasing insulin concentration and muscle contraction on glucose uptake are additive, suggesting that insulin and exercise increase glucose transport through different mechanisms. Thus, insulin does not appear to be an essential requirement for increasing glucose

uptake and enhancing anaerobic glycolysis during exercise. Other hormones such as cortisol can play a minor role in the regulation of anaerobic glycolysis by indirectly increasing blood glucose concentration. Cortisol is a strong stimulator of tissue catabolism. This process could supply additional substrate for an increase in blood glucose concentration through gluconeogenesis in the liver.

Anaerobic glycolysis provides ATP for contracting skeletal muscle during high-intensity exercise. Anaerobic glycolysis can be regulated by the enzymes glycogen phosphorylase and phosphofructokinase, the concentration of blood glucose and availability of muscle glycogen, and the hormone epinephrine. The increase in anaerobic glycolysis during exercise is tightly regulated so that ATP production matches ATP utilization.

See also: anaerobic glycolysis – response to exercise; anaerobic glycolysis – response to training; carbohydrate metabolism; carbohydrates; glycogenolysis

Further reading

Dawson, B., Fitzsimmons, M., Green, S., Goodman, C., Carey, M. and Cole, K. (1998) 'Changes in Performance, Muscle Metabolites, Enzymes and Fibre Types after Short Sprint Training', *European Journal of Applied Physiology* 78: 163–9.

Spriet, L.L. (1995) 'Anaerobic Metabolism During High-intensity Exercise', in M. Hargreaves (ed.) *Exercise Metabolism*, 1–39, Champaign IL: Human Kinetics.

Turner, M.J., Howley, E.T., Tanaka, H., Ashraf, M., Bassett, D.R. and Keefer, D.J. (1995) The Effect of Graded Epinephrine Infusion on Blood Lactate Response to Exercise, *Journal of Applied Physiology* 79: 1206–11.

JEFFREY A. POTTEIGER

ANAEROBIC GLYCOLYSIS – RESPONSE TO EXERCISE

During the initiation of exercise and during moderate-to high-intensity exercise, considerable energy is produced from anaerobic glycolysis. The contribution of anaerobic glycolysis to energy production, while difficult to measure accurately in the contracting muscle, is believed to be dependent on several factors, including the intensity and duration of the exercise, the training status of the individual, and the skeletal muscle fibre type activated during exercise.

During the initiation of exercise, there is an increase in the breakdown of muscle adenosine triphosphate (ATP). This decrease, combined with increases in other modulators, serves to increase anaerobic glycolysis. With the start of intense exercise, there is an immediate increase in muscle glycogen utilization and blood glucose uptake. During near maximal, maximal, and supramaximal exercise, the predominant fuel for skeletal muscle contraction in muscle glycogen. As exercise intensity is decreased there is an increased uptake of blood glucose by the contracting muscle. The enzymes glycogen phosphorylase, hexokinase, and phosphofructokinase catalyze reactions that help regulate energy production from anaerobic glycolysis. Glycogen phosphorylase cleaves glycosyl units from muscle glycogen to be used in anaerobic glycolysis. In response to muscle contraction, the activity of glycogen phosphorylase is increased. During the process of excitation-contraction coupling there is an increased release of calcium from the sarcoplasmic reticulum in active skeletal muscle. This calcium serves to stimulate the binding of actin and myosin proteins and increase glycogen phosphorylase activity. Additional increases in the intramuscular concentrations of adenosine diphosphate (ADP), adenosine and inosine monophosphates (AMP, IMP), and inorganic phosphate, which occur during high-intensity exercise, may also increase glycogen phosphorylase activity. Hexokinase is the enzyme that works in conjunction with the glucose transport proteins to assist the muscle fibre

with glucose uptake from the blood. The activity of this enzyme is increased in response to muscle contraction and an increase in the rate of anaerobic glycolysis. Phosphofructokinase is generally considered the rate-limiting enzyme in anaerobic glycolysis. This enzyme catalyzes the conversion of fructose 6-phosphate to fructose 1,6-bisphosphate. The most prominent mechanism for allosteric control of phosphofructokinase is through an ATP-induced inhibition. When skeletal muscle is at rest and ATP concentrations are high, ATP is responsible for inhibition of phosphofructokinase. During the initiation of physical activity, the concentrations of fructose 6-phosphate, ADP, AMP, inorganic phosphate, and fructose 1,6-bisphosphate increase. As physical activity is continued or as the intensity of exercise is increased, the concentration of ATP in the cell begins to decrease while the IMP and ammonia concentrations increase. Anaerobic glycolysis continues as the combination of decreasing ATP concentration, increased fructose 6-phosphate concentration, and increasing concentrations of ADP, AMP, inorganic phosphate, ammonia, and fructose 1,6-bisphosphate serve to stimulate phosphofructokinase.

During the initial 10 s of high-intensity exercise, anaerobic glycolysis is estimated to provide approximately 44 per cent of the total ATP production. As high-intensity exercise continues to 30 s duration, the ATP provision from anaerobic glycolysis increases to approximately 49–56 per cent. As high-intensity exercise duration is increased to 90 s, anaerobic glycolysis is estimated to contribute approximately 36–54 per cent of the ATP to muscle contraction. It is evident that as the exercise duration increases, the percentage of total energy that is provided by anaerobic glycolysis decreases. This is probably due to several factors, including an increase in the metabolic waste products – primarily lactic acid – associated with anaerobic glycolysis contributing to a decrease in force-generating capacity within the muscle, and an increase in the delivery of oxygen to the working tissues by the cardiovascular system, thereby increasing the contribution of aerobic metabolism to energy production.

The training status of an individual can also influence the contribution of anaerobic glycolysis to ATP production during exercise and physical activity. During the initiation of low-to-moderate-intensity exercise, untrained individuals rely more on anaerobic glycolysis to supply ATP for muscle contraction than do trained individuals working at the same relative exercise intensity. This is probably caused by an inability of the pulmonary and cardiovascular systems in untrained individuals to deliver oxygen to contracting skeletal muscle, thereby causing a greater reliance on anaerobic glycolysis. Trained individuals have the capability to meet the needs of aerobic metabolism at the initiation of exercise because the pulmonary and cardiovascular systems of trained individuals have a greater capacity to deliver oxygen to the working tissues. At exercise intensities considered high to maximal, trained individuals produce more ATP through anaerobic glycolysis than untrained individuals. The benefits of being trained are probably apparent through increases in muscle glycogen concentration, greater activity of glycogen phosphorylase and phosphofructokinase, and increases in muscle glucose uptake from the blood.

Muscle fibre type may also influence how energy is derived from anaerobic glycolysis. Investigations using single muscle fibre preparations have allowed for the determination of how different fibre types influence energy production from all metabolic pathways. Data from these investigations have provided important insight into energy production from anaerobic glycolysis in contracting skeletal muscle. Resting muscle glycogen concentration has been shown to be significantly higher in type II fibres compared to type I fibres. This

would lead to a greater capacity for energy production from anaerobic glycolysis in type II compared to type I fibres. Additionally, higher rates of muscle glycogenolysis have been observed in type II fibres than in type I fibres. Research has indicated that glycogenolysis in type II fibres may be between six and thirty-five times greater than that observed in type I fibres. During high-intensity exercise, glycogenolysis in type I fibres has been shown to be approximately 60 per cent of the rate for type II fibres. It has been clearly demonstrated that the existing fibre type in muscle may play a critical role in the capacity of that muscle to produce energy from anaerobic glycolysis.

Finally, the carbohydrate status of the individual may affect the rate of energy production from anaerobic glycolysis. Elevated pre-exercise concentrations of muscle glycogen have been shown to increase the energy produced from anaerobic glycolysis at the initiation of exercise. Conversely, as muscle glycogen and blood glucose concentrations decrease, in response to poor nutrition or prior exercise, the ability of anaerobic glycolysis to produce energy to support muscle contraction decreases. This is particularly true at exercise intensities near maximal.

See also: aerobic glycolysis – response to exercise; anaerobic glycolysis – regulation and hormonal control; anaerobic glycolysis – response to training; carbohydrates

Further reading

Bogdanis, G.C., Nevill, M.E., Lakomy, H.K.A. and Boobis, L.H. (1998) 'Power Output and Muscle Metabolism During and Following Recovery From 10 and 20 s of Maximal Sprint Exercise in Humans', *Acta Physiologica Scandinavica* 163: 261–72.

Esbjornsson-Liljedahl, M., Sundber, C.J., Norman, B. and Jansson, E. (1999) 'Metabolic Response in Type I and II Muscle Fibres During a 30 s Cycle Sprint in Men and Women', *Journal of Applied Physiology* 87: 1326–32.

Hogan, M.C., Gladden, L.B., Grassi, B., Stary, C.M. and Samja, M. (1998) 'Bioenergetics of Contracting Skeletal Muscle After Partial Reduction of Blood Flow', *Journal of Applied Physiology* 84: 1882–8.

Spriet, L.L. (1995) 'Anaerobic Metabolism During High-intensity Exercise', in M. Hargreaves (ed.) *Exercise Metabolism*, 1–39, Champaign IL: Human Kinetics.

Ward-Smith, A.J. (1999) 'Aerobic and Anaerobic Energy Cconversion During High-intensity Exercise', *Medicine and Science in Sports and Exercise* 31: 1855–60.

JEFFREY A. POTTEIGER

ANAEROBIC GLYCOLYSIS – RESPONSE TO TRAINING

The two primary modes of exercise training are aerobic and anaerobic. Aerobic training involves repetitive, submaximal-intensity muscular contractions performed for durations longer than 2–3 min. Anaerobic training typically involves performing maximal-intensity muscular contractions for short durations generally less than 2 min. While there are many studies of the effects of aerobic training on physiological function, there are far fewer investigations of the effects of anaerobic training on physiological function and performance. This is due in part to the difficulty in performing various measures of physiological function at the level of the intact muscle fibre. In general, invasive measures, such as muscle biopsies, must be made to assess changes in those factors that may influence anaerobic glycolysis. Measures of enzyme activity within the pathway of anaerobic glycolysis are performed before and after training using muscle homogenates. This process is typically used to assess the effectiveness of training on energy production from anaerobic glycolysis.

The adaptations resulting from training begin with the first training session, and are specific to the training stimuli and the genetic potential of each individual. The **principles of training**, including intensity, frequency, duration, and specificity, will impact the specific physiological adaptations that occur. Variations of the training programme principles will dictate the responses that occur in anaerobic glycolysis. The limits of an individual's genetic potential will also establish how much change will occur in the systems of the body in response to the training programme. As individuals become more trained, alterations in the training principles will have to be made to ensure further adaptation. Further, as an individual reaches his or her genetic potential, the physiological responses will become smaller. It must also be remembered that each person responds differently to individual training programmes.

Anaerobic glycolysis is used mostly during very high-to-moderately high-intensity work with a duration of 10–120 s or during steady state exercise at 75–90 per cent of maximal aerobic power. Improvements in the ability to produce energy through anaerobic glycolysis are typically achieved through high-intensity anaerobic training. This is particularly true for training protocols and sports that dramatically disrupt acid–base balance through high concentrations of lactic acid. This would include sports or activities that are performed at near maximal effort for durations of 2 min or less. One of the most profound training responses to high-intensity training is an increased ability to tolerate high acid conditions in the tissues of the body. Generally, about 6–8 weeks of training is required to increase the body's buffer systems allowing for a better maintenance of acid–base balance.

When examining the effects of training on anaerobic glycolysis, it is important to identify the substrate used and the end product produced, as these factors will be influenced by the type of training performed. Anaerobic glycolysis can use either circulating blood glucose or stored muscle glycogen as a substrate. The primary end product from anaerobic glycolysis is lactic acid. Anaerobic training can have an influence on substrate utilisation by increasing the availability of the substrate or by increasing the activity of the enzymes responsible for regulating substrate utilisation. High-intensity anaerobic training increases the use of muscle glycogen as an energy substrate because this type of training tends to increase intramuscular glycogen concentrations. It has been suggested that high-intensity anaerobic training will result in a small increase in the utilisation of blood glucose when the exercise is performed at intensities slightly less than maximal effort. High-intensity anaerobic training will result in an increase in the activity of the glycolytic enzymes, particularly glycogen phosphorylase and phosphofructokinase. Anaerobic training increases the concentration of these enzymes, and may also increase the sensitivity of the enzymes to the intramuscular changes in the adenosine triphosphate: adenosine diphosphate ratio (ATP:ADP). High-intensity anaerobic training may also affect the activity of the enzyme lactate dehydrogenase (LDH). This enzyme occurs in muscle in two different isozyme forms, LDH heart type (LDH_h) and LDH muscle type (LDH_m). The enzyme kinetics of LDH_h promote the conversion of lactic acid to pyruvic acid, while the enzyme kinetics of LDH_m promote the conversion of pyruvic acid to lactic acid. There is actually a continuum of isozymes so that the following subtypes can be identified: LDH_{h4}, LDH_{h3m1}, LDH_{h2m2}, LDH_{h1m3}, and LDH_{m4}. The LDH_h type is more prominent in slow twitch skeletal muscle and cardiac muscle, while the LDH_m type is more prominent in fast twitch skeletal muscle. Training appears to shift the continuum of isozymes. High-intensity anaerobic training results in an increase in the LDH_{m4} isozyme and a decrease in the LDH_h subtypes. This would result in an increased production of lactic acid but, at the same time, would increase the amount of ATP being produced from anaerobic glycolysis. Although high-intensity anaero-

bic training may increase the production of lactic acid during exercise, it will probably also increase the ability of the body to clear lactic acid by other less active skeletal muscle, through oxidation, and the liver, by gluconeogenesis. High-intensity anaerobic training will also increase the buffer systems of the body and thereby help the body withstand the decreases in intramuscular hydrogen ion concentration (pH). Increases in intramuscular and extramuscular buffers after training will allow for a better control of pH during high-intensity exercise.

Conversely, most traditional forms of aerobic training, at less than 75 per cent of maximal oxygen consumption, have little effect on energy production through anaerobic glycolysis. This type of training does not appear to influence significantly the concentration or activity of the enzymes glycogen phosphorylase or phosphofructokinase. Aerobic training performed at moderate to high intensity – 75–90 per cent of maximal oxygen consumption – may increase the activity of hexokinase, which would help facilitate entry of glucose into the cells. This may result in a greater utilization of blood glucose as a substrate and spare the use of muscle glycogen. Aerobic training decreases LDH_m activity in fast twitch muscle and influences the LDH isoenzyme to be more like the heart type (LDH_h). Aerobic training may also increase the ability of some muscles to take lactic acid out of the blood and utilise it as energy substrate through aerobic metabolism.

See also: aerobic glycolysis – response to training; anaerobic glycolysis – regulation and hormonal control; anaerobic glycolysis – response to exercise; carbohydrates; glycogenolysis

Further reading

Harmer, A.R., McKenna, M.J., Sutton, J.R., Snow, R.J., Ruell, P.A., Booth, J., Thompson, M.W., Mackay, N.A., Stathis, C.G.,

Cramer, R.M., Carey, M.F. and Eager, D.M. (2000) 'Skeletal Muscle Metabolic and Ionic Adaptations During Intense Exercise Following Sprint Training in Humans', *Journal of Applied Physiology* 89: 1793–1803.

Linossier, M.T., Dormios, D., Perier, C., Frey, J., Geyssant, A. and Denis, C. (1997) 'Enzyme Adaptations of Human Skeletal Muscle During Bicycle Short-Sprint Training and Detraining', *Acta Physiologica Scandinavica* 161: 439–45.

MacDougall, J.D., Hicks, A.L., MacDonald, J.R., McKelvie, R.S., Green, H.J. and Smith, K.M. (1998) 'Muscle Performance and Enzymatic Adaptations to Sprint Interval Training', *Journal of Applied Physiology* 84: 2138–42.

Spriet, L.L. (1995) 'Anaerobic Metabolism During High-intensity Exercise', in M. Hargreaves (ed.) *Exercise Metabolism*, 1–39, Champaign IL: Human Kinetics.

Tabata, I., Nishimura, K., Kouzaki, M., Hirai, Y., Ogita, F., Miyachi, M. and Yamamoto, K. (1996) 'Effects of Moderate-Intensity Endurance and High-Intensity Intermittent Training on Aerobic Capacity and VO_2max', *Medicine and Science in Sports and Exercise* 28: 1327–39.

JEFFREY A. POTTEIGER

ANATOMICAL TERMINOLOGY

When referring to movements of the body or locations of anatomical structures in the body, specific terminology is used. The cardinal planes and axes of the body are used to describe movements meaningfully and unambiguously. However, the relative locations of parts of the body with respect to the whole also need to be described unambiguously.

The relative location of a point on the axial or appendicular skeleton is indicated by the use of either proximal or distal. A point that is more proximal lies closer to the axial skeleton than one that is more distal on the extremity. For example, the elbow lies proximal to the wrist. Similarly, a point that is more cranial is closer to the head than one that is caudal to it. So, the sternum – breastbone – is cranial to the pelvis. Superior and inferior are used to describe

points that are above and below each other, respectively. For example, the thoracic spine is superior to the lumbar spine. Whether a point is on the front or the back of the body or a segment is indicated by the use of dorsal and ventral respectively, such that the pectoral – chest – muscles lie ventrally on the thorax and the trapezius muscle on the back of the neck lies dorsally. Anterior and posterior are alternative anatomical terms for the front and the back of the body, for example, the anterior and posterior regions of the deltoid muscle.

To determine on which side of a segment a point lies, medial is used to indicate a point that is closer to the midline of the body, and lateral indicates that a point is further away from the midline. For example, the medial malleolus is the bone on the inside of the ankle, closer to the midline, and the lateral malleolus is the bone on the outside of the ankle, further away from the midline. Finally, to indicate how close to the bone in the middle of a segment a point lies, the terms superficial and deep are used, such that skin is superficial to muscle.

See also: appendicular skeleton; axial skeleton – structure and function; cardinal planes and axes

Further reading

Williams, P.L., Bannister, L.H., Berry, M.M., Collins, P., Dyson, M., Dussek, J.E. and Ferguson, M.W.J. (eds) (1995) *Gray's Anatomy: the Anatomical Basis of Medicine and Surgery*, Section 1, Edinburgh: Churchill Livingstone.

CLARE E. MILNER

ANGULAR MOMENTUM – GENERATION, TRANSFER, AND TRADING

To alter the angular momentum of a sports performer requires a net external turning effect – or torque – acting on the performer. Traditionally, in sports biomechanics, three mechanisms of inducing rotation have been identified, although they are, in fact, related.

A force couple consists of a parallel force system of two equal and opposite forces (F) which are not collinear – they are a certain vector distance apart (r, see Figure 2(a)). The net translational effect of these two forces is zero and they cause only rotation. The net moment of the couple, the torque, is: $T = r \times F$. The moment, or torque, vector has a direction perpendicular to and out of the plane of this page. Its magnitude is the magnitude of one of the forces multiplied by the perpendicular distance between them ($F.r$). The torque, or moment of the force couple, can be represented as in Figure 2(b) and has the same effect about a particular axis of rotation wherever it is applied along the body. In the absence of an external axis of rotation, the body will rotate about an axis through its **centre of mass**. Someone floating in water is acted upon by a force couple of his or her weight acting downwards at the centre of mass and an equal, but opposite, buoyancy force acting upwards at the centre of buoyancy, which does not generally coincide with the centre of mass.

An eccentric force ('eccentric' means 'off-centre') is effectively any force, or the resultant of a system of forces, that is not zero and that does not act through the centre of mass of an object. This constitutes the commonest way of generating rotational motion, as in Figure 2(c). The eccentric force here can be transformed by

adding two equal and opposite forces at the centre of mass, as in Figure 2(d), which will have no net effect on the object. The two forces indicated in Figure 2(d) with an asterisk can then be considered together and constitute a force couple – anticlockwise – that can be replaced by a torque T as in Figure 2(e). This leaves a 'pure' force acting through the centre of mass. This force F causes only **linear motion**, $F = d(mv)/dt$, where v is the velocity of the centre of mass of the object of mass m, and t is time; the torque T causes only **angular motion (rotation)** ($T = dL/dt$), where L is the angular momentum of the object. The magnitude of T is $F.s$. This example could be held to justify the use of the term 'torque' for the turning effect of an eccentric force although, strictly, torque is defined as the moment of a force couple. The two terms, torque and moment, are often used interchangeably.

Checking of linear motion occurs when a body that is already moving is suddenly stopped at one point, about which it then rotates. An example is the foot plant of a javelin thrower in the delivery stride, although the representation of such a system as a quasi-rigid body is of limited use. This, as shown in Figure 2(f), is merely a special case of an eccentric force.

Transfer of angular momentum

The principle of transfer of angular momentum from segment to segment is

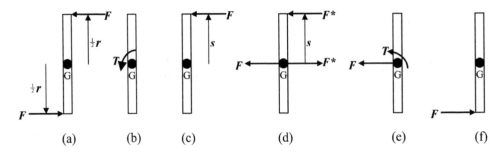

Figure 2. Generation of Angular Momentum, here.

often considered to be a basic biomechanical principle of movement. Consider a diver performing a simple piked dive. The diver can be represented by two 'gross' body segments attached in the pelvic region, about which they mutually rotate by muscular contractions evoking the torque-countertorque principle (see **laws of rotational motion**). Here, take-off is followed by contraction of the trunk and hip flexors, generating a clockwise – forward – angular momentum in the trunk and an anti-clockwise angular momentum in the legs, equal in magnitude but opposite in direction from that in the trunk. These, respectively, add to and subtract from the take-off values, so that angular momentum has been transferred from the legs, which remain more or less fixed in space, to the upper body. Thereafter, the leg and trunk extensors contract to transfer angular momentum from the trunk to the legs. During this second phase of angular momentum transfer, the orientation of the trunk in space remains fairly constant. Before water entry, the take-off angular momentum values are more or less restored. A more complex example is the long jump hitch kick technique, in which the arm and leg motions transfer angular momentum from the trunk, to prevent the jumper from rotating forwards too early.

Trading of angular momentum

This term is often used to refer to the transfer of angular momentum from one axis of rotation to another. Consider a diver or gymnast taking off with angular momentum only about the somersault – frontal – axis, to perform a twisting somersault. The diver then adducts his or her left arm – or performs some other asymmetrical body movement, such as a hip swing – by a muscular torque, which evokes an equal but opposite counter-rotation of the rest of the body to produce an angle of tilt of the

somersault axis to its original direction. No external torque has been applied so the angular momentum is still constant about the original, frontal, axis but now has a component about the twisting axis. The diver has 'traded' some somersaulting angular momentum for twisting – longitudinal – angular momentum and will now both somersault and twist. It is often argued that this method of generating twisting angular momentum is preferable to generating twist during ground contact, as it can be more easily removed by re-establishing the original body position before landing. This can avoid problems in gymnastics, trampolining, and diving caused by landing with residual twisting angular momentum. The crucial factor in generating airborne twist is to establish a tilt angle and, approximately, the twist rate is proportional to the angle of tilt. In practice, many sports performers use both the contact and the airborne mechanisms to acquire twist (see for example Yeadon 1993).

Rotational movements in airborne sports activities in diving, gymnastics, and trampolining, for example, often involve three-dimensional multi-segmental movements. The three-dimensional dynamics of even a rigid or quasi-rigid body are far from simple. For example, in two-dimensional rotation of such bodies, the angular momentum and angular velocity vectors lie on the same line – they are collinear. If a body with principal moments of inertia that are not identical – as for the sports performer – rotates about an axis that does not coincide with one of the principal axes, then the angular velocity vector and the angular momentum vectors do not coincide. The movement known as nutation can result, as in bar clearance in high jumping. Nutation also occurs, for example, when performing an airborne pirouette with asymmetrical arm positions. The body's longitudinal axis is displaced away from its original position of coincidence with the angular momentum vector – sometimes called the axis of momentum – and will describe a cone around that vector.

See also: angular motion (rotation); biomechanical principles of movement

Reference

Yeadon, M.R. (1993) 'The Biomechanics of Twisting Somersaults', *Journal of Sports Sciences* 21: 187–225.

Further reading

Yeadon, M.R. (1993) 'The Biomechanics of Twisting Somersaults', *Journal of Sports Sciences* 21: 187–225.

ROGER BARTLETT

ANGULAR MOTION (ROTATION)

As noted elsewhere in this encyclopedia, in **kinematics**, motion in sport can be linear, rotational or, more generally, a combination of both. Rotation, or angular motion, is motion in which all parts of the body travel through the same angle in the same time in the same direction about the axis of rotation. The movement of a body segment about a joint is motion of this type. An object that retains its geometrical shape, for example a cricket bat, can be studied in this manner and is known as a rigid body, the motion of which is studied through rigid body mechanics. Human body segments, such as the thigh and forearm, are often considered to be close approximations to rigid bodies. All human movement involves rotation.

The location of an object in space can be specified by its position vector, a linear vector, and its orientation, a rotational vector. The angular orientation of a body segment in two dimensions can be specified by the angular orientation of its longitudinal axis to a horizontal line drawn from its centre of mass towards the right. When an object changes its orientation, in rotational motion, the change is known as angular displace-

ment. Angular displacements are considered to be positive if they are anticlockwise when viewed from the positive direction of the axis of rotation towards the origin of the coordinate system. For angular position and displacement the SI unit is the radian (rad). However, degrees (°) are still used widely. A radian is equal to $180/\pi$ degrees, where π is approximately equal to 3.1417, so that one radian is approximately 57.3°.

Angular motion quantities are vectors, the direction of the vector being given by the right hand rule; if the fingers of the right hand are curled in the direction of rotation, the extended thumb – out to the side of the hand – points in the direction of the angular motion vector. Unlike other motion vector quantities, angular displacements do not follow the rules of composition – addition – and resolution. This, among other things, makes the specification of the angular orientation and motion of a body segment in three dimensions vastly more complex than for two-dimensional rotation or for three-dimensional linear motion. In three-dimensional analysis of the orientations of body segments, the angles between adjacent body segments can be defined by reference to coordinate systems attached to each segment, one considered to be moving relative to a fixed position of the other. The resulting Euler or Cardan angles correspond to anatomical angles. The rotational motion of the moving segment is represented by three ordered angles of rotation about its coordinate system; the rotation angles are dependent on the sequence of rotations, one of the main problems of using Euler–Cardan angles to define segment orientations.

The rate of change of angular displacement with time is known as angular velocity. The SI unit for angular velocity is rad s^{-1}. The convention for positive and negative angular velocities is similar to that for angular displacement above. The rate of change of angular velocity with time is known as angular acceleration. The convention for positive and negative angular accelerations is similar to those for angular displacement above. A positive angular acceleration vector indicates that an object has a positive angular velocity, the magnitude of which is increasing, or a negative angular velocity, the magnitude of which is decreasing. The opposite applies to a negative angular acceleration vector. The SI unit for angular acceleration is rad s^{-2}.

See also: cardinal plane movements; kinematics; linear motion; rigid body mechanics

Further reading

Bartlett, R.M. (1997) *Introduction to Sports Biomechanics*, ch. 2, London: E&FN Spon.

ROGER BARTLETT

ANGULAR MOTION SENSORS

The relationship between displacement, velocity and acceleration is given in linear motion sensors. The equivalent relationships for angular motion are from angular orientation – or position to angular velocity to angular acceleration by differentiation; the reverse way round for integration (see also **angular motion (rotation)**). The same caveats in applying these transformations apply as in the linear case: differentiation has the effect of amplifying noise and integration is susceptible to drift and uncertainty about initial conditions. Integration and differentiation may be performed electronically or in software.

Sensors to measure orientation

The combination of three independent measurements of linear position allows the orientation of an object to be calculated. However, sensors are available that measure orientation directly. The simplest is the rotary potentiometer, an electrical device that changes its resistance as a shaft rotates. Potentiometers are often used to measure the angle at human joints, such as the knee, in which case they are called electrogoniometers (see also **goniometry**). Two or three potentiometers may be combined to measure rotation in multiple planes. The centre of rotation of the potentiometers must be aligned with the centre of rotation of the object. This is particularly a problem where the centre of rotation moves during the course of a movement. The flexible goniometer, a device marketed by Biometrics Ltd, avoids this problem by summing the bend along a length of a flexible substrate giving the absolute angle between the ends of the device. The goniometer will measure the angle between the ends without requiring alignment with the centre of rotation. Where continuous rotation must be monitored, for example to measure bicycle crank position, potentiometers are not suitable as they have an electrical 'deadzone' once per revolution, for which they give no output. An alternative is to use optical shaft encoders; these devices are more expensive but give a digital output specifying shaft position over a full 360°. Optical shaft encoders can be absolute, outputting angular position, or incremental, outputting change in angular position.

Light transmitted along an optical fibre is attenuated as it bends. The transmission changes in a predictable way with angle of bend and can produce a very thin, lightweight sensor. One company, Measurand Inc., has combined several fibre-optic sensors on to a thin flexible substrate to produce a sensor called 'shape tape', which can track its bend and rotation at several positions along its length. Computer processing allows the end orientation and displacement to be determined relative to the start point.

Accelerometers are small, lightweight sensors that can be used as inclinometers to detect angle relative to the earth's gravitational field. They are also sensitive to acceleration and so can only be used in applications where accelerations are negligible or can be filtered out. They are not able to measure rotation about a vertical axis. Magnetic flux sensors allow orientation to the earth's magnetic field, which varies according to latitude, to be measured. They are not able to measure rotation about the magnetic field vector. The latter two sensors can be combined into one device that overcomes the disadvantages of both to measure orientation in three planes, at the price of increased complexity and cost. Magnetic position sensors measure orientation as well as displacement. They are discussed in the entry on **linear motion**.

Angular velocity

Rate gyroscopes are devices that output a signal proportional to their rate of rotation, or angular velocity. One particular device measures the Coriolis force on a micro-engineered tuning fork as it rotates; the magnitude of this force is proportional to angular velocity. Advances in electronic fabrication have made rate gyroscopes more widely and inexpensively available. Their output can be converted to change in angle by integration.

See also: accelerometry; amplification and signal conditioning; electronics; signal display and storage

Further reading

Webster J.G. (ed.) (1999) *The Measurement, Instrumentation, and Sensors Handbook*, Boca Raton FL: CRC Press.

BEN HELLER

ANKLE AND FOOT

The ankle and foot form a complex region containing many joints, which provide flexibility and enable the foot to adapt to its environment. This flexibility of the foot is essential because it is the point of contact between the ground and the body; it must be able to adapt to changes in terrain with minimum perturbation of the body system

as a whole. The many bones and joints in the foot enable it to play multiple roles during activity; it is a flexible shock-attenuating structure during the early part of the stance phase of gait, and then becomes a rigid lever during push-off at the end of the stance phase. This change in dynamic function is achieved by activity of the invertor and evertor muscles of the foot, rotating it about its longitudinal axis from a flexible pronated position to a rigid supinated position.

Owing to the foot's position as the most distal segment in the body, the ankle and foot region is subjected to high loads, particularly during running and jumping activities. It is also subjected to large shear forces during cutting and other side-step activities that occur in sports. As a result of these high loads and extreme positions, the ankle and foot is at high risk of overuse injury, although sometimes injuries related to ankle and foot risk factors manifest themselves higher up the kinetic chain – in the lower leg, knee, or hip. Overuse injuries related to foot and ankle structure and mechanics include plantar fasciitis, patellofemoral pain, tibial stress fractures, and chondromalacia patellae.

See also: bones of the ankle and foot; foot arches; joints of the ankle and foot; muscles of the ankle and foot

Further reading

Williams, P.L., Bannister, L.H., Berry, M.M., Collins, P., Dyson, M., Dussek, J.E. and Ferguson, M.W.J. (eds) (1995) *Gray's Anatomy: the Anatomical Basis of Medicine and Surgery*, Section 6, Edinburgh: Churchill Livingstone.

CLARE E. MILNER

ANKLE INJURY

This entry focuses on the definition and current concepts of management and controversies of common ankle injuries

An ankle sprain is the most common injury in most sports. It should be stressed that a sprain is an injury mechanism, not a diagnosis. Most athletes who sprain their ankle do not seek medical care, but simply rest for a few days up to two weeks before resuming sports. In these cases, we consequently do not know the real grade of the injury. Despite the severity of injury, the recommended treatment in the acute phase, minutes to hours after the injury, has two main objectives. These are to prevent and alleviate pain and to optimize the healing conditions despite the exact diagnosis. The primary aim is to prevent swelling. 'RICE' is a well known concept of acute management, comprising Rest, Ice, Compression and Elevation. Ninety-five per cent of the blood flow is suppressed within a few seconds, if a firm bandage is applied. The muscle blood flow decreases linearly with the increase in pressure of the bandage. Icing is well anchored in the soul of sports people and is often applied on the field in form of spray or a gel package. It is obvious that we get a decrease in blood flow from application of ice, but it takes a relatively long time and it is also uncertain if it is of any importance in counteracting the bleeding *per se*. The maximal reduction of blood flow may occur within ten minutes after application of ice but only a maximum of 65–70 per cent of the initial blood is actually suppressed. On the basis of this, in the best case we would expect a 35 per cent reduction in the blood flow, which can probably not lead to any appreciable reduction in the blood flow in the injured tissue. The other aspect of the ice effect, which is well documented, is to reduce the pain by affecting skin receptors, and is of course another important issue to consider. After surgery, the combination of pressure and ice is frequently used in form of cryo-cuff applications with documented good clinical effect, reducing both swelling and pain. Elevation of the leg is also one of the recommended measures in the acute management. This is of course only applicable if the injury occurs in an organised environ-

ment, hardly if it happens when out running. It is well known that one must raise the injured site 30 cm above the level of the heart to get any effect of this measure. At 30 cm, the blood flow is still 100 per cent due to auto-regulation. At 50 cm the blood flow drops to 80 per cent, and at 70 cm it is still 65 per cent of the flow at heart level. Rest probably has no great effect in the acute situation at all in reducing the bleeding. If a muscle works with maximal blood flow, this flow does not decrease during the first minutes after one has stopped the work.

Do we gain anything by an early detailed patho-anatomic diagnosis after an ankle sprain? Yes: intra-articular injuries to the cartilage can occur in many of these cases. It should also be stressed that a sprain can cause damage to several structures such as joint capsule, ligaments, cartilage and bone. Whilst cartilage and bony injuries often give later symptoms of pain, ligament injuries cause instability if not healed properly. Schäfer and Hintermann examined 110 patients with at least two ankle sprains and duration of symptoms of more than six months. They found a complete anterior tibiofibular (ATF)-ligament rupture in 64 per cent, a rupture of the calcaneo-fibular (CF)-ligament in 41 per cent and a rupture of the deltoid ligament in 6 per cent. In 54 per cent of these cases they reported cartilage lesions on the talus, the majority of the cases localised on the medial side. The etiology for these medial injuries is probably mechanical. Noguchi showed with a three-dimensional model that the loading of the medial compartment in the talocrural joint increased markedly due to instability caused by a lateral ligament injury. All medial ligament injuries presented by Schäfer and Hintermann were associated with chondral lesions. The clinical relevance or risk of further progression of the chondral lesions is not clearly understood.

To what extent will medial ligament ruptures result in long-term dysfunction, instability or pain? Some textbooks claim that acute medial ligament injuries seldom needs to be repaired, while others claim that an open repair is to be recommended. Many symptomatic cases with recurrent instability are found to have partial or total deltoid ligament ruptures with no obvious chondral lesion. When should we then conclude that a sprain is severe enough to warrant an arthroscopy or even a ligament reconstruction? Ferkel and Scranton claimed that non-operative treatment should continue for at least three months after an acute ankle sprain before arthroscopy is performed. It may be argued that for an athlete, three months of persistent pain and/or dysfunction is a very long time to wait without a clear diagnosis. Most symptoms after an uncomplicated sprain disappear or decrease dramatically the first few weeks. A common rule is that persistent pain for more than 2–3 weeks after a sprain, swelling and dysfunction is a valid indication for further investigation and intervention.

The medial ligament injuries are usually caused by eversion-type sprains or associated with fractures. These are outnumbered quantitatively by lateral ligament injuries. But it is important not to miss these, since they usually are more severe and often require specialist attention. Only about 10–20 per cent of inversion ligament injuries require surgical treatment, due to functional instability and recurrent dislocations. Furthermore, chronic lateral ligament repair shows very good results using open or semi-open techniques, a so-called modified Brostrom procedure. There are several other operative methods described in the literature, but the anatomic reconstruction is usually preferred. With the use of mini anchor techniques, the morbidity after these operations is very low. The use of arthroscopic reconstruction is controversial. Recurrent instability should seldom be treated operatively before a thorough physiotherapeutic intervention for at least 10–12 weeks. The indications for acute

arthroscopy on inversion sprains may thus be argued. However, Van Dijk and coworkers examined thirty consecutive patients with acute open repair of the lateral ligaments. During operation, arthroscopy revealed a fresh injury to the cartilage in twenty cases, nineteen of them to the medial anterior aspect of talus. In six patients, loose cartilage bodies were found. In confirmity with this, an arthroscopy is suggested in direct conjunction with the open ligament repair.

It is evident that it may be difficult to participate in vigorous sports with an unstable ankle joint. Education of athletes and coaches in acute management to stop the bleeding is helpful in reducing the absence from training from this very common injury. Taping and orthotics should be considered only as temporary measures during rehabilitation, even though they are used extensively for prophylactic use in many sports. Re-injuries are common and occur mainly in insufficiently rehabilitated cases. Non-operative treatment with a controlled proprioceptive and strength training programme should start immediately after injury. The surgical cases should be selected from the 10–20 per cent of failures with recurrent instability and pathologic laxity after this regime.

See also: Anterior drawer test; sports injuries; Talar tilt test

Further reading

Marder, R.A. and Lian, G.J. (1997) *Sports Injuries of the Ankle and Foot*, New York: Springer. ISBN 0-387-94687-X

CHRISTER ROLF

ANKYLOSING SPONDYLITIS

Ankylosing spondylitis (AS) is an inflammatory disorder of unknown cause that mainly affects the axial skeleton, peripheral joints, but extra-articular structures may also be involved. It is an important condition to consider in sports medicine for two reasons. First, it most commonly presents with lower back pain that is insidious in onset, and it affects young males and the diagnosis can therefore be missed unless the sports physician is aware of its clinical features. Second, exercise activity is an important component of the treatment of this condition.

The disease can affect a number of organs. Sacroiliitis is the earliest manifestation, followed by disease of the lumbar spine. Other areas of involvement of the disease are peripheral arthritis, enthesitis, acute anterior uveitis (iritis), aortic insufficiency and inflammatory lesions of the bowel. The cause of the disease is not well understood, but immune-mediated mechanisms, enteric bacteria and a direct role of HLA B27 have been implicated.

Ankylosing spondylitis presents, usually in late adolescence or early childhood and more commonly in males, as dull pain, insidious in onset, felt deep in the lower lumbar or gluteal region. It is accompanied by low-back morning stiffness of up to a few hours' duration that improves with activity and returns following periods of inactivity. Pain can occur at other sites of musculoskeletal involvement. Occasionally patients present with predominantly constitutional symptoms such as fatigue, anorexia, fever, weight loss, or night sweats. Rare manifestations are acute anterior uveitis, aortic insufficiency, and symptoms of inflammation in the colon or ileum.

The most specific findings on clinical examination are loss of spinal mobility, tenderness in the sacroiliac joints, tenderness upon palpation at the sites of other bony areas, and paraspinous muscle spasm. Decreased chest expansion on maximal inspiration may also be a feature. Clinical examination should include assessment of the other organs that may be affected (eyes, cardiovascular and gastrointestinal system).

The diagnosis of ankylosing spondylitis can be made on the basis of radiographic sacroiliitis plus any one of the following three criteria: (1) a history of inflammatory back pain; (2) limitation of motion of the lumbar spine in both the sagittal and frontal planes; and (3) limited chest expansion, relative to standard values for age and sex. Clinical features that are helpful in distinguishing the inflammatory back pain of ankylosing spondylitis from other causes of back in athletes are its insidious onset not related to sports activity, associated morning stiffness, and improvement rather than aggravation by exercise or activity.

The HLA-B27 gene is present in approximately 90 per cent of patients, and most patients with active disease have an elevated erythrocyte sedimentation rate and an elevated level of C-reactive protein. Rheumatoid factor and antinuclear antibodies are uniformly absent.

X-rays show blurring of the cortical margins of the subchondral bone of the sacroiliac joints, followed by erosions and sclerosis. Lumbar spine X-rays show straightening, reactive sclerosis, erosion, 'squaring' of the vertebral bodies, progressive ossification of the superficial layers of the annulus fibrosus and eventual formation of marginal syndesmophytes.

Treatment of ankylosing spondylitis should be under the care of a rheumatologist, who can prescribe appropriate medication. In addition to pharmacological intervention, the participation by the patient in an exercise programme designed to maintain functional posture and to preserve range of motion is most important. There is evidence that exercise increases mobility and improves function. Surgery is indicated for severe hip joint arthritis, the pain and stiffness of which are often dramatically relieved by total hip arthroplasty. Acute iritis can be treated with local glucocorticoid administration in conjunction with mydriatic agents. Coexistent cardiac disease may require pacemaker implantation or aortic valve replacement.

See also: lower back injury

MARTIN SCHWELLNUS

ANTERIOR CRUCIATE LIGAMENT INJURY IN WOMEN

No person in the United States shall, on the basis of sex, be excluded from participation in, be denied the benefits of, or be subject to discrimination under any educational program or activity receiving federal financial assistance.

From the preamble to Title IX of the Education Amendments of 1972

In 1972, a single legislative act dramatically changed the athletic landscape for female athletes throughout the United States. Title IX of the Education Amendments of 1972 created a level field of opportunity for female athletes in government assisted education programs. Elementary through university level programs were required to provide female athletes with the same sporting opportunities, level of coaching, and athletic facilities as their male counterparts. In 1971, 300,000 girls participated in high school athletic programs. Today there are over 2.7 million female high school athletes, a ninefold increase. A parallel sixfold increase in participation has occurred at the collegiate level.

As the number of female athletes has increased over the past three decades, an alarming trend has been noted by coaches, trainers, therapists, and physicians. Certain injuries were recognized to occur at a much higher rate in female athletes than male athletes. One such disabling knee injury is the anterior cruciate ligament (ACL) rupture (see **anterior cruciate ligament tear**). Studies conducted by the National Collegiate Athletic Association over the past fifteen years document a threefold higher rate of ACL injury in female soccer and basketball players as compared to males in similar sports. Similar studies evaluating high school age athletes noted ACL injury rates eight times greater in females than males. The mechanism of ACL injury, risk factors for injury, and injury prevention will be reviewed as they pertain to the female athlete.

A review of game videos over the past fifteen years has revealed that the typical female ACL injury occurs in the absence of player-to-player contact. Up to 70 per cent of all female ACL injuries are caused by this non-contact mechanism. The classic non-contact ACL tear results from an awkward landing, rapid deceleration, pivoting, or cutting maneuver performed in response to a sudden change in the direction of play (i.e. unanticipated, deflected pass). The hip internally rotates, the knee collapses toward the midline, and the ACL ligament tears.

In response to the alarmingly high rate of non-contact ACL injury in female athletes, several researchers have evaluated possible risk factors for this common injury. A consensus conference was held in 1999 in Hunt Valley, Maryland, USA. Experts in the fields of athletic training, physical therapy, sports medicine, and orthopaedic surgery reviewed the current literature and identified four categories of risk factors for non-contact ACL injury in female athletes.

Environmental factors include knee bracing and player-surface interface. Knee bracing to prevent ligament injury gained popularity during the late 1970s and 1980s. Early reports indicated a decrease in **medial collateral ligament tear** knee injuries though bracing in high school and collegiate athletes. More recent studies have not only shown no benefit to bracing, but a slight increase in knee injury rates with brace use. Currently there is no reliable evidence to suggest that knee bracing prevents non-contact ACL injuries in female athletes.

Player-surface interface has recently gained attention as a possible contributing factor to ACL injury. A high degree of friction between the player's shoe and playing surface has been shown to increase the rate of ACL injury in multiple sports including team handball and American football. In addition, non-contact ACL injuries occur most frequently on dry playing surfaces. While these factors certainly influence the rate of ACL injury, player-surface interface is not a gender-specific risk factor, and alone does not account for the higher rate of non-contact ACL injury in female athletes.

Female athletes differ structurally in many ways from their male counterparts. The pelvis is wider in women, the hip alignment differs, there is a greater amount of tibial external rotation or torsion, and the feet tend to pronate to a greater degree. Hyperlaxity of ligaments is more prevalent in the female population, and the ACL ligament and space for the ligament known as the 'femoral notch' tend to be smaller in women. In spite of these very obvious structural differences, none of the above-mentioned anatomic factors have been shown to directly correlate with a higher incidence of non-contact ACL injury.

With the discovery of estrogen and progesterone receptors on ACL cells in 1996, several investigators were prompted to evaluate the effect of the female menstrual cycle on non-contact ACL injury rates. Results of this research have been conflicting, with different authors showing higher rates of non-contact ACL injury during different phases of the menstrual cycle. Further clouding the issue are studies showing no effect of oral contraceptive pills on injury rates, and animal studies demonstrating no effect of estrogen on ligament mechanical properties. While female hormones most likely play some role in ligament homeostasis, no consensus statement can be made regarding their effect on non-contact ACL injury.

Joint stability is achieved through static and dynamic structures. Static contributors to joint stability include bony congruency, ligaments, and the joint capsule. Dynamic joint stability is provided by all muscle-tendon units crossing a particular joint. In addition, muscle groups proximal or distal in the kinetic chain indirectly stabilize the knee by providing an optimal foundation for hamstring and quadriceps function and by avoiding vulnerable positions. Dynamic stability is controlled though both voluntary and involuntary muscle activity. Mechanical receptors within the muscle-tendon unit sense joint position in space, also called 'proprioception'. Proprioception is feedback utilized by the central nervous system to control involuntary muscle activity and to keep the knee out of high-risk positions. Studies have documented a measurable difference in speed and strength of muscle contraction in response to proprioceptive input between male and female athletes. Female athletes recruit key ACL agonists such as the hamstring muscles at a slower rate and with less strength than male athletes. This difference in ability to respond to proprioceptive input results in a gender-specific decrease in dynamic knee joint stability in female athletes.

Numerous studies involving jumping, landing, electromyography, and muscle strength testing have documented key gender differences in neuromuscular control of the knee joint. Female athletes, in general, demonstrate weaker core strength allowing for anterior pelvic tilt and compensatory lower extremity rotation that places the ACL at risk. Hip extensors, abductors and external rotators (i.e. hamstrings, gluteal muscles, and short external rotators) tend to be weaker, placing the femur and knee in an adducted, internally rotated valgus position. This valgus or 'collapsed knee' position allows for high rotational forces across the knee during activity which results in non-contact ACL injury. In addition to poor positioning resulting from muscle weakness, the female athlete tends to jump and land in a more straight-leg/flat-footed position. Specifically, female athletes land with approximately 5° less knee flexion, 9° less hip flexion, and 9° greater knee valgus than their male counterparts. This places the center of gravity posterior to the knee joint, induces strong quadriceps ACL antagonist activity, prevents the hamstring muscles from optimally stabilizing the knee joint, and subjects the ACL to undue levels of stress.

Consensus regarding the cause of increased rates of non-contact ACL injury in female athletes has directed prevention strategies toward improvements in proprioception and neuromuscular control. Several successful, sport-specific programs have been developed to reduce injury rates. While differing in details, all successful prevention programs share common components. In general, programs focusing on improvement of proprioception though use of balance boards or balance drills, core strengthening, hip extensor, abductor and external rotator strengthening, hamstring strengthening, improvement in landing position by avoiding a 'collapsed knee' or flat-foot position, and use of plyometrics have been most successful in reducing non-contact ACL injury rates in female athletes. Prospective jump training programs have shown more than a threefold reduction in non-contact knee injuries at the high school level. A prospective, sport-specific soccer prevention program demonstrated an 88 per cent reduction in non-contact ACL injury in a study population of over 2,000 female high school soccer players. The same program was shown in a randomized, prospective study to reduce the rate of non-contact ACL injury by 77 per cent in collegiate level women soccer players. All successful programs stress the importance of compliance and good form when executing the various training maneuvers.

With the increasing number of female athletes, it is clear that certain injuries occur at a higher rate in the female athletic population. One of the more disabling injuries is the non-contact ACL rupture. Focused research incorporating epidemiology, video analysis, and biomechanics has identified a gender difference in neuromuscular control as the primary factor dictating the higher rate of non-contact ACL

injury in female athletes. Very specific prevention programs have evolved in response to this research, and have dramatically decreased the rate of injury in the female athletic population. Prevention programs will continue to take on an expanding role in athletic training, and further collaboration in the scientific community will identify additional injury risk factors and allow for the application of future prevention concepts.

Further reading

Ardent, A. and Dick, R. 'Knee Injury Patterns Among Men and Women in Collegiate Basketball and Soccer', *The American Journal of Sports Medicine* 23, 6: 694–701.

Griffin L.Y., *et al.* 'Non-contact Anterior Cruciate Ligament Injuries: Risk Factors and Prevention Strategies', *Journal of the American Academy of Orthopaedic Surgeons* 8, 3: 141–50.

Hewett, T.E., Lindenfeld, T.N. *et al.* 'The effect of neuromuscular training on the incidence of knee injury in female athletes', *The American Journal of Sports Medicine* 27, 6: 699–706.

Ireland, M.L. 'The Female ACL: Why Is It More Prone to Injury?', *Orthopaedic Clinics of North America* 33: 637–51.

JOHN C. FRANCO
BERT R. MANDELBAUM

ANTERIOR CRUCIATE LIGAMENT TEAR

This entry focuses on the definition and concepts of management of injuries to the anterior cruciate ligament of the knee

Injuries to the anterior cruciate ligament (ACL) are common, especially in contact sports. The diagnosis of a total ACL rupture is established clinically with the Lachman test and can be verified with help of arthroscopy or MRI. Despite this, the diagnosis is often delayed, which can have serious consequences.

What consequences does an ACL injury have? The natural course is determined by the patient's activity grade, motivation, rehabilitation programs of varying qualities, different advice from physicians, and also the criteria used for evaluation. Despite the fact that there are many studies on the natural history of anterior cruciate ligament injuries, there are no prospective randomized studies that compare the best non-operative treatment with the best operative treatment. Some reports may convince one that ACL injuries should be treated surgically. However, there are other studies showing contrary evidence, which makes it very confusing. It is, however, obvious that there is a greater proportion of more physically active individuals in the surgical than in the non-surgical studies.

There are a number of studies attempting to compare operative treatment with non-operative treatment. These investigations are often biased, and it is misleading to conclude that non-operative treatment for an ACL rupture is better than surgical treatment on this basis. Physically active patients probably choose surgical treatment, whilst the calmer patients choose non-operative treatment, reduce their activity level, and do not subject their knee to extensive strain, gaining a good functional result. In one randomized study, suturing of the acute ACL injury followed by immobilization with a cast was compared with immobilization with a cast alone. In other words two poor treatment methods were compared to each other. However, if one should carry out an acute ACL reconstruction in one group and immediately train the other group by following an active rehabilitation program, and then follow both groups for five years, one can perhaps approach a solution to this problem. The Linköping group in Sweden headed by professor Jan Gillquist has done more randomized studies than any other group. They have also compared operative treatment with non-operative treatment of ACL ruptures in a prospective randomized study. Unfortunately, they operated on all their patients with an open surgery technique, which is not the modern standard. Every

other case was operated with ACL reconstruction and in the rest of the cases only the peripheral injuries were treated followed by immobilization with a cast over a period of time. This study consequently did not give a clear indication of the best treatment available today – to operate or to immediately start an extensive training program. How should we find an answer to this question? Professor Ejnar Ericson from Sweden gave his view on this during a consensus symposia in Sweden in 1997. If one has a twenty-year-old male football player who weighs 85 kg, is 178 cm tall and has a defined high-activity grade, these data can be fed into a common database. The computer then randomly decides if this patient should be treated non-operatively and prints out a rehabilitation program that the patient takes with him to the physiotherapist. At other clinics which are linked to the same computer network, there may be a corresponding patient who is treated surgically, for example, with the best surgical option, followed by an active rehabilitation. Such a multi-centre study with matching of patients could likely lead us to discover which treatment gives the best results. In the light of Ericson's suggestion, you could ask why leading sports surgeons have not conducted this 'perfect' study during the last century.

It seems that some sports, such as football and rugby, are more unforgiving for an ACL injury than others such as ice hockey, volleyball or downhill skiing. It is generally not possible to continue contact sports on high level with a ruptured ACL. Operative treatment can make it possible for players to continue. With modern operation techniques, there is a reasonably high probability that a highly motivated person can return to any kind of sports. Therefore, one can probably treat athletes in a satisfactory manner from this aspect. Whether this is optimal for the knee joint itself in the long run is a different question. One investigation based on all licensed football players in

Sweden (Folksam Insurance register) who during 1986 were reported to have an ACL injury found that 33 per cent of the patients played football three years after the injury, and 15 per cent after seven years. This can be compared to data on the natural course of events after an ACL injury showing that about 50 per cent would still have played football seven years after the injury. It was also noted that none of the players at the elite level who suffered an ACL rupture in 1986, still played at the elite level seven years later, whilst 30 per cent of the uninjured players still played at this level at this point in time. The type of treatment, whether operative or non-operative, did not influence the number of players still playing three and seven years following the injury. This study reflects the effect of treatment at a national level; the patients were treated at many different hospitals by more or less experienced surgeons. The operative technique that was used in the majority of these cases, is not used today. The results are in line with those presented by Engström showing that only very few elite football players return fully to the original sport one year after an ACL injury.

The treatment of these injuries has been discussed extensively during the last twenty-plus years. What is new in anterior cruciate ligament surgery in 1995 compared with 1985? The biomechanical knowledge has increased. The surgical technique has improved. Rehabilitation is started earlier and morbidity is low. The patient selection may be different. Today we have knowledge on isometry, how the substitute graft should be placed and stretched, and we also have new methods of fixing the substitute. The techniques today also cause less damage to the soft tissues.

What is unchanged in 1995 compared to 1985? Injury type, graft material, rehabilitation techniques, and evaluation have not changed dramatically, except for the use of allografts and that physiotherapy is begun earlier than before. The evaluation techniques are similar with the exception of the introduction of stability measurements. How have these differences influenced the results of the operation as presented in published studies? To answer this question, studies from 1980 to 1985 were compared with those from 1990 to 1995. In general there has been no change in the frequency of excellent/good (70–100 per cent) results between the periods of time investigated in the present study, despite the fact the knowledge of the knee joint has increased and the evaluation standards seem to be the same. The results from studies published in 1996 did not change these findings.

Experimental studies show that the biomechanics of the knee and the substituted ligament are far from normal after reconstruction. Despite this, clinical studies show that 70–100 per cent of patients have excellent results. Why? The reason for this may be that the clinical evaluation tends to show a false improvement in the results or that patients adapt to a less perfect functioning. It is still not known what consequences such an adaptation may have in the long run.

During the periods studied, knowledge of knee and ligament mechanics, anatomy, and function has increased dramatically. Despite this there is no difference in the excellent/good results between the periods studied. Why? It may be that the reconstruction techniques are tested in an unsystematic and unprofessional scientific manner which gives rise to bias in the results. The evaluation methods are still marred by great uncertainty and allow relatively free interpretations.

See also: anterior drawer test; knee injury; Lachmann test

Further reading

Renstrom, P. and Lynch, S. (1998) 'An Overview of Anterior Cruciate Ligament Management', in Chan, K., Fu, F., Maffulli, N.,

Rolf, C. and Liu, S., *Controversies of Orthopedic Sports Medicine*, 5–27, Williams and Wilkins Publishers. ISBN 962-365-025-7.

CHRISTER ROLF

ANTERIOR DRAWER TEST

The Anterior drawer test is an established clinical test of the knee and of the ankle to verify an abnormal anterior translation of tibia in relation to femur for the knee, or correspondingly talus in relation to fibula of the ankle. A pathologic anterior translation without a clear end point is caused by a tear of the anterior cruciate ligament in the knee or a tear of the anterior talofibular ligament in the ankle.

The knee test is performed with the patient in supine position. The knee is flexed to 90° and the foot is fixed onto the bench. The examiner's hands hold the proximal lower leg just below the joint line. In a muscle-relaxed position the lower leg is moved in an anterior direction. Normally the anterior cruciate ligament restricts this movement by a definite end point at the end of the translation. If the anterior cruciate ligament is ruptured, the translation of the lower leg will exceed the normal limits without a definite end point. If the posterior capsule and associated structures are also damaged, the anterior drawer test will be more or less pronounced in external or internal rotation of the lower leg. The anterior drawer test is clinically not as sensitive as the Lachmann test in discriminating an anterior cruciate ligament tear.

For the ankle, the patient should be placed in supine, relaxed position. The ankle joint should be examined in different positions around neutral, which is around 90° of flexion. One hand fixates the heel behind and around the calcaneus, the thumb being placed in front of the ankle to support the subtalar joint. The calcaneus and talus is then gently moved in anterior direction whilst the other hand stabilizes the lower leg. Normally, a definite end point should occur. If the ligament is ruptured the end point is gone. In both situations for the knee and ankle the other side has to be compared because individuals normally differ in laxity.

See also: ankle injury; knee injury

Further reading

Renstrom, P. and Lynch, S. (1998) 'An Overview of Anterior Cruciate Ligament Management', in Chan, K., Fu, F., Maffulli, N., Rolf, C. and Liu, S. *Controversies of Orthopedic Sports Medicine*, 5–27, Williams and Wilkins Publishers. ISBN 962-365-025-7.

Lynch, S.A. and Renstrom, P. (1999) 'Treatment of Acute Lateral Ligament Rupture in the Athlete', *Sports Med* 27: 61–71.

CHRISTER ROLF

ANTERIOR GLENOHUMERAL INSTABILITY

This entry focuses on anterior glenohumeral instability, as seen in clinical practice, observed in diagnostic procedures and evaluated by shoulder function scores.

The history and clinical examination are the most important instruments for evaluation of the injured shoulder, but the anatomy and biomechanical function is very complex. In patients with recurrent anterior glenohumeral instability, a detailed history, clinical examination and plain radiographs with standard projections can, in most cases, provide the correct diagnosis. On the basis of this information further management can be decided. Anterior glenohumeral instability is defined as increased anterior laxity in the joint combined with subjective symptoms of instability. Thus, if the patient complains of corresponding symptoms, the glenohumeral anterior stability can be assessed by the anterior apprehension test with the patient sitting in relaxed position on a chair or in supine position. The shoulder is passively abducted to 90° with external rotation of 0°. The elbow is flexed to 90°. The examiner stands or sits behind the patient and puts his hand over the acromion. The thumb presses lightly on the humeral head from behind while the forefinger rests on the clavicle. With the other hand, the examiner externally rotates the patient's forearm. If the patient reacts with apprehension, the test is positive. The relocation test is then used to verify that the reaction is caused by the anterior instability. The patient lies supine on an examination couch. The arm is abducted to 90° and maximally internally rotated with the arm flexed 90° at the elbow. From this position, the arm is externally rotated till the patient shows apprehension. The grade of external rotation at which pain or apprehension is experienced, is registered. In this test the position of the humeral head is normalized with external rotation. It is important not to uncontrollably release the pressure on the patient's upper arm since the shoulder can dislocate. This test was described by Frank Jobe in 1989 He mostly discussed the patient's pain reaction. In 1994 Speer reevaluated this test and found that if the patient reacts with pain alone, it is difficult to assess whether it is a subtle instability or if other injuries are causing the symptoms. However, there is a good correlation between the instability verified from surgery and that assessed by the apprehension test. It is important to elicit the direction of increased laxity and instability. Posterior instability can be differentiated by the posterior apprehension test. The patient lies on a level examination couch and the arm is held at 90° elevation with the elbow flexed at 90° and 0° of internal rotation. A backwards pressure is applied by putting one hand over the proximal humerus and pressing it downwards. It is important that the patient is relaxed when this is carried out. A patient with a posterior instability shows apprehension. If this happens the test is positive. Sulcus sign should always be considered to

limit the risk of misdiagnosing a multi directional laxity. The patient is seated on a chair or examination couch. The examiner applies a downwards traction on the arm by pulling the arm downwards. A sulcus will appear under the acromion in patients with multiplane instability and with increased laxity. The sulcus can be graded according to American Shoulder and Elbow Surgeons score (0 = no sulcus; 1 = 0–1 cm translation; 2 = 1–2 cm translation or to the glenoid cavity rim, 3 = >2 cm translation or above the glenoid cavity rim). Henry and coworkers presented an analysis of these instability tests, where they tried to evaluate the precision in these compared to the operation findings. The best test was the sulcus sign with a sensitivity of 97 per cent, specificity of 99 per cent in differentiating patients with one plane instability from patients with multiplane instability. Finally, the Carter-Wilkinson index is used to assess and differentiate hypermobility.

The way we evaluate anterior laxity and instability may differ. There are many scoring systems available, reflecting the fact that there is no uniform way yet to assess shoulder function. The Constant scoring system is the official score of the European Shoulder and Elbow Society. It is developed for measurement of the shoulder function irrespective of diagnosis. Even though this is the official scoring system, it has been evident for a long time that this is not satisfactory as the only scoring system for assessing patients with instability problems. The American Shoulder and Elbow Society developed their own scoring system. Another scoring system has been developed in Japan. There are also many different evaluation systems developed by different institutions around the world. Some other systems are specifically developed to evaluate an unstable shoulder, such as the Rowe score and modified Rowe score. According to the Constant scoring system, the range of movement is measured with the patient in the sitting position on a chair or examination couch with symmetrical loading. No rotation of the upper part of the body is allowed during the examination. Only the active pain-free range of movement is assessed. It is the grade at which the pain occurs that is measured, not the maximal range. The American scoring system measures even the passive range of movement with the patient in the lying position. The active movement according to the American system is not as clearly defined with regards to pain. In the Constant scoring system, flexion, abduction, internal rotation and functional external rotation are measured. In the American scoring method, the elevation, external rotation at various degrees of abduction, and posterior internal rotation, as well as a movement termed cross body adduction, are measured. Flexion occurs when the arm is lifted forwards and upwards. The American scoring system measures instead elevation. This involves the arm being lifted obliquely forwards and upwards at the scapula level. Abduction means that the arm is lifted straight from the side with the thumb pointing forwards till one has reached 90° abduction. At this point the thumb is then rotated up toward the ceiling for the rest of the abduction. External rotation is measured according to a point system depending on where the elbow is in relation to the head. It should be observed that the hand should not touch the head, and every part of movement that the patient manages is noted and graded. At the end, the points are summed. In the American system, external rotation is measured in degrees with the arm at 0° of abduction and also with the arm in 90° of abduction. In the Rowe scoring system, stability, range of movement, and function are assessed. The disadvantage with this score is that pain or strength is not taken into consideration. This scoring system has since been changed and is now called the modified Rowe scoring system. In this, pain, stability, range of movement, and function are taken into consideration. More

emphasis is put on function and return to sports. In other words this is better for evaluating the results of instability surgery in athletes who have high demands on function. One advantage with Constant scoring system is that every step in the objective evaluation is defined in detail to minimize the risk of variation in results that can arise when the method of evaluation differs between studies. The Constant score is not sensitive in evaluating instability of the shoulder: one should complement with another evaluation method. Since the modified Rowe score has been used in many studies, it is suitable to use this to assess instability.

In summary, the shoulder is difficult to assess with objective measures because of the complex anatomy and biomechanical function. This is reflected by a lack of international consensus regarding evaluation scores, making communication and interpretation of published data difficult, and consequently the clinical management is an issue for the experienced surgeon.

See also: shoulder injury

Further reading

Hawkins, R. and Saunders, W.B. (1996) *Shoulder Injuries in the Athlete. Surgical Repair and Rehabilitation.* ISBN 0-443-08947-7.

CHRISTER ROLF

ANTERIOR KNEE PAIN

The term 'anterior knee pain' covers a number of diagnoses, different etiological factors and a variety of patho-anatomical correlates. The terminology and definitions vary considerably in the literature.

It is obvious that any traumatic injury such as an anterior meniscus tear, or previous surgery in the area such as graft taking from the patella tendon during reconstructive surgery of the anterior cruciate ligament, can cause anterior knee discomfort and pain.

If there is a significant trauma in the history, these patients often see a specialist to rule out the need of further investigation or surgical intervention.

Anterior knee pain which is not caused by trauma includes the patello-femoral pain syndrome. Fairbank reported that 31 per cent of 446 British schoolchildren suffered from this syndrome, while Hording found a 10 per cent incidence in fifteen-year-olds. These data are based on history and clinical findings. In his Ph.D. thesis of 1997, Thome stated that the patello-femoral pain syndrome is the clinical presentation of anterior knee pain excluding intra-articular injuries as well as peri-patellar tendinitis and bursitis. This definition is not easy to compare with that used in other reports. It requires, in principle, that one has carried out an arthroscopy or an MRI to exclude intra-articular pathology, and a histopathological investigation to exclude tendinitis. Lindberg defined the patello-femoral pain syndrome, including a history of pain from around the kneecap and at least two of the following symptoms: pain on stair-climbing; pain on knee-bending; pseudo-locking, pain, or stiffness after sitting for a long time. This definition is simple, but cannot exclude intra-articular pathology as suggested by Thome. Werner defined a patello-femoral pain syndrome excluding chondromalacia, as that is a patho-anatomical diagnosis in principle requiring an arthroscopy. Many authors have, however, shown that chondromalacia changes are *per se* not directly related to anterior knee injuries. A common ground from recent studies is that these patients have anterior knee pain which becomes worse with loading. Speculations on the causes of this syndrome have been made throughout the twentieth century. Budinger described patellar chondral injuries without osteoarthritis from arthrotomy undertaken as early as 1906. The concept of chondromalacia patellae was described by Aleman in 1928. It was believed that the injuries found with arthrotomy were caused by trauma. Today it is known that these types of chondral changes, detected by arthroscopy, may occur without any correlation to anterior knee pain. This does not rule out that mechanical loading or trauma is of importance for cartilage injuries or for knee pain. Hirsch discussed the mechanical characteristics of the patella cartilage, and suggested that overloading could cause softening. Anatomical anomalies, non-alignment, patellar instability, and patella maltracking in combination with abnormal tightness of the lateral retinaculum, have all been suggested as important etiological factors for anterior knee pain and chondromalacia.

More or less heroic treatments have been used in the past, including removal of the patella, which was described by Mac Fellander in 1951. Other methods are lateral release and transposition of the tuberositas tibiae, but the value of these treatment methods has not been clearly evaluated. A careful clinical examination is very important for determining the optimal treatment because the symptoms vary between patients. Adequate documentation of the history is also important in finding the cause of the knee problems in any individual case. The clinical examination involves a careful assessment of the lower extremities. Presence of increased femoral anteversion with compensatory tibial torsion, genu recurvatum, valgus position of the knee and overpronation of the subtalar joint may be of importance. Measurement of the Q angle should be included in the examination protocol, even if the correlation between an increased Q angle and the symptoms described may be questioned. The patella's position in the patello-femoral joint is evaluated for patella alta, patella baja, tilted patella, subluxated or rotated patella. Tilted patella with medial opening is believed to be relatively common in the patello-femoral pain syndrome. This may depend on a tight lateral retinaculum and/or atrophy of the vastus medialis obliqus muscle. Control of the patella mobility should also be done. Normal patella mobility is 10 mm in both the lateral and medial directions. To assess whether the patient needs an external patella support (taping or orthotics) as part of the treatment, it is important to examine patella steering during concentric and eccentric knee extension – the so-called patella tracking test. The thigh muscles, especially the quadriceps muscles, are often weak in these patients. Atrophy of the vastus medialis muscle is an important clinical finding. This in turn can lead to muscular imbalance between the vastus medialis muscle and the vastus lateralis muscle. Both these muscles are most active at the end of extension and in normal cases they are equally active. Muscular imbalance between quadriceps and hamstrings are also commonly present, which is especially due to weakness in the quadriceps muscles. In the patello-femoral pain syndrome, the hamstrings are relatively more activated than the quadriceps. Muscle tightness, most often of the lateral muscles as well as hamstrings, should also be noted. Tightness of the lateral retinaculum may also be important. The symptoms can be evaluated objectively with simple functional tests such as squatting and climbing stairs combined with a subjective evaluation such as the visual analog scale (VAS). Patients should be informed that treatment can take months. As each patient is unique, the same treatment can have a varying effect in different individuals. In view of this, a careful examination, and an individually directed non-operative treatment can be prescribed, depending on the patients symptoms. If no improvement is seen within 3–6 months, the patient should be referred to an orthopedic surgeon for further evaluation.

A typical treatment program for patello-femoral pain syndrome can, stepwise, be as follows. Since muscle atrophy and decreased activity of the vastus medialis muscle often occurs, the treatment should initially be directed to restoring the function of this muscle. Training of the vastus medialis muscle can be initiated by electric stimulation. Once the function of the vastus medialis muscle has improved and there is a good balance between vastus medialis and vastus lateralis, proprioceptive training is started. This should be carried out with the knee in flexion. Progressive strength training of the quadriceps can be carried out when there is a balance between vastus medialis and the vastus lateralis muscles. In most cases, the greatest need is for eccentric quadriceps training. This can be done as isokinetic training, which should be done with moderate angular velocity of $90° s^{-1}$. Isokinetic apparatus can also be used for concentric quadriceps training, and is preferably done at a slightly faster angular velocity. Patients showing displacement of the patella from a patellar tracking test, should not exercise at high angular velocity during eccentric muscle work due to an increased risk of patella dislocation. The advantage of isokinetic training (open chain) in the patello-femoral pain syndrome, apart from giving a rapid muscular effect, is that it provides specific eccentric training without impact. Closed chain exercises are usually well accepted. When the muscle strength of the quadriceps has been improved, functional training can be started with progressive increments of knee-loading exercises. If patella hypermobility is present, the training of coordination, muscle strength and knee function can preferably be done with the patella taped or using a patella-stabilizing orthotics.

See also: knee injury

Further reading

Grelsamer, R.P. (2000) 'Patellar Malalignment, Current Concepts Review', *JBJS (Am)* 82: 1639–50.

Rolf, C. and Chan, K.M. (2001) 'Knee Injuries', *FIMS Team Physician Manual*, 15: 365–95, Lippincot, Williams and Wilkins. ISBN 962–356 – 029-X.

CHRISTER ROLF

ANTERIOR SHOULDER DISLOCATION

Anterior shoulder dislocation is the most common type of shoulder dislocations (90–95 per cent). This injury is most common in overhead and contact sports such as rugby, but occurs frequently also from falls during downhill skiing or from bicycles. Dislocation occurs when the arm is abducted and forced backwards in external rotation. The anterior part of the glenoid socket is injured. Its surrounding ligament (labrum) and the anterior capsule is ruptured, in particular the inferior glenohumeral ligament is torn. This is called a Bankart lesion, after an American surgeon who described this injury a long time ago. The humeral head dislocates anteriorly out of the joint and is locked in this position, a painful experience for the patient. Whilst passing the sharp edge of the anterior glenoid socket, an impression fracture often occurs at the posterior superior aspect of the humeral head. This fracture was described by Eve (1880) but is most often called Hills-Sachs lesion, after the author who wrote about this fracture in 1940. The Bankart injury occurs in more than 80 per cent of the patients with anterior dislocation. The simultaneous stretching/rupture of the joint capsule is probably of greater importance for recurrent dislocation than was been earlier believed. What is the complication from an anterior dislocation? In younger people, recurrent dislocation is the most common complication after a first-time dislocation, whilst in the elderly it is common to find stiffness and pain, caused by deterioration through degenerative changes in the joint. In the young, the joint capsule probably has a different elasticity and constitution, which possibly increases the risk of recurrent dislocation. The literature provides no direct evidence why the recurrent dislocation frequency is highest around twenty years of age, nor whether the activity level is of importance. The anterior apprehension test is usually painful up to two weeks after an acute dislocation. Thereafter it is a useful test for increased laxity and recurrent instability. The shoulder is passively abducted to 90° with external rotation of 0°. The elbow is flexed to 90°. The examiner stands behind the patient and puts his/her hand over the acromion. The thumb is pressed lightly on the humeral head from behind while the forefinger rests on the clavicle. With the other hand, the examiner externally rotates the patient's forearm. If the patient reacts with apprehension the test is positive. The relocation test is then used to verify that the anterior instability is the real cause of the positive apprehension. The patient is placed in a supine position on an examination couch. The arm is abducted to 90° and internally rotated with the elbow flexed 90°. From this position, the arm is externally rotated until the patient shows apprehension. The position of external rotation at which pain or apprehension is experienced is registered. Applying a firm anterior pressure, simulating stable anterior structures, the apprehension test should be possible to perform further without inconvenience. If so, the relocation test is positive. Any pain reaction during the test should, however, be noted. Pain alone does not mean that there is an instability problem: it can rather indicate associated injuries to other structures. Even though this is a straightforward diagnosis there are pitfalls to be recognized. In patients with hereditary multidirectional instability, which means joint laxity with function impairment, the sulcus sign is positive. This patient can dislocate or rather subluxate the shoulder anteriorly without having a Bankart or Hill Sachs injury. Sulcus sign should thus always be evaluated. The patient is seated on a chair or an examination couch. The examiner applies a downward traction on the arm by pulling the arm downward. A sulcus will appear under the acromion in patients with multiplane instability and with increased laxity. The sulcus can be graded according to the American Shoulder and Elbow Surgeons standard (0 = no sulcus; 1 = 0–1 cm translation; 2 = 1–2 cm translation or to the glenoid cavity rim; 3 = >2 cm translation or above the glenoid cavity rim). The Carter-Wilkinson index is used to assess general joint laxity, which refers to hypermobility, another condition which has to be recognized in the management of these patients. A plain X-ray is recommended for first-time dislocation and patients with relatively fragile bones such as growing children and the old. MRI is not routinely indicated after a first-time dislocation. There is no evidence that immobilization reduces the risk of recurrent dislocation. An arm-shoulder sling can be used for a day or so. Before returning to sports, the patient should have regained full function, have strength equal to the other shoulder, and have a negative apprehension test.

Acute reconstructive surgery after primary dislocation is not routinely indicated for an average patient. In a ten-year perspective, every other patient younger than twenty-five years is operated on unnecessarily if they are operated on after the first dislocation. However, young patients engaged in throwing sports, with the dominant shoulder involved, should be considered for surgery after a primary dislocation. In many younger patients, recurrent dislocations and subluxations are certainly unpleasant but are often fully compatible with both work and recreation activity. When the subjective problems of instability are no longer tolerated by the patient, and the preferred activity level therefore reduced, there is an indication for surgery. The original Bankart operation is the method recommended in the first place for recurrent anterior shoulder instability. This is a reliable method that in most hands results in further recurrent dislocation in less than 10 per cent of cases. An earlier non-operated unstable shoulder with dislocation arthropathy is managed in relation to the symptoms. If this is caused by instability, the shoulder is stabilized. If the symptoms are caused by osteoarthritis, shoulder replacement is considered. No

studies have shown that early stabilization reduces the risk of osteoarthritis. The primary objective of stabilization surgery is to improve mobility, and not to reduce the risk of osteoarthritis in the future. Arthroscopic stabilization is today the standard method in most sports medicine centers. With development of technical support, the indications for arthroscopic procedures are rapidly increasing. There are, however, cases which require open surgery.

In some injury situations, such as a forceful tackle in rugby, the shoulder is often dislocated with the arm in high abducted position, pushing the humeral head toward the superior structures rather than toward the inferior anterior labrum. The combination of a Bankart injury and a SLAP (superior labrum anterior to posterior) tear is therefore commonly seen in injured rugby players. The use of arthroscopy has allowed the diagnosis and treatment of this injury. The SLAP can not be visualized and examined with open surgery. In elderly patients the combination of anterior shoulder dislocation and rotator cuff tear is not to be underestimated. This is probably caused by the lack of elasticity, an increased stiffness and thus fragility of these collagen structures over time. The clinical examination is thus of extreme importance even when a straightforward anterior dislocation is present. If missed in the first instance, patients with these combination injuries, besides having a sense of recurrent instability, often typically complain of pain and weakness during certain activities, which points in the direction of these diagnoses.

See also: anterior glenohumeral instability; apprehension test; rotator cuff rupture; shoulder injury; SLAP

Further reading

Hawkins, R. and Saunders, W.B. (1996) *Shoulder Injuries in the Athlete. Surgical Repair and Rehabilitation.* ISBN 0-443-08947-7.

CHRISTER ROLF

ANTHROPOLOGY

Anthropology emerged and began to take shape as an academic discipline at the same time that the modern **Olympic Games** were revived. However, although anthropology and large-scale international sports events were born out of the same intellectual impulse, they parted ways soon after that and sport never became a topic of central concern to anthropologists.

Anthropology at the 1896 and 1904 Olympic Games

John MacAloon, the originator of the anthropology of Olympic sport, analyzed the origins of the modern Olympic Games in *This Great Symbol,* his biography of their founder, Pierre de Coubertin. He located Coubertin's philosophy of 'internationalism' (see **international perspectives**) – a respect for each national culture based on the festive performance of difference – within the turn-of-the-century emergence of an imagination of global culture that was also manifested in scholarly and popular ethnography (see **ethnocentricity**). The ethnographic imagination was evident in the Olympic Games from the start. For example, the organizing committee of the first Olympic Games in Athens in 1896 originally proposed that folk dancing and reenactments of customs of 'free' Greeks in Greece and 'enslaved' Greeks in the Ottoman Empire should take place between the athletic contests or in the evenings. The goal of the performances was to show to the spectators not only the antique glories of Greece as embodied in the revived Olympic Games, but also the current conditions of Greeks from the far corners of the world. The proposed reenactments included a Wallachian wedding with the capture of the bride, the kidnapping of a Greek maiden by Turkish Janissary troops, and the revival of the Olympic Games of Ortaköy in Asia Minor during the Byzantine period. However, these plans encountered the resistance of the dancers and in particular the women from the proposed cities and villages, who refused to appear in the stadium before a large crowd. Eventually the plans were dropped because of budget cuts.

From 1851 on, the forces of imperialism, nationalism, and globalization had converged to generate a new kind of public event: the international exposition or world's fair. The 1900, 1904, and 1908 Olympic Games were held in conjunction with world's fairs. In the turn-of-the-century expositions, anthropological exhibits and sporting events played important roles in illustrating the march of progress: anthropological exhibits illustrated the evolution of civilization from savagery to industrial society, and athletic contests the superior physical achievements of civilized men. From the mid-1800s German folklorists had shown an interest in folk games, including athletic games, and the strong German influence on American anthropology was seen in works on games by American anthropologists. Stewart Culin, one of the founders of the American Anthropological Association (est. 1902), organized an exhibition on games of the world at the 1893 Columbian Exposition in Chicago, and later published two books on North American Indian and Oriental games and numerous articles on games. Within North American anthropology, folklore occupies an ambiguous position; folklorists are commonly employed by anthropology departments, but in a few universities folklore is a distinct department. Continuing the German tradition of interest in games, folklorists have typically paid more attention to sports over the last century than have cultural anthropologists.

Anthropology and sport converged at the 1904 Louisiana Purchase Exposition (world's fair) in St Louis. There, the first president of the American Anthropological Association, William McGee, collaborated with the president of the Amateur Athletic Union, James Sullivan, to organize 'Anthropology Days,' in which members of the ethnic groups from the 'living displays' on the exposition grounds competed with each other in running, jumping, throwing, climbing, archery, tug-of-war, and pole-climbing. This experiment was an outgrowth of the exhibit of anthropometry, in which measurements were taken on the assembled ethnic groups in public view for the education of the visitors. The purpose of Anthropology Days was to 'scientifically' test the idea – perhaps inspired by the earlier accounts of savage games – that savages were physically superior to civilized men in speed, stamina, and strength by comparing the Anthropology Days performances to those of the Olympic Games. The lesser performances of the untrained savages were used to support the conclusion that 'savages' were inferior to civilized men, with the exception of a few events such as pole-climbing and bolo-throwing.

Although he did not personally attend the St Louis games, Pierre de Coubertin denounced Anthropology Days as 'inhuman' and 'embarrassing', and the negative reaction to this combination of anthropology and sport on the European-dominated **International Olympic Committee (IOC)** contributed to the separation of indigenous sports from the Olympic Games, with displays of cultural difference largely restricted thereafter to the opening and closing ceremonies and the Cultural Olympiad. This also marginalized anthropology's involvement in what would become the central trend of development in global sports.

State-sponsored ethnography and minority sports in the Soviet Union and China

Anthropologists were, however, involved in the indigenous sports on the margins of the world sports system. Russia had a long anthropological tradition dating to before

the revolution, with Soviet 'ethnography' heavily influenced by German folklore. After 1917, both ethnography and sports were employed in the service of Leninist policies that called for the integration of formerly 'backward' ethnic groups – or 'nationalities' – into the new state. The Tashkent Games of 1920, also called the First Central Asian Games, were designed to draw the mainly Turkic peoples of what were then independent republics into the Soviet order at a time in which the Soviet state had very little real power on its Central Asian frontiers. In accord with Marxist theory (see **Marxism**), the games were also to demonstrate the superiority of **socialism** to the formerly oppressed Turkic minorities both in the republics and across the border in Turkey, Persia, Afghanistan, China, and Mongolia. This sports event preceded scientific studies to produce an ethnographic map of the area in 1924, which resulted in the delimitation of several sovereign states that one-by-one joined the Union of Soviet Socialist Republics over the next decade. Under the heading of 'folklore,' games and sports played a minor role in defining such ethnic groups, along with weightier categories such as language and religious practice. In its rejection of bourgeois competitive sport, the USSR also included demonstrations of folk games and dancing in the opening ceremonies of conventional sports events, including the First Workers' Spartakiad of 1928. The People's Republic of China imitated the Soviet model but gave minority nationality sports an even more prominent place: in 1953 the First National Minority Games were held in Tianjin, and the first two Chinese National Games in 1959 and 1961 included several ethnic minority sports, such as wrestling, polo, horse racing, and swinging, as official or exhibition events. In 1982 the Chinese National Minority Games began to be held at regular intervals of several years. Through ethnographic fieldwork, Chinese ethnologists identified the representative sporting practices of the ethnic minorities in China and catalogued them along with other traits (dress, language, marriage practices, and so on) used to classify each of the fifty-five minority nationalities that were officially recognized by the Chinese state. The National Minority Games were used by the Communist Party to showcase its support for the preservation of minority nationality culture and their integration into the Chinese nation.

Sport in 1970s–1980s North American anthropology: Victor Turner and Clifford Geertz

Perhaps due in part to the overall lack of politicization of indigenous sports in North America until 1990, sports did not attract a great deal of attention among North American anthropologists. Despite the fact that sports, loosely defined, are found everywhere in the world that anthropologists work, the anthropology of sport never congealed into a substantial subfield. Sport studies remained peripheral in anthropology. This may be partly attributed to an elitist bias: sports in non-Western societies have not received as much attention from anthropologists (or folklorists) as have the analogues of European 'high culture', such as painting, sculpture, dance, music, and theater.

From the early 1900s to the 1980s, only a handful of anthropologists and folklorists wrote about games and sports, with Native American sports receiving the most attention. Victor Turner was one of the few major theorists of the 1970s and 1980s who dealt with sports, albeit briefly, in his works on 'liminoid genres'. By this he meant activities that, because of their separation from the structural world of work, contain the potential for creativity and social change (Turner 1982). John MacAloon, who was his student at the University of Chicago, applied Turnerian ideas specifically to sports and developed the concept of

'ramified performance genres'. He argued that the Olympic Games can be analyzed as a series of nested performances: the 'frames' of game, ritual, festival and spectacle, taken together, constitute the phenomenon of the Olympic Games (MacAloon 1984). This notion has received wide application among scholars of the Olympic Games.

Clifford Geertz's 'Deep Play: Notes on The Balinese Cockfight' (1973), is one of the most widely-read anthropological essays of our time. Although cockfights are rather distant from the ideal kind of sport, the concept of 'deep play' that is used to read the cockfight as a text about Balinese culture could easily apply to sports involving human competitors as well. However, this article, despite its popularity, did not motivate researchers to go out and do research on other sports, although it has occasionally proven useful to anthropologists of sport, such as G. Whitney Azoy (1982). Azoy, a student of Victor Turner, wrote an ethnography of the traditional game of buzkashi in Afghanistan, utilizing concepts from Geertz and Turner to show that traditional buzkashi games were not merely games, but were political arenas in which local khans strove to increase their prestige and power; while government-sponsored buzkashi games were arenas in which the provincial governors asserted their power over the khans.

The local/indigenous sport movement in 1980s Europe: Henning Eichberg

In the 1980s there began a world-wide wave of international competitions and sports festivals designed to celebrate local and ethnic identities as alternatives to the rigid national identities expressed in conventional international sports. This included the First Games of the Small Countries of Europe, the First Inter-Island Games, the First Eurolympics of Minority Peoples, and so on. This paralleled a development in international scholarship, including the establishment in 1987 of a French-Danish-German network known as the Institut International d'Anthropologie Corporelle (IIAC), and several conferences in Europe on traditional games (Eichberg 1998: 132–3). The key figure in this trend was Henning Eichberg, who used the notion of 'body culture' (*Körperkultur*) to look at the body primarily as cultural, emphasizing the multiple roles of the body in social process and historical change (Eichberg 1998: 11–27). This concept is undergirded by a political agenda intended to recuperate the body/self from the fragmenting effects of professionalized, competitive sports that characterized the use of *Körperkultur* (commonly translated as 'physical culture') in the East German sports regime before the fall of the Berlin Wall. The concept of body culture has been useful to a few sport anthropologists because it places sport firmly within the context of culture, and thus within the dominant paradigm of cultural anthropology. It does this by linking sports with other kinds of body techniques, so that sports are no longer a separate, peripheral category, but may be linked with other bodily activities such as ritual and theater, as well as everyday practices such as table manners or bodily decorum.

The revival of interest in folk sports in Europe was spurred by the decline of socialism in the Eastern Bloc and the concomitant questioning of state-sponsored, nationalist physical culture. By comparison, the politicization of indigenous sports in North America lagged slightly behind, finally appearing with the organization of the first North American Indigenous Games in 1990. The relationship between indigenous peoples and the Olympic Games, and the use of indigenous cultural practices in the ceremonies and symbols surrounding the games, were a subject of much popular and scholarly debate during the 2000 Sydney Olympic Games, because of the problematic history of the treatment of aboriginal populations.

The Anthropology of Sport *and the Association for the Study of Play*

In Anglophone anthropology, the publication of Kendall Blanchard's and Alyce Cheska's *The Anthropology of Sport* in 1985 marked the fledgling emergence of the anthropology of sport as a subfield. This book was the product of a development that had begun at a conference in 1973, when Cheska gathered together the group of scholars who founded the Association for the Anthropological Study of Play in the following year. The group has held an annual meeting every year since then, but it is symptomatic that in 1987 it changed its name to the Association for the Study of Play (TASP), acknowledging that its members came from a variety of disciplines beside anthropology. Over the years TASP published several proceedings, annuals, and journals. However, while TASP brought together scholars from many disciplines who shared an interest in play, sport, and games, it did not establish a strong presence within the discipline of anthropology itself. *The Anthropology of Sport* discussed ways of looking at sport from the perspective of the conventional subfields of British/American anthropology: physical anthropology, cultural anthropology, archaeology, and linguistics. It also developed an evolutionary model for analyzing sports by reference to level of social complexity (band, tribe, chiefdom state). While it succeeded in showing how an anthropologist trained in conventional anthropological theories might view sports, this book made little original contribution to those theories themselves, and thus failed to capture the attention of the discipline as a whole. The publication of *The Anthropology of Sport* helped to create an identity for the anthropology of sport, and it sold enough copies that it was reprinted in 1995, but there is still no professional journal devoted to the subfield. There is no international organization of scholars; there is no commission on sport among the twenty commissions of the International Union of Anthropological and Ethnological Sciences. There is not an association for the anthropology of sport among the thirty-five sections recognized by the American Anthropological Association, although since 1997 there have been a few panels organized at its national meetings with the purpose of beginning to delineate a subfield.

The anthropology of sport, 1990s to 2003

Many of the best anthropologists of sport turned to their colleagues in sociology and other disciplines for intellectual exchange. Alan Klein published books on such varied topics as baseball in the Dominican Republic, bodybuilding, and minor league baseball on the Texas-US border. An anthropologist by training, Klein found intellectual comrades in the North American Society for Sport Sociology (NASSS), culminating in his election as president for 1998–9. Many anthropologists looked outside their own discipline to networks with sociologists, physical educators, and historians for intellectual exchange because, lacking a solid foothold within the discipline, anthropological studies of sport were marginalized by other anthropologists.

This finally started to change in the 1990s with the advent of new approaches in anthropology drawn from post-colonial studies (see **post-colonialism**), postmodernism, practice theory, **feminism**, and transnational theory. In addition, there was the vast interdisciplinary literature on 'the body' and the acceptance of studies of popular culture into the disciplinary mainstream. As was much discussed in critiques of the discipline, until recent decades anthropologists tended to study societies as if the twentieth century did not exist. Colonial governments were often nearly invisible in ethnographic accounts; affairs of the nation-state ignored, transnational

flows of culture erased. Because they were so entangled with the modern era, Olympic sports were neglected, too. It was not until the discipline turned its attention to post-colonialism, transnationalism, and the world system of nation-states, that sports studies could be located within central disciplinary concerns. As was most forcefully elucidated by Eichberg and the Institut d'Anthropologie Corporelle, and in a less concentrated way by sport ethnographies from the mid-1990s on, the 'modern' sports that comprise the Olympic Games are products of a specific history involving the rise of modern nationalism and the imperialist use of sports as 'civilizing' disciplines by colonialists (particularly the British) and missionaries (particularly the YMCA). Indigenous sports are implicated in these processes because they die out due to neglect in formal physical education programs that emphasize 'modern' sports for nation-building, or they are 'sportized' and promoted internationally in strategies to legitimate national cultures in the international arena, or they fiercely defend their 'traditional' authenticity against the threat of the loss of local identities before the force of Westernization.

The combination of the new theoretical directions in anthropology with the new identity politics of sport produced an increasing number of sport ethnographies as well as edited collections intended as overviews of the state of the field or as textbooks. Certain publishers, such as Berg and Frank Cass, developed series and published a large selection of offerings in sports studies with an anthropological perspective. However, the majority of sport anthropologists still wrote for an audience that shared either their theoretical or area concerns, not for an audience that shared their interest in sport; and in 2003 the anthropology of sport was still not officially legitimated by a national or international association.

References

Azoy, G.W. (1982) *Buzkashi: Game and Power in Afghanistan,* Prospect Heights IL: Waveland Press (2nd edn 2003).

Eichberg, H. (1998) *Body Cultures: Essays on Sport, Space and Identity,* London and New York: Routledge.

Geertz, C. (1973) 'Deep Play: Notes on The Balinese Cockfight', in *The Interpretation of Cultures,* 512–53, New York: Basic Books.

MacAloon, J. (ed.) (1984) 'Olympic Games and the Theory of Spectacle in Modern Socie-ties', in *Rite, Drama, Festival, Spectacle: Rehearsals Toward a Theory of Cultural Perfor-mance,* 241–80, Philadelphia PA: Institute for the Study of Human Issues.

Further reading

Blanchard, K. and Cheska, A. (1985) *The Anthropology of Sport: An Introduction,* South Hadley MA: Bergin and Garvey (2nd edn 1995).

Dyck, N. (ed.) (2000) *Games, Sports and Cul-tures,* Oxford: Berg Press.

Klein, A.M. (1991) *Sugarball: The American Game, the Dominican Dream,* New Haven CT: Yale University Press.

MacAloon, J. (1981) *This Great Symbol: Pierre de Coubertin and the Origins of the Modern Olym-pic Games,* Chicago: University of Chicago Press.

Turner, V. (1982) *From Ritual to Theatre: The Human Seriousness of Play,* New York: Per-forming Arts Journal Publications.

SUSAN BROWNELL

ANTHROPOMETRIC MODELS

These can be used in computer simu-lation models and in calculating body segment inertia parameters. The following three examples illustrate many important points.

Hanavan's human body model

Hanavan's (1964) work was part of the USA space programme designed to improve the performance of self-manoeuvring space-craft through a mathematical model to pre-dict the inertial properties of the human in several quasi-static postures. The model was based on experimentally determined mass distributions and the anthropometry of the person concerned. No account was taken of changes in inertial properties during a change in body position. The model consisted of fifteen segments of simple geometry – the head was a circular ellipsoid of revolution, the two trunk segments were elliptical cylin-ders, the hand was a sphere and the other segments were all frustums (truncations) of circular cones. Twenty-five anthropometric measurements were needed to dimension the model.

The model was validated in a series of relatively simple, symmetrical body posi-tions for which experimental results were available from sixty-six people for the whole body inertial parameters. With the exception of one of the positions studied, where the experimental controls appeared to be poor, the values of whole body mass centre location were such that only 50 per cent of the predicted model horizontal and vertical locations were within 1.3 cm and 1.8 cm respec-tively of the experimental data. The errors in the moment of inertia values were greater, with only half of the values about the two horizontal principal axes being within 10 per cent of experimental values, even ignoring the two worst positions. For the vertical axis, a discrepancy of less than 20 per cent occurred for only half of the data.

The model had simplicity and the small number of measurements needed to specify its parameters as plus points. Its weaknesses were the substantial errors in segment volumes and moments of inertia, arising largely from oversimplified segment geo-metry and the constant density assumption. It also did not permit movements between the head and trunk segments and made no attempt to model the dynamically distinct segments of the shoulder girdle.

Hatze's anthropometric model

The major assumption in the model of Hatze (1980) was the necessary one of segmental rigidity, estimated to result in a maximum error of 6 per cent. The model had the same segments as that of Hanavan above plus the two shoulder girdle segments; it was dimensioned through 242 anthropometric measurements.

The segments in the model were subdivided into subsections of known geometric structure, each having a specified density; by this means the model incorporated density distributions along and across segments. Lower legs and forearms were composed of ten elliptical cylinders of equal heights and different densities; the thighs and upper arms were similar, but with modifications to represent the moving parts of the buttocks and the head of the humerus respectively. The hands were modelled in the grip position, and consisted of a prism and a hollow half-cylinder to which an arched rectangular cuboid was added to represent the thumb. The feet consisted of 103 unequal trapezoidal plates, each having non-linearly varying density. The head–neck segment consisted of an elliptical cylinder to represent the neck and a general body of revolution for the head. The latter was used in preference to the ellipsoidal model of the head, claimed to underestimate the mass of that segment by 23 per cent.

Validation data were reported from two young male athletes, one female tennis player and one twelve-year-old boy. The maximum discrepancies between model and measurements obtained were 5.2 per cent for segment volume and 5.0 per cent for the principal moment of inertia about the frontal cardinal axis. These were attributed, at least in part, to the validating data, swimming trunks trapping air in immersion measurements, and the inability of the participants to relax fully during oscillation experiments.

The strengths of the model were clearly the very small errors reported between predicted and measured parameter values, the incorporation of the dynamically distinct shoulder girdle segments, the allowances for varying segment density, and the personalisation the model offered. However, it is overparameterised – the requirement for 242 anthropometric measurements, taking 80 min to collect, limits its practical use.

Yeadon's mathematical inertia model of the human body

The body segments in the model of Yeadon (1990) were, as in the model of Hatze above but unlike that of Hanavan, subdivided into subsegments (forty in total). Except for the cranium, the body subsegments were represented as stadium solids – solids shaped like a sports stadium – for the five trunk and the hand and foot subsegments or, for the other limb and the head subsegments, as truncated circular cross-section cones. The cranium was represented by a semi-ellipsoid of revolution, the inertia parameters of which are standard.

The dimensioning of the model was provided by a series of simple measurements at the boundaries of the subsegments. The boundary positions were measured using anthropometric callipers, so that the subsegment heights could be calculated. The boundary perimeters, measured with a tape, were used to define most of the truncated cone subsegments of the head, arm, and leg. At the shoulder of the torso, depth was measured as the perimeter could not be. For the other stadium solids of the trunk, hand, and foot, the boundary widths were measured. It should be noted that the error in obtaining cross-sectional areas for these solids was reduced if the perimeter and width were used to define the geometry rather than the depth and width. The model required ninety-five measurements to define it – which Yeadon claimed could be completed in 20–30 min – considerably more measurements than the twenty-four needed for Hanavan's model but far fewer than the 242 required by Hatze's model.

The density values in this model, like those in both of the other models discussed in this entry, were derived from cadaver studies. This is a limitation of all of these models. Each of the major limb segments had a constant density, as did the head–neck segment and the three trunk segments. The variable segmental densities in Hatze's model are probably a closer approximation to reality.

The evaluation of the model involved three trampolinists – two male, one female. The total body masses from the model were compared with those obtained by weighing, and resulted in errors close to 2 per cent for all three trampolinists, which is worse than the value obtained by Hatze. The error was attributed to the effect of breathing on torso measurements. No attempt was made to carry out any evaluation of the accuracy of the segment inertia parameters, although many segmental volumes and centres of volume can be easily measured. Hanavan and Hatze also used measurements of whole body moment of inertia in their evaluations. Yeadon's argument that the evaluation of his model is effectively performed in the motion simulations he carried out slightly sidesteps the issue. In all other respects this model seems an excellent compromise between that of Hanavan, the errors in which are too large and which is oversimplified for modelling and simulating sports motions, and the overparameterised model of Hatze.

See also: body segment inertia parameters; computer simulation models

References

Hanavan, E.P. (1964) 'A Mathematical Model of the Human Body', *AMRL Technical Report*, 64–102, Wright Peterson Air Force Base, Dayton OH.

Hatze, H. (1980) 'A Mathematical Model for the Computational Determination of Para-

meter Values of Anthropometric Segments', *Journal of Biomechanics* 13: 833–43.

Yeadon, M.R. (1990) 'The Simulation of Aerial Movement – II. A Mathematical Inertia Model of the Human Body', *Journal of Biomechanics* 23: 67–74.

Further reading

Bartlett, R.M. (1999) *Sports Biomechanics: Reducing Injury and Improving Performance*, London: E&FN Spon.

ROGER BARTLETT

ANTICIPATION

Following the information processing approach, detection of an early cue within an invariant sequence of events provides a means of reducing the time to response, as all events subsequent to this particular cue become redundant and, therefore, by definition, carry no uncertainty or information-processing load. Essentially, anticipation is a way of reducing the time, or even the stages, of processing that would normally be involved in responding to an unanticipated stimulus. Literature distinguishes between spatial, or event, and temporal anticipation. Spatial anticipation means that the performer knows what kinds of stimuli are going to be presented and what kinds of responses will be required. Temporal anticipation means that the performer knows when some stimulus is going to appear.

If several response alternatives exist in a performance task and one alternative is more predictable than the others, reaction time will be shorter than it would if all the alternatives were equally likely. Experiments have shown that even novice performers, when given advance information or pre-cues about characteristics of an upcoming stimulus, such as its location, reduce their choice reaction time. Researchers presume they organize their movements in advance, completing some of the information processing activities that are usually conducted in the stages after the appearance of the stimulus. If sufficient information is given so that all the aspects can be selected in advance, a response selection stage is not used. Specifically, researchers found that participants start to make a cost-benefit trade-off, according to the probability of the advance information's correctness. When there is a 50–50 chance of the precues being correct, performers respond as if the task is a two-choice reaction time task. When the precue is probably correct, performers' reaction time is faster than if they have not biased their response. However, when the precue is probably wrong, performers' reaction time is slower than it is in the 50–50 condition. Schmidt and Lee (1999) contended that the costs of a wrong anticipation are usually higher than the benefits of a good anticipation.

For temporal anticipation, researchers stipulated that 'foreperiod' is the time between a warning signal, indicating that the stimulus to respond will occur shortly, and the real stimulus. If this interval stays the same for every trial, reaction time can become very short. Researchers contend that this phenomenon happens because the performer can prepare the required action in advance of the stimulus, such that the actual initiation of it begins before the stimulus. However, when the foreperiod is constant but very long – a few seconds or more – and various features of the response are known in advance, subjects apparently cannot shorten reaction times to zero even with extensive practice. The reaction times in tasks with long but regular foreperiods seem to be as long as those in which the foreperiod is short but irregular, thus preventing an early response. Researchers' interpretation is that the internal 'timing' of short durations is much less variable than for long durations.

Anticipations are explained through the motor programs, where the program must be structured completely, before the movement can be initiated. However, Gibson (1994) argued that intentional behavior is prospective in nature, since it must be prepared for any action possibilities offered by the environment. To perceive action possibilities requires detection of both the opportunities offered by the environment and the dynamic properties of the performer. Thus, anticipation might not be solely determined by the properties, such as motor programs, of the performer.

See also: attention and performance; memory motor representations

References

Gibson, E.J. (1994) 'Has Psychology a Future?', *Psychological Science* 5: 69–76.
Schmidt, R.A. and Lee, T. (1999) *Motor Control and Learning, Third Edition*, Champaign IL: Human Kinetics.

Further reading

Schmidt, R.A. and Lee, T. (1999) *Motor Control and Learning, Third Edition*, ch. 4, Champaign IL: Human Kinetics.
Williams, A.M., Davids, K. and Williams, J.G. (1999) *Visual Perception and Action in Sport*, ch. 4, London: E&FN Spon.

DUARTE ARAÚJO

ANTI-DOPING AGENCIES

Until the late 1990s, doping control efforts represented a fragmented approach to an international problem. In part because of the 1998 Tour de France scandal, the International Olympic Committee embarked on a program that would coordinate theses efforts into a single, independent agency. The result of the 1999 Lausanne World Conference on Doping in Sport was the creation of the World Anti-Doping Agency (WADA) that was established in November 1999 and is currently housed in Montreal, Canada. In three years of operation, WADA has reached agreements with thirty-four international sports federations that oversee Olympic sports, and conducts unannounced, out of competition testing.

WADA has a great deal of roles and responsibilities in conducting effective doping control. Its two main purposes are to protect the athlete's fundamental rights to participate in doping-free sport and to ensure harmonized, coordinated and effective anti-doping programs at the international and national level. It is charged with maintaining the List of Prohibited Substances and Methods, as well as accrediting laboratories that test for such substances. WADA must collaborate with affected stakeholders in doping control to maximize the effectiveness of its programs and monitor those programs. WADA develops educational materials for all concerned parties so that the policies and procedures are clear to all. WADA is also given the responsibility to promote, conduct, and fund research in the field of anti-doping

The creation of WADA led to the birth of national anti-doping agencies throughout the world, such as the United States Anti-Doping Agency (USADA) that began operations in October 2000. USADA, like other national anti-doping agencies, was created as an entity that is independent of its national Olympic committee, although must work in close cooperation to achieve its mission. It is recommended that each national agency adopt and implement anti-doping rules, direct and collect samples, manage test results and conduct hearings. The national agencies also implement policies consistent with the international code, maintain athlete whereabouts and assist other anti-doping agencies. Finally, they are designated to develop anti-doping educational programs and promote research.

Anti-doping agencies have the potential to dramatically improve the cooperation and consistency of doping control efforts through standardization and international agreement. Instead of an assortment of organizations with inherent conflicts and agendas, independent agencies can operate in a method of fairness, transparency, consistency and trust. While there has been initial success at the Olympic level, the incorporation of professional leagues remains a challenge.

Further reading

USADA (2003) *United States Anti-Doping Guide,* Colorado Springs CO: USADA.
WADA (2003) *World Anti-Doping Code,* Montreal: WADA. March.

GARY GREEN

ANXIETY AND AUTOMATICITY

Anxiety has been defined as feelings of nervousness and tension that are associated with activation or arousal of a person. Anxiety reactions have been suggested to result from demands placed on a person that are interpreted as threatening or beyond their ability to respond. Anxiety can be either a temporary mood state, state anxiety, or a more stable personality trait, trait anxiety. More specifically, state anxiety is associated with transitory fluctuations in feelings of apprehension and tension in specific circumstances, while trait anxiety is defined as a general predisposition to interpret conditions as threatening and to respond by exhibiting state anxiety.

Anxiety, overall, has a negative influence on performance in general and sports performance in particular. However, anxiety does not always have a negative influence on performance. Automatic processes are less influenced by anxiety than effortful or strategic processes. A process is considered automatic if it requires very few or no cognitive resources or effort, does not require attention − it can occur unconsciously, and is involuntary. By contrast, a process is considered strategic when it requires cognitive resources, requires conscious attention, and is under voluntary control.

The Processing Efficiency Theory (PET) proposed by Eysenck and Calvo (1992) was developed to account for anxiety influences performance. Additionally, it can be used to speak to the relationship between anxiety and automaticity. According to PET, state anxiety, which is typified by worry – also known as cognitive anxiety, and manifests itself as self-preoccupation, concern over evaluation, and concern over performance, occupies a portion of the total processing capacity of the working memory specific to executive functions. Working memory capacity, which is assumed to be limited, is, therefore, reduced by elevations in cognitive anxiety, leaving fewer resources for task-related processing.

An implication of PET is that tasks that require a large amount of working memory capacity are more influenced by anxiety than tasks that require less working memory capacity. This has been supported by studies of participants' performance on various tasks, such as a driving simulator, table tennis, the Stroop Task, and analogical reasoning. The performance of highly anxious individuals was found to be more negatively affected on high working-memory tasks than on low ones. Given that automatic tasks require few or no cognitive resources, performance on automatic tasks should not be influenced by anxiety occupying a portion of the available working-memory capacity. A variety of studies have provided evidence that processes that have become automatized, such as a golf putt, sentence comprehension, or addition of two simple numbers, are little influenced by anxiety compared to strategic processes that require cognitive capacity.

It is clear that anxiety can influence performance; however, the extent to which this happens is determined by the cognitive effort needed to perform the task. If the task requires a lot of cognitive effort, anxiety will have a greater influence on performance than if the task requires less cognitive effort. Performance on tasks that have become automatized and do not require cognitive capacity will be little influenced by anxiety.

See also: trait anxiety

References

Eysenck, M.W. and Calvo, M.G. (1992) 'Anxiety and Performance: The Processing Efficiency Theory, *Cognition and Emotion* 6: 409–34.

MAREIKE WIETH

ANXIETY AND EXPERIENCE

Experience is one of the many factors influencing the effects of anxiety on individuals in sport. Prior experience in sport shapes subsequent cognitive, behavioural, and somatic responses to anxiety. Sport experience is influenced by skill, personality, and attribution style. Highly skilled sport participants typically cope with anxiety better than less skilled participants. Trait anxiety, or neuroticism, a personality predisposition, will adversely affect individuals' responses to anxiety in sport. An individual's experience in sport can be specific to the type of sport, certain tasks within the sport, such as dribbling or shooting, or to specific circumstances occurring in sport, for example, relegation matches or tryouts. The outcomes associated with each of these experiences will influence confidence either positively, e.g. success, or negatively, e.g. failure. The greater the importance, uncertainty, and consequences associated with these outcomes, the greater is the potential for anxiety.

The way in which sport participants attribute or account for sport experiences will also play a role in the effect they have on anxiety. For example, sport participants who experience success in sport and attribute it entirely to internal factors, such as skill and effort, may reduce their anxiety in future performances. However, sport participants who experience success and attribute it to external factors, such as luck or weaker competition, will not necessarily deal with anxiety more effectively in the future. Therefore, successful past performances increase self-confidence and decrease anxiety, but only when they are attributed to an internal locus of control, one that is under the control of the individual. Failures in sport performance that participants attribute to a mix of internal and external factors are more likely to decrease anxiety than failures that are attributed to internal factors, which result in an increase in anxiety, or attributed solely to external factors, which result in a lack of control over future performance outcomes.

Experience in sport also helps individuals cope with and interpret somatic symptoms associated with anxiety and arousal. For instance, an experienced sport participant is more likely than a less experienced one to be familiar with, and to identify, an increase in heart rate and muscle tension before a competition as part of the normal physiological process. In fact, many experienced sport participants view these characteristics as an indication of their preparedness for competition. In contrast, the inexperienced sport participant may interpret these same symptoms as an indication of nervousness and anxiety. This, in turn, may result in an elevated optimal arousal for an experienced sport participant, which suggests that the experienced sport participant performs better under higher arousal than the inexperienced participant. Therefore, an individual's optimal arousal in sport will vary, in part, based on their experience. Consequently, the interpretation of anxiety will influence the effect it has on sport participants more than the intensity of anxiety.

Individual differences in a sport participant's interpretation of anxiety are often overlooked by coaches, who do not consider the varying experience among sport participants when providing them with motivational talks before sport competition. Hence, inexperienced individuals may become over-aroused during these pre-competition motivational strategies, whereas more experienced individuals may view them as unnecessary or insufficient. Sport participants can enhance their experience of anxiety by increasing their awareness of appropriate and expected anxiety responses in sport and developing cognitive strategies, such as imagery, and physiological ones, such as controlled breathing, to cope with anxiety.

See also: arousal and activation; anxiety states; trait anxiety

ANTHONY P. KONTOS

ANXIETY STATES

Anxiety states are current or 'right now' emotional states characterized by feelings of apprehension and tension. These states occur when individuals are highly activated and consciously perceive this activation as unpleasant. This unpleasantness comes from uncomfortable bodily responses such as increased sweating, muscular tension, rapid and shallow breathing, and shakiness, as well as unpleasant cognitive responses such as worry, self-doubt, and fear. People respond with state anxiety when they are confronted with threatening circumstances. The threat that causes anxiety comes from different sources, including fear of failure, fear of evaluation, feelings of inadequacy, fear of not performing well, and fear of physical harm.

Even though anxiety involves unpleasant feelings and thoughts, individuals vary in how facilitative or debilitative these feelings and thoughts are for performance. That is, although its symptoms are unpleasant, anxiety can be helpful or facilitative for some athletes. This is especially true in preparation for competition, where athletes have stated that anxiety is helpful to them, seemingly to aid their focus and the urgency of preparation. In general, each individual has his or her own optimal pre-performance anxiety zone, within which performance will be optimal. Conversely, if the performer's anxiety lies outside this zone, then performance will be impaired. Interestingly, elite, successful, and more highly confident athletes interpret their anxiety states as more facilitative for performance as compared to non-elite, less successful, and less confident athletes.

Whether anxiety states are perceived as facilitative or debilitative is based on athletes' perceptions of control, specifically whether they believe they have the ability to cope with the symptoms of anxiety so as to attain their goals. Thus, state anxiety can enhance performance when people are able to maintain a favorable expectancy about goal attainment. However, state anxiety interferes with performance when worry consumes significant portions of the individual's attentional resources, such that the attentional capacity for the task is reduced. For example, when highly state anxious, attentional focus is narrowed to the point at which task-relevant cues are unable to be processed. In addition, anxiety can influence athletes' attention and subsequent performance by increasing controlled processing, or the deliberate effortful and conscious focus on actual performance execution that is used in learning skills. In competition, athletes typically engage in automatic processing, which is the unconscious, effortless, and smooth performance of well learned skills. State anxiety has the potential to move athletes from automatic to controlled processing as they become consciously aware of their performance and try to control it directly. As an example of this, state anxiety has been shown to hurt performance by interfering with the smooth coordination of agonist and antagonist muscles necessary for performance control and success.

The control of anxiety states is a very salient factor in elite performers' abilities to produce peak performances at important competitions. Strategies that elite performers have reported using to help them control their anxiety states include mental focus plans, pre-performance routines, attentional strategies such as centering, self-talk, or reframing, and emotional control

strategies such as imagery, conscious muscle control, and breathing control. Interventions specifically targeted to control specific anxiety states have been shown to be effective for athletes.

See also: arousal and activation; attention and anxiety; competitive state anxiety and performance; multidimensional anxiety; unidimensional anxiety

Further reading

Gould, D., Greenleaf, C.A. and Krane, V. (2002) 'Arousal-anxiety and Sport Behavior', in T.S. Horn (ed.) *Advances in Sport Psychology, Second Edition,* 207–42, Champaign IL: Human Kinetics.

Woodman, T. and Hardy, L. (2001) 'Stress and Anxiety', in R.N. Singer, H. Hausenblas and C.M. Janelle (eds) *Handbook of Sport Psychology, Second Edition,* 290–318, New York: Wiley.

ROBIN S. VEALEY

APPEAL PROCESS

The right to a fair appeal process is an integral part of any anti-doping program. While athletes at all levels consistently support drug testing, they do insist that it is performed in a just manner and applied equally. Although various organizations conduct appeals differently, almost all of them provide an avenue for athletes to have their cases heard in an impartial manner. The hallmark of an appeal is that it be conducted in a transparent and fair review so that similar cases are decided without respect to an athlete's competitive ability.

For most organizations, the first step in an appeal process is analysis of the 'B' sample. This is generally performed after the 'A' sample has been confirmed and the athlete has been notified of the result. The 'B' sample, which is sealed immediately after the sample is collected, is opened and analyzed. If the 'B' result does not match the 'A', the case is generally dismissed at that point. It is rare however, that the results do not match and a positive test is assigned to the athlete. At this point, the athlete has a choice of accepting the result and subsequent penalty or seeking an appeal. According to the World Anti-Doping Agency (WADA), the athlete, their national federation or Olympic committee, any anti-doping agency, international federation or IOC, can request an appeal.

Many sports organizations, including the international and national anti-doping agencies that oversee Olympic athletes, have adopted a standard of 'strict liability' for the purposes of positive tests. The criterion for strict liability is the mere presence of a prohibited substance is found in the athlete's urine. It is important to note that the manner in which the substance entered the body is largely irrelevant in appeals based on strict liability. Strict liability has the advantage that arbitrators do not have to consider subjective and often unverifiable circumstances that led to the positive test. In an appeal, the burden of proof is on the anti-doping agency to establish that a doping offense has occurred.

Before the advent of **anti-doping agencies**, appeals were heard by the national or international Olympic committees which had the potential for conflicts of interest. WADA now utilizes the Appellate Division of the international Court of Arbitration for Sport (CAS) to hear its appeals and represents a more independent process. The United States Anti-Doping Agency (USADA) first convenes an independent review panel in positive cases to review written materials only and assess whether or not a doping offense has occurred. The athlete can either accept the sanction or proceed to appeal either directly to CAS or first to the American Arbitration Association using arbiters from the North American CAS. If the latter is selected, either the athlete or the international federation has the option of appealing to CAS.

Other sports organizations have their own unique processes for appeal. For example, the National Collegiate Athletic Association (NCAA) of the US conducts appeals in a blinded manner whereby the identity of the athlete and his/her institution is unknown to the appeal panel. All appeals are conducted by conference telephone call and identities are protected. In order to serve the needs of the NCAA's 1,000 schools and 350,000 athletes, strict liability is not followed and extenuating circumstances are occasionally considered.

The appeal process is a key component in any doping program, and must be conducted in a fair and transparent manner that satisfies the needs of all involved stakeholders.

References

Olympic Movement Anti-Doping Code, Prohibited Classes of Substances and Prohibited Methods 2003. http://www.wada-ama.org/docs/web/research_science/prohibited_substances/Prohibited%20Classes%20of%20Substances%20and%20Prohibited%20Methods%202003.pdf

USADA (2003) United States Anti-Doping Agency, Protocol for Olympic Movement Testing, Colorado Springs CO: USDA.

GARY GREEN

APPENDICULAR SKELETON

The appendicular skeleton consists of the bones of the upper and lower limbs and those of the shoulder and pelvic girdles, through which the limbs attach to the axial skeleton. The bones of the upper limb can be divided into the bones of the shoulder, arm, wrist, and hand. Similarly, the bones of the lower limb can be divided into the bones of the hip, leg, and foot.

The upper limb bones are the humerus in the upper arm, the ulna and radius in the forearm, and the carpals, metacarpals, and phalanges of the hand. The shoulder girdle consists of the clavicles, or collarbones, which attach to the sternum medially, and the scapulae, or shoulder blades, which are connected to the trunk by muscular attachments only. The major joints of the upper limb are the shoulder, elbow, wrist, and the articulations of the individual digits.

The shoulder is a ball and socket joint. The ball is the proximal end of the humerus, which sits in the shallow socket of the scapula known as the glenoid cavity. This enables the shoulder to be extremely versatile in its movements and it is capable of multiaxial rotation. The humerus is held in place by strong ligaments and tendinous attachments. The elbow joint is a hinge joint formed by the articulation of the humerus and ulna and, therefore, has only one main axis of rotation, for flexion-extension. The radius does not contribute to the elbow joint. However, the articulation between the radius and the ulna is responsible for pronation and supination of the hand. With the elbow flexed to 90° from the anatomical position, the hand is in a supinated position when it is palm up and pronated when palm down. This movement is achieved by the radius crossing over the ulna in the forearm. The wrist lies between the ulna and radius of the forearm and the metacarpal bones of the hand. This joint is biaxial, permitting flexion-extension and abduction-adduction.

The lower limb bones are the femur in the thigh, the patella, or kneecap, the tibia and fibula in the calf, and the tarsals, metatarsals, and phalanges in the foot. The pelvic girdle is made up of the hip-bones, the *os coxae*, each of which comprises the ilium, ischium, and pubis; it is a much more rigid structure than the light and mobile shoulder girdle. The major joints of the lower limb are the hip, knee, ankle, the subtalar joint, and the metatarsophalangeal joints of the toes.

There are some similarities between the upper and lower limbs. The hip joint is a ball and socket joint, like the shoulder, but the femur is more deeply set into the hip-bone. The hip is similarly capable of multiaxial rotation and is the most mobile joint

of the lower extremity. When bearing weight, the knee appears to be a hinge joint, like the elbow; its major movement is flexion-extension. Only the larger bone of the calf, the tibia, contributes to the knee joint; the fibula only contributes to the ankle joint. The ankle is also a hinge joint: rotation of the foot about the other two axes of rotation is achieved through the oblique subtalar joint of the hind foot, or rear foot.

See also: ankle and foot; axial skeleton – structure and function; cardinal planes and axes; elbow and forearm

Further reading

Williams, P.L., Bannister, L.H., Berry, M.M., Collins, P., Dyson, M., Dussek, J.E. and Ferguson, M.W.J. (eds) (1995) *Gray's Anatomy: The Anatomical Basis of Medicine and Surgery*, Section 6, Edinburgh: Churchill Livingstone.

CLARE E. MILNER

APPREHENSION TEST

The apprehension test is a common clinical test used to evaluate the presence of anterior shoulder instability.

Glenohumeral anterior shoulder instability is caused by a previous anterior shoulder dislocation, which often is associated with a significant trauma. Recurrent instability occurs as a consequence in a majority of younger patients sustaining this injury, in particular if they participate in overhead sporting activities. It can be assessed by the anterior apprehension test, which reflects an anterior translation of the humeral head in relation to the glenoid socket, possible due to the typical Bankart injury which is an avulsion of the anterior labrum from its normal position at the anterior edge of the glenoid caused by the acute dislocation. A Bankart injury occurs in an absolute majority of traumatic anterior dislocations.

The apprehension test is performed either with the patient sitting in a chair or in supine position. It is important that the shoulder muscles are relaxed, whatever technique is used. The shoulder is passively abducted by the examiner to 90°, initially with no external rotation. The elbow is flexed to 90°. The examiner stands or sits behind the patient and puts one hand over the test shoulder's acromion. The thumb is pressed lightly onto the tissues overlying posterior humeral head, 2 cm low and 1 cm medial to the posterior lateral corner of the acromion, whilst the forefinger rests on the clavicle. With the other hand, the examiner abducts and externally rotates the patient's forearm. If the patient reacts with apprehension (attempting to move in other direction and protect the shoulder) or shows a subluxation tendency during this maneuver, the apprehension test is positive. This reflects symptoms caused by an increased anterior laxity and translation of the humeral head out of the joint. To verify the validity of this test the relocation test is used. The patient and examiner maintain the same starting positions. The arm is abducted to 90° and internally rotated with the arm flexed 90° at the elbow. From this position, the arm is externally rotated until the patient shows apprehension. The grade of external rotation at which apprehension is experienced is registered. By applying an anterior support with one hand over the anterior part of the shoulder in order to support the anterior shoulder structures, the shoulder is again moved into external rotation which now is allowed further without apprehension if the relocation test is positive. It is important not to release the anterior pressure with the hand until the arm is internally rotated again; otherwise the shoulder joint can dislocate and the test can cause severe discomfort. This test was described by Frank Jobe in 1989. Later Speer reevaluated the test and found that if the patient reacts with pain alone, it is difficult to assess whether it is caused by a subtle instability, or an associated rotator cuff or labrum injury. Doing this test with

patients with multidirectional joint laxity or general joint laxity can show a significant anterior translation of the humeral head, as if it was subluxating, but with little subjective discomfort. Chronic anterior recurrent instability can also be complicated by stiffness and concomitant injuries to the shoulder which blur the outcome of the apprehension test. In acute traumatic anterior shoulder dislocation, the apprehension test will of course be painful due to the acute tissue trauma and concomitant inflammatory reaction. Thus the test has its best potential in patients with recurrent anterior instability.

See also: anterior glenohumeral instability; Bankart injury; shoulder injury

Further reading

Hawkins, R. and Saunders, W.B. (1996) *Shoulder Injuries in the Athlete. Surgical Repair and Rehabilitation.* ISBN 0-443-08947-7.

CHRISTER ROLF

AROUSAL AND ACTIVATION

The construct of activation is an athlete's ability to respond to a task demand based on their arousal. Arousal is the general excitation of an organism, based on a continuum from deep sleep to extreme excitement. This continuum reflects the relationship that exists between arousal and athletic performance. For example, a low arousal, when one is drowsy, is not conducive to the demands of physical exertion in sports. An athlete who exhibits a high arousal, however, could run the risk of being too excited to perform effectively. A concomitant factor with this continuum of activation is that arousal is a combination of physiological and psychological activity in an athlete. Physiological signs such as muscle tension, increased blood pressure, and physical relaxation as well as psychological factors such as motivation, anxiety, and self-talk can all affect the arousal of an athlete. The balance of these physiological and psychological factors in one's activation state can have a significant impact on performance.

Arousal and activation, in relation to performance, have been examined using many theories. One of the earliest theories to try to explain the impact of arousal on performance was the inverted-U hypothesis. Other theories of the arousal-performance relationship are cue utilization, multidimensional activation, drive theory, and reversal theory. All of these explanations examine the effects of arousal on standard of performance and readiness for competition. Because each of these theories has strengths and weaknesses, understanding the precise relationship between arousal and performance has become an important topic in sport and exercise psychology research.

See also: arousal and activation – individual differences; arousal and activation strategies; cue utilization; reversal theory; self-talk; Yerkes-Dodson Law

Further reading

Hardy, L., Jones, G. and Gould, D. (1996) *Understanding Psychological Preparation For Sport*, ch. 5, Chichester: John Wiley.

R.A. HEDSTROM

AROUSAL AND ACTIVATION – EFFECTS OF EXPERIENCE

The relationship between experience and arousal has been commonly discussed within the context of arousal and performance. It has been commonly assumed within the academic community of sport psychology that the arousal deemed optimal for performance interacts with the experience or skill of the performer. Indeed, most introductory textbooks contain a section within the arousal-performance chapter that highlights this notion. In addition, a great deal of anecdotal evidence exists from coaches.

Owing to the common acceptance and anecdotal evidence, limited research has been directly conducted on this topic. Evidence of research interest evidence is found in related topics. For instance, Zajonc (1965) discussed the importance of skill within the context of social facilitation and Drive theory. The most important determinant of performance in Drive theory is the dominant response. Most dominant responses are thought to be impacted by skill or experience. The dominant responses of experienced athletes are assumed to be correct or best for complex task performance, whereas the dominant response for inexperienced athletes is assumed to be detrimental for complex task performance. More specifically within the social facilitation literature, the effects of the audience are hypothesized to be detrimental to novice individuals performing a complex task. In contrast, expert or experienced individuals in the same conditions are hypothesized to perform well. Unfortunately, although most social facilitation experiments have demonstrated the effect of skill on performance under differing conditions, arousal was not always measured or inconsistent findings occurred with the palmar sweat index of arousal.

In addition to social facilitation research, psychophysiological research has reported differences with experience using corresponding arousal measurements. Several researchers in the last twenty years have extensively examined the physiological patterns associated with performance. These investigations either provide training to novice performers or use elite, or experienced, and novice, or inexperienced, performers in a cross-sectional experimental design to gain an understanding of potential physiological adaptations to training. Findings consistently demonstrate that experienced performers are less aroused, as indexed by heart rate, than their novice counterparts in a variety of performance tasks, ranging from pistol shooting to parachute jumping.

Although the relationship between experience and arousal is commonly accepted, intuitive, and empirically supported, one must not generalize this to all performers. For instance, within experienced performer research, evidence exists that the age of the performer moderates the experience-arousal relationship. Molander (1989) examined heart rate patterns of highly experienced younger – age range 22–36 years – and older – age range 47–58 years – miniature golfers. Although all performers were highly experienced and skilled, the heart rate patterns of the older players before execution of the putting stroke demonstrated an acceleration pattern that was deemed to be detrimental to performance. The heart rate patterns of the highly experienced and skilled younger performers decelerated before executing the putting stroke. The deceleration pattern is typically believed to be beneficial to performance of skills such as putting and pistol shooting. Hence, performer experience does affect arousal, but this relationship within experienced performers may be moderated by age.

See also: arousal and activation – effects of personality; Yerkes-Dodson law

References

Molander, B. (1989) 'Age Differences in Heart Rate Patterns During Concentration in a Precision Sport: Implications for Attentional Functioning', *Journal of Gerontology* 44: 80–7.
Zajonc, R.B. (1965) 'Social Facilitation', *Science* 149: 269–74.

Further reading

Fenz, W.D. and Jones, G.B. (1972) 'Individual Differences in Physiologic Arousal and Performance in Sport Parachutists', *Psychosomatic Medicine* 34: 1–8.

Pijpers, J.R., Oudejans, R., Holsheimer, F. and Bakker, F.C. (2003) 'Anxiety-performance Relationships in Climbing: A Process-oriented Approach', *Psychology of Sport and Exercise* 4: 283–304.

MARC LOCHBAUM
DEBBIE J. CREWS

AROUSAL AND ACTIVATION – EFFECTS OF PERSONALITY

The relationship between personality and performance has been extensively examined for over forty years, with much attention being paid to this topic from the late 1950s to the early 1980s. Underlying the notion that certain personalities are optimal for sport performance is the belief that the personality affects the relationship between performance and arousal or activation. Sport psychologists differ over the exact distinctions between arousal, activation, and motivation. These definitional differences are important for gaining a better understanding of sport performance, although they may confuse the reader. Within the sporting environment, many researchers operationalize arousal and activation within the motivation framework. For this entry, readers should view the arousal and activation constructs as synonymous, and are referred to Landers and Boutcher's (1988) operational definition of arousal as an energizing function that harnesses of the body's resources in preparation for and during intense and vigorous activity.

The most popular personalities that have been conceptually linked to, or gained research support as affecting, the arousal-performance relationship are extraversion-introversion and trait anxiety. These personalities have traditionally been conceptualized within the **Yerkes-Dodson law.** Based on earlier work of Royce, Eysenck *et al.* (1982) are best known in sport psychology for their discussions of the potential impact of the personality super factor, extraversion-introversion. The extraversion-introversion hypotheses are based on the underlying cortical arousal of these personalities. More specifically, they hypothesized that extraverts are cortically under-aroused and, thus, are better able to handle higher arousal in performance-oriented contexts. In contrast, introverts are chronically over-aroused and, hence, hypothesized to have difficulty handling higher arousals. Hence, writers of sport psychology textbooks have typically suggested that the Yerkes-Dodson law is modified based on these personalities. More specifically, the extravert's inverted-U arousal-performance relationship shifts to the right, whereas the introvert's inverted-U arousal-performance relationship shifts to the left.

In addition to the extraversion-introversion super factor, research attention has focused on the effects of trait anxiety on the arousal-performance relationship. High trait-anxious performers are hypothesized to have greater state anxiety under performance conditions and thus to be more highly aroused. In addition to interacting with arousal, anxiety is theorized to interact with task complexity. For instance, high-anxious individuals are hypothesized to perform better on simple tasks when the effects of high arousal are beneficial when compared to low-anxious individuals, whereas, with a complex task, low-anxious performers are hypothesized to outperform their high-anxious counterparts. For instance, Weinberg and Raglan (1978) demonstrated that indeed high-anxious individuals perform complex tasks better under low arousal conditions, whereas low-anxious individuals perform complex tasks better under high arousal conditions.

Investigations of the effects of personality on sport performance have endured since the late 1950s. Unfortunately, most of this research was conducted over twenty years ago, with more than 600 published articles between 1960 and 1980. Because few of these research investigations have specifically and systematically investigated the effects of personality on arousal-performance theories, the basic hypotheses have remained unchallenged for decades.

See also: arousal and activation – effects of experience

References

Eysenck, H.J., Nias, D.K.B. and Cox, D.N. (1982) 'Sport and Personality', in S. Rachman and T. Wilson (eds) *Advances in Behaviour Research and Therapy*, 1–56, New York: Pergamon Press.

Landers, D.M. and Boutcher, S. (1988) 'Arousal-performance Relationship', in J. Williams (ed.) *Applied Sport Psychology: Personal Growth to Peak Performance*, 197–236, Mountain View CA: Mayfield.

Weinberg, R.S. and Raglan, J. (1978) 'Motor Performance Under Three Levels of Stress and Trait Anxiety', *Journal of Motor Behavior* 10: 169–76.

Further reading

Landers, D.M. and Arent, S. (2001) 'Arousal-performance Relationship', in J. Williams (ed.) *Applied Sport Psychology: Personal Growth to Peak Performance*, 206–28, Mountain View CA: Mayfield.

Thompson, R. and Perlini, A. (1998) Feedback and Self-efficacy, Arousal, and Performance of Introverts and Extroverts, *Psychological Reports* 82: 707–16.

MARC LOCHBAUM
DEBBIE J. CREWS

AROUSAL AND ACTIVATION – INDIVIDUAL DIFFERENCES

Activation is an athlete's ability to respond to the demands of a task based on their arousal at the time of performance. This arousal can range from low, during sleep, to high, when extremely excited. The relationship that exists between activation and athletic performance is mediated by the athlete's individual personal characteristics. Because of the idiosyncratic factors associated with the activation-performance link, individual differences are found during fluctuations in arousal.

One individual difference that has a major impact on arousal is experience. An athlete who understands the task demands could experience a different response to arousal owing to familiarity. This individual difference will affect both physiological and psychological responses to athletic performance. For example, an athlete who is unfamiliar with the task at hand might experience signs of arousal that could hinder performance, for example increased heart rate, negative self-talk, or increased muscle tension. Because of these symptoms, an athlete may not be able to perform in his or her individual zone of optimal functioning. Experienced athletes have a better chance to adjust their physiological and psychological symptoms of appropriate arousal to attain their individualised zone through several techniques.

Individual differences in arousal and activation also exist between sports. Team sports and individual sports place different demands on athletes, resulting in various arousal states. For example, singles tennis players do not need to adjust their arousal to compensate for a team-mate. They do, however, rely solely on their individual zone of optimal functioning for performance.

Further reading

Hardy, L., Jones, G. and Gould, D. (1996) *Understanding Psychological Preparation For Sport*, ch. 5, Chichester: John Wiley.

R.A. HEDSTROM

AROUSAL AND ACTIVATION STRATEGIES

The relationship between activation and arousal is an important topic within applied sport psychology research. An athlete's ability to be ready for a performance task is defined as his or her activation. One's arousal can impact this activation. Arousal is a combination of physiological and psychological factors that influence an athlete's excitation. Athletes have used certain strategies in an attempt to affect this relationship between arousal and activation.

Strategies used to affect the extent of activation and arousal include physiological, cognitive, and behavioural techniques. Performance practices include **relaxation training** – physiological, **self-talk** – cognitive, and **goal setting** – behavioural. Another practice used by athletes is the development of pre-performance routines, allowing athletes to develop contingency plans for handling their fluctuating activation throughout a competition. Each of these techniques can influence the factors associated with arousal. For example, if an athlete is experiencing muscle tension, this could affect his or her ideal performance and activation. By using a strategy, such as relaxation training or self-talk, an athlete can influence his or her ability to be properly activated for the performance task. Further, athletes can devise pre-performance routines to develop an overall strategy for counteracting factors that impede low activation.

All of these strategies can be used by an athlete to perform at his or her desired activation. Incorporating activation strategies into performance training can allow athletes a comprehensive approach to dealing with the physiological and psychological factors associated with the arousal-activation relationship.

See also: arousal and activation; arousal and activation – individual differences

Further reading

Hardy, L., Jones, G. and Gould, D. (1996) *Understanding Psychological Preparation For Sport*, ch. 5, Chichester: John Wiley.

R.A. HEDSTROM

AROUSAL AND ACTIVATION THEORIES

Activation refers to an athlete's preparedness to respond to a task or demand. This activation is influenced by the athlete's individual arousal, measured on a continuum from sleep to extreme excitement.

An athlete's activation state is a combination of physiological and psychological factors affecting their overall readiness to perform at a desired standard.

Several theories have been used to understand better the affect of activation state and arousal on performance. The inverted-U hypothesis (Yerkes-Dodson law) has examined the relationship of activation and performance in a curvilinear manner. The inverted-U hypothesis takes into account only the physiological responses to arousal. Several other theories used to investigate this construct are cue utilization theory, multidimensional activation, drive theory, and reversal theory. Multidimensional activation refers to the impact of arousal on the cognitive processes of an athlete. This theory states that multiple processes affect an athlete's ability to properly reach a desired activation (see **individual zones of optimal functioning**). Multidimensional activation stresses the importance of cognitive strategies such as self-talk and pre-performance routines. Drive theory views the arousal-performance relationship as a linear association. As arousal is increased, performance also increases. Conversely, low arousal and activation state lead to lower standards of performance. Each of these theories, while consisting of methodological strengths and weaknesses, have aided investigation of the relationship between activation state and performance. Understanding this association between activation and performance could allow athletes to experience an enhanced control over physiological and psychological responses to arousal.

See also: arousal and activation; arousal and activation – individual differences; cue utilization; reversal theory; Yerkes-Dodson law

Further reading

Hardy, L., Jones, G. and Gould, D. (1996) *Understanding Psychological Preparation For Sport*, ch. 5, Chichester: John Wiley.

R.A. HEDSTROM

ART

From prehistoric times to the present, innumerable artists have attempted to depict athletes in action and to express their sense of the cultural significance of sports. Among the first images that are certainly about sports (rather than noncompetitive physical movement) are the images of wrestlers on the walls of ancient Egyptian tombs. Far more numerous than the scattered images documenting sports in Egyptian, Minoan, and Mycenean cultures were the many thousands of vase paintings, statues, and statuettes from Greek and Roman antiquity. The black-figured and red-figured vases awarded to the victors at the Panathenaic Games offer an especially impressive set of athletic images. *The Discus-Thrower*, by the fifth-century BC sculptor Myron, is among the world's most widely recognized works of art. Few examples of Roman sports-related art have survived, most of them mosaics picturing gladiators or charioteers. Ancient images of female athletes are especially rare, but a fourth-century AD mosaic in Sicily's Villa Armerina shows ten young bikini-clad women engaged in an athletic contest.

Organized sports were far less important during the Middle Ages than were the sports of antiquity, and they attracted fewer artists, but the illustrations of medieval manuscripts like the Manasseh Codex picture jousting knights. Archery matches, which were the pastime of choice for the urban middle classes, were sketched by draftsmen of limited skill, while defter artists were attracted by the colorful pageantry of Renaissance tournaments. As tournaments fell out of favor, fencers began to appear in drawings like Willem Swanenburg's *The Fencing Hall*, which carefully placed them in geometrically defined space.

In eighteenth-century English sporting art, horse races figure prominently, as they did a century later in the work of Edgar Degas and other Impressionists. Cricketers are portrayed in innumerable works, none finer than Benjamin West's *The Cricketers* (1763), which depicts five young aristocrats from Virginia and South Carolina, all five presumably proud to play a game that marked them as culturally English.

Sports figure much less prominently in Asian art than in European and American, but polo – 'the sport of kings' – is an exeptional case. Sixteenth- and seventeenth-century Persian and Indian painters adorned manuscripts with miniature depictions of the game. Chinese sculptors of the T'ang dynasty produced countless terracotta statuettes of male (and female) polo players. Japanese aristocrats were fond of archery contests, images of which abound on scrolls and screens. Inexpensive nineteenth-century woodblock prints are more likely to show the hugely muscled sumo wrestlers whose grapplings delighted the masses.

Baseball and other sports appear in the Currier and Ives lithographs that were the American equivalent of the Japanese prints, but the most memorable work was done by Thomas Eakins. His pictures of oarsmen include the masterpiece, *Max Schmitt in a Single Scull* (1871). Like his European contemporaries, Eakins was also fascinated by wrestlers, whose straining muscles brought to life his anatomy charts. Henri Rousseau's charmingly primitive *Rugby Players* (1908) is among the best-known paintings of the era. Women appeared mainly as tennis or croquet players, as they did in John Lavery's *A Rally* (1885), Max Liebermann's *Tennis Players at the Seaside* (1901), Edouard Manet's *Croquet Party* (1873), and a series of oils by Winslow Homer (1865–9).

In the twentieth century, as sports became as important as they had been in ancient Greece, the number of images of athletes increased exponentially. Hardly a single major artist failed to produce at least one or two depictions. If we think of runners, Pablo Picasso's *The Race* (1922), Robert Delaunay's *Runners* (1926) and Willi Baumeister's *Female Runner* (1927) come quickly to mind. That the action and excitement of modern spectator sports are thematically attractive is clear from Lionel Feininger's *The Bicycle Race* (1912), Max Beckmann's *Rugby Players* (1929), and Nicholas de Stael's *Soccer Players* (1952). More leisurely sports, enjoyed without spectators or mass-media coverage, appear in quieter works such as Henri Matisse's *A Game of Bowls* (1908) and David Inshaw's *Badminton* (1972–3). George Bellows exposed the shadowy side of sports with *Both Members of the Club* (1908) and a number of other pictures of boxers at their bloody work.

The closest Andy Warhol came to the genre of sports in art seems to be his silkscreen print, *Torso* (1977), but his pop-art contemporaries made up for the deficit. Roy Lichtenstein's *Girl with a Ball* (1961) is a good example. The century's most prolific producer of sporting canvases was probably LeRoy Neiman, whom one might categorize as a belated Expressionist. *Volvo Masters* (1983) can serve as a representative example of his work.

Paolo Gioli's *Eakins' Man* (1982), which mimicks a set of multiple photographic exposures of a naked runner, suggests that photographers, who have frequented sports grounds since the late nineteenth century, have now taken over the exacting task of fixing for all time the ephemeral moments of sport.

Reference

Kühnst, P. (1996) *Sports: A Cultural History in the Mirror of Art*, trans. Allen Guttmann., Dresden: Verlag der Kunst.

Further reading

Bickford, L. (1994) *Sumo and the Woodblock Print Masters*, Tokyo: Kodansha International.
Boggs, J.S. (1998) *Degas at the Races*, New Haven CT: Yale University Press.
Coombs, D. (1978) *Sport and the Countryside in English Painting, Watercolours and Prints*, Oxford: Phaidon.

Cooper, H.A. (ed.) (1996) *Thomas Eakins: The Rowing Pictures*, New Haven CT: Yale University Press.

ALLEN GUTTMANN

ARTHROSCOPIC SURGERY

The concept of arthroscopic surgery is to perform the surgical procedures through keyhole incisions with the highest precision and accuracy. Arthroscopic surgery has seen great advancement since it was first introduced by Professor Takagi of Tokyo, who became the first to examine the interior of the knee joint in 1918. Since then many researchers from Europe have published their experiences, but one of the major contribution was made by Watanabe, who published his *Atlas of Arthroscopy* in 1957, which was later revised in 1969. He also developed Watanabe arthroscopes, which were used widely.

The principles of modern arthroscopy are quite simple. An arthroscope is connected to a light source and a camera. The camera is also connected to a monitor so that the interior of the joint can be seen on the monitor. The scope is introduced into the joint through a small incision. Another small incision is made into the joint and other instruments such as scissors and graspers can be introduced through it. The arthroscope comes in different sizes depending on the joint for which the arthroscopy is being done. The camera comes with different angles but a 30° angle scope is most commonly used.

The scope also has an inflow for the fluid to enter the joint. This distends the joint and makes visualization better. Normal saline is the fluid of choice: it is isotonic and does not cause damage to the articular cartilage. Arthroscopy can be performed on most joints of the body, which have a potential space for insertion of an arthroscope. The most common joints for which arthroscopy is done routinely nowadays are the knee, shoulder, elbow, ankle, and wrist.

The other joints where arthroscopy is done less commonly are the hip joint and the metatarsophalyngeal joints.

The visualization improves with a good light source and sufficient distension of the joint. Many fluid pumps are available in the market – these maintain a constant pressure in the joint. This facilitates not only the visualization but also any surgical procedure that may be required. Easy-to-use power instruments are now widely available and have revolutionised arthroscopic surgery.

The arthroscopy of the knee, ankle and small joints of the foot can be performed either with or with out tourniquet control. The advantage of the tourniquet is that it produces a completely bloodless field, which aids in visualisation. However the tourniquet can only be applied for a limited duration, which is around a maximum of two hours for the lower extremity. However this is usually enough for most arthroscopic procedures carried out in the lower limb joints. The tourniquet can lead to neuroparesis.

Many surgeons like to carry out the arthroscopy without a tourniquet, and apply it only if bleeding is encountered during the procedure.

Arthroscopy can be done under general anaesthesia, spinal anaesthesia, or local anaesthesia. All three are quite safe and depend on the condition of the patient, the preference of the patient and anaesthetist, and the surgeon's level of comfort and familiarity with the type of procedure.

The advantages of arthroscopy are numerous but mainly there is reduced postoperative morbidity, smaller incisions, less inflammatory response, precise diagnosis and accurate surgery. There is also a lessened complication rate, decreased rehabilitation time and reduced hospital costs as most patients who have arthroscopic surgery can be discharged to their homes the same day. There are some disadvantages as well. The foremost is a steep learning curve. Arthroscopic surgery requires a triangulation technique, which has to be learnt in order to perform the procedures. It could therefore be time-consuming at first. The instruments are also expensive. However, these disadvantages are few and the benefits far outweigh them.

The commonest shoulder arthroscopic procedure is possibly the subacromial decompression, which has reduced morbidity and prolonged rehabilitation, associated with open subacromial decompression.

The shoulder arthroscopy has improved our understanding of SLAP (superior labrum anterior to posterior) lesions. These lesions are likely to be missed if an open anterior stabilisation procedure is being performed. With the improvement of surgical techniques and development of modern arthroscopic instruments it is now easily possible to repair these lesions. Instruments have to be small to pass through small holes, yet must be strong and durable in order to resist breakage. Small absorbable screws are now available which come with sutures to fix such lesions. The greatest advancement seen in the arthroscopic surgery of the shoulder is perhaps the anterior stabilisation of the shoulder. Many open procedures have been carried out to stabilise the shoulder for this purpose in the past. The lesion involves the capsule as well as the glenoid labrum, which is detached from the glenoid rim, creating a potential space in front of the neck of the scapula to accommodate the dislocated humeral head. Use of endoscopic instruments and small diameter screws and other implants can accurately and securely repair this lesion. The results of anterior stabilisation of the shoulders done arthroscopically are now comparable to the results of open stabilisation. This has marked effect on early rehabilitation, which is vital for elite athletes who want to return to their sporting activities as soon as possible.

The repair of rotator cuff is also done arthroscopically now, a procedure which is technically more demanding but has shown encouraging early results. There has also been the development of new user-friendly instrumentation, and stronger and better suture material for the repair of rotator cuff tears.

In the knee joint the most common procedure remains anterior cruciate ligament reconstruction (ACL) and excision or repair of meniscal tears. These are done as day case procedures. The visualisation of the meniscal tear is complete and an excision or repair can be done with modern implants and instrumentation. Recently darts or arrows have been used for fixation. All inside suturing techniques are also available and depend on the expertise and preference of the surgeon. Arthroscopic ACL surgery has also shown favourable results. The grafts most commonly used are the patellar tendon bone graft or the hamstring tendons. The strength of these two types of graft is almost the same, with almost no difference in the results reported in the literature. The success of the procedure depends on a number of factors. Surgical technique has to be precise, with accurate placement of the femoral and tibial tunnels and adequate notchplasty if required. Patients follow an extensive rehabilitation programme after surgery.

In the ankle joints the loose bodies are easily removed, and osteochondritis dissecans lesion can be likewise treated. A loose ankle can also be better evaluated with an arthroscopic procedure.

Hip arthroscopy is mainly done for labral tears and removal of loose bodies or for evaluation of a painful joint with no obvious cause.

Similarly, the elbow joint can have loose bodies taken out through the scope rather than via open procedure.

Arthroscopic surgery is certainly the way forward, but familiarisation with open techniques is important, as sometimes an open approach may be required for the benefit of the patient; for example, a difficult rotator cuff tear may not be amenable

117

to arthroscopic repair. Similarly, a revision procedure for failed arthroscopic anterior stabilisation may be better treated with an open procedure.

Arthroscopic surgery continues to expand as new instruments and better techniques are developed. This seems to be the future of many other procedures, which are at present carried out in a conventional manner.

CHRISTER ROLF

ASIAN GAMES

The Asian Games are a comprehensive sports competition for Asian countries that materialised at India's instigation. The first Asian Games took place in 1951. The Asian Games are held every four years in the interval between the Olympics. With the involvement of many traditional Asian sports that are not included in the Olympics, such as muay Thai and sepak takraw, the popularity of the Asian Games continues to grow with each passing event. At the fourteenth Asian Games in Pusan, South Korea, held in 2002, all forty-three member countries and regions of the Olympic Council of Asia, including North Korea, were represented. The first Winter Asian Games took place in 1986, in Sapporo, Japan. The fifteenth Asian Games are scheduled for Doha, Qatar.

MUNEHIKO HARADA

ASIAN SPORTS

While many of the sports in comprehensive sporting events, as typified by the Olympics, are of European or American origin, there are some sports that have their roots in Asia. Out of these, judo, tae kwon do, and keirin will be included in the 2004 Olympic Games in Athens. At the 2002 Asian Games in Pusan, these sports were joined by others such as kabaddi, karate, sepak takraw, bujutsu, and soft tennis. Sports that are seeking to gain international

competitive status include sumo, kendo, and naginata, all with their origins in Japan. These sports all have their own world competitions. Kick-boxing, a fighting sport modelled after the Thai national sport muay Thai (Thai kick-boxing), was created in Japan. The International Wushu Federation is aiming to introduce wushu events, including women's tai chi, at the 2008 Olympic Games in Beijing.

MUNEHIKO HARADA

ASSET-BASED SECURITIZATIONS (ABS)

ABS financing was first used to capitalize the construction of the Pepsi Center Arena, which opened in 1994 as the new home of the Denver Nuggets NBA team and the Colorado Avalanche NHL team. The private developer of the new arena raised $139.8 million to underwrite a significant share of the construction costs. Shortly thereafter, the Los Angeles Arena Corporation used ABS financing to borrow $315 million to build the Staples Center, which also opened in 1999 and hosts two NBA teams, the Los Angeles Lakers and Los Angeles Clippers, and the NHL's Los Angeles Kings. To date, securitizations have been used to build at least twelve major sport facilities, totaling more than $1 billion in the US.

With ABS, the most creditworthy revenue streams projected to emanate from a structure are bundled into a financial security and sold to private, usually institutional, investors. The major difference between ABS financing and standard private-placement debt agreements is that the asset-backed approach does not require all revenue produced by a facility to be pledged to debt repayment. For example, the Pepsi Center agreement required only four of the ten multi-million, multi-year sponsorships and the facility's suite leases be pledged as security for the ABS bonds. Typically in private-placement arrangements, the team or facility operator is required to commit all future venue income as collateral for construction loans. The attraction of the ABS option is that only a portion of a new facility's revenues must be pledged as security.

To date, ABS bonds have been secured from such contractually obligated income sources as long-term naming rights agreements, luxury suite leases, concession contracts and long-term corporate sponsorship deals. The revenue produced form these contractually binding sources can be considerable. The Staples Arena is a prime example. The downtown Los Angeles arena contains 160 suites that lease from $197,500 to $307,500 annually; the ten 'founding' corporate sponsorship agreements net $50 million, and the naming rights contract is worth $105 million. These three assets alone produce an estimated $40 to $45 million annually. The ability of facilities like the Staples Center to generate such substantial cash flows makes them attractive candidates for ABS.

Another feature of ABS financings which differentiates them from standard private borrowing arrangements is that the contractual ownership of the specific revenues are first sold into a trust which in turn issues notes to investors. The trust structure is created to make the possibility of bankruptcy more remote, so that if the arena or stadium owner should declare bankruptcy, the assets of the trust remain inviolable. This 'bankruptcy remote' feature of the ABS transaction makes them more attractive to prospective institutional investors. Typically, an established financial institution will establish and administer the trust. The trust sells investors the ABS bonds secured by the future income from contracted revenue streams, together with the renewal rights to any of the selected revenue streams. The commitment of renewal rights is an important feature of ABS transactions because it means investors have a

long-term claim on revenue sources that are often short-term in nature. For example, the initial contract term for many luxury suites and corporate sponsorships does not extend beyond 3–5 years. By conveying the right to access revenues from subsequent contract renewals of suite leases, concession contracts, etc., investors have greater assurance of timely repayment.

With an asset-backed transaction, the independent trust acts as the transaction agent. The trust first collects the promised facility revenues pledged by the facility operator, and then redistributes them to each investor on a pro rata basis to meet guaranteed principal and interest payment obligations.

Both the Pepsi Center and Staples Center asset-backed bonds sold out quickly. In the case of the Pepsi Center, the $139.8 million ABS notes were sold at a 6.94 per cent rate of interest for twenty-one years to five institutional investors. The bonds were secured by revenues produced from three contracted asset sources: luxury suites, concessionaire contracts, and four of ten corporate sponsor packages. The interest rate was 1 per cent above the ten-year US Treasury Note rate at the time of the transaction. The company developing the arena proclaimed that the lower interest rate saved up to $3 million annually (approximately 10–15 per cent of the Denver Nuggets' and Colorado Avalanche's annual operating revenues) compared to the cost of traditional financing. In addition, the facility operator and its principal tenants (the Nuggets and Avalanche) have unrestricted rights to all revenues not dedicated to repaying the ABS bonds.

The Spanish soccer club, Real Madrid, one of the world's elite teams, sold $70 million worth of bonds secured solely by its membership fees (Real has 75,000 fans who pay to be official club members) and ticket sales which typically amount to $40 million a year. The team used the proceeds to acquire top players. The ABS is perceived to initiate a circle of events, i.e. the club uses the money to buy players who help them become more successful. This, in turn, means they get more people in the stadium and more television revenue, so there is additional income to pay the bonds. Previously Real Madrid had securitized the team's $10 million annual footwear and apparel sponsorship agreement with Adidas, which enabled them to sell $50 million of bonds to investors.

JOHN L. CROMPTON

ASSOCIATIVE AND DISSOCIATIVE STRATEGIES

The attentional strategies of athletes when confronted with pain and discomfort can often be categorised as either dissociative or associative. Some athletes use an associative strategy, in which their focus is internal and is used to remain acutely aware of bodily sensations yet unaware of the environment. This strategy might include focusing on the athlete's breathing or muscle tension. Other athletes might use a dissociative strategy, in which they maintain an external focus by tuning into environmental distractions and stimuli, such as music or scenery, as opposed to their bodily sensations. Dissociation tries to prevent the athlete's recognition of their body's feedback. The timing and effectiveness of each of these techniques may vary according to individual preferences; however, the strengths of each technique seem to counterbalance the other's weakness. It is possible that these techniques are most effective when used in combination.

For instance, the use of association may help athletes, such as distance runners, maintain appropriate effort in competition by allowing them to monitor the status of their body sensations and using these to set their pace. An internal focus would allow a runner to tell if he or she was running too fast or not fast enough. Additionally, this type of monitoring may help prevent injuries, as athletes are more in tune to pains and abnormal sensations occurring in their body. For example, a runner would use an internal focus to note light-headedness or that a hamstring was overly tight and would readjust his or her pace, or even stop if necessary. In contrast, using association may also prove detrimental once an athlete has been injured or is recovering from an injury, as the athlete might focus too much attention on favouring the injury or protecting it from re-injury, failing to note appropriate task demands during competition. For example, an American football player, who is worried about re-injuring his shoulder, might focus solely on how his shoulder is feeling after each tackle, so much so that he neglects to hear the called signals for the next play.

Conversely, dissociation can help injured athletes by allowing them the external focus needed for the demands of competition. A dissociative focus would have helped the football player hear the play calls. As well, when faced with difficult or painful tasks, athletes often find it easier to be preoccupied with external stimuli, such as pleasant surroundings, chants, and music, all of which serve to distract the athlete from feelings of fatigue and discomfort. Thus, athletes can train harder and for longer periods. However, in contrast to those using an associative strategy, these athletes might be subject to injury as their external focus prevents them from noticing important internal signals, such as a tight hamstring or dizziness.

Both associative and dissociative techniques can be used in combination with each other, which may be the most beneficial for elite athletes. For instance, distance runners might find using an associative strategy helpful early in a race, when they can use the internal information to help set their pace, and periodically thereafter to check for pain or potential injuries. The remainder of the time might be most productively used with a dissociative strategy to distract the athlete from fatigue and boredom and assist in the maintenance of harder effort.

TIFFANYE M. VARGAS-TONSING

ATTENTION – FOCUSED AND DIVIDED

Attention and performance are clearly linked, with errors of attention – such as losing concentration, becoming distracted, and attending to the wrong cues – resulting in poor performance. For this reason, there has long been interest, both in psychology and, more recently, in the sport sciences, in understanding more about attention and its many components. In the psychology literature, the term 'attention' has been used in many different ways. One context in which attention has been used is to refer to a person's capability to remain alert, or concentrate, over an extended period. Humans can sustain peak concentration for only a few seconds, with this alertness being influenced by a range of factors including arousal and activation. A second context in which attention has been used is in relation to the limited capacity people have for processing information, particularly when it arises simultaneously from multiple sources. Because processing capacity is limited, the optimal use of available capacity is essential for successful performance of many tasks. Depending on the nature of the task and the skill of the performer, optimal performance may be achieved either by focusing attention – to apply maximum resources to a particular task element, or by dividing it in an attempt to spread available resources concurrently between multiple tasks or task elements.

Focused, or selective, attention provides a means by which certain information can be preferentially selected for detailed processing while other information can be ignored. Performance is optimal if attention can be focused in such a way as to ensure that all relevant information is processed

and all irrelevant or potentially distracting information is not. For example, a basketball player attempting a free throw has the greatest chance of success if attention is focused on task relevant cues, such as the target position on the backboard or the 'kinaesthetic feel' of the correct movement pattern, rather than on task irrelevant cues, such as the distracting sounds and movements of the opposing team's fans. Both the relevant and irrelevant information may arise from sources external to the performer or internal – kinaesthetic feedback, mental images, thought patterns.

Several methods have been developed to determine to what cues or sources of information performers selectively attend in performing particular tasks. Behavioural methods have included selective masking or occlusion of particular cues to determine the impact on performance. Physiological methods have included the recording of people's eye movements – or visual search strategies – and measurements of brain activity as people perform the task of interest. Cognitive methods have included people self-reporting on their attentional focus and attentional style. The use of multiple methods is increasingly favoured as each method in isolation is imperfect. Self-report methods, for example, may be unreliable as people need not necessarily be consciously aware of the particular cues to which they are attending. Studies of focused attention have consistently revealed systematic differences in the allocation of attention between highly skilled and less skilled, or novice, performers. Experts typically have been shown to be able to pick-up information from cues that are additional, and usually earlier occurring, than those on which novices rely for their performance. For example, in soccer experienced players spend less time than inexperienced players attending to the ball or the ball carrier and more time attending to other features, such as the movement of other players.

In contrast to focused attention, divided attention necessitates the sharing of processing resources between two or more concurrent activities. For example, a basketball player dribbling the ball down the court needs not only to ensure that relevant information for the control of the ball is processed but also must, at the same time, process information about the position and movement of team-mates and opponents to execute a successful play. It has been well documented since the late nineteenth century that humans have some very significant limitations in capability to perform two tasks at the same time, although the extent of this limitation appears to be dependent upon the specific nature of the tasks and the skill of the person performing the task. Concurrent tasks that require the same sensory or motor system to perform, such as two tasks dependent on vision or two tasks dependent on response by the hands, or tasks that share some competing organisational structures, such as two tasks with different timing requirements, are particularly troublesome. However, extensive practice appears to remove some of these constraints.

The typical approach that is used to examine divided attention involves a dual-task methodology in which participants are required to perform a secondary task, such as a reaction time task, while simultaneously performing a primary task to the best of their ability. In sport settings, the primary task is typically a fundamental skill, such as ball control. Secondary task performance – relative to conditions in which the secondary task is performed alone – provides a measure of the attention demand of the primary task and the capability of the performer to divide attention effectively between the competing tasks. Superior secondary task performance is generally evident when the primary task is relatively simple or the performer is highly practised and skilled. For example, in the skill of juggling, the more competent jugglers demonstrate better secondary task performance than do those less competent, and secondary task performance improves as the juggling skill becomes more proficient. Methods have also been developed to estimate overall attentional workload using self-report measures and physiological correlates such as pupil diameter, cardiac acceleration-deceleration and variability, and electrical activity in various regions of the brain.

Two fundamentally different forms of information processing underpin aspects of both focused and divided attention (Schneider and Shiffrin 1977). Controlled processing occurs consciously, is slow, occurs in strict steps, and requires significant processing resources. Automatic processing occurs without conscious awareness, is rapid, can occur in parallel rather than in series, and appears to require very limited processing resources. With practice, more processing appears to become automatic, or at least more automatic than in the early stages of learning, and it is this progression that allows the skilled person to perform better than a novice when attention is divided. The challenge confronting researchers is to understand in greater detail how experts make more effective use of attention than lesser-skilled performers and to seek out means by which the acquisition of expert control of attention can be facilitated.

See also: arousal and activation; attention – theoretical aspects; skill-acquisition stages – control.

Reference

Schneider, W. and Shiffrin, R.M. (1977) 'Controlled and Automatic Human Information Processing, I: Detection, Search, and Attention, *Psychological Review* 84: 1–66.

Further reading

Abernethy, B. (2001) 'Attention', in R.N. Singer, H.A. Hausenblas and C.M. Janelle (eds) *Handbook of Sport Psychology, Second Edition*, 53–85, New York: John Wiley.

Abernethy, B., Summers, J.J. and Ford, S. (1998) 'Issues in the Measurement of Attention', in J.L. Duda (ed.) *Advances in Sport and Exercise Psychology Measurement*, 173–93, Morgantown WV: Fitness Information Technology.

Moran, A.P. (1996) *The Psychology of Concentration in Sports Performers: A Cognitive Analysis*, Hove: Psychology Press.

BRUCE ABERNETHY

ATTENTION – THEORETICAL ASPECTS

Attention is the ability to focus on one cue while ignoring others. Attention research is characterised by three theoretical approaches: information processing, social psychological, and psychophysiological. Information processing approaches are focused on the role of attention and other information-focused psychological processes such as perception, memory, and decision-making. Scholarship within this theoretical approach has provided information about individuals' ability to focus on certain cues while screening out others. Information processing theorists have also examined issues such as alertness and the amount of information to which an individual can attend. Social psychological approaches to attention have examined the impact of social factors, such as distraction, on attentional processes. A large body of research within the social psychological approach has focused on attentional style. Attentional style research assumes individuals possess unique capacities to attend to information in different settings. Attentional style varies along two dimensions: width – broad to narrow – and direction – internal to external. Psychophysiological approaches have examined the relationship between attention and physiological variables such as the electroencephalogram (EEG) or heart rate. A lot of quantitative research on attention within each theoretical approach has been conducted. It is recommended that future research utilises broader multi-theoretical approaches and explores qualitative methodologies.

See also: attention – focused and divided; attention and anxiety; attention and performance; attention and performance model; attention theories; attentional narrowing; attentional style; attentional training

Further reading

Boutcher, S.H. (1992) 'Attention and Athletic Performance: An Integrated Approach', in T.S. Horn (ed.) *Advances in Sport Psychology*, 251–63, Champaign IL: Human Kinetics.

CHRISTINA JOHNSON

ATTENTION AND ANXIETY

Anxiety, in its state form, is a negative emotional feeling that is characterised by nervousness, distress, and tension. Anxiety over a competition can influence performance in various ways. One way is through changes in attention. Based on the theory of cue-utilisation, as an athlete's anxiety increases, his or her perceptual field narrows to the point where he or she cannot utilise task-relevant cues needed to execute performance successfully. Not only do anxious athletes reduce their perceptual field, they also scan their field less often. Another way in which anxiety can affect attention is by reducing an athlete's ability to rapidly shift his or her attentional focus as circumstances demand. For instance, a soccer goalkeeper may need to shift from a broad-external focus towards many potential strikers to a more narrow focus as the shot is coming so as to make the save. Performance anxiety may reduce this attentional flexibility. Anxiety can also cause an athlete to attend to inappropriate cues, such as focusing on worry, one's physiological responses, spectators, and becoming more self-aware. An increase in self-awareness can be disruptive to well-learned tasks that typically run through automatic processes. Finally, anxiety can affect attention by taking up a portion of one's processing capacity of working memory. This leaves an athlete with fewer resources for processing the demands of the task at hand.

See also: attention and performance model; attentional style; concentration and attention strategies; controlled and automatic processing; cue utilization.

Further reading

Boutcher, S.H. (1992) 'Attention and Athletic Performance: An Integrated Approach', in T.S. Horn (ed.) *Advances in Sport Psychology*, 251–63, Champaign IL: Human Kinetics.

DEBORAH L. FELTZ

ATTENTION AND PERFORMANCE

The research within 'attention and performance' has sought to illuminate basic questions about the human mind by examining human performance in relatively simple tasks. When the term is used in the context of human performance, attention refers to engagement in the perceptual, cognitive, and motor activities associated with performing skills. Researchers investigating human performance have shown that humans have attention-limits that influence their performance, such as the difficulty of performing more than one task at a time. The most popular attention theories propose that we have a limited capacity to process information. Some theories consider this limitation to be a central pool of attentional resources. Multiple resource theories arise from an alternative view that proposes several resources from which attention can be allocated.

From an information-processing approach, the term attention is used to refer to three different processes. First, the construct of attention has been postulated to explain the selectivity of attention – focused attention. Second, it relates to our ability to distribute attention across several concurrent tasks – divided attention. Third, it refers to our state of alertness or readiness for action.

One issue that involves reaction time measurements is that they are usually studied in highly unrealistic settings. One important component of these is that the participant is seldom allowed to anticipate future-near events. Clearly, under these conditions, humans will be very limited in information processing, violating the tenets of rationality. Providing both spatial and temporal anticipation allows early regulation, whereas providing real environmental information leads to more accurate and faster response.

See also: anticipation; information processing approach; serial and parallel processing.

Further reading

Schmidt, R.A. and Lee, T. (1999) *Motor Control and Learning, Third Edition*, ch. 4, Champaign IL: Human Kinetics.
Williams, A.M., Davids, K. and Williams, J.G. (1999) *Visual Perception and Action in Sport*, ch. 2, London: E&FN Spon.

DUARTE ARAÚJO

ATTENTION AND PERFORMANCE MODEL

More that a century after William James described attention as: 'the taking possession by the mind, in clear and vivid form, of one out of what seem several simultaneously possible objects or trains of thought' (James 1890: 404), there is a general consensus that attention is fundamental to skilled motor performance. Despite this seemingly obvious contention, the specific mechanisms responsible for attention's affect on performance remain poorly understood.

According to Boutcher (2002), our current understanding of how variations in attention impact sport performance is largely derived from research conducted from three theoretical perspectives – social psychological, information processing, and psychophysiological. Social psychological theorists and researchers tend to emphasise the extent to which internal or external distractions – such as worry, self-awareness, negative thoughts, and spectators – and individual attentional predispositions, such as attentional style, result in attention being focused on cues that are relevant or irrelevant to the task at hand. In contrast, information processing theorists view attention through a 'stimulus-processing-response' model, in which information enters the body through the sensory system and is processed either consciously, effortfully, slowly, and inefficiently – control processing – or unconsciously, effortlessly, quickly, and efficiently – automatic processing. Although all sport performances require a combination of control and automatic processing, their relative use depends on the task demands and on the extent to which the task has been learned. Generally, a static task environment allows for automatic processing, whereas tasks performed in a dynamic environment require more conscious thought and effortful attention. Similarly, novices often find it necessary to engage in a lot of conscious effortful attention to perform the skill properly. The skill of dribbling a basketball can be used as an illustration. When first learning to dribble, the novice expends much attention in the completion of this task. Even the slightest lapse will result in a performance error. In contrast, when the task is well learned, the performance becomes automatic, requiring very little conscious effortful thought, thus allowing the performer's attention to be directed towards other task-relevant cues, such as position of team-mates and opponents. Another advantage of automatic processing over control processing is the 'attentional capacity', which appears to be associated with control processing and means that attending consciously to multiple tasks or dividing attention among various cues may impair performance. Both social psychological and information processing perspectives embrace the notion, initially set forth by Easterbrook (1959),

that high arousal reduces the perceptual field and, thereby, reduces the processing of environmental cues. The psychophysiological perspective uses physiological changes, such as cortical and cardiac activity, as markers of attention. For example, certain cortical activity measured by electroencephalography can be interpreted as an indicator of attentional focus.

By synthesising various research paradigms and theoretical perspectives used in studying attention, Boutcher was able to construct a model of the attention-performance relationship, integrating the most salient aspects from each. Figure 3 illustrates that the theoretical perspectives complement each other to describe more fully the attentional process and how it influences performance. Specifically, the social psychological perspective contributes to the understanding of how internal and external factors, such as enduring dispositions, task demands, and the environment, contribute to arousal. The information processing perspective then describes how this arousal may be channelled into control or automatic processing of information. The relative appropriateness with which control and automatic processing are used will, in turn, determine performance quality. Finally, the psychophysiological perspective is used to monitor physical responses as indicants of attention.

See also: attentional narrowing; attentional style; Yerkes-Dodson law

References

Boutcher, S.H. (2002) 'Attentional Processes and Sport Performance', in T.S. Horn (ed.) *Advances in Sport Psychology, Second Edition*, 441–57, Champaign IL: Human Kinetics.

Easterbrook, J.A. (1959) 'The Effect of Emotion on Cue Utilization and the Organization of Behavior', *Psychological Review* 66: 183–201.

James, W. (1890) *Principles of Psychology: Volume 1*, New York: Holt.

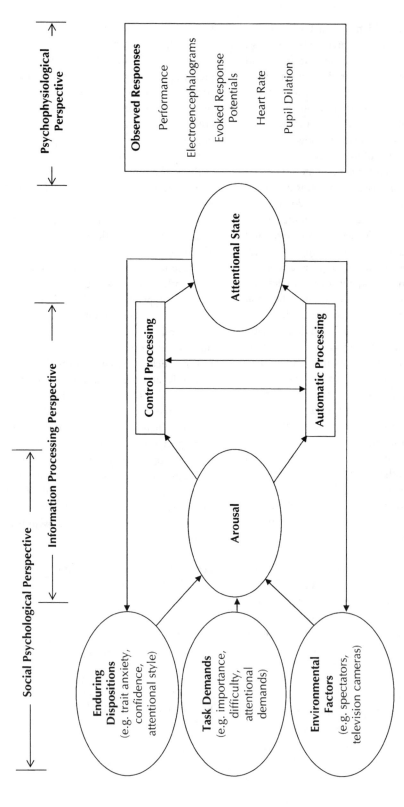

Figure 3. Theoretical and research perspectives contributing to various aspects of Boutcher's model of internal and external factors and attentional processing. Adapted, by permission, from S.H. Boutcher (2002) 'Attentional processes and sport performance', in T. Horn (ed.) *Advances in Sport Psychology, Second Edition*, 441–57, Champaign, IL: Human Kinetics, p. 449.

Further reading

Csikszentmihalyi, M. (1975) *Beyond Boredom and Anxiety*, San Francisco CA: Jossey-Bass.

Gould, D., Eklund, R.C. and Jackson, S.A. (1992) '1988 US Olympic Wrestling Excellence, II. Thoughts and Affect Occurring During Competition, *The Sport Psychologist* 6: 383–402.

RICK ALBRECHT

ATTENTION THEORIES

A basic assumption of the information processing approach is that there is a limitation on the amount of information that can be processed at one time. As a consequence performers need to be selective in what they process to avoid cognitive overload. Therefore, several theories have emerged assuming different characteristics, such as fixed or flexible capacity, selectivity by available processing resources or selectivity for controlling action.

Some researchers have argued that there is a bottleneck somewhere in the information-processing system that allows performers to perceive only a part of what is available in the environment. Much of the early research was concerned with identifying the location of the bottleneck in the processing sequence and under what conditions attention could be divided between two or more tasks. These theories assumed that attention was a fixed capacity for processing information and that performance would deteriorate if this capacity was approached or exceeded by the task requirements. However, evidence supporting an attention mechanism located both early and late in the processing sequence has argued against attempts to locate attention selection at a particular stage of processing.

In contrast with bottleneck theories, attention can be viewed as a general, flexible capacity, as was argued by the Nobel Prize laureate Daniel Kahneman. Thus, the amount of available attention, a limited resource, can vary depending on certain conditions related to the individual, the tasks being performed, and the context. Kahenman's theory could explain why different bottlenecks emerge for different individuals and for different task combinations. This approach also differed from fixed capacity models by suggesting that parallel processing occurs in all the processing stages, but with some demanding of attention at the same time. However, flexible capacity theories could not explain, for example, inconsistent interference when different secondary tasks are coupled with the same primary task, since, according to the theories, the interference should be consistent.

A different view of attention is as multiple resource modules, each with their own unique capacities and resource-performance relationship. Within such a perspective, attention can be committed to separate stages of processing at the same time. Wickens contended that interference could then be explained in the extent to which the two tasks use common resource features. In this model, no special selective attention mechanism is proposed; rather selection is viewed simply as the process of allocating resources.

A criticism of the previous models has been that instead of relating attention to the analysis and interpretation of sensory information, it should be related to the control of action. Neumann (1996) argued that when a person has the intention to attain some goal, many received stimuli are processed, the final product being the selection of a certain action. Then, as a result of this selection, certain processes are prevented from occurring. Neumann suggested that it is the selectivity of action that explains why capacity is limited, contrary to the traditional view that selection is needed owing to the restricted capacity to process information. Selective attention is required because of physical constraints that require performers to select between competing actions. These constraints require that performers select the most relevant information to control action. Thus, selection for action is the most fundamental process of attention, not resources or capacity. The selected action requires certain sub-processes or structures for its completion, and preventing some other action from using them would ensure that the selected action would, in fact, have a good chance of being completed and of having its goal fulfilled.

See also: attention and performance; information processing approach; serial and parallel processing

Reference

Neumann, O. (1996) 'Theories of Attention', in O. Neumann and A.F. Sanders (eds) *Handbook of Perception and Action, Volume 3: Attention*, 389–446, San Diego CA: Academic Press.

Further reading

Williams, A.M., Davids, K. and Williams, J.G. (1999) *Visual Perception and Action in Sport*, ch. 2, London: E&FN Spon.

DUARTE ARAÚJO

ATTENTIONAL NARROWING

Drawing upon early findings that increased arousal tends to reduce the field of cue utilisation, Easterbrook (1959) developed a theory of performance based on an individual's range of cue utilisation. This theory also tried to reconcile the apparently contradictory findings about the relationship between arousal and performance – that at low arousal, an increase in arousal tends to be associated with a facilitation of performance, yet at higher arousals such an increase generally has an opposite disruptive effect. The theory of cue utilisation not only assumes that a shrinkage of the perceptual field takes place as arousal increases but also hypothesises further that, as cue utilisation is reduced, task-irrelevant cues are excluded from perception before task-relevant cues, and the simultaneous use of task-irrelevant and task-relevant cues tends to disrupt performance. Further, the complexity of different tasks will vary in the number of perceptual cues that must be used simultaneously to achieve a desired behaviour.

Given these basic assumptions, performance on a given task may be attributed, at least in part, to the congruence between the perceptual demands inherent in that task and the performer's range of cue utilisation. The bottom portion of the figure illustrates how the reduction in the size of the perceptual field may relate to task performance. If an individual's range of cue utilisation is relatively broad for the perceptual demands of the task, response effectiveness is reduced by the simultaneous use of task-relevant and task-irrelevant cues that are contained in the relatively broad perceptual field. At the other extreme, it is possible that one's perceptual field becomes narrowed to such an extent that it excludes not only those task-irrelevant stimuli in the environment, but some task-relevant cues as well. When this occurs, performance again deteriorates. This time, however, the decrement is not the result of distraction caused by attending to both relevant and irrelevant cues, but occurs from a loss of task-relevant cues within the perceptual field.

Easterbrook hypothesised that the extent of cue utilisation, therefore, may be used as a possible explanation for the curvilinear relationship between arousal and performance. As illustrated in Figure 4, very low arousal results in a peripheral field so broad that it includes virtually all environmental cues available to the performer. At this point, there is little discrimination between those cues that are relevant to the performance of the task at hand and those that are totally irrelevant. As arousal becomes moderate, the perceptual field gradually narrows, with only secondary, or task–irrelevant, cues initially being excluded from the performer's range of cue utilisation. At the same time, primary, or task–relevant, cues are retained within the perceptual field, thereby offering an explanation for the optimal performance generally observed at intermediate or moderate arousal. However, as arousal increases beyond 'moderate', the range of cues being used continues to shrink until even those cues that are relevant to the central task become excluded from the performer's perceptual field. Accompanying this failure to incorporate all necessary task-related cues is a logical corresponding decrease in overall performance.

Attentional narrowing has not only been identified as a possible mechanism in the disruption of performance under high stress, but also it has more recently been incorporated into a predictive model of athletic injury. Simply put, high arousal results in attentional narrowing that, in turn,

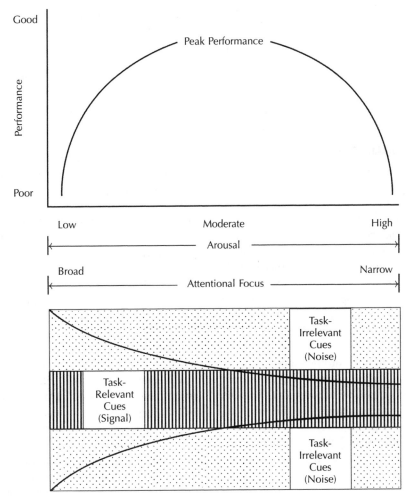

Figure 4. Attentional narrowing and the arousal-performance relationship. Adapted, with permission, from Landers, D.M. (1980) The arousal-performance relationship revisited, *Research Quarterly for Exercise Science and Sport* 51: 77–90. Copyright 1980 by the American Alliance for Health, Physical Education, Recreation and Dance, 1900 Association Drive, Reston, VA 20191.

results in failure to pick up vital – potentially injurious – cues in the environment.

See also: attentional style; attentional training

References

Easterbrook, J.A. (1959) 'The Effect of Emotion on Cue Utilization and the Organization of Behavior', *Psychological Review* 66: 183–201.

Further reading

Anderson, M.B. and Williams, J.M. (1988) 'A Model of Athletic Injury: Prediction and Prevention', *Journal of Sport and Exercise Psychology* 10: 294–306.
Nideffer, R.M. (1976) 'Test of Attentional and Interpersonal Style', *Journal of Personality and Social Psychology* 34: 394–404.

RICK ALBRECHT

ATTENTIONAL STYLE

Common admonitions by coaches, athletes, and spectators, such as 'pay attention' or 'keep your eye on the ball', imply that the ability of athletes to focus their attention on task-relevant cues, while ignoring task-irrelevant stimuli, is at least partly responsible for the difference between success and failure in sport. One possible explanation for the relationship between attention, arousal, and performance in athletics is Nideffer's theory of individual attentional style (Nideffer 1976a; 1976b).

Drawing heavily on previous research into cue utilisation theory, the concepts of broad and narrow attention, and individual perceptual style differences in internal and external scanning ability, Nideffer developed a parsimonious theory of individual attentional style and human performance. According to this theory, at any single moment an individual's attentional focus may be described by its position along the two dimensions of attentional breadth and direction. Breadth of attention refers to the amount of information to which an individual is attending and ranges along a continuum from narrow to broad. At the same time that attention is focused in this generally broad or narrow manner, it is also primarily directed towards either internal thoughts and feelings or external sources of stimuli. According to the theory, although most individuals possess, to some extent, the ability to shift their attentional focus along each of these continua, there is a natural predisposition to spend an inordinate time functioning within a relatively limited range along each of these two dimensions of attention. As a result of this personal inclination towards a standard type of attention, it becomes theoretically possible to categorise an individual's personal attentional 'style' as being predominantly broad-external, broad-internal, narrow-external, or narrow-internal. In an effort to assess the attentional constructs contained in his theory, Nideffer (1976a) developed the Test of Attentional and Interpersonal Style (TAIS), which contains nine subscales ostensibly measuring 'interpersonal' traits, two that reflect behavioural and cognitive control, and six subscales purporting to measure individual attentional style. Although the psychometric properties of the interpersonal subscales have rarely been examined, the attentional scales have been subjected to considerable empirical investigation – with generally mixed results.

Superimposed on this foundation, that everyone possesses a preferred attentional style, is the basic assumption that various behavioural tasks make different situational demands on a performer's attention. Nideffer organized these demands into four distinct categories reflecting the theoretical types of attentional style – broad-external, broad-internal, narrow-external, and narrow-internal. The more one's personal attentional style 'matches', or is congruent with, the specific situational demands of a given task, the better one is likely to perform that task. An example of a task that is frequently cited in the sport science literature as requiring a narrow-external attentional focus is that of hitting a baseball. The theory of attentional style would predict that batters with a narrow-external individual attentional style, thereby corresponding to the situational task demands, will tend to perform this task more effectively than those hitters possessing a relatively broad-external, broad-internal, or narrow-internal attentional style.

Arousal also interacts with attentional style to impact on performance. As arousal increases, one is unable to shift rapidly one's attentional focus from one type to another, for example, from narrow-internal to broad-external. This lack of attentional flexibility typically results in a rigid adherence to one's predisposed attentional style, even though it may not match the attentional demands required by given circumstances, leading to a decrement in performance.

See also: attention and performance model; attentional narrowing; attentional training

References

Nideffer, R.M. (1976a) 'Test of Attentional and Interpersonal Style', *Journal of Personality and Social Psychology* 34: 394–404.
—— (1976b) *The Inner Athlete*, New York: Thomas Crowell.

Further reading

Easterbrook, J.A. (1959) The Effect of Emotion on Cue Utilization and the Organization of Behavior, *Psychological Review* 66: 183–201.

RICK ALBRECHT

ATTENTIONAL TRAINING

It is difficult to imagine any single factor impacting more fully on athletic performance than the ability to ignore the thousands of task-irrelevant cues in one's internal and external environment while attending to the mere handful of cues essential to the performance. To some extent, this ability may reside in 'hardwired' information-processing tendencies that performers bring with them to the task. These relatively stable attentional traits are the basis for the perception that the inclination to focus attention effectively or ineffectively is, for the most part, an unchangeable natural endowment: 'you either have it or you don't'. Fortunately, a more malleable aspect of attention also exists – one lending itself to systematic attentional training.

Attentional training programmes are largely based on the premise that individuals possess innate and learned attentional predispositions, or styles, that either are or are not consistent with the attentional demands required for the successful execution of a given task. An essential first step in attentional training, therefore, involves the assessment of individual attentional strengths and weakness, including one's tendency to gravitate to a particular type of attentional deployment when experiencing high physiological or psychological arousal. There is also the need to identify attentional demands inherent in the task. This identification of individual attentional style and recognition of task-relevant and, thereby, task-irrelevant cues provides the basis for the development of individualised programmes designed either to decrease the attention given to task-irrelevant cues in the environment or to increase the attention directed towards task-relevant cues.

The main tenet of attentional training programmes involves indirectly improving attentional focus by enhancing interrelated psychological skills that are assumed to be associated with effective attentional deployment. Therefore, training in arousal regulation, mental rehearsal, confidence building, goal setting, and cognitive restructuring are frequently used to improve attentional focus.

Arousal regulation is a central feature in many attentional training programmes because high arousal is hypothesised to impact negatively on attention in three ways. First, as arousal increases, peripheral cues tend to be excluded from the attentional field. This phenomenon, known as 'attentional narrowing', often results in 'tunnel vision' whereby the performer fails to attend to essential environmental cues. High arousal also tends to increase the attention devoted to internal – and frequently negative – thoughts and feelings. Not only is inordinate attention focused inward, thus rendering it unavailable in the detection of important external stimuli, but also these negative internal thoughts tend to interfere with task-related confidence. Finally, arousal reduces attentional flexibility, making it difficult to adjust to changing attentional task demands. Therefore, use of arousal regulation techniques, such as progressive relaxation, breath control, biofeedback, and meditation, presumably reduce the likelihood of attention becoming inappropriately restricted, internally focused, or rigid.

Mental rehearsal – mental imagery, mental practice, and visualisation – is another common component in many attentional training programmes. The rationale for its inclusion is that mentally rehearsing the task should assist the athlete to identify, and attend to, relevant cues associated with performance. Frequent repetition of a successful performance – even a mental performance – can also result in enhanced task-related confidence. Increases in an individual's confidence should, in turn, reduce the occurrence of distracting negative thoughts.

Effective goal setting strategies are yet another psychological tool used in attentional training. Setting process goals, something the athlete can focus on and control, as opposed to outcome goals, often beyond the athlete's control, serves to reinforce the need to concentrate on the present rather than become distracted by past or future events.

Although intuitively appealing because of their sound theoretical underpinnings,

attentional training programmes have yet to demonstrate empirically any benefits for sports performance.

See also: attentional narrowing; attentional style; goal setting; mental practice and imagery; self-confidence

Further reading

Nideffer, R.M. (1976) 'Test of Attentional and Interpersonal Style', *Journal of Personality and Social Psychology* 34: 394–404.
Nideffer, R.M. and Sagal, M.S. (1998) 'Concentration and Attention Control Training', in J.M. Williams (ed.) *Applied Sport Psychology: Personal Growth to Peak Performance, Third Edition*, 296–315, Mountain View CA: Mayfield.

RICK ALBRECHT

ATTRIBUTIONS

Attributions are perceived causes that individuals provide for an event related to their own or someone else's behaviour. Perceptions of success and failure are subjective, meaning winning does not always result in perceptions of success and losing does not always equate with perceptions of failure. Attribution theory allows researchers to understand why there are individual differences in perceptions of success and failure by focusing on how individuals explain performance outcomes in sport. The theoretical premise is that after an achievement outcome, individuals are motivated to engage in a causal search to determine why a particular outcome occurred, which in turn, motivates future behaviour.

According to attribution theory, an outcome of a performance may generate certain positive or negative psychological and behavioural responses. Attributions may be classified into three categories: stability, locus of causality, and locus of control. Stability refers to the extent to which an individual attributes the cause of behaviour to factors that are stable or unstable. For example, an athlete wins a race for stable reasons, such as, personal ability or talent, or may win owing to unstable reasons, such as luck. Locus of causality reflects whether an individual perceives the cause of behaviour as internal or external. For example, a coach believes his athlete won the race because of the athlete's hard effort – internal – or because of the easy competition – external. Locus of control reflects whether an individual perceives the cause of behaviour to be within his or her personal control. For example, a reason within the athlete's control may be personal preparation, whereas a factor out of the athlete's control may be the opponent's preparation.

By combining each of the three dimensions, different combinations yield different attributional patterns or styles. For example, an athlete who perceives a successful outcome is due to internal, controllable, and stable reasons may attribute the outcome to personal ability. These combinations may be used to measure the accuracy of self-ascribed and other-directed attributions, or what is also known as attributional bias. A self-directed attributional pattern, the self-serving bias, demonstrates how individuals externalise failure and internalise success. Related to other-directed attributions, the fundamental attribution error describes how individuals accentuate the importance of internal causes and de-emphasise the importance of external causes. Although individuals may feel they are providing an accurate appraisal of the outcome, research demonstrates that people are capable of making errors in their attributions.

When studying attributions in sport, researchers may use a general attribution measure or sport-specific measure of attributions. A general attribution inventory, the Causal Dimension Scale-II (CDS-II), consists of twelve items that measure four causal dimensions – locus of control, stability, personal control, and external control. A more sport-specific measure, the Sport

Attributional Style Scale (SASS), presents the individual with sixteen sport scenarios and reports the most likely cause of the event. Five dimensions are measured – locus of causality, stability, controllability, intentionality, and globalisation. The SASS allows individuals to interpret subjectively success and failure, ascribe a variety of causal attributions to the outcome, classify these outcomes into dimensions, and distinguish among positive and negative attributions.

Using these measures, attributions of coaches, athletes, and spectators have been examined to predict behavioural and psychological outcomes in sport. Bond et al. (2001) examined the relationship between attributions and self-efficacy beliefs in competitive female golfers. Results demonstrated that after a successful outcome, self-efficacy beliefs were predicted by attributional stability, whereas no attributional categories emerged as significant predictors of efficacy under conditions of failure. Golfers who experienced an increase in efficacy beliefs also reported using more internal and stable attributions for their performances.

In a series of studies, Graham et al. (2002) examined attributions as predictors of positive emotions, such as joviality and self-assurance, and negative emotions, such as sadness, hostility, and guilt, after. The findings from their first study conducted in an experimental setting revealed that stability and controllability emerged as predictors of joviality and self-assurance. For negative emotions, locus of causality significantly predicted sadness and guilt, while stability negatively predicted hostility and guilt. In their second study, the authors measured the same relationships in the competitive context of swimming and athletics and found stability predicted joviality and self-assurance, while controllability predicted joviality. For negative emotions, all three attributions emerged as significant predictors of hostility and guilt. Although Weiner (1986) proposed

133

specific relationships between attributions and emotions, the authors concluded that, consistent with previous research in sport, their findings on the attribution–emotion relationship yielded mixed results. The authors recommended that future research should continue to explore these relationships and, in particular, examine the discrete emotions that emerge in specific athletic contexts when the causal dimensions are evident.

In addition to measuring athletes' self-directed attributions, sport researchers have examined attributional bias in coaches. After poor performances in the first half on the season, football coaches were asked to rate the ability and effort of their players. The authors hypothesised there would be individual differences attributional bias, owing to the different roles and responsibilities between the head coach and the assistant coaches. Because the head coach was responsible for the recruitment of athletes, he was hypothesised to rate athlete ability more favourably, and attribute poor performance to lack of effort. In contrast, because assistant coaches were responsible for further developing the skills of the athletes, they were hypothesised to attribute poor performances to low ability rather than low effort. Consistent with the hypotheses, the head coach rated the players high in ability and low in effort, while the assistant coaches reported lower ratings of ability and higher effort.

Attributional bias has also been measured in sport fans and spectators. Wann and Schrader (2000) examined the relationship between team identification and self-serving bias in sport spectators. Their results demonstrated that spectators who highly identified with their teams reported internal attributions after a win and external attributions after a defeat. Thus, highly identified fans viewed their teams as almost as an extension of themselves and considered their support as central to their self-concept. As a result these spectators feel better about themselves when they feel better about their team.

Sport attribution theorists and researchers advocate future research to expand the conceptualisation and understanding of attributions and their relationship to various psychological and behavioural outcomes. Biddle and Hanrahan (1998) recommend that future research consider the examination of attributions that are spontaneous. Although spontaneous attributions are more difficult to measure, it is important for researchers to better understand the attributional process as it occurs during performance. Also, they suggest that future research adopt a more qualitative approach to the study of attributions. Through the use of in-depth qualitative interviews, researchers may expand beyond the findings gathered with quantitative studies and use individuals' rich detail and personal accounts to better understand why certain outcomes occurred, and how these outcomes affect future psychological and behavioural patterns in sport.

References

Biddle, S.J.H. and Hanrahan, S.J. (1998) 'Attributions and Attributional style', in J.L. Duda (ed.) *Advances in Sport and Exercise Psychology Measurement*, 3–19, Morgantown WV: Fitness Information Technology.

Bond, K.A., Biddle, S.J.H. and Ntounamis, N. (2001) 'Self-efficacy and Causal Attribution in Female Golfers', *International Journal of Sport Psychology* 32: 243–56.

Graham, T.R., Kowalski, K.C. and Crocker, P.R.E. (2002) 'The Contributions of Goal Characteristics and Causal Attributions to Emotional Experience in Youth Sport Participants', *Psychology of Sport and Exercise* 3: 273–91.

Wann, D.L. and Schrader, M.P. (2000) 'Controllability and Stability in the Self-serving Attributions of Sport Spectators', *Journal of Social Psychology* 140: 160–8.

Weiner, B. (1986) *An Attributional Theory of Motivation and Emotion*, New York: Springer-Verlag.

Further reading

Biddle, S.J.H., Hanrahan, S.J. and Sellars, C.N. (2001) 'Attributions: Past, Present, and Future', in R.N. Singer, H.A. Hausenblas and C.M. Janelle (eds) *Handbook of Sport Psychology, Second Edition*, 444–71, New York: John Wiley.

Carver, C.S., DeGregorio, E. and Gillis, R. (1980) 'Field-study Evidence of an Ego-defensive Bias in Attribution Among Two Categories of Observers', *Personality and Social Psychology Bulletin* 6: 44–50.

T. MICHELLE MAGYAR

ATYPICAL MOTOR DEVELOPMENT – ASSESSMENT

Atypical motor development can be detected by motor milestones, fundamental motor patterns, and performance outcome assessments. If the statistical norms are established for these assessments, the results of the assessments can be expressed by the deviation from the mean. Of many performance outcome assessments, the Movement Assessment Battery for Children is specifically designed for the identification of motor impairment. On the performance test of this battery, the results above the sample means are scored zero indicating an absence of motor impairment.

To determine whether the motor development of an individual is normal or not on the basis of age norms, it is necessary to set border lines on the normal distribution, such as the second percentile, two standard deviations, or the motor quotient 70. Although which side of the border line an individual is placed may lead to serious consequences, border lines are often determined arbitrarily and lack theoretical grounds.

Atypical motor development can be also assessed without any normative data. For example, atypical gait patterns may be recognised by foot drags at the swing through phase. The International Paralympic Committee classifies athletes with disabilities on the basis of the functional ability to perform basic tasks in each sport.

See also: adapted physical activity; motor development – atypical; paralympics

Further reading

Stack, D.M. and Minnes, P.M. (1989) 'Aberrant Motor Development in Three Disabilities: Directions for Research and Practice', *Early Child Development and Care* 43: 1–14.

MOTOHIDE MIYAHARA

AUTHORITARIANISM

Authoritarianism is a system of government in which absolute obedience is required by rulers of subjects or citizens. This is not exactly synonymous with totalitarianism in the sense that authoritarian rulers may demand obedience only in restricted spheres (such as politics and the economy), leaving other areas of civil society (such as sport and culture) to other parties. Totalitarian rule, however, implies the exerting of control over all spheres of social, political and economic life.

One defence of authoritarianism is that states subject to authoritarianism are more likely to be economically successful than democratic countries. Examples cited in support of this argument are South Korea, Taiwan, Singapore, and Malaysia, which were authoritarian in their period of rapid economic growth. Nevertheless, Spain under Franco and countries such as the Philippines and Indonesia provide examples of authoritarian states which have failed to promote economic growth while, in the Asian context, India enjoyed rapid growth in the 1990s while under democratic rule.

While authoritarian rule implies some freedom of civil society from political control (where its activities do not challenge the system of political and economic power), sport has been used by many authoritarian governments to legitimate their role. The

135

successes of the Real Madrid football club in the European Cup competition in the 1950s and early 1960s were seen as useful for the Franco regime in breaking down its international isolation, and Taiwan (the Republic of China) found sport a useful tool in its battle to exclude the People's Republic of China from international cultural exchange through sport, successfully countering Communist China's involvement in the Olympic movement for much of the post World War II period in the last century. Communist China meanwhile has found sport a useful vehicle for demonstrating its progress and effectiveness in the cultural production (of athletes). The introduction of professional football in China in the 1990s also illustrates an aspect of authoritarian strategy. China has allowed some liberalisation of economic activity (the introduction of capitalism in restricted elements of the economy) while maintaining tight political control.

When South Korea became in 1988 the second Asian country to host the Olympic Games, part of the attraction was for the country to announce its emergence as a world economic power, and the process of staging the games was used as an occasion to liberalise and loosen some of the controls on civil society.

IAN P. HENRY

AXIAL SKELETON – STRUCTURE AND FUNCTION

The axial skeleton consists of the vertebral column and skull plus the ribs and associated bones of the thorax. It is the central part of the skeleton, and the appendicular skeleton attaches to it through the shoulder and pelvic girdles. The vertebral column contains thirty-three vertebrae in four regions; moving distally from the head, these are the seven cervical, twelve thoracic, five lumbar, five sacral, and four coccygeal vertebrae. Vertebrae within a region

are numbered in ascending order in a proximal-to-distal direction. The sacrum and coccyx are made up of fused vertebrae, whereas the vertebrae in the other regions are true moveable vertebrae. The vertebral column is not simply a stack of vertebrae, but has four curved regions: the cervical curve is convex anteriorly; followed by the thoracic curve, which is concave anteriorly; the anteriorly convex lumbar curve; and the anteriorly concave pelvic curve. Since the vertebrae protect the spinal cord, injuries to this region are potentially very severe. Depending on the vertebral level at which the spinal cord is damaged, more or less of the body may be paralysed. As a result, most sports have rules that are designed to minimise the risk of spinal cord damage. For example, American football has banned tackles made with the head of the tackler as the first point of contact with the opponent. This rule was introduced after changes to protective headgear led to a large increase in cervical spine injuries because of an increase in the use of this tackling technique.

The bones of the thorax, or chest, form a protective cage around the major organs of the chest cavity, principally the lungs and heart. Each vertebra of the thoracic region has two ribs associated with it. Of the twelve pairs of ribs, ten are attached to the sternum, or breast bone, anteriorly by costal cartilage. The most distal two pairs are not secured anteriorly and are, therefore, known as floating ribs. As the link between the upper and lower body, the bones of the thorax can be subjected to large forces in those sports that call for power to be transferred from one part of the body to another. For example, rib stress fractures are relatively common in rowers. During the rowing stroke, a rower must drive his or her legs against the foot plate of the boat and subsequently transfer the power generated at the feet to the oar handle and propel the boat through the water. For the force developed at the foot plate to be transferred effectively to the blade, the trunk must provide a rigid link between the lower and upper body. The tension necessary to achieve this places great strain on the ribs and may result in a stress fracture. This injury tends to occur during winter training when the rower is training at a lower stroke rate, but generating more force with each stroke.

The skull consists of the cranium, the large dome that houses and protects the brain, and the bones of the face. It is made up of eight cranial and fourteen facial bones. All of these, except the mandible or jawbone, are attached rigidly to each other in the adult by interlaced articulations called sutures. Injuries to the skull tend to be acute trauma from contact with another athlete, equipment, or the ground.

See also: joints of the lumbar spine and pelvis; joints of the thoracic region; muscles of the lumbar spine and pelvis; muscles of the thoracic region; structure of vertebrae; thoracic region – pectoral girdle, thoracic spine and ribs

Further reading

Williams, P.L., Bannister, L.H., Berry, M.M., Collins, P., Dyson, M., Dussek, J.E. and Ferguson, M.W.J. (eds) (1995) *Gray's Anatomy: the Anatomical Basis of Medicine and Surgery*, Section 6, Edinburgh: Churchill Livingstone.

CLARE E. MILNER

B

BALANCE IN SENIOR ATHLETES

Ageing population is a severe challenge to many developed countries, Hong Kong, as a modern city, is with no exception. According to the World Health Organization, life expectancy will have risen from 66 to 73 by the year 2025. It is estimated that the percentage of people aged over sixty-five in Hong Kong will increase drastically from 14 per cent today to 40 per cent in the coming fifty years. Morbidity accompanied with ageing has imposed huge financial burden to both the health care system and broader community; expenditure on the treatment of bone fracture is an example of this. The cost of rehabilitation after bone fracture is HK$1,300,000,000 annually. Given that falls represent the most common cause of bone fracture among the elderly, fall prevention and maintenance of balance are therefore urgent problems that demand immediate action.

Statistics show that numerous seniors suffer from disabilities and prolonged hospital stays as the result of a fall. It is computed that by the age of eighty-five, approximately half of all injury-related deaths arise from falls, with between one third and a quarter of all those over sixty-five reporting a fall in the previous year (Blake *et al.* 1988). A recent Australian study of community-dwelling adults aged over seventy proved that in a one-year period, 49 per cent of the subjects fell, 23 per cent fell more than once, 9 per cent had fractures and 10 per cent strains or other moderate injuries as a result of the fall. Predisposition to falling not only contributes to heavy placement of people in institutional care, but also degrades the quality of life of the elderly. In the light of this, it is crucial to figure out the reasons that lead to failure of balance maintenance, so that the condition can be alleviated.

It is generally accepted that this alarming situation results from multiple factors, both environmental such as trip and slip hazards, as well as biological, such as age-related changes in strength, coordination and sensory system (Lord 1996; Stelmach and Worringham 1985). With reference to the musculoskeletal system, decreased joint range of motion and muscle strength, together with alterations in anthropometric variables, such as decreased height and increased kyphosis, are all age-related effects that affect postural stability during rest stance and gait. At the same time, age-related changes to the sensory and motor systems also contribute to increased postural instability and predisposition to falls.

Moreover, the maintenance of balance while standing and walking also relies on intact visual, proprioceptive, vestibular and motor systems. Vision has an important role in controlling balance, especially in compensating for the loss or degradation of other senses. Common visual disorders like age-related maculopathy have demonstrable effects on balance; in addition, of all the sensory inputs, proprioception is the most crucial for normal balance control. Proprioceptive function not only deteriorates with normal ageing, it is also impaired by various diseases, notably diabetic peripheral neuropathy; next, a range of vestibular dysfunctions can impair balance as well as giving rise to vertigo and other symptoms. Among the three most common disorders, namely vestibular neuritis, Meniere's disease and benign paroxysmal positional vertigo, the latter is not only the most prevalent, but also has the strongest association with advancing age; further, central processes and the organisation of balance-related motor commands can be disrupted by neurological disease of the CNS, notably those affecting the basal ganglia and cerebellum; furthermore, although decreased muscle strength has minimal effects on some balance tasks, it can impose significant limitations on others. The rate of force production, rather than simple maximal isometric strength, is an important factor. Impaired muscle function is associated with instability during gait and with impairments in tasks such as rising from a chair.

In conclusion, maintenance of balance is a serious problem among the elderly population. Yet, with clear guidelines and appropriate assistance, senior athletes can still enjoy the benefits and fun of sports participation; remaining physically active is the only way to achieve healthy ageing.

References

Blake, A.J., Morgan, K., Bendall, M.J. *et al.* (1988) 'Falls by Elderly People at Home: Prevalence and Associated Factors', *Age and Ageing* 17: 365–72.

Lord, S.R. (1996) 'Instability and Falls in Elderly People', in C. Lafont, A. Baroni, M. Allard *et al.* (eds) *Facts and Research in Gerontology (Falls, Gait and Balance Disorders in the Elderly)*, 125–139, New York: Springer.

Stelmach, G. and Worringham, C. (1985) 'Sensorimotor Deficits Related to Postural Stability: Implications for Falling in the Elderly', *Clinics in Geriatric Medicine* 1: 679–94.

KAI MING CHAN

BALL AND SURFACE DEFORMATION

In sport, balls impact on different surfaces, such as relatively rigid walls, as in squash, or complex deformable surfaces, such as turf in golf. The ball impacts are characterised by the relative stiffness between the ball and the surface. In the case of hollow pressurised sports balls, as in football, squash, and tennis, the surfaces are generally much stiffer than the balls and most of the deformation occurs in the latter In golf, the stiffness of the ball is much greater than the grass on which it lands and almost all the deformation takes place in the turf, creating a pitch mark, which may or may not reform over time. There are some impacts in which the relative stiffnesses of the ball and surface are similar, and the deformations are shared. Examples of these are cricket balls on a cricket pitch and tennis balls on a tennis racquet.

When substantial deformation of the surface takes place, then the depression or pitch mark causes the angle of rebound to increase owing to the rebound of the ball off the inside face of the pitch mark. For impacts in which the surface does not deform appreciably, the dominant characteristic is the surface roughness.

In oblique impacts, classical theory categorises the impact as either slipping or rolling when the ball rebounds. If the ball slips throughout impact, any increase in the roughness of the surfaces makes the ball rebound steeper and slower. If the friction of the surface and the impact conditions dictate, the ball might roll off the surface and a further increase in roughness has no effect. In practice, the specific value of rolling spin is just one point on a continuous spectrum of values and a rebounding ball can 'overspin', i.e. gain more spin than rolling.

The stiffness of natural surfaces, such as turf, will depend upon parameters characterised by the turf's moisture content, organic matter content, grass type, and soil type. In normal use, clay-rich soils tend to be softer than sandy soils and produce a slower, steeper bounce with relatively deep pitch marks. In contrast sandy soils produce long, shallow pitch marks, in which the ball slides throughout impact.

Artificial surfaces are often designed to bridge the gap between soft natural surfaces and hard surfaces, such as concrete and bitumen. Artificial turfs try to simulate natural turf and have to ensure that the bounce of the ball and its speed as it rolls across the surface are correct. They do this by incorporating sand, water, or rubber granules into the long fibres of the artificial grass to try to simulate the energy loss seen during interaction with natural turf.

At the opposite extreme, the hardest sports surfaces are concrete and bitumen, which may have their characteristics modified through coatings of acrylic paint impregnated with sand particles. These coatings only vary the coefficient of friction, regardless of the number of coatings used. Rubber crumb layers may be used between the rigid surface and the paint layer to give a softer feel for players, such as 'Rebound Ace' in tennis. As regards the ball bounce, however, they are effectively rigid and the coefficient of friction is still the dominant characteristic.

A formula for the 'speed' of relatively hard sports surfaces has been suggested and is given by: speed $= 100(1 - \Delta v_x / \Delta v_y)$, where Δv_x and Δv_y are the changes in horizontal and vertical velocity, respectively, for a standard impact. Interestingly, the term $\Delta v_x / \Delta v_y$ is the Newtonian definition of the coefficient of friction for a non-deforming impact, implying again that the friction is dominant in impacts on hard sports surfaces.

See also: normal impact; oblique impact; sports surface characteristics – athlete perception; sports surfaces characteristics – measurement

Further reading

Haake, S.J. (1998) 'Impact Problems of Balls in Tennis and Golf', *Transactions of the Japanese Society of Mechanical Engineering* 64: 2318–27.
International Tennis Federation (1997) *Initial ITF Study on Performance Standards for Tennis Court Surfaces*, London: International Tennis Federation.

STEVE HAAKE

BALL AND SURFACE IMPACTS

The significance of surface impacts in ball sports is self-evident. Generally, a ball game begins with an impact with an implement or with a part of the body, the ball flies through the air and subsequently impacts with a surface, whether it is the ground, a wall, or barrier of some sort. The rebound from the surface is affected by several factors: the **coefficient of restitution** of the ball on the surface, the coefficient of friction between the ball and the surface, and the velocity, angle, and spin at impact. Surface impacts are dominated by two factors – deformation and friction. In some ball sports, the ball undergoes most of the deformation, as in tennis and squash, and the properties of the ball dominate. In this scenario, the only property of the surface that matters is its coefficient of friction with the ball. At the opposite extreme, for example golf balls landing on a golf green, the surface undergoes most of the deformation while the ball remains effectively rigid

In the simplest analysis, both the ball and the surface are assumed not to deform and any energy loss is taken into account by the coefficient of restitution. Two cases are then considered in which the ball either slips throughout impact or rolls by the end of it. The type of impact is dependent on the characteristics of the surface and the impact velocity parameters. Generally, however, such an analysis is too simplified for the relatively complex interactions in which the ball, surface, or both deform significantly. Then, it is necessary either to resort to non-linear models, often using viscoelasticity, or to use finite element analysis codes, in which the material parameters of the ball and surface can be defined. In the latter case, however, determining the appropriate dynamic material constants for a ball impacting with a semi-plastic sports surface at high speed can be difficult.

See also: ball and surface deformation; normal impact; oblique impact

STEVE HAAKE

BALL SWING AND REVERSE SWING

The phenomena of 'swing' and 'reverse swing' are typically observed with sports balls that exhibit some kind of asymmetry, most famously in cricket where they are used by bowlers to confuse a batsman. Rather than the ball travelling in a straight line towards the batsman, when viewed from above, the ball follows a curved trajectory, either swinging towards or away from the batsman. The asymmetry of the cricket ball causes the flow of air to be different about either side, causing a pressure difference and a lateral force. Conventional swing is caused by a difference in separation of the **boundary layer** on either side of the ball, owing to the flow being laminar on one side and turbulent on the other (see **laminar and turbulent flow**). Reverse swing occurs when the flow is turbulent on both sides, but there still remains a difference in **boundary layer separation**.

A cricket ball differs from balls used in other sports, notably tennis, football, and golf, owing to its asymmetry caused by a proud equatorial seam and one side often being rougher than the other. During the course of a match, the fielding players will take great care in ensuring that one side of the ball remains smooth and polished while the other side – separated by the seam – is allowed to become rough. It is this asymmetry that leads to the phenomenon of 'swing'. A proficient swing bowler is able to deliver the ball towards the batsman with the seam in a vertical plane, but at a slight angle to the direction of flight. In other words, when viewed from above the seam is pointing to the left or the right of the batsman. Some backspin is usually applied to the ball in the plane of the seam, which helps to keep it stable in the air. The combined effect of the seam and the difference in roughness on each side of the ball causes it to swing.

As the air flows around either side of the ball, the speed of the air just outside the boundary layer varies, reaching a maximum at a particular point where the corresponding pressure is now at its minimum (see **Bernoulli's equation**). After this point, the pressure increases so that the net pressure opposes the forward flow on elements in the boundary layer. This stage is known as an adverse pressure gradient, as it opposes the flow of air. The air closest to the surface has the least momentum and this momentum is reduced further by the adverse pressure gradient. As the airflow travels around the ball, the momentum of the air nearest to the surface continues to reduce until it is eventually reversed, causing eddies – irregular motions of air that make up the region behind the ball known as the wake. At this point, the boundary layer is said to have separated. Separation occurs with both laminar and turbulent boundary layers, but laminar boundary layers are more prone to separation because the increase in speed in the boundary layer, away from the surface, is less rapid. Hence, it is easier for the adverse pressure gradient to slow down the air nearest to the surface.

In conventional swing, the cricket ball is delivered with one side rougher than the other and the seam pointing at a slight

141

angle away from the smooth side, when viewed from above, so that the smooth area first comes into contact with air flowing around the ball. On the rough side of the ball the boundary layer is tripped into turbulent flow as the air flows over the seam. Because this turbulence allows mixing to occur, the boundary layer has sufficient energy to remain in contact with the ball and does not separate until quite late, when it is a significant distance around the ball. On the smooth side of the ball the boundary layer remains laminar and separates earlier. The difference in separation points on both sides of the ball leads to unequal pressure distribution and a resultant side force causing the ball to swing towards the rough side. In other words, the wake behind the ball is deflected to be more in line with the seam.

Much research has been carried out on this topic, using cricket balls mounted in wind tunnels as well as computational fluid dynamics. These studies have examined, among other things, the effect of ball speed, back spin, seam angle – the angle of the plane containing the seam, relative to the direction of travel – and atmospheric conditions – cricketers often report that the ball swings more when the atmosphere is 'heavy', if it is cloudy, or when playing near the sea. One study found that a new ball with a seam at $15°$ to an airflow of $30 \, \mathrm{m \, s^{-1}}$ experienced a side force equivalent to 45 per cent of its weight. It is widely accepted that, with new balls, the seam is able to trip the boundary in the range of speeds from 15 to $30 \, \mathrm{m \, s^{-1}}$. Above $30 \, \mathrm{m \, s^{-1}}$ (66 miles per hour), the side force begins to decrease. At this speed, the Reynolds number (see **non-dimensional groups**) in typical conditions would be about 1.5×10^5. The optimum seam angle for swing, however, is generally found to be around $20°$.

One final complication on this topic is 'reverse swing', when the ball swerves in the air in the opposite direction from that which would normally be expected. This phenomenon occurs when bowling at speeds up to $38 \, \mathrm{m \, s^{-1}}$ (85 mph). This will only happen on balls with quarter seams, as used in first class cricket, owing to the extra roughness of the surface. When a ball is bowled fast enough, the boundary layers on both sides of the ball become turbulent. In this case the seam acts like a ramp to thicken the boundary layer on the rough side, so it separates sooner. On the smooth side, as the boundary layer contains turbulence, it separates later, in the same way as on the rough side for conventional swing. The pressure difference on both sides of the ball is now reversed and the ball will swing in the opposite direction. It has also been shown that reverse swing can be achieved at speeds of just $30 \, \mathrm{m \, s^{-1}}$, simply by bowling the ball with the rough side facing forward, rather than the smooth side.

Cricket is not the only sport that uses a difference in boundary layer separation to affect the flight of balls through the air. A pitch in baseball, known as a 'knuckleball', is a comparatively low speed pitch, typically, $30 \, \mathrm{m \, s^{-1}}$, for which the ball is thrown with little or no spin. Research has shown that the separation point 'jumps around' when it occurs at the seam. If the ball is rotating slowly, the seam will coincide with the separation points on either side of the ball several times, causing a fluctuating pressure difference. This effect causes the erratic flight of the ball and makes the job of striking the ball much harder for the hitter.

Further reading

Massey, B.S. (1992) *Mechanics of Fluids*, London: Chapman and Hall.

Mehta, R.D. (1985) 'Aerodynamics of Sports Balls', *Annual Review of Fluid Mechanics* 17: 151–89.

MATT CARRÉ

BANKART INJURY

The typical pathologic anatomic correlate to an anterior glenohumeral (shoulder) dislocation, and most likely the main reason for recurrent anterior shoulder instability following this injury, is called a Bankart lesion after an American surgeon who described this injury in 1947. The mechanistic background is that the humeral head dislocates in anterior direction out of the joint whilst the arm is forced in excessive abduction and external rotation. Whilst the humeral head passes the sharp edge of the anterior glenoid socket, the mid- and inferior part of the anterior labrum is detached from its bony insertion. Normally the labrum controls the steering of the humeral head to the glenoid socket with support of a negative intra-articular pressure. When the labrum is ruptured in any direction this important steering is lost and the humeral head will start wobbling during movements of the arm. The most important anterior passive stabiliser in this capsular complex is the inferior glenohumeral ligament and the anterior capsule. The muscular support is irrelevant. Even a heavy weight rugby player cannot respond quickly enough with his muscles to support the structures in the rapid movement of a dislocation. It is obvious that this injury varies in severity depending on the forces applied and the quality of the tissue surrounding the joint. Bankart injury occurs in more than 80 per cent of the patients with anterior dislocation. Correspondingly, the original Bankart operation was described as a means of reinserting and stabilising the anterior labrum. This is currently the method which is recommended in the first hand for surgery on patients with recurrent anterior shoulder instability. It is a reliable method that in most hands results in recurrent dislocation in less than 10 per cent, and is preferably undertaken with arthroscopic techniques.

See also: anterior glenohumeral instability; anterior shoulder dislocation; shoulder injury

Further reading

Hawkins, R. and Saunders, W.B. (1996) *Shoulder Injuries in the Athlete. Surgical Repair and Rehabilitation*, ISBN 0-443-08947-7

CHRISTER ROLF

BEGINNING AN EXERCISE PROGRAM IN SENIORS

Many countries are now facing the challenge of a growing elderly population. This problem has become a global issue that requires attention world-wide. With improvements in living conditions, nutrition, social services, and medicine, the World Health Organization projects that life expectancy will have risen from 66 to 73 by 2025. The percentage of people aged over sixty-five is predicted to increase drastically, from 14 per cent today to 40 per cent in the next fifty years. Possible outcomes this will bring to society include escalating medical costs, increased housing problems, and inadequate social services and public facilities. Therefore, ways to deal with this trend should be worked out without delay.

Beginning an exercise program and working toward the concept of 'Active Living' is one of the most effective ways to alleviate the situation. The advantages of physical activities in enhancing a person's cardiovascular capacity, endurance, strength, balance, and flexibility, as well as providing us with a sense of inner harmony, and insights about ourselves and the world around us, have been widely recognized. That means physical activity is crucial in shaping individuals' lives and the wider social system. Yet, the concept of Active Living exceeds the notion that exercise is good for the body only. It offers physical activity a humanistic and subjective view by recognizing that exercise contributes to an increased sense of well-being and quality of life. It advocates the idea that physical activity is good for the whole person, emphasizes the linkages between mind, body, and spirit, together with the interaction of an individual with others and with the environment. In other words, Active Living involves the meaningful integration of physical activity into every dimension of life, regardless of physical capability or economic situation. Incorporating exercise into daily life can not only improve the health of the elderly, reducing the financial burden on the medical system, but can also provide individuals with the chance of happiness and self-fulfilment, and benefit their psychological, mental, emotional, and spiritual aspects of life. In this sense, both government and non-government organizations should work together to promote the concept of Active Living among the elderly population. Depending on different economic and cultural backgrounds, every community should begin exercise programs for seniors and develop its unique form of Active Living.

Hong Kong is one place that is encountering the challenge of an ageing society. Given the alarming situation, the HKSAR government and the Chinese University of Hong Kong have put immense effort into promoting the idea of Active Living, aiming to better the health condition of elderly citizens, to lower their dependence on the public medical system and to improve their overall quality of life.

In June 1998 the HKSAR government launched a three-year territory-wide health-promotion event, namely the Healthy Living Campaign, co-organized with the Department of Health, the Health and Welfare Bureau, the Home Affairs Bureau, and the Housing Department and Social Services Department, to promote an active as well as healthy lifestyle in the community. It is hoped that with the help of this health-enhancing campaign, the benefits of physical activity will be integrated into the daily life of the entire population, thus leading to the enhanced well-being of the individual and society. Under the main theme of

'Healthy Living into the Twenty-first Century', various publicity and educational activities were implemented to highlight the key message emphasized in each year of the campaign period, such as 'Healthy living starts with me' in 1998, to 'Join hands to raise hygiene standards' in 1999–2000, and 'Build a healthy city' in 2000–2001. Extensive media coverage, including specially produced advertisements on TV and radio, posters, leaflets, and newsletters were also distributed to educate the public on the importance of 'Healthy and active living'.

A year-long project on Healthy Exercise for All was another focus of the Healthy Living Campaign. It was jointly organized by the Department of Health and Leisure and Culture Services Department to promote active living for all ages, and aimed at enhancing public awareness of the benefits of participating in sports and exercising on a regular basis. A number of simple exercises were devised by the government, in collaboration with other professional bodies, to meet the needs of the community. Exercise materials were produced in the forms of posters, leaflets, as well as video compact disc, which were widely distributed to social centers for senior citizens, to encourage them to exercise regularly by implementing a self-attainment award scheme. The aged were given a logbook to record the pattern and frequency of physical exercise, so as to motivate participants to maintain a good habit of exercising. Outreach promotional activities on healthy exercise were also available, whereby qualified instructors visited the integrated service centers for the elderly, the day care centers, and homes for the aged, to offer instruction to senior citizens and their carers in how to exercise.

The HKSAR government raised the concept of Active Living to the international level by designating 1999 as the International Year For Older Persons (IYOP). Together with the Elderly Committee, over 700 activities involving about

300,000 elderly were organized during the year. The IYOP not only provided an opportunity for the public to pay tribute to the elderly for their contributions to society, but also encouraged seniors to take an active role in community affairs.

As well as the government, non-government organizations also put huge efforts into founding exercise programs among the elderly. The Chinese University of Hong Kong is the pioneer in the development of sports medicine and sports science, as well as promotion of the idea of Active Living. In 1998, with support from WHO and several overseas health-promoting universities like Lancaster University, the University of Central Lancashire, the University of Newcastle and the University of Portsmouth in Great Britain, the idea of developing a health-promoting scheme at CUHK University was put into practice by launching the Wellness CUHK program. The concept of the Wellness CUHK program was to integrate health into the culture, processes, and policies of the university, and provide a health-conducive environment for all students and staff. In 1999, the Hong Kong Center for Sports Medicine and Sports Science of CUHK was invited by the World Health Organization (WHO) to host an expert meeting on active ageing, to consolidate experiences in promoting active ageing and identify a global strategy for the next millennium. Also, in 2001, organized by the WHO Collaborating Center for Sports Medicine and Health Promotion, the International Conference on Tai Chi was held. Over thirty-five scientific papers were presented, and there was a fruitful exchange of experience and expertise among scientists, researchers and clinicians. A Tai Chi Extravaganza was held, and this established a Guinness world record of more than 10,000 people simultaneously practicing Tai Chi for half an hour.

In addition, the Hong Kong Center for Sports Medicine and Health Promotion initiated the project titled Active Living – The Way to Healthy Ageing. It aimed at raising the self-efficacy of the elderly by encouraging physical activities in daily life and participation in recreational activities. The project also hoped to provoke a change in daily lifestyle, and to encourage seniors to stay active and independent. It was hoped that the message of Active Living would be spread to over 400 contact points, with the potential to reach over 100,000 elderly in Hong Kong.

Apart from actions initiated by government and non-government organizations, the implementation of physical activities among the elderly depends on cultural factors as well, so that a distinctive style of Active Living can be established. In Hong Kong, crowded living conditions and limited open space for outdoor activities make morning walks and Tai Chi favorable choices of exercise for the aged, as both of these are low-cost and self-controled activities and do not need large spaces. They are also effective in improving balance control, muscle strength, flexibility, and function of the cardiorespiratory system. Practicing these kinds of exercise in groups not only enables seniors to enjoy physical interdependence and social interactions with others, but also enables them to seek assistance and support from other seniors facing similar health problems.

In conclusion, the promotion of exercise programs for the elderly is a global concern, and relies on the atmosphere jointly created by both government and non-government organizations. Incorporating the unique cultural factors of a society, the idea of Active Living can be promoted to the entire community, thus enhancing its health and quality of life.

KAI MING CHAN

BENCHMARKING

Benchmarking has gained in popularity since the last decade of the twentieth century. Today, it has become a common language in both commercial and public sectors because of its importance in providing standards for comparing performances and also for its insights into ways of improving performance. Legislation can play an important part in stimulating an interest in benchmarking in the public sector, an example being Best Value policy in the UK, legislated by the Local Government Act 1999, through which local authorities are required to secure continuous improvement in exercising all their functions, with due regard to economy, efficiency and effectiveness.

A benchmark is a reference point for comparisons established from the value for a performance indicator (PI). There are two principal types of benchmarking: data benchmarking and process benchmarking. Data benchmarking concerns quantitative comparisons of performance outcomes across different facilities (cross-section) and/or different time periods (time-series). Process benchmarking involves qualitative exploration of the reasons for differences in performance between facilities within the same industry, i.e. the processes which cause performance differences. Data processing is an essential prerequisite for process benchmarking.

There are a number of performance measurement systems within the sports sector, including Sport England's 'National Benchmarking Service' (SENBS), the University of South Australia's 'CERM performance indicators', and the Association of Public Service Excellence's 'Performance Networks'. These systems are largely quantitative data benchmarking systems. In addition there is a variety of benchmarking clubs which are groups of organisations which exchange information on an ad hoc basis in order to derive industry-specific indicators for comparison among the participating members. Benchmarking clubs are more likely to include process benchmarking.

SENBS can be used to illustrate the structure of a data benchmarking system.

It employs quantitative data collection methods that include customer market research, a centre's utilisation and financial records, and population data for the local catchment area. There is typically a tight protocol to follow in the collection of information in a benchmarking exercise (e.g. Sport England 2002). It is vital to maximise the consistency of the data used for benchmarking, and there are many dangers of inconsistency, not simply in market research sampling and administration but also in different organisations' systems for recording utilisation and financial information. Benchmarking data is assembled from subscribers to the service – whose results are able to be compared with the existing benchmarks. Then, when around a hundred new centres have provided information, the data can be used collectively to estimate new national benchmarks.

The array of performance indicators used in the SENBS represents four dimensions to service performance: access by different population groups to the service; overall utilisation of facilities; financial performance; and customers' scores for their satisfaction with, and the importance of, a number of service attributes. The benchmarks are presented for three different family categories of sports centres, to facilitate 'like for like' comparisons for individual centres. Three families are used by SENBS. The first is different types of sports centre, i.e. whether or not it has a main hall, swimming pool, and outdoor facilities, which has an influence on the type of visits that are attracted to a centre, and the costs and income of a centre. The second family is different socio-economics of catchment populations, which is represented by the percentage of the local population in the lowest socio-economic groups – a good variable to represent a variety of social exclusion factors – which has a significant influence on both usage and income. The third family is different sizes of centre (using internal floor space), which causes significant differences in utilisation, income and cost performance.

In SENBS, three benchmarks are reported for each performance indicator: 25 per cent, 50 per cent and 75 per cent scores in the distribution of centres' scores in each family type. Below the 25 per cent benchmarks are the worst performing quartile of centres; the 50 per cent benchmark is the mid-point score, the median; whilst above the 75 per cent benchmark are the best performing quartile of centres. The median is a better mid-score than the mean when the distribution of scores is not normal but skewed, as is often the case with performance data. It is important to relate an individual centre's scores for any performance indicator to the whole range of performance in the appropriate family types, not just the best performing centres in the top quartile. Very often the 75 per cent benchmark for a performance indicator will not be achievable for a centre because of problems endemic to its design or location, so that more modest target is appropriate, e.g. the median benchmark.

Sports facility benchmarking services such as SENBS, CERM, and Performance Networks are facilitating services. They do not reduce performance to a simplistic single scoring system. Instead they allow an individual participating organisation/authority to select the most important performance indicators for their objectives, compare their scores to the benchmarks, and then use the comparisons in their plans to improve their services. Unlike other performance systems, such as health and education in the UK, sports benchmarking services do not publish 'league tables' for centres, so there is no 'naming and shaming' of poorly performing centres.

According to Taylor and Godfrey (2003), there are numerous uses and benefits from benchmarking. Comparison of an individual centre's performance with the relevant benchmarks provides baseline data for centres to review their service objectives and stra-tegic options for achieving them. Sometimes, these can involve quite fundamental changes in direction, such as making a case for facility closure and replacement. By incorporating knowledge of local circumstances, managers can identify which weaknesses are actionable and which are unavoidable without major investment/locational decisions. Common outcomes from the process of interrogating the results are varied and cover three main purposes: reporting performance to stakeholders; long-term strategic planning; and shorter-term tactical decisions. They include informing inspections by government agencies, internal service reviews, strategies, performance plans, business plans, contract specifications, and public-private-partnership specifications. Benchmarks have been used as the basis for targets for performance-related contract payments.

Other less tangible benefits from benchmarking include more accurate and increased awareness of the state of the service, sometimes challenging preconceived ideas; increasing awareness of further information needs, which contributes to the development of a more evidence-based management culture; and a greater realism in setting objectives and targets. Benchmarking services put client sports services on a steep learning curve in terms of the skills and processes required for generating the right information, interpreting the results, especially in the context of local circumstances, and utilising the results in performance planning, in particular being carefully selective in their use of performance indicators. Benchmarking complements broader quality management systems, such as the sports-industry-specific quality system QUEST in the UK. Quality systems typically concentrate on evaluating systems and processes, which is complementary to the evidence on service outcomes provided by benchmarking.

See also: performance indicators

References

Sport England (2002) *Best Value Through Sport: National Benchmarking Service for Sports Halls and Swimming Pools, Guidance and Survey Documentation*, London: Sport England.

Taylor, P. and Godfrey, A. (2003) 'Performance Measurement in English Local Authority Sports Facilities', *Public Performance and Measurement Review* 26, 3: 251–62.

SHIA PING KUNG
PETER TAYLOR

BERNOULLI'S EQUATION

Bernoulli's equation is widely used in fluid mechanics to express the energy contained within, or the work done on, a fluid. The terms in the equation relate to the pressure energy of the fluid and its gravitational potential energy, as well as the kinetic energy owing to the velocity of the fluid. For an ideal fluid, which is frictionless and of constant density, the sum of these three terms is said to remain constant during the flow of the fluid.

If the velocity of a section of fluid changes then, from Newton's First Law, this change in velocity must be associated with a force or system of forces acting on the fluid section. In fluid mechanics, the force exerted is most easily expressed in terms of pressure. If one considers a small element of fluid within a stream-tube, one can apply Newton's Second Law to the flow. It is assumed that the flow is steady and the forces acting on the element are caused by the fluid pressure acting all around it as well as gravitational effects. Other forces, such as those resulting from viscosity, surface tension, electricity, and magnetism, for example, are all assumed to be negligible. If the density of the fluid also remains constant, the resulting equation is: $p/\rho + v^2/2 + gz =$ a constant, where p is the fluid pressure, ρ is its density, v is the velocity of the fluid flow, g is the acceleration due to gravity and z is the height of the fluid at a particular time. This equation, in various different forms, is known commonly as 'Bernoulli's equation', named in honour of Swiss mathematician Daniel Bernoulli (1700–82) who published one of the first works on fluid flow in 1738.

The first term of the equation represents the amount of potential work due to 'pressure forces' associated with a unit mass of the fluid. It can be thought of as the work that would be done if the fluid moved from a point where the pressure was p to another point where the pressure was zero. The second term simply represents the kinetic energy of unit mass of the fluid and the third term corresponds to the work that would be done on the fluid by raising it to a particular height above an arbitrarily chosen datum. For a frictionless fluid with constant density undergoing steady flow, the sum of these three terms will remain constant, but only within a single stream-tube. The equation shown above is often re-written after dividing all the terms by g. In this case the three terms are referred to as 'pressure head', 'velocity head', and 'gravity head', with the constant term, being the 'total head'. For describing the behaviour of gases, whose density is relatively small, the first and second terms often dominate and the gravity term may be neglected.

This relatively simple equation can be used in a variety of fluid flows to assess the relationship between velocity and pressure, as long as the relevant assumptions hold. For instance, a stream-tube of frictionless fluid travelling at near constant height – so that the third term remains constant, but whose velocity decreases, will increase in pressure so that the changes in the first and second terms cancel each other out. If the density remains constant, the equation shows that a reduction of velocity by half will be accompanied by a fourfold increase in pressure. Similarly, an increase in velocity would be accompanied by a decrease in pressure. This understanding can be used to help explain the behaviour of fluids in **boundary layer**s travelling over curved surfaces, such as when a sports ball is in flight.

See also: ball swing and reverse swing; boundary layer separation; laminar and turbulent flow; Magnus and negative Magnus effects

Further reading

Massey, B.S. (1992) *Mechanics of Fluids*, London: Chapman and Hall.

MATT CARRÉ

BETA-2 RECEPTOR AGONISTS

Beta-2 agonists are a specific class of sympathomimetic amine **stimulants** that deserve special mention. They are commonly used as therapeutic drugs for their bronchodilator effects in the treatment of asthma, but are potentially ergogenic aids at high doses. Beta-2 agonists are a major source of contention for sports organizations because a significant portion of the population has either asthma and/or exercise-induced asthma (EIA) and would not be able to compete effectively without these drugs. However, abuse does occur and some athletes utilize these drugs for the sole purpose of increasing their performance. Indeed, in 1998 some countries at the Winter Olympics requested inhaled beta-2 agonists for one third of their athletes.

Asthma is a common condition in the general population, and participation in athletics does not protect against asthma. Exercise itself is a stimulus for bronchospasm in approximately 80 per cent of known asthmatics. In addition, exercise can provoke an asthmatic response in individuals without underlying asthma. Depending on the criteria, studies have revealed 10–50 per cent of athletes have exercise-induced asthma (EIA), although the actual incidence is likely closer to 10 per cent. Asthmatic response can also be influenced by environmental conditions such as airborne allergens and cold, dry air.

Beta-2 agonists are a mainstay in the treatment of asthma and EIA in athletes. Their main mechanism of action is smooth muscle relaxation and bronchodilation, and they are usually given by inhalation 15–30 min before athletic participation.

Many studies have examined whether or not selective beta-2 inhalers are ergogenic at normal doses. The data have been conflicting and the IOC has allowed the use of albuterol, formoterol, salmeterol, salbutamol and terbutaline in the form of inhalers for the treatment of asthma or EIA. In the past, athletes were required to produce a physician's note verifying the underlying disease and need for treatment. The IOC now requires evidence of asthma or EIA on the basis of eucapnic voluntary hyperpnea testing. In order to use these inhalers and compete at the Olympic Games, an independent medical advisory board must review the athlete's case.

Much of the controversy regarding beta-2 agonists stems from the drug clenbuterol. Clenbuterol came to attention prior to the 1992 Summer Olympics, and six athletes were disqualified for using it at those Games. Although technically a beta-2 agonist and available for the treatment of asthma, it is considered a 'repartitioning' agent because of its theoretical ability to increase muscle mass, and thus classified as an anabolic agent (see **anabolic agents**). Owing to the supposition that this is likely mediated through beta-receptors, it is felt that other beta-2 agonists may possess similar ability. However, it is likely that in order to act as a partitioning agent, clenbuterol (and potentially other beta-2 agonists) would need to be given in large oral doses. The significant beta-2 effects at this level would likely limit the dosage.

The use of beta-2 agonists highlights the difficulty of determining what a legitimate (therapeutic use) medical use is and what constitutes unethical use.

GARY GREEN

BETA-BLOCKERS

Beta-blockers are prohibited only in certain sports, such as shooting and other sports that require fine motor control. Research results suggest that they enhance shooting performance mainly by reducing hand tremor. Testing for beta-blockers is conducted only at competitions.

Beta-blockers are widely used in conventional medicine to treat high blood pressure (hypertension), insufficient blood flow to the heart (angina), and heart rhythm disturbances (arrythmias). They are also prescribed for less common conditions such as tremors, migraines, eye diseases (glaucoma), or overactive thyroid glands (thyrotoxicosis). They are called beta-blockers because they block the effect of natural stimulants produced in the human body on beta receptors located in the heart, lung, and blood vessels. Beta-blockers limit the heart rate, and reduce anxiety and tremor. They are used by performers and public speakers to control stage fright. Adverse effects of beta-blockers include fatigue, depression, nightmares, cold fingers and toes, low blood sugar (hypoglycemia), heart failure, and they can trigger an asthma attack.

Beta-blockers first appeared on the list of substances prohibited by the **International Olympic Committee (IOC)** in the mid-1980s when it was shown that using them substantially improved shooting performances. Shooters are trained to pull the trigger between heart beats to avoid the slight motion of the outstretched arm that occurs with each beat. At first it was thought that beta-blockers improve shooting performance because they keep the heart rate down and give the shooter more time to aim. More recent research suggests that another likely mechanism is the reduction of hand tremor. Shooting scores improvement by beta-blockers has been demonstrated clearly in properly designed scientific studies. Beta-blockers are also prohibited in other sports that require fine muscle control.

As of 2003, the Olympic Movement Anti-Doping Code lists beta-blockers under 'classes of prohibited substances in certain sports' and states that 'Where the rules of the governing body so provide, tests will be conducted for beta-blockers.' Oftentimes, the governing body is the International Federation. Examples of sports subject to beta-blocker testing include archery, bobsled, diving, sailing (match race helms only), shooting, synchronised swimming, and certain skiing sports. Testing for beta-blockers is unlikely in endurance skiing events where beta-blockers would limit heart rate and cardiac output, and therefore decrease exercise capacity, perhaps with catastrophic consequences. Testing for beta-blockers is conducted only at competitions.

Some examples of beta-blockers are acebutolol, alprenolol, atenolol, labetalol, metoprolol, nadolol, oxprenolol, propranolol, sotalol, and related substances. There is no reporting cutoff for beta-blockers. In other words, the presence of any amount of beta-blocker is a doping violation, and the actual urinary concentration (see **urinary concentrations**) need not be measured, nor is it relevant.

Athletes with a legitimate medical need for beta-blockers can still control their conditions by asking their physicians to prescribe alternative medications that are not prohibited or by seeking a therapeutic use exemption from the International Olympic Committee Medical Advisory Committee.

See also: drug testing

References

Catlin, D. (1999) 'Beta Blockers', in *Doping: An IOC White Paper*, 43, Lausanne: International Olympic Committee.

Catlin, D.H. and Hatton, C.K. (1991) 'Use and Abuse of Anabolic and Other Drugs for Athletic Enhancement', *Advances in Internal Medicine* 36: 399–424.

Olympic Movement Anti-Doping Code, Prohibited Classes of Substances and Prohibited Methods

2003. http://www.wada-ama.org/docs/web/research_science/prohibited_substances/Prohibited%20Classes%20of%20Substances%20and%20Prohibited%20Methods%202003.pdf [accessed 5 August 2003].

CAROLINE K. HATTON

BIOCHEMISTRY OF EXERCISE

The discipline of exercise biochemistry includes cellular function, bioenergetics, and metabolism. The study of cellular function involves examination of how changes in muscle cell structures – membranes and organelles – are altered by exercise, and includes the study of exercise responses at the molecular level. Bioenergetics is the study of energy production in tissues, particularly skeletal muscle. Metabolism refers to carbohydrate, lipid – fat, and protein utilisation in response to various exercise stimuli.

Cellular function

Skeletal muscle comprises thousands of specialised fibres, the muscle cells, organised in a connective tissue matrix. The unique structure of the muscle cell makes it possible for contraction to occur, the cell to be maintained, and sufficient energy to be generated. Contractile proteins are arranged into units called myofibrils that run the length of the fibre. The contractile protein apparatus of the myofibril is held together by an elaborate series of proteins called the cytoskeleton.

Muscle cells are multinucleated, attesting to the great need for protein synthesis for cell maintenance. The nucleus contains the cell's genetic material – deoxyribonucleic acid (DNA) – as well as ribonucleic acid (RNA) components required to transcribe the DNA code. Outside the nucleus, in the cytoplasm, other RNA components translate that code into the protein product. Research has examined gene expression in skeletal muscle in response to exercise (see gene expression responses to exercise) to determine the molecular mechanisms responsible for muscle function and adaptation.

Because of the great energy demands associated with contraction, the muscle contains an intricate **mitochondria** system that forms a reticulum around myofibrils. Mitochondria are the cell organelles containing all the chemical pathways responsible for aerobic metabolism – energy production that requires oxygen. The sarcoplasmic reticulum also surrounds myofibrils and functions to sequester and release calcium to control muscle contraction. Around each muscle fibre is a branched series of **capillaries** needed to deliver nutrients, remove waste products, and to provide gas exchange. Located approximately in the centre of the fibre is the endplate, where the motor neuron innervates the muscle cell.

Muscle contains fibres that have different contractile and metabolic properties. Type 1 fibres, also called slow twitch fibres, have a slower contraction and relaxation speed and specialise in aerobic metabolism; they have more mitochondria and capillaries. Type 2 fibres, also called fast twitch fibres, have a faster contraction and relaxation speed and specialise in anaerobic metabolism and force generation. These are broad categories, and it is likely that a continuum exists between the two.

Endurance and **resistance training** result in specific adaptations in the muscle fibre. The main adaptation with endurance training is an increase in the capillary-to-fibre ratio and an increase in the volume of mitochondria, to supply more energy to the contracting muscle. The main adaptation to resistance training is an increase in the diameter of the fibres such that more tension can be developed. This increase in diameter leads to muscle hypertrophy – increased size. While both resistance and endurance training appear to enlarge the endplate, endurance training has a profound effect, increasing the endplate size by 30 per cent

151

and condensing the distribution of neuro-transmitter receptors.

Bioenergetics

Bioenergetics refers to the study of the energy conserving processes in living systems. Energy is stored chemically as adenosine triphosphate (ATP) and then converted to mechanical energy for muscle contraction. The breakdown of ATP yields energy for muscle contractile proteins in the myofibril to 'slide together', generating a contraction. The breakdown of ATP is an exergonic reaction, meaning that it releases energy, which happens because of the hydrolysis of the last phosphate group, which is called a high-energy phosphate. The energy released is known as free energy. This energy is capable of being converted to mechanical energy, coupled to another reaction that requires energy – endergonic, or lost as heat.

In skeletal muscle, ATP is hydrolysed to adenosine diphosphate (ADP) and inorganic phosphate. Phosphocreatine then reacts with the ADP, donating its high-energy phosphate, producing ATP and creatine. Hydrolysis of ATP occurs at the site of the myosin head, which functions as an ATPase enzyme. The release of energy is captured and used to complete the process of contraction, involving myosin and actin interactions. Because only ATP can be used to fuel muscle contractions directly, ATP must be continually replenished for exercise to continue.

When the muscle begins to contract, the small stores of ATP are rapidly depleted, and the phosphocreatine reaction takes place to regenerate more ATP. Once phosphocreatine stores are depleted or reduced, which occurs in the first few minutes of exercise, ATP must be regenerated through other sources. During short-duration, high-intensity exercise, anaerobic glycolysis (see later) provides the needed ATP; during long-duration, moderate-intensity exercise, aerobic glycolysis and fat oxidation (see later) provide the ATP needed for muscle contraction to continue.

Creatine is the most popular nutritional ergogenic aid targeted to enhance the ATP-phosphocreatine system. Creatine supplementation has been shown in many, but not all, research studies to enhance exercise performance in repetitive high-intensity exercise bouts. There seems to be some variability in the response, such that not all individuals show a benefit.

Metabolism

Metabolism refers to all chemical reactions and pathways that store, utilise, and derive energy from organic molecules. Carbohydrate, fat, and protein are the principal organic molecules that are ingested in the diet, stored in the body, and broken down to produce ATP in skeletal muscle.

Carbohydrate in the human diet is mainly derived from plants and is a combination of carbon, hydrogen, and oxygen atoms. These carbohydrates are digested into to simple sugars such as glucose and fructose, or fruit sugar. Simple sugars are called monosaccharides and contain six carbon atoms. Disaccharides are two simple sugars linked together; an example is sucrose, or table sugar, which is composed of glucose and fructose. Polysaccharides consist of many monosaccharides linked together. Starch is the polysaccharide found in plants, and glycogen is the polysaccharide found in animals, particularly meat. The human diet is about 50 per cent carbohydrates, but 55–70 per cent is recommended for those participating in strenuous exercise.

Glucose is the main monosaccharide used in metabolism. It is transported from the gut to the liver and skeletal muscle, where it is taken up and stored as glycogen, a combination of many glucose molecules. Cells take up glucose with the assistance of the hormone insulin, although exercise will also promote glucose uptake into muscle cells. Glucose is transported into the muscle with the help of special transporter proteins called glucose transporter-4 (GLUT 4) proteins. When glucose enters the cell, it is immediately phosphorylated to glucose-6-phosphate, essentially trapping it in the cell. At this stage, it can either be used to produce energy through the metabolic pathway called glycolysis or stored as glycogen. The main storage sites for glycogen are the liver ($\sim$100 g) and skeletal muscle ($\sim$350 g).

The liver plays an important role in regulating blood glucose concentrations. It is essential that blood glucose concentrations are kept fairly constant, because nerve cells depend on blood glucose as their primary energy source. When blood glucose concentrations fall, such as occurs during fasting or exercise conditions, the liver increases glucose release into the circulation. The glucose can then be taken up by skeletal muscle to assist with ATP production. When blood glucose concentrations rise, such as after a meal, the liver increases uptake of glucose from the circulation and stores it as glycogen. These processes are under tight hormonal control.

Glycogen in muscle is broken down into glucose to supply energy as ATP for muscle contraction. Glucose can be metabolised either anaerobically to provide energy for high-intensity exercise or aerobically to provide energy for endurance exercise. These processes require a sequence of enzymatic reactions, those chemical reactions that are facilitated, or catalysed, by enzymes. Anaerobic metabolism of glucose occurs in the cytoplasm; aerobic metabolism of glucose occurs in the mitochondria of the cell. The terms anaerobic and aerobic will be used here, although some investigators call these processes fast glycolysis and slow glycolysis, respectively.

During anaerobic metabolism, glucose is converted to pyruvic acid and then to lactic acid (see also **anaerobic glycolysis**). Anaerobic metabolism occurs during periods of reduced oxygen availability, such as during high-intensity activity. Lactic acid will accumulate in the muscle, increasing the intracellular hydrogen ion concentration (decreasing pH), which, in turn, inhibits the glycolytic enzymatic reactions and directly interferes with muscle contraction. The end result will be a decrease in energy availability and reduced contractile force. Glycolysis produces two molecules of ATP per molecule of glucose; thus, while the rate of ATP production is fast, the amount of ATP is limited. The hormone epinephrine plays an important role in regulating anaerobic glycolysis by activating enzymes in the metabolic pathway. This effect is thought to be mediated by beta-adrenergic receptor action.

High-intensity exercise relies on ATP production through anaerobic glycolysis, such that the first 10 s of exercise obtains 44 per cent of ATP from anaerobic glycolysis, 30 s of exercise obtains 49–56 per cent, and 90 s of exercise obtains 36–54 per cent. As exercise duration increases, the intensity of exercise will decrease and, thus, the reliance on anaerobic production of ATP will decrease. Trained individuals rely less on anaerobic production of ATP than untrained individuals who are working at the same relative exercise intensity. Because trained athletes work at a higher intensity, they will generate more lactic acid overall. However, training increases the ability of the body to clear lactic acid, and improves the body's buffer systems to withstand decreases in pH, which occurs with lactic acid accumulation.

Because of this increase in lactic acid, athletes have used nutritional ergogenic aids as 'body buffers'. Bicarbonate loading – soda loading, or citrate loading involves ingesting 0.3 g per kg body mass of sodium bicarbonate or 0.3–0.5 g per kg body mass of sodium citrate 1–2 h before exercise. The large variability in the results of studies that have examined these ergogenic aids, suggests variability in individual responses; not everyone benefits under all conditions.

Research has shown that caffeine can also boost anaerobic performance.

Glucose derived from muscle glycogen can also be metabolised aerobically. When exercise is of low-to-moderate intensity, glucose is broken down to pyruvic acid, which enters the mitochondria. Pyruvate then enters the tricarboxylic cycle (TCA), also known as the citric acid cycle or the Krebs' cycle, a series of enzymatic reactions to break pyruvate into carbon dioxide (CO_2) and hydrogen atoms. The CO_2 enters the circulation and is expired through the lungs. Hydrogen atoms are carried to the electron transport system located on the inner mitochondrial membrane. One mole of glucose yields 38–39 moles of ATP. One of the final reactions of the electron transport system is the combination of oxygen with hydrogen atoms to form water. As long as adequate oxygen is present, aerobic breakdown of glucose will continue.

Much of the regulation of aerobic metabolism occurs through the changing concentrations of the adenine nucleotide pool of ATP, ADP, and adenosine monophosphate (AMP), representing the energy of cell. Also the concentration of TCA intermediates can control the flux of substrates through the TCA cycle. Several hormones play significant roles in regulating aerobic energy metabolism, such as insulin, glucagon, epinephrine, and norepinephrine.

At the onset of exercise there is a fall in phosphocreatine and an increase in ADP, thereby lowering the ratio of ATP to ADP. In turn, this lower ratio activates glycolysis, the TCA cycle, and oxidative phosphorylation, producing an increase in carbohydrate oxidation and oxygen consumption. Pyruvate dehydrogenase is key to the regulation of carbohydrate oxidation during exercise, and this enzyme is responsive to pyruvate concentration and the ATP : ADP ratio. Also, the TCA pool expands with the onset of exercise. Lowering the ratio of phosphocreatine to creatine, as happens during exercise, may raise the sensitivity of oxidative phosphorylation.

Adaptations to endurance training include increases in oxygen delivery to exercising muscle and increased activity of the TCA cycle and other oxidative enzymes. There are structural adaptations as well, such that there is greater capillary density in the muscle and an increase in mitochondrial volume. Also, there is a shift in substrate utilisation to a greater reliance on metabolism of fat to provide energy, which results in less utilisation of muscle glycogen.

In lipid metabolism (see **lipolysis**), dietary fats are digested and absorbed into the circulation and transported to adipocytes, the main storage site for fat, as well as to other tissues, such as skeletal muscle. Fat is stored as triglyceride, which is a molecule of glycerol and three fatty acid molecules. Fatty acids can be metabolised aerobically in muscle cells to provide energy. They are the primary fuel under resting conditions and can generate a significant proportion of ATP during exercise at low-to-moderate intensities. Lipid molecules contain hydrocarbons, either in the aliphatic chain or aromatic ring form. Fatty acids are hydrocarbon chains (CH_3-CH_2-CH_2-) with a carboxylic acid (-COOH) at one end.

Phospholipids are similar in structure to the triglyceride molecule except that one of the fatty acid of the triglyceride is replaced with a phosphate (PO_4^{2-}) molecule or phosphate bound to another small molecule, such as choline or inositol. Phospholipids form a lipid bilayer that is the basis of plasma membranes surrounding cells and most intracellular organelles. Sphingolipids function as cellular second messengers, in mediating cell growth, and in cell-to-cell adhesion. Steroids consist of three six-carbon and one five-carbon ring covalently bound to form a rigid and planar structure. Cholesterol is a prominent steroid molecule that provides rigidity to the plasma membranes and is used as a base in the synthesis of bile acids and hormones, including oestrogen, testosterone, aldosterone, and cortisol. Cholesterol also serves as a precursor for vitamin D.

Lipolysis is the process of breaking triglyceride down to its constituents, three fatty acid molecules and one glycerol molecule. Triglycerides are stored predominantly in adipose tissue but also in skeletal muscle. Fatty acids released from adipose tissue are transported by the circulation to skeletal muscle. Specific proteins function as transporters to carry fatty acid into the muscle fibres. Fatty acids in the muscle, derived either from adipose tissue or from muscle triglycerides, will enter the mitochondria through a carnitine-associated transport system, where the breakdown typically involves the sequential removal of two-carbon acetyl groups (CH_3-C=O), a process known as beta-oxidation (β-oxidation). The acetyl groups enter into the TCA cycle, where they are broken down into CO_2 and hydrogen, which pass the electrons through the electron transport chain to reduce molecular oxygen to combine with hydrogen and form water. The number of ATP molecules produced by fatty acid oxidation varies according to the number of carbons in the fatty acid; for example, an 18-carbon fatty acid yields 147 molecules of ATP, and a fatty acid with fewer or more carbons will yield fewer or more ATP, respectively.

Fatty acids from adipocytes are oxidised at a maximum rate during low to moderate exercise intensity, approximately 25–65 per cent of maximal aerobic capacity; this rate decreases with higher exercise intensity. As exercise intensity increases, and the oxidation of fatty acids from adipocytes plateaus or decreases, the use of intramuscular triglycerides increases. At about 65 per cent of maximal aerobic capacity, the maximal oxidation rate occurs of all fatty acid sources combined.

Endurance-trained individuals are able to maintain a higher proportion of energy from fatty acids at any given relative intensity compared with untrained individuals. The main adaptations influencing fat metabolism are:

- an increased oxygen delivery to exercising muscles by increased blood flow and increased capillary density;
- a maintenance or increase in the rate of fatty acid release from adipose tissue at higher exercise rates and relative intensities, which reflects maintenance of blood flow to adipose tissue at these intensities;
- a higher rate of transport of fatty acids into muscle cells by specific transporters;
- an expansion of enzymatic capacity for oxidising fatty acids inside muscle cells, which can be explained by increased mitochondria volume and content.

As fat is an important energy source during endurance exercise, several nutritional ergogenic aids have been developed to enhance this process. Carnitine is widely marketed and purported to increase fatty acid transport into the mitochondria. However, research studies have found that carnitine supplementation does not increase muscle carnitine concentrations or enhance performance. Medium-chain triglycerides are fats composed of fatty acid chains of about 6–10 carbon atoms. Because medium-chain triglycerides are more easily digested in the intestines and absorbed into the circulation than are other fats, they are purported to be an easily oxidised fuel for muscle. However, there is little evidence to support their use as an ergogenic aid. Caffeine is known to enhance endurance performance. It was once thought this ergogenic effect was caused by caffeine's role in enhancing fat use as a fuel. However, recent studies suggest that caffeine may act predominantly on the central nervous system.

The human diet should contain about 10–15 per cent protein (see also **protein metabolism**). Protein is composed of twenty different amino acids, and nine of these are essential – they cannot be made in the body and must be obtained from the diet. Dietary protein is digested into amino acids and transported to tissues by the circulation. Protein digestion and absorption can take up to 2–3 h. After entering the cells, the amino acids are reformed into specific proteins, as there are no stored amino acid pools. Excess ingested protein is broken down, oxidised, or converted to fat or glucose for storage. Proteins contain carbon, hydrogen, oxygen, and nitrogen. Protein breakdown involves the removal of the nitrogen group from the amino acid. The nitrogen is converted to ammonia, which is then converted to urea in the liver and excreted by the kidneys. Various hormones, such as growth hormone, testosterone, and thyroxine, control the rate of protein synthesis.

Because of their ability to take on various shapes, proteins serve myriad important roles in the body. Skin, bones, muscle, and hair are predominantly composed of protein for structural purposes. Protein in muscle functions in producing the muscle contraction, as proteins such as myosin and actin link and slide together. Antibodies that play important roles in immune function are proteins. Enzymes that catalyse all chemical reactions in the body are proteins. Many hormones are proteins, for example, insulin, growth hormone, glucagon, and antidiuretic hormone. Proteins' function is maintaining the body's pH and fluid balance, and they are important in transporting substances in the circulation. In times of starvation or extreme exercise, protein can be used as a supplementary fuel for muscle.

Protein is not a major energy source for muscle during exercise. However, protein can produce up to 10 per cent of energy during prolonged physical activity, serving as an auxiliary fuel. To provide energy, muscle proteins are first broken down into their constituent amino acids. Some of these amino acids can then be metabolised

in the mitochondria to produce ATP. Both endurance and resistance trained athletes require more protein, around 1.2–1.4 g per kg body mass, than non-exercising individuals, who need only 0.8 g per kg body mass. For endurance athletes, the extra protein is needed because some protein is being metabolised for energy during exercise. For resistance-training athletes, the extra ingested protein is needed to repair and build muscle mass.

Protein and amino acid supplements are perhaps the most popular nutritional ergogenic aids. Because most athletes are ingesting the recommended amount of protein in their diets, there is probably no need for protein supplementation. Certain amino acids, such as branched chain amino acids, have been purported to provide extra energy or reduce fatigue, yet scientific studies do not confirm this. Further, excess dietary protein could prove harmful, since high protein concentrations increase calcium loss in the urine.

Further reading

Brooks, G.A., Fahey, T.D., White, T.P. and Baldwin, K.M. (2000) *Exercise Physiology: Human Bioenergetics and Its Applications, Third Edition*, Mountain View CA: Mayfield.

Powers, S.K. and Howley, E.T. (2000) *Exercise Physiology: Theory and Application to Fitness and Performance, Fourth Edition*, Madison WI: Brown and Benchmark.

Williams, M.H. (2002) *Nutrition for Health, Fitness, and Sport, Sixth Edition*, Boston MA: McGraw Hill.

PRISCILLA M. CLARKSON

BIOENERGETICS

Bioenergetics is the science that studies the energy-converting processes within living or biological systems. Energy is neither created nor destroyed but only converted from one form to another; this is known as the first law of thermodynamics. Therefore, energy can be stored chemically as adenosine triphosphate (ATP) and can be converted to mechanical energy by muscle contraction. The energy that is utilised in this case not only results in the interaction of the muscle proteins but also helps move the protein filaments, to result in muscle contraction; it can also build molecules, such as proteins. Typically, in these processes, the useful energy stored as ATP in biological systems is used to produce mechanical energy. The energy stored in the chemical bonds of ATP can be liberated when the molecule is partially broken down. Typically, the breaking down of the ATP molecule will result in the last phosphate group being hydrolysed from the rest of the molecule forming adenosine diphosphate (ADP), inorganic phosphate (P_i), and energy. The amount of energy released or liberated during this process is known as the free energy available from this reaction. If this free energy is capable of being utilised, it can be converted to mechanical energy or help direct or push a reaction in a specific direction. The energy within the bonds of the ATP molecule can then be used to help in biological processes when liberated. In these processes, heat is also produced since no thermodynamic process is completely efficient. Unfortunately, biological systems cannot convert heat energy to mechanical energy. Biological systems are also sensitive to small changes in temperature and the rates of enzymatic biological reactions are temperature dependent. If the temperature of the system is increased, the rate of the reactions is often increased, within a finite temperature range; beyond a certain temperature ($>45°C$), proteins can be degraded. Enzymes are specific types of proteins that help to speed up biochemical processes. The Q_{10} effect is the rate of change of the reaction when the temperature is increased $10°C$. For example, if the Q_{10} is 3 the rate of the reaction has increased threefold.

Further reading

Hill, T.L. (1977) *Free Energy Transductions in Biology*, New York: Academic Press.

Lehninger, A.L. (1973) 'Bioenergetics', in A.L. Lehninger, *Biochemistry, Second Edition*, 387–416, New York: Worth.

ALLAN GOLDFARB

BIOMECHANICAL PRINCIPLES OF MOVEMENT

We can describe the biomechanical principles of coordinated movement as general laws based on physics and biology that determine human motion. These principles may be subdivided into the following categories. Universal principles are valid for all activities; principles of partial generality are valid for large groups of activities, for example, force, endurance, and precision or accuracy tasks; particular principles are valid for specific tasks.

It should be noted that, although the coordination of joint and muscle actions is often considered to be crucial to the successful execution of sports movements, too few of the underlying assumptions have been rigorously tested. For example, the transfer of angular momentum between body segments is often proposed as a feature of vigorous sports movements. However, several investigators (e.g. Sørensen *et al.* 1996) have shown that, in kicking, angular momentum is not transferred from the thigh to the shank when the thigh decelerates. Instead, the performance of the kick would be improved if the thigh did not decelerate. Its deceleration is caused by the motion of the shank through inertia coupling between the two segments. The scarcity of systematic research into the applicability of the principles of coordinated movement to sport should be borne in mind.

Universal principles

Use of pre-stretch or the **stretch-shortening cycle** of muscular contraction

In performing many activities, a segment often moves in the opposite direction to the one intended (see also **temporal and phase analysis**). This initial counter-movement is often necessary simply to allow the subsequent movement to occur. Other benefits arise from the increased acceleration path, initiation of the stretch reflex, storage of elastic energy and stretching the muscle to optimal length for forceful contraction, which relates to the **muscle tension-length relationship**.

Minimisation of energy used to perform a specific task or the principle of limitation of excitation of muscles

There is some evidence to support this as an adaptive mechanism in skill acquisition, for example, the reduction in unnecessary movements during the learning of throwing skills. The many multi-joint muscles in the body support the importance of energy efficiency as an evolutionary principle.

Principle of minimum task complexity or control of redundant degrees of freedom in the kinematic chain

The kinematic chain – now more commonly referred to as the kinetic chain, and this term will be used throughout the rest of this encyclopedia – proceeds from the most proximal to the most distal segment. Coordination of that chain becomes more complex as the degrees of freedom – the possible axes of rotation plus directions of linear motion at each joint – increase. A simple kinetic chain from shoulder girdle to fingers contains at least seventeen degrees of freedom. Many of these would seem to need to be controlled to permit movement replication. For example, in a basketball set shot the player keeps the elbow well into the body to reduce the redundant degrees of freedom so that forces are applied in the required direction of motion. This principle may explain why skilled movements look so simple. The temporal and spatial characteristics of the relevant kinetic chains

are often the main focus of many quantitative biomechanical analyses. The relationship between this principle and recent observations of kinematic variability, even within the movement patterns of skilled sports performers, has not yet been fully explored.

Principles of partial generality

Sequential action of muscle (summation of internal forces; serial organisation; transfer of angular momentum along the kinetic chain)

This principle is most important in activities requiring speed or force, such as discus throwing. It involves the recruitment of body segments into the movement at the correct time. Movements are generally initiated by the large muscle groups, which are usually pennate and which produce force to overcome the inertia of the whole body plus any sports implement. The sequence is continued by the faster muscles of the extremities, which not only have a larger range of movement and speed but also improved accuracy owing to the fewer muscle fibres innervated by each motor neuron – the innervation ratio. In correct sequencing, proximal segments move ahead of distal ones; this ensures that muscles are stretched to develop tension when they contract. This principle is partly negated by long axis rotations, which do not reach peak speeds in the proximal-to-distal sequence, for example, in the tennis serve and squash forehand drive (Marshall and Elliott 2000).

Minimisation of inertia (increasing acceleration of motion)

This is most important in endurance and speed activities. Movements at any joint should be initiated with the distal joints in a position that minimises the moment of inertia, to maximise rotational acceleration. For example, in the recovery phase of sprinting, the hip is flexed with the knee also flexed; this configuration has a far lower moment of inertia than an extended or semi-flexed knee. This principle relates to angular momentum (see **angular momentum generation, transfer and trading**) generation, transfer, and trading, which are affected by changes in the moment of inertia.

Principle of impulse generation-absorption

This principle is mainly important in force and speed activities. It relates to the **impulse-momentum relationship**: impulse = change of momentum = average force × time force acts. This shows that a large impulse is needed to produce a large change of momentum; this requires either a large average force or a long time of action. In impulse generation, the former must predominate because of the explosive short duration of many sports movements, such as a high jump take-off, which requires power – the rapid performance of work (see below). In absorbing momentum, e.g. catching a cricket ball, the time is increased by 'giving' with the ball to reduce the mean impact force, preventing bruising or fracture and increasing the chances of making a successful catch.

Maximising the acceleration path

This principle arises from the **work – energy relationship** – $\Delta E = F_m s$ – which shows that a large change in mechanical energy (ΔE) requires a large average force (F_m) or the maximising of the distance (s) over which we apply force. This is an important principle in events requiring speed and force, for example, a shot-putter making full use of the width of the throwing circle.

Stability

A wide base of support is needed for stability; this applies not only for static activities

but also for dynamic ones, where sudden changes in the momentum vector occur (see **equilibrium and stability**).

See also: equilibrium and stability

References

Marshall, R.N. and Elliott, B.C. (2000) 'Long Axis Rotation: The Missing Link in Proximal-to-Distal Sequencing', *Journal of Sports Sciences* 18: 247–54.

Sørensen, H., Zacho, M., Simonsen, E.B., Dyhre-Poulsen, P. and Klausen, K. (1996) 'Dynamics of the Martial Arts High Front Kick', *Journal of Sports Sciences* 14: 483–95.

Further reading

Bartlett, R.M. (1999) *Sports Biomechanics: Reducing Injury and Improving Performance*, London: E&FN Spon.

ROGER BARTLETT

BJD (BONE AND JOINT DECADE) GLOBAL INITIATIVE

The Bone and Joint Decade officially commenced in January 2003, based on the goals and objectives agreed between various health organizations world-wide. Its primary purpose is to raise awareness of the impacts that musculoskeletal disorders have had on individuals and societies as a whole globally. It aims to promote valuable guidelines on prevention and treatment of diseases such as osteoporosis, osteoarthritis, age-related lower back pain, and other bone and joint diseases that are causing problems world-wide. Its cost-effective programs aim to help minimize the deleterious economic effects of these diseaseses. In addition, the BJD also plans to carry out extensive research on various musculoskeletal disorders, seeking improvements in diagnosis, prevention and treatment. With an abundance of health professionals within the project, a great amount of information can be provided relating to various musculoskeletal disorders. This will be done through publication of brochures, research papers, and magazine articles, as well as more interactively, via symposia. These education campaigns should greatly benefit those who initially lack knowledge and understanding of the problem of bone and joint diseases. Within the decade, the goal is to complete the mission through cooperation with governments and other health organizations that are aware of the potential severity of the problem for populations world-wide. Previously, the Decade of the Brain (1990–2000) was very successful in addressing disorders related to the human brain. Thus there is a good chance that the promotion of the Bone and Joint Decade (2000–2010) will be equally successful.

There are many facts that exemplify the prevalence of bone and joint diseases. In the United States, musculoskeletal disorders are the leading cause of disability, accounting for 131 million patients annually. Likewise, in various developing countries, 10–15 million people are injured or disabled annually from road accidents (The Bone and Joint Decade 2000).

However, in order for their mission to complete successfully within the next five or six years, many other different health and educational related organizations have partnered up with them to provide support and resources. For example, Pharmacia's involvement in the Bone and Joint Decade has been greatly concentrated in the global concern of arthritis. This pharmaceutical company definitely has a strong historical background in the development of new drugs and therapies towards patients with arthritis, reducing the amount of pain that patients suffer. In addition, they contribute towards development of educational programs which allow the patient to learn more about arthritis and also provides patients with some basic health knowledge to help minimize their pain, therby assisting patients to enjoy a higher quality of life (The Bone and Joint Decade, 2000).

Until now, The Bone and Join Decade has been quite successful on their mission. The global concern of bone and joint diseases has drawn the populations' attention, recognizing the seriousness of these musculoskeletal disorders. However, there are many people around the world unable to receive any educational support through the government because of the problem of poverty and starvation in developing countries. The Bone and Joint Decade may be able to give these countries aid, providing the population with relevant information about bone and joint diseases, but this is not a simple task. There is still a long way to go, and hopefully cooperation between The Bone and Joint Decade and other health organizations can seek solutions to the major problem of musculoskeletal disorders among countries worldwide.

Reference

N.A. (2000) *The Bone and Joint Decade*, http://www.boneandjointdecade.org.html (accessed 24/10/2003).

VICTOR W.T. HO

BLOOD DOPING

Throughout human history, magical powers have been ascribed to blood. Ancient warriors would drink the blood of their conquered foes to increase their own strength. Although it was known that aerobic endurance is dependent on oxygen-carrying capacity, it was not until the 1940s that studies were demonstrated an increase in performance with the addition of exogenous red blood cells. United States military studies reported that the infusion of 2,000 cc of freshly drawn blood into matched donors resulted in increased VO_2 max. This technique was limited by transfusion technology of the time and this did not become a popular until the advent of modern techniques of blood storage. Further studies revealed that transfusions resulted not only in increased hemoglobin levels, but elite runners improved their maximal oxygen consumption and total run time to exhaustion.

Improvements in transfusion technology created a host of options for endurance athletes to surreptitiously increase their VO_2 max. The most common method was autologous blood doping, in which an athlete would remove 1–2 units of their own blood at least six weeks before a competition. They would store the concentrated red blood cells and then reinfuse them just before an event. In this manner, the athlete would get the benefit of the infused blood along with their own newly produced cells. Athletes could also transfuse matched donor cells via heterologous blood doping and then were spared the period of relative anemia while waiting for their red cell mass to re-equilibrate. The biggest scandal involving this method was the 1984 United Stated Olympic Cycling team in which several members confessed to blood doping.

The use of blood doping as an ergogenic aid is severely limited by potential disastrous complications. Even under rigorous hospital conditions, the incidence of serious immune reactions in matched transfusions approaches 3 per cent. In addition, the risk of infectious complications such as HIV and hepatitis B and C are significant risks to heterologous blood doping. Autologous blood doping should reduce the infection risk, but complications can still result from improper storage.

Although many considered blood doping allowable in sports because it does not represent a foreign substance, especially the autologous variety, the International Olympic Committee specifically prohibits a physiologic substance that is taken in abnormal quantity or by abnormal route of entry in order to increase performance. Clearly, blood doping falls under that prohibition despite the fact that there was initially no clear method of detection. The use of blood testing, which has been used to combat exogenous **Erythropoietin (EPO)/**

Darbepoetin use, can also be used to detect blood doping by determining the presence of different populations of red blood cells. Genetic testing can obviously detect heterologous blood doping. In addition, many sports organizations, such as the Union Cyclist International (UCI) have banned athletes that have hematocrits greater than 50 per cent. This is an indirect method of deterring blood doping. However, the advent of recombinant erythropoietin (EPO) in the late 1980s and attendant risks of transfusions severely reduced the use of blood doping as an ergogenic aid. However, it will be interesting to note if the improvements in drug testing for EPO and darbepoetin lead to a resurgence in the use of blood doping.

GARY GREEN

BODY

The 'Return of the Body' movement, which originated in the 1970s, signalled a crisis of modern industrial society to which people responded with an increased striving for identity, authenticity and distinction as well as by devoting more attention to the body. Rapid processes of modernisation and globalisation – above all those of technological progress and the new media – have led, on the one hand, to a growing detachment from a body which, in the age of the cellular phones and the internet, vanishes into 'virtual reality'. On the other hand, one can observe a revaluation, even a growing fetishism, of the body. Fitness and health, a slim figure, youth and 'sex appeal' have become the credo of modern society and the paradigm of middle-class popular culture. The new model body must be firm and flawless and exude good health – in short, a body is not allowed to show the slightest trace of work, illness, age, childbirth or, generally, of life.

The body as social construct

Parallel to the rise of this 'body culture', there was an increasing scientific interest in the body which was no longer confined to biologists and the medical profession but also spread to historians and social scientists. The starting point of historical and social scientific analyses was the realisation that the body is a historical and social construct.

While the body has a biological foundation, it is the medium of human interaction, of social relationships and of dealing with the environment. Moreover, it not only sends and receives signals; it is itself a signal. The body is not only the basis of our physical existence but also the site of social control and the outward expression of cultural moulding and remoulding. How we perceive our body, how we manage it, use it and judge it differs according to our cultural context. We are subjected to physiological needs; we must eat or sleep, but what we eat and how we sleep, the daily ritual of body care and somatic culture generally are wholly dependent on the prevailing social structures.

Body ideals and body practices, its use as a medium of communication and as an anchor for identity, the regulation and control of physical conditions and functions and the attitudes and behaviour patterns related to all this, are therefore never authentic, static, and universal but shaped by culture. The norms, rules and, ideals which a society affixes to the body and, oriented to these, the proper management of the body in a given culture are considered natural and taken for granted, meaning, however, that precisely these processes of normalisation and naturalisation hinder any conscious critical appraisal of the status quo. This is also true of the 'gendering' of the body. In academic disputes concerning sport, the body and gender approach proposed by Connell is of especial interest. According to Connell, bodies are both objects and agents in social practice. 'The practices in which bodies are involved form social structures and personal trajectories which in turn provide the conditions of new practices in which bodies are addressed and involved' (Connell 2002: 47).

Social processes, and participation in sport in particular, are invariably connected with bodily activities and these bodily activities are connected, in turn, with social norms and interpretations. Connell calls this process 'social embodiment' or 'body-reflective practice', and presents numerous examples to demonstrate how social embodiment functions and how biology and culture are inseparably interwoven with each other.

Men's and women's bodies are subjected to patterns of interpretation and social norms which reflect the dichotomous and hierarchic gender order. On the one hand, the gendered distribution of power and the corresponding division of labour inscribe different signs on the bodies of men and women. On the other hand, 'female' and 'male' physical characteristics and practices are of crucial importance for the construction and legitimisation of the social order.

Numerous studies undertaken in history studies and the social sciences have revealed that ideas, needs, emotions and practices related to the body are influenced not only by the social but also by the gender order. Hence, men and women develop a gender-specific 'somatic culture': typical habits of eating and dressing, typical body ideals as well as typical daily rituals of taking care of and presenting the body. The body strategies and the body language of the sexes, which come into play, for instance, in the appropriation of space, in postures and gestures, and in movement and expression, are a reflection of the prevailing gender relationships. Further, heath and illness, physical fitness, and weakness are not entirely biologically ordained but display cultural and gender-typical patterns.

Sporting bodies

As sport is based on the body, it always involves the presentation of the body and its accomplishments and is to a large degree connected with bodily changes. Accordingly, the movement cultures prevailing in a given society are closely related to the build of the body. The minuet and the graceful figures of its dancers, for example, used to reflect the refined life-style of the court; whereas, with their stiff, upright bearing, the followers of Friedrich Ludwig Jahn and his German gymnastics enacted soldierly masculinity. In different movement cultures and in different sports certain bodily techniques are required and thus trained, and participation in sport is strongly influenced by the ethos of the body, i.e. by bodily ideals, for example, but also by thresholds of inhibition.

Modern sport, which began to spread in the nineteenth century, is associated with a specific construction of the body, namely with a rational management of its processes as well as its optimisation and instrumentalisation, based on the knowledge of the link between body build, physiological processes and sporting performance. In this respect the parallel developments of sport, industrial society and science and technology are closely interwoven. The continuous increase in standards of achievement and growing competition led not only to an expansion of sport science but also its division into areas ranging from the study of movement to the psychology of sport, the focus always being the greatest possible use of the body's resources.

Bodies and meanings

But it is not only the body as a guarantee of great sporting performance that is the focus of attention. Today the growing fetishism of the body and the increased striving for individualisation and distinction have led to a rise in the demand for all kinds of physical activity. Not only have sports clubs enjoyed a steady growth in membership figures; the demand for anti-stress training and body therapies as well as dance-related and

health-oriented physical activities has also increased at a tremendous rate. Moreover, the craze for excitement and thrills and the longing for authenticity and identity have led to an upsurge of activities, such as parachute-jumping or white-water rafting, which expose the body to risk. Also experiencing a boom are types of sport which offer conspicuous consumption, like golf or tennis, or the presentation of (subcultural) identity, like skateboarding. Underlying the modern body-and-health cult is the conviction that the body, being infinitely manipulable, is no longer a matter for fate but is one's own responsibility. The form and function of the body are today considered to be the product of individual effort in which money, time and energy must be invested in order to create a work of art independent of time and matter. Hence, on the one hand, today's bodies appear alienated, detached from the self; on the other, the body can be used as a way of presenting the self, as a symbol of creativity and modernity, as a means of social distinction or as a way of demonstrating vigour, efficiency, and self-discipline.

The unity of fitness, health and beauty – in fact, the whole new artificially designed conception of the body – is today one of the most important means of creating and expressing social inequality. Body, fitness, and health are signs of social status; they are resources and privileges as well as symbolic and cultural capital in Bourdieu's sense of the term. The body has been accorded a place of unsuspected eminence in our lives, not only in its own management and in dealing with others but also as a commercial product in economic discourse, for example in the health and fitness industry.

Nevertheless, there are huge discrepancies between our desires and reality, between the bodies presented in the media and our own bodies, between the promises of sport providers and the actual effects of exercising.

There is much evidence to suggest, however, that problems people have with

163

their bodies cannot be solved solely by taking up a sport. This is because, frequently, negative images of the body are reinforced, for example by the awareness of one's own shortcomings when one compares the ideals presented in and the sporting feats glorified by the media. The organisers of gymnastics and fitness classes are marketing women's (and also increasingly men's) dreams of health and beauty and, by attempting to shape the body to the requirements of the 'abstract male gaze', are only continuing the manipulations of the female body encountered in other areas of society, for instance in the mass media. In this respect, however, women (and men) are by no means the victims, at any rate not in a superficial sense; on the contrary, they take an active part in the construction of body, body culture, society, and gender.

Reference

Connell, R. (2002) *Gender*, Cambridge: Polity Press.

Further reading

Bordo, S.R. (1993) *Unbearable Weight. Feminism, Western Culture, and the Body*, Berkely/Los Angeles/London: University of California Press.
Laqueur, T. (1990) *Making Sex: Body and Gender from the Greeks to Freud*, Cambridge MA: Harvard University Press.
Pope, H., Phillips, K. and Olivardia, R. (2000) *The Adonis Complex: The Secret Crisis of Male Body Obsession*, New York: Free Press.

GERTRUD PFISTER

BODY COMPOSITION

Human body composition is influenced by genetics and nutrition and can be affected by factors such as exercise training, disease, and diet. The assessment of body composition is important in medicine, health and fitness, child growth, and anthropology.

Body composition can be described in various ways. In a chemical description, the body is divided into fat, water, protein, and ash or bone mineral. Another common description is a two-compartment model where the body is divided into fat and fat-free mass. In this model, fat-free mass represents all the tissue in the body other than the fat tissue; that is muscle, blood, bone, and connective tissue. The water content of the fat-free mass is about 70–75 per cent.

Fat occurs beneath the skin and around the internal organs. Fat is also found within tissues such as bone and muscle. Fat can be divided into non-essential and essential compartments. Fat tissue insulates and protects organs and is a stored form of energy and metabolic substrates. The composition of fat may vary, with the density ranging from about 920 to $960 \, \text{kg m}^{-3}$. Fat mass may vary from about 6 to 40 per cent of body mass.

Muscle occurs in three forms: skeletal, cardiac, and smooth. Skeletal muscle is the predominant form of muscle tissue. Skeletal muscle is important for locomotion and thermogenesis, and is a reservoir for amino acids. The density of muscle is relatively constant at $1,065 \, \text{kg m}^{-3}$. Muscle mass can vary from about 40 to 65 per cent of body mass, with an anorexic person and body builder with hypertrophied muscle being at opposite ends of the spectrum.

Bone is a specialised type of connective tissue. Bone is a dynamic tissue responding to stimuli by changing its shape and density, albeit at a much slower rate than fat and muscle tissue. The density of bone varies considerably from 1,180 to $1,330 \, \text{kg m}^{-3}$ depending on sex, age, and physical activity status. Bone mass varies from 10 to 20 per cent of total body mass.

Further reading

Hawes, M.R. and Martin, A.D. (1996) 'Body Composition, Proportion and Growth', in R.

Eston and T. Reilly (eds) *Kinanthropometry and Exercise Physiology Laboratory Manual*, 7–46, London: E&FN Spon.

MIKE LAMBERT

BODY COMPOSITION ASSESSMENT

Body composition can be assessed chemically as fat, water, protein, and ash. Most other methods of body composition assessment are based on the model in which the body consists of two chemically distinct compartments: fat and fat-free mass. Body composition can be assessed by many different methods; each method relies on certain assumptions and has varying accuracy.

Fat-free mass can be predicted from total body water, which occurs in a relatively fixed proportion of 72–74 per cent in fat – free mass and does not occur in fat. Total body water can be estimated from isotope dilution techniques, such as doubly labelled water. Total body potassium is an intracellular cation present in constant proportions in fat-free tissue while being absent in fat tissue. A measurement of total body potassium, such as potassium[40], can also be used as an estimate of fat-free mass (see **body composition assessment – whole body counting**).

Densitometry is a body composition technique that has been used as the 'gold standard' for many years (see **body composition assessment – densitometry**). This method assumes that the body is composed of two compartments, fat and fat-free mass, and is based on the assumption that fat has a density of $900 \, \mathrm{kg \, m^{-3}}$ at $37°C$ and fat-free mass has a density of $1.1 \, \mathrm{kg \, m^{-3}}$ at $37°C$. However, bone density may vary, introducing an error of about 3–4 per cent into this assumption. The most widely used method of calculating density is by measuring body volume by applying Archimedes' principle, which states that the volume of an object submerged in water equals the volume of water the object displaces. A more recent technique calculates body volume

and then body density by air displacement plethysmography.

Anthropometry is a technique that uses measurements of skinfold thicknesses and limb circumferences in multiple regression equations to predict body density and to calculate body fat and fat-free mass. There are several hundred equations that have been developed for specific populations by sex, age, ethnic group, and physical activity status (see **body composition assessment – anthropometry**).

Bioelectrical impedance is another method of body composition assessment, which became popular in the 1980s (see **body composition assessment – electrical impedance**). A small electrical current is passed between two electrodes, usually placed on the hand on foot of the person being assessed. The resistance to the current is based on the water and electrolyte distribution in the tissue between the electrodes. Equations have been developed that predict fat content from impedance.

Dual-energy X-ray absorptiometry (DEXA) can measure total bone-mineral content, lean tissue, and fat. A whole body DEXA scan can provide assessments of body composition both regionally and for the whole body (see **body composition assessment – dual energy X-ray absorptiometry**).

See also: body composition assessment – imaging techniques; body composition assessment – statistical methods

Further reading

Hawes, M.R. and Martin, A.D. (1996) 'Body Composition, Proportion and Growth', in R. Eston and T. Reilly (eds) *Kinanthropometry and Exercise Physiology Laboratory Manual*, 7–46, London: E&FN Spon.

Lukaski, H.C. (1987) 'Methods for the Assessment of Human Body Composition: Traditional and New', *American Journal of Clinical Nutrition* 46: 537–56.

MIKE LAMBERT

BODY COMPOSITION ASSESSMENT – ANTHROPOMETRY

Anthropometry is the science involving measurements of size, girth, bone diameters, and skinfold thicknesses to calculate body composition, dimensions, and proportions – somatotype. These techniques have application in medicine, health and fitness, and monitoring training status for participation in sport. The measuring instruments most often used in anthropometry are:

- Steel tape designed for non-extensibility and flexibility.
- Anthropometer to measure lengths and breadths.
- Skinfold callipers to measure skinfold thickness. The most commonly used good quality callipers are the Holtain, Lange, and Harpenden callipers. These callipers all have a constant pressure of 10 kPa exerted by the jaws, irrespective of the thickness of the skinfold layer. They have a measurement accuracy of 1 mm or less.
- Bone callipers to measure the width of the humerus and femur.
- Weighing scale, up to 150 kg body mass.
- Stadiometer for measuring stature.

An anthropometrist is someone trained in recording these measurements with a very low measurement error. The International Working Group in Kinanthropometry (IWGK) holds certification courses and workshops designed to train investigators to have a low measurement error and high repeatability in their measurements. The major cause of low tester measurement reliability is incorrect location and measurement of the skinfold sites.

The main reason for measuring skinfolds is to estimate general fatness. This is based on the assumption that subcutaneous fat represents total body fat. Although this is a reasonable assumption, there will always be some differences between individuals. The first equation using skinfold techniques was published in 1951. Since then several hundred equations, which predict body density from a series of well defined skinfold measurements, have been published in the scientific literature. The locations of these skinfold measurement sites are based on bony landmarks, which make their location accurate and repeatable. Typically, the studies that have developed regression equations to predict body density from skinfold measurements have used several participants who have had their body densities measured accurately using the so-called 'gold standard' procedure of underwater weighing (see **body composition assessment – densitometry**). Various skinfold sites are also measured, and then a mathematical equation describing the best-fit relationship between skinfold measurements and body density is calculated. The most accurate prediction equations take the sex and age of the participant into account, as these are factors that affect the relationship between subcutaneous fat and body density most significantly. For example, females have a higher proportion of internal fat than males. From an age perspective, bone density increases up to the age of twenty years and then starts reducing after fifty years. This change in bone density has an effect on total body density. Equations developed on young people and applied to older participants generally underestimate body density.

The error associated with predicting body fat from skinfold measurements can be accounted for by the biological variation in the proportions of subcutaneous fat, ± 2.5 per cent error, biological variation in the distribution of subcutaneous fat, ± 1.8 per cent error, and technical measurements errors, ± 0.5 per cent error. The advantages of using skinfolds for assessing body fat are that the equipment is inexpensive and the procedure is non-invasive. Further, the measurements can be conducted either in a laboratory or in the field. A disadvantage of using skinfolds is that the measurement technique does require training and the inter-measurer variation may be unacceptably high if the measurers are not well trained.

Procedure for measuring skinfolds

The skinfold thickness is a measurement of a folded layer of skin and the subcutaneous fat in the fold. The measurement of the skinfold is made by first marking the site. The sites are clearly defined using bony landmarks as reference points. Then the skin and underlying fat is grasped firmly 1 cm above the marked site and pulled away from the underlying muscle. The callipers are placed at a depth of about 1 cm over the fold, to measure the thickness. The callipers must be placed at right angles to the fold. The fat tissue has compressibility so it takes a few seconds for the reading to stabilise in an obese subject. To standardise the reading it should be recorded after 4 s. Three measurements should be recorded at each site, in rotational order, and the average reading should be used for the calculation.

Selection of an equation

It is important to select an equation that has been derived from a population whose characteristics are similar to those of the participant in biological sex, age, ethnicity, physical training, and health status. Furthermore, it is better to select an equation with skinfold sites including the arm, trunk, and legs to account for differences in fat patterning.

An alternative approach

A current trend is to express body fat as a sum of skinfolds rather than converting it

into a percentage of body fat. This method avoids relying on assumptions that are not always met. Examples of the calculation:

Men: Body density = 1.112
$-0.00043499(X_1)$
$+0.00000055(X_1)^2$
-0.00028826(age in years)

Women: Body density = 1.097
$-0.00046971(X_1)$
$+0.00000056(X_1)^2$
-0.00012828(age in years)

Where X_1 = sum of 7 skinfolds (mm) - chest, midaxillary, abdominal, suprailiac, subscapular, triceps, and thigh.

The body density is then substituted into the following equation to predict body fat per cent:

Body fat per cent = [(4.95/body density) $-4.50]\times100$ (Siri 1961).

The absolute fat mass (kg) and fat free mass can be calculated from the following equations:

Absolute fat mass (kg) = [body fat per cent × body mass (kg)]/100

Fat free mass (kg) = body mass (kg) − absolute fat mass (kg).

See also: body composition; body composition assessment; body composition assessment – electrical impedance; body composition assessment – imaging techniques; body composition assessment – statistical methods; body composition assessment – whole body counting

Reference

Siri, W.E. (1961) 'Body Composition from Fluid Spaces and Density', in J. Brozec and A. Henschel (eds) *Techniques for Measuring Body Composition*, 223–44, Washington DC: Academy of Sciences.

167

Further reading

Jackson, A.S. and Pollock, M.L. (1978) 'Generalised Equations for Predicting Body Density of Men', *British Journal of Nutrition* 40: 497–504.

Jackson, A.S., Pollock, M.L. and Ward, A. (1980) 'Generalised Equations for Predicting Body Density of Women', *Medicine and Science in Sports and Exercise* 12: 175–82.

Lohman, T.G. (1981) 'Skinfolds and Body Density and Their Relation to Fatness: A Review', *Human Biology* 53: 181–225.

Ross, W.D. and Marfell-Jones, M.J. (1991) 'Kinanthropometry', in J.D. MacDougall, H.A. Wenger and H.J. Green (eds) *Physiological Testing of the High Performance Athlete, Second Edition*, 223–308, Champaign IL: Human Kinetics.

MIKE LAMBERT

BODY COMPOSITION ASSESSMENT – DENSITOMETRY

Body composition, and in particular body fat, can be estimated from body density. As fat tissue is less dense than bone and skeletal muscle, the body density of a person with a high proportion of fat will be less than the body density of a lean, muscular person. There are two published equations that predict body fat percentage from body density. Both equations give very similar results. These equations are:

Body fat per cent = ((4.57/body density) −4.142) × 100 (Brozek *et al.* 1963)

or

Body fat per cent = ((4.95/body density)−4.5) × 100 (Siri 1961).

Assumptions

The assumptions associated with using body density to predict body fat are that fat tissue has a density of $900 \, kg \, m^{-3}$ and fat free mass has a density of $1,100 \, kg \, m^{-3}$, and that these densities are constant between individuals. The first assumption is mostly true. The fat component consists primarily of triglycerides, which have a density of $900 \, kg \, m^{-3}$. Other lipids, such as those occurring in the nervous system and cell membranes, have different densities but occur in relatively small quantities, making their contribution to the total fat density insignificant. The density of fat free mass varies with a standard deviation of about $20 \, kg \, m^{-3}$. This can be attributed to the varying bone density, which decreases in females from the age of about 40–50 years and in males from about the age of fifty years. If the fat free mass density is less than $1,100 \, kg \, m^{-3}$, the body fat will be overestimated, and if the fat free mass density is more than $1,100 \, kg \, m^{-3}$, the body fat will be underestimated. There are also ethnic differences in bone density, which will invalidate this assumption of a constant fat free mass density of $1,100 \, kg \, m^{-3}$. The measurement error around the varying density of fat free mass can affect the prediction of body fat by about 5 per cent. Body density can be determined by underwater weighting and air-displacement plethysmography.

Underwater weighing

Density is equal to mass/volume. Body volume can be determined by submerging the body underwater and measuring the body weight underwater. This method applies Archimedes' principle, which states that, 'the upthrust on a body fully submerged in a fluid is equal to the weigh of the fluid'. Stated differently, the loss of weight measured underwater, compared to the weight measured on land, is directly proportional to the volume of water displaced by the body volume. This technique therefore requires weighing the participant on land, followed by weighing the participant underwater. The air in the body, in lungs and gastrointestinal tract, also has to be taken into account and corrections made for them, as they will affect the calculation of density.

Procedure

The underwater measurement is made with the participant sitting on a chair or frame suspended from a scale above a water tank. The water tank should be at least 1 m deep. More accurate readings are obtained if a load cell is attached to the chair or frame to determine weight. The participants should be weighed in their bathing costumes and should empty their bladders and defecate before the measurement to eliminate gas from their gastrointestinal tracts. Participants should also rub themselves when they are wet to remove the air bubbles attached to their skin. Participants should avoid eating food within 2 h before the measurement. Being weighed in the fasted state reduces the measurement error by about 1 per cent.

The participant needs to be weighed while completely submerged. An obese person may have difficulty in submerging completely. If this is the case, he or she can be given a mass of about 3 kg to hold tightly on his or her lap. The underwater weight will obviously have to be corrected accordingly. The participant should be asked to exhale maximally coinciding with the measurement. Failure to do so will result in an erroneous reading, as the buoyancy of the air in the lungs will contribute to an underestimation of body density and an overestimation of body fat. The correction for residual volume can be made either simultaneously while the participant is being weighed, or outside the tank coinciding with a maximal exhalation.

Residual volume is measured using a nitrogen washout technique, during which the participant breathes within a closed system that contains a known amount of oxygen. As nitrogen is not involved in oxidative metabolism, the quantity of nitrogen inhaled and exhaled does not change and the quantity of nitrogen in the lungs after a maximal exhalation is representative of the residual volume. Residual

volume can also be predicted from age, height, and sex. The error between predicted and measured residual volume is about 2–4 per cent, which introduces an error of about 2 per cent in the final calculation of body fat per cent.

The equations for predicting residual volume are:

Men: residual volume = 0.0115 (age in years) + 1.9 (height in m) − 2.240

Women: residual volume = 0.0210 (age in years) + 2.3 (height in m) − 2.978 (Boren *et al.* 1966).

The calculation for density and fat is done through the following formulae:

Density = weight in air (kg)/(volume − (residual volume + 100 ml)),

where the 100 ml is an adjustment for gastrointestinal gas, and:

Volume = (weight in air (kg) − weight underwater (kg))/density of water: the temperature of the water should be recorded and the density of water adjusted according to the temperature).

Therefore:

Density = weight in air (kg)/[[(weight in air (kg) − weight underwater (kg))/ density of water] − (residual volume + 100 ml)].

This technique is relatively time consuming, the participant needs to be unafraid of submerging underwater, and the technique is difficult to use with certain populations, such as the obese, elderly, and disabled.

Air-displacement plethysmography

More recently the underwater weighing technique of measuring body volume and body density has been replaced by a method of gas displacement. During this technique the participant is immersed not in water but in a closed and sealed air-filled chamber. This has become possible through a commercial system called the BOD POD (Life Measurement Instruments Inc., Concord, California). This system consists of a test chamber, volume 450 l, in which the participant sits. This chamber is separated from a reference chamber, volume 300 l, by a thin diaphragm. When the participant enters the test chamber and the door is closed and sealed, the pressure changes. The diaphragm vibrates or oscillates with the change in pressure. The relationship between gas pressure and volume at a controlled temperature is applied and body volume is calculated.

An advantage of this technique over body density determined by underwater weighing is that the participant does not have to submerge himself or herself under water. A common problem this technique shares with underwater weighing is the assumption of a common fat free density for all participants when body density is calculated; as discussed above this assumption is not always true, resulting a some measurement error. In comparative studies the air displacement technique has been shown to be reliable and valid.

See also: body composition; body composition assessment; body composition assessment – anthropometry; body composition assessment – electrical impedance; body composition assessment – imaging techniques; body composition assessment – statistical methods; body composition assessment – whole body counting

References

Boren, H.G., Kory, R.C. and Syner, J.C. (1966) 'The Veterans Administration – Army Cooperative Study on Lung Function II: The Lung Volume and Its Subdivisions in Normal Men', *American Journal of Medicine* 41: 96–114.

Brozek, J., Grande, F., Anderson, J.T. and Keys, A. (1963) 'Densitometric Analysis of Body Composition: Revision of Some Quantitative Assumptions', *Annals of the New York Academy of Sciences* 110: 113–40.

Siri, W.E. (1961) 'Body Composition from Fluid Spaces and Density', in J. Brozec and A. Henschel (eds) *Techniques for Measuring Body Composition*, 223–44, Washington DC: Academy of Sciences.

Further reading

Hawes, M.R. and Martin, A.D. (1996) 'Body Composition, Proportion and Growth', in R. Eston and T. Reilly (eds) *Kinanthropometry and Exercise Physiology Laboratory Manual*, 7–46, London: E&FN Spon.

MIKE LAMBERT

BODY COMPOSITION ASSESSMENT – DUAL ENERGY X-RAY ABSORPTIOMETRY

Although dual energy X-ray absorptiometry (DEXA) was first developed to measure bone mineral content, the technology has evolved and it is now considered a useful tool for the measurement of fat, bone, and fat free mass. The DEXA method is based on the principle that, when an X-ray source is placed on one side of an object, the change in the intensity of the beam is related to the thickness, density, and chemical composition of the tissues in the object. The X-ray signal is converted into an electronic signal by the detector and is then translated into an image.

The DEXA equipment consists of a bed on which the participant lies. A dual energy X-ray beam is passed through the participant from under the bed to detectors above the participant. The beam and the detectors move over the supine participant allowing for regional and whole body measurements. The attenuation of the beam through bone, lean, and fat tissue is different. Furthermore, the attenuation of the signal with low-energy and high-energy beams is also different. Thus DEXA uses two separate sets of equations for the low- and high-frequency beams. The measurement of the whole body takes about 10–20 min, depending on the type of beam and detectors. The total X-ray exposure during a test is about the same exposure as one gets during a dental X-ray.

The earlier DEXA models had pencil beams with single detectors. The more recent designs use a fan-beam X-ray source and multi-element detectors. This improves the precision and also the speed of the scanning that occurs during the measurement.

Until recently, body density determined by the method of underwater weighing (see **body composition assessment – densitometry**), was regarded as the gold standard. This model divides the body into two compartments, fat mass with a density of $900.7\,kg\,m^{-3}$, and fat free mass with a density of $1{,}100\,kg\,m^{-3}$. This model assumes that these densities are constant. However, the fat free mass density may vary, particularly in individuals with varying bone density, and, therefore, underwater weighing may be inappropriate for these people. Body composition analysis by DEXA does not violate these assumptions and, therefore, is becoming accepted as a more accurate method. The comparison of percentage fat measured by underwater weighing and DEXA show differences that correlate well with differences in bone density.

Dual energy X-ray absorptiometry is also calibrated against external standards and is relatively independent of hydration, which also reduces the error. Although the DEXA method of body composition assessment overcomes some of the limitations of the underwater weighing techniques, some fine tuning for the differences between manufacturers, beams, and processing software is still required before it can be accepted as the 'gold standard'.

See also: body composition; body composition assessment; body composition assessment – anthropometry; body composition assessment – densitometry; body composition assessment – imaging techniques; body composition assessment – statistical methods; body composition assessment – whole body counting

Further reading

Ellis, K.J. (2000) 'Human Body Composition: In Vivo Methods', *Physiological Reviews* 80: 649–80.

MIKE LAMBERT

BODY COMPOSITION ASSESSMENT – ELECTRICAL IMPEDANCE

Living cells have electrical properties. This characteristic has been described and used in medicine for centuries. A more recent application of this property has been to measure bioelectrical impedance of tissue. Bioelectrical impedance is a safe and relatively effective method for assessing fat free mass, per cent body fat, total body water, and changes in extracellular fluid. The method became accepted from a clinical perspective after the work of Nyboer in the early 1970s. Nyboer showed that changes in electrical impedance in the body were caused by changes in blood volume. Further work showed that a current passes through blood and other tissues simultaneously. In fact the human body acted like any other electrical conductor, which has a relationship between the volume of the conductor – the human body, the conductor's length – the participant's height, the components of the conductor – fat or fat free mass, and its impedance. Fat and fat free tissues have different electrical properties and abilities to conduct an electrical current. The hydrous fat free mass contains virtually all the water and electrolytes and, therefore, this tissue accounts for the conduction of an electrical current. Therefore, the overall conduction is closely related to lean tissue.

Impedance to the flow of the current is a function of the resistance and reactance of the conductor. However, the reactance is very low in biological systems, so in this context the terms 'impedance' and 'resistance' can be interchanged.

First principles

Ohm's law states that between two points of a conductor, $R = V/I$, where R is the resistance, V is the voltage, and I is the current. In a symmetrical conductor, R is directly proportional to its length, L, and inversely proportional to cross sectional area, A. Therefore, R, or the impedance, $Z = \rho L/A$, where ρ is the specific resistivity; in the SI system, ρ is measured in ω m, and volume, $v = LA$. Rearranging the impedance equation by multiplying by L/L, $Z = \rho L^2/LA$; simplifying, $Z = \rho L^2/v$.

This estimation assumes that the conductor is a perfect cylinder, with a uniform cross-sectional area. However, in the human body this relationship is not perfect. In reality the human body can be described as five cylinders – trunk, two arms, and two legs, excluding the head. Each cylinder has a different cross-sectional area and, therefore, contributes a different resistance to the total resistance. Further, the differences in cross-sectional area are not proportional to differences in the per cent body mass. For example, the trunk contributes about 46 per cent to the total body mass, but only influences whole body resistance by 3 per cent. Despite the deviations from the assumptions, because the human body is not a perfect cylinder, the application of bioelectrical impedance to measure fat free mass, per cent body fat and total body water can be done so with reasonable accuracy.

Measurement

Bioelectrical impedance is measured while the participant lies down on a non-conducting surface. The participant's legs should be spread with the thighs not touching, and all metallic jewellery should be removed. Four adhesive electrodes are positioned in the middle of the dorsal surface of the ipsilateral hand and foot, proximal to the metacarpophalangeal and metatarsophalangeal joints. A current of about 800 μA, at a frequency of about 50 kHz, is passed through the outer pair of electrodes for a few seconds. The decrease in voltage across the body is measured using the inner pair of electrodes. The impedance is determined from this measurement and used in an appropriate equation to estimate body fat. Many equations have been developed for different sub-groups, differentiated by ethnic group, age, and biological sex. The positioning of the electrodes is important as a change in the conductor path length changes the resistance.

The following criteria should be controlled to reduce the experimental error of the measurement:

- no food or drink for 4 h before the measurement;
- no exercise for 12 h before;
- urinate 30 min before the test;
- no alcohol within 48 h of the measurement;
- no diuretics within seven days.

The following factors should be controlled as they also affect the measurement error:

- menstrual cycle;
- skin temperature;
- use of oral contraceptives;
- exercise-induced dehydration;
- prior food;
- different body positions;
- electrode placement and configuration (bipolar or tetrapolar).

Criterion measurements

The analysis of body fat using bioelectrical impedance has been compared to criterion techniques such as hydrodensitometry (see **body composition assessment –**

densitometry). These criterion methods are not free of error and, therefore, some of this error is incorporated into the bioelectrical impedance technique. The reported R^2 values range between 0.74 and 0.99 and the standard error of the estimate ranges between 1.81 and 4.02 kg. If these factors are controlled, the measurement error of body fat can be maintained within 3–5 per cent.

The advantages of measuring body composition with bioelectrical impedance are the speed of operation, portability, safety, lack of intrusion, and low inter-measurer variability.

See also: body composition; body composition assessment; body composition assessment – anthropometry; body composition assessment – densitometry; body composition assessment – imaging techniques; body composition assessment – statistical methods; body composition assessment – whole body counting

Further reading

Brodie, D., Moscrip, V. and Hutcheon, R. (1998) 'Body Composition Measurement: A Review of Hydrodensitometry, Anthropometry, and Impedance Methods', *Nutrition* 14: 296–310.

Ellis, K.J. (2000) 'Human Body Composition: In Vivo Methods', *Physiological Reviews* 80: 649–80.

Hawes, M.R. and Martin, A.D. (1996) 'Body Composition, Proportion and Growth', in R. Eston and T. Reilly (eds) *Kinanthropometry and Exercise Physiology Laboratory Manual*, 7–46, London: E&FN Spon.

Lukaski, H.C. (1987) 'Methods for the Assessment of Human Body Composition: Traditional and New', *American Journal of Clinical Nutrition* 46: 537–56.

Nyboer, J. (1970) *Electrical Impedance Plethysmography, Second Edition*, Springfield MA: Charles C. Thomas.

Van Loan, M.D. (1990) Bioelectrical Impedance Analysis to Determine Fat-free Mass, Total Body Water and Body Fat', *Sports Medicine* 10: 205–17.

MIKE LAMBERT

BODY COMPOSITION ASSESSMENT – IMAGING TECHNIQUES

Body composition can also be assessed using imaging techniques. These techniques measure tissue – fat, bone, and muscle – directly. An advantage of imaging techniques over techniques such as densitometry, anthropometry, and bioelectrical impedance are that imaging techniques can measure whole body or regional tissue and they provide visual images of different types of tissue. A disadvantage is that the techniques are usually expensive and some techniques have a small risk associated with exposure to ionising radiation. Examples of imaging techniques are dual energy X-ray absorptiometry, computed tomography, and magnetic resonance imaging

Dual energy X-ray absorptiometry (DEXA)

This imaging technique was first developed to measure bone mineral content. The technology has evolved and it is now considered a useful tool for the measurement of fat, bone, and fat free mass. The DEXA method is based on the principle that when an X-ray source is placed on one side of an object, the change in the intensity of the beam is related to the thickness, density, and chemical composition of the object's tissue. The X-ray signal is converted into an electronic signal by the detector and is then translated into an image. (See also **body composition assessment – dual energy X-ray absorptiometry**.)

Computed tomography

Computed tomography (CT) imaging, also known as CAT scanning (Computed Axial Tomography), was invented in 1972 by a British engineer Godfrey Hounsfield and South African-born physicist All Cormack. Tomography is derived from the Greek words *tomos*, meaning 'slice' or 'section', and *graphia*, meaning 'describing'.

The first clinical CT scanners, which were only able to scan heads, were first used in 1974. Larger scanners for the whole body became available in 1976. Computed tomography scanning works on a similar principle to an X-ray scan. The CT technique uses X-rays that are collimated – focused – to provide a fan-shaped beam that is passed through the body, or the section of the body, to be measured. The tissue causes the intensity of the beam to be attenuated. Detectors on the other side of the body, or section of the body, measure the attenuation of the transmitted radiation. Different types of tissue have varying effects on the attenuation. The X-ray source and detectors are rotated 360° around the participant while the measurements are recorded throughout the rotation. During each rotation, the detector records about 1,000 images. Other designs of CT devices have a full circle of detectors around the body, or a section of the body, and the X-ray source is rotated.

Complex algorithms are applied to the stored cumulative signals from the detector. These signals are converted and reconstructed into a two-dimensional cross-sectional image of the body section scanned. The images of the different tissue types are contrasted and clearly separated. Experiments have shown that, when the mass of the separate tissue types are added and compared to total body mass, the error of measurement is less than 1 per cent. Computed tomography scanning can separate abdominal fat into superficial and deep compartments using the fascia superficialis as an anatomical landmark. Lean tissue can also be divided into skeletal muscle and visceral tissue. Bone can also be separated into cortical or trabecular bone.

Magnetic resonance imaging

The first magnetic resonance imaging (MRI) procedure on a human took place in 1977; MRI is a radiology technique that uses magnetism, radio waves, and a computer to produce images of structures in the whole body. An MRI scanner is a large tube surrounded by an even larger circular magnet. This technique is based on the principle that the earth has a very weak magnetic field of 0.5 gauss. Under these conditions, the atoms and molecules in the body are in random orientation. When the body is placed in a strong magnetic field, which is greater than the magnetic field of the earth, the nuclei which are made up of neutrons and protons, act as little magnets and align themselves. Hydrogen ions are particularly sensitive to re-alignment. The hydrogen ion is simply a proton and has a very high abundance in tissue, of 98 per cent. When the nuclei re-align they absorb energy. When the magnetic field is removed, or altered, the nuclei lose their alignment and release their stored energy in the form of another radio frequency signal. The time taken for the nuclei to release the radio frequency-induced energy and return to their natural orientation is called the relaxation time (T_1) state. The T_1 for protons varies in different types of tissue. For example, the relaxation time for adipose tissue is much faster than the relaxation time in muscle. As with the CT technique, complex algorithms convert these signals into a series of cross-sectional images. The process can be repeated at regular slices throughout the body until the whole body is mapped. Magnetic resonance imaging can also separate total fat tissue into visceral components and subcutaneous tissue.

In contrast to images produced by X-ray radiography and computed tomography, MRI does not use ionising radiation, but rather a strong magnetic impulse. The measurement takes about 30 s per slice. For the measurement of the whole body, a series of multiple scans are made systemically along the body. This takes about 30 min. There are no known side-effects from an MRI scan; therefore, the procedure can be used on foetuses and children.

However, patients with heart pacemakers or metal implants cannot be scanned with MRI because of the effects of the powerful magnet.

The accuracy of estimating total and regional body composition using CT and MRI is similar. MRI is preferred in intervention studies, in which repetitive measurements are made and when it is important to measure both regional and total changes in fat and skeletal muscle mass.

See also: body composition; body composition assessment – statistical methods; body composition assessment – whole body counting

Further reading

Ellis, K.J. (2000) 'Human Body Composition: In Vivo Methods', *Physiological Reviews* 80: 649–80.

Lukaski, H.C. (1987) 'Methods for the Assessment of Human Body Composition: Traditional and New', *American Journal of Clinical Nutrition* 46: 537–56.

MIKE LAMBERT

BODY COMPOSITION ASSESSMENT – STATISTICAL METHODS

Research into body composition can be classified into one of the following categories: a study of differences in body composition between groups, or differences in body composition before and after some form of intervention, such as an exercise or diet programme, or the relationship between variables that predict body composition

Differences between groups are usually accepted as being significantly different if the statistical test, for example an independent *t*-test for a two group study design or an analysis of variance for more than two groups in the study design, yields a level of significance of 5 per cent or less, that is $P < 0.05$. This can be explained as a 95 per cent probability that the differences between the means of the two groups are real or, conversely, there is a 5 per cent probability that the differences occur by chance. For this type of research design, it is important that the participants are randomly selected from the population that they represent and that the sample size is sufficiently large to reduce the risk of a type II error – not finding differences when in reality there are differences. This is in contrast to a type I error, which describes the risk of finding differences that, in reality, do not exist. The measurement error of the various methods of body composition assessment also needs to be considered in the analysis.

A research design for studies examining differences before and after intervention needs to consider the seasonal changes in body composition and, therefore, includes an appropriate control group. Also, body composition assessment techniques with sufficient measurement precision should be used. For example, it is not appropriate to use a measurement technique with, for example a 3 per cent measurement error, if the expected change in body composition is less than 3 per cent. This will also increase the risk of causing a type II error.

Studies on the relationship between variables use either bivariate or multivariate statistics. A Pearson's product moment correlation is an example of a statistic used for analysing bivariate relationships, and calculates a correlation coefficient (r), which ranges between -1 and $+1$. This describes an association between the variables. A positive correlation coefficient reflects a direct relationship between variables, and a negative correlation coefficient describes an inverse relationship. The closer the coefficient is to $+1$ or -1, the stronger the direct or inverse relationship respectively. A strong association does not imply causality.

A multivariate statistic is used when one variable – the dependent variable – is related to more than one independent variable. This procedure calculates a regression equation that describes the best relationship between the variables. Examples of this procedure are represented by the equations that have been derived from a variety of skinfold measurements to predict body density. The coefficient of multiple regression (R) is an index describing the closeness of the relationship between the variables; it is derived from the relationship between the predicted and actual values. The closer R is to 1, the better the independent, or predictor, variables are able to predict the dependent variable. The standard error of the estimate is an indication of the confidence with which the variables can be predicted. This is calculated from the standard deviation of the differences between the predicted and actual values.

See also: body composition; body composition assessment; body composition assessment – anthropometry; body composition assessment – densitometry; body composition assessment – electrical impedance; body composition assessment – imaging techniques; body composition assessment – whole body counting

Further reading

Vincent, W.J. (1999) *Statistics in Kinesiology, Second Edition*, Champaign IL: Human Kinetics.
Winter, E.M., Eston, R.G. and Lamb, K.L. (2001) 'Statistical Analyses in the Physiology of Exercise and Kinanthropometry', *Journal of Sports Sciences* 19: 761–75.

MIKE LAMBERT

BODY COMPOSITION ASSESSMENT – WHOLE BODY COUNTING

Body composition can be assessed indirectly by measuring different chemical components in the body that have a fairly constant appearance and then enabling inferences about the total body composition to be made. Examples of whole body counting are total body water, total potas-sium, neutron activation analysis, and creatinine and 3-methylhistine excretions.

Total body water

Water is not present in triglyceride tissue. The remaining combined tissue, the fat free mass, consists of about 73 per cent water. Therefore, by measuring the total body water, one can calculate the fat free mass. Isotopes – tritium, deuterium, and oxygen-18 – have been used to calculate the total body water. This dilution technique is based on the principle that a tracer is administered, either orally or intravenously, and then after a period of equilibration the concentration of the tracer is measured in a fluid sample of blood, saliva, or urine. This technique is based on the assumptions that the tracer is equally distributed in the water pool in a relatively short time, and that the tracer is not metabolised during the equilibration period. The measurement of the tracer requires expensive equipment. For example, a radioactive β-counter is needed to measure for tritium and a mass spectrophotometer measures oxygen-18. Deuterium can be measured using mass spectrophotometry or gas chromatography. For each tracer method, the error of measurement is about 1.4 kg for absolute fat mass. A concern about this technique is that the total body water is not constant across all ages and, also, varies depending on health status.

Total body potassium

Potassium is an intracellular cation found in all tissue except triglyceride tissue. There is approximately 2.5 g potassium per kg fat free mass in men and 2.3 g potassium per kg fat free mass in women. Potassium-40 is an isotope of potassium, and occurs with a constant distribution of 0.012 per cent in this tissue. Potassium-40 emits a gamma ray at 1.46 MeV. If this emission is measured the total potassium can be estimated and then the fat free mass can be predicted. A whole body counter is needed to measure the gamma rays. This is a sophisticated device, which has to have adequate shielding to prevent contamination by background emissions. The counting time varies from a few minutes to an hour.

Neutron activation analysis

This technique assesses body composition by measuring hydrogen, oxygen, carbon, nitrogen, calcium, phosphorous sodium, chlorine, and potassium in vivo. When the body is exposed to neutrons, the nuclei of the various atoms are made unstable. The result is that gamma rays are emitted immediately and for some time thereafter. The decay rate permits identification of the isotope. These isotopes can be detected outside the body using a whole body counter similar to the counter used for the measurements of potassium-40. The accuracy of neutron activation is as good as the analysis of the chemicals using traditional wet chemical techniques. A major disadvantage of this technique is the radiation exposure associated with each test and the scarcity of the equipment.

Creatine excretion

Creatine is synthesised in the liver and kidneys, but about 98 per cent of the creatine in the body is absorbed into skeletal muscle and stored in the form of creatine phosphate. Creatinine is formed by the hydrolysis of free creatine liberated during the dephosphorylation of creatine phosphate. There is a relationship between creatinine excretion in the urine and muscle and fat free mass. Approximately 1 g of creatinine is excreted per 20 kg of fat free mass. However, more recently it has been shown that this relationship varies and that urinary excretion is, to some extent, independent of body composition. Another limitation using creatinine excretion as an estimation of fat free mass is that meat intake can increase the creatinine excretion by 20 per cent compared to days when no meat is eaten.

3-Methylhistidine excretion

3-Methylhistidine is an amino acid found mostly in muscle and made by the post-translational methylation of specific histidine residues in actin and myosin. After catabolism of myofibrillar protein, 3-methylhistidine is not re-utilised or metabolised and is excreted. As with creatinine excretion, 3-methylhistidine excretion is also affected by the intake of meat; 3-methylhistidine excretion is almost twice as high on days when meat is eaten than on days when the diet is free of meat. Another limitation with this technique is that non-skeletal muscle turnover may also contribute to the pool of 3-methylhistidine that is excreted.

See also: body composition; body composition assessment; body composition assessment – anthropometry; body composition assessment – densitometry; body composition assessment – electrical impedance; body composition assessment – imaging techniques; body composition assessment – statistical methods

Further reading

Ellis, K.J. (2000) 'Human Body Composition: In Vivo Methods', *Physiological Reviews* 80: 649–80.

Lukaski, H.C. (1987) 'Methods for the Assessment of Human Body Composition: Traditional and New', *American Journal of Clinical Nutrition* 46: 537–56.

MIKE LAMBERT

BODY SEGMENTS AND INERTIAL PROPERTIES

Various inertia parameters of body segments are used in sports biomechanics. The mass of each body segment and the segment centre of mass position are used in calculating the position of the whole body **centre of mass**. These values, and segment moments of inertia, are used in calculations of net joint forces and moments using the method of inverse dynamics. The most accurate and valid values available for these inertia parameters should obviously be used. Ideally, they should be obtained from, or scaled to, the sports performer being studied. The values of body segment parameters used in sports biomechanics have been obtained from cadavers and from living persons, including measurements of the performers being filmed.

Cadaver studies have provided very accurate segmental data. However, limited sample sizes throw doubt on the extrapolation of these data to a general sports population. They are also highly questionable because of the unrepresentative nature of the samples in sex, age, and morphology. Problems also arise from the use of different dissection techniques by different researchers, losses in tissue and body fluid during dissection, and degeneration associated with the state of health before death. Segment mass may be expressed as a simple fraction of total body mass or, more accurately, as a linear regression equation with one or more anthropometric variables. Even the latter may cause an under- or over-estimation of total body mass by as much as 4.6 per cent.

Studies on living people have been very limited. Body segment data have been obtained using gamma-ray scanning or from imaging techniques, such as **computerised tomography (CT)** and **magnetic resonance imaging (MRI)**. These may eventually supersede the cadaver data that are still too often used in sports biomechanics. Obtaining body segment parameter data from sports performers may require sophisticated equipment and a great deal of the performer's time. The immersion technique is simple, and can be easily demonstrated by any reader with a bucket,

a vessel to catch the overflow from the bucket, and some calibrated measuring jugs or weighing device. It provides accurate measurements of segment volume and centre of volume, but requires a knowledge of segmental density to calculate segment mass. Also, as segment density is not uniform throughout the segment, the centre of mass does not coincide with the centre of volume.

Several 'mathematical' models calculate body segment parameters from standard anthropometric measurements, such as segment lengths and circumferences (see **anthropometric models**). Some of these models result in large errors even in estimates of segment volumes; some require too many measurements for field use. All these models require density values from other sources, usually cadavers, and most of them assume constant density throughout the segment, or throughout large parts of the segment.

The greatest problems in body segment data occur for moments of inertia. There are no simple yet accurate methods to measure segmental moments of inertia for a living person. Many model estimations are either very inaccurate or require further validation. A relative error of 5 per cent in segmental moments of inertia may be a conservative estimate. Norms or linear regression equations are often used, but these should be treated with caution as the errors involved in their use are rarely fully assessed. It may be necessary to allow for the non-linear relationships between segmental dimensions and moment of inertia values.

Further reading

Mungiole, M. and Martin, P.E. (1990) 'Estimating Segment Inertial Properties: Comparison of Magnetic Resonance Imaging with Existing Methods', *Journal of Biomechanics* 23: 1039–46.

ROGER BARTLETT

BONDS – GENERAL OBLIGATION AND REVENUE

The ability of public jurisdictions in the US to finance the construction of sport facilities has depended on their ability to borrow substantial amounts of money over an extended period of time. They do this through the sale of bonds, which are a promise by the borrower (the public jurisdiction) to pay back to the lender (the financial institution) a specified amount of money, with interest, within a specified period of time.

Most public agencies finance major capital development projects in the same way individuals purchase new homes or cars. Rather than paying the entire purchase price in advance, or 'up front', government agencies pay for the cost of a new facility over several years. The needed capital for home construction is borrowed from a lending institution, typically a bank, that then requires the borrower to repay or retire the debt in a series of scheduled payments that may stretch out over thirty years. In the case of publicly-funded sports facilities, the revenues pledged to repay the debt obligation are derived from either taxes imposed by government agencies, or revenues emanating from the facilities.

Using taxes collected over a period of years to pay the debt charges emanating from major capital development projects like stadiums and arenas is usually preferred to up-front payments for three reasons. First, by spreading the payments over an extended time period, the annual tax burden borne by taxpayers in any single year is less onerous. For example, in a county that imposed a half-cent general sales tax increase to fund a new stadium, a household which spent $15,000 a year on taxable goods and services in the county would pay an additional $75 in taxes. Hypothetically, if 200,000 households were to spend at the same level on average, the general sales tax would produce $15 million in new revenues. That amount, if perceived by lending institutions to be a stable stream of revenue, could secure a construction loan for as much as $150 million. This approach is likely to be more palatable than asking each of those 200,000 households to pay $750 in additional taxes in one year to pay for the facility, which would be required if the $150 million facility was funded by a one-time, up front payment.

Second, from a political perspective, debt financing is a desirable approach. For many elected officials guided by their preeminent goal to be re-elected, financing that shifts the cost of a new facility as far forward as possible is an attractive option. This extended payment approach pushes most of the potential political penalties associated with increased taxes well into the future, so they become problems for political successors. Meanwhile, politicians responsible for the facility reap the benefits of creating a new community asset.

Third, a system which defrays taxpayer payments over many years accommodates the reality that population turnover is a constant. If cities used alternatives to borrowing, such as making a one-time payment in full, then some present residents would pay the full cost of the facility, but if they later left the community they would receive only partial benefit from their investment. Conversely, others moving into the community would receive benefits from an asset to which they had made no financial contribution. With debt financing, some measure of equity is achieved, as all residents contribute tax dollars and pay their share of the amenity to which they have access.

Debts which are full-faith and credit obligations of a government entity have an unlimited claim on the taxes and other revenues of the jurisdiction borrowing the funds. The burden of paying these debts is spread over all taxable property within the issuing government's geographical boundaries. The most common

179

type of these obligations is a general obligation bond.

When it issues general obligation bonds, a government unit makes an unconditional promise to the bondholder (usually a commercial bank) to pay back the principal and interest it owes through its authority to levy taxes. When general obligation bonds are issued by local governments (e.g. cities, counties, school districts), payment is usually secured by property taxes. State governments, which rely on non-property tax sources, usually pledge revenue streams from sales or income taxes to repay general obligation bonds.

General obligation bonds offer a number of advantages. Because of their full faith and credit backing, they are the most secure of any of the available long-term debt instruments. Consequently, the borrowing costs associated with general obligation debt are considerably cheaper than any of the other debt financing options. The difference in interest rates between general obligation bonds and non-guaranteed tax-exempt bonds maybe as much as 1 per cent or 2 per cent. In other words, it may cost 7 per cent to finance a project using non-guaranteed bonds as opposed to 5 per cent if general obligation bonds were used. The additional cost over the full period of the loan may be substantial. The difference between paying 5 per cent and 7 per cent on a 20-year, $5-million dollar issue is almost $1,500,000.

The government body's unconditional pledge of full tax support makes general obligation bonds easier to sell. The reduced risk associated with the almost certain probability of reimbursement increases the attractiveness of general obligation bonds to a greater range of potential lenders. Because the sale of general obligation bonds represents an obligation that all taxpayers must meet, the government body desiring to issue them must first obtain approval by a majority of voters in a public referendum on the project.

In recent years, there has been resistance by voters to full-faith and credit obligations for building major facilities for professional sports teams (but not for smaller facilities for use by local amateur sports players). Hence, these major projects have increasingly used non-guaranteed funding mechanisms and revenue bonds are the most common type of these. These are not backed by the full-faith and credit of the government entity. Rather, they are sold on the basis that repayment will be forthcoming from other designated revenue sources. If revenue from the designated sources falls short of what is required to make the debt payments, the government entity is not obligated to make up the difference.

Non-guaranteed debt instruments have two major advantages. First, in most states, direct voter approval is not required because the general taxpayers are not being asked to pay these debts. Second, if the revenue accrues directly from the project, then the people who most benefit from the facility pay for it.

Revenue bonds are particularly appropriate when a new facility is capable of generating enough revenue to pay for its own operations and any debt obligations incurred in its construction. Because revenue bonds are repaid from income produced by the facility and not from property or sales taxes, no referendum is required. They are secured by the revenues of the project being financed. In the case of stadiums and arenas, the bonds would be payable solely from income generated from venue operations such as ticket sales, parking, and the sale of in-venue advertising. If no general fund pledge is provided as security, revenue bonds will typically have to pay higher interest charges because investors who purchase the bonds incur more risk.

Revenue bonds have become a popular approach to financing the construction of a range of revenue-generating sports facilities, including golf courses, indoor tennis centers, athletic fields, and marinas. For these kinds of facilities, the revenue usually is generated from a variety of non-contractually obligated sources such as admission fees, concession income, and user fees. The fundamental requirement for the use of revenue bonds is that the facility has the means to generate sufficient income to cover both operating and maintenance costs as well as annual principal and interest payments. If the project has the ability to operate on a financially self-supporting basis, then revenue bonds are likely to be the preferred debt instrument.

Sport facility developers have attempted to make revenue bond financing a more attractive option to lending institutions by issuing 'Lease Revenue Bonds'. In an effort to enhance the security of the bond transaction, the borrower (the city or county issuing the bonds) pledges repayment from stadium or arena revenue sources that are specified in a long-term facility lease. Venue revenues frequently pledged as repayment for lease revenue bonds include:

- facility naming rights (15–25 years)
- luxury suites/club seats (3–9 years)
- food/beverage concession contracts (5+ years)
- corporate sponsorship agreements (3–5 years)

All of these 'contractually obligated income' (COI) streams are secured by long-term contracts of varying lengths and as a result, are considered relatively stable and credit worthy.

What makes lease revenue bonds attractive to lenders is that the revenue streams pledged to repay the debt are contractually obligated *prior* to executing the bond agreement. The lender is assured in advance that a significant share of the facility's revenues will be committed to repaying the bonds, thereby reducing the risk of default.

JOHN L. CROMPTON

BONE

There are 206 bones in the human skeleton, of which 177 engage in voluntary movement. The functions of the skeleton are to protect vital organs – such as the brain, heart, and lungs – to provide rigidity for the body, to provide attachment points for muscle-tendon unit – allowing muscles to move the bony levers about the joints – to enable the manufacture of blood cells, and to provide a storehouse for mineral metabolism. The skeleton is often divided into the axial skeleton – the skull, lower jaw, vertebrae, ribs, sternum, sacrum, and coccyx – which is mainly protective, and the appendicular skeleton – the shoulder girdle, upper extremities, pelvic girdle, and lower extremities – which functions in movement.

The surface of a bone is rich in markings that show its history. Some of these can be seen at the skin surface, such as the medial and lateral malleoli at the ankle, while many others can be easily palpated (felt). These landmarks are often the anatomical locations used to estimate the axes of rotation of the body's joints, which are important for the biomechanical investigation of human movements in sport and exercise. Lumps known as tuberosities or tubercles – the latter are smaller than the former – and projections, or processes, show attachments of strong fibrous cords, such as tendons. Ridges and lines indicate attachments of broad sheets of fibrous tissue – aponeuroses or intermuscular septa. Grooves (furrows or sulci), holes (foramina), and notches and depressions (fossae) often suggest important structures, for example grooves for tendons. A rounded prominence at the end of a bone is called a condyle, the projecting part of which is sometimes known as an epicondyle, for example, on the medial and lateral surfaces of the humerus near the elbow joint. Special names may be given to other bony prominences: the greater trochanter on the lateral aspect of the femur and the medial malleolus on the medial aspect of the distal end of the tibia are examples.

The loading of living bone is complex, because the loads applied are usually combinations of tension or compression with shear, torsion, or bending, and because of the irregular geometric structure of bones. For example, during the activities of walking, and jogging, the tensile and compressive stresses along the tibia are combined with transverse shear stresses, caused by torsional loading associated with lateral and medial rotation of the tibia. Most bone fractures are produced by such combinations of several loading modes.

After fracture, bone repair is effected by two types of cell, osteoblasts and osteoclasts. Osteoblasts deposit strands of fibrous tissue, between which ground substance is later laid down, and osteoclasts dissolve or break up damaged or dead bone. Initially, when the broken ends of the bone are brought into contact, they are surrounded by a mass of blood. This is partly absorbed and partly converted, first into fibrous tissue then into bone. The mass around the fractured ends is called the callus. This forms a thickening, for a period of months, which will gradually be smoothed away, unless the ends of the bone have not been correctly aligned. In that case, the callus will persist and will form an area where high mechanical stresses may occur, rendering the region susceptible to further fracture.

See also: bone classification; bone growth; bone injury; bone structure and properties

Further reading

Nigg, B.M. and Herzog, W. (1999) *Biomechanics of the Musculoskeletal System*, ch. 2, Chichester: Wiley.

ROGER BARTLETT

BONE CLASSIFICATION

Macroscopically, there are two types, or classifications, of bone tissue: cortical or compact bone and trabecular or cancellous bone. The first forms the outer shell, the cortex, of a bone and has a dense structure. The second has a spongy structure of a loose latticework of trabeculae or cancelli; the interstices between the trabeculae are filled with red marrow in which red blood cells form. Cancellous bone tissue is arranged in concentric layers, or lamellae, and its osteocytes – bone cells – are supplied with nutrients from blood vessels passing through the red marrow. The lamellar pattern and material composition of the two bone types are similar. Different porosity is the principal distinguishing feature, and the distinction between the two types might be considered somewhat arbitrary. Biomechanically, the two types of bone should be considered as one material with a wide range of densities and porosities. Bone can be classified as a composite material in which the strong but brittle mineral element is embedded in a weaker but more ductile one consisting of collagen and ground substance (see also **bone structure and properties**). Like many similar but inorganic composites, for example, glass- or carbon-reinforced fibres important in **sports equipment**, this structure gives a material whose strength-to-weight ratio exceeds that of either of its constituents.

Bones can be classified by their geometrical characteristics and functional requirements, as follows. Long bones occur mostly in the appendicular skeleton and function for weight-bearing and movement. They are much longer than they are wide. They consist of a long, central shaft, called the body or diaphysis, the central cavity of which is the medullary canal, filled with fatty yellow marrow. At the expanded ends of the bone, the compact shell is very thin and the trabeculae are arranged along the lines of force transmission. In the same region, the periosteum – the membrane surrounding bone – is replaced by smooth hyaline articular cartilage. This has no blood supply and is the residue of the cartilage from which the bone formed. Examples of long bones are the humerus, radius, and ulna of the upper limb; the femur, tibia, and fibula of the lower limb; and the phalanges of the fingers and toes.

Short bones are composed of cancellous tissue and are irregular in shape; they are small, chunky and roughly cubical. Examples are the tarsal bones of the foot and the carpal bones of the hand. Flat bones are, basically, a sandwich of richly veined cancellous bone within two layers of compact bone. They serve as extensive flat areas for muscle attachment and, except for the scapulae, enclose body cavities. Examples are the sternum, ribs, ilium, and most of the bones of the skull. Irregular bones are adapted to special purposes and include the vertebrae, sacrum, coccyx, ischium, and pubis. They all have complex shapes and consist mostly of cancellous bone enclosed in thin layers of compact bone. Sesamoid bones form in certain tendons – the most important is the patella; these bones can be considered as a special type of short bone. Some, for example the patella, alter the line of pull of a muscle tendon (see **muscle mechanics**).

See also: bone growth; bone injury

Further reading

Nigg, B.M. and Herzog, W. (1999) *Biomechanics of the Musculoskeletal System*, ch. 2, Chichester: Wiley.

ROGER BARTLETT

BONE GROWTH

Bone grows by a process known as ossification or osteogenesis, which involves the deposition of mineral salts in an organic collagenous matrix, after the matrix has been laid down. If the process occurs in existing connective tissue, intermembranous ossification occurs, and the resulting bone is a membrane bone. If the process occurs within hyaline cartilage, intercartilaginous ossification occurs and results in a cartilage, or endochrondral, bone. The latter occurs for short bones, the former, for example, for the clavicle and skull bones. Long bones, in which both mechanisms are involved, are used here to illustrate the process of bone growth.

Bone begins to grow in the embryo. In long bones and others that experience intercartilaginous ossification, calcium phosphate is deposited in hyaline cartilage, a process known as calcification. Cells called osteoblasts appear around the middle of the shaft of calcified cartilage and result in the replacement of cartilage by bone. In this formative period of growth (5–12 weeks embryo age), ossification proceeds in all directions from the primary ossification centre, or diaphysis. Simultaneously, the bone collar ossifies intermembranously within the periosteum – the connective tissue that surrounds and nourishes the bone – forming the outside of the bone.

By birth, ossification has almost reached the ends of the cartilage; at each end a new secondary ossification centre, or epiphysis, appears, from which bone now develops. This is the characteristic feature of the growth period, during which the bone develops to adult length. The ends of the bone are separated from the main shaft of bone by the epiphyseal plates of cartilage. The bone lengthens; as new bone forms on the shaft – diaphyseal – side of the epiphyseal plate, new cartilage arises on the epiphyseal surface and the epiphyseal plate moves away from the diaphysis. The most recently formed bone at the end of the diaphysis is called the metaphysis. Diametral growth proceeds by the periosteum producing concentric rings of bone while some bone is reabsorbed in the medullary canal at the centre of the bone, increasing its diameter.

During the consolidation period (14–25 years), the entire epiphyseal plate eventually ossifies and the diaphysis and epiphysis fuse. An elevated ridge, the epiphyseal line, is left on the bone surface. Approximate ages of epiphyseal closure vary from 7–8 years for the inferior rami of the pubis and ischium to twenty-five years for the bones of the spinal column and thorax. Before epiphyseal closure, the strength of the capsule and **ligaments** around a joint may be two to five times greater than the strength of the metaphyseal-epiphyseal junction; therefore, injury is more likely at this site. **Fractures** or **dislocation**s involving epiphyses may lead to cessation of bone growth. This can be used as an argument against stressful contact sports until bone maturity has been achieved (about 17–19 years).

Bone ceases to grow, or atrophies, when no stresses are applied to it, as in a period of prolonged rest, for example, in a plaster cast. The reduction of circulation may be as important in this process as the absence of mechanical stress. One result is a thinning of, and reduction in, the number of trabeculae, reducing the strength of the cancellous tissue.

See also: bone classification; bone injury; bone structure and properties

Further reading

Nigg, B.M. and Herzog, W. (1999) *Biomechanics of the Musculoskeletal System*, ch. 2, Chichester: Wiley.

ROGER BARTLETT

BONE INJURY

Injury to the bone occurs when either the bone is inherently weak as to be unable to sustain physiological strain, or due to external trauma the force of which exceeds the strength of the bone.

Bone is the strongest tissue in the body. Its primary function is to sustain the entire weight of the body. The bones are made up of organic and inorganic material.

There are various pathological processes which make the bone weak and predispose it to injury or fractures.

The bone mass decreases with age and the elderly are more prone to fractures from a minor fall than young adults, who have a greater bone mass. The bones continue to go through a process of remodeling throughout their lifetime. The osteoblasts and the osteocytes are responsible for the formation of bone and collagen synthesis, while the osteoclasts are responsible for bone resorption. This process is in balance so that the bone mass is maintained.

There are many factors which are responsible for loss of bone mass. Prolonged immobilization can lead to osteopenia; this is seen in patients who are bedbound for a long period of time. Lack of exercise, alcohol, smoking, and female gender are other factors which can decrease bone mass. In females bone loss increases after menopause. Estrogen levels decrease by 80 per cent after menopause, which accelerates bone loss to 2–3 per cent per year for the next 8–10 years. The use of hormonal replacement therapy has been shown to decrease this bone loss. The use of corticosteroids leads to decrease in protein synthesis in general and inhibits calcium absorption from the intestine.

Patients with osteopenia usually present with generalized or localized bone pain but may also present with a fracture. The common site of the fracture is the vertebral bodies, the femoral neck, or the pubic rami, but any site may be involved. A thorough history of the patient along with clinical examination is required. Laboratory tests should be carried out to ascertain calcium levels, vitamin D level, serum alkaline phosphatase, and testosterone and estrogen level. Urine can also be examined to determine if the bone mass is static, increasing or decreasing.

Radiographs are essential. They can show osteopenia, but only when the bone has lost 30–50 per cent of minerals. Dual X-ray absorptiometery (DEXA) is the gold standard for detection of osteoporosis.

Osteomalacia in adults and rickets in children are the result of lack of calcium, which has many causes. These include dietary deficiency, renal problems, metabolic problems, lack of absorption from the gastrointestinal tract, and lack of sunlight. The lack of adequate mineralization of the bone can result in many fractures of the bones from minor falls, and at times these fractures occur even without a history of fall or trauma, as the bones are very osteopenic and weak.

In rickets the growth plates are affected. There is widening of the physis. The bone growth is affected and there is deformity of various bones. There may be valgus deformity at the knees. The hips may also show deformity. The feet and the hands may also be affected. The fractures can occur in any bone but most commonly the femur and the tibia, which are the weight-bearing bones affected. Treatment of these fractures is dependent on the site and their displacement. Surgical treatment requires careful planning as the bones are soft, and any form of fixation may not be as stable. If there is any concomitant deformity present, like bowing of the femur, then it can be addressed at the time of fixation of the fracture, or if the patient presents with the deformity only then osteotomies can be performed to correct the deformity. The medical treatment is instituted as soon as the diagnosis is made with the endocrinologist or the metabolic disease physician.

Osteomalacia is the adult form of the disease. Again there is lack of mineralization of the bones, which are predisposed to many fractures in the spine as well as the long bones. The treatment revolves around the use of calcium as well as vitamin D. This helps rebuild calcium level and improve bone mineralization. The fractures are treated operatively or non-operatively, and again this is dependent on the site as

well as the displacement. There is no contra-indication to operative stabilization. The growth plates are not affected in this disease as it occurs in the adult population.

Osteogenesis imperfecta is a form of bone disease in which collagen synthesis is impaired. There are various types of osteogenesis imperfecta. There may also be involvement of teeth and sclera. Other organs may be involved. Certain types are fatal and afflicted babies die soon after birth or even before birth. In other types children survive but their bones are very weak and frequently fracture. There may be multiple fractures involving almost any bone in the body. There may also be bony deformities, which may need correction. The medical treatment has shown some benefit in the form of pamidronate, which inhibits bone resorption.

Osteopetrosis is a disease process where there is decreased function of the osteoclasts. The osteoclasts are either absent or reduced in number. In other forms they are present in large numbers but are abnormal. They lack their ruffled borders and are not found in Howship's launae. The function of the osteoclasts is resorption of bone, whereas the osteoblasts lay down new bone. This is a coupling mechanism and the bone continues to remodel throughout its life. In ostoepetrosis the osteoclasts lose their function, with the result that bone is not resorbed and bone deposition continues without any resorption. The disease may present as either the congenital form or the adult form.

The congenital form is the autosomal recessive form and is the most severe form of the disease. Patients die during childhood. They have organomegaly and cranial and optic nerve palsy. The adult form is the mild form. The patients have a normal lifespan and have a history of fractures. They may have anemia as well as thrombocytopenia. Radiography reveals increased bone density. The metaphysis of the long bones are widened with a characteristic pattern of transverse sclerotic bands alternating with lucent bands. The vertebral bodies also develop sclerotic bands underlying the endplates and give the spine a rugger jersey appearance. Bone marrow transplantation is successful in some patients and vitamin D3 has been given to the patients along with a restriction of calcium. The fractures pose a difficult problem in this group of patients. The bones are very sclerotic and fixation of fractures may become difficult, as it is harder to drill through these bones. In long bone fractures any intramedullary device may not be possible as there may be virtually no intramedullary canal.

Paget's disease is a very common metabolic bone disease second only to osteoporosis. It has three stages. In the first stage there is increased osteoclastic activity. The radiographs show increased radiolucency. In the second stage there is increased osteoblasitc activity and the bone is dense and sclerotic. In the third stage there is increased activity of both the osteoclasts and the osteoblasts with a mixed picture. The radiographs show enlarged bones with areas of radiolucency as well as radio-densities. There is enlargement of different bones; patients may observe an increase in their hat size. They may present with deafness, high-output cardiac failure and pathological fractures. The disease may involve vertebral bodies and can have neural compression, or may involve the acetabulum, leading to arthritis, and may need hip arthroplasty. About 1 per cent of patients develop sarcoma, the commonest being osteosarcoma. The treatment relies on biphosphonates and calcitonin. Fractures require operative intervention.

IMRAN ILYAS

BONE STRENGTH/OSTEOPOROSIS PREVENTION

Osteoporosis, as defined by a World Health Organization study group as 'a disease characterized by low bone mass and microarchitectural deterioration of bone tissue leading to enhanced bone fragility and a consequent increase in fracture risk', is an important public health crisis that affects millions of people world-wide and has already reached an alarming state. Since 1990, there has been an almost fourfold duplication in osteoporosis hip fracture, with Asia set to suffer the most dramatic future increase mainly due to the estimated large increase in its aged population. Currently, it impinges on over seventy-five million people in Europe, Japan, and the US alone, with an estimated lifetime risk for wrist, hip, and vertebral fractures of around 15 per cent. It is projected that the global burden of osteoporosis hip fracture will exceed six million by the year 2050. Not only does the growing seriousness of the problem impose a huge financial burden on the health care system, but it also degrades the quality of life and independence of the elderly population. Therefore, osteoporosis programs targeted at high-risk individuals should no longer be delayed; among these, exercise practice is one of the most cost-effective responses, with multiple health benefits.

Groups with a high risk of fragility fractures include:

- individuals with a previous fragility fracture
- individuals under prolonged corticosteroid treatment
- women who have undergone a hysterectomy or who have experienced premature menopause
- individuals with risk factors such as liver or thyroid disease
- individuals with a body mass index $<19\,\mathrm{kg\,m^{-2}}$
- smokers
- individuals with a history of falling

Early detection of osteoporosis is a crucial way to prevent fracture. Validated diagnostic tools are available to measure bone mineral density (BMD) for the prediction of fracture tendency. Dual energy X-ray absorptiometry (DXA) at the hip and lumbar spine is the gold standard for BMD measurement. Less costly technologies such as peripheral DXA, and ultrasound at sites such as the radius and heel can also be employed. For those vertebral fractures that do not come to clinical attention, radiographic diagnosis is considered to be the best way for the identification and confirmation of their presence, while their severity can be determined visually from radiographs using semi-quantitative grading criteria.

Despite the existence of technology for the detection of osteoporosis, physical activity is still highly recommended as the first step in its prevention. The preventive value of physical exercise lies not only in its potential to reduce bone loss and improve muscle strength, but also in its profound benefits in preventing falls and reducing bone fractures. There are strong indications that early start of physical activity contributes to higher peak bone mass. Peak bone mass and subsequent bone mineral maintenance are largely affected by the interplay between mechanical stress, body composition, nutrition, and bone metabolism. Regular physical exercise places physical stress on the body, helps stimulate bone growth and preserve bone mass, and provides excellent general health benefits, the foremost being an increase in BMD. Activities such as resistance training and weight-bearing exercises are likely to be more beneficial as they help to build bone and preserve bone mass. Exercises that require muscles to work together against gravity without putting too much stress on bones and joints include hiking, weightlifting, and dancing. Also, recent evidence proves that some forms of physical activity can help to maintain or even increase BMD in selected populations. Many studies have confirmed that physical activity, in particular programmed weight-bearing exercises, may protect postmenopausal women

against rapid decline in bone mass, and decrease BMD loss in the distal radius and tibial regions. Besides, regular exercise has the benefit of enhancing coordination and strengthening muscles, both of which serve to reduce the risk of falling.

Falling is a major risk factor for osteoporosis – the most frequent cause of morbidity and mortality arising from the condition; therefore, practicing exercises that lower the risk of fall and fracture is another way to control osteoporosis. Randomized clinical trails have shown that regular exercise can reduce the risk of falls by approximately 25 per cent. Among all kinds of physical activities, weight-bearing exercises that can increase bone strength and improve balance are particularly beneficial; tai chi is one of the very good examples. The gentle and slow body movements practiced in this form of exercise help to relax muscles, strengthen bones, train endurance, and improve balance, flexibility, and coordination, thus lessening susceptibility to falls. It is reported by Wolf *et al.* that its regular practice not only reduces the risk of multiple falls by 47.5 per cent in the elderly, but that it also reduces responses associated with fear of falling and intrusiveness. It should therefore be an integrated and effective part of strategies designed to reduce the incidence of osteoporosis fracture.

In short, physical activity is vital for maintenance of healthy bones throughout life and is decisive in preventing osteoporosis, reducing falls and decreasing the risk of fracture. So, national and local policies, as well as campaigns should be devised to improve public awareness of the need for active living, accompanied by well conceived programs to make physical activity easier and more rewarding.

References

Assessment of Fracture Risk and Its Application to Screening for Post-menopausal Osteoporosis

(1994) report of a World Health Organization Study Group, Geneva: World Health Organization. WHO Technical Report Series no. 843.

NIH consensus development conference statement: 'Osteoporosis Prevention, Diagnosis, and Therapy', 27–9 March 2000. Available from: http://consensus.nih.gov/cons/111/111_intro.htm

Qin, L., Au, S.K., Choy, Y.W., Leung, P.C., Neff, M., Lee, K.M. *et al.* (2002) 'Regular Tai Chi Exercise May Retard Bone Loss in Postmenopausal Women: A Case-control Study', *Archives of Physical Medicine and Rehabilitation* 83; 1355–9.

Wolf, S.L., Barnbart, H.X., Kutner, N.G., McNeely, E., Coogler, C. and Xu, T.S. (1996) 'Reducing Fraility and Falls in Older Persons: An Investigation of Tai Chi and Computerized Balance Training', *J Am Geriatr Soc* 44, 5: 489–497.

KAI MING CHAN

BONE STRUCTURE AND PROPERTIES

Bone contains 25–30 per cent water, a protein – collagen – that accounts for 25–30 per cent of the bone's dry weight, and minerals – 65–70 per cent of the bone's dry weight. The collagen gives bone its resistance to tensile loading; the minerals provide resistance to compression and give bone its properties of hardness and rigidity. The protein content contributes ductility or flexibility – the ability to deform – and toughness – resistance to shock loading. Bone is a highly specialised form of connective tissue. It consists of a multitude of cells, osteocytes, which contribute only a small fraction of the bone's weight, within an organic, extracellular matrix of collagen fibrils. The tissue fluid and a gelatinous ground substance of protein polysaccharides are interspersed among the collagen fibrils. This ground substance serves to cement layers of mineralised collagen fibrils. All the organic material is impregnated with minerals, the distinguishing feature of bone.

Many bones, particularly long bones, consist of a periphery of cortical, or compact, bone surrounding a core of cancellous bone.

Cortical bone is an anisotropic viscoelastic material, which is non-homogeneous, brittle, and weakest under tensile loading. The structural unit of cortical bone is the osteon, an elongated cylinder that runs parallel to the bone's longitudinal axis and functions as a weight-bearing pillar. Each osteon is made up of concentric tubes of bone matrix, in each of which the collagen fibres run in a single direction. However, this fibre direction reverses in adjacent matrix tubes, improving the resistance of the bone cortex to torsional stress.

Cancellous bone, by contrast, appears to have a less well-organised structure, which is cellular or porous. The cancelli, or trabeculae, are rod- or plate-like and have various spatial orientations, corresponding to the direction of tensile and compressive stresses, and are roughly orthogonal. The trabeculae are more densely packed in those parts of the bone that have to transmit the greatest tensile or compressive stresses. The sponginess of cancellous bone helps to absorb energy but gives a lower strength than cortical bone.

The overall structure of long bones gives an optimal strength-to-weight ratio, made possible by the requirement for greatest stress resistance at the periphery of the bone and by the internal struts of the trabeculae. A narrower middle section in long bones reduces bending stresses and minimises the chance of fracture. Bone is relatively inelastic, experiencing only a small elongation before breaking. Above a certain load it behaves plastically; however, it is elastic in its normal, or physiological, range of deformation. It is also viscoelastic; it returns to its original shape over time and its properties depend on the strain rate. Because of its non-homogeneity, the type and region of the bone also affect its mechanical properties. Bone is also anisotrophic – its properties also vary with the direction in which the load is applied – for example, cortical bone has twice as large an elastic modulus along the long axis than across it.

At higher rates of loading, compact bone increases slightly in strength and stiffness and it fails at a lower strain. Compact bone is characteristically brittle at higher load rates, when less energy is absorbed before it fails. Its brittleness is caused by the mineral content, which makes bone susceptible to shock loads. Because of its brittleness, bone often fails before other biological materials when deformed.

See also: bone classification; bone growth; bone injury

Further reading

Nigg, B.M. and Herzog, W. (1999) *Biomechanics of the Musculoskeletal System*, ch. 2, Chichester: Wiley.

ROGER BARTLETT

BONES OF THE ANKLE AND FOOT

The ankle and foot contain many bones and joints, giving the region high mobility. As the first point of contact between the body and the ground, this flexible segment enables the individual to adapt easily to changes in terrain. The bones of the ankle joint are those of the distal part of the leg – the tibia and fibula – and the talus. The twenty-six bones of the foot are the talus, calcaneus, navicular, cuboid, and the three cuneiforms – these are the tarsal bones – plus the five metatarsal bones and the phalanges.

The talus is common to both the ankle and the foot, forming the distal part of the ankle joint and the proximal part of the subtalar joint. The distal ends of the tibia and fibula, the malleoli, form the proximal part of the ankle joint and can be used to approximate the ankle joint axis in vivo. The ankle joint axis passes just distal to the tips of the malleoli; according to Inman (1976) the axis lies, on average, 5 mm distal to the tip of the medial malleolus, and 3 mm distal and 8 mm anterior to the tip of the lateral malleolus. During on-line motion analysis and video analysis, biomechanists use the line between the tips of the malleoli as an approximation to the ankle joint axis.

The bones of the foot and ankle are at risk of stress fracture, particularly in runners and military recruits. Stress fractures commonly occur in the navicular, metatarsals and the distal third of the tibia. There is some evidence that the incidence of these overuse injuries is higher in those individuals who have narrower tibias, since these bones are less able to resist the bending forces to which the leg is subjected when the foot contacts the ground on every stride. Further, stress fractures occur twice as often in females than in males, although the reasons for this difference are unclear. Owing to the seriousness of stress fractures, which require several weeks rest from training and physical activity until the bone is healed, they are an important research topic for sports biomechanists and physical therapists. Factors that are thought to be related to the risk of stress fracture include structural anatomy, functional mechanics, footwear and training surface, training load, training frequency, and sex.

After fracture healing, several measures are available to try to prevent recurrence of the stress fracture. The most easily manipulated risk factor is training load and frequency; individuals should restart their training programmes conservatively and be cautious about increasing either the length or intensity of individual sessions, or the number of sessions. Similarly, softer training surfaces can be chosen and appropriate footwear with adequate shock absorption capabilities and support should be worn. Other options include orthotics, which are fitted into the footwear and realign the position of the foot.

See also: accelerometry; ankle and foot; foot arches; footwear and injury; force measurement; joints of the ankle and foot; muscles of the ankle and foot

Reference

Inman, V.T. (1976) *The Joints of the Ankle*, Baltimore: Williams and Wilkins.

Further reading

Williams, P.L., Bannister, L.H., Berry, M.M., Collins, P., Dyson, M., Dussek, J.E. and Ferguson, M.W.J. (eds) (1995) *Gray's Anatomy: the Anatomical Basis of Medicine and Surgery*, Section 6, Edinburgh: Churchill Livingstone.

Sarrafian, S.K. (1993) *Anatomy of the Foot and Ankle: Descriptive, Topographic, Functional, Grant's Anatomy*, chs 2 and 10, Philadelphia: Lippincott.

CLARE E. MILNER

BONES OF THE ELBOW AND FOREARM

The elbow is a hinge joint between the humerus in the upper arm and the ulna in the forearm of the upper extremity; its motion is sagittal plane flexion-extension. The entire joint comprises three articulations between the three long bones of the upper limb. These are the hinge joint already described, the secondary hinge joint between the radius of the forearm and the humerus, which is constrained by the annular ligament, and the radioulnar articulation that enables flexion-extension of the elbow to be combined with pronation and supination of the forearm and the hand. Contrary to the bony structure of the lower limb, both bones of the distal segment contribute to the elbow joint, but only the radius contributes to the wrist joint. Stabilisation of the joint is provided by both the distal end of the humerus – the trochlea – sitting in the trochlear notch of the ulna, and by the soft tissue structures of the joint capsule and collateral ligaments, and the annular ligament that maintains the position of the proximal end of the radius at the elbow.

The location of the elbow joint centre is approximated by sports biomechanists during on-line motion analysis or video analysis to enable the movements of the elbow to be calculated as the included angle between two lines. In video analysis, the first of the two lines usually run from the centre of the humeral head to the midpoint of the line joining the humeral epicondyles. The second line joins the latter point to the midpoint of the line joining the epicondyles of the wrist. An alternative schema, often used in on-line motion analysis, has one line passing from a bony landmark approximating the shoulder joint centre to the lateral epicondyle of the distal humerus, which approximates the elbow joint centre; the second line passes from this approximation of the elbow joint centre to a landmark at the wrist. The lateral epicondyle can be palpated on the lateral side of the elbow joint as a flat region with very little soft tissue between the skin surface and the underlying bone. This landmark is easiest to palpate with the arms abducted out to the sides of the body and parallel to the ground with the elbows flexed to 90° while maintaining the upper arm parallel to the ground.

Tracking the pronation-supination motion of the forearm is more complex, as it requires at least three markers on the upper arm and on the forearm to fully define their locations in three-dimensional space. There is no standard marker set for tracking this movement, but sport and exercise biomechanists are currently developing a suitable marker set. This will improve the use of on-line motion analysis in investigating complex motions of the upper body, such as the movements of the arm that occur in throwing sports. A true three-dimensional representation of upper extremity motion is necessary to study such sports meaningfully.

Traumatic injuries to the forearm are relatively common in team sports such as soccer. A player may fall and land awkwardly with the arm extended to cushion the impact of the fall. Such a fall can result in either fracture of the forearm or dislocation of the shoulder joint.

See also: elbow and forearm; joints of the elbow and forearm; muscles of the elbow and forearm

Further reading

Bird, S., Black, N. and Newton, P. (1997) *Sports Injuries: Causes, Diagnosis, Treatment and Prevention*, Cheltenham: Stanley Thornes.

Williams, P.L., Bannister, L.H., Berry, M.M., Collins, P., Dyson, M., Dussek, J.E. and Ferguson, M.W.J. (eds) (1995) *Gray's Anatomy: the Anatomical Basis of Medicine and Surgery*, Section 6, Edinburgh: Churchill Livingstone.

CLARE E. MILNER

BONES OF THE HEAD AND NECK

The bones of the head and neck comprise the bones of the skull and the seven vertebrae of the cervical spine. The bones of the skull, which are fused in the adult, are the cranium – the large dome that houses and protects the brain – and the bones of the face. The skull is made up of eight cranial and fourteen facial bones. All of these, except the mandible, or jawbone, are attached rigidly to each other by interlaced articulations called sutures. The bones of the skull are not fully fused at the sutures until old age and do not begin to close until aged twenty-two years, with the process being mostly complete by the age of thirty. This should be taken into consideration when younger athletes suffer from traumatic injury to the head, since the skull serves to protect the delicate tissues of the brain. Damage to the bones of the skull tends to be caused by acute trauma from contact with another athlete, equipment, or the ground.

The cranial bones are the occipital bone at the back of the head, the two parietal bones forming the sides and top of the cranium, the frontal bone of the forehead, the two temporal bones at the sides below the parietal bones in the region of the ears, the sphenoid bone at the base of the skull extending laterally in front of the temporal bones, and the ethmoid bone that forms the walls of the superior part of the nasal cavity. The facial bones are the two nasal bones – the bridge of the nose, the two maxillae of the upper jaw, the palatine bone behind the maxillae – forming parts of the roof of the mouth, the floor of the nasal cavity, and the floor of the eye orbit, the two inferior nasal conchae – the lateral walls of the nasal cavity, the two vomers that are also part of the nasal cavity, the two lacrimal bones – part of the eye orbit, and the two zygomatic, or cheek, bones.

Injuries to the head and neck tend to be traumatic and often occur as a result of unintentional contact between two players in team sports such as soccer. Typical injuries include nosebleeds, broken noses, concussion, and fracture of the facial bones, and may be severe enough to require hospitalisation. In some sports, such as cycling, protective headgear can be worn to reduce the risk of severe head trauma in the case of unintentional contact with the ground. Cyclists can also suffer from overuse injury in this region; neck pain may occur as a result of excessive hyperextension of the neck and typically affects the three cervical vertebrae closest to the skull. The risk of overuse injury of the neck can be minimised by appropriate setting up of the bicycle for the individual.

Racquet sports are notorious for eye injuries and are responsible for over half of all sports-related eye injuries (Bird *et al.* 1997). Squash is the biggest contributor, followed by badminton and then tennis. Such injuries are caused by the racquet, ball, or shuttlecock. The best protection from these injuries is to wear eye guards that prevent objects from entering the eye from all angles.

See also: head and neck; joints of the head and neck; muscles of the head and neck

Reference

Bird, S., Black, N. and Newton, P. (1997) *Sports Injuries: Causes, Diagnosis, Treatment and Prevention*, Cheltenham: Stanley Thornes.

Further reading

Williams, P.L., Bannister, L.H., Berry, M.M., Collins, P., Dyson, M., Dussek, J.E. and Ferguson, M.W.J. (eds) (1995) *Gray's Anatomy: the Anatomical Basis of Medicine and Surgery*, Section 6, Edinburgh: Churchill Livingstone.

CLARE E. MILNER

BONES OF THE HIP

The hip is the most proximal joint of the lower extremity and has the greatest multi-axial range of motion of all the lower extremity joints. It is formed between the hip-bone, which is part of the pelvis and consists of the ilium, ischium, and pubis; and the femur, the long bone between the hip and the knee. The hip is a ball and socket joint and, as such, makes the thigh and lower limb very mobile with respect to the pelvis. Because of its bony configuration, the joint is stabilised by both the cup-like acetabulum of the hip-bone and the strong ligamentous attachments between it and the femur.

The femur has a long and cylindrical diaphysis. Proximally, it has a short neck inclined to the long axis of the bone and an approximately spherical head that sits in the acetabulum of the pelvis. Distally, the femur thickens into the femoral condyles that make up the proximal part of the knee joint. Differences in the bony anatomy of the femur can affect lower extremity kinematics and, like other lower limb structural abnormalities, are thought to be related to the incidence of overuse injuries of the lower extremity.

The major structural abnormalities of the femur are femoral anteversion and Q angle. The Q angle expresses the geometric relationship between the pelvis, femur, patella, and tibia. It is measured as the acute angle between a line drawn from the anterior superior iliac spine of the pelvis to the centre of the patella and a line drawn from the centre of the patella to the tibial tubercle. It provides an indication of the medial angulation of the femur between the hip joint and the knee joint, which accommodates the difference between the width of the pelvis and the base of support at the feet. This angle is typically higher in women as a result of their wider pelvis. The Q angle is one of the structural measures that have been investigated by sports biomechanists in an attempt to determine the cause of lower extremity overuse injuries, such as those that occur during running.

Femoral anteversion is medial torsion of the femur, the internal rotation of the distal end of the femur relative to the proximal end. This changes the alignment of the bones at the knee and can lead to knee overuse injuries caused by malalignment of the femur relative to the patella and tibia, such as chondromalacia patella. Observing the static standing posture of an individual can identify femoral anteversion; the patella, or kneecap, is turned inwards instead of pointing straight ahead, and the toes are often turned in too. It is possible to correct the anteversion of the femur surgically, although this is only necessary if the anteversion is severe enough to interfere with daily activities.

Typical overuse injuries that occur in runners and which might be related to femoral anteversion or the Q angle include chondromalacia patella, patellofemoral pain, iliotibial band friction syndrome, and tibial and femoral stress fractures.

See also: cardinal plane movements; hip; hip joint; knee injury; muscles of the lumbar spine and pelvis; muscles of the thigh

Further reading

Williams, P.L., Bannister, L.H., Berry, M.M., Collins, P., Dyson, M., Dussek, J.E. and

Ferguson, M.W.J. (eds) (1995) *Gray's Anatomy: the Anatomical Basis of Medicine and Surgery*, Section 6, Edinburgh: Churchill Livingstone.

CLARE E. MILNER

BONES OF THE KNEE

The knee joint has the greatest sagittal plane range of motion (flexion-extension; see **cardinal plane movements**) in the lower extremity. The joint is formed between the two major long bones of the lower limb: the tibia, lying between the knee and the ankle, and the femur, lying between the knee and the hip. Although the fibula contributes to the ankle joint, it is not part of the knee joint. However, there is a third bone present at the knee: the patella or kneecap, which forms the patellofemoral joint by running along a groove in the femur. Stabilisation of the joint is predominantly by soft tissue structures – the anterior and posterior cruciate ligaments, the medial and lateral collateral ligaments, and the medial and lateral menisci. The distal end of the femur – the femoral condyles – rests on the tibial plateau.

The primary knee joint axis runs in a mediolateral direction, although its absolute position varies with knee flexion. The knee joint axis is approximated by sports biomechanists during **on-line motion analysis** and **video analysis** as running between the medial and lateral femoral condyles. These bony landmarks can be palpated easily and provide a good functional approximation to the knee's flexion-extension axis. There are also lesser amounts of rotation in the other two – secondary – planes, with abduction and adduction occurring around the anteroposterior axis and internal and external rotation occurring around the longitudinal axis of the tibia. Historically, these secondary planes of motion have been considered insignificant in the investigation of the cause of overuse injury at the knee. However, as sports biomechanists begin to have access to more advanced equipment for on-line motion analysis, more research is focusing on these subtle joint movements. It is hypothesised that slight malalignments in the bones of the lower limb may change the amount and pattern of motion around the secondary axes of rotation at the knee, and that these small changes, when repeated over the thousands of repetitions that occur during walking or running, may contribute to the development of overuse injuries at the joint.

Malalignment of the bones at the knee can lead to osteoarthritic deterioration of the condyles of the joint, with varus alignment leading to deterioration of the medial compartment and valgus alignment leading to deterioration of the lateral compartment. Biomechanics researchers are interested in conservative measures to improve the functional ability of individuals with knee osteoarthritis, such as in-shoe orthotics to correct the alignment of the bones at the knee joint and reduce the pressure on the arthritic side. These measures can improve the quality of life and the ability to remain physically active of an osteoarthritic individual, delaying or removing the need for surgery. If knee osteoarthritis progresses beyond the limit at which these conservative measures can provide relief, total knee joint replacement is the surgical option. This involves replacing the distal end of the femur and the proximal end of the tibia with metal and polyethylene components. The prosthesis typically lasts for fifteen years and individuals can return to most sports activities, even skiing, after recovery from surgery.

See also: joints of the knee; knee; knee injury; muscles of the knee

Further reading

Williams, P.L., Bannister, L.H., Berry, M.M., Collins, P., Dyson, M., Dussek, J.E. and Ferguson, M.W.J. (eds) (1995) *Gray's Anatomy: the Anatomical Basis of Medicine and Surgery*, Section 6, Edinburgh: Churchill Livingstone.

CLARE E. MILNER

BONES OF THE LUMBAR SPINE AND PELVIS

The pelvis is the junction between the trunk and the lower extremities. It supports the spine and rests on the lower limbs. The pelvis is strong and sturdy and is made up of four bones: the two hip bones, plus the sacrum and coccyx of the distal spine. The bones form a ring with a large aperture in the middle; in females this aperture is the birth canal. The hip bones themselves are made up of three fused bones, the ilium, ischium, and pubis. The lumbar spine sits immediately on top of the sacrum and comprises five individual vertebrae. There are several differences in the structure of the male and female pelvis. The female pelvis has a wider and more rounded pubic arch, situated ventrally and distal to the pubic bone, and the anterior superior iliac spines are more widely separated.

The pelvis consists of several articulations, between the sacrum and the ilium, the sacrum and the ischium, the sacrum and the coccyx, and between the pubic bones. However, only very limited movement occurs between the sacrum and the coccyx, at the sacrococcygeal joint, between the bones of the coccyx itself, and between the two pubic bones at the pubic symphysis. The lumbar spine is the most mobile part of this region, particularly in extension and flexion.

The pelvic region is a site of overuse injuries. In particular, stress fractures of the pelvis occur in runners. The exact mechanism of these fractures is unclear. Why, for example, do some runners suffer stress fractures more distally in the lower extremity whereas, in other cases, forces are transmitted up through the lower extremity without injury to its tissues and cause a stress fracture in the pelvis? Stress fractures through running can occur in most of the bones of the lower extremity, and the reasons why they manifest themselves in different places in different runners are the subject of ongoing research in sports biomechanics. Women are more susceptible to pelvic stress fractures than males, but the reasons for this are also unknown. The difference in the incidence of injury may be related to anatomical differences or other factors related to the sex of the person involved. Sports biomechanics researchers use advanced techniques, such as **on-line motion analysis**, to investigate these relationships and have been studying the interrelationships between anatomical, physiological, and training factors and the occurrence of overuse injuries in running for more than twenty years.

Another group of athletes at risk of overuse injury in the lumbar and pelvic region are rowers, who commonly suffer from low back pain. Relationships between the dynamic position of the lumbar spine during rowing and low back pain have been the subject of investigation by sports biomechanists and physical therapists in recent years. However, as with running overuse injuries, it remains unclear which factors are most important in this injury and, therefore, which individuals are most at risk. Possible causes of injury include hip flexor tightness and lack of hip joint flexibility.

See also: bones of the hip; hip joint; joints of the lumbar spine and pelvis; lumbar spine and pelvis; muscles of the lumbar spine and pelvis

Further reading

McGregor, A., Anderton, L. and Gedroyc, W. (2002) 'The Assessment of Intersegmental Motion and Pelvic Tilt in Elite Oarsmen', *Medicine and Science in Sports and Exercise* 34: 1143–9.

Williams, P.L., Bannister, L.H., Berry, M.M., Collins, P., Dyson, M., Dussek, J.E. and Ferguson, M.W.J. (eds) (1995) *Gray's Anatomy: the Anatomical Basis of Medicine and Surgery*, Section 6, Edinburgh: Churchill Livingstone.

CLARE E. MILNER

BONES OF THE SHOULDER

The shoulder, or glenohumeral, joint is the most proximal joint of the upper extremity and has the greatest multiaxial range of motion of all the upper extremity joints. It is formed between the scapula, or shoulder blade, and the humerus, the long bone in the upper arm that contributes to both the shoulder and the elbow joint. The shoulder is considered to be a ball and socket joint and, as such, makes the arm very mobile with respect to the torso. The joint has only a shallow socket in the glenoid cavity of the scapula for the humerus to sit in, but is protected against displacement by strong ligament and tendinous attachments. The shoulder complex comprises the glenohumeral joint plus the acromioclavicular joint, between the scapula and the lateral end of the clavicle, or collarbone, and the sternoclavicular joint, between the medial end of the clavicle and the sternum, or breastbone.

The humerus is the longest bone of the upper limb and consists of a long diaphysis with a hemispherical head proximally at the shoulder joint. Distally the bone thickens out into the articular condyle that forms the distal part of the elbow joint. Overuse injuries of the upper extremity are less common than in the lower extremity, since the upper body is not subjected as frequently to high repetitions with high loading. However, overuse injuries of the upper extremity do occur in throwing and hitting sports, and those that involve repetitive stereotyped movements; particularly at the glenohumeral joint, which relies heavily on soft tissue structures to maintain its integrity. Traumatic injuries to the bones of the shoulder are relatively common and typically result from a fall.

A common traumatic injury to the clavicle is fracture of the proximal or middle third of the bone. The most common mechanism of fracture is falling onto the outstretched arm and hand or directly onto the end of the shoulder. This particular injury may appear to be relatively minor, but it has the potential for serious complications because several important structures lie just below the bone: the top of the lung, the subclavian blood vessels, and a nervous structure known as the brachial plexus. To minimise the risk of this injury, learning how to fall properly in contact sports such as rugby and judo is essential, and should be taught from the earliest stage of player development.

Another traumatic shoulder injury common to those contact sports is shoulder subluxation, or partial dislocation, more accurately described as acromioclavicular sprain. This injury tends to occur when the athlete falls directly onto the end of the shoulder. The severity of the injury depends on how much of the ligamentous structure spanning the joint is disrupted. The injury can result in the damaged joint becoming more prominent, even after complete rehabilitation, but this rarely has any lasting effect on the joint's functional ability, and is only of concern cosmetically.

See also: muscles of the shoulder; shoulder injury; shoulder joint; shoulder rehabilitation

Further reading

Bird, S., Black, N. and Newton, P. (1997) *Sports Injuries: Causes, Diagnosis, Treatment and Prevention*, Cheltenham: Stanley Thornes.

Williams, P.L., Bannister, L.H., Berry, M.M., Collins, P., Dyson, M., Dussek, J.E. and Ferguson, M.W.J. (eds) (1995) *Gray's Anatomy: the Anatomical Basis of Medicine and Surgery*, Section 6, Edinburgh: Churchill Livingstone.

CLARE E. MILNER

BONES OF THE THORACIC REGION

The bones of the thoracic, or chest, region are the thoracic vertebrae, sternum, and ribs, plus the costal cartilages; the last of these are not bones, but are integral to the structure of this region. This region contains the heart and the lungs, around which the bones of the thorax form a protective cage. There are twelve thoracic vertebrae, each of which has two associated ribs. The ten upper pairs are each attached to the sternum – breastbone – ventrally by the costal cartilage. The remaining two pairs are the floating ribs, which do not have an anterior attachment and are attached only to the eleventh and twelfth lumbar vertebrae respectively. The first seven pairs of ribs articulate with the sternum through costal cartilage and are true ribs; the remaining three pairs of anteriorly secured ribs articulate only with the costal cartilage of the rib above.

The sternum is divided into three parts. The manubrium is the most caudal and articulates with the first ribs and the clavicle; the body is the largest piece and articulates with the second to sixth ribs and part of the seventh rib. The seventh ribs also articulate partly with the small xiphoid process that lies at the distal end of the sternal body.

The basic structure of a rib consists of two extremities and a body or shaft. The dorsal, or vertebral, extremity articulates with a vertebra. The ventral extremity of the true ribs articulates with the sternum, that of the false ribs articulates with the costal cartilage of the adjacent ribs, and that of the floating ribs does not articulate with other bony structure. The ribs increase in length from the first to the seventh; their length then decreases from the seventh to the twelfth. The body of the rib is grooved where the intercostal muscles of the thorax attach. Ribs are highly vascularised bones and consist mainly of cancellous bone inside a thin layer of compact bone (see **bone structure and properties**). The costal cartilages of the thorax are bars of hyaline cartilage that extend the length of the ribs ventrally (Williams *et al.* 1995).

Athletes who participate in contact sports are at risk of traumatic injury to the ribs.

Although painful, these injuries are rarely serious and heal rapidly because the bone is highly vascularised. Overuse injuries can also occur in the thoracic region. This type of injury may occur when the thoracic region is under tension and forms a rigid link between the upper and lower body for the transfer of load. For example, stress fractures are relatively common in competitive rowers and are thought to be related to the forces transmitted through the body from the feet pushing against the foot stretcher of the boat to the oar in the hands (see **axial skeleton – structure and function**).

See also: core stability; joints of the thoracic region; muscles of the thoracic region; thoracic region – pectoral girdle, thoracic spine and ribs

Reference

Williams, P.L., Bannister, L.H., Berry, M.M., Collins, P., Dyson, M., Dussek, J.E. and Ferguson, M.W.J. (eds) (1995) *Gray's Anatomy: the Anatomical Basis of Medicine and Surgery*, Edinburgh: Churchill Livingstone.

Further reading

Williams, P.L., Bannister, L.H., Berry, M.M., Collins, P., Dyson, M., Dussek, J.E. and Ferguson, M.W.J. (eds) (1995) *Gray's Anatomy: the Anatomical Basis of Medicine and Surgery*, Section 6, Edinburgh: Churchill Livingstone.

CLARE E. MILNER

BONES OF THE WRIST AND HAND

The wrist and hand contain many bones and joints, giving the region high flexibility. The hand is the major point of contact between the body and objects in the surrounding world; the flexibility of this region enables an individual to adapt easily to different holding and gripping requirements. The wrist and hand are also strong enough to support the body in sports such as gymnastics. The bones of the wrist joint are those of the forearm, and the sca-phoid, lunate, and triangular bones of the carpal region of the hand. The bones of the hand are the eight carpals, five metacarpals and the fourteen phalanges of the digits – the thumb has two, whereas the fingers each have three.

The proximal bones of the wrist are the radius and ulna of the forearm. Although the ulna does not directly articulate with the carpals at the wrist, it contributes to this joint through the articular disc that lies between it and the lunate and triangular carpal bones. The eight carpal bones are the scaphoid, lunate, triangular, pisiform, tra-pezium, trapezoid, capitate, and hamate. These bones are arranged in two rows; the first four are more proximal and the last four more distal. The scaphoid and lunate bones articulate with the radius.

The metacarpals of the hand are equiv-alent to the metatarsals of the foot. They are long slender bones with a body and two articulating ends. The first metacarpal is that of the thumb and it articulates with the trapezium of the wrist. The second meta-carpal articulates with the trapezium and the trapezoid as well as the third meta-carpal. The third metacarpal articulates with the capitate of the wrist and the second and fourth metacarpals. The fourth metacarpal articulates with the third and fifth meta-carpals, the capitate, and the hamate. The fifth metacarpal articulates with the fourth metacarpal and the hamate.

Although relatively uncommon, fracture of the scaphoid, the largest wrist bone, can occur as a result of a fall onto the out-stretched hand. A fall of this nature can result in fracture of either the scaphoid of the wrist or the radius of the forearm, depending on the position of the wrist and hand at the moment of impact. If the wrist is fully flexed, the scaphoid will fracture; lesser flexions will result in fracture of the distal part of the radius. Acute fracture of the scaphoid may also occur as a result of striking an opponent in contact sports, such

as rugby and American football, or in striking the ground or equipment with a hyperextended wrist in gymnastics. Although rare, this injury is potentially serious and may even be career-ending for the profes-sional sports person, as it has a high risk of complications such as delayed union, non-union, and, in the worst case, avascular necrosis where the broken fragment loses its blood supply and the bone tissue dies and collapses (Garrick and Webb 1999).

See also: joints of the wrist and hand; mus-cles of the wrist and hand; wrist and hand

Reference

Garrick, J.G. and Webb, D.R. (1999) *Sports Injuries: Diagnosis and Management*, Philadel-phia PA: W.B. Saunders.

Further reading

Williams, P.L., Bannister, L.H., Berry, M.M., Collins, P., Dyson, M., Dussek, J.E. and Ferguson, M.W.J. (eds) (1995) *Gray's Anat-omy: the Anatomical Basis of Medicine and Sur-gery*, Section 6, Edinburgh: Churchill Livingstone.

CLARE E. MILNER

BOOSTERS/SUPPORTERS CLUBS

The centerpiece for most annual donor programs to college sports is the booster or athletics supporter group (ASG) club. The fund-raising capabilities of these organiza-tions are substantial. There is evidence that a winning sports program has a major impact on the giving behavior of suppor-ters. Many of those who belong to ASGs are business owners and individual fans who were never students of the university. Businessmen 'boosting' athletic programs have long been a tradition in college athletics. Some argue that these boosters have little concern for the educational mission of the school, often viewing their five- and some-times six-figure donations as 'investments' in their favorite programs. In their opinion, this money not only grants them certain perks – the best seats, special parking spaces, the ear of the athletic director and of the coaches – but also entitles them to a say on how the college sports franchise should be run.

Unfortunately, recent history is replete with many instances in which prominent boosters have used ASGs to further their own interests independent of any kind of athletic department authority or overall institutional control. The desire of some overzealous boosters to win at any cost even if it involves breaking NCAA regulations has created serious problems for many universities and their athletic programs. Major institutions continue to be penalized severely for unethical practices by their boosters, typically for not controlling supporters who made illegal gifts to athletes such as cash payments to prospective athletes and large merchandise discounts to current student-athletes. Research indicates that being placed on probation can negatively impact charitable donations directed to both athletics and academics, further raising the importance of bringing boosters under institutional control.

ASGs commonly are organized as either *private foundations* or *athletic department-operated clubs*. Under the first arrangement, the support group incorporates as a non-profit, tax exempt foundation independent of the university. Private foundations have been both a blessing and a blight to athletic programs. On the positive side, some of the most successful ASGs have operated as private, nonprofit fund raising organizations. For example, in 2002, Fresno State's Bulldog Foundation and Clemson University's Foundation raised $7 million and $9 million, respectively, in support of athletic programs at their affiliate universities. Unfortunately, on the negative side, the independent status of these external booster groups can allow them to get out of control. Operating without any formal report-

ing responsibility to the university or the athletic department to which they are nominally affiliated, some work or have worked in a clandestine manner, violating rules, and making end runs around the athletic director's attempts at exercising institutional control. The alternative form of booster club organization is for the athletic department to establish its own 'in-house' ASG. Under this arrangement, the club 'resides' within the department and is staffed by departmental personnel.

JOHN L. CROMPTON

BOUNDARY LAYER

When a solid object, such as a sports ball, travels through a fluid, such as air, the air on the surface of the object has a velocity, relative to the surface, of zero. Well away from the surface, the air has a relative velocity equal to the velocity of the object. The region where the relative air velocity changes from zero to the maximum velocity is the boundary layer, in which viscous forces exert a noticeable influence on the motion of the fluid. In most cases this layer is very thin and not visible to the naked eye, but for instances where large objects, such as ships, pass through water, a change in relative fluid velocity can be observed. A change in fluid velocity with distance from the object means that there must be relative movement between fluid particles, and viscosity effects mean that shear stresses are present. In thin boundary layers, the velocity gradient is high, so high shear forces are experienced. It is difficult to define exactly where the boundary layer ends, but a convenient method is to use the point where the fluid velocity is 99 per cent of the maximum velocity. Ludwig Prandtl was once of the first to properly define boundary layers in 1904. He suggested that flow could be considered so that the boundary layer is the region in which shear stresses are of prime importance, whereas beyond this region velocity gradients are so small that the effect of viscosity is negligible.

The boundary layer can be examined by the flow of fluid across a smooth flat plate. As the flow reaches the plate, the fluid next to the surface is retarded, forming a boundary layer that is entirely laminar, that is, it contains stable flow. As the flow progresses over the plate, the boundary layer thickens as more and more of the fluid is slowed down by viscous shear forces. The laminar flow then begins to become unstable as the motion within the boundary layer becomes disturbed. After a period of transition, the boundary layer flow becomes turbulent and the thickness of the layer develops more rapidly. The velocity gradients in the two types of boundary layer, laminar and turbulent, are quite different. A laminar boundary layer contains, for the most part, a near-linear velocity gradient, with the relative velocity of fluid steadily increasing away from the surface. In a turbulent boundary layer, however, there is mixing of the flow between streamlines, which means that the velocity gradient near the surface is much higher. In other words, the velocity increases rapidly to begin with, moving away from the surface, until it reaches the maximum value at the edge of the boundary layer.

Boundary layer behaviour has a significant impact on the forces experienced by projectiles as they travel through the air. In sport, this can affect the drag that slows down golf balls as they fly through the air or swimmers as they move through water. Transverse forces observed in 'swinging' cricket balls are due to the different ways that laminar and turbulent boundary layers behave. Whereas the curved trajectories seen in topspin lobs in tennis and soccer free kicks are due to the Magnus effect, which is the result of the separation of boundary layers from spinning balls.

See also: ball swing and reverse swing; Bernoulli's equation; boundary layer separation; drag forces – pressure, skin friction, and wave drag; laminar and turbulent flow

Further reading

Massey, B.S. (1992) *Mechanics of Fluids*, London: Chapman and Hall.
Mehta, R.D. (1985) 'Aerodynamics of Sports Balls', *Annual Review of Fluid Mechanics* 17: 151–89.

MATT CARRÉ

BOUNDARY LAYER SEPARATION

As a solid object travels through a fluid, a thin layer forms adjacent to the solid surface that is known as the boundary layer. In this layer, viscous forces exert a noticeable influence on the motion of the fluid and there is a change in velocity moving away from the surface – a velocity gradient. As the air flows around the object there is a change in pressure just outside the boundary layer and this affects the behaviour of the fluid. At a particular point on the surface of the object, an adverse pressure gradient occurs and the boundary layer separates from the surface. During this process, re-circulating eddies form a wake region behind the object.

If the flow of air is considered over a curved surface, such as that of a sports ball in flight, the air is deflected around the surface accelerating to the point where the speed of the air, just outside the boundary layer, reaches a maximum. At this point the corresponding pressure is now a minimum. In this first stage, the negative pressure gradient is said to be favourable because the net effect of the pressure force in the forward direction counteracts the viscous effects of the boundary layer trying to slow the fluid down. However, as the flow continues around the curved surface, the pressure increases so that the net pressure opposes the forward flow on elements in the boundary layer. The pressure gradient in this stage is said to be 'adverse', is practically the same throughout the boundary layer, but has most effect on the air nearest the surface. Here, the air has the least momentum and is most easily brought to a standstill by the adverse pressure gradient. As the airflow travels further around the ball, the momentum of the air nearest to the surface continues to reduce until it is reversed and essentially 'breaks away' from the surface. At this point the boundary layer is said to have separated. The reversed flow at this point causes large irregular motions of air known as eddies. The eddies form a wake behind the curved object and the energy within them is dissipated as heat, so that the pressure remains relatively constant further downstream. Laminar and turbulent boundary layers both separate in this way, but laminar boundary layers are more prone to separation because the increase in speed in the boundary layer, away from the surface, is less rapid and the adverse pressure gradient can more easily take effect. In a turbulent boundary layer, the air close to the surface moves relatively faster because of mixing between elements of the fluid flow. Hence, it is harder for the adverse pressure gradient to slow down the air nearest to the surface.

In sport, boundary layer separation is the fundamental mechanism that affects the way balls fly though the air. The drag force acting on a ball is greater for a smooth ball that typically experiences a laminar boundary layer and separation occurs early, creating a large wake. A golf ball has dimples to cause turbulent behaviour in the boundary layer. Late separation results in a small wake behind the golf ball and less pressure drag. Cricket ball swing is the result of differences in boundary layer separation on either side of the ball, with a turbulent boundary layer on one side causing late separation and a laminar boundary layer on the other causing early separation (see **ball swing and reverse swing**). The Magnus effect observed for spinning sports balls, such as baseballs and footballs, is also due to boundary layer separation being different on both sides of the ball, this time caused by a different relative flow velocity.

See also: Bernoulli's equation; drag forces – pressure, skin friction, and wave drag; laminar and turbulent flow; lift forces – fundamentals; Magnus and negative Magnus effects

Further reading

Massey, B.S. (1992) *Mechanics of Fluids*, London: Chapman and Hall.
Mehta, R.D. (1985) 'Aerodynamics of Sports Balls', *Annual Review of Fluid Mechanics* 17: 151–89.

MATT CARRÉ

BOYCOTTS

The occasion of the twenty-second Olympic Games, held in Moscow, USSR, from 19 July to 3 August 1980 (203 events for 21 sports; participation by 5,283 athletes from 80 countries and regions), was the first time Japan voluntarily refused to participate in the Olympic Games. The decision was made on 24 May 1980 by the Board of the Japanese Amateur Sports Association (JASA) and by the Japanese Olympic Committee (JOC), and marked the first time that Japan had voluntarily declined to be represented at the Olympics, having sent its athletes to every Olympiad since the fifth Games in 1912 – with the exception of the three Games that were cancelled because of war, and the fourteenth Olympiad in 1948, to which Japan was not invited because of being held responsible for WWII. The decision to boycott the Moscow Games resulted from the Japanese government following the lead of US President Jimmy Carter, who had urged his Western allies to join his political strategy aimed at objecting to the Soviet Union's invasion of Afghanistan. The Japanese government imposed its political will on the JOC, and the JASA capitulated. By deciding to boycott the Games, JASA strayed from its principles as an autonomously managed sports organisation, independent of politics. It became painfully obvious that JASA and the other amateur sports associations were, in reality, bound hand and foot by political forces. In addition to these organisations' financial dependence on state subsidies to cover the cost of training athletes, their organisational structures had been reduced to being mere subcontractors for the government or the Ministry of Education, upon which they also relied for the supply their executive personnel. The politically motivated boycott of the Moscow Olympic Games went against the Olympic Charter, and served to highlight the lowly social status of athletes and coaches and the weakness of their positions. It became clear that there was an urgent need for JASA, and the main amateur sport associations beneath its umbrella, to transform themselves into independent, autonomous entities.

MUNEHIKO HARADA

BROADCASTING RIGHTS

The most significant change in the sport industry over the last twenty years has been the increasing importance of broadcast demand for sport, which has led to massive escalation in the prices of broadcasting rights for professional team sports and major sports events. At the beginning of the twenty-first century, for the major professional team sports in both the USA and Europe, income from the sale of broadcasting rights has become more important than the amount of income generated by selling tickets to spectators at the stadia. These developments first emerged in the United States in the 1980s but Europe started to catch up in the 1990s. Although there are close similarities between the price escalation for broadcasting rights for professional team sports in both the USA

and Europe, there are important differences between the two continents in the way these rights are distributed over different categories of television channel.

Quirk and Fort (1997) chronicle the early years of televised professional team sports in the USA and focus on the trade-off between new income from television and lost revenues from reduced attendances. In 1950, the Los Angeles Rams signed a contract involving the televising of six home games to viewers in the Los Angeles area. The contract specified that the sponsor would make up any loss resulting from lower attendances resulting from the live transmissions. The two home games that were not televised generated an average revenue of $77,000. The six televised games averaged only $42,000, resulting in the sponsor having to pay $198,000 in compensation. The contract was not renewed in 1951.

In these early years of televised professional team sports in the USA, this perceived negative impact on attendances was a major constraint on the development of more television coverage. In the 1960s, however, increased competition amongst the three major networks, CBS, NBC, and ABC, led to more television coverage of the four major team sports: American football, baseball, basketball, and ice-hockey. ABC, in particular, led the way with an aggressive attempt to broaden the interest in televised sport beyond the normal male audience, introducing technical innovations such as slow motion replays, close-ups, and split screens. Increasing advertising revenues generated through televised sport drove the networks to extend their coverage.

By 1970, the NFL earned $49 million a year from the sale of broadcasting rights, and this had increased to $167 million by 1980 (Quirk and Fort 1997). It was in the 1980s, however, that growth in the size of deals for sports broadcasting rights accelerated dramatically. Quirk and Fort (1997) estimated that in 1991 broadcast revenue accounted for 25 per cent of NHL revenues, 30 per cent of NBA revenues, 50 per cent of AL and NL revenues, and 60 per cent of NFL revenues.

The escalation in the price of broadcasting rights continued during the 1990s. In early 1998, American broadcasters agreed to pay $17.6 billion for the rights to the NFL for eight years. The previous deal, for 1995–8, was for $1.58 billion. In America, the major funding for these television deals has come from free-to-air channels. Sport attracts massive audiences. American football is definitely the number one sport. Nine of the all-time top-ten television programme audiences in the USA are Super Bowl finals. The record is held by 1996 Super Bowl final, which attracted a TV audience of 138.5 million viewers. In terms of ratings, the record is held by the 1982 Super Bowl finals, which achieved a rating of 49.1 per cent of US TV-households, which is number four on the all-time rating list. In recent years, MLB and NBA have competed for the number two status, while NHL is ranked as number four among the professional leagues.

Television companies bid for such games in order to be able to sell advertising slots at hugely inflated prices during their coverage of these games, coverage which lasts two or three times longer than the equivalent in Europe, and is broken more frequently by advertising slots than is the case in Europe.

In contrast to the USA, there was little or no competition in the European television market in the early post-war years. Although European countries differ substantially in the development of sport and broadcasting, there are common trends, and this can be illustrated this by looking at the UK position. In the UK, for instance, until 1955 there was only one channel, the BBC, a non-commercial public service broadcaster. Over this period the BBC developed extensive televised sports coverage in Britain, televising most of the major national sporting spectacles. Over this period, how-

ever, there was no live television coverage of the matches in the main professional team sports because of fears by these sports that live television coverage would reduce attendances at matches.

Whannel (1992) suggests that there were good economic reasons for the BBC to put so much emphasis on sport. He indicates the inequality of market power between the buyers and sellers of broadcasting rights for sports events that existed in the early part of the post-war period, with one buyer, the BBC, faced by a large number of suppliers of sports events, leading to low broadcasting rights fees and cheap programming costs for the BBC's sport coverage.

The arrival of ITV, a commercial public service broadcaster, in 1955, destroyed the BBC's monopoly on the buying side of the market and increased the level of fees. However, the BBC continued to dominate the broadcasting of sport, with ITV only really competing to televise football.

Throughout the 1970s football coverage was handled by negotiation between the BBC and ITV, and the Football League and the Football Association. The two TV channels cooperated to share coverage rather than competing against each other. This cosy relationship was shattered in the late 1980s when ITV pushed up the price of broadcasting rights for football for the 1988–92 period by 250 per cent and outbid the BBC to obtain exclusive rights.

It was not, however, until BSkyB, a pay service satellite broadcaster, entered the scene, most notably with its bid for football's Premiership matches for the 1992–7 period, that the landscape of sports broadcasting in Britain changed dramatically. BSkyB, with its owners Rupert Murdoch's News Corporation (owners of Fox), used to the much stronger competition for sports broadcasting rights in the United States, simply raised the price for the rights from its artificially depressed level.

For BSkyB, however, sport became much more important economically than it ever was for the BBC. The BBC received its revenue from the licence fee and had a responsibility to provide a breadth of programmes to satisfy 'the national interest'. This included prominence for sport because of the historically important role of sport in British culture. However, the BBC could never dedicate that share of its income (over 40 per cent) that BSkyB dedicates to sport, as this would be regarded as unbalanced for a public service provider.

These UK developments were mirrored in other European countries. The result has been that soccer has become the dominant TV-sport in Europe, both in terms of rating figures and rights fees. In 1998, a World Cup year, a soccer match topped the television programme popularity ranking lists in 75 per cent out of of fifty European countries. In Germany and France, 86 and 73 respectively of the top 100 programmes

were soccer-related. Six of the top ten TV programmes in the UK were soccer matches from the World Cup finals.

In the rest of Europe, as in the UK, the price escalation took off during the 1990s. This growth, however, did not correspond with the rate of growth in the rest of the economy, as Figure 5 reveals. In each of the big-five soccer nations, the UK, Spain, Italy, Germany, and France, the value of sports rights increased considerably more than the gross domestic product. For example, Italian soccer rights increased by almost 250 per cent, in a period where the activity in the overall economy decreased by 4 per cent. In Italy, soccer absorbed 64 per cent of the total amount spent on sport rights in 2000. This proportion was 51 per cent in the UK and Spain, 41 per cent in Germany and 39 per cent in France.

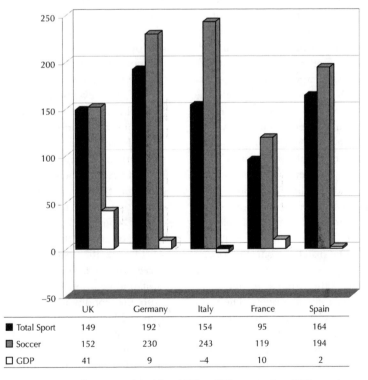

	UK	Germany	Italy	France	Spain
■ Total Sport	149	192	154	95	164
■ Soccer	152	230	243	119	194
□ GDP	41	9	−4	10	2

Figure 5. Percentage increase in European sports rights 1992 to 1997 compared to GDP growth over same period
Source: Kagan World Media Ltd (1999): European Media Sports Rights.

We can therefore see major differences between the European situation and that of the USA with regard to sports broadcasting over the post-war period. In Europe, professional team sports programmes were mainly broadcast on public service broadcasting channels until late in the 1980s. In recent years this pattern has changed. Pay channels have acquired a large slice of the most attractive soccer rights, while public service channels and other channels with maximum penetration have been restricted to highlights programmes. As an example, live matches from the domestic premier leagues in the 'big-five' European soccer nations are only screened on pay channels.

The discussion above indicates that European prices were significantly cheaper than American prices for sport broadcasting rights until the 1990s. The main reason for this was a lack of competition, combined with the strict regulation of European broadcasting which made it impossible for the channels to spend the same amount on sports rights as the US networks. This pattern changed late in the 1980s when European broadcasting was commercialised. Over the years, a large number of profit-maximising TV channels entered the scene and acquired sports rights in order to strengthen their market position. Advertising channels have given priority to programmes which are able to achieve high ratings figures. Pay service channels have concentrated on acquiring sports rights which attract a sufficient number of viewers willing to pay to watch. The latter channels have especially been successful in acquiring the rights to live matches from the domestic soccer leagues, pushing soccer way ahead of the other sports in terms of income from broadcasting rights. The main reason for the price escalation in Europe was the deregulation in the broadcasting market in the 1980s, creating much greater competition for sports broadcasting rights, turning a buyer's market into a seller's market.

References

Quirk, J. and Fort, R. (1997): *Pay Dirt: The Business of Professional Team Sports*, Princeton NJ: Princeton University Press.

Whannel, G. (1992) *Fields in Vision: Television Sport and Cultural Transformation*, London: Routledge.

CHRIS GRATTON
HARRY SOLBERG

BURNOUT

Athletic burnout is a psychophysiological condition, in which athletes involved at high levels lose interest and motivation to continue participating in their chosen sport, often resulting in withdrawal from competition. Junior athletes are equally susceptible to this condition, but burnout is most frequently observed when athletes are at, or nearing the peak of their athletic careers. When the rigours of training for **professional team sports** or individual sports are combined with a comprehensive competition schedule, the risk associated with injuries and 'mental fatigue' is elevated. Burnout is not an acute condition: the manifestation of various factors over a period of time eventually causes exhaustion. Raedeke *et al.* (1997) has suggested that the psychology of performance is based upon rewards, costs, satisfaction, investment, and alternatives; positive experiences in any of these five factors result in enthusiasm and enjoyment of the activity, while negative adaptation results in entrapment and, ultimately, burnout. The multidimensional nature of athletic burnout makes isolation of the specific issues difficult; however, three primary factors – psychological, physical, and emotional – have been identified with this condition (Smith 1986) and are outlined below.

The psychological aspect of athletic burnout may arise from many different stimuli. Personal intervention may be the most harmful; for example, coaches setting unrealistic goals, parents placing undue pressure on their children, or friends and spouses creating stress from personal relationships. From a young age, talented athletes may be subjected to pressure from their parents, who wish to seek consolation for their own unfulfilled sporting dreams through their children. The growing prevalence of specialisation among young athletes has potentially increased the risk of burnout. The large training demands placed on underdeveloped musculoskeletal systems in association with pressure from parents and coaches with unrealistic objectives, have the potential to reduce the intrinsic motivation for athletes, leading to burnout. It has also been recognised that the structure of highly competitive sport does not permit young athletes to spend sufficient time with their peers, resulting in a perceived lack of control and chance of withdrawal from the sport (Coakley 1992). Psychological pressure also arises with undue emphasis on competition success as an outcome measure at the expense of intrinsic fun, satisfaction, and relative improvements in various skill components related to age.

Further sources of psychological distress for athletes include activities of the **media**, situational issues and loss of **self-confidence**. Media activity can have a profound effect on an athlete's psyche, and even the most experienced athlete may find it difficult to cope with poor publicity, or the constant media spotlight, with their status in the community as role models, whether it is chosen or not, demanding that the media be dealt with in a professional manner. In addition to these personal issues, situational predicaments may severely impact upon the athlete's psyche, with travel demands and commitments to sponsors becoming an imposition on the individual mindset and affecting concentration on the athletic task at hand. These psychological issues and an athlete's over-exposure to the sport can contribute to a loss of interest, along with a devaluation of the athlete's ability,

decreased motivation to train, decreased self-confidence and an increase in perceptions of fatigue. Compounding these issues can be a lack of ability to cope with the downward spiral of events that may be occurring. Without the necessary support network, this spiral may eventually lead to withdrawal from the sport.

There are many physical symptoms associated with burnout, some of which are similar to over-reaching and **overtraining**. When year-round training is involved, particularly without consideration of optimal periodisation (see **training methods**), there is a distinctly elevated risk for developing symptoms of athletic burnout. Various physical, immunological and hormonal variations are associated with training overload, including an increase in viral infections, resting heart rate and muscle soreness. Furthermore, burnout may also result in a reduction in sleep capacity, appetite, body mass, and aerobic power. Athletes who are suffering from burnout may be susceptible to a greater risk of injury and encounter constant feelings of fatigue and lethargy.

Athletic burnout is one manifestation of overtraining. Overtraining refers to the physiological and psychological maladaptions to chronic periods of excessive physical work. When an athlete is diagnosed with overtraining syndrome, a long-term period of rest is usually required to return the body to a homeostatic condition. However, due to the presence of a distinct devaluation of personal achievement and loss of interest in competition, often with other emotional and psychological difficulties, it is evident that burnout is a complex issue associated with more factors than overtraining alone. It appears that athletic burnout contains a far greater capacity to reduce physical performance than overtraining.

Emotionally, one major factor contributing to athletic burnout is a shift in life priorities. A perceived need to focus on the future often arises in athletes following unsuccessful participation in competition. This shuffling of goals may be detrimental to future performance, as the athlete may wish to lead a life that is perceived as 'normal'. Elite athletes who devote their lives to competition may have difficulties socialising with the non-athletic population. As nutritional discipline and adequate rest are two primary contributors to performance, social outlets may be limited. Furthermore, the repetitive and routine nature of training produces boredom in some athletes, and the individual nature of some activities may reduce the level of social support received from peers. Despite often being outwardly confident, individual athletes may feel isolated and without a support network. In situations such as these, early identification by coaches is necessary to prevent the development of long-term, perhaps irreversible, problems. Without such support athletes may feel isolated and turn their back on their sporting endeavours.

Athletic burnout does not necessarily result in withdrawal from the particular sport. Resulting from a large investment of time and physical and emotional energy, and the prospect of future success in the sport, the athlete may feel unable to quit (Schmidt and Stein 1991). Following long-term participation in a sport, the athlete may perceive that his or her identity lies with the sport, and that, in quitting, they would be surrendering their identity.

The methods recommended to prevent or overcome burnout are similar to those used for overtraining. The most effective method of preventing athletic burnout appears to be the prescription of an appro-priately periodised training plan, incorporating adequate recovery and scheduled time away from the sport. If symptoms of over-training and burnout appear, there are several exercises to perform to minimise or even reverse the effects. These include: setting short term goals that are achievable; avoiding monotony by incorporating a fun element into various training drills; learning imagery and self-talk techniques; dissociation from the activity; physical **relaxation training** techniques; communication of negative feelings to members of a support network; and maintaining physical condition and nutrition. It is also necessary to monitor progress in relation to goals during recovery from burnout. It is the responsibility of coaches to ensure that the training load follows a sensible progression, while it is the responsibility of athletes to ensure that they communicate their feelings to their peers and support network.

References

Coakley, J. (1992) 'Burnout Among Adolescent Athletes: A Personal Failure or Social Problem?', *Sociology of Sport Journal* 9, 2: 271–85.

Raedeke, T.D. (1997) 'Is Athlete Burnout More Than Just Stress? A Sport Commitment Perspective', *Journal of Sport and Exercise Psychology* 19, 4: 396–417.

Schmidt, G.W. and Stein, G.L. (1991) 'Sport Commitment: A Model Integrating Enjoyment, Dropout, and Burnout', *Journal of Sport and Exercise Psychology* 8, 2: 254–65.

Smith, R.E. (1986) 'Toward a Cognitive-affective Model of Athletic Burnout', *Journal of Sport Psychology* 8, 1: 36–50.

ARON MURPHY
MARK WATSFORD

C

CALCANEAL APOPHYSITIS (SEVER'S DISEASE)

The most frequent cause of heel pain in prepubertal schoolchildren is repeated microtrauma to the heel causing calcaneal apophysitis, irritation of the heel bone growth plate. Symptoms decrease with heel cushioning and calf muscle stretching.

The calcaneal apophysis, attached to the primary ossification center by growing cartilage, caps the back, sole and sides (posterior only) of the heel bone. The Achilles tendon inserts into the posterior superior aspect of the apophysis and the plantar fascia to the inferior (sole) distal portion. The mechanical tension from the Achilles tendon and plantar fascia press the apophysis firmly against the primary ossification so avulsion fracture of this apophysis is very rare.

Most children with calcaneal apophysitis have poor flexibility of the gastrocnemius, postulated to be an etiologic factor. Many do have normal flexibility, however, and impact alone can cause pain. Children with flat feet rarely suffer from calcaneal apophysitis, probably because their feet flatten rapidly with walking or running, leading to load-sharing by the entire foot rather than load acceptance by a small spot on the heel in the normal or cavus (high-arched) foot configuration.

Most cases are bilateral, but unilateral symptoms may occur. Unilateral heel pain is more likely than bilateral to be caused by infection, tumor or stress fracture. Infection is often preceded by a minor injury such as stepping on a tack. Intraosseous cyst or lipoma within the calcaneus may cause pain, especially after a single, hard impact or during rapidly increasing sport training. Calcaneal stress fracture occurs in older athletes, when the growth plate is near closure or has closed.

Some children note their greatest pain and tenderness at the Achilles insertion. Others hurt at the plantar fascia origin, center of the plantar surface, or the medial and lateral apophyseal lines. Some hurt in all these areas. Focal swelling suggests contusion or infection. Skin and subcutaneous tissue redness, swelling, and tenderness are related to infection. A broad calcaneus may result from an expansile tumor, an acute fracture, or – very rarely – a slipped apophysis. Gastrocnemius flexibility is tested by dorsiflexing the child's ankle with the knee straight and the heel in varus (subtalar joint inverted). In this position, ten degrees of dorsiflexion above the neutral position should be possible.

When symptoms are bilaterally symmetric, diagnostic imaging may be omitted if the child responds rapidly to treatment. For unilateral cases or atypical bilateral cases, lateral and axial radiographs of the calcaneus are recommended. Radionuclide bone scan, magnetic resonance imaging or computed tomography may occasionally be needed for further evaluation of abnormal physical examination or X-ray findings.

Treatment of symptomatic calcaneal apophysitis includes gaining normal flexibility (if it is abnormal at presentation) and decreasing heel impact. Viscoelastic heel pads made from silicone or similar materials often bring immediate, nearly complete relief when used in a well padded sneaker with a firm heel counter. Gymnasts or other athletes who perform barefoot may find relief with an integrated air-heel cushion device or a viscoelastic pad attached to an ankle sleeve. Occasionally a child requires a removable walking boot that immobilizes the ankle and foot to become asymptomatic. Viscoelastic heel pads may be placed in the boot. Very rarely a well molded below-knee walking cast is needed for 3–4 weeks.

Rehabilitation includes strengthening the calf, posterior tibial, and foot intrinsic muscles. Running and landing mechanics should be evaluated for excessively hard heel strike, followed by optimizing the running and landing patterns. Any training errors noted in the history should be corrected, and a gradually progressive return to sport program designed. As with other apophysitis symptoms, calcaneal apophysitis may recur until the vulnerable stage of development has passed.

See also: physeal (growth plate) fractures; stretching

Reference

Micheli, L.J. and Ireland, M.L. (1987) 'Prevention and Management of Calcaneal Apophysitis in Children: An Overuse Syndrome', J Pediatr Orthop 7, 1: 34–8.

ANGELA D. SMITH

CANNABINOIDS

The term cannabinoids refers to compounds containing the active ingredient Δ-9-tetrahydrocannabinol (THC), such as marijuana and hashish. Although difficult to classify pharmacologically, this psychoactive substance is considered a euphoriant and its effects have been documented for many centuries by a variety of cultures. THC is lipophylic and easily absorbed by a variety of routes including oral, inhalation and combustion. It is the second most commonly used drug by athletes (after alcohol) and is primarily utilized as a recreational drug.

The effects of THC encompass a multitude of bodily systems, with the central nervous system being the target organ of the user. Although the athlete is obviously using THC to obtain a euphoriant effect, the actual effects demonstrate large individual variability and often depend on the route of administration and prior experience of the user. The most consistently observed effect is on the cardiovascular system, in which THC causes tachycardia, lowered upright blood pressure, elevated supine systolic blood pressure and conjunctival erythema. All of these effects are seen following the acute ingestion of THC; chronic use may increase plasma volume through an unknown mechanism.

Owing to the fact that THC usually enters through the lungs following combustion, the acute and chronic effects on the pulmonary system have been widely studied. Acute ingestion produces bronchodilation and can increase oxygen consumption at rest. With chronic inhalation, THC can produce bronchitis, air flow obstruction, asthma and hyper-reactivity of the airways. There is also the potential for lung cancer since the tar produced by marijuana smoke is more carcinogenic than an equivalent weight of tobacco smoke.

Although marijuana is used extensively by athletes, there are few studies on the effects of THC on exercise. Given the above effects and the fact that THC impairs motor coordination, it is not surprising that studies have demonstrated an attenuation of exercise capacity following THC ingestion. Studies using athletes have demonstrated lowered peak exercise performance, a decreased maximum work capacity and an increased metabolic rate. Additional studies of acute THC ingestion revealed a decrement in reaction time and the ability to perform psychomotor tasks. The mixture of alcohol (see **alcohol – doping and nutrition**) and marijuana demonstrates an additive effect in terms of performance reduction, a significant finding given that the two are often used in combination. The existing literature clearly demonstrates the ergolytic effects of marijuana.

Many sports organizations have banned the use of THC and include it in their drug-testing programs. Although it is clearly not ergogenic, the ban is often justified because (1) athletes are considered role models; (2) to discourage the use of a substance that reduces performance; and (3) for athlete safety. THC is a strongly lipophylic substance and as a result can be detected for several weeks after ingestion. Most organizations set a cut-off level of 12–15 $ng\,ml^{-1}$ for THC. These levels are high enough to distinguish between passive inhalation of marijuana smoke and actual use. Owing to its half life of two weeks and popularity, a positive test for THC is frequently encountered in the athletic population. When evaluating an athlete with a positive drug test for THC, it is incumbent on the professional to thoroughly review the athlete's drug history and not merely focus on marijuana use. In the author's experience, athletes with a positive test for THC are more likely to have a problem with drugs other than THC, such as alcohol or cocaine. It is not unusual for an athlete to test positive for THC due to its long half life, but to have a significant cocaine problem that did not show up because of its short half life.

GARY GREEN

CAPILLARIES

The primary function of the vascular system is to deliver blood carrying essential gases and nutrients to tissue, and to remove metabolic by-products from the tissue. The arteries and arterioles function to deliver blood, while venules and veins return blood to the heart. However, the exchange of nutrients and gases – oxygen and carbon dioxide – between the blood and tissues occurs exclusively within the capillaries. Among the components of the vascular system, the capillaries exhibit several unique features. Unlike the arteries, arterioles, venules, or veins, the walls of the capillaries are not surrounded by smooth muscle. Additionally, the walls of these vessels are only a single cell thick. Flattened and rounded endothelial cells make up the capillary walls.

Beyond the thin walls of the capillaries, the extracellular matrix is more porous than at other sites of the vascular system. This, too, contributes to the considerable diffusive capacity that is essential to the function of capillaries. This diffusion can occur directly across the endothelial cells, or through clefts found within the junctions that join together these cells. For example, lipid soluble molecules – including oxygen and carbon dioxide – simply move through the endothelial cells according to their concentration gradients. Thus, at metabolically active tissue, oxygen leaves the blood and enters the interstitium before crossing into the cells. In contrast, carbon dioxide produced by the tissue, first diffuses into the interstitium before passing through the lipid-based membrane of the endothelial cells and into the blood.

Electrolytes and other hydrophilic substances may also be exchanged with the blood at the capillaries by diffusion, but must do so by passing between the endothelial cells at the junctions. Because the structure of these intercellular junctions varies among different tissues, so does the capillaries' diffusive capacity for substances that are not lipid soluble. For example, in the central nervous system 'tight' junctions join endothelial cells together. These junctions feature no intercellular clefts and, accordingly, are impermeable to any substance. Thus, only molecules that can diffuse through endothelial cells – carbon dioxide, oxygen, water – and those that have specific transporters can be exchanged between the blood and cerebral spinal fluid. It is the presence of these tight junctions that is the basis of the 'blood-brain barrier' that enables robust homeostatic control of the central nervous system's environment. Conversely, at the liver – which demonstrates a rich exchange of substances with the blood – capillary endothelial cells are joined loosely by junctions, resulting in wide intercellular clefts. These clefts tolerate a high rate of diffusion into and out of the capillaries and permit the exchange of sizable molecules. In skeletal muscle, the permeability of endothelial cell junctions is moderate and sufficient to allow intermediate sized molecules, such as glucose and most electrolytes, to diffuse effectively through capillary walls. Throughout the body, the unhindered exchange of water between blood and tissues is due to water moving both across endothelial cell membranes and between the cells through junction clefts.

Other anatomical features of the capillary system permit effective exchange of materials between the blood and tissue. Each artery gives rise to six to eight arterioles, each of which then divides into two to five capillaries. As a result of this branching, a total of approximately ten billion capillaries in the body provide a surface area of 500–700 m^2. Since the rate of blood flow through the vascular system is inversely proportional to total surface area, the transit time of circulating erythrocytes and nutrients through the capillaries is dramatically increased. For example, flow rate at the aorta is roughly 500 mm s^{-1}, but at the capillaries

this rate is diminished to 0.5 mm s^{-1}. This, in turn, greatly enhances the potential for oxygen and nutrient extraction from the blood and into the tissue.

The diameter of capillaries is so small, about 7 μm, that much of the erythrocyte is directly in contact with the walls of the capillary. This close physical contact also improves gaseous exchange. Finally, because of the extensive branching of the body's capillary network, no cell within the body is separated from a capillary by more than 20–30 μm. Such proximity is imperative for gaseous exchange, since passive diffusion is the means by which movement can occur.

Because of the many capillaries distributed through the body, it is impossible to perfuse simultaneously all capillary beds fully without causing systemic shock. Accordingly, the number of capillaries transporting blood is determined by the metabolic activity – the oxygen demand – of any particular tissue. Moreover, as oxygen uptake varies in any one area of tissue, so too does the number of capillaries recruited for blood perfusion. In resting skeletal muscle, for example, blood flows through only about one tenth of the capillaries present. This proportion increases concomitantly with the increase in oxygen demand.

Although diffusion is the primary mechanism used by capillaries to exchange substances with tissue – through the interstitium – it is not the only one. Both bulk flow and transcytosis contribute to the movement of molecules and fluid between the blood and the interstitium. In transcytosis, vesicles carry specific molecules, usually large ones, through the endothelial cells comprising the capillary. Even larger substances pass between the endothelial cells in transiently formed channels that are derived from pits lining the basal surface of the endothelial cells. In both cases, the exchange of substances between the blood and surrounding tissue is permitted by the formation of membranous vesicles, and both modes are termed transcytosis. This process is of vital importance, because it enables blood-borne cytokines and proteins that are essential to inflammation to leave the blood in specific areas to assist in maintaining the health of local tissue.

In contrast to transcytosis, mainly fluid, along with small molecules, are exchanged across the capillary wall in bulk flow. In contrast to diffusion, in which each molecule in question moves according to its own specific concentration gradient, and independently of the transport of others, bulk flow entails the exchange of substances across the capillary in unison. Here, all movement of water and solute occurs in the clefts separating the constituent endothelial cells of the capillary. The direction of this movement, into or out of the capillary, depends on the potency of the opposing hydrostatic pressure and colloid osmotic pressure. These pressures are exerted both by the blood within the capillary and by the interstitial fluid surrounding the vessel. Hydrostatic pressure exerts force away from the source while colloid osmotic pressure yields an attractive force acting to inhibit the movement of water from the same source. Obviously, the rate and direction of net flow will depend on the sum of hydrostatic and colloid osmotic pressures inside the capillary compared to the sum of those pressures within the interstitium.

Near the arteriole end of the capillary there is a net pressure that favours filtration of fluid out of the capillary and into the interstitium. Yet the result of this movement, combined with the increased resistance to blood flow along the length of the capillary, causes a sharp drop in hydrostatic pressure within that capillary as it approaches the vein. As a result, there is a net pressure favourable to the re-uptake of fluid back into the capillary – absorption – along its venous end. Under normal conditions, however, there is a net efflux of plasma from the capillaries to the interstitium at a rate of two to five litres per day. This fluid

is then taken up by, and circulated through, the lymphatic system before being returned to the bloodstream, thus maintaining proper blood volume.

Further reading

Guyton, A.C. and Hall, J.E. (1996) *Textbook of Medical Physiology*, ch. 16, Philadelphia PA: W.B. Saunders.
Sherwood, L. (1997) *Human Physiology: From Cells to Systems*, ch. 10, Belmont CA: Wadsworth.

MICHAEL R. DESCHENES

CARBOHYDRATE METABOLISM

Glucose is transported to the tissues of the body by the circulatory system; take-up by the various tissues of the body occurs through insulin and the use of carrier proteins known as glucose transport proteins. Once glucose has entered the muscle fiber it is either stored or utilized depending upon the energy needs of the fiber. After entering the muscle fiber, glucose is phosphorylated into glucose 6-phosphate. At this point the glucose is either utilized to produce energy or stored as glycogen. Glycogen is the primary storage form of carbohydrate and can be used as an energy substrate. The primary storage sites for glycogen are the liver ($\sim 100\,g$) and muscle ($\sim 350\,g$). Concentrations of muscle and liver glycogen can be affected by both training and dietary manipulations.

Carbohydrates are the only fuel source that can be utilized to generate energy without the use of oxygen. Thus, the use of carbohydrates as an energy source during anaerobic metabolism is important. The extent to which anaerobic and aerobic metabolism are active depends on the intensity and duration of the activity.

The glycolytic energy system involves the process by which carbohydrates are broken down to produce adenosine triphosphate (ATP). The enzymes needed in glycolysis are readily available in the sarcoplasm of muscle fibres. The process of glycolysis is commonly broken down into aerobic – with oxygen – and anaerobic – without oxygen. These terms originated from early research, which found that, in the presence of oxygen, glycolysis proceeds at a slow rate and forms pyruvic acid; therefore, aerobic glycolysis is also termed slow glycolysis. When oxygen is not present in sufficient amounts, glycolysis produces lactic acid rapidly; therefore, anaerobic glycolysis is also termed fast glycolysis. The initial steps of glycolysis are identical, only the end products of fast and slow glycolysis are different. The end products of both forms of glycolysis occur as a result of the energy demands of the cell. When a high rate of energy production is needed, such as during high-intensity exercise, fast glycolysis is the primary supplier of energy.

Aerobic glycolysis utilizes the end product of slow glycolysis, pyruvate, which is passed into the mitochondria to be metabolized. Once in the mitochondria, the pyruvate is metabolized through the Krebs cycle, which is a series of enzymatic reactions that continues the oxidative process begun by glycolysis.

See also: carbohydrate supply; carbohydrate types

Further reading

Hargreaves, M. (1995) 'Skeletal Muscle Carbohydrate Metabolism During Exercise', in M. Hargreaves (ed.) *Exercise Metabolism*, 41–72, Champaign IL: Human Kinetics.
Spriet, L.L. (1995) 'Anaerobic Metabolism During High-intensity Exercise', in M. Hargreaves (ed.) *Exercise Metabolism*, 1–39, Champaign IL: Human Kinetics.

JEFFREY A. POTTEIGER

CARBOHYDRATE SUPPLY

The three **carbohydrates** that are significant as dietary sources for the body are starch, sucrose, and lactose. These sources of carbohydrates are found in grain products, fruits, vegetables, some diary products, and sugar cane. The average American consumes approximately 40–50 per cent of his or her total caloric consumption from carbohydrates. It is recommended that individuals who are engaged in heavy training consume between 55–70 per cent of their daily caloric consumption from carbohydrates.

Polysaccharides such as cellulose, hemicellulose, and pectins are not digestible and are the primary components of dietary fiber. Inulin, galactogens, mannosans, and raffinose occur in some fruits and vegetables and are partially digestible to monosaccharides. Starches that are glucose polymers are the only polysaccharides found in foods that are completely digested. For the body to utilize carbohydrates they must be broken down into monosaccharides.

Digestion of carbohydrate begins in the mouth, where food is broken down into smaller particles. Breaking down the food exposes more surface area to the salivary juices, which contain the enzyme amylase. Amylase initiates the breakdown of polysaccharides to monosaccharides, including starches to maltose, and disaccharides to two molecules of the monosaccharide glucose. As the food moves into the stomach, the low hydrogen ion concentration (pH) of the stomach contents inactivates amylase. Minimal amounts of carbohydrates are broken down in the stomach as a result of acid hydrolysis. After passing through the stomach the food moves into the duodenum of the small intestine. Pancreatic enzymes facilitate the digestive process of breaking down carbohydrates into maltose, maltotriose, and a mixture of dextrins. Eventually all carbohydrates are broken down into the monosaccharides glucose, galactose, and fructose. Glucose is the major monosaccharide used in energy metabolism; any galactose or fructose that is absorbed into the blood is converted to glucose by enzymes present in the liver.

Glucose is transported to the tissues of the body by the circulatory system. Glucose uptake by the various tissues of the body occurs through the use of carrier proteins known as glucose transporters. The glucose transporters used by skeletal muscle are referred to as glucose transport proteins 1 and 4.

Exercise of the presence of insulin stimulates an increase in glucose transport. Insulin is secreted by the β-cells of the islets of Langerhans located within the pancreas. Insulin release is increased when blood glucose is high to accelerate the transport of glucose into the cell. The increase in glucose transport into the cell stimulated by insulin occurs through the glucose transporter protein 4, which is the major isoform for the transport of glucose into muscle. Once glucose has entered the cell it is either stored or utilized depending upon the energy needs of the cell. After entering the cell, glucose is immediately phosphorylated into glucose 6-phosphate. The phosphorylation of glucose to glucose 6-phosphate effectively traps glucose in the cell. At this point, the glucose is either utilized through glycolysis or stored as glycogen. The phosphorylation of glucose is controlled by the enzymes glucokinase in the liver and hexokinase in the muscle fibers.

Glycogen is the primary storage form of carbohydrate in muscle and is used as an energy substrate for exercise. Limited stores of glycogen are available during exercise. The primary storage sites for glycogen are the liver and muscle. The liver contains about 100 g of glycogen, while skeletal muscle contains about 350 g. Glycogen concentrations of both the muscle and liver under resting conditions can be affected by training and dietary manipulations.

See also: carbohydrate metabolism; carbohydrate types; carbohydrates and the liver

Further reading

Febbraio, M.A., Chiu, A., Angus, D.J., Arkinstall, M.J. and Hawley, J.A. (2000) 'Effects of Carbohydrate Ingestion Before and During Exercise on Glucose Kinetics and Performance', *Journal of Applied Physiology* 89: 2220–6.

Febbraio, M.A., Keenan, A.J., Angus, D.J., Campbell, S.E. and Garnham, A.P. (2000) 'Preexercise Carbohydrate Ingestion, Glucose Kinetics, and Muscle Glycogen Use: Effect of the Glycemic Index', *Journal of Applied Physiology* 89: 1845–51.

JEFFREY A. POTTEIGER

CARBOHYDRATE TYPES

Carbohydrates are groups of molecules that are created from carbon (C), hydrogen (H), and oxygen (O). The simple stoichiometric formula $(CH_2O)_n$, where n is a positive integer, is generally accepted as representing the chemical make-up of carbohydrates. Carbohydrates can be divided into three main categories: monosaccharides, oligosaccharides, and polysaccharides.

Monosaccharides are the simplest of all the carbohydrate molecules. The monosaccharide classification of carbohydrates can be further subdivided into three major categories: glucose, fructose, and galactose. All of the three major monosaccharides contain six carbon, twelve hydrogen, and six oxygen atoms. Glucose and fructose are widely present in nature, occurring in fruits and honey. The simplicity of the glucose molecule makes it easy for the body to break down. Therefore, the glucose molecule is the most common carbohydrate found in the circulatory system. Galactose does not exist freely in nature. It is found in combination with glucose as the molecule lactose, the sugar found in milk.

When monosaccharides bond together, they can form the more complex molecules that create both oligosaccharides and polysaccharides. Oligosaccharides are generally disaccharides that are created from two to ten monosaccharides chemically bonded together. The three main disaccharides in biological functions are sucrose, lactose, and maltose. The combination of the monosaccharides glucose and fructose yield the disaccharide sucrose, which is found in refined cane and beet sugar. Lactose is created by the bonding of glucose and galactose and is found in milk. Maltose is created by the bonding of two molecules of glucose, and is found in grains. The breakdown of maltose, sucrose, or lactose yields glucose.

Polysaccharides are considered to be complex carbohydrates. They are composed of ten or more monosaccharides bonded together in a linear or complex branching chain. Starch and glycogen are a type of polysaccharide with a primary function of carbohydrate storage in plants and animals. Glycogen is a storage form of carbohydrates and is found in the liver and muscles of animals.

The three carbohydrates that are significant as dietary sources are starch, sucrose, and lactose. These sources of carbohydrates are found in grain products, fruits, vegetables, some diary products, and sugar cane. The average American consumes about 40–50 per cent of his or her total caloric consumption from carbohydrates. It is recommended that individuals who are engaged in heavy exercise consume between 55–70 per cent of their total caloric consumption from carbohydrates.

Polysaccharides such as cellulose, hemicellulose, and pectins are indigestible and are the primary components of dietary fiber. Insulin, galactogens, mannosans, and raffinose occur in some fruits and vegetables and are partially digestible to monosaccharides. Starches that are glucose polymers are the only polysaccharides found in food that can be completely digested. For the body to utilize carbohydrates they must be broken down into monosaccharides.

Digestion of carbohydrate begins in the mouth, where food is broken down into smaller particles. Breaking down the food exposes more surface area of the food to the salivary juices, which contain the enzyme amylase. Amylase initiates the breakdown of polysaccharides to monosaccharides, including starches to maltose and disaccharides to two molecules of glucose. As the food bolus moves into the stomach, amylase is inactivated by the low hydrogen ion concentration (pH) of the stomach contents. Minimal amounts of carbohydrates are broken down in the stomach as a result of acid hydrolysis. After passing through the stomach the food moves into the duodenum of the small intestine. Pancreatic enzymes facilitate the digestive process of breaking carbohydrates into maltose, maltotriose, and a mixture of dextrins. Eventually all carbohydrates are broken down into the monosaccharides glucose, galactose, and fructose. Glucose is the major monosaccharide used in energy metabolism; any galactose or fructose that is absorbed into the blood is converted to glucose by enzymes present in the liver.

See also: carbohydrate metabolism; carbohydrate supply

Further reading

Febbraio, M.A., Chiu, A., Angus, D.J., Arkinstall, M.J. and Hawley, J.A. (2000) 'Effects of Carbohydrate Ingestion Before and During Exercise on Glucose Kinetics and Performance', *Journal of Applied Physiology* 89: 2220–6.
Febbraio, M.A., Keenan, A.J., Angus, D.J., Campbell, S.E. and Garnham, A.P. (2000) 'Preexercise Carbohydrate Ingestion, Glucose Kinetics, and Muscle Glycogen Use: Effect of the Glycemic Index', *Journal of Applied Physiology* 89: 1845–51.

JEFFREY A. POTTEIGER

CARBOHYDRATES

All living tissues contain carbohydrates. Plants provide the major source of carbohydrates in the human diet. Carbohydrates contain carbon and water. The combination of carbon (C), hydrogen (H) and oxygen (O) atoms forms a molecule of carbohydrate with the general formula $(CH_2O)_n$, where n equals between three to seven carbon atoms. The hydrogen and oxygen are attached by single bonds. Carbohydrates with five and six atoms are of the most interest nutritionally. Glucose is the most common carbohydrate and has the formula $C_6H_{12}O_6$. Carbon bonds not linked to other carbon atoms are able to accept hydrogen and oxygen, or an oxygen-hydrogen combination. Fructose and galactose, two other simple sugars, have the same chemical formula as glucose, but with a slightly different carbon-to-hydrogen-to-oxygen linkage. Fructose and galactose each have their own biochemical characteristics.

Four types of carbohydrates exist: monosaccharides, disaccharides, oligosaccharides, and polysaccharides. The most common monosaccharides are glucose, fructose, and galactose. Glucose occurs naturally in food, but can be derived from the breakdown of more complex carbohydrates and from gluconeogenesis. Fructose occurs in fruits and honey. Galactose does not occur freely in nature, but is found in milk sugar. Disaccharides contain glucose as the principal component. The three disaccharides of nutritional significance are sucrose, lactose, and maltose. Sucrose is the most common dietary disaccharide and contains glucose and fructose. It is found in sugars, syrups, and honey. Lactose is found only in milk and consists of glucose and galactose. Maltose is composed of two glucose molecules. It is found in beer, cereals, and germinating seeds. Oligosaccharides are formed by combining between three and nine monosaccharides. Polysaccharides consist of from ten to thousands of monosaccharides linked together. Starch is the form of polysaccharide found in plants, with glycogen as the form of polysaccharide found in animals. Fibre is classified as a non-starch polysaccharide and includes cellulose, a material that resists breakdown by human digestive enzymes.

See also: carbohydrate supply; carbohydrate types

Further reading

Febbraio, M.A., Chiu, A., Angus, D.J., Arkinstall, M.J. and Hawley, J.A. (2000) 'Effects of Carbohydrate Ingestion Before and During Exercise on Glucose Kinetics and Performance', *Journal of Applied Physiology* 89: 2220–6.

Febbraio, M.A., Keenan, A.J., Angus, D.J., Campbell, S.E. and Garnham, A.P. (2000) 'Preexercise Carbohydrate Ingestion, Glucose Kinetics, and Muscle Glycogen Use: Effect of the Glycemic Index', *Journal of Applied Physiology* 89: 1845–51.

JEFFREY A. POTTEIGER

CARBOHYDRATES AND THE LIVER

The liver is responsible for regulating blood glucose concentrations in the body. When glucose concentrations are elevated, for example after a meal, the liver helps to regulate blood glucose by increasing the conversion of glucose to fatty acids. When glucose concentrations are reduced, as during fasting, starvation, or exercise, the liver will increase glucose release into the circulatory system by glycogenolysis or gluconeogenesis. About 90 per cent of gluconeogenesis occurs in the liver. Gluconeogenesis is the formation of glucose from non-carbohydrate precursors, including lactate, pyruvate, glycerol, and the carbon skeletons of amino acids. Gluconeogenesis is basically a reversal of glycolysis with the exception of three irreversible reactions involving the enzymes pyruvate kinase, phosphofructokinase, and hexokinase or glucokinase. There are, however, reactions in gluconeogenesis that can circumvent these three irreversible reactions and allow for glucose formation.

Both glycolysis and gluconeogenesis occur in the cytosol of the liver and, therefore, must be tightly regulated so that simultaneous activity of both pathways does not occur. Two hormones reciprocally regulate glycolysis and gluconeogenesis – insulin, which stimulates glycolysis, and glucagon, which stimulates gluconeogenesis. During conditions of elevated blood glucose, for example after a meal, insulin concentrations are elevated and glucagon concentrations are reduced and glycolysis is stimulated. During conditions of low blood glucose – such as starvation, fasting, and prolonged exercise – insulin concentrations are reduced while glucagon concentrations are increased and this favors gluconeogenesis. Cortisol, a hormone released by the adrenal cortex during periods of prolonged exercise or carbohydrate depletion, can also influence gluconeogenesis. Cortisol promotes protein breakdown, which increases the number of amino acid precursors available for participation as gluconeogenic precursors in the liver.

During exercise, an increased release of glucose from the liver is important to maintain blood glucose concentrations within acceptable ranges and thereby avoid hypoglycaemia. Hepatic glucose production increases two-to tenfold during moderate-to high-intensity exercise. Hepatic glucose output rises linearly with exercise intensity up to 50–60 per cent of maximal aerobic power (VO_2 max), and then increases exponentially with the relative intensity, despite a gradual decline in blood flow to the liver. During moderate-intensity exercise at less than 60 per cent VO_2max, blood glucose concentration remains relatively constant, despite a marked rise in glucose uptake in contracting skeletal muscle. This indicates that hepatic glucose output is closely matching muscle glucose uptake. This occurs as long as sufficient stores of carbohydrate are available in the liver. As exercise becomes more intense (>60 per cent VO_2 max), blood glucose concentration is usually found to increase in humans, indicating that the hepatic glucose output exceeds glucose uptake by contracting skeletal muscle.

During the transition from rest to exercise, liver glucose production increases owing to an increase in both liver glycogenolysis and gluconeogenesis. During moderate-to high-intensity exercise of short duration – less than 30 min – 85–95 per cent of the increase in liver glucose output is caused by an increase in glycogenolysis. Hepatic gluconeogenesis contributes only about 5–15 per cent of the total liver glucose output during the first 60 min of exercise. When exercise is continued for longer durations – greater than 60 min – liver gluconeogenesis contributes 20–25 per cent of liver glucose output. Clearly the relative contribution of **glycogenolysis** and gluconeogenesis in the liver is determined by both the intensity and duration of exercise.

It is generally believed that the main regulatory mechanism for hepatic glucose production is a change in blood glucose concentration. A decrease in plasma insulin and an increase in glucagon concentrations result in an increase in glucose production by the liver. Exercise-induced increases in hepatic glucose production are also paralleled by a rise in plasma epinephrine and norepinephrine. Cortisol and growth hormone may also play a minor role in stimulation of hepatic glucose production during exercise by increasing the availability of gluconeogenic precursors.

See also: carbohydrate metabolism

Further reading

Kjaer, M. (1995) 'Hepatic Fuel Metabolism During Exercise', in M. Hargreaves (ed.) *Exercise Metabolism*, 73–98, Champaign IL: Human Kinetics.

JEFFREY A. POTTEIGER

CARBON ISOTOPE RATIO TESTING

Carbon isotope ratio (CIR) testing is part of **anabolic-androgenic steroid testing** that helps detect the misuse of **anabolic-**

androgenic steroids normally produced in the human body (endogenous steroids) or of their precursors. Most carbon atoms are ^{12}C, but approximately 1.1 per cent of them are ^{13}C, and the CIR is the ratio of $^{13}C/^{12}C$ or delta value. There is a measurable difference in ^{13}C content between endogenous and pharmaceutical testosterone (T) because they arise from different pathways. CIR testing is done by gas chromatography-combustion-isotope ratio mass spectrometry of urine extracts. All carbon atoms in the compound of interest are oxidized to carbon dioxide. The end result is not the absolute $^{13}C/^{12}C$ ratio, but the difference, or delta value, between the $^{13}C/^{12}C$ ratio of the sample and that of an international standard. For example, a delta value of −24 per mil for natural T means that it contains that much less ^{13}C than the standard: 24 fewer parts per thousand. Pharmaceutical T contains less ^{13}C than endogenous T and has a lower delta value, for example −31 per mil.

Before CIR testing was applied in sport, the analytical methods in use could not distinguish pharmaceutical T from endogenous T. Since the early 1980s, the **International Olympic Committee (IOC)** rule has based the detection of T administration on the ratio of T to an analog, epitestosterone (E), in urine. As of 2003, the Olympic Movement Anti-Doping Code states that a urinary T/E greater than six 'constitutes an offence unless there is evidence that this ratio is due to a physiological or pathological condition'. Drug tests based on T/E may miss cases with T/E < 6 in which T (or both T and E) might have been used, or lead to reporting cases in which the elevated T/E might be natural. Additional approaches to distinguishing T users from non-users include measuring related urinary hormones or subjecting the individual to a diagnostic 'ketoconazole' test, an endocrine evaluation, or follow-up T/E tests. The T/E in drug-free adult males is stable over time, and a spike indicates abuse.

CIR testing can help resolve far more than cases of suspected T abuse. Following pharmaceutical T administration, the delta values of urinary T metabolites will drop. In contrast, the delta values of T precursors, or of endogenous steroids not involved in T **metabolism**, will not change. Such compounds can be used as endogenous references. A gap in delta value between T or its metabolites and an endogenous reference compound indicates abuse of T or of any steroid in its metabolism. Looking for such gaps is a superior approach because the delta value of T itself in a non-user might be affected by factors such as diet and be difficult to interpret alone, and because such gaps reveal the abuse of any one of many T precursors and metabolites. CIR testing has indeed been applied to various T precursors, T metabolites, and endogenous reference compounds. Mostly the test is done to obtain additional information to consider when deciding whether an elevated T/E, perhaps together with T/E values over time, other urine tests, or a medical history, are consistent with the misuse of male hormones.

See also: anabolic-androgenic steroid testing; prohormone supplements

References

Becchi, M., Aguilera, R., Farizon, Y., Flament, M.-F., Casabianca, H. and James, P. (1994) 'Gas Chromatography/Combustion/Isotope-ratio Mass Spectrometry Analysis of Urinary Steroids to Detect Misuse of Testosterone in Sport', *Rapid Commun. Mass Spectrom.* 8: 304–8.

Olympic Movement Anti-Doping Code, Prohibited Classes of Substances and Prohibited Methods 2003. http://www.wada-ama.org/docs/web/ research_science/prohibited_substances/ Prohibited%20Classes%20of%20Substances %20and%20Prohibited%20Methods% 202003.pdf [accessed 28 August 2003].

Shackleton, C.H.L., Roitman, E., Phillips, A. and Chang, T. (1997) 'Androstanediol and 5-Androstenediol Profiling for Detecting Exogenously Administered Dihydrotestosterone,

Epitestosterone, and Dehydroepiandrosterone: Potential Use in Gas Chromatography Isotope Ratio Mass Spectrometry', *Steroids* 62: 665–73.

CAROLINE K. HATTON

CARDIAC REHABILITATION

Cardiac rehabilitation can be defined as a comprehensive long term program that is designed to limit the physiological and psychological effects of cardiovascular disease, control cardiac symptoms and to reduce the risk of subsequent events by stabilizing or partially reversing the underlying arteriosclerosis process through risk factor modification. A modern day cardiac rehabilitation program will include patients who have had coronary artery bypass surgery, coronary angioplasty, myocardial infarction, pacemaker implantation, cardiac transplantation, valve replacement, and also patients with evidence of cardiovascular disease such as a positive stress test, or angina pectoris.

What are the aims of modern day cardiac rehabilitation?

The main aim of cardiac rehabilitation is to prevent the progression of arteriosclerosis and partially reverse arteriosclerosis through aggressive improvements in the reversible risk factor profile (cigarette smoking, hypertension, hyperlipidaemia, obesity, physical inactivity, diabetes mellitus) of the patient. Other aims are to improve functional capacity, control symptoms, reduce the risk of sudden death, reduce the risk of reinfarction and new CAD events, improve the quality of life and vocational status, and reduce costs of long-term medical care in these patients.

How is cardiac rehabilitation conducted?

Cardiac rehabilitation should start in hospital, and must become a lifelong activity.

Modern day cardiac rehabilitation is undertaken by a multi-disciplinary team comprising a sports medicine specialist, cardiologist, physiotherapist, biokineticist, nursing staff, nutritionist, and psychologist. Traditionally, cardiac rehabilitation has been divided into four phases, but it is important to see these phases as a continuum.

Phase I – inpatient cardiac rehabilitation

The purpose of Phase I is to reduce deconditioning caused by prolonged bed rest. The indications to start Phase I cardiac rehabilitation are: young age, small infarction, stable blood pressure, absence of cardiac failure, no dyspnoea at rest, no chest pain, or no arrhythmias.

Patients can begin exercising within forty-eight hours of the onset of myocardial infarction or a revascularization procedure. Exercise training consists of range-of-motion exercises, intermittent standing or sitting and walking, and is conducted by a physiotherapist or cardiac sister. Psychological and life-style counseling are also important. At this stage, the details of the further phases of cardiac rehabilitation can be discussed with the patient and the family.

Phase II – few days post-discharge up to six weeks

This phase represents a transition phase from the time of discharge from hospital until the patients is mobile and can attend a formal outpatient program. The duration of this phase can vary from days (for example in the case of a patient with no myocardial infarction but who underwent an uncomplicated angioplasty) to weeks (following coronary artery bypass grafting). This phase should be initiated as soon as possible after hospital discharge, and the exercise prescription is based on the results of a low-level exercise test before discharge from the hospital. This test is not always performed and patients are often discharged only with the instruction to undertake gentle walking exercise until the patient is entered into a formal cardiac rehabilitation program (Phase III).

Phase III – outpatient supervised for twelve weeks

Phase III cardiac rehabilitation is usually conducted at a dedicated venue with facilities for exercise training and resuscitation. Prior to entering this phase patients undergo a full medical assessment, including a musculoskeletal assessment, dietary consult, and psychological screening. In addition, a maximal exercise stress test is performed, and baseline muscle strength, flexibility, and endurance tests are conducted. The results of these tests are important as they are used for levels of risk stratification and exercise prescription.

Once baseline assessment and risk stratification is complete, patients start with formal attendance and rehabilitation. Patients are encouraged to start training three times per week, which is later progressed to training on most days of the week. Exercise training sessions are typically conducted for 30–60 min. Activities include a warm-up and cool down phase, stationary cycling (early in the program), walking or jogging, aqua-aerobics, circuit weight training, relaxation classes and aerobics classes.

Each patient is given an individualized training program based on their exercise test results, their functional test result and their musculoskeletal limitations. Patients are also taught how to exercise safely and to monitor exercise intensity by using heart rate monitoring or the rating of perceived exertion (RPE).

An important component of this phase is to monitor all the risk factors through regular (1) blood pressure checks at rest and during exercise once per week; (2) blood lipid profile checks (every three months);

(3) body mass index or per cent body fat (every month); (4) blood glucose monitoring before and after exercise (in diabetic patients); (5) psychological screening and monitoring; and (6) smoking cessation programs. The minimum duration of a Phase III program is three months, after which a repeat medical and functional assessment is performed. At this stage the patient undergoes a re-evaluation of the risk stratification, and high-risk patients are encouraged to continue with the Phase III program under medical supervision. Intermediate and low-risk patients can continue to the Phase IV rehabilitation.

Phase IV – unsupervised, lifelong program

Phase IV cardiac rehabilitation is an extended, unsupervised ongoing maintenance program and hopefully is of lifelong duration. Following the repeat assessment which is conducted after Phase III, patients who are stratified as low or intermediate risk can be given an exercise prescription, which can be followed in an unsupervised manner (home training or at an exercise facility). Regular re-assessments followed by alteration in the exercise prescription should be conducted on these patients (every six months for 1–2 years and then annually thereafter). In future, monitoring and adjustment of exercise programming will likely occur using information technology. There are already facilities in some countries where information from a heart rate monitor can be downloaded to a central facility where the information can be processed, and exercise prescription can be monitored and adjusted.

What are the benefits of regular exercise training in phases II, III, and IV of cardiac rehabilitation?

The following are the proven benefits of longstanding cardiac rehabilitation:

- improved functional capacity and exercise tolerance
- improved cardiovascular efficiency
- reduced cardiac symptoms or symptoms of heart failure
- reduction in risk factors for cardiac disease
- increased serum HDL concentrations
- decreased body weight and per cent body fat
- decreased serum triglyceride concentrations
- decreased blood pressure
- improved glucose tolerance
- reduced fibrinogen concentrations
- reduced platelet
- increased release of t-PA
- increased nitric oxide (NO) or endothelium derived relaxing factor (EDRF) release
- arrhythmia stabilization with reduced risk of ventricular fibrillation
- improvement in coronary blood flow, reduced myocardial ischaemia and severity of coronary arteriosclerosis
- reduction in risk of cardiovascular disease mortality
- improvement of psychosocial well being, quality of life and vocational status of patients
- early detection of symptoms and signs of progressive disease

Are there any risks during cardiac rehabilitation?

Provided sound scientific and medical guidelines are followed, the risk of complications during cardiac rehabilitation is low. In a large study it was found that for any particular rehabilitation program, the complication rate was one non-fatal myocardial infarction per 294,000 patient-hours of exercise, and one fatal event per 784,000 patient-hours of participation.

See also: hyperlipidaemia; pulmonary rehabilitation

220

References

Leon, A.S. (2000) 'Exercise Following Myocardial Infarction. Current Recommendations', *Sports Med* 29: 301–11.

Stewart, K.J., Badenhop, D., Brubaker, P.H., Keteyian, S.J. and King, M. (2003) 'Cardiac Rehabilitation Following Percutaneous Revascularization, Heart Transplant, Heart Valve Surgery, and For Chronic Heart Failure', *Chest* 123: 2104–11.

MARTIN SCHWELLNUS

CARDINAL PLANE MOVEMENTS

Flexion is the movement in the sagittal plane about the frontal axis away from the middle of the body (see **cardinal planes and axes**), in which the angle between two body segments decreases – a 'bending' movement. The movement is to the anterior, except for the knee, ankle, and toes. Hyperflexion is sometimes used to describe flexion of the upper arm beyond the vertical. Extension is the return movement from flexion. Continuation of extension beyond the reference position is called hyperextension, the return movement from which is usually referred to as flexion (the more precise anatomical term, reduction of hyperextension, is rarely used in sport and exercise biomechanics). Dorsiflexion and plantar flexion are used, respectively, to define ankle joint extension – the foot moving towards the anterior surface of the leg – and flexion – the foot moving towards the posterior surface of the leg. These are best defined relative to the dorsal and plantar surfaces of the foot to correspond to flexion and extension of the wrist. Some textbooks define dorsiflexion as flexion, based on it being a closing of the angle between the two relevant segments. This inconsistency in terminology is unhelpful to students of sports biomechanics.

Abduction is the sideways movement in the frontal plane about the sagittal axis away from the middle of the body or, for the fingers, away from the middle finger.

Radial flexion, or radial deviation, denotes the movement of the middle finger away from the middle of the body and can also be used for the other fingers. Hyperabduction is sometimes used to describe abduction of the upper arm beyond the vertical. Adduction is the return movement from abduction, towards the middle of the body or, for the fingers, towards the middle finger. Ulnar flexion, or ulnar deviation, denotes the movement of the middle finger towards the middle of the body and can also be used for the other fingers. Continuation of adduction beyond the reference position is called hyperadduction, the return movement from which is usually called abduction (the more precise anatomical term, reduction of hyperadduction, is rarely used in sport and exercise biomechanics).

Lateral flexion to the right or left defines the sideways bending of the trunk to the right or left and, normally, the return movement from the opposite side. Eversion and inversion refer to the raising of the lateral and medial border of the foot, respectively. Eversion cannot occur without the foot tending to be displaced into a toe-out – abducted – position and, likewise, inversion tends to be accompanied by adduction. Pronation of the foot is a combination of eversion and abduction, along with dorsiflexion of the ankle. Supination involves inversion, adduction, and plantar flexion. These terms should not be confused with pronation and supination of the forearm (see later).

Lateral, or external, rotation describes the inward rotation of the leg or arm in the horizontal plane about the vertical axis; medial, or internal, rotation describes the outward rotation of the leg or arm in the horizontal plane about the vertical axis. Lateral and medial rotations of the forearm are referred to, respectively, as supination and pronation. Rotation to the left and right are the rather obvious terms for horizontal plane movements of the head, neck, and trunk. Horizontal flexion, or horizontal abduction, and horizontal extension, or horizontal adduction, define the rotation of the arm about the shoulder, or the leg about the hip, from a position of 90° abduction. Movements from any position in the horizontal plane towards the anterior are usually called horizontal flexion and those towards the posterior horizontal extension.

See also: cardinal planes and axes; joints

Further reading

Bartlett, R.M. (1997) *Introduction to Sports Biomechanics*, ch. 1, London: E&FN Spon.

ROGER BARTLETT

CARDINAL PLANES AND AXES

To specify clearly and unambiguously the movements of the human musculoskeletal system in sport, exercise, and other activities, we need to define an appropriate scientific terminology. While 'raising arms' may be acceptable in everyday language, it is ambiguous; the movement could be to the side, to the front or in any diagonal plane. A description of human movement requires the definition of a reference position or posture, from which these movements are specified. Two are used. The fundamental position is familiar as it closely resembles the military 'stand to attention'. With the exception of the forearms and hands, the fundamental and anatomical reference positions are the same. In the fundamental position, the forearm is in its neutral position, neither pronated nor supinated. In the anatomical position, the forearm has been rotated from the neutral position so that the palm of the hand faces forwards: as the name implies, this is anatomically the basic reference position. Movements of the hand and fingers are defined from this position, movements of the forearm around the radioulnar joints are defined from the fundamental position and movements at other joints can be defined from either.

Various terms are used to describe the three mutually perpendicular – orthogonal – intersecting planes in which many, though not all, joint movements occur. Obviously, many such orthogonal systems can be described, depending on their common point of intersection. This point is most conveniently defined as either the centre of the joint being studied or the **centre of mass** of the whole human body. In the latter case, the planes are known as cardinal planes. The sagittal plane is a vertical plane passing from posterior to anterior, rear to front, dividing the body into left and right halves; it is also known as the anteroposterior plane. The frontal plane is also vertical and passes from left to right, dividing the body into posterior and anterior – back and front – halves; it is also known as the coronal plane. The horizontal plane divides the body into superior and inferior – top and bottom – halves; it is also known as the transverse plane.

Movements at the joints of the musculoskeletal system are largely rotational, and take place about a line perpendicular to the plane in which they occur. This line is known as an axis of rotation. Three axes can be defined by the intersection of pairs of the above planes of movement. The sagittal axis passes horizontally from posterior to anterior and is formed by the intersection of the sagittal and horizontal planes. The frontal axis passes horizontally from left to right and is formed by the intersection of the frontal and horizontal planes. The vertical or longitudinal axis passes vertically from inferior to superior and is formed by the intersection of the sagittal and frontal planes.

In three-dimensional kinematic analysis of the orientations of body segments, the angles between adjacent body segments can be defined by reference to coordinate systems attached to each segment, one considered to be moving relative to a fixed position of the other. The resulting Euler or Cardan angles correspond to the anatomical angles discussed above and in **cardinal plane movements**. The rotational motion of the moving segment is represented by three ordered angles of rotation about its coordinate system; the rotation angles are dependent on the sequence of rotations, one of the major problems of the Euler-Cardan angle method of defining segment orientations.

See also: joints; kinematics

Further reading

Bartlett, R.M. (1997) *Introduction to Sports Biomechanics*, ch. 1, London: E&FN Spon.

ROGER BARTLETT

CARDIOVASCULAR ADAPTATIONS TO TRAINING

Training induces changes in the heart, blood, and haemodynamics. The effect of a prolonged training programme on the heart is that, anatomically, the wall of the left ventricle becomes thickened and the left ventricle enlarged, with overall mild cardiac hypertrophy – an increase in the volume of the heart. This returns towards normal when the training programme is stopped. The enlargement of the ventricle and thickened wall makes the heart a more powerful pump, and we therefore see an increase in stroke volume – the amount of blood ejected with each heart beat – during submaximal and maximal exercise as well as at rest. Besides the cardiac enlargement – increased stroke volume – enhanced myocardial contractility contributes to this adaptation.

Related to the increase in stroke volume, is an increase in maximal cardiac output – the volume of blood pumped each minute – with aerobic training. Since cardiac output equals stroke volume multiplied by heart rate, resting heart rate is reduced as a consequence of the increased stroke volume because the total cardiac output remains unchanged at rest. That is, the same cardiac output can be achieved with a lower heart rate owing to the higher stroke volume. It is common to find that the submaximal exercise heart rate is lowered by 10–20 beats min^{-1} for the same reason. At maximal exercise, the cardiac output is increased, even though maximal heart rate may be slightly reduced or unchanged, again because of the substantial increase in stroke volume that occurs. The increase in cardiac output enhances oxygen delivery to, and removal of metabolites from, the active muscle.

Plasma volume increases after just a few training sessions, which may be a method to facilitate oxygen delivery to the muscles during exercise. There is also a small increase in the amount of oxygen extracted from the blood on its passage through the muscles, particularly during maximal exercise. This can be measured as a small increase in the arteriovenous oxygen difference after training but, generally, this measure changes very little with training. Although plasma volume increases, there is no corresponding increase in red cell mass. Therefore, haematocrit and haemoglobin concentrations may actually decline slightly after training. This could be mistaken for a clinically 'low' haemoglobin concentration, but may be within normal range for a well trained individual.

Both systolic and diastolic blood pressures at rest are slightly reduced by regular training. Therefore, aerobic training is a potentially useful means to reduce blood pressure in hypertensive patients. During exercise, there is both systolic and diastolic blood pressure decrease at the same submaximal exercise load. At maximal exercise, systolic blood pressure shows no effect of training, but diastolic pressure may be lowered. Coronary blood flow is reduced

both at rest and during submaximal exercise as a consequence of training, but maximal flow, such as during maximal exercise, is unchanged or slightly increased. In the muscle, blood flow through the active muscles is unchanged or slightly decreased during submaximal exercise after training, but there is a substantial increase in blood flow through the active muscle mass during maximal exercise.

See also: cardiac rehabilitation

Further reading

Brooks, G.A., Fahey, T.D., White, T.P. and Baldwin, K.M. (2000) *Exercise Physiology: Human Bioenergetics and Its Applications*, Mountain View CA: Mayfield.

Noakes, T.D. (2003) *Lore of Running: Discover the Science and Spirit of Running*, Cape Town: Oxford University Press.

ANDREW BOSCH

CARDIOVASCULAR ISSUES FOR SENIORS

Anatomical and neurological changes affecting the heart and blood vessels as we grow older reduce cardiovascular function, which has the knock-on effect of decreasing aerobic exercise capacity. At the level of the heart, changes in left ventricular diastolic function and a reduction in maximum heart rate lead to a decline in maximum cardiac output. However, the conduit vessels needed to transport blood to the exercising muscles also undergo anatomical and functional changes. A decline in elasticity, coupled with an increase in wall thickness and an impaired vasodilatory capacity of medium and large arteries with advancing age, can act to reduce limb blood flow during exercise. Since aerobic exercise needs to be supported by a good supply of oxygen, and oxygen transport to the exercising muscles is dependent upon adequate blood flow, these age-related cardiovascular changes

223

which limit blood flow during exercise also reduce aerobic exercise capacity. Studies have shown that cardiorespiratory capacity declines at the rate of 10 per cent per decade from early adulthood, which can drastically reduce sustainable exercise intensity in later years. Regular aerobic exercise in middle to old age can evoke good improvements in cardiac function and arterial compliance, thereby improving blood flow and 'putting the brakes on' the age-related decline in cardiovascular function. However, no amount of exercise training can totally reverse the age-related cardiovascular changes that have an adverse impact on exercise performance.

Blood pressure has a tendency to rise with increasing age in most Western societies. A combination of genetic and environmental factors influence the rise in blood pressure with advancing age, and determine whether blood pressure increases beyond normal limits. If resting systolic blood pressure rises above 140 mm Hg and/or resting diastolic blood pressure rises above 90 mm Hg, this is classified as hypertension. Hypertension is a major risk factor for cardiovascular events such as stroke and myocardial infarction, two of the leading causes of death in Western society. Regular physical activity can help to control resting blood pressure, and can have an important role in the treatment of hypertension. Research has shown that aerobic exercise training which utilises large muscle groups in a dynamic and rhythmical fashion elicits reductions in resting blood pressure, or at least helps to retain blood pressure within normal limits as we age. Aerobic exercise training is also recommended for individuals with mild hypertension. Even though it is a normal response for systolic blood pressure to increase during moderate intensity aerobic exercise, blood pressure should not rise to dangerous levels in mild hypertensive individuals during this type of activity. Elderly hypertensive individuals have been shown to respond positively to

regular aerobic exercise training, with reductions in resting blood pressure being reported. A lowering of cardiac output and peripheral vascular resistance at rest, together with a reduction in circulating catecholamines and renin, are possible mechanisms by which regular exercise exerts its blood-pressure lowering effect.

Resistance training (weightlifting exercise) as an exercise intervention by itself has not consistently been observed to produce a blood-pressure lowering effect. However, as an adjunct to aerobic exercise training, mild-to moderate-intensity resistance training can improve muscular strength and endurance (thereby helping to prevent or manage musculoskeletal conditions associated with increasing age) and can modify coronary risk factors. As blood pressure can be increased alarmingly during intense static (isometric) muscular contractions with large muscle groups, performance of high force isometric (or dynamic) muscle actions, such as those performed during one-repetition maximum strength testing, should be avoided in individuals with elevated blood pressure.

Older individuals who have previously experienced chest pain, irregular, rapid or fluttery heart beats or severe shortness of breath should seek the advice of a physician before engaging in a programme of exercise training. Alternatively, the physical activity readiness questionnaire (PAR-Q) is a screening tool that can be used to identify individuals requiring a physician's evaluation before participation in physical activity. An appropriate warm-up before exercise provides a period of cardiovascular and metabolic adjustment that older individuals must incorporate into all training sessions. The warm-up should last for at least 10–15 min and should engage the same muscle groups in activities that are similar to the muscular movements to be performed in the main exercise session. This can be immediately followed by 3–5 min of gentle mobility exercises, in which relevant joints are moved through their range of motion. An adequate warm-up can improve exercise performance and the gradual 'mobilisation' of the cardiovascular system from the resting state can decrease the risk of ischemic or dysrhythmic events. This latter point is particularly important for older individuals.

An appropriate cool-down should also be used after a period of exercise training to help clear metabolic waste products such as lactic acid, and prevent the effects of post-exercise hypotension (lowering of blood pressure). Post-exercise hypotension can be encountered immediately after aerobic exercise with large muscle groups, resulting in a feeling of 'light-headedness'. During exercise, the rhythmic contraction and relaxation cycles of active muscles help to 'massage' blood back to the heart. However, if exercise stops suddenly and the heart continues to pump high volumes of blood into the dilated blood vessels of muscles that are no longer contracting, this can lead to a 'pooling' of blood in the muscles and a diminished return of blood back to the heart. The immediate consequence can be a reduction in blood pressure that compromises blood flow to the brain, leading to feelings of light-headedness. Some individuals are more susceptible to this than others. However, to reduce the likelihood of this happening, the large active muscles should always be kept moving during rest cycles within the training session (particularly the large leg muscles), fluids should be liberally consumed to ensure maintenance of blood volume and a proper 'cool-down' should be implemented at the end of training that gradually brings the heart rate back to resting levels.

JOHN M. SAXTON

CARRYING CAPACITY

The term carrying capacity originates in animal husbandry, referring to the amount of livestock which can be carried per hectare of land, and is also used in regard to the ability of countries or continents to sustain human populations. The principles involved in the use of the term in the area of sport and recreation are similar. In this context carrying capacity, or recreation carrying capacity, is generally used in relation to natural areas of land or water and refers to the amount of sporting or recreational use which a site can accommodate sustainably – that is, without causing long-term or irreversible damage to the site. Conceptually this is a simple idea, but complexity arises in seeking to measure usage and sustainability and hence in arriving at a measure of carrying capacity. The situation is further complicated by the fact that the impact of sporting and recreational use on the environment can be modified by design and management practices. It has been suggested that there are a number of types of carrying capacity: psychological, economic, ecological, and physical.

Psychological, or perceptual, carrying capacity relates to the issue of crowding, as perceived by users of a site. This idea is particularly relevant to sparsely used areas – for example, wilderness areas, where hikers or mountaineers may feel their experience to be less enjoyable if they consider that the number of other users of the site is excessive. However, some activities – for example many forms of motor sport – have traditionally required crowds for maximum enjoyment. Some sources refer to this particular notion of carrying capacity as 'social' carrying capacity, since perceptions are partly shaped by social conditions – thus the level of use which is considered to be 'crowded' or 'congested' will vary among cultures and age-groups.

Economic carrying capacity refers to a level of usage which is commensurate with an economically sustainable operation. For example, the point at which a particular level of sporting activity causes so much wear and tear to a site that the on-going costs of maintenance become greater than the revenue available from user fees, could determine the economic carrying capacity of the site.

Ecological carrying capacity refers to the ability of the flora, fauna, and other natural systems of a site to withstand the effects of sporting and recreational impacts.

Physical carrying capacity is particularly relevant to organised sporting activities – for example, the capacity of a white-water rafting facility will be limited, at least in the medium term, by the number of craft and leaders available and possibly by available overnight accommodation. The physical capacity of sports pitches is determined by the number of players in a team, the length of matches, the physical quality of the surface, and the availability of floodlighting.

In practice all four come together when the recreational carrying capacity of a site is considered. Three dimensions must be taken into account: the level of use, the type of use, and the type of resource – as shown in Figure 6. The Recreation Opportunity Spectrum (ROS) terminology is used here to indicate a range of resources from the highly developed (ROS category 'modern'), such as a sports pitch or urban park, to the most natural (ROS category

'primitive'), such as a wilderness. Beaches and national parks of varying levels of use and development fall into the intermediate categories. 'Activity impact level' refers to the innate characteristics of a sporting activity and its consequent likely impact on the environment – thus, for example, hiking and canoeing are generally seen as low-impact activities, while motorised sports are generally high-impact activities. An activity which is 'high impact' in one type of area may be 'low impact' in another – for example, activities involving motorised vehicles are likely to be high impact in an area without hard surface tracks, but may be low impact where such tracks are available. What constitutes high, medium, and low usage levels will also vary according the type and size of the site.

Situation A presents little difficulty for management, even though the usage level and activity impact level are both high, since the capacity of a 'modern' facility or site is generally determined by its design and management and can be modified as required. Situation C is at the other extreme, with low activity impact, low usage and a 'primitive' site, but in general should also present few challenges to management. Situation B, with high usage and

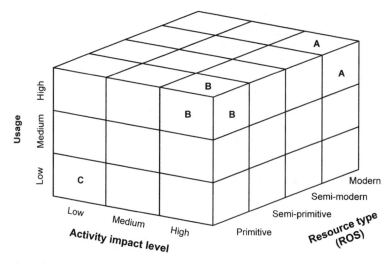

Figure 6. Relationship between usage level, impacts and resource type.

high activity impact level in a primitive area is likely to present particular difficulties if the resource is suffering damage. Typically, in a primitive area, the option of increasing carrying capacity is limited or non-existent since measures such as the provision of hard-surface tracks or measures to stabilise banks in a water area, would alter the intrinsic nature of the resource. The only solution is to restrict the quantity and/or type of usage – at least in peak periods.

All the above statements are qualified, since there are no hard and fast rules. Thus even a 'modern' site may reach a point where its capacity cannot, or should not, be increased and even apparently very low usage levels at some 'primitive' sites can be damaging. Ultimately, a scientific judgement must be made as to the likely physical effects of a given level of usage on a site. When that is known, a managerial or political decision must be made as to whether to do nothing and accept the damage to the resource, to restrict user access or to modify the site to increase its effective capacity.

Further reading

Lindberg, K., McCool, S.F. and Stankey, G. H. (1997) 'Rethinking Carrying Capacity', *Annals of Tourism Research* 24, 2: 461–4.

Pigram, J. J. and Jenkins, J. M. (1999) *Outdoor Recreation Management*, 90–6, London: Routledge.

A.J. VEAL

CARTILAGE INJURY

The joints are covered with articular cartilage, which is supported by underlying subchondral bone. A synovial lining surrounds the joints with an external layer of capsule and surrounding ligaments and muscles. A layer of synovial fluid is normally present in the joint, which is primarily responsible for decreasing friction and providing nutrition for the chondrocytes. The principal function of articular cartilage is load transmission as well as smooth motion of the joint.

The articular cartilage is made of cellular and extracellular components. The cells are called the chondrocytes, which secrete extra cellular matrix and are quite active. The extra cellular matrix is made up of water, proteoglycans, and collagen. Water makes up to 60–80 per cent of the wet weight. The collagens are proteins that give strength to the cartilage. In the cartilage primary collagen is type II but other types of collagens are also present. The collagens form a framework in which is trapped proteoglycans, which are either keratan sulphate or chodroitin sulphate.

The cartilage is an avascular structure. It is also aneurgenic and has no lymphatics. The metabolic function of chondrocytes is dependant on the movement of fluid across the articular cartilage, which also provides nutrition to these cells. The cartilage has the property of deformation or compression in which the fluid exudes out in to the joint. In this way the cartilage not only remains well nourished but it also helps in even weight distribution through the joint.

The articular cartilage is made up roughly of four layers: the superficial, middle, deep, and a calcified layer. The orientation of collagen in these layers is different, with more parallel arrangement of collagen in the superficial layers and vertical orientation in the deeper layers.

The articular cartilage is prone to injury, and as it is avascular the repair process is slow as well as incomplete. This also is dependent on the type of injury. The acute injury, which includes intra-articular fractures as well as blunt trauma, disrupts the continuity of the articular cartilage. The subacute or chronic injuries are produced due to intrinsic failure or abnormal distribution of weight. The type of injury to the cartilage also varies from a slight abrasion to complete disruption down to the subchondral bone.

227

The superficial lesions of the articular cartilage do not heal at all, as there is no vascular supply and no inflammatory response occurs. The deeper defects go right down the subchondral bone, where the inflammatory process is generated leading to the production of different cells and collagen which is type I rather than the type II which is normally found in the healthy cartilage. This alters the biomechanical properties of the articular cartilage, which can result in pain and loss of motion.

The size of the lesion also has a role in the future reparative process and the prognosis of joint lesion. If the defect is greater than a centimetre than it is likely that it will be covered with a fibrocartilage rather than the original cartilage.

In the acute cases where there has been an intra-articular fracture, it is vital to restore the joint congruity. Many studies have shown development of early degenerative changes in the articular cartilage if there is a step or a gap in the articular surface. Also, early fixation of these fractures allows early motion in the joint, which is vital for the nutrition and repair of the articular cartilage.

In chronic cases the cartilage wears out, and this may be due to many different pathologies like osteoarthritis, rheumatoid arthritis, metabolic diseases, septic arthritis, malalignment of limbs, ligament dysfunction, or a variety of congenital problems like developmental dysplasia of hips seen in the newborn. Septic arthritis is an emergency. Once the diagnosis is made with aspiration and gram staining then a thorough wash-out of joint is a must. Patients are also started on broad-spectrum antibiotics until the definitive culture result is back, at which time the antibiotics are changed according to the sensitivities.

Inflammatory arthritis, like rheumatoid arthritis, affects many joints and also the cervical spine. Patients can present with major disabilities. The treatment of these patients requires a multidisciplinary approach.

Rheumatologists need to be consulted for these cases, as there are anti-inflammatory medications which can help in decreasing the inflammation and possibly prolonging the life of the joint. Other conditions like ankylosing spondylitis affect the spine, which requires evaluation and possible treatment. Skin disorders may also be associated with inflammation of the joints like psoriasis. Extra care is required while performing joint replacements in this subgroup of patients, as there is a higher risk of infection.

All these conditions lead to acute or gradual wear of the articular cartilage. The disruption of the cartilage means that the subchodral bone is exposed. Bone-on-bone motion is painful and there is restriction of movement. The soft tissues around the joint also contract and various deformities occur. The process continues with loss of subchondral bone leading to marked stiffness and pain, and ultimately loss of mobility. Patients present with pain, limp, restriction of joint motion, and use of a support with limitation of general mobility. The clinical examination needs thorough evaluation of the patient as a whole, with examination of other joints as well as spine examination. The involved joint is usually but not always swollen. There is restriction of movements, which may also be very painful. The integrity of soft tissues around the involved joint needs evaluation, as they may also be affected and need addressing at the time of surgery. Fixed flexion deformities occur in both the knee and the hip arthrosis. The patient should have laboratory investigation. Radiographs can show the formation of subchondral sclerosis, cysts, loss of joint space, or osteophytes in cases of osteoarthritis, and may show osteopenia in cases of rheumatoid arthritis. In the early stages magnetic resonance imaging can delineate areas of cartilage injury.

Abnormal force transmission may also result from deficiency of ligaments such as the anterior cruciate ligament in the knee joint. This produces abnormal motion in the joint, which can damage the meniscus and also lead to future degeneration of the articular cartilage. Likewise a menisectomy can produce supraphysiological load transmission and development of abnormal contact and degenerative changes.

For younger patients and those with early stages of cartilage degeneration there are many options. These include simple debridement, microfracture, autologus chondrocyte implantation, mosaicplasty, fresh osteochondral allografts, osteotomies, and even total replacement of the joint if all else fails.

In the late stages of cartilage degeneration total joint replacement is an excellent option. It relieves pain and restores function. Patients are able to regain the quality of life they once enjoyed. The prosthesis has seen a major improvement in design and material. The survival rate of these implants has increased and thus even young patients are able to benefit from joint replacement.

The articular cartilage is a very unique structure and is frequently affected in younger patients suffering from trauma or sporting injury. This can lead to future increased morbidity, with loss of working days and huge costs to the health services, as the cost of joint replacement is high. Cartilage transplantaion is done in many centres around the world. Fresh osteochondral allograft addresses the problem of both bone loss and cartilage loss. However, long-term results are still awaited to confirm the reliability of the procedure.

IMRAN ILYAS

CATASTROPHE MODELS

The catastrophe paradigms were originally derived by Thom and developed by Zeeman as mathematical models for describing discontinuities that occur in the physical world. Thom believed that natural phenomena are seldom symmetrical or well ordered but instead are characterised by sudden transformations and discontinuities. It was primarily dissatisfaction with the symmetrical orderly decline in performance suggested by the inverted-U hypothesis that led Hardy and associates (e.g. Hardy 1990) to apply a catastrophe model to the anxiety – performance relationship.

Although several catastrophe models have been developed, the most commonly used in practice is the cusp catastrophe model. The cusp catastrophe model is three-dimensional and tries to explain the interactive effects of cognitive anxiety and physiological arousal upon performance (see Figure 7). The model predicts that increases in cognitive anxiety will have a facilitative effect upon performance at low physiological arousal, but a debilitative effect upon performance at high physiological arousal.

More specifically, with low cognitive anxiety, or worry, increases in physiological arousal are related to performance by an inverted-U relationship (the back part of the figure). However, with increases in cognitive anxiety, increases in physiological arousal can improve performance to an optimal point, beyond which additional arousal causes a dramatic or catastrophic decline in performance (the front part of the figure). Once such a performance decrement has occurred, it can only be reversed by a significant

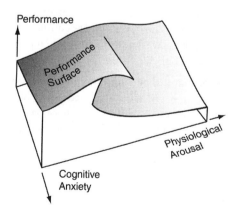

Figure 7. The cusp catastrophe model of anxiety and performance.

reduction in physiological arousal beyond where the original decrement in performance occurred. Recovery will probably require an element of physical relaxation and some form of cognitive restructuring followed by controlled reactivation towards optimal functioning.

According to the cusp catastrophe model, an athlete's best absolute performance will occur under conditions of moderate to high cognitive anxiety. This would indicate to practitioners that cognitive anxiety or worry is not necessarily bad or debilitative to performance; the model predicts that you will perform better with some worry, provided that physiological arousal does not also become too high. Performance only really deteriorates under the combined conditions of high worry plus high physiological arousal.

Hardy (1990) has also proposed a higher-order model, called a butterfly catastrophe. This model incorporates self-confidence. The model hypothesises that self-confidence can help protect against cognitive anxiety by moving the point of catastrophe – at the front of the figure – further towards the right. This proposal not only advocates the independent nature of cognitive anxiety and self-confidence, but also indicates that self-confidence could play a powerful role in athletic performance.

The strengths of these models involve their ability to explain complex interactions between variables and how they may affect performance; however, their complexity can also be a weakness because this makes the model difficult to test.

See also: arousal and activation; arousal and activation – effects of experience; arousal and activation – effects of personality; arousal and activation – individual differences; arousal and activation strategies; arousal and activation theories; Yerkes-Dodson law

Reference

Hardy, L. (1990) 'A Catastrophe Model of Performance in Sports', in J.G. Jones and L. Hardy (eds) *Stress and Performance in Sport*, 81–106, Chichester: John Wiley.

Further reading

Hardy, L., Jones, G. and Gould, D. (1996) *Psychological Preparation for Sport: Theory and Practice for Elite Performers*, Chichester: John Wiley.

IAN MAYNARD

CATCHMENT AREA

The term 'catchment area' derives from the phenomenon of river catchments – that is the area from which water drains into a river system. By analogy, the idea has been applied to sports facilities to mean the geographical area from which the facility draws its users or members. The idea is used in planning for sport, since the size of the typical catchment area of a facility determines the number and distribution of facilities required in a given planning area. It is also used in marketing, which may be concentrated on the existing catchment area or may be deliberately aimed at seeking to extend the catchment area. Indeed, an alternative term for the catchment area of a facility is its 'market area'.

Most sports facilities, such as swimming pools, sports centres and golf courses, attract some users from considerable distances. This might be because people move away from a neighbourhood but wish to remain in touch with their friends, or because people may have business in an area which demands periodic visits; some users may even be tourists. In practice therefore, the catchment area is usually defined as the area from which most users travel to visit a facility. Some arbitrary figure, such as 75 per cent, is typically used to define 'most'. The term 'travel from' is used, since, while most users of most facilities travel from home, some may travel to the facility from their place of work or education. Such work-based or education-based users can be particularly significant for city centre-based facilities.

The size of catchment areas varies depending on the type of facility and type of user. Thus specialised facilities, such as purpose-built rowing courses, have larger catchment areas than standard facilities such as public swimming pools. Larger, newer facilities are generally more attractive to users and so tend to have larger catchment areas than smaller, older facilities. Facilities used mainly by adults will tend to have larger catchment areas than those of facilities used mainly by children. Within facilities, different types of user may have different catchment areas from others – for example, the pensioners' keep fit session will have a different catchment area from the keep fit sessions attended by young professionals.

It is possible to establish the catchment area of a facility by means of a user or visitor survey – interviewing users of existing facilities to discover where they have travelled from. Although a user survey is desirable it is not always necessary, at least for initial appraisals: it is possible to infer catchment areas from user surveys carried out at similar facilities elsewhere. Thus, for instance, it has been found that about 75 per cent of users of urban public swimming pools in the UK travel from within one mile of the pool, so in planning, an approximate assessment of requirements using one-mile radius circles is a possibility.

In cases where all users of a facility must be members, membership records can be utilised as the basis for estimating catchment areas – the membership form becomes, in effect, a questionnaire for gathering data. The problem with membership records, however, is that the spatial distribution of *membership* may not reflect the distribution of *regular users* – for example, people who live close to a facility may use it more frequently than people who live far away. This information would, however, be captured in situations where records are kept of actual attendances of members rather than simply records of membership. To deal with the phenomenon of users travelling from their place of work or school rather than from their home address, the membership form must also include this information.

Further reading

Veal, A.J. (2002) 'Planning Methods', in *Leisure and Tourism Policy and Planning*, ch. 7, 116–53, Wallingford, UK: CABI Publishing.

A.J. VEAL

CAUSE-RELATED MARKETING

Cause-related marketing is often said to be a win-win-win proposition. Corporations earn money and goodwill. Nonprofit sport organizations gain money and exposure. Consumers spend money and feel good about it. In cause-related marketing, capitalism becomes a philanthropic tool.

Cause-related marketing strives to achieve two objectives – to improve corporate performance and to help worthy causes – by linking donations to a cause (in this context, related to sport) with the purchase of the company's products or services. It aligns the financial objective of increasing sales with corporate social responsibility.

Cause-related marketing is defined as the process of formulating and implementing marketing activities that are characterized by an offer from a business to donate a specified amount to a designated cause or organization when customers purchase a given product or service. Most often this is done through the use of cents-off coupons; for each coupon redeemed, the business donates a fixed amount, frequently up to a pre-established ceiling, to the sport organization.

American Express coined and copyrighted the phrase cause-related marketing to differentiate campaigns that tie charitable contributions directly to product promotions, from standard corporate donations in which dollars are given outright to a charitable cause. Every time somebody used its products, the company made a cash contribution to its nonprofit partner. The nonprofit partner received not only the cash contribution but also extensive publicity. The company's promotional effort typically included an extensive advertising campaign that stressed the programs and community benefits that the nonprofit organization delivered, together with ways in which the public could assist the organization.

The rationale of American Express for using cause-related marketing was that local civic pride was a powerful stimulant to the sale and use of the company's products and services. At the same time, American Express gained the goodwill of a grateful community. In the words of their chairman: 'cause-related marketing is our way of doing well by doing good'.

American Express has been the most visible advocate of this approach; however, the principles that this company used have been applied on a smaller scale by local businesses in all sizes of communities, and can be adapted readily to meet the needs of sport organizations.

The chief executive officer of American Express has stated:

> The program works. At first, we didn't know whether we'd found a new way to help business or just an interesting formula for giving money away. It's both. The increase in business we've seen in our cause-related markets proves the concept is as successful as any marketing program we've ever tried. We're doing good deeds, and we're also pleased with the commercial results.

Each cause-related marketing program initiated by American Express began with an announcement that the company would donate a small sum to the cause each time one of its clients in the area:

- used the American Express card,
- purchased American Express travelers checks,
- purchased a travel package of $500 or more (excluding air fare) at an American Express vacation store, or
- applied for and received a new American Express card.

Thus, the size of donation to the selected cause depended on business done by the company in a specific geographic area during a set time period, which was typically three months.

However, it was the program's most distinctive feature – a tailor-made advertising campaign that described both the cause and the way in which American Express clients could help it – that most dramatically linked the two. Most sport organizations cannot afford either expert creative talent to write and design first-rate advertising or the money for placing advertisements that reach the target audience. When a cause-related program was implemented, the same talent and experience that went into other advertising efforts of American Express were harnessed to explain both the cause and program to clients.

The approach is particularly effective if other businesses also cooperate in the effort. An executive of American Express, commenting on the success of the whole cause-related marketing program, stated:

> One of the most gratifying aspects of the whole program was the way our business partners rallied around. Banks that were selling other brands of travelers checks began to prefer ours. Restaurants and retailers that never accepted any cards began accepting the American Express card. And hundreds of these businesses in many markets not only displayed point-of-purchase material but often participated by making marketing donations of their own.

The optimal length of a cause-related campaign is difficult to assess. A fine line exists between maximal exposure and customer fatigue. The most common timeframe is three months. That is long enough to generate sufficient publicity, establish a strong presence in consumers' minds, and give them time to buy. It is short enough that the campaign does not lose its novelty. It also corresponds with a calendar quarter, making it easy to track results.

In some cases companies have linked with annual events so that they reinforce previous campaigns in customers' minds. For example, Proctor and Gamble carried out a cause-related marketing campaign with the Special Olympics annually and raised millions of dollars for the cause. The repetition of the campaign cemented the association between the company and the Special Olympics and produced residual benefit to the company even at other times of the year.

Partnerships of this type also have emerged between banks that issue credit cards and sport organizations. Again, the banks are seeking to capitalize on the goodwill of people for the sport group with which they identify. For example, Manchester United offers a Visa affinity card to its supporters. Each time the card is used, the team receives 1 per cent of the amount charged. The club's marketing manager said, 'We find the card a good way for fans to support the club without paying any extra. This service gives fans the opportunity to support Manchester United.' In essence, a sports organization challenges its supporters to ask the question, 'Why use a bank card that just gives money to the bank, when you can use one that gives money to the organization you support?' By tapping people's loyalty to causes this way, banks have an opportunity to encourage card-switching and to increase their market share. The cost to the banks is relatively small because these payments reflect a small portion of what they earn from annual fees and the interest that they charge card holders. It is also a small part of the percentage of each transaction, which ranges from 1.5 per cent to 6 per cent, that they charge their participating merchants.

Cause-related marketing has opened an entirely new channel of monetary support for sport organizations. At the same time, and perhaps more importantly, cause-related marketing also harnesses the creative promotional talents of private companies to improve awareness levels and heighten interest in the sport organization.

JOHN L. CROMPTON

CELL STRUCTURE MODIFICATIONS WITH EXERCISE AND TRAINING

It has long been appreciated that the stimulus of exercise training results in significant morphological remodelling of muscle cells. However, the structural modifications observed are dependent upon the specific mode of exercise – endurance or resistance training. In sum, the changes elicited by endurance training will improve the muscle cell's potential for aerobic metabolism and, consequently, its capacity to perform submaximal contractions over a lengthy exercise duration. Conversely, the outcome of structural alteration induced by resistance training is an increased content of contractile proteins within the cell, allowing for greater maximal force production.

Typical adaptations to the muscle cell after endurance training include enhanced capillarity, an increased concentration of myoglobin, and greater mitochondrial density. The first two adaptations allow greater oxygen delivery to, and uptake by, the muscle cell. The improved mitochondrial content provides greater activity for the enzymes of the Krebs cycle and electron transport chain, augmenting the cell's ability to manufacture adenosine triphosphate (ATP) by oxidative phosphorylation. Endurance training has also been associated with an increased calcium channel density of the sarcoplasmic reticulum, improving calcium kinetics during muscle contractions. Combined, these modifications serve to delay the onset of muscle fatigue during prolonged exercise.

Resistance training stimulates protein accretion within the active muscle cells. These proteinaceous materials are used to synthesize myofilaments, which, in turn, are assembled into myofibrils. The greater number of androgenic hormone receptors noted in weight-trained muscle may assist this process. As the newly formed myofibrils are arranged in parallel to those already present within the muscle cell, the cross-sectional area of the cell is amplified, along with its capacity to generate contractile force. But as a result of this area expansion, the muscle cell's capillary and mitochondrial densities diminish.

MICHAEL R. DESCHENES

CELLULAR FUNCTION

The modern study of biology is based upon cell theory. Because of this overriding concept, all living organisms share a common construct and unifying theme. The basic principles of cell theory are:

- all organisms consist of cells and their products
- new cells and life arise only from pre-existing cells
- all cells feature the same essential chemical composition and metabolic processes
- the functional activities of each cell depend upon the specific structural properties of that cell
- the organism's structure and function are determined by the structural characteristics and functional capabilities of its cells

The cells of humans are categorized as eukaryotic since they possess a nucleus and other membrane-bound organelles. In contrast, prokaryotic cells, such as those of bacterial organisms, do not contain membrane-bound subcellular structures. In addition to the nucleus, virtually all eukaryotic cells possess six organelles: the endoplasmic reticulum, the Golgi complex, lysosomes, peroxisomes, mitochondria, and vaults. The nucleus and organelles exist within a gel-like medium, which itself is maintained within the cell by the lipid bilayer plasmalemma. This cytosol accounts for over 50 per cent of the cell's volume. Within the cytosol is a proteinaceous scaffolding referred to as the cytoskeleton. This cytoskeleton is composed of microfilaments, microtubules, and intermediate filaments. In most cells, the primary function of the cytoskeleton is to provide shape and structural integrity. In muscle fibres, however, the microfilaments are arranged in a unique design allowing for the specialised contractile function of muscle tissue.

In addressing the function of subcellular structures, the nucleus, which is not considered to be an organelle, will be discussed first. A rather porous double-layered membrane called the nuclear envelope binds the nucleus. Sequestered within the nucleus is the cell's genetic material – the deoxyribonucleic acid (DNA) – as well as the ribonucleic acid (RNA) needed to assemble the proteins encoded by the DNA. Indeed, all three forms of RNA – messenger RNA, ribosomal RNA, and transfer RNA – can be found within the nucleus, although each form must be translocated out of the nucleus through nuclear pores in the envelope before protein assembly can occur in the cytosol. The nucleus is also vital to the process of cell reproduction since the formation of a new cell begins with the doubling of the mother cell's DNA.

Among the organelles, the endoplasmic reticulum is perhaps the most extensively distributed throughout the cell. It resembles a continuous folding of flattened fluid-filled membrane sheets. The appearance, and function, of the endoplasmic reticulum can be categorised into rough or smooth. In rough endoplasmic reticulum, ribosomes are attached to the outer surface of the membrane; no ribosomes are found on smooth endoplasmic reticulum. At the site of the rough endoplasmic reticulum, ribosomes manufacture proteins that are released into the lumen of the endoplasmic reticulum for further processing and transport. In addition to proteins, various lipids are synthesised by the endoplasmic reticulum. Indeed, cells that specialise in lipid, particularly steroid, production are abundant in smooth endoplasmic reticulum, although lipid assembly may also occur within rough endoplasmic reticulum. Besides the synthesis of proteins and lipids, the endoplasmic reticulum may provide other important functions. For example, in muscle cells it serves as a storage depot for the calcium required to initiate contraction, while in the liver detoxifying enzymes are concentrated in the endoplasmic reticulum.

Located at the terminal segment of the endoplasmic reticulum, and operating in conjunction with that organelle, is the Golgi complex. Like the endoplasmic reticulum, the Golgi complex consists of flattened, fluid-filled membrane. But, unlike the endoplasmic reticulum, the membranous structure is organised as a collection of individual sacs known as a Golgi stack. Molecules newly synthesised by the endoplasmic reticulum are delivered to the neighbouring Golgi stacks to undergo the final stages of processing. At the completion of this task, the final product is packaged in a vesicle that is pinched off from the membrane of the Golgi complex. Once lodged within the vesicle, the contents can then be directed to other organelles within the cell, or secreted from the cell by exocytosis.

Lysosomes are organelles that contain as many as fifty different digestive enzymes that are capable of breaking down intracellular debris. Lysosomes also destroy bacteria and other foreign materials that may enter the cell. Most cells possess roughly 300 lysosomes, although the cells of the immune system – which functions to protect the organism from potentially infectious agents – contain considerably more of these organelles. Much like lysosomes, the membrane-bound peroxisomes mainly contain enzymes. But rather than the hydrolytic enzymes found in lysosomes, oxidative enzymes fill the cell's peroxisomes. These enzymes serve to detoxify normally occurring cellular waste products, as well as potentially toxic matter that may enter the cell.

Mitochondria are unique organelles in that they are separated from the cytosol by a double, not a single, layered membrane. This is essential to the primary purpose of the mitochondria, which is to produce energy – adenosine triphosphate, ATP – by aerobic respiration. In brief, the movement of protons from the mitochondrial matrix into the intermembrane space separating the two layers of membrane, and then back into the matrix, is the basis of the oxidative phosphorylation process that satisfies about 90 per cent of the body's energy needs. Two important pathways participate in aerobic respiration. The enzymes of the Krebs cycle are housed within the mitochondrial matrix, while the cytochromes and enzymes of the electron transport chain are located along the infoldings, or cristae, of the inner mitochondrial membrane.

The subcellular organelles that have been most recently characterised are the vaults, which were only discovered in the 1990s. A single cell may contain thousands of vaults but, because they cannot be visualised with standard staining procedures, their identification proved troublesome. Currently, it is believed that these vaults serve as shuttles to transport molecules synthesised by the nucleus through the pores of the nuclear envelope into the cytosol. These molecules may include messenger RNA and ribosomal subunits.

The specific organelles that dominate a cell's structure determine the functional specialisation of that cell. For example, muscle cells, myofibres, have a plasma membrane – the sarcolemma – that is replete with ionic channels since these cells are excitable and, therefore, require the exchange of ions with the extracellular fluid. Owing to the largeness of the myofibre, the sarcolemma also displays invaginations that have been termed 'tranverse tubules' (see also **skeletal muscle – structure and function**). The presence of these transverse tubules allows electrical excitation to reach even the deep myofibrils that make up the myofibre.

Muscle cells are specialised to contract and generate mechanical force (see also **muscle contraction mechanics**). Accordingly, the microfilaments actin and myosin are highly organised and abundant in the myofibre. Indeed, more than 50 per cent of the myofibre's protein content is accounted for by actin and myosin. Because a sharp increase in cytosolic calcium concentration is needed to trigger contraction, the myofibre's endoplasmic reticulum – better known as the sarcoplasmic reticulum – has been modulated to function as a calcium depot and is richly developed, particularly at the terminal cisternae regions.

The energy demand of working muscle is extremely high and, as a result, the mitochondrial content of myofibres is large. But perhaps the unique feature of the muscle cell is that it is multi-nucleated. This derives from its development, during which many precursor cells – myoblasts – fuse together, each adding its own nucleus to the differentiating myofibre. This pool of nuclei within the mature cell is important, in that it appears that each nucleus is responsible for the maintenance of a certain segment of the myofibre's cytoplasm. This 'nuclear domain' theory is critical to our understanding of myofibre hypertrophy and atrophy, as well as the essential repair processes that are a consequence of the normal 'wear and tear' experienced by active muscle cells.

MICHAEL R. DESCHENES

CENTRAL AND PERIPHERAL NERVOUS SYSTEMS

The underlying principle of physical activity is that muscle contraction causes movement. Several different muscles are used during any task. The spatial and temporal coordination of these different muscles, which produces controlled function during physical activity, is initiated and regulated by the central and peripheral nervous systems.

The central nervous system consists of the brain, brainstem, and spinal cord. Motor commands are generated in the motor cortex of the brain and pass either directly to the spinal cord or to the brainstem, where they modulate motor regulatory centres, which also send projections to the spinal cord. These motor commands are also regulated by the cerebellum and basal ganglia, which do not send projections to the spinal cord. Simple reflexes are controlled at the spinal cord level.

The peripheral nervous system consists of the peripheral nerves, neuromuscular junctions, and muscle contractile apparatus. A peripheral nerve and all the muscle fibres it innervates are called a **motor unit**. Once the final motor command generated by the central nervous system moves from the spinal cord to the motor unit, it cannot be altered.

Further reading

Kandel, E.R., Schwartz, J.H. and Jessell, T.M. (2000) *Principles of Neuroscience, Fourth Edition*, New York: McGraw-Hill.

ALAN ST CLAIR GIBSON

CENTRAL AND PERIPHERAL NERVOUS SYSTEMS – HISTORICAL BACKGROUND

There is currently no unifying theory of how neural activity in the central nervous system leads to voluntary complex movements. Before the 1700s it was assumed that the brain functioned as a type of gland, based on the theory of the Greek physician Galen. In this model, the nerves conveyed fluids from the brain to the peripheral tissues.

In the 1800s, using staining techniques and the recently developed light microscope, Cayal and Golgi showed that neural tissues were a network of discrete cells and that individual neurons are responsible for information processing. Around the same time, Galvani showed that muscles and neurons produce electricity, and von Helmholtz and other German physiologists showed that electrical activity in one nerve cell affects activity in another neuron in a predictable manner.

Two conflicting views of how the brain uses these electrical-based neuronal systems to send commands to the peripheral nervous system were developed in the 1800s. The first was reductionist, suggesting that different brain regions control specific functions. This work was based on the work of Joseph Gall, who also suggested continuous use of these different brain regions for specific functions caused regional hypertrophy. Gall suggested that this regional brain hypertrophy created bulges in the skull, which could be associated with the specific function of the underlying brain tissue. Although this skull theory has been disproved, in the late 1800s Brodmann described fifty-two separate regions of the cortex that were anatomically and functionally distinct, and Hughlings Jackson showed that in focal epilepsy patients, convulsions in different parts of the body were initiated by activity in different parts of the cerebral cortex. These findings were supported by the work of Penfield, who used small electrodes to stimulate different areas of the motor cortex in conscious neurological patients and induced movements in different anatomical regions of the body.

The opposing view was that that all brain regions contribute to every different mental task and motor function. This theory was based on the work of Flourens in the 1800s, and was described as the aggregate-field view. Although this theory fell into disfavour in the 1900s, recent work has suggested that this theory may be valid, as large areas of the brain communicate with each other continuously using electromagnetic waves of different frequency during any task. Further support for the aggregate-field view comes from the concept that no activity is simple and that every motor task is the final common output of multiple behavioural demands such as emotional context, prior experience, sensory perception, and homeostatic requirements. Although this argument has not been completely resolved, one certainty is that the brain functions as a parallel processor, with multiple tasks being performed at any time.

Although the function of the central nervous system is still not completely clear, peripheral nervous system function has been fairly well described. In the early 1900s, Sherrington used the term **motor unit** to define a basic unit of function consisting of a motor neuron and all the muscle fibres to which it connects. Later work showed that the muscle fibres of a single motor unit have unique properties such as contractile speed, force output capacity, and muscle fibre composition, that are different from other motor units. The basic information processing was shown to be related to the action potential moving down the motor nerves to the muscle, which was controlled by sodium and potassium ion concentration changes through ion channels in the peripheral nerves and muscle sarcolemmal tissue.

There is still some controversy about how motor unit recruitment is controlled during complex movements. In the early 1900s, Bernstein examined multiple joint movements by taking photographs of the motion of the upper arms of workers using hammers to strike a spike located at a specific distance from the workers. He found that although the workers consistently hit the spike, the trajectory of the hammer was different during each blow. He concluded that a different sequential pattern of shoulder, elbow and wrist joint function must have been used for each blow, but that these different patterns created a similar task output. Latash later described this phenomenon as motor abundancy, as different strategies for motor unit recruitment must have been used to create these different multi-joint patterns, which led to similar outcomes. The purpose of this motor abundancy is presumably to prevent the development of excessive fatigue, which may occur if the same motor units are continuously recruited during the task. Furthermore, in the 1950s, Hebb suggested that individual motor tasks share similar characteristics when performed in different ways. He used the example of handwriting, which is similar in an individual when they produce either large or small letters or when writing in different seated positions. He called this motor equivalence, and suggested that a movement is represented as an abstract form in the brain in its completeness, and that different motor unit recruitment strategies were used to create the same style of handwriting.

During simple muscle contractions, motor units appear to be recruited dependent on size. This theory was developed by Denny-Brown and Henneman in the mid-1900s. They suggested that at low force output, motor units consisting of smaller type I – slow twitch – muscle fibres and smaller diameter nerves are initially recruited. As more force output or greater speed of movement is required, motor units with larger type II – fast twitch – muscle fibres and larger nerve diameters are additionally recruited. When force output and speed requirements decrease, the recruitment order is reversed. Although some later studies have validated this earlier work, in the late 1900s, Westgaard and De Luca suggested that motor units are rotated or substituted in an on/off manner during muscle activity. This method would require a more complex control system then would occur if the size principle theory were correct. Further work is needed to assess the validity of this rotation–substitution theory.

Further reading

Kandel, E.R., Schwartz, J.H. and Jessell, T.M. (2000) *Principles of Neuroscience, Fourth Edition*, New York: McGraw-Hill.

Latash, M. (1998) *Progress in Motor Control, Volume 1 – Bernstein's Traditions in Movement Studies*, Champaign IL: Human Kinetics.

ALAN ST CLAIR GIBSON

CENTRAL GOVERNOR – EVIDENCE FOR

A central debate in the exercise sciences is the cause of the fatigue that develops particularly during high-intensity exercise of short duration. The most popular theory holds that this form of exercise is limited by a peripherally based metabolite-induced failure of skeletal muscle contractile function, independent of reduced muscle activation by the central nervous system, so-called peripheral fatigue.

This theory arose originally from studies undertaken by Nobel laureate, Sir Archibald Vivian Hill, and colleagues in Manchester, England in the 1920s. In turn their interpretations were crucially influenced by the earlier 1907 findings of Sir Frederick Gowland Hopkins, Nobel laureate for his discovery of vitamins, and Walter Morley Fletcher. They showed that the lactate concentrations of frog skeletal muscle, initially stimulated to contract to exhaustion in vivo – in the body, fell when the muscle was excised and incubated in vitro – outside the body, literally in a test tube – in an oxygen-enriched environment, whereas concentrations rose when incubated in an oxygen-free environment. Accordingly

Fletcher and Hopkins (1907) concluded that lactic acid was spontaneously developed, under anaerobic conditions, in excised muscle and that fatigue due to contractions was accompanied by an increase of lactic acid. Later Hopkins wrote that: 'the accumulation of lactic acid in muscle occurs only in the conditions of anaerobiosis. With a proper oxygen supply it fails to accumulate at all', and that the 'great importance of this work was that it started the study of muscle fermentation and its relation to muscular contraction'.

Hill (1926) acknowledged the dependence of his own theory on this interpretation: 'An isolated muscle stimulated in nitrogen soon fatigues and never recovers: an isolated muscle stimulated in oxygen may go on contracting for days.' These observations by Fletcher [sic] led to the 'lactic acid story'. Accordingly Hill and his colleagues proposed that performance during high-intensity exercise was terminated by the development of skeletal muscle anaerobiosis as a result of a limiting skeletal muscle blood flow that followed the development of myocardial ischaemia. Such anaerobiosis ultimately prevented the neutralisation of the lactic acid that, Hill believed, initiated muscle contraction. As a result lactic acid accumulation in maximally working anaerobic skeletal muscle impaired skeletal muscle relaxation, causing the involuntary termination of exercise. But the crucial effect of this logic is that it has produced a single dominant theoretical model of the factor determining maximal exercise performance (see Figure 8).

Thus, this model predicts that a single factor, oxygen supply to the active muscles, determines their exercise capacity. Further the model predicts that exercise always terminates as a result of the catastrophic consequences of physiological and biochemical events initiated when the safe biological limits of the body are exceeded, with a resulting loss of intracellular homeostasis; the original 'catastrophe theory' of Edwards (1983). According to Hill, a failure of oxygen delivery to the active muscles caused a catastrophic increase in muscle 'lactic acid' concentrations, which impaired muscle relaxation, leading to the termination of exercise. This is an example of a simple, linear model of exercise control in which the increase in a single variable – metabolite – produces absolute system failure from which a period of absolute rest is required while that metabolite is removed, allowing the body to recover its exercise capacity.

The core weakness of this model is that it can apparently function without any input from the brain. Indeed, the missing and unstated assumption in this model is that motor unit recruitment in the active muscles is always maximal at the point of exhaustion, allowing the peripheral inhibitory metabolites to act on all the recruited motor units. For, if this is not the case, so that there are quiescent non-recruited motor units in the exercising muscles at exhaustion, then it cannot be presumed that a factor other than the brain determines the exercise performance; for the reason that any additional recruitment of those quiescent fibres by the brain would increase the 'maximum' work rate and, hence, the cardiac output and the maximum oxygen uptake (VO_2 max) as a consequence.

Indeed, an absolutely fundamental teaching in muscle physiology is that the principal mechanism for increasing skeletal muscle force production is to increase the number of motor units that are recruited in the active muscles. Yet there is no evidence to support the belief that all the motor units

A
Skeletal muscle blood flow/
oxygen delivery

B
Exercise performance

Figure 8. Cardiovascular-anaerobic model of factors determining maximal exercise performance.

are active during voluntary exercise in humans, inviting the conclusion that human muscle fatigue does not simply reside in muscle.

Accordingly, the opposing Central Governor Model of Exercise posits that the exercise performance is regulated by a third factor (C, see Figure 9), which then explains an apparently causal but spurious relationship between A and B; that is, in this model, the arrow of causality linking A to B is reversed. In this model, factor C is the number of motor units and, hence, the number of skeletal muscle fibres in the active muscles that are recruited by the central nervous system (CNS).

Accordingly, the Central Governor Model proposes that exercise performance is regulated by the brain specifically to ensure that catastrophic failure of any organ system does not occur during any form of voluntary exercise. In this model there is a 'governor' in the subconscious brain that monitors the state of all the bodily organs during exercise. In response to the information from those organs, the brain predetermines, before the onset of exercise, the number of muscle fibres that it can recruit to ensure that the proposed exercise bout can be completed safely. Sensory feedback from those organs during exercise then produces changes in muscle recruitment patterns on a moment-to-moment basis, explaining why the pace during exercise is never completely constant but changes continuously.

There is substantial evidence to support this Central Governor Model. In the first place, there are predictions of the traditional Hill model, for which the available evidence proves the opposite.

First, there is no evidence that the exercising muscles ever become 'anaerobic' during maximal exercise testing used to measure VO_2max.

Second, there is no evidence that lactic acid is anything other than an excellent fuel for muscle metabolism, so that it enhances, rather than impairs, muscle function.

Third, there is no evidence that all the available skeletal muscle fibres in the active muscles are ever fully recruited during maximal exercise; without full muscle recruitment, the traditional model of peripheral fatigue cannot work, since peripheral fatigue can only ever be present when all the muscle fibres in the active limbs recruited.

Fourth, this model cannot explain three fundamental observations: that athletes pace themselves during exercise at different speeds, not only at one pace corresponding to the lactic acid concentration that 'poisons' the muscles; that athletes frequently reach their maximum effort in the last 5 per cent of a competitive event, the so-called 'finishing spurt', when their lactic acid concentrations should be the highest; and that interventions such as hypnosis, music, verbal deception, **motivation**, training, and **drugs** that act only the CNS, all influence exercise performance, yet they cannot produce an effect by any mechanism predicted in Figure 8.

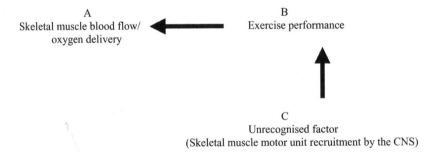

Figure 9. Governor (brain) model of factors determining maximal exercise performance.

In contrast, the evidence to support the Central Governor Model can be summarised as the following:

First, with a few remarkable exceptions, there is no evidence that exercise causes a failure of bodily homeostasis; rather the evidence is that the body defends its homeostasis as rigorously during exercise as it does at rest.

Second, there is now solid evidence that exercise terminates in various circumstances without full recruitment of all available muscle fibres in the active muscles, indicating that 'peripheral fatigue' is not the predominant cause of exercise termination.

Third, there is evidence that the exercise pace is regulated 'in anticipation' of the future and not simply in consequence of some physiological failure.

Fourth, the very presence of the sensations of fatigue must indicate that the CNS regulates exercise performance, because such sensations are without value if exercise performance is regulated in the periphery. For sensations, such as fatigue, that inform the brain that the muscles are exhausted are of no biological value if the brain is unable to influence the outcome. But if fatigue is a sensation that informs the body of how close it is approaching its capacity to defend its homeostasis, and if it increases the likelihood that the athlete will either reduce the exercise intensity or even terminate the exercise, then it is a sensation with a biological value.

Thus it is concluded that there is little published evidence supporting the theory that fatigue occurs only after physiological homeostasis fails in the periphery according to the 'catastrophe theory' of Edwards. Rather, the evidence supports the theory that fatigue in any form of exercise may form part of a regulated anticipatory response coordinated in the subconscious brain, the ultimate goal of which is to preserve homeostasis in all physiological systems during exercise.

See also: physiology of exercise

References

Edwards, R.H.T. (1983) 'Biochemical Bases for Fatigue in Exercise Performance: Catastrophe Theory in Muscular Fatigue', in H.G. Knuttgen, J.A. Vogel and J. Poortmans (eds) *Biochemistry of Exercise*, 1–28, Champaign IL: Human Kinetics.

Fletcher, W.M. and Hopkins, F.G. (1907) 'Lactic Acid in Amphibian Muscle', *Journal of Physiology* 35: 247–309.

Hill, A.V. (1926) 'The Scientific Study of Athletics', *Scientific American* April: 224–5.

Further reading

Gandevia, S.C. (2001) 'Spinal and Supraspinal Factors in Human Muscle Fatigue', *Physiological Reviews* 81: 1725–89.

Nielsen, O.B., de Paoli, F. and Overgaard, K. (2001) 'Protective Effect of Lactic Acid on Force Production in Rat Skeletal Muscle', *Journal of Physiology* 536: 161–6.

Noakes, T.D. (2003) 'Oxygen Transport and Running Economy', in T.D. Noakes, *Lore of Running*, 23–91, Champaign IL: Human Kinetics.

St Clair Gibson, A., Baden, D.A., Lambert, M.I., Lambert, E.V., Harley, Y.X.R., Hampson, D., Russell, V. and Noakes, T.D. (2003) 'The Conscious Perception of the Sensation of Fatigue', *Sports Medicine* 33: 167–76.

TIM NOAKES

CENTRAL PLACE THEORY

'Central places are broadly synonymous with towns that serve as centres for regional communities by providing them with central goods like tractors and central services like hospitals' (Haggett 1975: 363). Central place theory (CPT) is a normative and static theory, the origins of which can be found in studies in rural sociology and geography in the early twentieth century. The development of CPT is widely credited to the German economic geographers Walter Christaller (1933) and August Losch (1954). CPT is about location and space rather than land use; it attempts to explain the hierarchy of settlements according to their size and distribution, and the concentration of economic activity. The formulation and application of CPT represent a major contribution to locational analysis and studies in urban geography, particularly up until the mid-to-late 1970s.

There are several assumptions in Christaller's original CPT concerning retailing functions: towns are located on an isotropic and unbounded plain; the landscape is homogeneous; there are many small sellers producing the same product; population and purchasing power are evenly distributed; all goods and services are purchased by people from their closest central place or node; the transportation network is uniform in all directions, so that all central places are equally accessible; there is a constant range of any one central good or service from whatever central place it is offered; towns are hierarchically ordered; central places do not make excessive profits. In simple terms, once a certain distance is reached from the point of supply, the transportation costs for the consumer are so great that when they are added to the costs of the goods and services to be purchased, demand ultimately falls to zero or thereabouts. The point at which this happens varies because people are prepared to travel further for certain goods and services based on the value of those goods and services – high value/ higher order or low value/lower order.

Christaller argued that businesses locate as close to their customers as possible. In doing so, they minimise customers' transport costs and maximise expenditure at their business/point of sale. With a uniform population distribution, the centrality requirement results in a hinterland in which central places are located within a hexagonal network (hexagons exhaust a territory without any overlap and are the most efficient means of doing so). Several systems or models evolved in Christaller's research based in Southern Germany, where he suggested there were seven levels of the hierarchy.

The first settlement hierarchy is commonly referred to as the market optimisation case or principle, or $k = 3$ system (see Figure 10). In the $k = 3$ system, the central place of each hexagonal space either serves itself as well as two lower-order places, or serves itself and shares lower-order places with two immediate neighbours.

The second settlement hierarchy is the traffic optimising or transportation case or principle, or $k = 4$ system (see Figure 10). In this system, Christaller shifted the settlements so as to locate them at the centre of each side. This shift located settlements on transport routes linking larger towns. Each central place serves itself as well as either three lower-order settlements or sharing its six neighbours with another central place of the same order.

The third settlement hierarchy is the administrative optimising case or principle, or $k = 7$ system (see Figure 10). In this system, Christaller shifted each lower-order

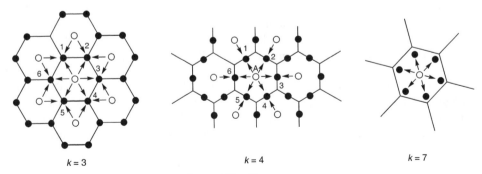

$k = 3$ $k = 4$ $k = 7$

Figure 10. Three Different Arrangements of Central Place Theory.

centre to within the trade boundaries of the higher-order centre so that all the six lower-order places in the hexagon are served by the central place. Such an arrangement is considered more stable than one where settlements are in competition or are divided.

CPT has been criticised on several grounds. Two main criticisms are that the theory is based on a special case (i.e. southern Germany) and that it was conceived as a closed system. Subsequently, Christaller's original CPT, with its fixed tiers of the hierarchy, has been explored, adapted and modified by many, with perhaps the most renowned work being that of August Losch, who combined the retailing *and* manufacturing functions in his modification of an urban system. Losch's system is more flexible than Christaller's. It is based on hexagonal units like those in Christaller's model, but he extended the concept of k hierarchies and introduced variation within the hinterland, because not all settlements possess all the functions of smaller settlements; in other words, there are areas, or discrete wedges, of city poor and city rich. Losch arrived at his system by taking all the hexagonal networks above and superimposing them on a dominant city or hub. The networks were rotated until the maximum number of higher-order services coincided and thereby reduced transport lines and distances between settlements to a minimum.

Christaller's and Losch's theories are concerned with interactions of thresholds (or conditions of entry of firms) and range or market areas (the drawing power of firms). In brief, firms of the same type and scale reach a competitive locational equilibrium and firms of different types agglomerate in urban centres.

There have been many more recent efforts to apply the systems devised by Christaller and Losch. Allen Philbrick (1963), for instance, even extended their models to a system of world regions: the

exchange world; transitional regions; subsistence regions; and unoccupied regions.

CPT helps explain the hierarchical development of settlements as discrete types of agglomerations which are:

> organized into an urban hierarchy of places connected by patterns of dominance of the smaller centres by the larger in a regular, nested arrangement. These assumptions lead to deductions about the increased polarization of activities in the larger urban centres. Structural changes in the economic environment, such as technological advances in agriculture, may cause marginal firms at different levels in the hierarchy to fail. In this event, the market is likely to be captured by the output of more efficient firms at higher levels in the hierarchy, the competitive process thus leading to further centralization. (Berry 1967)

Berry and Garrison (1958) undertook studies which demonstrated how hierarchies emerge within both individual metropolitan areas and the overall settlement system. They showed a hierarchical distribution of: small, isolated corner stores; neighbourhood shopping centres; district shopping centres; regional shopping centres; and the central business district (CBD). Their work concerning broader theories of tertiary activity, introduced the notion of: (a) a threshold or the minimum level of demand needed to support business activities; and (b) the range of a good or the maximum distance consumers are prepared to travel to purchase a product. A hierarchical pattern develops, but without constraints tied to hexagonal arrangements. CPT has been used as a tool for formulating the size and distribution of urban and regional shopping centres in the UK, and as a tool for evaluating existing arrangements.

In the early 1960s, Christaller theorised that centrifugal forces, involving decentralisation and a push away from expensive, congested, and polluted cities, promoted a growth in tourism activity in the hinterlands or peripheries. This is an interesting diversion because in CPT industrial and service activities were attracted and linked to central places. Christaller, in fact, believed that tourists were looking for outdoor recreation in pleasant landscapes and hence the peripheries were attractive places to visit and for the development of recreational facilities. Since Christaller put forward this view, there have been tremendous transformations and developments in transport and communications, urbanisation and gentrification, and counter-urbanisation. These forces have markedly increased the complexity of modern leisure, recreation, and tourism. And in modern sports, for example, globalisation has brought about unheralded growth in national and international sporting contests.

People will travel further as the value of the goods and services they wish to purchase increases and as the efficiency (speed, comfort, cost) of the transportation system increases. These developments will affect the size and shape of the catchment area of a good or service, and thereby alter Christaller's ideal market or landscape. Furthermore, while it is generally considered reasonable to assume that a market diminishes with distance, recent urban studies have highlighted a 'doughnut effect', with the city centre as a big hole surrounded by a population bulge that diminishes towards the urban peripheries. This 'doughnut effect' is an important consideration in locating recreational and sporting facilities.

Hierarchical principles such as those developed in Christaller's CPT are employed in a wide range of functions for developing standards for the provision of recreational and sporting facilities and in the broader development of centres, serving more traditionally as an organisational principle for services related to education and health. Whilst it is difficult and risky to generalise, with a concentration of major goods and services and transportation in larger cities, it is perhaps unsurprising to see many large-scale sporting events largely confined in space

(e.g. Olympic and Commonwealth Games), as opposed to those which are smaller or on the move (e.g. cycling events such as the Tour de France), located in large urban centres. Further, as Bale (1994: 11) points out:

> the stadium, the swimming pool or the route of a cycle race may be landscapes given over to sport but they can also be viewed as but part of intricate economic or physical systems. A sports stadium, for example, does not exist in isolation; it generates flows of people and spatial interactions over an area much greater than that of the stadium itself.

The traditional ideas of CPT are still in use, even if only implicitly, as people look to supply goods and services in a specified 'area' (whatever its size) or market. People consider, among other things, the area's location, its population, its administrative and political functions, its services, and its links to transportation networks and nodes.

References

Bale, J. (1994) *Landscapes of Modern Sport*, Leicester: Leicester University Press.

Berry, B.J.L. (1967) *Strategies, Models and Economic Theories of Development in Rural Regions*, Agriculture Economic Report No.127, Department of Agriculture, Washington DC: US Government Printing Office.

Berry, B.J.L, and Garrison, W. (1958) 'The Functional Bases of the Central Place Hierarchy', *Economic Geography* 34: 145–54.

Christaller, W. (1933/1966) *Central Places in Southern Germany*, trans. C.W. Baskin, Englewood Cliffs NJ: Prentice Hall.

—— (1964) 'Some Considerations of Tourism Location in Europe: The Peripheral Regions – Underdeveloped Countries – Recreation Areas', *Papers, Regional Science Association* 12, 1: 95–105.

Haggett, P. (1975) *Geography: A Modern Synthesis*, 2nd edn, New York: Harper and Row.

Losch, A. (1954) *The Economics of Location*, New Haven CT: Yale University Press.

Philbrick, A. (1963) *This Human World*, New York: John Wiley.

JOHN M. JENKINS

CENTRE OF MASS

The centre of mass of an object is the unique point about which the mass of the object is evenly distributed. The effects of external forces upon the human body can be studied by the **linear motion** of the whole body centre of mass and by **angular motion (rotation)** about that point. It is often found that the movement patterns of the centre of mass vary between athletes of different standards, providing a simple tool for evaluating technique. The position of the centre of mass of a human performer is a function of age, sex, and body build, and changes with breathing, ingestion of food, and disposition of body fluids. It is doubtful whether it can be pinpointed to better than 3 mm. In the fundamental or anatomical positions, the centre of gravity lies about 56–57 per cent of a male's height from the soles of the feet, the figure for females being 55 per cent. In this position, the centre of mass is located about 40 mm inferior to the navel roughly midway between the anterior and posterior skin surfaces. The position of the centre of mass is highly dependent on the orientation of a person's body segments. For example, in a piked body position the centre of mass of a gymnast may lie outside the body.

Historically, several techniques were used to measure the position of the centre of mass of the sports performer. These included boards and scales, and manikin – physical model – methods. The interested reader is referred to Hay (1993) for descriptions of these techniques. They are now rarely, if ever, used in sports biomechanics, having been superseded by the segmentation method. In this method, to calculate the position of the whole body centre of mass, we need to know the masses of the individual body segments and the locations of the centres of mass of those segments in the position to be analysed. The latter requirement is usually met by a combination of the pre-established location of each segment's centre of mass with respect to the endpoints of the segment, and the positions of those endpoints captured on a video, or other, image. For information on how the masses and other inertia characteristics of body segments are determined, see **body segments and inertial properties**. For the centre of mass to represent the system of segmental masses, the moment of mass – similar to the moment of force (see **kinetics**) – of the centre of mass about any axis must be identical to the sum of the moments of body segment masses about the same axis. The calculation can be expressed mathematically as: $ms = \sum m_i s_i$ or $s = \sum (m_i/m)s_i$, where m_i is the mass of segment number I, m is the mass of the whole body (the sum of all of the individual segment masses $\sum m_i$), m_i/m is the fractional mass ratio of segment number i, and s and s_i are the position vectors respectively of the mass centre of the whole body and segment number i. In practice, the position vectors are specified in terms of their three-dimensional (x, y, z) coordinates.

See also: anthropometric models; kinematics

Reference

Hay, J.G. (1993) *The Biomechanics of Sports Techniques*, Englewood Cliffs NJ: Prentice Hall.

Further reading

Bartlett, R.M. (1997) *Introduction to Sports Biomechanics*, ch. 3, London: E&FN Spon.

ROGER BARTLETT

CENTRE OF PERCUSSION AND THE SWEET SPOT

The term 'sweet spot' is used to describe the point or region of a racquet or bat where the ball should be hit for optimum results. The word 'sweet' is used to describe the location, because it feels sweet, or comfortable, for the player. It is generally accepted that there are two distinct definitions of this phrase, which leads to some confusion about its meaning. Each definition is based upon a different physical phenomenon. The two locations of the sweet spot are, first, where minimum shock load is transmitted to the player and, second, where minimum vibrations are excited. Each of these sweet spots is located on the longitudinal axis of the racquet – an axis of symmetry, because off-axis impacts cause the racquet to twist in the player's hand, resulting in an undesirable loading of the wrist.

The sweet spot that gives the least shock is found at the centre of percussion. A ball that impacts at this point will not cause any sudden translational motion of the handle either away from or towards the palm of the hand. Furthermore, the player will feel no linear impulse or 'jarring' on the hand; therefore, the shot feels 'good'. If the ball were to impact at a point of the racquet located between the tip and the centre of percussion, then the sudden shock loading at the handle would tend to move the handle out of the player's hand. In this case, the fingers remain gripped to the racquet, and the shock load acts to 'jerk' the player's hand and arm. Alternatively, if the ball were to impact between the centre of percussion and the throat of the racquet, the shock load at the handle would push the racquet into the player's palm. The location of the centre of percussion is determined from the inertial properties of the tennis racquet and is, therefore, different for each racquet on the market. The location can be calculated using the following equation: $d = I_p/am_r$, where d is the distance between the racquet's centre of mass and the centre of percussion, I_p is the mass moment of inertia of the racquet around its centre of mass, a is the distance between the centre of mass and the handle, and m_r is the mass of the racquet.

The centre of percussion is an important concept, and was fundamental in the development of the modern design of tennis racquets. In traditional wooden tennis racquets, with small head sizes, the centre of percussion was generally located close to the throat of the racquet. This is undesirable because the average player tries to strike the ball close to the centre of the string face. However, modern tennis racquets have larger head sizes, which inherently 'move' the centre of percussion closer to the centre of the head. Further, manufacturers have deliberately modified the inertial properties of the racquet in an attempt to move the centre of percussion closer to the centre of the head. This has been accomplished by the addition and subtraction of material – mass – from specific locations on the frame.

The sweet spot on the racquet or bat at which minimal vibrations are excited is located at a node point of a specific mode of vibration. For a tennis racquet, the dominant mode of vibration is that of the fundamental transverse mode. The node point for this mode is located close to the geometric centre of the head. If a ball strikes this point, the racquet will not vibrate, and the further from this point that the ball strikes, the greater the amplitude of vibration that is induced. These vibrations are transferred from the racquet to the player, causing discomfort.

For some sports equipment, like cricket bats, there is no unique location of the sweet spot that is associated with minimal vibrations. This is because several modes of vibration are excited during the impact, and each of these modes has its own nodal point. Therefore, the ball may strike the bat at a specific location that corresponds to a node point of one mode, but will excite vibrations of other modes. Manufacturers of cricket bats can modify the design of the bat to control the location of the node points, in an attempt to improve the performance of the bat. They can do this with modifications to the mass distribution along the axis of the bat blade and by changes to the stiffness of the handle.

A third location that is sometimes referred to as being a sweet spot is the point at which the ball comes off the racquet or bat with maximum speed (or power). However, it is contradictory to define this point as 'sweet' because, generally, this impact point induces large vibrations of the racquet or bat, as it is well away from the node of vibration. On a tennis racquet, the location that gives maximum power is close to the throat, on the longitudinal axis. The position can easily be obtained by holding the racquet in your hand and dropping a tennis ball onto the strings. The ball bounces highest off the throat and much lower from the tip. However, this is only the case when the racquet is held stationary. If the racquet is swung towards the ball, the point at which the ball comes off the strings with maximum speed moves towards the tip of the racquet. This is because, in a typical tennis swing, the tip of the racquet is moving faster than the throat.

This third definition of the sweet spot is that commonly used by the manufacturers in their marketing material. They generally specify the size of the sweet spot in terms of the area of the string bed that generates about 50 per cent or more of the maximum power. This is an arbitrary definition and purely based on marketing aims, so the educated reader should be aware of the limitations of the manufacturers' claims. Typical techniques used by manufacturers to increase the size of this sweet spot include the movement of the centre of mass closer to the tip of the racquet, and the use of peripheral weighting on the racquet frame to increase the polar moment of inertia. Professional players such as Pete Sampras are known to take this idea to the extreme and add a significant amount of lead to the tip of the racquet.

See also: moments of inertia – polar and transverse

Further reading

Brody, H., Cross, R. and Lindsey, C. (2002) *The Physics and Technology of Tennis*, Solana Beach CA: Racquet Tech Publishing.

SIMON GOODWILL

CEREBROVASCULAR DISEASE

Cerebrovascular disease, or stroke, is a local disturbance in the cerebral circulation causing a focal neurological deficit. Stroke (ischaemic stroke and haemorrhagic stroke) is one of the leading causes of morbidity and mortality in developed countries. Arteriosclerosis of the extracranial and intracranial arteries, which triggers thrombosis, is thought to be the underlying pathological basis for ischaemic stroke, whereas hypertension is the major determinant of haemorrhagic stroke.

What are the risk factors for cerebrovascular disease?

The risk factors for stroke can be subdivided into modifiable and non-modifiable risk factors (Table 3).

What are the general guidelines for the primary prevention of stroke?

The following are the general guidelines for the primary prevention of stroke:

- Management of modifiable risk factors, especially hypertension
- Oral anticoagulation with warfarin for selected high-risk patients with non-valvular atrial fibrillation
- Carotid endarterectomy for selected patients with carotid artery stenosis greater than 60 per cent
- Regular physical exercise
- Treatment with statin medications for patients who have coronary artery disease with or without hyperlipidemia

Table 3. Risk factors for stroke

Non-modifiable risk factors	Modifiable risk factors
Increased age	Hypertension
Male gender	Underlying cardiac disease
Positive family history	(atrial fibrillation, mitral
Ethnicity	valve abnormalities,
	patent foramen ovale,
	atrial septal aneurysm)
	Diabetes mellitus
	(including impaired
	glucose tolerance and
	insulin resistance)
	Hyperlipidaemia
	Cigarette smoking
	Increased alcohol
	consumption (moderate
	consumption appears to
	be protective)
	Obesity
	Lack of physical activity
	Others (increased
	fibrinogen, increased
	homocysteine)

- The routine use of antiplatelet medication has no proven role in primary stroke prevention, although aspirin is often prescribed for patients with vascular risk factors who have not yet had symptoms of either stroke or ischemic heart disease

What is the specific role of regular physical activity in the primary prevention of stroke?

It is well established that participation in regular physical activity reduces the risk of premature death and cardiovascular disease. More recently, the beneficial effects of physical activity have also been documented for stroke. In most studies, no distinction between ischaemic and haemorrhagic stroke were made. In one study the protective effect was shown in males for haemorrhagic stroke, and only a reduced risk of ischaemic stroke in smokers but not in non-smokers. This protective effect of physical activity

has been shown in men, women, blacks, and Hispanics.

However, there is no clear dose–response relationship between level of activity and risk of stroke. Vigorous physical activity compared with lower levels of physical activity has been shown to have either no effect or even deleterious effects, in some studies but not in others. Additional protection was observed with increasing duration of exercise; however, the prevalence of such activities in the elderly was quite low.

The protective effect of physical activity may be mediated in part through its role in controlling various known risk factors for stroke, such as hypertension, cardiovascular disease, diabetes, and body weight. Other possible mechanisms that are associated with physical activity include reductions in plasma fibrinogen and platelet activity, as well as elevations in plasma tissue plasminogen activator activity and HDL concentrations.

Current guidelines recommended for regular physical activity in the primary prevention of stroke are moderate-intensity exercise for at least 30 min on most, and preferably all, days of the week. It has been suggested that physical activity, as a modifiable behavior, requires greater emphasis in stroke prevention campaigns.

What are the general guidelines for the secondary prevention of stroke?

Secondary prevention is defined as the prevention of a recurrence after an initial cerebrovascular event. The following are the general guidelines for the secondary prevention of stroke:

- appropriate evaluation to identify the mechanism of the initial stroke
- carotid endarterectomy for patients with symptomatic carotid artery stenosis of 50 per cent or more
- oral anticoagulation with warfarin for patients with non-valvular atrial fibrillation

- use of various antiplatelet agents, including aspirin, ticlopidine, clopidogrel, and the combination of aspirin and slow-release dipyridamole
- treatment of risk factors may also reduce the risk of secondary stroke, but that requires further investigation.

What is the specific role of physical activity in the secondary prevention of stroke?

The primary effects of a stroke result from the upper motor neuron damage which causes paresis, paralysis, spasticity, and sensory perceptual dysfunction. Other secondary effects of stroke are also debilitating and include muscle atrophy and contracture that also contribute to poor quality of life.

Participation in a multidisciplinary rehabilitation program following a stroke has been shown to improve function and hasten return to work. The first step in such a program is focused on restoring self-care ability. However, endurance training is increasingly recognized as an important component of a comprehensive stroke rehabilitation program.

Participation in regular endurance training following stroke has been shown to have the following benefits:

- enhanced motor unit recruitment limiting the development of muscle disuse atrophy;
- increased physical work capacity;
- improvement in the lipid profile (increased serum HDL concentration, decreased triglyceride concentration);
- decreased platelet aggregation;
- increased fibrinolysis;
- weight loss;
- decreased resting and submaximal heart rate;
- decreased resting and submaximal blood pressure;

- delay in the onset of angina in symptom-limited patients;
- greater confidence in engaging in physical activities.

What are the guidelines for the prescription of endurance exercise in stroke patients?

All patients should undergo a full medical assessment, including a stress electrocardiogram (ECG) prior to commencing with an endurance-training program. Care must be taken to identify the nature and extent of neuromuscular abnormalities (weakness, spasticity, pain, loss of sensation) so that proper care can be taken during exercise testing and training activities.

Testing and training can be done on a modified cycle ergometer (chest braces, individually adjustable handle bars, adjustable toe clips, and large-base shoes to distribute the force over the pedal surface).

Exercise training should be conducted in a setting where there is medical supervision similar to that for cardiac rehabilitation. This program is ideally suited to be part of a standard program for Phase II cardiac rehabilitation.

General guidelines for exercise prescription are:

- commence activity at workloads equivalent to 40–60 per cent of maximum for 30 min and perform this at 3 days per week;
- gradually increase training intensity to the highest workload that can be tolerated without symptoms;
- perform regular measurements of blood pressure response during exercise training;
- limit rises in blood pressure during exercise to a maximum of 200/100 mmHg during training sessions;
- be aware of underlying cardiovascular disease;

249

- monitor all other risk factors for stroke (blood pressure at least weekly, blood glucose concentration in diabetics before and after every training session, lipid profile every 3 months) regularly during the program.

See also: cardiac rehabilitation; hyperlipidaemia; hypertension

References

Halar, E.M. (1999) 'Management of Stroke Risk Factors During the Process of Rehabilitation. Secondary Stroke Prevention', *Phys Med Rehabil. Clin N Am* 10: 839–56, viii.

Ingall, T.J. (2000) 'Preventing Ischemic Stroke. Current Approaches to Primary and Secondary Prevention', *Postgrad. Med* 107: 34–42, 47.

Wannamethee, S.G. and Shaper, A.G. (1999) 'Physical Activity and the Prevention of Stroke', *J Cardiovasc. Risk* 6: 213–6.

MARTIN SCHWELLNUS

CERTIFICATES OF OBLIGATION

In contrast to general obligation bonds, certificates of obligation do not require approval of the voters at a referendum. However, they may be still backed by the full faith and credit of a jurisdiction's tax base or, alternatively, by a specific revenue stream or streams, or by both. The legislative body is required to publish a legal notice in the local press announcing a public hearing of their proposed use so the public is informed. However, few people read official legal notices in their paper, so while the announcement meets the legal requirement for public disclosure, most of the public are uninterested in such arcane notices and remain ignorant of the debt to which their government is committing them. If the notice does arouse public opposition, then the electorate can petition the council requesting a public referendum on the use, but this rarely occurs.

These certificates usually are sold to local, rather than to regional or national, investors, and, as with general obligation bonds, the debt is retired over a given period of years with property tax revenues. In the context of sports facilities, these instruments typically are used in one of the following circumstances:

- If the capital investment is not made quickly, then the opportunity will be lost. There is insufficient time to go through the lengthy process of obtaining voter approval for the investment.
- In rapidly growing communities, new needs may emerge which were not anticipated when the last bond referendum was held, and in the judgment of the council immediate action is required.
- The legislative body has doubts that voters would approve the purchase, but its members are convinced strongly that the project is in the community's best long-term interest.
- They can be redeemed by designated income streams without recourse to property tax revenues.

There is a political risk to elected officials who support the issuing of certificates of obligation, because they are obligating taxpayers' money without requesting authorization to do so. This breach of accepted procedure may result in a backlash if the project does not have widespread public support, even if it meets one or more of the circumstances listed above. However, in the past decade many jurisdictions have passed limits on the length of time that individuals may hold an elected office. For example, city council members may be limited to two three-year terms in office. In these instances, there may be a temptation for 'lame duck' council members to promote the use of certificates of obligation to fund favored projects as tangible legacies of their elected term in office. Since they are not eligible for re-election, they are exempt from any voter backlash.

Voters in the city of College Station, Texas, approved at a referendum the expenditure of $2.12 million in general obligation bonds to fund the design and initial development of a new sports complex. However, during the design phase there was highly visible pressure from the sports community to expand the number of playing fields, so when bids for the work were received, they amounted to $2.985 million. Given the public pressure for the fields, the council approved the issuance of $865,000 in certificates of obligation to bridge the financial gap.

When the fields had been constructed, the sports community lobbied for floodlights to be installed so they could be used in the evenings. The cost was $700,000. Again, this was over and above the amount approved by residents in the bond referendum. Nevertheless, the council authorized the issuance of certificates of obligation to fund the lights.

Even though the issuance of these certificates of obligation led to a substantial increase in the tax rate from 43c to 48c per $100 property valuation, the council perceived that the visible public agitation for these projects provided them with sufficient justification and political support to defuse any potential voter backlash from the tax increase.

JOHN L. CROMPTON

CERTIFICATES OF PARTICIPATION

Certificates of participation (COPs) are a financing vehicle that utilizes the leasing authority of local governments. Four entities are involved in the COPs process. Their roles and the relationships between them are described in Figure 11.

The process starts with an intermediary organization, which may be a governmental agency or a public benefit nonprofit organization, selling COPs to a financial institution to raise the money to build the sports facility (flow 1 in Figure 11). The COPs are tax-exempt. The financial institution holds title to the facility as security for its loan, but confers 'possessory interest' rights to the intermediary through a long-term agreement. After receiving funds from the financial institution (flow 2), the intermediary contracts with a builder (flow 3) who constructs the facility (flow 4). The intermediary leases the facility to a facility operator (flow 5), for a lease fee (flow 6) which is sufficient to pay the annual debt charges on the COPs (flow 7). When the COPs are paid off, the title for the sports facility passes to the facility operator.

The use of COPs is growing rapidly, and the increase appears likely to continue. They are a means of surmounting legal and political impediments to the use of traditional bonds, so their growth has been particularly prominent in states severely

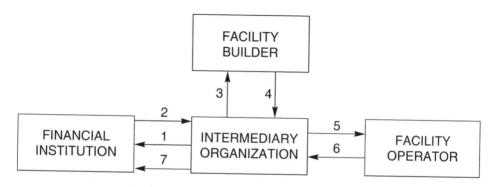

Figure 11. Steps in the issuance of certificates of participation.

constrained in their ability to borrow funds by tax limits or expenditure limitation statutes. For instance, California local governments can borrow only after receiving approval from two thirds of the voters in a referendum. Thus, one vote over a one-third minority can prevent a sports project coming to fruition despite a majority of voters supporting extra taxes to finance it. The COPs provide access to capital without a referendum. Given the size of the state and the pressures on state and local governments there to provide services, it is no surprise that California has the largest share of the COP market.

The ability to enter into these arrangements without voter approval is a controversial feature of COPs. In some jurisdictions, voters have opposed their use because they are not subject to citizen review. A referendum is not required because the lease agreement is not backed by the full faith and credit of the city. There is a moral, rather than a legal, obligation for the jurisdiction to pay the lease fee to the lender annually either from appropriations from the general fund or from a designated income stream. Hence, certificates tend to be viewed as higher risk than traditional bonds and so tend to have higher interest rates. Interest rates on COPs commonly run as much as 1 per cent higher than borrowing rates for general obligation bonds. Lending rates for COPs are often equivalent to rates charged for revenue bonds.

Two models of COPs have emerged: the public trust model and the public–private partnership model. The essential difference between them is that in the former arrangement, the facility operator is a public entity, whereas in the latter model, the intermediary leases the facility to a private company.

The public trust model

In the public trust model, if the lease fees are a revenue stream from a facility such as a sports arena or golf course and smaller than anticipated revenues accrue, then the public agency's general fund guarantees the debt service. The intermediary is usually a nonprofit organization acting as a public-benefit corporation, but in some circumstances it may be a different government entity. If a public-benefit corporation is used, its directors are likely to be public spirited citizens deemed acceptable to the government entity. When the debt is paid in full, then the sports facility becomes the jurisdiction's property. COPs tend to be used as alternatives to bonds and, thus, possess relatively long maturities (more than twenty years).

In the city of North Augusta, South Carolina, for example, the Riverview Park Sports Activity Center was funded by $2.4 million from the city's capital projects fund and $3.12 million in COPs. A corporation named Riverview Park Facilities Incorporated was established, and its directors constituted the five members of the North Augusta Parks and Recreation Advisory Board. The North Augusta City Ordinance No. 92–02 stated:

> Whereas, in order to finance the cost of the project, the City has determined to enter into a Base Lease Agreement whereby the City will lease the existing site whereon the Project will be constructed (the 'Land') to RIVERVIEW PARK FACILITIES, INC (the 'Corporation'), and contemporaneously with the execution of such Base Lease, the city will enter into a Project Lease Agreement whereby the Corporation will lease back the Project together with the land, as improved in the manner discussed above (the 'Facilities') to the City; and WHEREAS, the Corporation will assign its interest in the Project Lease Agreement to FIRST UNION NATIONAL BANK OF SOUTH CAROLINA, as Trustee for holders of Certificates of Participation in the Project Lease Agreement, which will provide the financing source for the project.

The public-private partnership model

In this alternative approach to using COPs, the local government agency assumes the role of intermediary. Rather than taking direct operational responsibility for the new facility as in the previous model, under this arrangement, the city or county engages a private company to manage the day-to-day operation of a new building. Using the services of a private operator is most appropriate when the project requires specialized know-how beyond the customary expertise of the local government unit. In the context of sports facilities, such amenities as golf courses, marinas, ice rinks, and stadiums are good candidates for this type of public-private collaboration.

In its role as broker of the development project, the city or county first procures the services of a qualified operator with a successful track record of managing the kind of facility the agency believes would be a community asset, such as a new ice rink, baseball stadium, or municipal golf course. The intent is to create a needed resource for the community. The inducement for the private operator such as a hotel management company or owner of a minor league baseball team, is that the city can borrow the construction capital to build the new asset at a much more favorable rate of interest through the use of COPs. Because of their tax-exempt status, COPs can be issued at significantly lower rates, as much as 3.5 per cent lower, than the cost charged to private companies for standard commercial bank loans. Access to such relatively inexpensive development capital by partnering with a government agency is a powerful inducement for a private company to seek collaboration.

A particularly innovative use of COPs was demonstrated in the financing of Arrowhead Pond Arena in Anaheim, California. The Arrowhead Pond Arena was a join venture between the City of Anaheim and Ogden Facility Management Corporation. The project to construct the Arrowhead Pond was funded by COPs. However, all of the debt service payments associated with the COPs are paid by Ogden Management Corporation, in return for which Ogden received a thirty-year contract to manage the arena, during which period the company retain all arena revenues excluding those associated with the National Hockey League's (NHL) Mighty Ducks. Ogden also received 7.5 per cent of gross gate revenues from the Mighty Ducks. At the end of the thirty-year period when the bonds are paid off, the arena is turned over to the City of Anaheim. The city paid for the land, infrastructure improvements and legal documentation, while Ogden's total cost was $126 million (including cost of debt service). Ogden anticipated losses in the first twelve years of operation, but they projected the profits in the last eighteen years would be more than the first twelve years of losses. Apart from the naming rights to the facility and approval of the annual budget, the city gave Ogden almost complete autonomy to operate the arena. The financing arrangement is unique in that Ogden is solely responsible for guaranteeing payment of the facility's debt service. In addition to the NHL's Mighty Ducks, the arena is the home of the Anaheim Bullfrogs, a franchise of the Roller Hockey International League. Arrowhead Pond also hosts indoor soccer and tennis events, and many concerts. The aggregate number of annual visitors exceeds 2 million.

JOHN L. CROMPTON

CERVICAL SPINE REHABILITATION

Cervical spine rehabilitation refers to the way neck pain is treated by members of the health care rehabilitation team. The rehabilitation team usually is led by a doctor who may have specialization in physiatry, neurology, orthopedics, or primary care medicine. Other members of the team include a physical therapist, athletic trainer, and occupational therapist. Neck rehabilitation consists of diagnosing the specific problem, treating the acute symptoms, restoring normal neck motion and strength, safely returning one to activity, and the prevention of reoccurrences.

The cervical spine consists of seven stacked bones (vertebrae) that begin at the base of the head and end at the level of the shoulders. The source of neck pain can come from one or a combination of different structures within a joint or series of joints. In a cervical joint, which is everything between two adjacent vertebrae, are tendons, cartilage, muscles, the spinal cord, nerves, and a disc. These structures work together pain-free in symmetry. This symmetry can be lost in a traumatic event (i.e. a collision in rugby) or can be lost over a period of time through sustained overuse and/or poor positioning of the neck.

If the neck is a source of symptoms, pain can be felt around the neck or it can be referred to the head, face, shoulder, down the arm to the hand, and to the upper back. A dysfunction in the neck can create symptoms of an ache or sharp pain, burning, numbness, loss of strength in the arm, and even dizziness and blurred vision.

Neck rehabilitation is divided into three phases. These phases are the acute phase, the recovery phase, and the functional or maintenance phase. In the initial phase (acute phase) of neck rehabilitation, the rehabilitation team examines the athlete to determine the source and severity of the symptoms. Based on the exam findings and the age and health of the patient, a treatment plan is formulated. In acute situations, where pain significantly interferes with function, a medical doctor may prescribe medications to control pain and or to reduce inflammation. Typically a medical doctor will also prescribe physical therapy.

A physical therapist aids in the reduction of pain and inflammation with the use of modalities, such as: ultrasound, electrical stimulation, massage, manual therapy, traction, and ice. A neck immobilizer/collar may be recommended at this time. If it is determined that conservative treatment alone cannot manage the patient's symptoms, more invasive treatment such as injections or surgery may be warranted.

Next, the recovery phase begins when the pain and inflammation are reduced. Under the guidance of a physical therapist, the athlete actively participates in controlling the symptoms through exercise and activity modification. The athlete strengthens and stretches specific muscles of the neck, shoulder blade and trunk to maximize the neck's optimal movement patterns. The athlete demonstrates cervical joint protection strategies that include correct posturing and proper body mechanics. These strategies enable the athlete to begin to independently manage their own symptoms.

The last phase is the maintenance phase. During this phase, the athlete becomes independent in recognizing how to prevent future re-injury. The athlete and the rehabilitation team analyze each activity of the athlete's sport. Changes are made that ensure the athlete returns to their activities and sport safely. The athlete is equipped with appropriate adaptive equipment (i.e. use of a mirror in cycling or a neck collar in American football) and demonstrates more complex activity modifications (i.e. positioning of the head and neck when running or with heading the ball in soccer). These changes enable maximum cervical protection.

References

Physical Medicine and Rehabilitation: Neck Pain and Problems. Houston TX: Methodist Health Care System. http://www.methodisthealth. com/rehab/neckpain.htm

Physical Medicine and Rehabilitation: Neck Pain Rehabilitation. American Academy of Physical Medicine and Rehabilitation. http://www.aapr.org/member/market/neckpain.htm

TIMOTHY NEEDHAM

CHAIN OF CUSTODY ISSUES

Chain of custody is a broad term used to describe the standards, procedures, or protocols that ensure the physical security of samples, data, and records. In sports drug testing, chain of custody usually describes any written procedures to ensure that the collection (see **collection issues**), transportation and laboratory analysis of urine, blood, or other specimens remain secure from outside tampering, review, or disclosure.

Sports drug-testing programs publish chain-of-custody protocols to provide athletes with assurance that their specimens' location, possession and security are known at all times. Although the true definition of 'chain of custody' is established by the organizations' published protocols, chain of custody usually includes three facets of the testing process: collection, transportation, and laboratory analysis.

Collection

Chain of custody begins with the notification of the athlete to be tested. Organizations must ensure that the correct individual is being selected and that person is indeed the individual who appears for testing. Sports organizations use couriers at the site of competition to ensure that the correct person is chosen for testing. In most cases, that courier remains with the athlete and escorts him/her to the testing area. In out-of-competition settings, other devices are used, including picture identification or the presence of an official to certify the identity of the athlete. Chain-of-custody protocols for sports drug testing limit who has access to the collection area, establish the secure nature of the collection supplies and describe how the athlete will be monitored while in the testing location.

In sports drug testing, the direct observation of urination is a chain-of-custody issue. Trained personnel observe the athlete to ensure that the specimen provided belongs to that athlete without any manipulation or tampering. After providing a specimen, the athlete packages the specimen for transportation or is required to observe the packaging and certifies by signature that all protocols were followed. The sports organization provides collection supplies that are tamper-evident or tamper-proof to ensure that the specimen remains secure until arrival at the laboratory.

Transportation

Specimen collectors are required to retain all specimens in their control until the specimens are transferred to a transportation agent for delivery to the laboratory. Computerized tracking systems by transportation companies can generally describe the location of the samples from the time the collector releases them until the specimens are delivered to the laboratory. Nevertheless, it is not possible nor is it necessary to account for each and every person who handles the specimens between the collection location and the laboratory.

Laboratory analysis

The laboratory plays a vital role in the chain of custody of a specimen. Only the laboratory can establish that a specimen arrived without any evidence of tampering. Laboratory personnel carefully document in writing the arrival and security status of every specimen before beginning analysis. These processes are not established by the sports organization but by the laboratory's standard operating procedure (SOP). The SOP also establishes the internal chain-of-custody controls in the laboratory to ensure access to specimens by authorized personnel and safeguard against sample labeling, accessioning and storage mistakes.

Sports drug testing generally utilizes split sampling techniques (i.e. a single void is divided into two separate specimens during packaging at the collection site) and the athlete may request that a second test of a sample be conducted. The athlete may also be present during the opening of this second portion of the split sample. This process reassures the athlete that the sample has been transported and analyzed under strict security protocols.

References

National Collegiate Athletic Association (2002) 'Drug-Testing Program 2003–04', August.
US Department of Transportation (2001) '49 CFR Part 40 Procedures for Transportation Workplace Drug Testing Programs', 21 February 2001.
World Anti-Doping Agency (2003a) 'Elements of An Anti-Doping Program', http://www.wada-ama.org/en/t3.asp?p=32332.25 November 2003.
—— (2003b) 'Wada Technical Document – TD2003LCOC,' http://www.wada-ama.org/docs/web/standards_harmonization/code/chain_custody_1_2.pdf. 25 November 2003.

FRANK URYASZ

CHILDREN

In the Western world childhood is an 'invention' of the Modern Age, as historians have now variously demonstrated. Whereas in the Middle Ages children shared in the lives of the adults and grew into their later duties, childhood developed as a separate sphere with its own specific rights and obligations as a result of economic and social changes which included the diffusion of cultural skills.

Childhood

Childhood, the first stage of life, is marked by great physical, intellectual, and psychical processes of change and ends with the onset of puberty. In development psychology childhood is divided into various phases from infancy to late childhood, characterised by changing motor, cognitive, and psychosocial requirements and skills.

The integration of children into society takes place through life-long **socialisation** processes, which can be regarded as the individual's active appropriation of the ecological and social environment. In these processes endogenous factors are interwoven with anthropological constants and socio-ecological influences. The tasks of socialisation in childhood are the development of not only basic emotional trust as well as intelligence but also of motor, language, and social skills.

Children and physical activities

In childhood movement plays a key role since it is through movement that children experience themselves and their environment, which they must 'grasp' – in a double sense. Depending on their stage of development, children acquire motor skills which range from the conscious grasping of objects in infancy to highly complex physical exercises in late childhood. Games, including movement games, are indispensable for the physical, psychical, and intellectual development of children; they are anthropological constants.

As early as in primary socialisation, which largely takes place in the family, children begin to appropriate space in play as well as gain experience of their bodies and movement, and it is here that the way is paved for socialisation in sport. Numerous studies have revealed a 'social heritage', in which parents hand down to their children their interest in sport by encouraging and supporting them as well as by serving as role models. Physical education at school also plays an important role in imparting not only motor skills and sporting abilities but also motives, interests, and attitudes relating to sports. However, traditional sports lessons, with their emphasis on performance and achievement, may also lead to negative experiences, especially on the part of children who are not very athletic, and thus to their rejection of sporting activities.

As children grow up it is then above all their peers who determine values and behavioural patterns. Especially boys play sports such as **football** or skateboarding in peer groups and, here, athleticism increases their prestige within the group. In addition, the mass **media** have a great influence on boys' socialisation in sport: virtually all boys know the great football or basketball stars, and for many of them players like Michael Jordan or David Beckham are idols whom they wish to emulate.

A great many children's games and sporting activities take place spontaneously and in an informal setting, although over recent decades considerable changes have been observable in childhood, children's experience and behaviour, as well as in recreational activities. Especially in large cities children find little space that they can appropriate for physical activities and games. However, a growing fascination for the new media is to be observed along with a decrease in spare time, so that today spontaneous play in peer groups seems to be the exception rather than the rule.

Today children tend to make use of the sporting activities provided by schools and clubs, the consequences of which are subjection to norms and discipline as well as, generally, a 'sportifying' of children's physical activities.

In countries with a sport system based on clubs, the sports club is the most important provider of sports besides schools. In Germany, for example, 60 per cent of all boys and 45 per cent of all girls between the ages of seven and fourteen are members of a sports club.

Even though the figures of girls and boys who are active in sports may not differ greatly in some age cohorts, a closer look reveals that girls and boys have different sports cultures. This applies above all to the types of sport chosen. Among girls horse-riding, dance, and gymnastics seem to be the most popular sports all over Europe, while boys continue to predominate in football as well as in streetball and skateboarding. However, it must not be overlooked that girls have now conquered the football pitches in many countries. Nevertheless, only certain girls are attracted to more risky or physical contact sports. In all this there are close links between sports culture, images, identities, and life experience of the two genders.

This also means that children's opportunities of playing sports depend, among other things, on social and ethnic background. Especially girls from immigrant families with a Muslim background are largely excluded from sporting activities. Although Islam does not prohibit the playing of sports on principle, it does demand that religious decrees are obeyed, such as keeping the body covered at all times or segregating the sexes – which largely makes it impossible for girls from traditional Muslim families to take part in sporting activities.

While socialisation processes, which can either promote or hinder participation in sports, have been well researched, the question whether (and, if so, how) sport contributes towards education and socialisation has not yet been answered. Ever since the nineteenth century, schools and sport organisations in many countries have hoped that sport would instil in young people numerous 'virtues' from discipline, dedication, and persistence to social skills. Today it is assumed that social learning can take place in sports settings, especially when this is the intended aim. Competence in communication and cooperation, coping with frustration and how to handle norms and **rules** are the most important educational goals which are aimed at in and through sport. The extent to which the competences acquired in sports settings can be applied to other spheres is as yet unknown.

Children and top-level sport

A controversial issue discussed in sport federations and the public sphere as well as in sport studies, at least in Europe, is the significance and the role of performance and contests in children's sports. When should and when can children begin to train systematically? What effects does training for competitive and top-level sports have on children's personalities and their development? In the USA competitive sport for children does not seem to be a contested issue, on account of the major importance of sporting success and the fact that competitive sport is firmly rooted in the education system. In many other countries, children and training cause controversial discussions. In many sports, top-level performance can only be achieved through extensive and focused training in childhood. This is especially true of sports which require a high degree of coordination, such as gymnastics on apparatus, rhythmic sportive gymnastics, and ice-skating. Advocates of children's competitive sport emphasise, among other things, the development of talent while its detractors refer to 'child labour' and point to the excessive strain put on children, the one-sided orientation of interests and experience, and the loss of a protected sphere to which they have a right.

On the basis of scientific data collated in the 1990s evidence was presented, on the one hand, for the great strain and exertion that children were exposed to in competitive sports training; on the other hand, it was revealed that such training did not inevitably result in either social, mental, or physical harm. Moreover, it was clearly shown that children did in fact take an active part in decision-making relating to a career in sport. Nevertheless, one should underestimate neither the role of parents, who not infrequently project their own aspirations and dreams onto their children, nor that of trainers and coaches, who are dependent on the success of their athletes. Preparing children for top-level competitive sport brings with it both opportunities and dangers. Parents, trainers, federations, and society as a whole must all shoulder this responsibility.

Further reading

Aries, P. (1962) *Centuries of Childhood: A Social History of Family Life*, New York: Philippe Knopf.

Daugs, R., Emrich, E. and Igel, C. (eds) (1998) *Kinder und Jugendliche im Leistungssport* [Children and Adolescents in Top-level Sport], Schorndorf: Hofmann.

Horne, J., Tomlinson, A. and Whannel, G. (1999) *Understanding Sport*, London/New York: E&FN Spon.

Rolff, H.-G. and Zimmermann, P. (2001) *Kindheit im Wandel. Eine Einführung in die Sozialisation im Kindesalter* [Changing Childhood: An Introduction to Socialisation in Childhood], Weinheim: Beltz.

Schmidt, W. (2002) *Sportpädagogik des Kindesalters* [Sport Pedagogy of Childhood], Hamburg: Czwalina.

GERTRUD PFISTER

CHOKING

Choking has been defined as performing more poorly then expected, given one's skill, when the desire to perform optimally creates feelings of performance pressure. Choking under pressure is thought to occur in any task in which incentives for optimal skill execution are at a maximum.

How does performance pressure lead to unwanted skill decrements? Two main theories have been proposed to explain the choking phenomenon. The first class of theories, often termed self-focus or explicit monitoring theories, propose that performance pressure increases anxiety and self-consciousness about performing correctly (Beilock and Carr 2001). This heightened self-consciousness enhances the attention that a performer allocates to their skill execution processes. For highly skilled individuals, whose performance execution is normally automated, this pressure-induced attention can serve to disrupt or slow down execution processes that normally run outside of conscious scrutiny – ultimately leading to less than optimal performance outcomes.

Distraction theories have also been proposed to account for choking under pressure. Distraction theories suggest that performance pressure creates worries about a situation and its consequences that distract attention away from skill execution (Wine 1971). Specifically, distraction theories propose that pressure creates a dual task, in which performance worries and skill execution compete for the attentional capacity once devoted solely to primary task performance. When attention is taken away from skill execution by pressure-induced worries, performance is thought to suffer.

Explicit monitoring theories appear to be best able to account for choking under pressure in sports skills. For example, in an attempt to test the two main theories of choking, Beilock and Carr (2001) examined performance under pressure in a golf-putting task. Participants were trained on a golf putting skill under one of three conditions. The first of these was a single-task condition, in which individuals putted in isolation. The second was a self-awareness condition, in which individuals putted while being videotaped for later analysis by golf professionals. This manipulation was designed to expose performers to having attention called to themselves and their performance in a way intended to induce explicit monitoring of skill execution. The third condition was a distracting condition, in which individuals putted while monitoring a series of verbally presented words for a specified target word. This manipulation was designed to expose performers to being distracted from the putting task by irrelevant thoughts in memory – the cause of performance decrements under pressure

according to distraction theories. All three groups were then exposed to the same high pressure. Pressure caused choking in those individuals trained in the single-task condition and in those individuals trained in the environment that simply created distraction. However, pressure did not lead to choking for individuals trained in the self-awareness condition. The authors concluded that training in an environment that prompted attention to skill parameters, the self-awareness condition, served to adapt these performers to the attentional focus that often occurs under pressure. That is, self-awareness training served to inoculate individuals against the negative consequences of paying too much attention to well learned performance processes – the precise mechanisms that explicit monitoring theories suggest are responsible for performance decrements under high pressure.

See also: anxiety and automaticity; yips

References

Beilock, S.L. and Carr, T.H. (2001) 'On the Fragility of Skilled Performance: What Governs Choking Under Pressure?', *Journal of Experimental Psychology: General* 130: 701–25.

Wine, J. (1971) 'Test Anxiety and Direction of Attention', *Psychological Bulletin* 76: 92–104.

Further reading

Baumeister, R.F. (1984) 'Choking Under Pressure: Self-consciousness and Paradoxical Effects of Incentives on Skillful Performance', *Journal of Personality and Social Psychology* 46: 610–20.

Beilock, S.L., Carr, T.H., MacMahon, C. and Starkes, J.L. (2002) 'When Paying Attention Becomes Counterproductive: Impact of Divided Versus Skill-focused Attention on Novice and Experienced Performance of Sensorimotor Skills', *Journal of Experimental Psychology: Applied* 8: 6–16.

SIAN L. BEILOCK

CHRONIC EXERTIONAL COMPARTMENT SYNDROME (CECS)

A compartment syndrome can be defined as 'a condition in which increased pressure within a closed space compromises neuromuscular function within that space'. Compartment syndromes can be classified into acute and chronic syndromes. Acute refers to a syndrome of rapid onset, usually precipitated by a specific event (most commonly trauma), which leads to rapid tissue necrosis. This is a surgical emergency and should be treated by open fasciotomy promptly. The term chronic exertional compartment syndrome (CECS) refers to the condition in athletes in which there is pain of gradual onset associated with alterations in neuromuscular function that interfere with performance. The CECS has been described mostly in relation to the lower leg but has also been reported in the hand, forearm, and thigh.

The traditional description of the lower leg compartments is that of four compartments: anterior, lateral, superficial, and deep posterior compartments. Within each compartment the important structures to consider are the muscles, nerves, and blood vessels.

Pathophysiology of CECS

The precise pathophysiology of the CECS is not well understood, but the following factors are thought to lead to increases in intra-compartmental tissue pressure during exercise:

- an inelastic fascial sheath;
- decreased venous return from the lower leg;
- increased skeletal muscle volume (by about 20 per cent during muscular exercise);
- other factors such as active muscle contraction, tissue oedema and the accumulation of glycogen and water during carbohydrate loading.

The cause of the pain that is experienced by athletes as a result of increased compartment pressure is not clear but muscle ischaemia, sensory receptor stimulation in the fascia when pressure is increased, sensory receptor stimulation in the periosteum when pressure is increased, and biochemical factors released due to increased pressure may contribute to the cause of pain.

Diagnosis of CECS

Pain in the lower leg is by far the commonest symptom. The pain of CECS is usually described as aching (85 per cent), tightness or squeezing (81 per cent), and in most cases it is bilateral (82 per cent). It is typically associated with exercise (94 per cent) and is severe enough to interfere with athletic performance (98 per cent). The common neurological symptoms are muscle weakness and sensory disturbances, and these relate to the muscles and nerves in the compartment that is affected.

At the time of clinical examination the following clinical signs may be elicited (best done before and after an exercise session): tenderness over the compartment, increased tissue pressure, swelling, fascial herniations, and neurological signs (weakness and sensory loss).

The determination of an increased tissue pressure above the normal is the 'gold standard' for the diagnosis of this condition. Increases in tissue pressure must be measured at rest, during exercise and for varying periods after exercise in patients with CECS.

Other special investigations such as radiography are not helpful in the diagnosis of CECS, except if it is used to exclude other causes of lower leg pain. A technetium bone scan is sometimes done to exclude tibial stress syndromes type II and I.

Nuclear magnetic resonance imaging (NMR), electromyography, and nerve conduction studies have also been used as additional investigations.

Treatment of CECS

The only effective long-term treatment is surgical decompression of the affected compartment. There is a place for trial of conservative treatment only if the diagnosis is not well established (for example if there are limited facilities for special investigations). A trial of non-operative treatment would include rest, tissue massage, and treatment for the condition that is considered to be the most likely alternative diagnosis.

Following subcutaneous fasciotomy the relief of symptoms and return to activity have been consistently reported as good. However, it has also been shown that decompression of all the affected compartments must be achieved (often the deep posterior compartment is missed).

See also: lower leg injury

MARTIN SCHWELLNUS

CIRCUIT TRAINING

Participation in physical exercise is increasing all the time. Men and women are more aware of the importance of good health and a favourable body composition and the many other positive effects that exercise provides. However, many people believe they do not have the time to achieve and maintain good fitness. Circuit training has thus evolved out of a need for people to experience the benefit of exercise, while achieving it in less time. Circuit training refers to a series of weight-training exercises of approximately 15–20 repetitions each, using moderate weights (± 40 per cent of a single maximal repetition – 1 RM). The person moves from station to station with a short 15–20 s rest.

Circuit training has been shown to improve cardio-respiratory endurance, body composition and strength in sessions lasting 25–30 min. Studies have shown that circuit training can improve aerobic endurance by 5 per cent, lean body mass by 1–3.2 per

cent, and strength by 7–32 per cent. Although improvements have been noted, they are not as substantial as if the person trained only that aspect of fitness. For example, improvements in aerobic performance range between 15–25 per cent when training only the aerobic component over a similar duration. Studies have also shown that improvements in endurance – maximal oxygen uptake, VO_2max – and strength are dependant on the work performed and not the equipment used.

The effects of circuit training on cardiovascular performance have been well documented. Wilmore *et al.* (1978) reported an improvement of 11 per cent in a group of women exercising for 30 s with 15 s rest over a 10-week period. Of particular interest in this study was that a group of men participating in the same programme did not show any improvement. The researchers explained this as being due to the women working at a higher percentage of maximum heart rate than the men – the men would have required more intensive training to increase their cardiorespiratory capacity, which this circuit did not provide. In a study designed to assess the duration of training, Gettman *et al.* (1978) found that minor improvements were seen between 11 and 20 weeks, but were not significantly greater. In this study, a 20-week running programme improved cardiovascular performance by 17 per cent.

Other studies have shown no improvement in cardiovascular performance. Allen *et al.* (1976), after a 12-week programme, found no improvement in cardiovascular performance. Their circuit consisted of 30 s of high-resistance, low-repetition sessions followed by 60 s recovery, with a total circuit time of 30 min. The lack of improvement witnessed was ascribed to the duration of the rest periods.

One of the other effects of circuit training is to influence body composition. Garfield *et al.* (1979) showed that lean body weight increased significantly, by 1–3.2 per cent, while per cent body fat dropped by 2 per cent. Circuit training, therefore, has a positive effect on body composition and weight control, although its role in reducing total body weight is not apparent, as the increase in lean body mass is offset by the loss of body fat.

The effects of circuit training on strength development have been well studied. Circuit training has been shown to compare favourably with traditional weight-training programmes in improving strength. Improvements ranging from 7–27 per cent have been seen when assessing 1 RM leg press, and 8–32 per cent when assessing 1 RM bench press in people using circuit training. Strength improvements seen in circuit training are on a par with those experienced in low-repetition, high-resistance weight-training – 12–38 per cent.

The benefits derived from circuit training are dependant on several factors. None is more important than the time spent exercising, the rest periods between each exercise, the duration of the programme, and the individual's initial fitness.

References

Allen, T.E., Byrd, R.J. and Smith, D.P. (1976) 'Hemodynamic Consequences of Circuit Weight Training', *Research Quarterly* 47: 299–306.

Gettman, L.R., Ayres, J.J. and Pollock, M.L. (1978) 'The Effect of Circuit Weight Training on Strength, Cardio-Respiratory Function, and Body Composition of Adult Men', *Medicine and Science in Sports* 10: 171–6.

Wilmore, J.H., Parr, R.B., Girandola, R.N., Ward, P., Vodak, P.A., Barstow, T.J., Pipes, T.V., Romero, G.T. and Leslie, P. (1978) 'Physiological Alterations Consequent to Circuit Weight Training', *Medicine and Science in Sports* 10: 79–84.

ANDREW GRAY

CITY MARKETING

It is conventional to refer to image as consisting of a mental reconstruction of a place in a person's mind. However, this traditional use of the term has been expanded to embrace a conceptualization of image as perceived reputation or character.

Cities consciously engage in what has become known as place marketing, which involves striving to sell the image of a place so as to make it more attractive to businesses, tourists, and inhabitants. The pervasive popularity of sport in the media has persuaded many cities that sport may be a useful vehicle through which to enhance their image. Some believe that major sports events and teams are the new 'image builders' for communities. In the construction years after World War II, this role was performed by tall buildings, tower skylines, large span bridges, or manufacturing industries (for example, Motor City or Steel City). Today, as the economy has switched to a service orientation, major sports events, teams, and facilities capture the imagination and help establish a city's image in people's minds. When the Houston Astrodome was built, it was the self-proclaimed 'eighth wonder of the world', and was an important element in the city's effort to recast its image from sleepy bayou town to space-age Sunbelt dynamo.

A professional sports team guarantees a significant amount of media coverage for the city in which it is located. It keeps the community's name in front of a national audience. If a city has a major league team, then each day across the nation when fans read their sports pages, the city's name will be there. A baseball owner noted, 'Tonight, on every single television and radio station in the USA, Seattle will be mentioned because of the Mariners' game, and tomorrow night and the next night and on and on. You'd pay millions in public-relations fees for that.' Further, sports teams usually generate favorable publicity plugging troubled cities into the good news network: 'We're OK', say the sports pages.

There is much public sympathy for the adage that no place really can be considered a 'major league city' or 'first tier city' if it does no have a major league sports team. The team often is positioned in people's minds as being symptomatic of a city's character, and as defining external perceptions of the city. Despite these claims, the legitimacy of the premise that major league team equates to a major league city is challengeable. It is doubtful that people view Charlotte, Jacksonville and Nashville to be big-time locations and Los Angeles an also-ran place because the former have NFL teams, while the latter does not. Large cities receive constant media attention. Their size ensures that a disproportionate number of newsworthy events occur there, both positive and negative. Hence, their image is molded by a host of symbols, events, people, and behaviors, so the incremental contribution of a sports event, facility or team to the image of those cities is likely to be relatively small. Their contribution to the image of smaller cities is likely to be proportionately more substantial.

People frequently make judgments about the competence of a city's administration and its quality of life by extrapolating from snippets of information or from symbols. A sports team is a highly visible symbol. Thus, another dimension of the image issue relates to perceptions of the community's status. A sports franchise may be considered by some as a symbolic embodiment of the city as a whole. Thus, while association with sports teams generally is perceived to enhance a city's image, there is some risk that if a team is poor then it could create, or at least reinforce, a negative image. For example, in the US the city of Cleveland had an image of failing city which possibly was reinforced by a series of losing seasons by its professional teams who played in old-fashioned, dingy stadiums. Similarly, if a city loses its team or the team is relegated it may create the impression that the community is declining or a 'loser'. Indeed, it may be worse for a city's image to lose a major event or have its team relegated than to have never attained major status at all.

Given the potential positive impact of a franchise on a city's image, those cities with most to gain from it are probably those which are in decline. They are most desperate to communicate signs of economic and social rejuvenation. The city of Cleveland shows that this can be a successful strategy. The city was widely known as 'The Mistake by the Lake' as a result of its river burning from its pollutants, racial riots, and a depressing and decaying downtown. The city invested $800 million in major leisure projects, including new major league facilities for the MLB Indians, NBA Cavaliers and NFL Browns. This stimulated a revitalization of the downtown area. The facilities attract 5 million people to events at a downtown that just one decade earlier was avoided. Downtown Cleveland is now seen as a desirable place that attracts residents, people from across the region and tourists.

JOHN L. CROMPTON

CIVIC PRIDE/PSYCHIC INCOME

Civic pride/psychic income is the emotional and psychological benefit residents perceive they receive from a sports team or event, even though they may not physically attend or participate in it and are not involved in organizing it.

People may avidly follow 'their' team through the media and engage in animated conversations with others about the team, but never attend a game. In this respect, it has been pointed out that the economics of sports is much different from the economics of, say, apples. An individual is unlikely to derive pleasure from knowing that somebody else in the community is eating apples, but may derive pleasure and a sense of civic pride from the performance of the community's sports teams.

When a business in a community is successful, elected officials and business leaders may get excited because it leads to more jobs and more income for the community's residents, but ordinary citizens do not because such benefits do not personally affect most of them. When a sports team or local athlete is successful, a much broader segment of the population becomes excited and identifies with it. A sports team is an investment in the emotional infrastructure of a community. Sports has been eloquently described as 'the "magic elixir" that feeds personal identity while it nourishes the bonds of communal solidarity'.

Sports are not like other businesses. It has been said they are about 'triumphs of the human spirit, community bonding, and family memories. They're about taking a break from the pettiness that divides us. They're about celebrating some of the things that make society whole: competition, victory, redemption.' Society has an emotional attachment to sports and receives a psychic income from them. The emotional involvement transposes some people from the dreary routines of their lives to a mode of escapism that enables them to identify with a team, personalize its success, and feel better about themselves. Life is about experiences, and sports teams help create them – albeit vicariously in most cases. When Tottenham Hotspur football club, based in north London, essentially went bankrupt in the late 1990s, their bank did not foreclose on the unpayable loan by closing the ground and selling it and the other team assets as they would have done with any other business. They realized if they took this action, they would alienate a large proportion of the London population, lose tens of thousands of accounts in London, and be stigmatized forever. The bank absorbed the team's losses and the team continued to operate.

Sports teams are a medium through which cities and their residents express their personality, enhance their status and promote their quality of life to a national audience. Sports teams and events are much more than enterprises with economic benefits and costs. They are cultural assets which for many communities exceed in importance such traditionally perceived cultural assets as art galleries, museums, and symphony orchestras. When viewed from this perspective, a case can be made that such organizations should be eligible to receive public subsidies if they are needed to remain viable in the same way that many performing arts, museums, and visual arts entities receive public subsidies. If they were removed from a community's social fabric, there would be a void.

The relationship between sports teams and their fans is often referred to as a 'love affair'. The pervasive influence of sports is exemplified by the extensive use of sports metaphors in everyday life. Knowing how to keep a straight bat; respond to a googly; bat on a sticky wicket; keep your end up; avoid being stumped; or duck a bouncer, are cricketing phrases that are endemic in the English language. Indeed, it has been suggested that the language of sports is the symbolic glue that holds together the entire social life world. This might be hyperbole, but sport is a central topic of conversation in many social contexts.

Sports teams or events provide a tangible focus for building community consciousness and social bonding. They are an important part of the collective experience of urban dwellers since they tie them together regardless of race, gender, or economic standing. They are one of the few vehicles available for developing a sense of community. One commentator concluded that fans who chant 'we're number one' are trumpeting the superiority of both their team and their town. In rallying around the home team, people identify more closely with a broader civic framework in cities that often are spatially, socially, and politically fragmented. They generate civic energy.

It has been suggested that sports is a theater where Kipling's twin impostors of triumph and disaster run side-by-side and impact large numbers of people. It provides a theater of emotions to fantasize about and to casually share. When a team or event is successful, benefits often accrue to the collective morale of all residents. A substantial proportion of a community emotionally identifies with 'their' team or event, and feels elation, anxiety, despondency, optimism, and an array of other emotions according to how the team performs. Some of these people may not understand the nature of the event or how the activity is performed. Nevertheless, the team constitutes a common identification symbol that brings together the citizens of the city.

Sports teams contribute to building a community's sense of place. The warmth people derive from their connections to a team, athlete, or event is difficult to quantify in monetary terms and sometimes gets lost in the cynical wranglings between millionaire players and billionaire owners.

It has long been recognized that the emotional identification with sports teams has an extraordinary impact on the morale of many people. In recent years a biological explanation for this has emerged. Winning and losing have a direct effect on the chemical composition of our brains, particularly on levels of a neuro-transmitter called serotonin. The social environment, not heredity, has been shown to be the critical determinant in serotonin levels. Winning raises levels and losing lowers them. This at least partially explains observations like 'Every time we win, we're like a different country. Everybody's happy. Football [soccer] can bring peace.' People with low serotonin levels are more depressed and aggressive than people with high levels. When individuals identify with the fortunes of their team and it loses an important game, unconsciously, they lose. They are more likely to feel depressed or become violent afterwards because their serotonin levels have dropped. Anti-depressant drugs, such as Prozac, work by raising serotonin levels.

The psychic income and civic pride that people experience often is used by elected officials who seek to exploit the popularity of sport by linking with it. For example, they invariably seek association with victorious teams by organizing parades and ceremonies for teams in which they feature prominently, hoping the 'feel-good factor' will spill over to aid their popularity as elected officials. Politicians can probably aid their re-election chances if they can arrange for the election to coincide with an important sporting success with which their constituents identify, because the raised serotonin levels of constituents is likely to create a 'feel-good factor'.

JOHN L. CROMPTON

CLINICAL FINDINGS

Clinical findings are at times so precise that a diagnosis of the pathology is easily made even without any supplemental imaging or other investigations. However, there are various injuries that occur in sports to joints, muscles, ligaments, nerves, and bones, which require detailed examination which is then supplemented with investigations.

Bone is a strong tissue but it is prone to injury and fractures. Any bone in the skeleton can fracture. The clavicle is fractured in contact sports like rugby and soccer; so are the long bones like the tibia and the femur. The humerus and the forearm bones are also often fractured in contact sports. A fall may cause axial force leading to fracture of the vertebral bodies. There is swelling at the fracture site; this may also be associated with bruising and discoloration of skin. This is due to the haematoma formation. The fracture site is also very tender. This is very obvious in acute fractures. However, in a fracture which is older this is an important sign to assess whether or not the fracture is healing. In nonunion there may be persistent fracture site tenderness. The nonunion may be obvious on the radiographs or may need further investigations to confirm the diagnosis. In acute fractures there may also be crepitus present. This sign, although quite diagnostic, is difficult to elicit because of pain. In older fractures when there is concern of a nonunion the clinical examination can give clues. Motion at the fracture site is sometimes present and there is little doubt about the union. The other findings are deformity at the level of the fracture; there may also be rotation or overlapping at the fracture. In hip fractures there may be shortening of the ipsilateral leg as well as external rotation of the foot. This finding is quite common, and usually just observing the position of the leg supplies a provisional diagnosis.

Joints are also injured in sporting activities. The knee is frequently affected in many sports, but most often in contact sports and those which involve cutting, turning, and sprinting. The knee is injured in a various positions. The knee may go into hyperextension with a valgus strain or may be flexed with a valgus or varus strain. There may also be a rotatory component in the injury mechanism. There may also be collision with another player, leading to a direct valgus/varus strain or antereoposterior force.

The clinical examination focuses on inspection of the knee. There may be bruising and swelling of the knee. The knee should be viewed from the front and also seen from the back to assess the popliteal fossa, which may also reveal bruising as well as swelling. The knee may reveal tenderness. If this is over the bone then a fracture is suspected. If there is tenderness around the joint line then a meniscal tear is suspected. McMurray's test is positive if there is tear of the medial or lateral meniscus. The knee is extended from a flexed position with fingers placed on the suspected meniscal tear. A valgus strain may be applied or the knee given a rotatory motion. The patients feel pain and there is tenderness. Appley's grinding test is also suggestive of a tear in the meniscus. The patients are placed prone and the knee flexed to 90°. Axial pressure is applied to the foot and the knee rotated. This causes pain because the torn meniscus catches between the femur and the tibia. The anterior cruciate ligament is torn in several sports, and its frequency has increased mainly due to better imaging and treatment options.

The knee swells within hours of the injury. This is due to haemarthrosis as the blood supply to the ACL is disrupted. Once the knee is settled, examination of the knee easily picks up the lesion. The anterior draw test is positive. This should always be compared with the uninjured side. If there is complete rupture of the ACL there is a soft end point to the anterior draw. If there is a bony end point to the anterior draw then a partial tear may be suspected. The anterior draw should also be elicited in both internal and external rotation of the foot to detect any rotatory instability, which may be associated with an ACL tear. Lachman's test is diagnostic of ACL rupture. This is performed with the knee flexed to 30° with one hand stabilising the thigh and the other hand rocking the leg anteriorly. A pivot shift test is pathogonomic of an ACL rupture. This test may be difficult to perform on a conscious patient as it can cause pain; it is usually performed with the patient under anaesthetic. A valgus strain is placed on the knee joint and the knee flexed from an extended position. The subluxed tibia reduces back with a jerk.

When collateral ligaments are injured this can cause instability of the knee joint. The collateral are tested with the knee extended and also flexed at 30°. If the knee joint opens up on valgus/varus testing in the extended position then there is usually injury to the collaterals; but also the ACL and the PCL may be ruptured. If there is laxity in 30° of flexion then only the collateral is injured, because at the 30° of flexion all other ligaments and the capsule are relaxed and the primary constraint is the collaterals.

The posterior cruciate ligament (PCL) when ruptured can present with a posterior sag. The legs are flexed to 90° and placed together. The leg with PCL deficiency reveals posterior sag. The tibial tuberosities should be seen from the side for assessment. A posterior draw test is also positive.

A posterolateral corner injury should be tested with the patient lying prone. The knee is flexed to 30° and then to 90°. The foot is externally rotated. There is a difference of almost 10° of rotation in cases with posteriolateral ligament injury. This is also called the dial test. The other test is the external rotation recurvatum test. The involved leg is lifted up holding the greater toe. The knee goes into hyperextension and varus position.

The shoulder joint can also show anterior instability with a positive apprehension test. The patient either lies supine or sits on a chair. The arm is externally rotated with abduction to 90°. The arm is gently externally rotated. The patient dislikes this and tenses his muscles to stop further external rotation. The anterior draw test is also positive in many of these cases. Other tests that are performed in shoulder examination are the speed test for the biceps tendon, the lift-off test for the subscapularis and O'Brien's test for SLAP (superior labral anterior to posterior) lesions.

The Jobes test assesses the rotator cuff. The patient is asked to abduct the arm against resistance. The patient is unable to do this and feels pain. The Hawkins and the Neers test determine the impingement. The Hawkins is performed by internal rotation of the shoulder at 90° of forward flexion. The patient feels sudden pain on the internal rotation as the rotator cuff impinges on the undersurface of the acromion.

The ankle joint can also present with chronic instability. A varus/valgus stress on the joint may reveal laxity of the ligaments.

The anterior draw test can also be performed on the ankle joint, which may show abnormal translation of the talus.

IMRAN ILYAS

CLOSED CHAIN

The concept of open and closed chain exercises was first described by Dr Arthur Steindler in 1955. Based on a kinetic mechanical engineering model, he described the body as a series of interconnected joints where the movement of one joint directly effects the movement of other joints above and below. He referred to a closed kinetic chain exercise as one in which the distal extremity meets considerable resistance that prevents or greatly restrains motion. Usually the distal limb is fixed in position by contact with a surface, such as the floor or a wall. In contrast, an open kinetic chain exercise is an exercise in which the distal extremity is free to move about in space. Typically, closed chain exercises involve the movement of multiple joints and are considered weight-bearing exercises. Technically, these exercises are performed when the force applied by the body is not strong enough to overcome the resistance against the body.

An example of a closed chain exercise is the squat. This exercise starts in the standing neutral position, with or without a weight bar over the shoulders. The individual then slowly flexes (or bends) the hip, knee and ankle joints while supporting the weight on the shoulders. In this example, the foot (or distal limb) remains fixed to the floor. Various examples of closed chain movements can be identified in numerous athletic activities and activities of daily living. Some phases of the push-off phase of the running cycle, push-up exercises, cycling, hand-stands in gymnastics, and movements of the legs during weightlifting are just a few of the many types of closed chain motions common in sports.

Generally, closed chain exercises are considered a multi-joint and multi muscle group exercise in which several joints are involved and the agonist (prime mover) and antagonist (opposing muscle group) muscles contract simultaneously. In the example above, during a squat the hip flexors, gluteal muscles, quadriceps, hamstrings, and gastrocnemious muscles all contract simultaneously.

The advantages of closed chain exercises are that they approximate functional activities and are therefore considered sports-specific activities. Closed chain exercises enable us to develop balance and proprioceptive skills (knowing where our body is in space). A typical prescription for a closed chain exercise routine focusing on upper body strengthening recommended by the American College of Sports Medicine might include 1 to 3 sets of 10 to 12 repetitions, 3 to 4 times per week of push-ups, triceps (chair dips) and pull-ups. In these exercises, the individual is using body weight as the resistance instead of an external weight. The individual should start with one set of 10–12 repetitions and work up to three sets of 10–12 repetitions, 3 to 4 times per week.

There has been significant controversy in the literature regarding the appropriate exercises necessary for rehabilitation after an anterior cruciate ligament (ACL) repair. Closed chain exercises appear to cause decreased shearing forces and increased compressive forces on the joints involved in the exercises as compared to open chain exercises. Shearing forces pull the tibia (leg bone) and femur (thigh bone) in opposite directions and thus place increased strain on the ACL. Compressive forces activate the hamstring muscles to prevent the anterior motion of the tibia and thus increase stability of the knee joint. This increased stability, decreases shearing and disruptive forces about the ACL and allows for better healing after surgery.

See also: open chain

Further reading

Paine, R.M. and Johnson, R.M. (2003) 'Section B Open and Closed Chain Exercises (Non-Weight-Bearing and Weight-Bearing Exercises)', in J.C. DeLee, D. Drez Jr and M.D. Miller (eds) *DeLee and Drez's Orthopedic Sports Medicine*, 2nd edn, 336–8, Philadelphia PA: W.B. Saunders.

JESSICA SCHUTZBANK

CLUB HEAD MASS AND CLUB INERTIA EFFECTS

A long held concept in those sports where implements are used is that the heavier the device then the faster the ball will travel. This apparently intuitive statement needs quantifying. The simple laws of the physics of collisions show that: $v_{ball} = v_{head} (1 + e)/(1 + m_{ball}/m_{head})$, where m and v are mass and velocity respectively and e is the **coefficient of restitution**, which measures the amount of energy supplied to the ball. Typically, for a golf ball and club head collision, this coefficient will be 0.78, meaning that about 20 per cent of the energy available in the club is lost in the impact by non-linear deformations of the ball, and some of the club head.

In most collisions, the mass of the ball is much less than that of the implement being used to hit it. The second term in the denominator of the above equation is, therefore, small compared to the first term, and the post-impact speed of the ball is mainly dependent on the coefficient of restitution. Even when this second term is included, the change in ball speed caused by an increase in head mass is disproportionally small. In golf, for instance, the mass of a driver head is around 200 g, and that of a ball 46 g. Measured coefficients of restitution average about 0.78. Thus an increase in head mass by 50 per cent to, say, 250 g would generate an increase in ball speed of only 3.7 per cent. Equally, a decrease to 150 g decreases the ball speed by only 6 per cent. These figures assume that the change in club head mass would not affect the pre-impact club head speed.

The equation shows that increasing the coefficient of restitution to, say, 0.85, that is by 9 per cent, would produce an increase in ball speed of 4 per cent, a much better return than altering the head mass. It is for this reason that much effort has been expended by manufacturers of the implements and the balls to decrease the energy lost in the collision. In modern developments, the heads are allowed to deform but designed to resume their original shape in a time frame that allows some of that movement to add energy to the ball. This is particularly true in golf, where the process is known as the 'trampoline effect'.

Inertia is defined both as the property that makes an object continue on its current path and as the resistance to motion away from or out of that path. In its simplest physical form, it is related to the acceleration of an object caused by the application of a force. For a given force, the higher the inertia, the lower the acceleration and vice-versa. By way of an example of this, consider a golf club accelerated by a golfer with the intention of generating a high club head speed. The larger the inertia of the club, the smaller the acceleration will be and, therefore, the smaller the speed achieved at impact. This inertia can be simply calculated as the product of the mass of the head and the square of the distance of that mass from the pivot about which it is rotating, namely the wrists. By making clubs longer, the manufacturer makes them more difficult to swing unless the mass of the head is reduced significantly to compensate.

Conversely, inertia can be used to maintain the club head on line during the impact with the ball. The measured impact forces peak at over 12 kN although, fortunately, for a duration of less than 0.5 ms. If the line of action of the impact is directly through the centre of mass of the head, then the head will suffer no rotation.

Unfortunately, and at any standard of golf, this perfect impact seldom occurs. The line of action of the force is usually offset from the centre of mass, and the head will rotate. If the rotational inertia of the head about the centre of mass is large, then the resulting rotation will be slow, and the effect on the ball over the period of impact will be less.

In new designs of club head, the metal titanium is used. This has the same specific strength as steel. As a result, the volume of the head can be made larger with consequential increases in the rotational inertia. Manufacturers also add mass in areas well away from the centre of mass for a similar effect. The same effects can be built into tennis racquets by adding mass to the periphery of racquets on the sides and, in cricket, by redistributing the mass of the cricket bat either to make it easier to swing, which is good for juniors, or to resist the impact of a fast ball.

See also: angular momentum – generation, transfer, and trading; ball and surface impacts; centre of mass; force measurement; impact between objects; impulse-momentum relationship; sports equipment

Further reading

Cochran, A.J. (1996) *Golf: The Scientific Way*, London: Central Books.
Cochran, A.J. and Stobbs, J. (1996) *Search for the Perfect Swing: The Proven Scientific Way to Fundamentally Improving Your Game*, Northam: Roundhouse.
Jorgensen, T. (1999) *The Physics of Golf*, New York: Springer-Verlag.

J.S.B. MATHER

COACHING

Coaching takes place within a wide variety of contexts: education, the arts, sport, and more recently in management consultancy. What is common to all these situations is that coaching ultimately is about improving performance, but the actual coaching experience may be very different for those taking part in each of these contexts.

One of the main factors in skill acquisition is practice, but for practice to be meaningful it needs to be organised and people need to be motivated to do it. The role of the coach then is to organise the environment in order to both motivate and allow athletes to develop and improve their performance in the chosen activity. The implication here is that coaching is much more than simply about the 'how to do it' aspects of skill acquisition. Coaching is a process that can only be truly understood if the context and the social interactions that exist within the coaching environment are taken into account. It is impossible to isolate the coach from these, and each context will demand different behaviours. Coaching then is a multi-faceted, multi-layered phenomenon that must be managed by the coach if coaching is to be effective (Lyle 1999; 2002).

Several coaching models have been suggested by various authors in an attempt to conceptualise the coaching process, but few have truly taken into account the social interactions and other contextual factors that are part of every coaching situation. What these interactions are, will vary depending on the level of coaching being practised. Coaching can take place at a variety of levels, ranging from participation coaching, where the coach is usually more concerned with the recreational aspects of sport and the encouragement of people to take part, through to elite performance coaching where peak performance is the ultimate goal. Coaches at the participation level will need different skills, have different demands, interface with different people and have different constraints, from those working at the elite level. Both, however, will be involved in a process of planning, managing, and controlling the numerous variables associated with their coaching in order to achieve their goals, be

it peak performance, athlete development or mass participation. Although within the coaching structure of most National Governing Bodies (NGBs) of sport these levels of coaching may be reflected in the various coaching awards, it is important to appreciate that these are not viewed as different levels of the same process but as two distinct processes (Lyle 2002).

How people experience the coaching process will then depend on the context in which it takes place. Added to this, different coaches in a variety of contexts may have different coaching styles and philosophies. A coach may have a preferred style of coaching, but may also vary that style or use alternative strategies depending on factors such as the age and ability of the athletes, the constraints of time and money imposed, the period of the training cycle, the relationship with the athlete, the needs and the goals of all concerned. This reflects the complex nature of coaching, and even though there is a vast array of literature on the subject, there is very little research which critically examines coaching practice (Lyle 1999). In fact, coaching as an area for academic study is relatively new, and to understand some of the reasons for this we need to look at the historical developments of coaching within the United Kingdom.

For many years athletes from various sport disciplines have sought the advice of others in an attempt to improve performance, yet it is only recently that 'coaching' has begun to emerge as a profession. Within the United Kingdom (UK) at least, the lowly status attached to coaching can be explained by several factors (see Lyle 2002), but perhaps the fundamental issue surrounding the development of coaching has been the emphasis on amateur sport. In the nineteenth century there was a distinct class divide between the working-class 'professional' coach/trainer and the 'gentleman player'. The Victorian 'amateur ethic' and the inherent values attached to this ideal have continued and, even today, sport in the UK could not function without its strong volunteer base.

In recent years within the UK coaching has started to become more 'professional'. Much of this drive to professionalise coaching has come from the increased recognition of sporting performance within our society. The importance attached to sport as a political tool by many nations and the strive to achieve Olympic gold has led to a greater emphasis being placed on sport by governments. At grass roots level too there has been support by the UK government, first in the 1980s with the 'Sport for All' campaign and more recently, in school sport, with the publication *Sport: Raising the Game* (1995) through which the government endeavoured to restore through physical education in schools particular versions of Englishness and citizenship by placing high emphasis on traditional games. Also within the education environment, the end of the twentieth century has seen the growth in initiatives such as sports colleges, where emphasis is placed on sporting performance.

Perhaps, however, one of the most important factors that has led to the advances and developments in coaching in the UK in recent years has been the National Lottery. The introduction of the National Lottery has meant that now both sporting organisations and individuals can be funded in order to allow the athlete to train full time. In addition, this funding has meant that athletes can be supported by specific programmes that have aimed to provide sports science support to both elite performers and those with the potential to become world class. Along with these initiatives has come a recognition of the need to develop coaching and coaches from grass roots to elite levels. As a result, financial help has been given to increasing and improving coach education and encouraging continued professional development. Lottery funding has also meant that performance coaches now may work alongside

various sport scientists – the biomechanist, physiologist, psychologist, physiotherapist, and team doctor – and sports coaching at this level has become an integrated, multi-disciplined affair.

Alongside these developments there has been an explosion within our universities of sports science programmes, and at undergraduate and postgraduate level coaching science has now become an area of academic study. While the emphasis of many of these programmes is on related, and certainly valuable, sub-disciplines like skill-acquisition, physiology of training or psychology of performance, there is a failure to really get to the heart of what coaching is about. To do this time needs to be spent on deconstructing the coaching process and to understand that although there may be general principles that need to be adhered to if coaching is to be effective, the process itself will vary depending on the context in which it takes place.

References

Lyle, J. W. B. (1999) 'The Coaching Process: An Overview', in N. Cross (ed.) *The Coaching Process: Principles and Practice for Sport*, 3–25, Edinburgh: Butterworth Heinemann.

—— (2002). *Sports Ccoaching Concepts. A Framework for Coaches' Behaviour*, London: Routledge.

DI BASS

COEFFICIENT OF RESTITUTION

The strict definition of the coefficient of restitution, often denoted by the symbol e, is the ratio of the relative speed of two elastic spheres after direct impact to that before impact. Generally the coefficient of restitution has been used to characterise the rebound of dissimilar objects, and particularly **ball and surface impacts**. The coefficient of restitution is a property of the two impacting surfaces, and is commonly assumed to be a constant regardless of impact speed and deformation. For instance, a tennis ball impacting normally onto a rigid surface will have a coefficient of restitution of approximately 0.75 at an impact speed of $5\,\mathrm{m\,s}^{-1}$. At higher impact speeds of up to $30\,\mathrm{m\,s}^{-1}$ the coefficient of restitution can drop to a value of approximately 0.3, depending upon the construction of the ball. The internal pressure in the ball, the ball's wall thickness, the properties of the materials of the ball, and the properties of the surface impacted upon all play a part in determining the value of the coefficient of restitution. When quoted, the coefficient of restitution should be qualified with the construction of the impacting objects and their impact speed.

The coefficient of restitution is usually measured by using light gates or high-speed video to measure the relative speeds before and after impact; estimates can be made for ball impacts onto a rigid surface by measuring the rebound (h_f) and drop (h_i) heights. The coefficient of restitution is then given by $e = \sqrt{(h_f/h_i)}$. In this case, air resistance is ignored and it may be found that values of coefficient of restitution given by high-speed video tests are slightly higher than the value calculated from the drop test.

See also: normal impact

STEVE HAAKE

COGNITIVE MOTOR CONTROL

One of the predominant perspectives of how the nervous system controls movement is based on hierarchical theories. These theories have in common some form of memory representation, such as a motor program, that provides the basis for organizing, initiating, and carrying out intended movement (see **memory motor representations**).

The time constraints imposed on the movement influence how movements can be controlled. Movements of relatively long duration, greater than one third of a second, can use feedback generated during the movement itself to assist in their closed-loop control. In contrast, very rapid movements require all the efferent commands to be structured in advance, in a so-called open loop, or programmed, control. In the closed-loop control, an original command for action starts the action by progressing through the stimulus–identification, response-selection, and response-programming stages, eventually leading to activation of the movement commands to the muscles. Then, in longer moments, in contrast with the open-loop system, a reference of correctness is allegedly generated that will serve as the model against which the feedback from the performance is compared. The reference mechanism then compares the value of the goal to that of the sample obtained from the environment, and an error is computed, representing the difference between the actual and intended states. New commands are then sent to the musculoskeletal system, producing changes in the movement as a result. These effects generate information that is sent back to the reference mechanism, to make new decisions about future movements in a continuous cycle. In this sense, humans are considered processors of information, with their performance being limited by this capability.

See also: information processing approach.

Further reading

Schmidt, R.A. and Lee, T. (1999) *Motor Control and Learning, Third Edition*, ch. 4, Champaign IL: Human Kinetics.
Swinnen, S. (1994) 'Motor Control', *Encyclopedia of Human Behavior* 3: 229–43.

DUARTE ARAÚJO

COHESION

Cohesion refers to the feelings of unity within a group or team. One of the earliest, and most parsimonious, definitions of cohesion was that it was the sum of all the forces operating on a group to remain united. Although this reflected the notion of team unity simply, it proved to be too vague to support much systematic research. The most widely used definition in sports psychology was put forth by Carron *et al.* (1998), who stated that cohesion was 'a dynamic process that is reflected in the tendency for a group to stick together and remain united in the pursuit of its instrumental objectives and/or for the satisfaction of member affective needs' (p. 213). This definition reflects a precise conceptual model of team cohesion. According to these authors, team cohesion in sports has four key characteristics – it is dynamic, multidimensional, instrumental, and affective. By noting that cohesion is dynamic, we can see that even if a team's make-up remains stable, perceptions of team unity can and do change from season to season and day to day. Sometimes a team will be highly united, at other times it will not. It is equally important to recognize that cohesion is multidimensional; no one all-encompassing reason explains why teams remain united.

Consistent with earlier conceptualisations, Carron *et al.* believed that, to understand the cohesiveness of teams, one must recognise a variety of factors for why teams are, or are not, cohesive. The most obvious distinction of different dimensions of cohesion is seen through task cohesion and social cohesion; these are, respectively, the instrumental and affective aspects of cohesion noted above. Task cohesion deals with how united teams are about the instrumental tasks they are trying to accomplish. Social cohesion refers to team unity around its members' affective needs. Thus, some teams may be largely task oriented, whereas others are more social oriented.

Although cohesion can be assessed through various qualitative and quantitative means, it is most commonly measured through self-report quantitative scales. The

Group Environment Questionnaire was designed for this purpose and is probably the most widely used measurement of cohesion. Typical of quantitative cohesion scales, it measures the individual team members' perceptions of both task and social unity within the team. It also measures individual perceptions of their attraction to the team, and the members' perceptions of the unity of the group as a whole.

Summarising the research on the topic, it is probably best to understand team unity as part of an input-throughput-output model, in which cohesion acts as a central mechanism mediating the impact of input, such as team structure, on output, for example, performance. The inputs into such a model would include environmental, social, group, and individual factors that affect cohesion. The outputs would include individual and team processes and attributes. Cohesion would act as a dynamic multidimensional go-between.

Factors influencing cohesion can be divided into those that operate at the group, the subordinate, and the super-ordinate levels. Subordinate antecedents are based on the attributes of the individual team members. Research has shown that, with respect to such issues, similarity enhances cohesion, although in some personality characteristics, such as dominance and submissiveness, compatibility is also important. At the super-ordinate level, issues such as the temporal and physical environment in which the team performs have been noted as influential. In particular, physical settings that facilitate increased interpersonal interactions, for example cramped locker rooms, increase cohesion. Group factors refer to those social and interpersonal processes that occur among teammates. Probably the most influential of these processes on cohesion include role clarity and role acceptance. Teams that have members whose roles are plainly established and accepted tend to be more cohesive than those whose members' duties are muddled.

Whereas certain factors may influence the amount of social or task cohesion a team displays, this team unity can subsequently affect a variety of significant outcomes. Because cohesion involves significant individual perceptions, as well as a sense of the group as whole, these outcomes include both individual and team issues. Outcomes of cohesion for the individual player include satisfaction with the team, adherence to the task, sacrifices to the team, and role acceptance. All increase with greater team cohesion. Although team performance has been the outcome of cohesion that has attracted most interest, other factors include team confidence, **social support**, stability, and resistance to disruption. More cohesive teams tend to be more confident and more resistant to team disruptions, offer more social support for team members, and have a lower turnover.

Of all the variables linked to team cohesion, probably the most significant is team performance. There is a wealth of literature on the relationship between team cohesion and performance, particularly on clarifying the direction of causality between the two, that is, does cohesion have a greater impact on performance than performance does on cohesion? It has been repeatedly shown that both social and task cohesion are related to team performance in a wide variety of sporting teams. The typical paradigm to address the causal nature of this relationship has used cross-lagged designs. Such designs assess both cohesion and performance in a small sample, such as one team, at various instants in time, for example, throughout a season. Thus, it is possible to determine the subsequent effect of one variable on a second variable. These studies have shown that, although both the effect of performance on cohesion and cohesion on performance are significant, there is probably a stronger effect of cohesion on subsequent performance. Thus, although winning teams

tend to be more cohesive than losing teams, highly cohesive teams will also outperform low cohesive teams, and this latter relationship is somewhat more likely.

Various team-building strategies have been proposed to enhance team cohesion, and indirectly accrue the benefits of improved team performance and other outcomes. These programmes tend to structure various aspects of the team in the hope of creating more cohesive teams. Typical focal points include communication patterns, team distinctiveness, uniqueness of the group, and team norms and roles. Strategies to enhance social cohesion might focus on making the team more distinctive, for example, through new team apparel. Interventions designed to enhance task cohesion may do so through team **goal setting**.

See also: group dynamics; social psychology

Reference

Carron, A.V., Brawley, L.R. and Widmeyer, W.N. (1998) 'The Measurement of Cohesiveness in Sport Groups', in J.L. Duda (ed.) *Advances in Sport and Exercise Psychology Measurement*, 213–26, Morgantown WV: Fitness Information Technology.

Further reading

Carron, A.V., Brawley, L.R. and Widmeyer, W.N. (1998) 'The Measurement of Cohesiveness in Sport Groups', in J.L. Duda (ed.) *Advances in Sport and Exercise Psychology Measurement*, 213–26, Morgantown WV: Fitness Information Technology.

Carron, A.V. and Denis, P.W. (1998) 'The Sport Team as an Effective Group', in J.M. Williams (ed.) *Applied Sport Psychology: Personal Growth to Peak Performance, Fourth Edition*, 127–41, New York: McGraw Hill.

PHILIP SULLIVAN

COLD USAGE IN REHABILITATION

Cold usage or cryotherapy is one of the most common modalities used in treating sports related injuries. Cryotherapy includes the usage of ice packs, ice cubes, vapocoolant sprays, ice soaked towels, and cold baths. This treatment reduces the skin temperature and causes vasoconstriction (narrowing of the blood vessels) around the area of injury. Reduction of blood flow helps to delay or prevent swelling and pain around the injured area and to decrease the local metabolic rate of the injured tissues by decreasing enzymatic function. In addition, cryotherapy helps to slow or eliminate nerve conduction, thereby blocking the sensory transmission of pain impulses. Cold is the agent of choice during the first 24–72 hours post-injury because it helps to limit the extent of secondary injury. In other words, by decreasing the local blood flow to the injured area it limits further damage to the injured area resulting from local inflammation and cell damage.

Conductive cooling (ice packs) can be applied for up to 15–20 min, and the cold effect will penetrate approximately 1–5 cm under the skin. The penetration will depend on the amount of subcutaneous fat, or skinfold thickness. If a cold substance is applied for too long it can cause hyperemia (reactive increase in blood flow) and damage due to excessive oxygen in the area of injury. Larger areas take longer to cool. The general rule of thumb is ice for 20–30 min every two hours during the first 2–3 days of injury (unless using the ice massage technique). The two hours between icing allows for re-warming of the tissues.

Commercial gel packs and cold baths (immersion of the injured area in cold water) are the safest method of cold usage at home. Ice massage cools the skin more quickly due to the lack of a protective barrier, and appears to be more effective than simply placing ice over the limb. A simple method of ice massage involves freezing water in a small cup and then tearing off the bottom of the cup. The ice is then applied to the skin directly and continuously moved in a circular motion around the area

of injury. Typically, these massages last for up to five minutes and should be stopped when the skin over the injured area becomes red, warm or numb.

Cold usage is beneficial both during phase I and phase II of the rehabilitation process. The area of injury determines the appropriate type of cold application. For small areas like the hands or feet, an ice pack or ice massage is most appropriate. For larger injuries like calves or thighs, ice baths may work better.

During the rehabilitation phase, and after the initial pain and swelling have decreased significantly, ice can be combined with active and passive range of motion. The ice could be used before and during the therapeutic exercise bout for 20–30 min twice a day. Between these exercise bouts, the injury site should be protected. (i.e. with a cast or taping). Once the pain and swelling secondary to initial exercise has subsided, the individual may progress to more vigorous exercise and functional activity, and ice is to be used after exercise for 20–30 min.

Cold usage should be avoided in individuals with cold intolerance, Raynaud's phenomenon, hypersensitivity, decreased sensation, compromised circulation or blood flow (individuals with diabetes) or over an area of wound healing. Cold sprays should be applied by professionals because of the potential for misuse leading to burns or frostbite. Finally, the application of cold should be avoided prior to vigorous exercise because it may cause a decrease of ligament elasticity and muscle flexibility that may lead to injury.

Further reading

Grana, W.A. (2003) 'Application of Cold', J.C. DeLee, D. Drez Jr and M.D. Miller (eds) *DeLee and Drez's Orthopedic Sports Medicine*, 2nd edn, 352–5, Philadelphia PA: W.B. Saunders.

JESSICA SCHUTZBANK

COLLAPSED ENDURANCE ATHLETE

There has been a large increase in the number of participants in endurance sports events world-wide, perhaps because regular physical activity has been shown to have numerous health benefits. As a result, the provision of medical care at such events has become extremely important. Medical staff are required to plan for medical emergencies at these events, and one of the most common clinical problems that they have to manage is that of an athlete who has collapsed.

What percentage of athletes participating in endurance events is likely to be admitted to the medical facility?

The estimated percentage of starters of various endurance events that will require admission to the medical facility is depicted in Table 4.

The percentages in Table 4 represent the likelihood of a collapse as well as other medical and orthopaedic conditions. It appears that the percentage admissions for medical conditions other than collapse are reasonably constant, whereas the prevalence of collapse is variable. Factors that increase the frequency of collapse after an endurance event are:

- running rather than cycling or swimming;
- poor level of fitness in the population;
- lack of previous competitive experience;
- increased duration of the event (race distance);
- adverse environmental conditions (increased temperature and humidity).

The percentage of starters who will have to be admitted to a medical facility following races of various distances under cool ($<24°C$) and hot ($>24°C$) conditions is depicted in Figure 12.

Race distance and environmental conditions are therefore two very important factors influencing the risk of collapse after running.

What are the common causes of collapse after an endurance event?

The following conditions are associated with collapse after prolonged physical exercise:

- exercise-associated collapse (heat syncope/exhaustion);
- exercise associated muscle cramping (EAMC);
- heatstroke;
- hypoglycaemia;
- hyponatraemia;
- cardiac arrest (most commonly due to myocardial infarction);
- other medical conditions (drugs);
- orthopaedic conditions;
- hypothermia (in cold environmental conditions).

The life threatening conditions within this group of causes are cardiac arrest, heatstroke, hyponatraemia, and hypoglycaemia. These are more likely to be encountered when the event takes place in hot and humid conditions.

Planning a medical facility at an endurance event

Clinical assessment of the athlete begins with designing an appropriate medical

Table 4. Expected percentage of race starters likely to be admitted to a medical facility

Endurance event	Percentage of race starters requiring medical care
42 km running race	2–20
21 km running race	1–5
Ultra-triathlon (>200 km)	15–30
Cycling	5
Cross-country skiing	5

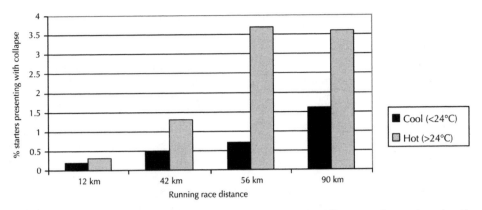

Figure 12. The percentage of race starters presenting with collapse after the different race distances in cool and hot conditions.

facility when planning the event. Such a facility must have a triage area where rapid assessment can be made, a general treatment area for the management of non-life threatening collapsed athletes, an intensive care area for the management of collapsed athletes with life-threatening conditions, a small functional laboratory and an appropriate administrative area. Appropriate facilities, trained staff, and equipment must be present. A typical medical facility will have sports physicians, a cardiologist or anaesthetist (in the intensive care area), physical therapists, nursing sisters, massage therapists and administrative staff. Minimum diagnostic facilities should include equipment to measure blood pressure, rectal temperature, ECG, and a laboratory for blood glucose and serum sodium concentrations (events>42 km). Treatment facilities should include cardiopulmonary resuscitation equipment (including drugs and defibrillator), cooling baths, and fans.

In addition to planning a medical facility at the finish of the event, it is also important to consider that accidents and medical emergencies can occur during the race. Therefore, first aid stations and medical facilities (including a rapid response medical team) must be provided.

Clinical assessment of the collapsed endurance athlete

In the triage area, a collapsed athlete must undergo a rapid assessment by an experienced medical practitioner to determine if this is a potentially life-threatening condition or not.

If possible, a medical history must be obtained from the athlete or fellow athletes (in the case of a runner who is confused or comatosed). One of the most important indicators of the severity of the collapse is whether the runner collapsed during the run (indicating a potentially life-threatening cause), or after the finishing line (indicating postural hypotension). The following additional aspects in the history should alert the doctor to the diagnosis: excessive or inadequate amount of fluid ingested during the run, amount of urine passed during the run, vomiting or diarrhoea before or during the run, carbohydrate ingestion before and during the run, the use of any drugs before or during the run, recent illness, race preparation (heat acclimatization, race preparation), and symptoms just prior to the episode of collapse.

The most important indicators on clinical examination of a severe, life-threatening condition are:

- altered level of consciousness (coma, confusion)
- supine systolic blood pressure <100 mmHg
- heart rate >100 beats/min
- core (rectal) temperature >40°C
- a body weight loss >5%
- any body weight gain
- visible swelling and palpable oedema of the limbs indicating fluid overload

All these athletes must be transported to the intensive care area immediately for further assessment. Additional investigations can be performed, including a blood glucose concentration ($<4\,\text{mmol}\,l^{-1}$ indicating hypoglycaemia), and serum sodium concentration ($<130\,\text{mmol}\,l^{-1}$ indicating hyponatraemia).

Management of the collapsed endurance athlete

The management of the collapsed endurance athlete will depend on making an accurate diagnosis. The general principles of treatment of the collapsed runner are depicted in Table 5.

See also: exercise in heat – medical aspects; exercise in cold – medical aspects; exercise associated muscle cramps, field-side medical care

References

Holtzhausen, L.M. and Noakes, T.D. (1997) 'Collapsed Ultraendurance Athlete: Proposed Mechanisms and an Approach to Management', *Clin J Sport Med* 7: 292–301.

MARTIN SCHWELLNUS

COLLECTION ISSUES

Collection protocols for sports drug-testing programs have many common elements. However, organizations adopt and modify their collection protocols based on experience working with specific groups of athletes. Accordingly, organizations develop their own unique standards, policies, and protocols that determine how specimen collection will be administered.

When athletes challenge the validity of positive drug-test results, the integrity of the collection process often is called into question. Therefore, it is important that sports organizations comply with their written protocols and institute training and quality control programs for sports drug-testing collectors. Although the collection process is often overlooked in quality-control programs, when mistakes occur, it often happens during collection. Fortunately, such mistakes can be corrected on-site with the full knowledge of the involved athlete.

Collection protocols should provide flexibility to accommodate different settings. For example, a collection may be conducted at an athlete's residence or place of employment. It can also be done as part of a competition, e.g. at pool, arena, or other venue. The sports drug-testing collector must be able to administer specimen collection according to policy and at the same time operate in facilities that usually are less than ideal.

The collection of urine specimens in sports drug testing is a sequential process with many steps. Such steps include but are not limited to: identification of the athlete to be tested; selection of a collection container by the athlete; the voiding process under the direct observation of a same-sex validator; specimen integrity checks (e.g. specific gravity, pH); specimen numbering and packaging by the athlete or by the collector under the athlete's watch; and the certification by all parties that the published collection process was followed.

Sports organizations utilize trained specimen collectors for their drug-testing programs. Often these collectors are medical professionals such as physicians, nurses, athletic trainers, or medical technologists. The collectors receive training in the collection process and the significant paperwork necessary to complete a thorough collection activity. The collectors are responsible for ensuring collection-facility security and following written **chain of custody** procedures to ensure specimen validity. The collector is the last person to see the specimens before transportation to the laboratory.

There are several differences between sports testing and most workplace drug testing programs. Athletes are under constant observation during the voiding process, whereas direct observation in the workplace is usually reserved for suspicion of specimen tampering or manipulation. Direct observation usually makes temperature measurement unnecessary and allows for the continued use of partial specimens until the athlete reaches the minimum amount necessary. In sports drug testing, urinary specific gravity and urinary pH are established on-site so that athletes who provide dilute or alkaline urine are detained until adequate specimens are provided. These readings are rarely used in the

Table 5. Principles of treatment of conditions associated with collapse in endurance athletes

Medical condition responsible for collapse	Principles of treatment
Exercise associated collapse	• Lie down the athlete and elevate the lower limbs • Oral fluids containing 5–10% carbohydrate and electrolytes are encouraged • Repeat assessment after 5–10 min
Exercise associated muscle cramps (EAMC)	• Passive stretching • Contraction of the antagonist muscle • Oral fluids containing 5–10% carbohydrate and electrolytes if desired by the athlete • Repeat assessment after 5–10 min
Heatstroke	• Admission to the intensive care area • Rapid cooling by placing the athlete in an ice-water bath for 5–10 min to reach a rectal temperature of <38°C as soon as possible • Increasing air flow over the athlete by using fans • Intravenous fluids (1–1.5 L saline) can be administered • Repeat assessment every 5–10 min • Possible admission to hospital for further observation and investigation
Hyponatraemia	• Admission to the intensive care area • Under no circumstances should intravenous fluids be administered • Fluid restriction • The use of diuretics may be considered • Repeat assessment every 5–10 min • Admission to hospital for further observation and investigation
Hypoglycaemia	• Admission to the intensive care area • Intravenous administration of glucose (50% solution) • Repeat assessment every 5–10 min • Admission to hospital for further observation and investigation
Cardiac arrest	• Admission to the intensive care area • Immediate cardiopulmonary resuscitation • Electrocardiographic (ECG) monitoring • Defibrillation if indicated • Intravenous line for drug administration • Repeat assessment every • Emergency admission to hospital for further treatment and investigation

workplace model. Specimens are assigned a unique code number at the collection site and the laboratory has no information about the athlete other than gender and sport.

In cases where a breach in collection protocol is recognized at the collection site, steps should be immediately taken to correct the violation. In rare cases, this may involve collecting another specimen from the involved athlete so that any irregularities in the collection are corrected before a sample is transported to the laboratory. An athlete who provides a specimen that leads to a positive case might call into question the veracity of the positive result if there are collection irregularities. It is important to head off such challenges by adhering to written collection protocols.

References

National Collegiate Athletic Association (2002) 'Drug-Testing Program 2003–04', August.

US Department of Transportation (2001) '49 CFR Part 40 Procedures for Transportation Workplace Drug Testing Programs', 21 February 2001.

World Anti-Doping Agency (2003a) 'Elements of An Anti-Doping Program', http://www.wada-ama.org/en/t3.asp?p = 32332. 25 November 2003.

—— (2003b) 'Wada Technical Document – TD2003LCOC,' http://www.wada-ama.org/docs/web/standards_harmonization/code/chain_custody_1_2.pdf. 25 November 2003.

FRANK URYASZ

COLLECTIVE EFFICACY

Collective efficacy is an extension of the construct of self-efficacy applied to groups. Whereas, self-efficacy refers to people's judgments of individual capabilities and efforts, Bandura (1997) defined collective efficacy as a group's shared beliefs in its capacities to organize and execute actions to produce a desired goal, which is reflected in individual members' perceptions of their group's capabilities. Collective efficacy beliefs are hypothesized to influence what sports teams or exercise groups choose to do as a group, how much effort they put into their group endeavors, and their persistence when collective efforts fail to produce quick results or encounter forcible opposition. Bandura also acknowledged, however, that a group's collective perceptions of efficacy are rooted within individual perceptions of self-efficacy. Thus, both perceptions should be examined when studying sports teams or exercise groups. When studying collective efficacy for the team or group, perceptual consensus must be considered. This means that to average individual data for use as group means, a researcher must demonstrate that group members perceive in the same way. This does not mean that there must be unanimity of beliefs across members, but there should be some shared congruence.

Bandura (1997) recommended two approaches for obtaining single estimates of a group's collective efficacy from individual members. The first approach involves assessing each member's belief in his or her personal capabilities to perform within the group – self-efficacy – and then aggregating these individual self-efficacy measures for the group. The self-efficacy beliefs of members within a group context are not detached from the **group dynamics** operating within it and, thus, individual self-efficacy measures can be aggregated for the group to provide a measure of a group's collective efficacy. The second approach involves assessing each member's belief in his or her group's capabilities as a whole, and then aggregating these individual measures for the group. The type of question asked in this approach is, 'How confident are you that your team can execute its game plan?' Bandura contended that aggregated collective efficacy would be more predictive of group performance than will aggregated self-efficacy when the group task is highly interdependent. For instance, in sports such as basketball and soccer, successful performance requires an interdependent effort, whereas, members of a golf team do not require such interdependence to accomplish a team success. Thus, an aggregate of individual efficacies may have sufficient predictive power for group outcomes for low-interdependent teams, such as golf teams, gymnastics teams, and swimming teams.

As with self-efficacy beliefs, Bandura predicted that performance accomplishments of the group are the most powerful source of information for collective efficacy beliefs. Groups that have a past history of success are more likely to develop a shared sense of strong efficacy among their members. Likewise, a series of performance failures could decrease the collective efficacy of its membership, which, in turn, could spiral into subsequent failures. However, it is also possible that teams may become overconfident as a result of past success because of complacency, lack of focus, and a willingness to take risks and try new strategies. The perceived collective efficacy of a team or group might also be influenced through a collective **social comparison** process with other teams, the group's confidence in the leadership, verbal persuasion by the coach or team captain, and the team's feelings of preparedness. Team cohesion and team goals also are considered sources of collective efficacy.

See also: self-efficacy and self-confidence

Reference

Bandura, A. (1997) *Self-efficacy: The Exercise of Control*, New York: Freeman.

Further reading

George, T.R. and Feltz, D.L. (1995) 'Motivation in Sport from a Collective Efficacy Perspective, *International Journal of Sport Psychology* 26: 98–116.

DEBORAH L. FELTZ

COLONIALISM

Colonialism is a product of modernity, in the form of Europe's seventeenth-to-nineteenth-century industrial (and political) revolution. It sought to replace group, clan, and dynastic (divine) sovereignty with the sovereignty of the modern nation-state, through direct military invasion and the occupation of lands, as well as domination of the colonised populations' memory and consciousness. The apology for colonialism was often couched in terms of modernising the non-modern, indigenous and traditional (non-Western) societies. The transformation (by force) of colonised societies from tradition to modernity, however, has come to be regarded as being for the sole benefit of the colonial (capitalist) society's 'settler' and metropolitan economies. Moreover, colonialism was accompanied by the establishment of a new history and geography denying the value (and often the existence) of pre-colonial structures and identity.

Colonial policy was based on the idea that in order for the 'Rest' to emulate 'the West', it had to be colonised, politically, economically, and culturally (i.e. to be 'taught' the political, cultural, and economic lessons of 'modernity'). This was to be achieved by:

1. The use of a rational (racial) process of institutional violence, known also as the politics of *la terre brulée* (scorched earth), *razzia,* or military expedition (raid, incursion, invasion, attack, aggression, conquest). The aim of this was to impose upon colonised populations a new military reality, and therefore an accepted de facto position of subordination.

2. Demographic restructuring (and resultant 'de-traditionalisation') often as a result of imposed urbanisation (ghettoising populations). This process usually resulted from the control by settlers of agricultural production

which provoked a forced migration of local population from rural areas to cities, and as consequence the annihilation of old tribal solidarities, languages, cultures, ecological equilibria, and customary codes (Arkoun 2000).

3. The 'deculturation' of the colonised population, which resulted from the colonial power's denial of the pre-colonial civilisation and its sources of identity (including art, culture, religion, and language). As an example of the effect of colonialism on local culture and collective memory, we can cite the case of French colonialism in Algeria, which according to Khan (1991: 286), worked not only to expropriate the Algerian tribes and destroy the rural economy, but also to wipe out handicraft and guild-type organisation, pillage the cities, suffocate the few extant intellectual élites, steal or burn archival documents and entire libraries, wage ceaseless war on Arabic language and Islam, and try to drive them into permanent inferiority by setting up a Native School system designed mainly to enhance a servile education necessary for the advancement of colonialism and a degree of acculturation apt to ensure the maintenance of foreign domination.

4. The imposition of an hegemonic relation of dominant/subordinate, colonial/colonised, or what Fanon refers to as the process of (scientific) subjugation of the colonised-subordinate by the colonial-master. This division between two societies was part of scientific process of colonisation. For Tocqueville, there have to be two very distinct forms of legislation in Africa, because there are two very separated societies. Absolutely nothing could prevent Europeans being treated separately. The rules that were made for them should be applied only to them. (translated from the French).

As a result of colonial domination, new forms of struggle and conflict emerged. This is not defined in terms of class struggle – using a Marxist approach – but as a conflict between the colonial and the colonised, where the objective of the colonised-subordinate is to access the privileges of the colonial-master. This process announced the beginning of a new stage, which was that of de-colonisation, which according to Fanon (1961), took different phases. First, the emancipation phase, which consisted of promoting national unity as the central idea in the anti-colonial struggle. In the second phase, national consciousness developed gradually in the course of armed action to achieve the integration and cohesion of the various social groups.

Sport, in parallel with other cultural phenomena (e.g. art, literature, and theatre), inspired by the struggle for integration or independence, became a privileged site for individual liberation but also sometimes as an instrument for subversion (Dine 1996). In other words, a space for identification as well as symbolic place for the gathering and manifestation of certain signs of community and religious identity allowing 'differentiation' from colonial society. It was also a space for political messages, created by a collective voice, addressed to outsiders, and intended to be heard by the colonial power. This specific niche (the sports club) was necessary for the social sustenance and political expression of the 'indigenous' population. Consequently, sport, 'l'Héritage de l'occupant' was used as a means for the affirmation of indigenous society in resistance to colonial cultural hegemony, in its own field. This process of absorption and then transformation of sport by nationalist movements is interpreted by Hannerz (1991) as being a form of 'creolization' of a global culture, as the nations of the 'periphery' transform or adapt metropolitan culture (sport) to their own specification.

References

Arkoun, M. (2000) *Intellectual Traditions in Islam*, London: I.B.Tauris in association with the Institute of Ismaili Studies.

Dine, P. (1996) 'Un Héroisme problématique: Le sport, la littérature et la guerre d'Algérie', *Europe* no.806–7 (July – June), 177–85.

Fanon, F. (1961) *Les Damnés de la terre*: Paris: Maspero.

Grandmaison, O.L. (2001) 'Les impasses du débat sur la torture en Algérie: Quand Tocqueville légitimait les boucheries', *Le Monde Diplomatique*, http://www.monde-diplomatique.fr/2001/06/LE_COUR_GRANDMAISON/15321. Retrieved 27.08.02

Hannerz, U. (1991) 'Scenarios for Peripheral Cultures', in D. King (ed.) *Culture, Globalisation and the World system*, 107–28, London: Macmillan and Department of Art and Art History, State University of New York at Birmingham.

Khan, A. (1991) 'Algerian Intellectuals: Between Identity and Modernity', in A. El-Kenz (ed.) *Algeria: The Challenge of Modernity*, London: CODEBRIA Books series.

MAHFOUD AMARA

COMMONWEALTH GAMES

The genesis of the Commonwealth Games is credited to the Reverend John Astley Cooper, born in Adelaide, Australia, but a long-time resident of England. Astley, writing in an article in the *Greater Britain* magazine in 1891, suggested that a 'Pan-Britannic festival', combining sporting, military, and literary events, would 'draw closer the ties between the Nations of the Empire'. Following this initial proposal, Richard Coombes, an Englishman living in Australia, a writer for the *Referee*, and a prominent sports administrator, carried on the cause over the next decades, despite periods of flagging support.

Ultimately, it was the sporting component of the proposed festival that captured the attention of the public and, as a result, in 1911 a sporting contest was held at the Crystal Palace, London, with athletes from the United Kingdom, Australia, South Africa, and Canada competing in nine events. This contest formed part of the 'Festival of the Empire', staged as part of the celebrations for the coronation of King George V.

As the twentieth century progressed and the political bonds of the British Empire began to weaken, paradoxically, its cultural bonds strengthened, in areas such as sport. This led to the first British Empire Games being staged in Hamilton, Canada, in 1930 after M.M. (Bobby) Robinson, the Canadian athletic team manager, had proposed their establishment while at the 1928 Amsterdam Olympic Games. Part of his rationale was to counteract the perceived domination of the United States at the Olympic Games, and also to continue the notion of 'amateurism' as the ideal in sport, an ideal which was thought to be diminishing outside the Empire.

Over 400 athletes, representing eleven countries, participated in the Hamilton games. A sum of $30,000 was provided by the City of Hamilton to help the teams defray their traveling costs. Since then, the Games have been conducted every four years (midway between Summer Olympic Games) except for 1942 and 1946 (when they were canceled due to World War II).

From 1930 until 1950 the Games were known as the 'British Empire Games', then, until 1962, as the 'British Empire and Commonwealth Games'; from 1966 to 1974 as the 'British Commonwealth Games'; and from 1978 as the 'Commonwealth Games'.

The Commonwealth Games Federation (CGF), established in 1932, is the body responsible for setting up and upholding the rules of the Games. It promotes them, establishes regulations for their conduct, and seeks to encourage amateur sport throughout the Commonwealth. Thus the role of the CGF stretches beyond facilitation of the games, to assisting with sport development and physical recreation throughout the Commonwealth. The games have grown in size and scope, to the extent that they now have little resemblance to the first celebrations. From the six sports and 400 athletes at Hamilton in 1930, to nine sports and 664 athletes in Vancouver in 1954, ten sports and 2,073 athletes in Auckland in 1990, and fifteen sports and 3,638 athletes in Kuala Lumpur in 1998, there were seventeen sports and approximately 3,700 athletes in Manchester in 2002. The 2006 Games will be held in Melbourne, Australia.

While the range of sports included in each Games has varied, athletics and swimming must always be included. Boxing is the only other sport which has been on every Commonwealth Games program. Currently the host country chooses at least eight other sports from: archery; badminton; bowls; boxing; canoeing; cycling; fencing; gymnastics; judo; rowing; shooting; squash; table tennis; tennis; ten pin bowling; triathlon; weightlifting; wrestling; and yachting. It also selects one or more team sports.

While the Commonwealth Games have had their detractors, currently they appear to be in a strong position, with two cities, Hamilton and Delhi, bidding to host the 2010 Games. Delhi was successful, beating Hamilton by 46 votes to 22. This will be the first time that India has hosted the event and, like the 1998 Kuala Lumpur Games, signals a widening of the hosts from the traditional Commonwealth sports powers.

Further reading

Commonwealth Games Federation website: www.tcol.co.uk/comorg/cgf.htm

Dheensaw, C. (1994) *The Commonwealth Games: the First 60 Years, 1930–1990*, Sydney: ABC Books (Australian Broadcasting Commission).

Phillips, B. (2002) *The Commonwealth Games: The History of all the Sports*, Manchester: Parrs Wood.

KRISTINE TOOHEY

COMMUNITY

A set of social relationships based on some common features or characteristics, usually accompanied by a sense of solidarity or identify. The concept is central to much nineteenth-century social analysis which sought to explain the characteristics of modern, urban, industrial society by contrast with traditional, rural, kinship-based forms of social organisation. Perhaps the best known account of this distinction is by Ferdinand Tönnes in his ideal-typical constructs of *Gemeinschaft* (community) and *Gesellschaft* (society).

The nature and value of community is perceived differently from different perspectives. Conservative notions of community emphasise common roots, kinship, and shared history, while socialist perspectives tend to characterise the notion of community as performing a hegemonic function, 'papering over the cracks' of divided societies – hence Benedict Anderson's description of national identity as 'imagined community'). Margaret Thatcher's purported statement that 'there is no such thing as society' reflects to some degree the neo-liberal view that there are only communities of interest, freely formed associations.

Sport may be associated with any or all of these different perspectives. Sporting conservatives may claim that there are innate qualities in a 'national' football team – e.g. the 'hard working English', 'Brazilian flair and tempo', 'German method'. Left-wing radicals may claim that national teams perform the function of promoting a false sense of unity, masking social divisions, while neo-liberals will point to sporting communities as merely communities of interest.

Sport is stressed, particularly by conservative theorists, as performing a variety of positive functions in modern societies, including providing a sense of identity beyond the family, or a source of social solidarity in an alienating or anomic environment. It can have a progressive function in overcoming social divisions (bringing different ethnic groups together for example in support of the team, or uniting Olympic and Paralympic sport in a broader movement). Nevertheless, identities are exclusive as well as inclusive, and sporting communities can be patriarchal, racist, and anti-egalitarian. Recent policy concerns with concepts such as social inclusion and in particular with the development of social capital, through sport reflect a concern to employ sport as a vehicle for building and sustaining social networks which form the basis of community interaction.

IAN P. HENRY

COMMUNITY RECREATION

The use of 'community' to qualify the noun 'recreation' is a product in the Anglo-Saxon tradition of the 1970s, but has taken on a somewhat different set of connotations in the last two decades. Community recreation followed on from the community development movement of the early 1970s which sought to foster community action to regenerate inner city areas in Britain in the light of local and central governments' failure to do so (Smith and Jones 1981). This movement was broadly associated with left-wing politics and in the domain of culture had its most radical expression in community arts (Kelly 1984), which valued art in terms not of aesthetic quality but rather by reference to its potential for promoting community development.

Community recreation developed in parallel, incorporating a wide range of public and voluntary sector recreation initiatives. It had three defining characteristics (though not all would be evident in any one initiative). The first of these was a concern with meeting the needs of disadvantaged groups (the unemployed, women, ethnic minorities) who were underrepresented as users of public sector facilities and services. The second was a concern with decentralisation and the move to more local units of provision, a move fuelled by recognition of the failure of large-scale, bureaucratic provision to display sensitivity to local needs. The third characteristic was that of self-determination, the involvement of members of the local community in local decision-making. Examples of community recreation schemes developed in British cities included the establishment of recreation programmes in Centres Against Unemployment, and Football and the Community schemes which sought to engage local communities through their emotional affiliation to local football clubs, and the promotion of priority zones for public sector investment in sport and leisure in the Urban Programme and the Sports Council's funding schemes. Thus the appeal of community recreation in this initial stage was in tackling recreation disadvantage, addressing alienation by large-scale bureaucracies, and combating local apathy. In addition there was an often unacknowledged concern to use recreation, particularly sport and active recreation, to combat delinquency and anti-social behaviour and to alleviate the threat of social disorder which in British cities became manifest in urban riots at the beginning of the 1980s (Scarman 1981).

The emphasis, in public sector management skills in relation to community recreation, was rather less on facility management or the development of a public sector business approach, than on understanding the specific nature and needs of local communities and the practice of community work skills.

In the later 1980s, however, with the receding threat of urban riots, and the growing confidence of the New Right in government under Margaret Thatcher, the connotations of the term 'community' shifted subtly. The slogan 'Care in the Community' reflects the nature of this change as government sought to roll back the state, reducing public provision of services by placing responsibility for delivery of services in the voluntary and private sectors. Public sector recreation provision was either to be commercialised in its operation, with its management sometimes taken over by the private sector (under legislation for Compulsory Competitive Tendering for example), or management of facilities and services was to be vested in the voluntary sector with the establishment of trusts to manage and operate facilities. The dangers of such policy shifts are that trusts are likely to operate most readily when serving well established (and often middle-class) communities, while the pressures to commercialise public sector services are said to result in the targeting of such services at more affluent market segments, with an emphasis on achieving financial rather than social goals.

Sports policy in the UK had moved on by the late 1990s, with the Conservative government's policy statement *Sport: Raising the Game* (Department of National Heritage 1995) consigning community recreation and the egalitarian concern for 'sport for all' to local government (while at the same time it sought to reduce local government expenditure), and focusing instead on elite sport, and the young and physical education. These themes recurred in the Labour government's policy statements *A Sporting Future for All* (Department of Culture Media and Sport 2000) and *Game Plan* (Department of Culture Media and Sport 2002), and though sport and recreation were part of the government's social inclusion agenda, and though Sport England has developed Sport Action Zones targeting the most deprived areas, community recreation approaches (in the sense developed in the 1970s context) have declined in significance. The change of thinking underpinning this is evident in direct comparison of the sports policy statements of the Labour governments of Harold Wilson

(Department of Environment 1975) and those of Tony Blair (Department of Culture Media and Sport 2000; 2002), and is also reflected in the shift from community development to the form of communitarianism (Etzioni 1993; Tam 1998) espoused in the rhetoric of New Labour's election campaigns of 1997 and 2001, the latter placing more emphasis on community obligations than on community rights.

Little material exists dealing directly with community recreation as a topic, Haywood (1994) being a significant exception.

References

Department of Culture Media and Sport (2000) *A Sporting Future for All*, London: DCMS.
—— (2002) *Game Plan*, London: DCMS.
Department of National Heritage (1995) *Sport: Raising the Game*, London: HMSO.
Department of the Environment (1975) *Sport and Recreation*, London: HMSO.
Etzioni, A. (1993) *The Spirit of Community: Rights, Responsibilities and the Communitarian Agenda*, London: HarperCollins.
Haywood, L. (ed.) (1994) *Community Leisure and Recreation: Theory and Practice*, Oxford: Butterworth-Heinemann.
Kelly, O. (1984) *Community, Art and the State*, London: Comedia.
Scarman, L. (1981) *The Brixton Disorders: Report of the Right Honourable Lord Scarman*, London: HMSO.
Smith, L. and Jones, D. (1981) *Deprivation, Participation, and Community Action*, London: Routledge and Kegan Paul.
Tam, H. (1998) *Communitarianism: A New Agenda for Politics and Citizenship*, Basingstoke: Macmillan.

IAN P. HENRY

COMPARATIVE ANALYSIS OF SPORT POLICY

Despite the appearance in recent years of a number of texts dealing explicitly with comparative (and transnational) analysis in the field of sport and leisure policy and management (cf. Bramham *et al.* 1993; Chalip *et al.* 1996; Houlihan 1997) this area of research is still sparsely populated. With these few exceptions there has been little discussion of methodological implications, and in particular of the epistemological difficulties which such forms of comparative analysis have encountered.

One might divide the approaches to comparative analysis into four major types:

Type 1: seeking (statistical) similarities

The first of the approaches involves those studies which operationalise some measure of participation or policy commitment to allow comparison along multiple cases of policy systems. In classic studies of this type, 'objective' data are subject to analysis to identify forms of statistical association between social, political, economic, or cultural conditions or context on the one hand (e.g. levels of GDP across comparator countries) and policy outcomes on the other (e.g. size of sports club or association membership). Typical dependent variables in such studies might be: frequency of participation in sport; levels of government expenditure in sport; numbers of hours spent on physical education in schools; time allocation to sport in time budget studies; or media data in respect of hours of sport broadcast.

The approach adopted in this type of research can be characterised as nomothetic, since it seeks to establish law-like generalisations. There may be an element of providing support for a particular theoretical base or position, for example the modernisation thesis might be supported where measures of increased bureaucratisation of sporting organisations provide evidence of an increasingly rational design set for sporting organisations in a diverse range of national contexts, though in other instances the statistical associations generated may simply provide the basis for qualitative exploration of associations discovered.

The strength of this type of approach is to be found in its ability to accommodate and summarise large numbers of cases, although operationalising the concepts one might wish to measure, such as 'sports equity', and the quality, availability, and comparability of data in such studies, will present significant difficulties. The approach of 'seeking similarities' thus tends to ignore cultural specificities in the search for universalisation or generalisation. The social meaning of an activity or of a definition of an expenditure category is sacrificed for the purposes of cross-case comparison.

A number of exemplar studies for this approach in the field of sport and leisure participation and policy provide illustrations of the strengths and weaknesses of this approach. Such weaknesses include: difficulties of operationalisation (Szalai 1972), comparability of data (Jones 1989), of measurement (Rodgers 1978), and of explanations of causality (Gratton and Centre 1999), weaknesses which in effect promote qualitative analysis to evaluate and explain associations between social, political, economic, and/or cultural conditions and policy outcomes.

Type 2: describing difference

The second approach to comparative analysis involves considering policy not as a set of statistically operationalised concepts, but rather as detailed qualitative accounts of individual policy systems and perhaps the interactions between those systems. Thus this approach is not nomothetic but ideographic in nature, since it lays emphasis on capturing the specific policy history and context rather than searching for general laws. The goal of explanation here is to account for how and why societies differ in terms of sports participation or policy. The danger of this approach, however, is the tendency to explain everything in terms of historical contingency. Comparison of a large number of exemplar states, or policy systems, is not possible because of the complexity of detailed analysis and description, and thus the core problem for the 'describing differences' approach is that of validation of interpretation, and moving beyond the descriptive. This approach generally is associated with theoretical accounts of a middle-range nature, often relying on 'ideal type' concepts to capture the essence of the national systems to be described.

Three policy studies might be selected to provide insights in to the approach and its strengths and weaknesses (Henry and Paramio Salcines 1999; Henry and Nassis 1999; Houlihan 1997). Each employs key concepts in the process of developing comparison – urban regimes, political clientelism, and policy networks. Such key concepts should of course be subject to evaluation in terms of their utility and robustness. Potential conceptual weaknesses in this approach are highlighted by Sartori (1991), who identifies four types of mistake in the logic of comparison which may be evident. These he terms: *parochialism* – tendency of comparativists to continually invent new terms or use old ones in unintended ways; *misclassification* – ignoring important differences and clustering together unlike phenomena; *degreeism* – to represent all differences as a matter of degree rather than qualitative difference; and *concept stretching* – removing aspects of the original meaning of the concept so that it can accommodate more cases.

The answers to whether or not such 'sins' have been committed in the adoption of a particular concept may not be absolute – but rather a matter for debate and empirical demonstration. There is no reason why, for example, urban regimes or policy networks might be found in every city or every policy system. In contrast, political clientelism, which tends to be assumed to be prevalent in certain types of society, may be more widespread than is often assumed. Thus Sartori's catalogue of potential errors provides a useful checklist

against which the concepts employed in characterising the policy system may be evaluated.

The difficulties associated with this type 2 approach therefore relate predominantly to the validation and interpretation of concepts to summarise complex qualitative data relating to what may be remarkably diverse policy systems.

Type 3: theorising the transnational – transnational rather than cross-national comparison

The third approach to comparative analysis might be termed 'theorising the transnational', and here the global context is the constraining/enabling frame of policy action within which the local/national context is produced and mediated. One of the problems of the first two types of comparative analysis is that both take as their unit of analysis nation-states as unique and bounded cases. They fail to take account of the increasing inter-linkages/ interactions between nation-states and the shared global context. Studies of globalisation, for example, have tended to evaluate intra-state, inter-state and trans-state phenomena. They seek to take account of both transnational (global) pressures and intranational (local) context, hence the coining of the term 'glocalisation'.

The strength of this form of comparative analysis is that it seeks to accommodate the global and local *structural* context (as with the type 1 approach of 'seeking (statistical) similarities') as well as the local nature of *agency* within this structural context (as with type 2, 'describing difference').

Two theoretical perspectives are cited here as illustrating the nature of the third approach (regulation theory[1] and figurational sociology) with three examples of such work in Joseph Maguire's (Maguire 1999) seminal contribution incorporating a range of empirical studies, and two studies invoking comparison at local (Dulac and

Henry 2001) and national (Henry and Uchiumi 2001) levels. Their core characteristics, at least in the way they are applied in the three studies highlighted here, are that they are:

- macro-theory oriented (though not meta-narratives);
- adopt strategies that link concerns with structure and agency;
- adopt neo-realist assumptions that social structures are socially constructed, but exist independently of the individual, and may have impacts which are not necessarily directly observable;
- and that since such structures are socially constructed they will be culturally relative.

In each of these three exemplars, although there are significant contrasts in theoretical basis or in the policy systems being compared, there is a shared logic of comparison: that refers to the need to focus on structural context and local interpretation of that context by policy actors; that looks to factors (and groups of actors) which operate across the boundaries of nation-states; and which looks to identify whether there are any 'interaction effects' between policy systems such as one group of policy actors learning from another. However, while such studies differ significantly from type 1 and type 2, they share with those earlier types the conception of policy as being used to address problems and issues in the wider context. Type 4 studies, which we label as 'defining discourse', seeks to understand the ways in which policy discourse defines the policy world and the problems it seeks to address.

Type 4: defining discourse

While studies of policy as discourse have grown over the last decade, relatively little work has been undertaken in relation to sports policy in this domain. It is perhaps worth distinguishing between discourse in policy and policy as discourse here. The former is concerned with evaluating language to identify an underlying reality (and tends therefore to be linked with a realist or a neo-realist ontology), while the latter is concerned with the construction of realities through language (and is thus related to the postmodern relativist ontological position). Examples of the former would include Chalip's critical theory-based analysis of policy discourse (Chalip 1996) and McKay's analysis of the ways in which the Australian Sports Commission has framed its gender equity policy in the mutually reinforcing hegemonic discourses of masculinity and corporate managerialism (McKay 1994).

A policy-as-discourse approach rejects the notion of an underlying reality and argues instead for the notion of socially constructed realities (Wood and Kroger 2000), constructed in this context through the discourse implicated in the development and articulation of policy. For example, policies dealing with urban poverty and deprivation which focus on addressing problems at the level of the individual (e.g. re-education and training projects, programmes developing social capital, etc.) define urban problems as being a matter of individual pathology, while policies which focus on improving the operational effectiveness of public or private sector bureaucracies in this field might be said to define the problem in terms of organisational failure. Policy discourse is thus seen as defining rather than simply responding to a problem.

It is claimed by advocates of postmodern inquiry that their approach to the discursive construction of policy has the potential to make a distinctive, democratising contribution to public policy analysis. Such an approach is adopted in Amara's (2003) review of how the policy of the 'professionalisation of sport' (launched by the Algerian government in 1998) is interpreted and expressed in the Algerian context, and how its expression in policy documents and in policy action defines the nature of the construction of the social world of sport.

The strengths of an approach such as that adopted by Amara include the highlighting of the exercising of power in the development of policy discourse. Such analysis is bound up with Foucauldian notions of power and, postmodern theorists argue, holds out the possibility of emancipatory outcomes, by highlighting the implications of defining reality through these types of discourse. However, this approach also opens itself to the consequences of a relativist epistemology in which it might be argued that policy problems only exist insofar as they are discursively constructed, and that issues of reliability and validity, and the privileging of one account over another, are similarly problematic.

Note

1. Although regulation theory has its roots in Marxist analysis, its application here is essentially neo-pluralist. Thus Fordist, neo-Fordist, post-Fordist systems are not functional requirements of an accumulation regime but rather ideal typical descriptions of the set of social relations which have accompanied particular changes in the economic structures of a society. Such sets of social relations and economic structures are the outcomes of the interaction of agency and structure.

References

Amara, M. (2003) 'Global Sport and Local Modernity: The Case of Professionalisation of Football in Algeria', Institute of Sport and Leisure Policy, School of Sport and Exercise Sciences, Loughborough: Loughborough University.

Bramham, P., Henry, I., Mommaas, H. and van der Poel, H. (eds) (1993) *Leisure Policies in Europe*, Wallingford, Oxon: CAB International.

Chalip, L. (1996) 'Critical Policy Analysis: The Illustrative Case of New Zealand Sport Policy Development', *Journal of Sport Management* 10, 3: 310–24.

Chalip, L., Johnson, A. and Stachura, L. (1996) *National Sports Policies: An International Handbook*, London: Greenwood Press.

Dulac, C. and Henry, I. (2001) 'Sport and Social Regulation in the City: The Cases of Grenoble and Sheffield', *Society and Leisure/Loisir et Société* 24, 1: 47–76.

Gratton, C. and Centre, L.I.R. (1999) 'COMPASS 1999: A Project Seeking the Coordinated Monitoring of Participation in Sports in Europe, UK Sport and Italian Olympic Committee', London: UK Sport.

Henry, I. and Paramio Salcines, J. (1999) 'Sport and the Analysis of Symbolic Regimes: A Case Study of the City of Sheffield', *Urban Affairs Review* 34: 641–66.

Henry, I. and Uchiumi, K. (2001) 'Political Ideology, Modernity and Sports Policy: A Comparative Analysis of Sports Policy in Britain and Japan', *Hitotsubashi Journal of Social Studies* 33, 2: 161–85.

Henry, I. P. and Nassis, P.P. (1999) 'Political Clientelism and Sports Policy in Greece', *International Review for the Sociology of Sport* 34, 1: 43–58 (16 pages).

Houlihan, B. (1997) *Sport, Policy and Politics: An International Comparison*, London: Routledge.

Jones, H. G. (1989) *The Economic Impact and Importance of Sport: A European Study*, Strasbourg: Council of Europe, Committee for the Development of Sport.

Maguire, J. (1999) *Global Sport: Identities, Societies, Civilizations*, Oxford: Polity.

McKay, J. (1994) 'Masculine Hegemony, the State and the Incorporation of Gender Equity Discourse: The Case of Australian Sport', *Australian Journal of Political Science* 29, 1: 82–95.

Rodgers, B. (1978) *Rationalising Sports Policies: Sport in Its Social Context: International Comparisons*, Strasbourg: Council of Europe.

Sartori, G. (1991) 'Comparing and Miscomparing', *Journal of Theoretical Politics* 3: 243–57.

Szalai, A. (ed.) (1972) *The Use of Time*, The Hague: Mouton.

Wood, L. and Kroger, R. (2000) *Doing Discourse Analysis: Methods for Studying Talk in Action and Text*, London: Sage.

IAN P. HENRY

COMPETITION PLANS AND PERFORMANCE ROUTINES

A competition plan is a detailed plan of action that athletes use before and during competition to improve performance. Also called performance routines, these plans help athletes prepare to perform by mentally rehearsing pre-competition and competition conditions that they will possibly encounter. Competition plans often involve a systematic series of psychological skills, such as **self-talk**, imagery, relaxation, affirmation statements, and goal setting, that assist athletes in feeling physically and mentally prepared. Psychological skills, such as self-talk and mental imagery, are commonly used in competition plans to improve attentional focus and facilitate arousal regulation. Overall, competition plans allow athletes to cope with and minimize distractions, and structure their time before competition so they are confident and prepared to perform at the beginning and during competition.

Before competition, athletes face many distractions; without a plan of action, many athletes lose focus and perform poorly. One goal of the competition plan is to help athletes prepare for distractions and assist them in paying attention to important or relevant thoughts rather than unimportant or irrelevant thoughts that interfere with performance. For example, the start of an event or match may be delayed. Athletes who have prepared for or rehearsed this delay will adapt quickly rather than focusing on why there is a delay or problems it may cause. They will continue with their pre-competition routine that keeps them focused on feeling mentally and physically prepared until the delay is resolved.

Athletes often use competition plans to regulate their arousal by rehearsing positive self-talk and mental imagery. Self-talk can be instructional or motivational cue words or phrases spoken internally to oneself or out loud. Athletes can eliminate negative thoughts that interfere with productive performance by adhering to positive comments and mental images. Imagery helps to regulate arousal, when athletes practice several mental rehearsals of performance of different strategies for different circumstances. Visualizing how to perform in ideal conditions with a successful outcome can improve performance. Visualizing how to overcome obstacles or unexpected circumstances can prepare athletes to succeed when problems do arise. In preparing a competition plan, athletes might think about the kinds of things that could happen or go wrong in important competitions and practice solutions through imagery. Imagery and self-talk allow athletes to prepare for adversity and to practice being successful during competition.

A competition plan may entail a routine that begins two hours before competition and lasts through the end of the event. Or, the plan may involve a routine for one single event within a competition, such as a high jump, dive, or basketball free throw. An example of performance plan for shooting a free throw in basketball might be: take the ball from official, dribble three times, place shooting hand on ball, look at basket, inhale and exhale a deep breath, say cue words 'over the rim', mentally imagine the ball going in, and shoot the ball. Athletes who use competition plans will be able to adjust to problems or changes in routine easily because they have rehearsed how to deal with adversity during competition. Athletes who use competition plans will be better prepared to perform optimally – at a peak – when the competition begins and throughout the event or game. Overall, competition plans and performance routines allow athletes to feel prepared and more confident about their performances.

See also: attention and performance; mental practice and imagery; mental preparation; stress management

Further reading

Weinberg, R.S. and Gould, D. (1999) *Foundations of Sport and Exercise Psychology*, Champaign IL: Human Kinetics.

Williams, J.M. (ed.) (2001) *Applied Sport Psychology: Personal Growth to Peak Performance*, London: Mayfield.

MELISSA A. CHASE

COMPETITIVE SPORTS – GLOBAL SCENE OF HEALTH PROMOTION

Competitive sports vary compared to recreational sports in the degree of their intensity. Further, both the frequency and the modes of training also vary. Based on more training and experience, competitive athletes do not just enjoy the fun of sport, but view sports as their career. The athletes truly understand the benefits of being physically active, but they also have an increased risk of being injured during the sporting event. Competitive athletes have personal trainers, physiotherapists, doctors, and other health care professionals to prepare them before games and assist them if injured. Team physicians are most interested in the study of these elite athletes' requirements, as they are the ones who will be on hand if the athlete is injured. Thus, team physicians must make clear decisions and assessments of the seriousness of the injury of the athlete, and be able to determine whether or not the athlete can return to play immediately. During competitive sport events such as the Olympics, athletes play to win, but there can be some problems. There are incidents where athletes take steroids to increase their strength and endurance in order to achieve their goal, and this leads to the loss of the meaning of sport. Fair play is important in competitive sport; athletes are brought together to share both the joy and the competitiveness of the game, while also demonstrating leadership, sportsmanship, and fair play to the youth and the global population. Based on a scientific article, it is believed that traditional doping increased greatly in the 1960s and is still widespread in most sports at elite level today. Thus, the ethical issue of doping is a major problem in competitive sports. Some of the prohibited classes of substances include stimulants, narcotics, anabolic agents, diuretics, and peptide hormones. As well as the problem of doping, sports injuries are more often seen in elite athletes because they have an increased risk of being injured. Therefore proper prevention and treatment processes are required to maximize their performance level during participation. The prevention and management of sports injuries can be divided into three phases: prevention, diagnostic, and management and rehabilitation. Further, to minimize the risk of being injured during games, protective equipment is used, such as helmets, pads, gloves, etc. These are especially important for most contact sports such as football, hockey, and lacrosse. Another issue that should be considered in competitive athletes is the proper warm up and cool down exercises before and after exertion.

With respect to warm up exercises, they involve various basic stretches and cardio warm up. These exercises help improve performance, relieve the aches and pains of intense athletic activity, and serve to prepare an individual for intensive exercises (Micheli *et al.* 2001). Furthermore, they also help loosen up ligaments, muscles, tendons, and joints to prevent common sports injuries. Ligaments and tendons are very susceptible to overuse injuries, and warm up exercises help increase the elasticity of ligaments and tendons, and as a result, minimize the risk of injury. Warm up exercises also help prepare an athlete for upcoming intense competition, especially with respect to the cardiovascular system. The duration of warm up exercises should be quite long for competitive athletes when compared to participants in recreational sports, since elite sports are more intense. Warming up in athletes should be supervised by team physicians, some as specific exercises may not be beneficial for the athlete. A well designed warm up program should be used by each elite athlete based on the team physician's advice. Thus, proper preparation for exercises is essential to enhance an individual's performance and minimize the risk of common sprains and strains.

Cool down exercises are done after the event. These involve jogging, stretching, etc. An important point to note is that after vigorous sports participation, one should not rest immediately, since the heartbeat will not yet have returned to the normal state, thus jogging, for example, will allow the heartbeat to return to homeostasis. Also, cool down exercises help relieve aches and pains caused by the accumulation of lactic acid in muscles.

The type of drink consumed is also an important issue to address for elite athletes. In games of high intensity such as basketball, hockey, American football and soccer, athletes require a great amount of liquid in order to replace the loss of body fluid through sweat. However, water is not efficient enough in vigorous sports because energy is lost quickly in competitive athletes' and sports drinks are a better option. Sports drinks provide extra energy for the athlete, so he or she can perform at their optimal level, while preventing dehydration. The consumption of liquid helps prevent hyperthermia in hot and humid environments. However, hypothermia is still a risk when athletes do not have proper clothing in cold environments. Globally speaking, Westerners have a higher risk of suffering from conditions such as hypothermia and frostbite, as the weather in their countries is relatively colder.

The final issue of importance in promoting health for athletes is sports nutrition. The total daily energy requirement for athletes participating in endurance, strength, and team sports is between 2,500 and 4,000 kcal for women and 3,000 and 6,000 kcal for men (Micheli *et al.* 2001). However, certain activities require a larger amount of energy intake during competition and intense training periods. The major nutri-

ent is carbohydrates, since they are what the body needs during vigorous sports; it is essential that the body has a rich store of carbohydrate. Sources of carbohydrate include breads, cereal, rice, pasta, etc. The normal recommendation for carbohydrate intake is about 50 per cent of daily energy intake. However, during preparation for a competition or intense training period, carbohydrate intake can be increased to 65 to 70 per cent of the daily energy intake. Generally, a low fat diet before competition is preferable. With respect to the micronutrients, vitamins and minerals are important during energy metabolism, and the intake of vitamins and minerals is positively related to energy intake. Calcium and iron are both very important macrominerals that are required for elite athletes.

In short, health promotion in competitive sports and recreational sports is very similar, but competitive sports require a better planned, precise, and unique program for each athlete. Elite athletes gain experience as they compete, and they learn to prevent injuries happening. Various national and international health care organizations have designed guidelines for these competitive athletes to follow, in order to compete at their best, and to demonstrate the meaning of sports, sportsmanship, leadership, friendship, and peace to the youth and the next generation.

Reference

Micheli, L., Smith, A., Bachl, N., Rolf, C. and Chan, K.M. (eds) (2001) *FIMS: Team Physician Manual*, Hong Kong SAR: Lippincott Williams and Wilkins Asia Ltd.

VICTOR W.T. HO

COMPETITIVE STATE ANXIETY AND PERFORMANCE

The relationship between competitive anxiety and performance has been an interest of sport psychologists for more than four decades. Competitive state anxiety is a maladaptive emotional condition that is specifically associated with competitive or performance tasks. It is not synonymous with arousal, but can be considered an extension of high arousal. State anxiety is characterized by aversive feelings of nervousness, distress, and tension before, during, or after competition. Competitive state anxiety is the result of negative thought patterns about competition, such as worry about defeat, how one will be evaluated, possible injury, or the inability to control one's stress in competition. These negative thought patterns may also be accompanied by physiological arousal, such as increases in muscle tension, heart rate, respiration rate, and galvanic skin response. The most often used measure of competitive state anxiety is the Competitive State Anxiety Inventory-2, which measures cognitive worry, perceptions of somatic anxiety, and competitive **self-confidence**, though the self-confidence dimension does not have conceptual basis for being a dimension of anxiety. Competitive state anxiety can result in various performance interruptions, including the **yips** (in fine motor tasks), **choking**, or distraction from the task.

Several theories have been put forward to explain the relationship between competitive anxiety and performance. Early research conducted on the sport anxiety-performance relationship was based on the inverted-U hypothesis This hypothesis posited a curvilinear relationship between physiological arousal and performance. Moderate arousal was generally associated with better performance, whereas too little or too much arousal led to poorer performance. Other anxiety theorists expanded the unidimensional approach of the inverted-U by examining multidimensional explanations of anxiety and performance, including **individual zones of optimal functioning**, **catastrophe models** of anxiety, and **reversal theory**.

See also: attention and anxiety; stress, anxiety and coping strategies; Yerkes-Dodson law

Further reading

Landers, D.M. and Arent, S.M. (2001) 'Arousal-Performance Relationship', in J.M. Williams (ed.) *Applied Sport Psychology*, 206–28, London: Mayfield.

Martens, R., Burton, D., Vealey, R.S., Bump, L.A. and Smith, D.E. (1990) 'Development and Validation of the Competitive State Anxiety Inventory-2 (CSAI-2)', in R. Martens, R.S. Vealey and D. Burton (eds) *Competitive Anxiety in Sport*, 117–207, Champaign IL: Human Kinetics.

DEBORAH L. FELTZ

COMPLEX SYSTEMS

The word 'complex' comes from the Latin word *complexus* meaning interwoven. A complex system in nature is any system with two or more interacting parts, which are free to vary in relation to each other. This characteristic describes any system with many degrees of freedom or with many levels, for example a sports team has many players involved and the human body has many muscles, joints, and a multitude of levels of analysis, including hormonal, endocrinal, physiological, anatomical, and psychological.

Systems are entities that can be studied in an holistic manner. Systems are often composed of subsystems that are also of intrinsic interest. Examples in the human body include the perceptual subsystems, including the visual, haptic, and acoustic apparatus, and the motor subsystems, such as those involved in locomotion, postural control, and reaching and grasping. Biological and physical systems can de differentiated by those that are animate, such as a flock of birds, school of fish, or the human body, or inanimate, such as a puddle of water. Typically biological systems inhabit environments composed of other similar systems. Biological systems are examples of complex open systems, with an internal state and an onboard source of energy, which receives a continuous stream of information sources as inputs from an environment, and has effectors for acting on their environments, such as negotiating their way around and effecting desired changes.

Complex systems in nature display many fundamental attributes, including:

- many independent degrees of freedom – roughly component parts, which are free to vary;
- many different levels to the system, such as neural, hormonal, and biomechanical in the human body;
- nonlinearity of behavioural output;
- capacity for stable and unstable patterned relationships between system parts to occur through system self-organisation – these systems can spontaneously shift between many coordinated states;
- the ability of subsystem components to constrain the behaviour of other sub-systems.

Examples of complex systems in the natural physical world include the weather, animal colonies including human societies, the economic markets and the human body. Note how all these systems possess many microscopic components, for example, molecules of vapour, individual organisms, or specific muscles and joints. However, it is important to note also that the behaviour of the whole system is best understood macroscopically, where the individual components combine together to form coherent patterns, such as a river, a colony of ants, or muscle-joint complexes in movement systems. In other words, the way that the individual elements form recognisable patterns over space and time is far more relevant than what any individual element is doing at any one moment.

See also: constraints; constraints-led perspective; open systems in sport

KEITH DAVIDS

COMPUTATIONAL FLUID DYNAMICS

It has long been accepted that understanding and modifying fluid flow phenomena fundamentally should lead to performance enhancement. It comes as no surprise then that elite sports people, sports teams, and **sports equipment** manufacturers are increasingly trying to derive competitive aerodynamic advantage from advanced flow modelling technologies. Computational fluid dynamics (CFD) is a modern simulation tool in computer aided engineering (CAE) that predicts aerodynamic and hydrodynamic effects in sport. It emerged from academia twenty years ago and it complements wind tunnel and experimental techniques for estimating forces derived from flows on or around sports equipment and athletes. It has the advantage of being more fundamental in the flow information it provides because it solves the constitutive equations of fluid flow – the Navier-Stokes equations – and thermal and materials transport for nearly any geometry and set of boundary conditions. In principle, it provides much more predictive data than conventional approaches with a deeper capability for interrogative visualisation.

Within CFD software, the Navier-Stokes equations are solved iteratively using complex computer algorithms. The net effect is to allow the user to model computationally any flow scenario, provided the geometry of the object being modelled is known and some initial flow conditions are prescribed. The output from CFD software can then be viewed graphically in colour plots of velocity vectors, contours of pressure, lines of constant flow field properties (see, for example, Figure 13) or as numerical data and graphs. There are three elements to the CFD modelling process; a computer aided design (CAD) geometry is first created, a computational 'mesh' or grid is superimposed on top of the geometry, the flow

Figure 13. Airflow lines around a Formula 1 racing car. Reproduced by kind permission of Advantage CFD, a division of Reynard Motor Sport.

properties of each mesh element being an output from the CFD software, and, finally, a CFD flow prediction is produced by the software's solver (see Figure 14).

The use of CFD in competitive sport began in earnest in the early 1990s when Formula 1 motor racing teams started to use the increasingly easy-to-use packages of commercial CFD software then on the market, their goal being to improve the aerodynamics of their racing cars. Until that time, they had been using a mixture of extensive, and expensive, wind tunnel testing, rules-of-thumb, aerodynamic intuition, and experience. Within the tight competitive timescales of Formula 1, wind tunnels tend to yield information on overall body forces, pitching moments, and a few pressure tappings at best. Ten years on, modern Formula 1 teams have optimised their design process to the extent that it is now all virtual, from CAD to stress analysis to CFD to creating a prototype that is then tested in the wind tunnel and on the

track. In competitive motor sport today, there are probably around 100 full-time CFD engineers engaged world-wide. Larger and larger computers and parallel supercomputers are being used in motor racing applications, doing full car simulations in a matter of hours or days on meshes of up to 100,000,000 computational elements.

Another area of extensive CFD usage in sport is yachting and yacht design. Here, the regular America's Cup Challenge has been a major driving force behind the use of CFD in the sport (see Figure 15). The goal has been to design keels and appendages that stay within the rules yet produce the best performance over a wide range of sea conditions; CFD has been used to design competitive hulls to within millimetre tolerances. Yachting teams are also exploring the use of CFD to evaluate various sail and mast configurations for optimal thrust and to assess boat-boat interactions for race tactics.

Other Olympic sports have been modelled using CFD. Swimmers have been assessed with CFD to help elucidate the propulsive and drag mechanisms during a swimming stroke. In Winter Olympic sports, considerable CFD interest has been focused on ski jumping, in particular the jumper's posture. Simulations have shown that the drag of a V-style jumper is almost the same as that of a jumper using a conventional parallel-ski jumping style, but the lift is 8 per cent higher for the V-style jumper, which leads to longer jumps. Bobsleigh is a Winter Olympic sport that has

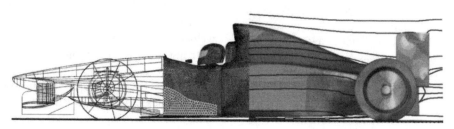

Figure 14. The three parts of the CFD process: CAD – grid – flow prediction illustrated by a generic Formula 1 racing car.

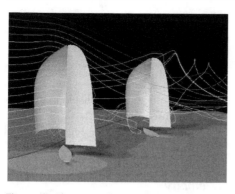

Figure 17. Flow pathlines around a soccer ball at 65 km h^{-1}. Reproduced by kind permission of University of Sheffield Sports Engineering Research Group.

Figure 15. Flow around two America's Cup yachts sailing downwind. Reproduced by kind permission of Alinghi and Ecole Politecnique Federale de Lausanne.

drawn the attention of CFD modellers to improve the aerodynamic shape of the sled. Cycling too has been open to CFD simulation (see Figure 16), which has systematically been applied, for example, to cycle aerodynamic design, helmet design, cyclist posture, and optimal cyclist drafting positions during team pursuit.

Another exciting CFD application in sport is that of modelling sports balls (see Figure 17). Here, CFD software has been used to model the effects of different roughness elements on the surface of a ball and the spin of the ball. When a trajectory calculation algorithm is coupled with the fundamental CFD simulations, the likely

path of a ball for a given set of initial kicking conditions, and transit conditions, can be predicted. On an American football, the impact of the laces on the surface of the spinning ball has been shown to be crucial in tripping the turbulent boundary layer and causing trajectory instabilities during flight. On a soccer ball, the turbulent to laminar boundary layer transition during its flight had the single biggest effect on the ball's trajectory and, in particular, large lateral movements of the ball in the air as the balance of forces on the ball suddenly changed.

In sports applications, CFD can provide accurate aerodynamic and hydrodynamic trends. It also provides flow data that can lead to fundamental insight into different flow scenarios in sport, and it allows for 'what if?' scenarios to be assessed relatively easily and cheaply on a desktop PC. Drawbacks to the use of CFD at present are as follows. It still cannot simulate boundary layer 'tripping' where fluid transitions occur from laminar to turbulent flow; these are critical in some sports applications. Moving body and multiphase modelling simulations, such as air–water flows, are very demanding of computational resources. Accurate modelling of boundary layer flow is dependent on good semi-structured boundary layer meshes normal to wall boundaries, and good quality empirical turbulence models in a given CFD code. For most 'real world' sports applications, only advanced commercial CFD codes tend to provide accurate sports flow simulations,

Figure 16. Flow pathlines around a cyclist with a disk rear wheel in a 30 km h^{-1} cross wind. Reproduced by kind permission of the UK Sports Institute.

and they cost typically tens of thousands of dollars per year to licence, which can be a stumbling block to usage; however, CFD is still much cheaper than wind tunnel and experimental approaches. There is a significant learning curve to the proper use of CFD codes, ranging from a few weeks to a few months dependent on the user, their know-how and experience; in reality, only engineers can use these high-end analysis tools effectively.

In the future, it is predicted that CFD will be used to help explain flow phenomena in both competitive and training sports scenarios; it will become standard in the design of better sports equipment. In short, CFD has already become an integral part of the emerging discipline of sports engineering, and the spectrum of CFD applications in sport will continue to grow rapidly as the technology evolves and its benefits are recognised.

See also: aerodynamics of sails; ball and surface deformation; ball swing and reverse swing; Bernoulli's equation; boundary layer; boundary layer separation; drag forces – pressure, skin friction, and wave drag; fluid dynamics; hydrodynamics of boat hulls; hydrodynamics of oars; javelin and discus aerodynamics; laminar and turbulent flow; lift forces – fundamentals; streamlines

Further reading

Hanna, R.K. (2002) 'Can CFD Make a Performance Difference in Sport?', in S. Ujihashi and S.J. Haake (eds) *The Engineering of Sport 4*: 17–30, Oxford: Blackwell.
http://dmawww.epfl.ch/Quarteroni-Chaire/NewResearch/americascup.php3

KEITH HANNA

COMPUTER INTERFACING

The conversion of physical quantities to voltages by sensors is described in **angular motion sensors**, **force and other sensors**, and **linear motion** sensors; the modification of these voltages to accentuate the signal of interest is described in **amplification and signal conditioning**. This entry details the data acquisition process by which these voltages are interfaced to a computer to allow subsequent **signal display and storage**. It consists of three stages: telemetry, anti-alias filtering, and analogue-to-digital conversion.

Telemetry

Telemetry is the process by which the signal is transferred from the site of collection to the site of recording. Telemetry links may be either analogue or digital. The former transmit analogue signals, which are then digitised at the far end of the link. Digital links digitise the analogue signal locally before transmitting the digitised data over the link. Analogue links are generally simpler, but digital links have greater noise immunity; once the signal is digitally encoded, any noise smaller than the minimum needed to swap between a 1 and a 0 will have no effect. Digital links can provide complete noise immunity by transmitting additional error-detecting data to verify that the signal is received correctly. A common and powerful technique is to break the data into small groups and to compute and transmit a sixteen bit – a bit is a binary digit – cyclic-redundancy code (CRC) for each. The receiving system uses the same algorithm to compute a CRC on the received data. The group is re-transmitted if the CRC values do not match. A further way to classify telemetry links is by the nature of the physical medium used to transmit the signal. They can be divided into two functional categories, tethered and un-tethered, or wireless, systems.

Tethered systems require a physical link between the sensor and the data-acquisition system; this can be a disadvantage for sensors that are body-worn as it may interfere with movement. Advantages include simplicity and the ability to transfer power to the remote sensor along the link.

Single-ended wired telemetry is the simplest telemetry system. Voltage is measured between one or more signal wires and a reference – common – wire. The signal wires can carry digital or analogue signals. This type of system is susceptible to picking up electrical noise; for long wire runs or in electrically noisy environments, shielded cable should be used. Multiple signals may be combined – or multiplexed – onto one wire to reduce the size of the cable; this is sometimes known as 'thin-wire telemetry'.

In differential wired telemetry, digital or analogue signals are carried using pairs of wires; the signal is extracted from the difference in voltage between the wires. Differential signalling improves noise performance, as noise that is common to both wires is cancelled. The wires are often bundled together in 'twisted pairs' to minimise noise caused by magnetic fields.

Fibre-optic telemetry encodes an analogue or digital signal onto a light carrier transmitted along a fibre-optic cable. This has the advantage of very high noise immunity, and increased safety owing to complete electrical isolation between a human participant and any mains-powered data-collection equipment. Disadvantages include the necessity to have electrical power, usually batteries, at the remote end, and the fragility of fibre-optic cables.

Untethered, or wireless, systems don't require a physical link between sensor and data-collection equipment. This can ease set-up, as there are no trailing wires, and does not constrain sensors placed on moving objects. They may also reduce noise and increase safety owing to electrical isolation. Disadvantages include added complexity and the need to have a power source at the remote end of the link.

Radio systems can transmit analogue signals using amplitude modulation (AM) or, better, frequency modulation (FM). Digital signals can be encoded in a proprietary manner or can use standard protocols, such as Bluetooth, Zigbee, Digital Enhanced Cordless Telecommunications (DECT), or Global System Mobile (GSM). The range varies from a few metres to several kilometres and is usually greater outdoors than indoors. Other wireless systems use infrared light, ultrasound, or magnetic pulses; these are often used to telemeter heart rate between a chest strap and a monitoring watch.

Data logging

Data logging is an alternative to telemetry in which the signal is stored locally in analogue or digital form and later downloaded to a computer. This has the advantage of complete freedom of movement, but does not allow real-time display.

Sampling and anti-alias filtering

The Nyquist sampling theorem states that only signals with a frequency less than half of the sampling frequency – the 'Nyquist frequency' – can be faithfully digitised. Higher frequencies will be 'aliased'; that is, they will appear to have a lower frequency. In the extreme case, a signal with a frequency equal to the sampling rate will be measured as a constant voltage, as it will be sampled at exactly the same point in each cycle. Once a signal has been aliased it cannot be recovered, so it is critical to sample at well over twice – usually five times or more – the highest signal frequency likely to be present. Any noise contamination usually has a wider frequency spectrum so is likely to have components above the Nyquist frequency. If these components are large enough to distort the signal of interest they must be low-pass filtered before sampling (see **amplification and signal conditioning**). This is called anti-alias filtering and must reduce the noise above the Nyquist frequency to an insignificant amount while passing all the signal of

299

interest. Sampling at the highest possible rate can ease the anti-alias filter's task by increasing the gap between the desired signal and the Nyquist frequency, or it may obviate the need for anti-alias filtering altogether. Averaging several samples together can reduce the resulting large file sizes, which also reduces high-frequency noise.

Analogue-to-digital conversion

This is the process by which an analogue voltage is converted to a digital number. One of the most important parameters for analogue-to-digital converters (ADCs) is the number of bits in the digital number, usually 8, 10, 12, or 16. For a converter with n bits the smallest measurable change in input voltage is $V_{range}/2^n$ where V_{range} is the input voltage range of the ADC. For example, a 10-bit ADC with an input range 0–5 V cannot measure a change smaller than 5/1024, or approximately 5 mV. If higher accuracy is needed, then an ADC with more bits can be selected or the signal can be amplified, ensuring that the largest value does not exceed the input range of the ADC.

In addition to the number of bits there are other parameters to consider when selecting an ADC: the method of interfacing to the computer, the maximum sampling rate, the number of input channels, the input voltage range, whether the inputs are differential or single-ended, and the overall accuracy. Overall accuracy is always less than the formula given previously, owing to ADC imperfections, such as non-linearity, channel-to-channel cross talk, and digital noise from other parts of the system. An overall figure of merit for an ADC is the 'effective number of bits' (ENOB). For example, the 10-bit converter considered above may only have an ENOB of 7.5 bits, increasing the error to almost 30 mV.

See also: electronics

Further reading

Webster, J.G. (ed.) (1999) *The Measurement, Instrumentation, and Sensors Handbook*, Boca Raton FL: CRC Press.

BEN HELLER

COMPUTER SIMULATION MODELS

Computer simulation modelling is essentially the running of experiments on mathematical models in a computer. The interrelationships between modelling, simulation, simulation evaluation, and optimisation are shown in Figure 18.

System modelling

In computer simulation modelling, the models used are mathematical ones based on physical laws, unlike statistical models that fit relationships to the data and are sometimes used in conjunction with hierarchical models (see **heirarchical modelling**). Mathematical modelling links the performer, or sports object, and its motions. It involves representing one or more of the characteristics of a system using mathematical equations. Every model is an approximation that neglects certain features of the system. The art of good modelling can be described as including in the model only enough complexity to allow its effective and meaningful use. All else being equal, the simpler the model, the better, as it is then easier to understand the behaviour of the model and its implications. The difficulty of interpreting the results, particularly for feedback to coaches and sports performers, increases rapidly with model complexity.

Computer simulation

Experiments measure what happens in the real world to real objects; a mathematical model forms a similar basis for computer experiments. Indeed, computer simulation

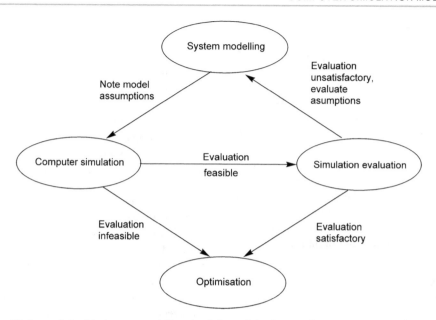

Figure 18. Inter-relationships between modelling, simulation and simulation evaluation.

can be defined as the carrying out of experiments under carefully controlled conditions on the real world system that has been modelled. It is much easier to control extraneous variables in a mathematical model than in the real world. Mathematical modelling transforms the real system into a set of equations; computer simulation involves the performance of numerical experiments on these equations, after which we transform the results back to the real system to understand reality.

The advantages of computer simulation are as follows. First, it is safe, as the athlete does not have to be involved in potentially hazardous experiments. Second, it saves lots of time, as many different simulations can be performed in minutes. Third, it is cost-effective, as it is far cheaper to run a simulation than, for example, to build a prototype javelin. Last, it offers the potential for predicting optimal performance. Its limitations are the problem of simulation evaluation (see later), the requirement for good mathematical and computer skills, and potential difficulties in 'translating' the results into a language that is intelligible to

practitioners. Of these, the problem of simulation evaluation is the most important.

Simulation evaluation

The need to add complexity to an existing simulation model should be revealed by continuously relating the results of the simulations on that model to physical measurements. This tests the model to see if it is an adequate approximation of the real world system, and to ascertain what new features need to be added. In many computer simulations, such simulation evaluations are not carried out; in some, they are not feasible. One approach to simulation evaluation, which has been widely reported for some simulation models of airborne sports activities, has been to combine modelling and empirical studies, so that the model results can be compared directly with the movements they model (e.g. Yeadon *et al.* 1990). This approach could be adopted in many more cases and would help both to relate the model to the real world and to communicate the simulation results to coaches and athletes.

Optimisation

Formally, optimisation is the method for finding the optimal value – this may be a mathematical maximum or minimum – of a function f of n variables. Finding the maximum for the function f is identical to finding the minimum for the function $-f$. For this reason, optimisation normally seeks to find the minimum values of the function to be optimised. Biomechanically, optimisation is an operation on the mathematical model to give the best possible motion, subject to model limitations. The process involves **forward dynamics and optimisation**.

Reference

Yeadon, M.R., Atha, J. and Hales, F.D. (1990) 'The Simulation of Aerial Movement. Part IV: A Computer Simulation Model', *Journal of Biomechanics* 23: 85–9.

Further reading

Bartlett, R.M. (1999) *Sports Biomechanics: Reducing Injury and Improving Performance*, ch. 6, London: E&FN Spon.

ROGER BARTLETT

COMPUTERISED TOMOGRAPHY (CT)

Computerised tomography (CT) is an imaging technique utilising the difference in attenuation of **bone** and soft tissues to produce a cross sectional image. Although **magnetic resonance imaging (MRI)**, with its superior ability to distinguish different soft tissues and multiplanar imaging capability, has displaced CT from many musculoskeletal indications it is still important, particularly in acute **traumatic injury**.

CT utilises a fine beam of X-ray radiation and sensitive detectors which rotate in a housing through which the patient is moved on a motorised couch. Fast computers calculate X-ray attenuation within the tissue irradiated and reconstruct a series of images in the same plane as the X-ray beam. X-ray attenuation is represented in the image on a grey scale so that higher attenuation tissue is lighter and lower darker. Using the current generation of multi-detector scanners it is possible to obtain further images in any chosen orientation with little loss of image quality.

CT scanning is rapid, only requiring complete immobility for a few seconds, there are few contraindications, it is accurate in the assessment of the abdominal, thoracic, and cranial contents, and provides good **bone** imaging.

Non-fatty soft tissues have only relatively small differences in X-ray attenuation; intra-abdominal and thoracic organs are largely outlined by fat, or in the case of lungs, air, allowing good visualisation. Intravenous water-soluble iodine containing compounds may also contribute by preferentially increasing the attenuation of vessels and more vascular soft tissues. CT is now the accepted gold standard in the assessment of thoracic and abdominal trauma.

Differences in X-ray attenuation between the grey and white matter of the brain and cerebrospinal fluid are small but adequate for good quality structural assessment of the cranial contents. Clotted blood is of relatively high attenuation and can be directly identified. CT provides the information required for decisions on clinical management following significant head injury (see **head and neck injury – global scene of prevention**).

Radiographs are projections of three-dimensional objects onto a two-dimensional plane as a consequence of which even experienced radiologists can be unable to fully assess many bony injuries. CT by producing a series of two-dimensional cross-sectional images allows analysis of even the most complex injury patterns with great accuracy. Surgical planning following complex bony injury, particularly of the pelvis, knee, ankle, and foot is one of the commonest CT indications. CT is also able to diagnose many fractures and joint sub-luxations which are not identified on conventional radiographs.

CT arthrography is performed by injection of liquid of high attenuation into a joint to outline articular cartilage, fibro-cartilage, ligaments, intra-articular bodies, and other articular structures. Although MRI has greatly reduced the indications for the technique it is routinely used in the surgical planning of shoulder stabilisation, where it can demonstrate bony and soft tissue Bankart lesions (see **Bankart injury**). Other indications include the elbow (see **elbow and forearm**) to identify loose bodies, the **hip joint** labral tears, and the ankle (see **ankle and foot**) osteochondral fractures/osteochondritis dissecans. In the presence of contraindications or restricted access to MRI, CT and CT arthrography assume increased importance.

References

Andre, M. and Resnick, D. (1996) 'Computed Tomography, in Bone and Joint Imaging', in D. Resnick (ed.) *Bone and Joint Imaging*, Philadelphia PA: W.B. Saunders.

Totty, W.G., McEnery, K.W., Renner, J.B., Robertson, D.D., Hsieh, P.S. and Hatem, S.F. (1998) 'Musculoskeletal CT', in J.T. Lee, S.S. Sagel, R.J. Stanley and J.P. Heiken (eds) *Computed Body Tomography with MRI Correlation*, Philadelphia PA: Lippincott Williams and Wilkins.

ROBERT COOPER

CONCENTRATION AND ATTENTION CONTROL

The ability to focus on the relevant cues in the environment, and to maintain that focus, is one of the most important skills for a performer to possess. Attention control in sport has been studied from three perspectives: information processing, social psychology, and psychophysiology. Information processing has two specific forms. Control processing requires effort and is both cum-bersome and slow, whereas automatic processing is effortless and efficient. Processes focusing on attentional selectivity, capacity, and alertness are typically examined. Social psychology has focused on individual differences and environmental influences, demonstrating how these can disrupt attention. Distraction theories – which focus on the loss of attention through focusing on inappropriate irrelevant cues, automatic functioning, and attentional style – an individual difference factor – are examined under this perspective. The psychophysiological approach examines the underlying mechanisms of attention by monitoring cortical and cardiac activity. Electroencephalograms, evoked response potentials, and heart rate primarily have been used to examine attention control and its relationship to performance in the psychophysiological approach. From an applied perspective, attentional strengths and weaknesses of performers are assessed and specific attention control programmes are established that are specifically related to the type of sport being played, for example, whether it is open or closed, or fine or gross.

See also: attention and performance; concentration and attention strategies

Further reading

Boutcher, S. (2002) 'Attentional Processes and Sport Performance', in T. Horn (ed.) *Advances in Sport Psychology*, 441–57, Champaign IL: Human Kinetics.

Carver, C.S. and Schier, M.F. (1981) *Attention and Self-regulation*, New York: Springer-Verlag.

ROBERT WEINBERG

CONCENTRATION AND ATTENTION STRATEGIES

Many attentional strategies have been developed to improve concentration and to help make the execution of the skill more automatic, including the following. Pre-performance routines involve self-regulation of thoughts and emotions to put the performer in an optimal emotional, highly self-expectant, and focused state immediately before execution, and to remain that way during the performance. Imaginal rehearsal allows the performer to focus on the relevant cues that are critical for successful performance and to narrow his or her focus to the task at hand. **Self-talk** can be either motivational or instructional and often involves cue words to trigger a particular response automatically, keeping performers in the present. In addition, non-judgmental thinking helps performers to focus on the task itself instead of evaluating their performance as good or bad. Simulation involves performing and practising the skill under similar conditions to those of competition. Biofeedback has been used to help performers control autonomic responses and to 'quiet' certain aspects of the mind and body. Competition plans require performers to design detailed plans of action to facilitate attentional focus on the process, the controllable factors, of performance. Overlearning skills will also help performance to be more automatic.

See also: attentional training; concentration and attention control

Further reading

Abernethy, B. (2001) 'Attention', in R.N. Singer, H. Hausenblas and C. Janelle (eds) *Handbook of Research on Sport Psychology*, Second Edition, 53–85, New York: John Wiley.
Moran, A. (1996) *The Psychology of Concentration in Sport Performers*, Hove: Psychology Press.

ROBERT WEINBERG

CONGESTION

Congestion arises when a facility or resource exceeds its carrying capacity. Congestion is often associated with traffic and traffic movement and delays, but extends more widely to recreation and sport participation and spectatorism and even business investment. For example, Whitson and Macintosh (1993) noted that local residents were concerned with road access and hence opposed the locating of Saddledome at Calgary's Stampede grounds. Others have noted that business investment in local areas may be discouraged by crowding and congestion (e.g. Baade and Dye 1990).

Levels of congestion are influenced by such factors as traffic volume, mode of traffic, the nature of the transport network (its structure and size) and supporting services. Congestion levels rise and fall and are generally associated with 'peak' periods of use.

Satisfaction with participation in activities tends to diminish with higher levels of congestion. Congestion generally creates frustration and annoyance (sometimes leading to incidents now widely reported now as 'rage' – as witnessed and publicised in relation to urban traffic and surfing), and gives rise to social and environmental costs through time delays, accidents, and pollution. Congestion may occur during participation in events (e.g. racing cars and bikes, yachting, skiing) and in some cases may be expected or even desired (also see crowding). It may occur in all or part of a sporting experience, for example in skiing, where congestion is mostly considered a negative factor in experiences, it may occur on the slopes or at ski lifts, with people waiting lengthy periods.

Congestion is frequently associated with costs and externalities. Transport congestion, for example, is widely considered an externality as the full costs of congestion are borne by both users and non-users of transport facilities. Large numbers of visitors making their way to sporting events may lead to delays in transport movement as well as limited or lower levels of accessibility of transport facilities for local residents. In other words, people not seeking to participate in an event will be affected by its conduct. Further, people may have special places they visit for consumptive sports such as fishing and hunting, and activities such as walking or surfing. Congestion, or the mere presence of activities perceived to be incompatible, may result in people substituting another site for their desired site, delaying their visit, or undertaking a different activity altogether.

Many ideas and strategies have been put forward to counter problems of congestion and associated costs and externalities. Access times can be restricted to certain groups. Use can be restricted completely (i.e. in numbers) or manipulated. Entrance fees may be used to limit demand. However, restricting the number of entrants will not necessarily result in an efficient utilisation of a facility or resource. According to Patrick and Lovejoy (1990: 6):

> Some visitors may not be willing to pay the marginal cost of congestion that they inflict on others, while others who would be willing to pay an additional fee for congestion may be excluded. Welfare improvement could be accomplished by charging entrance fees, the optimal price being equal to the external congestion cost of the marginal visit.

Of course, facility and site managers may wish to concentrate use, which will lead to congestion. This may necessarily occur at large sporting venues for the purposes of security checks and minimisation of direct costs. Where congestion occurs at large-scale events, similar strategies to those identified for crowding (see **crowding**) may be employed.

References

Baade, R.A. and Dye, R.E. (1990) 'The Impact of Stadiums and Professional Sport on Metropolitan Area Development', *Growth and Change*, 21, 2: 1–14.

Patrick, R.H. and Lovejoy, S.B. (1990) 'Rationing the Congested Recreational Facility: Market Versus Political Instruments', in J.D. Hutcheson, F.P. Noe and R.E. Snow (eds) *Outdoor Recreation Policy: Pleasure and Preservation*, 95–104, New York: Greenwood Press.

Whitson, D. and Macintosh, D. (1993) 'Becoming a World Class City: Hallmark Events and Sport Franchises in the Growth Strategies of Western Canadian Cities', *Sociology of Sport Journal*, 19, 2: 221–40.

Further reading

Bale, J. (1992) *Sport, Space and the City*, London: Routledge.

JOHN M. JENKINS

CONSERVATION

The idea of conservation – the protection of natural resources and the environment – can seem somewhat alien in advanced capitalist societies dominated by free market economics and consumer values, in which global sport now plays a significant role. The conservation of land to be used freely by society directly opposes the free market ideology of private ownership, production, and capital accumulation. However, it was the idea of an opposing force (against the acquisitive tendencies of capitalism) that conceived the conservation movement and the first political act to enshrine the protection of wild places in legislation.

To better understand the term conservation it is worth contrasting it with a similar term, preservation. Preservation means to protect an area in its 'primordial state', that is to keep something as it was before the impact of humankind. Conservation, on the other hand, means to 'sustain' and 'manage' a natural resource in a sustainable way. For example, a river flowing through a national park may be managed and sustained through the use of designated water sports and the annual introduction of fish stocks. Conservation and the conservation movement has influenced and effected society's gradual move from a mechanistic to an ecological worldview, and helped spawn the massive increase in the popularity of outdoor sports and recreation.

Historically, the notion of conservation as a concept and movement can be traced back to the nineteenth century, when a concerted push for the protection of natural resources occurred in the United States. There were three main reasons for this. First, the gradual closing of the frontier in the late 1800s caused anxiety in the nation because the frontier had supported a way of life that would now come to an end. No longer could freedom and opportunity be found by settling lands to the west. This led to a recognised need for areas of public land that could be used for outdoor recreation and sport and, in a sense, could create the idea of an endless frontier in the minds of the nation.

Second, there was a shift in the way society viewed and valued nature, particularly wild nature. The Puritans (the original settlers of the United States) did not value wild nature for its own sake. Yet the pioneer farmer of the seventeenth and eighteenth centuries, living on the frontier close to nature, embodied all of the virtues highly valued by the new settler society – rugged individuality, resourcefulness, strength, and independent thought. It was these virtues that were the foundation of Thomas Jefferson's democratic ideal. He dreamed of a society of farmers that worked close to the land and close to wilderness. After the 1700s certain sections of American society were increasingly influenced by the romantic writers of Europe who, as city dwellers, were repelled by the ill-effects of the industrial revolution, such as pollution and forced child labour in factories. These writers often expressed the desire for the simple life – for beauty, wholesomeness and happiness that must surely came from living close to nature. The desire for such simplicity and spiritual renewal found its expression in America in the writings of Henry David Thoreau's *Walden*.

Third, protection of natural resources and the environment came about through political leadership. In the USA, John Muir, the founder of the Sierra Club, stands out as an historical figure who most influenced the political leaders of his time (his relationship with Theodore Roosevelt was particularly instrumental) about the importance of protecting the nation's precious natural resources for their beauty, inspiration, and spiritual uplift.

As a result of the designation of Yellowstone National Park (the first national park in the world) in 1872, outdoor sports and recreation began to grow at a rapid rate, particularly with the advent of the automobile in the early 1900s. As the popularity of park visitation grew there was an alarming decline in wildlife because of a consumer desire to take home some sort of souvenir, or have something to show for money spent. Concern over the destruction of the United States' forests led to a report on the plight of the country's forests in 1876. This led to the formation of the United States Forest Service. In 1907 an inventory of natural resources was made and, as a result, the Weeks Act of 1911, which authorised the purchase of forestland for watershed protection, was introduced. The national forests of the eastern United States were established and acquired under this Act. With increasing amounts of land coming under the protection of federal legislation, the need to manage national parks soon arose. Pressure from other uses continued to threaten these parks, such as hunting and fishing, so in 1916 the National Parks Service was established.

Other countries followed the United States' example and a variety of conservation areas and parks were established world-wide. For example, The Royal National Park in Australia was established on the southern outskirts of Sydney in 1879. In 1924, the first dedication of a wilderness area occurred, the Gila Wilderness in New Mexico. From this point on there was a growing body of legislation designed to protect land from resource extraction and to institute and promote responsible management and visitor behaviour in protected public lands worldwide.

Much of the legislation relating to the conservation of natural resources was based on the provision of outdoor sports and recreation. The emphasis upon the recreational use of national parks dates from the original Yellowstone Act of 1872, which stated that the park should be dedicated and set apart as a 'pleasuring ground' for the benefit and enjoyment of the people. The Canadians followed the American example by legislating in 1887 to enlarge the Banff Hot Springs Reserve (1885) and designate it as the Rocky Mountains Park. The legislation defined the term 'park' as a public park and pleasure ground for the benefit, advantage, and enjoyment of the people of Canada. Today the Banff National Park (as it is now called) attracts hundreds of thousands of visitors from all over Canada and the world who come to enjoy the area's many sporting opportunities, including skiing, climbing, and kayaking.

Britain established its first national parks between 1950 and 1955 under the National Parks and Access to the Countryside Act 1949 (since replaced by the 1968 Countryside Act). Both Acts were orientated strongly towards outdoor sports and recreational use, and were directed towards the perpetuation of characteristic anthropomorphic cultural landscapes and the safeguarding of the public's access to the countryside, rather than the preservation of natural ecosystems.

Research indicates that participation in outdoor sports and recreation is the start of most individuals' movement towards conservation values, and is seen by many as the greatest single value derived from national parks and wilderness areas. Various lobby groups for outdoor sports and recreation (skiing, sports utility driving, bicycling, climbing, kayaking) have been instrumental in the formation of national park systems in the West, and national park policy worldwide. Parks around the world are now conserved and managed in a variety of ways, for example the national forest system in the United States is sustained for ongoing timber production and sporting/recreational use.

Further reading

Loland, S. (1996) 'Outline of an Ecosphy of Sport', *Journal of the Philosophy of Sport* 23, 1: 70–90.

STEPHEN WEARING

CONSTRAINTS

Self-organising dynamical systems achieve functional states of coordination only when under constraint. Constraints have been defined as boundaries or features that limit the form of a biological system engaged in a search for an optimal state of organisation. In this sense they have the effect of reducing the number of configurations available to a dynamical system at any instance. That is, constraints help to structure the state space of all possible configurations for a biological movement system. There are many classes of constraints that can shape the behaviour of a dynamical system, and it remains an important task in movement science to identify them. Constraints are specific to biological niches and can be found at many different levels of the system or the environment. For a species, they are allied to selection as part of the optimising evolutionary process, which guides biological organisms towards functionally appropriate behaviours in a particular niche or habitat. At the level of perception and action, constraints operate in the same way on the behaviour of movement systems during goal-directed activity. That is, selected coordination patterns in the human movement system emerge under constraint as less functional states of organisation are destroyed.

Constraints, therefore, are factors that influence the self-organisation of a movement system's degrees of freedom. The production of skilled movement behaviour in sport depends on a stability and flexibility in the behaviour of natural dynamical systems. Dynamical systems have been modelled as complex systems that are continuously evolving over different timescales. A dynamical system can be defined as any system whose changing states over time can be mathematically modelled as trajectories in a phase space with a rule of evolution, using differential equations. The term 'phase space' refers to all the hypothetical states of organisation into which a dynamical system can evolve. For example, the phase space of molecules of water adhering as a dynamical system involves just three attractor states, or forms of organisation, characterised as liquid, steam, or ice. Dynamical systems can evolve along different pathways, primarily because they are 'open' systems, meaning that their form can be influenced by many factors in the environment. In studying open dynamical systems, it has become clear that the influences that guide the form emerging from the system should be considered as constraints on system behaviour. The role of constraints in shaping motor behaviour became prominent from the 1980s, because it was realised that the stability of functional coordination patterns can be altered by task constraints imposed on performers, such as information to channel movement dynamics, equipment used for performing an activity, and the structural organisation of the performance environment including intentions and feedback

See also: constraints-led perspective; dynamical systems theory; environmental constraints; open systems in sport

KEITH DAVIDS

CONSTRAINTS-LED PERSPECTIVE

For many movement scientists, the central problem of investigation concerns how the many interacting biomechanical degrees of freedom of the human movement system are coordinated and controlled during goal-directed activity. Despite the proliferation of degrees of freedom, dynamical movement systems show a surprising amount of order, and it has been known for some time that functional coordination patterns emerge during self-organisation in individual performers to satisfy competing and cooperating task, informational, and **environmental constraints**. The model of how interacting **constraints** and self-organisation processes underpin coordination and control of actions has formed the basis of a principled constraints-led approach to practice in sport, suggesting that the main role of the coach or teacher is to manipulate key constraints on the learner to facilitate the search for functional movement behaviours.

In a constraints-led approach, there is a clear emphasis on discovery learning. Exploratory **practice** embraces problem-solving behaviours, because individuals must actively engage in learning rather than passively receiving information. Learners are encouraged to find and assemble their own unique solutions to motor problems during exploratory practice. Discovering various solutions to the task, whether successful or not, is essential in learning to experience various task solutions. Discovery learning occurs in a practice context similar to the performance context, enabling the individual to become more attuned to the available information sources. While an individual actively participates in learning, he or she is able to concentrate on exploring potentially important sources of information as, opposed to independently satisfying task demands prescribed by the coach. Exploratory practice is valuable at both the coordination and control stage of learning for different reasons (see **skill-acquisition stages – control**; **skill-acquisition stages – coordination**). Initially, exploratory practice is useful for learners to assemble functional and unique coordination structures to achieve a specific task goal, such as intercepting a ball. Later in learning, exploratory practice allows individuals to refine and adapt existing basic coordinative structures to enhance flexibility, such as to control a ball in different ways and under different conditions. In sport, exploratory behaviour can be encouraged by manipulating key task constraints to direct the learners' search for effective coordination solutions. An important issue concerns the nature of the constraints that learners have to satisfy during motor learning. Practice should provide opportunities for performers to learn how to soft-assemble adaptive behaviours in ways that robustly respond to local context and exploit the **variability** of intrinsic dynamics.

To exemplify, equipment design is an important factor that can influence acquisition of skill, while satisfying health and safety requirements of practice conditions. This point is particularly important in children's skill acquisition. Current theoretical models of **motor development** across the lifespan recognise that children should not be viewed as 'mini-adults', but as coherent, developing **complex systems**. Despite this view, commercialised sports equipment has rarely been engineered to facilitate motor skill acquisition and the physical fitness of young children. The result is that equipment in sport, such as balls, are typically too large or too heavy for children to grasp, throw, or kick, and striking implements are often too narrow, long, or heavy for children's use. This clearly increases the risk of injury, and could hamper skill acquisition.

KEITH DAVIDS

CONTROLLED AND AUTOMATIC PROCESSING

Bryan and Harter's work in the late 1800s, examining the acquisition of the telegraphic language, marked one of the first explorations of controlled and automatic processing. They studied telegraphic operators of various skills, who were required to translate a message written in English to Morse code and then tap a telegraph key to convey the message to another party. They found that the acquisition of telegraphic skill proceeded through distinct phases characterised by differences in the amount of controlled and automatic processes that supported execution. Although the performance of less skilled telegraphic operators was governed by controlled processes that took effort and time to execute, more skilled operators worked automatically. Telegraphy transmissions by skilled operators were fast and accurate and were less harmed by external distractions or disturbances than were those of their novice counterparts.

The idea that various degrees of controlled and automatic processing characterise different stages of learning can be seen in modern theories of skill acquisition. Fitts and Posner (1967) suggested that novice performance is governed by conscious or controlled cognitive processes that take time, effort, and attentional resources to initiate. With extended practice, performance is thought to reach an autonomous or automatic phase in which conscious attentional control is no longer required for successful performance. Here, performance is smooth, relatively effortless, and places little if any load on conscious attentional resources.

Differences in controlled and automatic processing are particularly apparent when novice and expert skill execution is examined under single-task conditions – when a skill is performed in isolation – and dual-task conditions – when a skill is performed simultaneously with a secondary task. Novice performance requires controlled processing that requires effort and attention to execute. Thus, the addition of a secondary task harms performance, because there are not enough attentional resources to allocate to both primary and secondary tasks simultaneously. In contrast, the automated performances of experts are thought to run largely outside of conscious awareness.

As a result, high skill execution is not harmed by the addition of secondary task demands, because such performance is not dependent on the attentional resources that a secondary task requires. In ice hockey, for example, instructing hockey players to skate and stick handle a puck through a slalom course of pylons while performing a secondary task, such as identifying geometric shapes projected onto a screen they could see from the ice, harms novice but not expert performance. Similarly, in soccer, adding a secondary task, such as monitoring a list of verbally presented words for a specific target word, to a soccer dribbling task leads to greater decrements in novice, but not experienced, performance than when the soccer task is performed in a single-task, isolated environment (see Beilock *et al.* 2002). These findings not only illustrate differences in novice and expert skill execution, but the degree to which controlled and automatic processes are differentially affected by demanding dual-task conditions.

References

Beilock, S.L., Carr, T.H., MacMahon, C. and Starkes, J.L. (2002) When Paying Attention Becomes Counterproductive: Impact of Divided Versus Skill-Focused Attention on Novice and Experienced Performance of Sensorimotor Skills, *Journal of Experimental Psychology: Applied* 8: 6–16.

Fitts, P.M. and Posner, M.I. (1967) *Human Performance*, Belmont CA: Brooks/Cole.

Further reading

Proctor, R.W. and Dutta, A. (1995) *Skill Acquisition and Human Performance*, Thousand Oaks CA: Sage.

SIAN L. BEILOCK

CONTUSION

Contusions are bruises or haematomas, which occur on or close to the surface of the brain.

Many patients who sustain a musculoskeletal injury also sustain a head injury. These injuries may be quite obvious or may be missed. Most head injuries occur as a result of motor vehicle accident but may also occur as result of fall from heights or recreational and sports injuries. Such sports include soccer, skateboarding, and baseball. Other causes of head injuries are stab, gunshot, and missile wounds.

The mechanism of injury to the patient should lead to a strong index of suspicion of head injury. Treatment of the patient starts at the site of the accident. The airway is maintained and the cervical spine stabilised. The patient needs immediate transfer to a health facility. In the emergency department a quick conversational attempt with the patient ascertains if he or she is conscious. A brief history may also be taken from the patient to get an idea of any amnesia. A history may also be taken from the paramedical team and also the treatment given to the patient. The immediate step is to maintain the airway if it has not been done before, and with it to stabilise the cervical spine. Respiration is maintained with an airway or even an intubation if the patient is not breathing at all. The cervical spine is stabilised with a hard collar if it has not already been applied. Sandbags can be placed at the sides of the cervical spine and tape placed around the head. This immobilises the spine. The head injury is often associated with a cervical spine injury, and failure to stabilise the cervical spine may lead to inadvertent upper cervical spine injury with complete paralysis in some cases. The next step is to make sure that breathing is not obstructed. The physician should palpate the trachea to note any shift, as well as auscultate the chest for adequate inflation of lungs and breath sounds. Road traffic accidents may also result in chest injury, which may be a flail chest, haemothorax, or pneumothorax. These need to be dealt immediately with a chest tube or intubation. The circulation is maintained next. A blood sample should be sent to the lab for examination and cross-match blood requested. The IV line is maintained and isotonic fluid given. All monitors are connected to measure the vital signs and other parameters. Any neurological deficit is recorded and a detailed examination of the patient is carried out. The thoracolumbar spine is examined by log rolling the patient and examining the entire spine for any bruise, haematoma, step or swelling. If the patient is conscious then any tenderness is noted

A series of radiographs are taken, usually the trauma series, which includes a cervical spine radiograph, a chest radiograph, and a pelvic radiograph. There may be other radiographs requested by the physician as required.

The Glasgow coma scale needs to be recorded at the time of injury and when the patient enters the emergency room. It will help in the diagnosis, management, and prognosis. The patient is assigned a score between 3 and 15. This is based on eye responses, motor responses, and verbal responses. The higher the score the less severe the injury. A score of three means that the patient is unresponsive, whereas a score of fifteen means that the patient is alert, oriented, and able to follow commands. Although the Glasgow coma scale is good for assessment of the brain and also its probable medical outcome, it is less predictable for neurobehavioral outcomes. The most reliable predictor of the neurobehavioral outcome is the duration of post-traumatic amnesia. If it is less then twenty-four hours then the head injury is classified as mild and the outcome is usually good. If the duration of post-traumatic amnesia is between twenty-four hours and seven days then the head injury is moderate, and if the post-traumatic amnesia is more then seven days then the head injury is severe.

Imaging techniques of choice are the CT scan and magnetic resonance imaging (MRI). These can provide valuable information as to the status of the brain. There may be an epidural haematoma, which is collection of blood between the duramater and the skull. This is usually due to tearing of the middle meningeal artery. These are quite serious injuries as they can cause sudden compression of brain and may be fatal. There is usually a short, lucid interval, which is followed by loss of consciousness. The subdural haematomas may be acute or chronic. This occurs secondary to vein tear and bleeding within the subdural space. They are accompanied by contusions and can cause focal damage to the cortex. Subarachnoid haemorrhage occurs in the subarachnoid space and does not cause any space-occupying lesion. It can be caused by trauma or a ruptured aneurysm. Intracerebral haematomas or haemorrhage can cause focal defects as well as brain herniation. An extradural haematoma or a subdural haematoma requires precise surgical intervention. The intracerebral haematomas may also require evacuation. The different lobes of the brain have different centres for speech, vision, and hearing as well as for motor function of the limbs. A clinical examination can evaluate the deficiency or impairment of a particular function.

There are many acute and chronic effects of injury to the brain. Patients with severe head injury are often comatose and obtunded. As the mental function recovers, cortical arousal returns but most patients display global cognitive dysfunction and are not able to execute higher tasks. Age also has a great influence on the duration of recovery. Children tend to recover more quickly then the older people. Many old people may already suffer from dementia or cerebrovascular disease with impaired memory. These patients have a prolonged rehabilitation time. Injury to the temporal lobes adversely affects speech, fluency, comprehension, naming, repetition, reading, and writing. Similarly, injury to the occipital lobe will affect vision, and many visual

311

deficits can be seen depending on the nature of the injury to various visual bundles.

Many psychiatric problems resut from contusions, depending on the precise nature of the injury and also the age of the patient. Children younger then ten have the propensity to develop attention deficit disorders, but they lack the hyperactive component. Adults tend to develop a range of disorders ranging from mild anxiety disorder to severe psychosis. Adolescents develop irritability, depression, and aggressive behaviour. In older patients there may be preexisting psychological problems, which may be exacerbated. A previous history of psychological disturbances as well as any psychiatric treatment should be noted.

Patients can continue to improve for as long as three years. However, there are residual deficits in attention, memory, and also in higher thought processes like planning, problem solving, and strategy formation. Long-term deficits that are common in adults and children are attention disorders, anxiety, and psychosis.

Management of contusion is a combined approach, which includes the general surgeon, the neurosurgeon and the psychiatrist.

IMRAN ILYAS

COORDINATION

Coordination can be thought of as groups of muscles functioning together in a harmonious fashion to complete a specific, functional task such as sports actions in gymnastics or synchronized swimming. Two aspects of motor function that are important in producing coordinated movements are motor control and motor learning. Motor control is the ability to use incoming sensory information in order to produce an accurate, appropriately timed movement. Motor learning, also known as motor plasticity, refers to a persistent change in the motor output that occurs in relation to a particular sensory signal. Athletes are often required to fine tune and sharpen their sport-specific skills in order to produce precisely coordinated outcomes. When a sports-related injury has occurred, deficits in coordination often accompany deficits in strength, power, flexibility, and endurance, requiring specific attention and retraining as part of the rehabilitation treatment plan. This can be caused by the injury itself or a consequence of detraining. Rehabilitation clinicians take advantage of motor learning when retraining patients with deficits in coordination.

Motor control and motor learning are mediated by the nervous system at multiple levels including the sensory receptors, afferent and efferent nerves, spinal cord, brainstem, basal ganglia, cerebellum, and cortex. Injury at any point can result in coordination deficits. In the setting of sports, injury most often occurs at the level of the sensory receptors located in articular structures. However, no discussion of coordination would be complete without particular attention to the role of the cerebellum.

It has long been known that the cerebellum plays a vital role in the production of smooth movements and the maintenance of stable posture. The clinical picture of cerebellar damage includes difficulty with starting and stopping movements and inability to control the force, direction, timing, and velocity of movements. This produces impairments in balance (ataxia), slurred speech (dysarthria), inability to reach to a target (dysmetria), and oscillation with attempted purposeful movements (intention tremor). Cerebellar damage may also impair the production of sequences of repetitive movements. Tasks once performed automatically may require intense mental concentration. The cerebellum is clearly important in motor learning as well as motor control. Studies of animals with cerebellar damage show deficits in adaptation of eye-head coordination, difficulty in learning skillful limb movements and decreased performance on reaction-time tests.

Although the contribution of the cerebellum is unique, to produce a coordinated outcome the peripheral and central nervous system must be functioning properly at multiple levels. At the most peripheral level, sensory receptors provide awareness of the position of the body and its parts in relation to the environment. Articular mechanoreceptors are the sensory receptors present in joints that mediate the proprioceptive sensations of kinesthesia, the awareness of joint motion, and joint position sense, the awareness of limb position. Conscious proprioception is necessary for the proper function of joints in sports, activities of daily living and occupational tasks. Unconscious proprioception modulates reflex joint stabilization and muscle function. Proprioception is mediated not only by sensory receptors in joints but also by muscle spindle receptors and cutaneous mechanoreceptors. The improvement in kinesthesia that occurs with use of a neoprene sleeve or brace wrapping an injured extremity can be attributed to the increased stimulation of cutaneous mechanoreceptors. Muscle spindle receptors play an important role in reflex muscle splinting during acute joint injury.

When articular structures are damaged, for example as the result of a sports injury, rehabilitation is necessary to reestablish dynamic joint stability. In addition to their mechanical role, articular structures provide sensory information required for joint stability during sudden changes in joint position common to sports activity. Deficits in neuromuscular control can lead to recurrent joint injuries. Joint surgery may restore the mechanical restraining function of joint structures, but proprioceptive input remains altered. Sports rehabilitation programs should focus not only on strengthening the muscles surrounding the involved joint in order to restore mechanical stability, but also on retraining the altered afferent pathways to enhance the sensation of joint movement.

Articular sensory receptors contribute to motor control at different levels of the central nervous system, and all of these must be addressed in the rehabilitation program. At the spinal level, reflex splinting provides protection from injury during conditions of increased stress about the joint. Muscle spindles adjust peripheral nervous system activity to provide joint stabilization by contraction of synergistic and antagonistic muscles. The injured athlete, therefore, must practice activities that require reflex joint stabilization during sudden alterations in joint position. At the level of the brainstem, joint proprioceptors, vestibular centers in the ears and visual input all provide information to help maintain erect posture and balance. Balance and postural activities with and without visual input help to address motor control at this level. At the highest levels of central nervous system function (the motor cortex, basal ganglia, and cerebellum), the conscious awareness of body position and movement allows voluntary movements to be planned and initiated. Rehabilitation techniques that focus on consciously performed joint positioning activities, especially at joint end ranges, will help to stimulate conscious motor programming.

Kinesthetic and proprioceptive training should begin early in the rehabilitation process with simple balance and joint repositioning tasks. Joint repositioning activities and unstable platform exercises while seated can be started before weight bearing is allowed. Once weight bearing is begun, single leg stance exercises performed on various surfaces are simple, yet effective balance retraining activities. This can progress to the use of an unstable platform, initially with both feet and finally with single leg stance. Exercises that include balancing on an unstable platform while performing a sports-specific skill integrate conscious and unconscious proprioceptive pathways

313

and are an example of higher-level kinesthetic rehabilitation activities.

As the rehabilitation program progresses, turning, cutting, and agility activities should be practiced. Running figure-eights in both directions can be used to initiate turning. Cross-over drills, four-corner running and reaction cutting maneuvers are frequently used for agility training. These should be begun at slow speeds and progressed to normal speed by the conclusion of the rehabilitation process. The final phase of kinesthetic training involves the practice of activities specific to the particular sport and should be uniquely tailored to the individual athlete. An understanding by the therapist of the demands of the sport and the position played is crucial to this phase of recovery. In order to avoid re-injury, return to sporting activities should not be considered until full sports-specific functional recovery has occurred.

Another aspect of motor control that deserves special mention is the area of eye-hand coordination; of particular importance in many sports such as archery, shooting, and basketball. The eyes and hands are anatomically removed from one another, yet are clearly linked on a neurological basis. The visual system and the motor control system share sensory information about objects' location in space in order to produce coordinated movements. The importance of this aspect of coordination is particularly relevant in sports that involve hitting an approaching ball, such as baseball and tennis. This perceptual–motor task requires the interaction of complex visual and spatial information to predict the trajectory and velocity of the oncoming ball. Although this type of coordination can be improved with practice, there are clearly individual differences in ability to perform such demanding tasks.

Further reading

Prentice, W.E. (ed.) (1994) *Rehabilitation Techniques in Sports Medicine*, St Louis MO: Mosby.

Rosenbaum, D.A. (1991) *Human Motor Control*, San Diego CA: Academic Press, Inc.

ALLISON BAILEY

COORDINATIVE STRUCTURES

Studying the processes of movement coordination is a key task for motor behaviour specialists. Understanding how the learner uses and constrains the many relevant degrees of freedom in the motor system, concurrently, during tasks like soccer kicking or tennis serving, is the crux of the issue. At a basic level of analysis, movement system degrees of freedom include the muscles and joints of the body. How does the learner cope with the task of coordinating the activity of over 700 muscles and 100 joints of the body? Based on the insights of the great Russian movement scientist Nicolai Bernstein, the acquisition of coordination can be viewed as the process of constraining the movement system degrees of freedom into functional and flexible coordinative structures, which convert a highly complex system – the human body – into a more controllable organisation.

The term 'coordinative structure' captures how coordination emerges between motor system components during goal-directed behaviour. Coordinative structures are functional relationships formed between important anatomical components of a performer's body designed for a specific purpose or activity, such as when groups of muscles or joints are temporarily assembled into coherent units to achieve specific task goals, such as hitting a ball or performing a T-balance.

The many degrees of freedom for the regulation of movements exemplifies that, typically, there is great abundance from which the central nervous system can select for the performance of motor tasks. On the face of it, the coordination of so many micro-components of the human body seems a very daunting task, but the abundance of motor system degrees of freedom is at once a resource and a problem for the human central nervous system during the process of learning a movement. For example, even a simple movement of reaching and grasping an object with the hand and arm could require the performer to regulate seven degrees of freedom of the arm, involving flexion-extension, abduction-adduction, and axial rotation of joints. Three of these degrees of freedom are at the shoulder, one at the elbow, one in the radioulnar joints, and two at the wrist. In addition, such an analysis might assume that the gripping motion of the hand acts as one degree of freedom. In fact, the fingers and thumb can be configured together in many different ways depending on task requirements. With this problem for the human central nervous system in mind, consider the number of degrees of freedom to be regulated in movements such as kicking a ball in soccer or the triple-salto in ice-skating.

In answer to the question of how learners cope with this embarrassment of riches, it has been proposed that many degrees of freedom become redundant in some actions, meaning that they do not actively contribute to the regulation of an action. The assembly of an immediately functional coordination solution is beyond the capacity of many learners, and so the problem of controlling the movement system is managed by overly constraining the available motor system degrees of freedom by producing rigidly fixed movements. Progressively, with learning and experience, the fixed characteristic of coordination is altered as movement system degrees of freedom are released and allowed to reform into coordinative structures, that is different configurations or synergies for specific purposes. Typically, as a result of extended practice, the initial strong couplings between system degrees of freedom are gradually unfixed and formed into task-specific coordinative structures, so that internal and external forces can be exploited to increase

movement economy and efficiency The formation of specific functional muscle-joint linkages or synergies is an important method of managing the many degrees of freedom to be controlled in the human movement system. Such functional groupings compress the physical components of the movement system and specify how the relevant degrees of freedom for an action become mutually dependent. Synergies between motor system components help to make it more manageable for learners when they discover and assemble strongly coupled limb relations to cope with the many movement system degrees of freedom. In this way, fluctuations in the number of degrees of freedom used over practice trials are managed by constraining variability in their implementation to a sub-space of the total number available. Coordinative structures emerge from the rigidly fixed configurations that learners use early on to manage the multitude of motor system degrees of freedom.

Therefore, athletes form synergies between motor system components during learning, and these coordination tendencies form the 'intrinsic dynamics' of each individual movement system. Intrinsic dynamics can be thought of as the spontaneous coordination preferences for, or the tendencies towards, specific modes of coordination that are available in any individual movement system whenever a new skill has to be acquired. Therefore, intrinsic dynamics are the basic building blocks of coordinative structures found in each individual performer, and are constrained by many factors including genes, anatomical and physiological characteristics, learning, previous experiences, and social influences.

The concept of the coordinative structure suggests that muscle collectives are organised into emergent and dynamic functional units, the behaviour of which is constrained by the immediate environmental demands. They soon become dynamic and flexible as learners gain experience. It is important to understand the relationship between the 'controllability' of the motor system and the flexibility of movement coordination. Once basic coordinative structures are formed and stabilised through practice, they need to be made adaptable so that performers can control their actions in changing environmental circumstances. By being open to information from the environment, coordinative structures can be tuned or adapted to function in each unique performance condition. As a result, each coordinative structure performs in a way that is activity-specific, with sets of coordinative structures combining to govern sequences of movement. Coordinative structures are tuned to function specifically in each unique condition by environmental information. Therefore, good quality perceptual information is necessary in assembling coordinative structures, because the details of their specific form or organisation are not completely pre-determined and emerge under the constraints of each performance condition. The assembly of coordinative structures is a dynamical process that is dependent on relevant sources of perceptual information related to key properties of the performer, such as haptic information from muscles and joints, and the environment, for example vision of a target or surface. Each coordinative structure may be slightly varied each time the performer constructs an action in dynamic environments. For example, novice soccer players learn to adapt the coordinative structure for a soccer pass flexibly, so that it can be used under changing conditions, for example, with soccer balls of different size and pressure, on pitches varying in dimensions, as weather conditions change, or as the motor system becomes fatigued.

See also: constraints-led perspective; learning process; learning theories and models; motor control; motor development; motor skills

KEITH DAVIDS

COPING IN SPORT

Coping in sport refers to changing cognitive and behavioural efforts to manage internal or external demands that are appraised as exceeding one's physical or cognitive resources. These efforts can be described as strategies, tactics, responses, cognitions, or behaviours. Since sources of sport-related stress can be either acute – physical or mental errors, criticism, pain, or opponent or crowd behaviour – or chronic, for example, daily pressure to succeed, career transitions, injury, poor coach or team relationships – coping effectiveness is contingent on using effective coping strategies.

Adaptive coping strategies enable athletes to ignore, or quickly recover from, stressful distractions by redirecting their energies. Coping does not necessarily infer effectiveness because strategies incongruent with specific circumstances can also be harmful. Such maladaptive coping strategies, such as hostility, seeking revenge, drug use, and smoking, can result in poorer concentration, negative **self-talk**, misdirected attentional focus, heightened state anxiety including muscle tension, and, ultimately, performance decrements. The long-term effects of maladaptive coping include chronic stress, **burnout**, disengagement, and attrition. Personality characteristics such as sensation seeking, **trait anxiety** and ego **goal orientation** have been associated with maladaptive coping strategies.

Coping has both dynamic and dispositional aspects but is a learned skill, not a personality attribute. Coping strategies involve the use of one or more cognitive or behavioural attempts at reducing the intensity of perceived stress. They are situation-specific, changing in response to the dynamic nature of the sport environment. In contrast, the term 'coping styles' refers to a disposition of preferring to use similar types of coping strategies over time, in response to common stressors, or after different types of stress. Coping styles include problem-focused and emotion-focused, approach and avoidance, sensitisation and desensitisation, and engagement and disengagement.

Problem-focused coping and emotion-focused coping are two widely accepted coping categories distinguished by task and stress management characteristics, respectively. Problem-focused coping involves altering or managing the problem causing the stress, whereas emotion-focused coping regulates emotional responses to the problem causing the stress. Problem solving, information gathering, goal setting, and time management skills are examples of problem-focused coping. Relaxation, meditation, and cognitive restructuring are examples of emotion-focused coping. Problem-focused coping is used more often in changing environments, while emotion-focused coping is used more often in conditions perceived as static.

Approach coping strategies involve persistently seeking to overcome the stressful condition mentally or physically and are preferred when athletes view conditions as controllable, know the source of stress, are receptive to and capable of communicating, have adequate time to address the issue, or will be disadvantaged by failing to resolve the issue. Forgetting about, or reducing the importance of, the stressor is considered avoidance coping, a style preferred under time constraints when conditions are perceived as uncontrollable, emotional resources are limited – for example, low self-confidence – or when there is little chance of resolving the stressful issue, for example, a referee's bad call. Identifying coping styles can enhance the effectiveness of coping interventions.

See also: coping strategies in adversity; coping theory; state anxiety – antecedents; stress management; stress and anxiety – antecedents

Further reading

Anshel, M.H., Kim, K.W., Kim, B.H., Chang, K.J. and Eom, H.J. (2001) 'A Model for Coping with Stressful Life Events in Sport: Theory, Application, and Future Directions', *International Journal of Sport Psychology* 32: 43–75.

Crocker, P.R.E., Kowalski, K.C. and Graham, T.R. (1998) 'Measurement of Coping Strategies in Sport', in J.L. Duda (ed.) *Advances In Sport and Exercise Psychology Measurement*, 149–61, Morgantown WV: Fitness Information Technology.

Hardy, L., Jones, G. and Gould, D. (1996) *Understanding Psychological Preparation for Sport: Theory and Practice of Elite Performers*, New York: Wiley.

EVA V. MONSMA

COPING IN SPORT MODEL

Coping models in sport are theoretically driven, mostly by theories generated in the psychology literature. In general, they illustrate the process of stress appraisals and emotion, stressful events in sport, injury risk prevention, or injury response. Cognitive appraisal models for describing responses to injury evolved from stage models describing grief and loss. Traditional theories of the coping literature differentiate between trait and transactional models. Trait models assume consistency of coping style across different circumstances, while transactional models propose a tendency to alter coping styles as a function of the context in which the stressor is experienced.

Lazarus and Folkman's (1984) model of stress, appraisal, and coping describes the response given by an individual to stress after they have appraised it in relation to their available resources. The process begins with an athletic encounter that is simultaneously appraised on what is at stake, primary appraisal, and what can be done about it, secondary appraisal. Emotions are then generated accompanied by cognitions, subjective feelings and physiological changes subsequently requiring management, or coping. Taking action by using problem-focused or emotion-focused coping strategies is the last phase of the model. Dispositional coping styles and social support moderate the relationship between appraisal and adaptation – performance or emotional well-being. The relationship between appraisal, coping, and emotion is bi-directional; moving through the process enables adaptation to subsequent stressors.

An alternative transactional model is that of Anshel et al. (2001) for coping with stressful events in sport. The following sequence is illustrated. First, the stressful stimulus or event is detected. Second, the athlete cognitively appraises, or interprets, the stimulus or event; the use of coping strategies as thoughts – cognitive strategies – or actions – behavioural strategies – follows. Finally, post-coping activity takes place – remaining on task, going off task, engaging in cognitive reappraisal of the stressor, or examining coping effectiveness. Coping strategies used by athletes are categorised as: approach-behavioural coping, such as **goal setting** or seeking **social support**, approach-cognitive coping, for example, **self-talk** or coping imagery, adaptive and maladaptive avoidance-behavioural coping, such as exercising or drug use, and avoidance-cognitive coping, for example self-deprecating humour or cognitive reappraisal.

Two models frequently cited in the sport injury literature are the stress-injury model, exemplifying injury risk, and the integrated model of response to sport injury, depicting injury response. In the context of a demanding practice or competition, the former exemplifies injury risk prevention by focusing on the independent or interactive contribution of personality characteristics, history of stressors, and coping resources to the stress response. The stress response is a bi-directional relationship between cognitive appraisals, both adaptive and maladaptive, and physiological or attentional changes. Risk of injury is highest when athletes, perceiving an imbalance between situational demands and their resources, experience muscle tension, narrowing of attention and increased distractibility. Interventions to prevent injury risk

ultimately target the stress response. The injury response model is less established, but suggests that responses to injury are influenced by pre-injury variables and post-injury variables.

See also: stress, anxiety and coping strategies; stress management

References

Anshel, M.H., Kim, K.W., Kim, B.H., Chang, K.J. and Eom, H.J. (2001) 'A Model for Coping with Stressful Life Events in Sport: Theory, Application, and Future Directions', *International Journal of Sport Psychology* 32: 43–75.

Lazarus, R.S. and Folkman, S. (1984) *Stress, Appraisal, and Coping*, New York: Springer.

EVA V. MONSMA

COPING STRATEGIES IN ADVERSITY

The dynamic nature of sport contributes to a variety of adverse conditions requiring effective coping strategies. Strategies are often categorised into more parsimonious sets of dimensions. Although the sport psychology literature often advocates matching coping strategies with specific conditions, theoretically driven models of coping suggest that multiple coping strategies from different dimensions can be used concurrently.

Cognitive and behavioural interventions for coping with sport-related stress can follow the acronym COPE: Controlling emotions, Organizing input, Planning a response, and Executing. When learning a new skill, using anticipatory coping strategies, such as coping models, can enable learners to cope with task demands and can lead to enhanced confidence, competency, and performance. Coping models demonstrate and verbalise negative cognitions, affects or behaviours that may precede performance, gradually showing progression from low coping ability to mastered performance. Coping imagery is another anticipatory strategy, in which coping with expected stress is rehearsed before the actual experience.

Another common adversity in sport is injury. Interventions to reduce injury risk ultimately target the stress response. Common **stress management** strategies include progressive relaxation and stress inoculation. By contrast, association – using pain as a cue for preparation – and disassociation – preoccupation with external events rather than internal feelings and sensations – coping strategies influence pain tolerance and can explain an athlete's ability to cope with the pain of injury. Other strategies used by experienced athletes include reinforcement statements and ignoring pain during critical moments.

The account-making model is a process for coping with career termination. It involves constructing a narrative containing the following seven steps towards closure: traumatic experience, outcry, denial, intrusion, working-through, completion, and identity change. Two central features of the model involve working-through each step and the completion of the last step. Confiding in others during the working-through step enables utilisation of feedback from significant others to modify and refine the account. The end of the process involves shifting self-focus towards others facing similar experiences. Other career-ending strategies include cognitive restructuring, constructive thought redirection, **goal setting** to facilitate determination and directions, stress management, time management, skills assessment and development, maintaining a routine of exercise and training, **social support**, and staying in contact with the sport. Several of these can also be applied to other sport-related stressors.

Problem- and emotion-focused coping are the most frequently cited dimensions of coping. Problem-focused coping refers to strategies geared at managing or alter a stressor through behaviours such as information gathering, goal setting, and problem-solving. Emotion-focused coping refers to attempts at regulating emotional responses resulting from a stressor through actions such as meditation, relaxation, and cognitive efforts to change the meaning an individual attaches to given circumstances.

Coaches can play an integral role in developing coping strategies, and should focus on helping athletes develop an arsenal of coping strategies to match situational characteristics. Attending to coping styles can help direct interventions.

See also: coping in sport; mental practice and imagery; self-talk

Further reading

Gould, D., Finch, L.M. and Jackson, S.A. (1993) 'Coping Strategies Used by National Figure Skaters', *Research Quarterly for Exercise and Sport* 64: 453–68.

Grove, J.R., Lavallee, D., Gordon, S. and Hardy, J.H. (1998) 'Account-making: A Model of Understanding and Resolving Distressful Reactions to Retirement from Sport', *The Sport Psychologist* 12: 52–67.

McCullah, P. and Weiss, M.R. (2001) 'Modeling: Considerations for Motor Skill Performance and Psychological Responses', in R.N. Singer, H.A. Hausenblas and C.M. Janelle (eds) *Handbook of Sport Psychology, Second Edition*, 205–38, New York: John Wiley.

EVA V. MONSMA

COPING THEORY

Three frequently cited theoretical frameworks from the psychology literature have helped to explain **coping in sport**. These are the transactional perspective (Lazarus 1991), social cognitive theory (Bandura 1997), and Krohne's (1993) two-dimensional coping. A common feature of these theories is the tendency to alter coping styles as a function of the context in which the stressor is experienced.

From the transactional perspective, coping is a process that begins with two degrees of situational appraisal that operate simultaneously. Primary appraisal involves motivation directed at evaluating the importance of the stressor relative to personal values, beliefs, situational intentions, and goal commitments. Secondary appraisal involves assessment of what can be done; in this appraisal, coping options, allocating responsibility of blame or credit, and future expectations are considered. For both forms of appraisal, conditions appraised as important result in an emotional response; the outcomes are evaluated through the extent of harm, threat, or challenge.

In contrast, coping is an implicit feature of Bandura's social-cognitive theory, which posits that the beliefs people have about themselves are key elements in controlling behaviour, such as stress responses. Self-systems enable individuals to exercise control over their thoughts, their feelings, and their actions because of abilities to symbolise, to learn from others, to plan alternative strategies, to regulate one's own behaviour, and to engage in self-reflection. Self-reflections are interpretations and evaluation of personal experiences that inform and alter both environment and self-beliefs, which, in turn, inform and alter subsequent behaviours – reciprocal determinism. Bandura's concept of self-efficacy, a self-reflection defined as beliefs in one's ability to organise and execute actions required for managing prospective stressors, and the coping process are parallel, involving personal and environmental appraisals for managing stressful events. Sources of efficacy include mastery experiences, vicarious experiences – modelling, social persuasion, and physiological states, such as stress; these can all affect choices, effort, perseverance, and resilience.

Krohne's (1993) view of coping separates behaviours from concepts, hierarchically organising them into two overlapping two-dimensional structures. At the bottom of the hierarchy is the behavioural level, composed of reactions, such as seeking information about a performance error, followed by several similar reactions called acts, for example, practising the skill correctly. Next, at the conceptual level, a set of acts reflects a particular strategy, such as practising the skill against opponents, divided into two super-strategies. The first of these is vigilance, or intensified intake and processing of threatening information, for example, developing strategies using the mastered skill; the second is cognitive avoidance, or turning away from the threat-related cues, for example, abandoning strategies that continually fail. These various states exist as a result of intolerance of uncertainty and intolerance of arousal (see **arousal and activation**). For example, as intolerance of uncertainty and arousal increase, anxiety causes coping to fluctuate because vigilance and cognitive avoidance are high. Applied to tennis, players switching from stepping into a shot to an open stance have heightened awareness of their stroke mechanics and avoid making risky shots. Subsequently, the coping strategy of using regular positive self-statements becomes intermittent. Most theoretical explanations of coping are neutral with regard to, and independent of, outcome. Coping efforts, then, may prove to be either adaptive or maladaptive.

References

Bandura, A. (1997) *Self-Efficacy: The Exercise of Control*, New York: W.H. Freeman.

Krohne, H.W. (1993) 'Attention and Avoidance: Two Central Strategies for Coping with Aversiveness', in H.W. Krohne (ed.) *Attention and Avoidance*, 3–18, Seattle WA: Hogrefe and Huber.

Lazarus, R.S. (1991) *Emotion and Adaptation*, London: Oxford University Press.

Further reading

Zeidner, N. and Endler, N.S. (eds) (1996) *Handbook of Coping: Theory, Research, Applications*, New York: John Wiley.

EVA V. MONSMA

COPING WITH ADVERSITY

The dynamic nature of sport contributes to a variety of adverse conditions requiring effective coping skills. However, coping is necessary only in response to circumstances or events interpreted as adverse or unpleasant. Since adversity is contingent on negative cognitive appraisals, the ultimate goal of coping skills is to prevent negative appraisals. If conditions are negatively appraised, then athletes must decide which appraisal is most beneficial for circumventing the stress.

Harm or loss, threat, and challenge appraisals are most common in stress management. Feelings of harm or loss reflect, first the damage that has already occurred, frequently followed by maintaining situational control, and, last, modifications to performance, emotion, strategy, and participation reduction or discontinuation. Threat appraisals consist of expectations of future harm and are associated with state anxiety. Challenge appraisals represent confidence to deal directly with, learn from, or even benefit from, the stressor, for example, competing against a highly skilled opponent might be interpreted as threatening, however, it can also be viewed as an opportunity to demonstrate competence.

Adverse conditions can be categorised as changeable, for example, poor coach-team relationships, or mental and physical errors, or unchangeable, for example, injury or career termination. Adverse conditions can arise as early as initial sport involvement, when skills or strategies may be perceived as difficult or fearful, for example, aerial rotation skills. Problem-focused and approach coping strategies are often used when athletes perceive they can cognitively or behaviourally change stressful circumstances; emotion focused and avoidance strategies are used when stressful conditions are perceived as unchangeable. However, both can be used in any given circumstances. Threatening conditions can heighten the likelihood of reduced performance quality, chronic stress, **burnout**, and, eventually, quitting the activity.

See also: coping strategies in adversity; state anxiety – antecedents; stress management

Further reading

Gottlieb, B.H. (1997) 'Conceptual and Measurement Issues in the Study of Coping with Cchronic Stress', in B.H. Gottlieb (ed.) *Coping With Chronic Stress*, 3–42, New York: Plenum.

EVA V. MONSMA

CORE STABILITY

The core region of the body is the pelvis and lower torso. This area has become the focus of attention in injury prevention and rehabilitation strategies. The main concept of core stability is that the trunk (see **axial skeleton – structure and function**) must be stable if the extremities that are attached to it (see **appendicular skeleton**) are to be used safely and effectively.

If the core region is not stabilised effectively, excessive movement of the pelvis and lumbar spine may occur during activity. If this happens during demanding and repeated sports movements, the lower back is put under increased strain and overuse injuries resulting in lower back pain can occur. A strong and stable core is essential in most sporting activities. The role of the trunk is obvious in power transfer in sports such as rowing, in which power generated in the legs must be transferred through the body to the arms, but a stable core is also important in sports without an obvious transfer of power through the torso, such as running. The role of the core muscles in running is to stabilise the pelvis as the body is supported alternately on each leg during the running stride. This is important in enabling the lower extremity to be in correct alignment when it is loaded during ground contact, an important factor in overuse injury prevention (see **hip joint**). This function of the core muscles is also important in team sports that involve rapid cutting movements and changes in direction.

The major muscles involved in stabilising the core are the transverse abdominis on the front of the abdomen, multifidus in the lower back, and gluteus maximus and medius in the pelvic region. Athletes often mistakenly focus on strengthening the surface muscle of the abdomen – rectus abdominis – in an attempt to stabilise this region. This sheet of muscle runs proximally to distally along the torso and is involved in trunk flexion; it does not provide the deep circumferential support of the lower torso for which the core muscles are responsible.

In athletes with a weak core, these core muscles may not be automatically activated to provide trunk stabilisation when needed. The athlete must be trained to activate the muscles consciously during the preparatory stage of a movement to protect and stabilise the lower back. With practice, the core muscles will start to activate whenever the body is loaded and a strong core is needed.

While learning to activate the correct muscles, the athlete should sit or lie with the pelvis in a neutral position and think about drawing the navel up and in towards the spine. This is a subtle movement and, therefore, may require a different sort of body awareness than the power athlete is used to. Although the movement is small, it has a significant effect on the stability of the whole body. Another way to determine whether the transverse abdominis is being activated is to locate the place on the front of the pelvis where the muscle can be felt at the surface. On the front of the pelvis are two bony protuberances, the anterior superior iliac spines (see **bones of the lumbar spine and pelvis**) that can be felt anteriorly just below the top of the iliac crests laterally on the pelvis. Approximately

30 mm medial to these bony protuberances is the soft tissue region where the transverse abdominis can be felt. To learn how this muscle feels when activated, an individual should cough with their fingertips against this region – he or she should feel the muscle tighten and relax. When the transverse abdominis is consciously contracted, the same tension should be felt under the fingertips. This is a good test to use during core stability training to determine whether the correct muscles are being activated.

See also: lumbar spine and pelvis; muscles of the lumbar spine and pelvis

CLARE E. MILNER

CORTICAL CELL ASSEMBLIES

One of the significant challenges in neuromotor control is to understand the relationship between movement behaviour and the biology that underpins it. Knowledge of muscular mechanisms and the capability of muscle to generate force are well established, as is knowledge of the neuromuscular junction – the interface between the nervous system and muscle. In contrast, understanding the nature of the relationship between behavioural processes of motor preparation and the role of the brain in these processes remains tentative. The association between motor programmes and preparation and performance of voluntary movements is well known. Although motor programmes, like long-term and working memory, can be viewed as products of the work of the brain, knowledge of the neurobiology of the former appears considerably less than knowledge of the latter.

The idea of cortical cell assemblies provides a starting point from which the neurobiology of motor programme processes can be explored. Donald Hebb introduced cell assembly theory in 1949 as a proposed bridge between neurophysiology and neuropsychology. Hebb described a cell assembly as 'a diffuse structure comprising cells in the cortex and diencephalon (and also, perhaps, in the basal ganglia of the cerebrum), capable of acting briefly as a closed system, delivering facilitation to other such systems and usually having a specific motor facilitation' (Hebb 1949: xix). Cell assembly theory has provided impetus to development of a vast literature on learning and memory and the evolution of terms such as long-term potentiation (LTP) and long-term depression (LTD) and identification of specific circuits in the hippocampus, for example, in which LTP and LTD can be observed.

Although a neuromotor affiliation to cell assemblies is alluded to in Hebb's original proposal, it was not pursued in the motor control field directly until recently (see, for example, Wickens *et al.* 1994). Although the concept of a motor programme had been used as a basis for understanding many empirical results related to motor preparation, its explanatory power was diminished in the absence of an underlying neurobiological mechanism. Cortical cell assembly theory offered a possible neural mechanism for motor programming. From this perspective a motor programme may be conceptualised as a cell assembly represented as strengthened synaptic connections between cortical pyramidal neurons. The strengthened synaptic connections determine which combinations of corticospinal neurons are activated when the cell assembly is ignited. At a biological level, the conditions for cell assembly formation and activation can be specified through specific and quantifiable features of the anatomy and physiology of the motor cortex. At a behavioural level, cell assembly activation dynamics can be associated with operational quantities such as reaction time and the nature and number of parameters in a motor-preparation precuing paradigm. Thus, a cell assembly can represent the planning and preparation as well as the execution of the response. One prediction of cell assembly theory is that the time taken for a cell assembly to become fully ignited, or activated, is related to the information available about the nature and number of parameters to be specified in the forthcoming motor response. The nature of parameters is described by characteristics such as the 'direction' in which the response is to be initiated and the extent, or distance, to a target location. Number refers to the number of parameters that remain to be specified when the imperative stimulus occurs, as would occur in a choice reaction time experiment.

For example, a participant is seated, grasping a manipulandum attached to a pointer that is to be moved from a central rest position to one of four possible targets, two each side of the central rest position. For a given trial, the targets, red light emitting diodes (LEDs) serve as precue providers and the source of the imperative stimulus. The precue is presented for 500 ms, followed by a variable foreperiod, then the signal to move – the imperative stimulus. A precue consists of the illumination of 1, 2, or 4 LEDs for 500 ms before the variable, 500–2,000 ms, foreperiod. This arrangement provides for five different precue conditions. In condition one, illumination of one light provides precue information including both the nature – the direction and distance – and the number (0) of parameters needed to plan the entire response before stimulus onset. This is similar to a simple reaction time condition as all the parameters are contained in the precue. In conditions 2–4, two targets are illuminated to provide one of three two-choice reaction time settings. The first is direction precued – left or right – and extent uncertain – short or long; the second is extent precued, direction uncertain, and the third is a mutually conditional combination of direction and extent – either left short, right long or left long, right short. In condition 5, all four targets are illuminated, neither direction nor extent precued in a 4-choice reaction time setting.

In this paradigm, the dependent measure, reaction time, indicates the time needed to specify the remaining parameters and to initiate movement at stimulus onset. Not surprisingly, reaction time is shortest when the precue completely specifies the response – simple reaction time – and longest when neither direction nor extent is precued and both are presented in a 4-choice reaction time setting. For the two-choice conditions in which direction or extent is precued, reaction time is shorter when the precue specifies direction – extent programmed after stimulus onset – than when the precue specifies extent with the direction programmed after stimulus onset.

These results are consistent with the predictions of cortical cell assembly theory. When direction is precued, neurons representing direction-specific muscles can be preselected at precue presentation and preparation of extent, after stimulus onset, is achieved by altering the gain in those preselected neurons. In contrast, when extent is precued, the activation of neurons representing direction-specific muscles cannot be increased until the stimulus occurs; thus, the time for cell assembly ignition is increased and this is reflected in the lengthened reaction time.

The robustness of cell assembly theory as a biological mechanism underpinning the process of motor programming will depend on rigorous testing that involves different and additional parameters such as 'hand' along with an increase in the number of alternatives. If 'hand' was added to the paradigm, and extent and direction retained, the maximum number of choices would be eight – 2 hands × 2 directions × 2 extents – providing a stringent test of cortical cell assembly theory. The combination of neurophysiological and neuropsychological knowledge provides an exciting avenue in neuromotor control through which the unsolved mysteries of motor preparation can be explored.

See also: neuromotor control – motor programs; neuromotor control – movement outcomes

References

Hebb, D. (1949) *The Organisation of Behavior*, New York: John Wiley.

Wickens, J., Hyland, B. and Anson, G. (1994) 'Cortical Cell Assemblies: A Possible Mechanism for Motor Programs', *Journal of Motor Behavior* 26: 66–82.

Further reading

Churchland, P.S. (2002) *Brain-Wise: Studies in Neurophilosophy*, Cambridge MA: MIT Press.

J. GREG ANSON

COUNCIL OF EUROPE

The Council of Europe is the continent's oldest continent-wide political organisation, and was founded in 1949. It groups together forty-five countries, including twenty-one countries from Central and Eastern Europe, and is distinct from the twenty-five-nation European Union. It has its headquarters in Strasbourg, in north-eastern France, and shares its parliament building with the European Parliament of the EU for part of each month.

The Council was established with the following aims:

- to defend human rights, parliamentary democracy and the rule of law;
- to develop continent-wide agreements to standardise member countries' social and legal practices;
- to promote awareness of a European identity based on shared values and cutting across different cultures.

The Council's role changed substantially with the demise of the Eastern bloc. Since 1989, its role has been that of:

- acting as a political anchor and human rights watchdog for Europe's post-communist democracies;
- assisting the countries of Central and Eastern Europe in carrying out and consolidating political, legal, and constitutional reform in parallel with economic reform;
- providing know-how in areas such as human rights, local democracy, education, culture, and the environment.

The Council of Europe's Vienna Summit in October 1993 recognised this new role and set out new political aims, casting the Council of Europe as the guardian of democratic security – founded on human rights, democracy, and the rule of law.

The main component parts of the Council of Europe are: the Committee of Ministers, composed of the forty-five foreign ministers or their Strasbourg-based deputies (ambassadors/permanent representatives), which is the organisation's decision-making body; the Parliamentary Assembly, grouping 626 members (313 representatives and 313 substitutes) from the forty-five national parliaments and Special Guest delegations from the two candidate states; the Congress of Local and Regional Authorities, composed of a Chamber of Local Authorities and a Chamber of Regions; and the 1,800-strong secretariat.

The budget of the Council of Europe is considerably smaller than that of the European Union. In 2003 this stood at €175,490,000. The Council has developed some 193 legally binding European treaties or conventions on topics ranging from human rights to the fight against organised crime, and from the prevention of torture to data protection or cultural cooperation. It also has developed recommendations to governments setting out policy guidelines on such issues as legal matters, health, education, culture, and sport.

The Council defines its role in sport as falling under two principal headings: pro-

moting sport for all as a means of improving the quality of life, facilitating social integration and contributing to social cohesion, particularly among young people; and fostering tolerance through sport and defending sport against the serious threats currently facing it. The Council's major policy documents relating to sport are thus the **European Sports Charter** (and its Code of Ethics in Sport), the Anti-doping Convention, and the European Convention against Spectator Violence and Misbehaviour.

Through its Committee for the Development of Sport (CDDS) the Council operates seminars on moral or organisational issues relating to sport (such as on good governance of sporting organisations, women in sport, countering spectator violence) as well as supporting some humanitarian efforts through sport (such as a scheme to support sports camps for displaced children in the former Soviet Union Republics, undertaken in 2004). However, given its limited budget the Council is, unlike the European Union, unable to fund interventions in sport to any degree, relying instead on moral persuasion of other parties and its influence with its member states.

IAN P. HENRY

CREATINE

Creatine is one of the most widely used nutritional supplements by athletes and has been touted for its ability to increase strength and power. The average diet contains 1–2 grams/day of creatine and it is also endogenously produced by the liver, pancreas, and kidneys from the amino acids methionine, glycine, and arginine at a rate of 1–2 grams/day. Although 90 per cent of creatine is stored in skeletal muscle as free creatine ($^1/_3$) and phosphocreatine ($^2/_3$), it is also found in the brain and testes.

The initial justification for oral creatine supplementation was the 1992 finding by Harris of a 20 per cent increase in skeletal muscle creatine following a seven-day loading dose. Skeletal muscle phosphocreatine is rapidly depleted during 10–20 seconds of maximum exercise, but half is resynthesized after sixty seconds with full restoration in five minutes. ATP is reduced to ADP with maximum muscle contraction and regenerated anaerobically with the assistance of phosphocreatine. Phosphocreatine is the rate-limiting step, and oral creatine should increase phosphocreatine stores and thus power.

Whether creatine supplementation actually provides ergogenic benefit has been the subject of great debate. Juhn and Tarnopolsky reviewed studies of (1) single-bout, high-intensity exercise; (2) repeated bouts of maximal exercise; (3) weightlifting/strength; (4) submaximal exercise and maximal exercise lasting >60 seconds; and (5) running and swimming. Their conclusion was that oral creatine could only increase performance in repeated 6–30 seconds bouts of maximal stationary cycling where there are recovery periods of twenty seconds to five minutes (#2). They found no benefit in the other above situations. There is little evidence that these laboratory gains translate into improved athletic performance.

Another factor complicating creatine is the variation in individual response. Muscle-biopsy studies demonstrated that subjects with lower levels of both muscle creatine and phosphocreatine tended to have greater increases in creatine and phosphocreatine after supplementation. One factor in this is that skeletal muscle cannot exceed a creatine concentration of 150–160 mmol kg^{-1}. Thus, athletes who consume less dietary creatine, e.g. vegetarians, may benefit more from creatine supplementation. There is also likely little value to high-dose creatine supplementation. If creatine is to be used, most authors recommend 0.3 g kg^{-1} day^{-1} loading for five days, followed by 0.03 g kg^{-1} day^{-1} maintenance.

Another area of controversy is that of adverse effects. Creatine causes muscle-water retention and there was a great fear of subsequent dehydration, muscle cramping, and heat injury. Although there are anecdotal reports, controlled studies do not seem to support a large increase in these symptoms nor related gastrointestinal cramping. Another fear was that once creatine muscle stores were saturated, excess creatine would unduly tax the kidneys and result in renal injury. While urinary creatine and creatinine excretion does increase with supplementation, there have been few reported incidents of renal failure in subjects with normal baseline renal function. It would seem prudent to restrict creatine supplementation in those with either existing renal disease, or at high risk for its development.

The most worrisome complication is the development of lower-extremity compartment syndromes. Radiographic studies demonstrated increased muscle size due to water retention, and there are anecdotal reports of acute compartment syndromes and rhabdomyolysis. Potteiger performed a well controlled experiment using calf compartment pressures and found significant increases at rest, immediately after and in the post-exercise period. This is an important concern given the large numbers of creatine users.

Creatine is allowable by sports organizations and there is currently no testing for it. Although it is a physiologic substance, oral supplementation could be considered an 'abnormal quantity' and banned. It can only be considered potentially ergogenic under very limited circumstances.

Reference

Juhn, M.S. and Tarnopolsky, M. (1998) 'Oral Creatine Supplementation and Athletic Performance: A Critical Review', *Clin J Sport Med* 8: 286–97.

GARY GREEN

CRIME

Crime may be defined as 'an action or omission which constitutes an offence and is punishable by law' (*New Oxford Dictionary of English* 1998: 434). One problem facing researchers and policy-makers is that only a proportion of crimes are detected, and some are judged not guilty or rejected for reasons of mental health/diminished responsibility or of failures in detection/ evidential processes. Also, politicians change definitions of crime and tariffs for penalties, as they perceive changes in society or take more retributional or lib-eral/reformist views. Thus the USA and UK incarcerate a larger proportion of citizens (the former more than 2 million), while many European states put more effort into non-custodial and rehabilitation pro-grammes. Thus, records may vary over time and be non-comparable between nations or within federal states, and comparative studies are a minefield. Long-term increases in crime (especially against property) may relate to growing affluence but may be an artefact of improved record keeping.

Custody is extremely expensive, and evidently not very effective: in Britain 78 per cent of prisoners re-offend by twenty-four months after release. Most people offend only once, but given the multiplicity of internal/personal factors, and structural/ societal factors known to influence criminality, no justice/home affairs system has found a model to predict accurately committal of crime, and have focused instead on trying to prevent crime by dealing with its context (e.g. by lighting and TV surveillance of spaces, or securing property including cars, credit cards, and mobile phones).

The justice, insurance, and personal costs of crime are substantial, and there are concerns in many post-industrial societies that youth crime is growing, and to intervene so that it does not become a way of life. In

Britain for example, the Audit Commission (1996: 12) recorded: 'a disproportionate amount of crime is committed by young people, especially young males. In 1994, two out of every five known offenders were under the age of 21, and a quarter were under 18.' Moreover, there is a hard core of repeat offenders – in Britain 6 per cent commit 7 out of 10 known crimes, and many programmes focus on trying to rehabilitate them (what is known as tertiary intervention), rather than secondary inter-ventions targeted at 'at risk' youngsters and primary interventions aimed at prevention, part usually of multiple-agency pro-grammes aimed at regeneration.

Sport and outdoor activities have long been seen as activities that might form part of rehabilitation, because of being seen as character-forming, fitness-conveying, and self-esteem and confidence-building. Thus they have played a large part in the work of uniformed youth organisations, of Outward Bound (Kelly and Baer 1968), and of police and probation programmes across the world (see Collins 2003 for examples from UK, North America, France, and Australasia). Most anecdotes and first-hand qualitative experiences suggest positive outcomes from sport and physical activity for individuals, though Begg *et al.*'s (1996) study with 1,700 teenagers in New Zealand was one of the few to find that the more active were more likely to be delinquent.

Three British examples of interventions with associated effects (it is overstating the case to call them outcomes) are set out in Tables 6–8.

Table 6 shows a primary intervention scheme. With such young children, research had to be by observation and informal on-site discussions, and interviews with community stakeholders. Long-term measures of crime prevention (i.e. negative evidence) are very difficult to obtain.

The problem with such schemes as shown in Table 7, however, is that they are resurrected each holiday, often with

327

Table 6. Primary intervention scheme

Scheme	Effects
(1) Primary – Streetsport, Stoke on Trent (McCormack 2000) Football and other sports on open spaces for 8–14 year olds in the evenings and weekends in deprived parts of an old industrial city, sustained by city for over a decade	• reduced 'hanging about'/noise • gaining skills/commitment – form teams • fewer problems in local school, youth centre • fewer incidents with police • greater confidence in self and community

Table 7. Secondary intervention scheme

Scheme	Effects
(2) Secondary – SPLASH summer vacation schemes 2000–2 (CGEY 2003) Home Office match-funded sport, music, drama, and art schemes for 13–17 year-olds in 300 high-crime estates in school vacations	• 7.4% reduction in local crime over 2001 • low cost per attendance – £1.63 per hour • but sizeable support per individual child • noise/nuisance hardly increased relative to 13% in other areas.

Table 8. Tertiary intervention scheme

Scheme	Effects

(3) Tertiary – Solent Sports Counselling (McCormack 2000)
One-to-one scheme started by Sport England, taken
over by the County Council, reduced in duration
and then ended after over thirteen years when
probation service finances were cut.
	• reduced likelihood of re-offending
	• improved social skills and integration replacing
	  'impoverished leisure'
	• new sports skills and participation
	• better physical and mental health, less or no
	  drugs

different leaders and children; and there is no mechanism to sustain work. And what also is not known is whether crime is displaced to neighbouring areas which do not have the benefit of leaders and support. Coalter (2001) and Collins (2003) have criticised such programmes for being unclear about the purpose of their intervention, or trying to meet too many objectives likely only to divert offending to other places,or times not joining up with other agencies to provide comprehensive care, and/or having too few resources or too short a timescale without follow up to produce long lasting results.

More concentrated and sustained (Positive Futures) schemes are being promoted

in other areas by the Home Office (see Table 8).

A rarely used technique known as life history analysis was used to relate life events to sports and leisure activity, which for these youngsters was sporadic, fragmentary, and isolated.

McCormack (2000), and Witt and Crompton (1997) identified factors and behaviours that put young people at risk of offending, and suggest that interventions should focus on these, but Coalter (2001) has pointed out the frequent lack of clear objectives to evaluate, the lack of resources for studying control or lapsed groups, and the lack of long-term follow-up on recidivism/reoffending, a costly and difficult task when rootless youngsters move on – though all these aspects were undertaken two decades earlier in Segrave and Hastad's (1985) ground-breaking study in the USA.

References

Audit Commission (1996) *Misspent Youth*, London: The Audit Commission.

Begg, D.J., Langley, J.D., Moffitt, T. and Marshall, S.W. (1996) 'Sport and Delinquency: An Examination of the Deterrance Hypothesis in a Longitudinal Study', *British Journal of Sport Medicine* 30: 335–41.

Cap Gemini Ernst and Young UK plc (2003) *SPLASH 2002 Final Report to Youth Justice BoardII*, London: CGEY plc.

Coalter, F. (2001) *Realising the Potential of Cultural Services*, Sport London/Local Government Association. Available at http://www.lga.gov.uk/OurWork.asp?lsection=59&ccat = 376

Collins, M.F. (2003) *Sport and Social Exclusion*, London: Routledge.

Kelly, F.J. and Baer, D.J. (1968) *Outward Bound Schools as an Alternative to Institutionalisation for Adolescent Delinquent Boys*, Boston MA: Fandel.

McCormack, F. (2000) 'Leisure Exclusion? Analysing Interventions Using Active Leisure with Young People Offending or At-risk', unpublished Ph.D. thesis, Loughborough University.

Segrave, J. and Hastad, D.N. (1985) 'Three Models of Delinquency', *Sociological Focus* 18, 1: 1–17.

Witt, P.A. and Crompton, J. (1997) 'The Protective Factors Framework: A Key to Programming for Benefits and Evaluating for Results', *Journal of Park and Recreation Administration* 15, 3: 1–18.

MIKE COLLINS

CROSS-CULTURAL RESEARCH

Cross-cultural research examines topics that integrate societies, nations, and cultures, by providing strategies for the systematic testing of theories about human society and behaviour. Despite the involvement of diverse ethnic and cultural groups in sport and exercise, sport and exercise scientists often tend to overlook culture and, therefore, their theories and conclusions lack universality and applicability across different ethnic and cultural groups. To encourage valid and reliable cross-cultural research, several cross-cultural research strategies are introduced in this entry: first, the importance of defining culture; second, the types of cross-cultural research; and third, cultural equivalence in research methods.

The definition of culture is critical to the validity of cross-cultural studies. In prototype cross-cultural studies, researchers often use 'categorical cultures' in which they divide cultures by nationality, race, or ethnicity. Betancourt and Lopez (1993) cautioned that defining cultures simply by using typical and dichotomous cultural categories could pollute research findings. Because ethnicity could include a common nationality, culture, race, or language – and even race is a biological characteristic-based definition – such categorical cultures have little to do with the 'culture' that an individual has absorbed. To overcome this caveat of categorical cultures, Triandis (1996) suggested 'conceptual culture', which incorporates the specific cultural elements such as shared attitudes, beliefs, social norms, and values. Such underlying cultural elements are called 'cultural syndromes', which vary in cultural dimensions – individualism and collectivism – and can be used as parameters in psychological theories. Four different attributes – the meaning of the self, the structure of goals, accepted behaviours as a function of norms and attitudes, and the needs of the in-group or social exchanges – are the main elements determining cultural dimensions. Although different cultural dimensions could coexist within one culture, and individuals may select these themes at different times and in different circumstances, a cultural group tends to focus on a prominent theme and this pattern varies cross-culturally.

Second, cross-cultural research typically involves two or more categorical culture-comparison studies. Here, researchers look for the existence of differences in some psychological variables among cultures. Betancourt and Lopez (1993), concerned that mere categorical comparison studies would not sufficiently explain why such differences exist, suggested cross-cultural research strategies that were more systematic and theory-based, i.e. bottom-up and top-down. These theoretically based approaches identify how cultural differences are associated with cultural processes, such as culture-specific or culture-general. When a bottom-up strategy is adopted in a study, a researcher first observes a phenomenon or a psychological process in one culture and then examines the phenomenon or process cross-culturally to test a theory of human behaviour developed in a specific culture. A top-down strategy introduces cultural elements to an existing theory to broaden its theoretical universality; when adopting this strategy, the researcher progresses from mainstream psychological theory to the study of cultural variables pertinent to the theory, and explores potential universality.

Third, when conducting cross-cultural research, researchers should carefully examine equivalence of measurements and research protocols across cultures. Equivalence in cross-cultural research contributes to the significance of research findings by demoting potential bias in cross-cultural research. Helms (1992) eloquently summarised equivalence issues in cross-cultural research as functional, conceptual, linguistic, psychometric, testing condition, contextual, and sampling equivalence.

Functional equivalence refers to the meaningfulness of test scores. That is, psychological variables of interest are well reflected in test scores in different cultures and occur with comparable frequencies through different cultures in the research. Conceptual equivalence addresses concerns of psychological constructs that are measured by questions and items. Often, different cultural groups may not understand the questions asked on a measure, resulting in a different interpretation. To minimise

both functional and conceptual non-equivalence, cross-cultural researchers proposed the adoption of both emic and etic approaches; the former identify unique characteristics of a cultural perspective and the latter compare that culture with other cultural perspectives.

Linguistic equivalence entails whether the research protocols or language used in the assessment are linguistically equivalent and reflect a similar meaning across cultural groups. Often, the true meaning of questions or words can be altered in translation and interpretations of words and slang reflect the translator's socialisation experience. Back translation is one of most commonly used methods to improve linguistic equivalence. It involves one individual translating a measurement from source language to target language while a second person, who is unfamiliar with the original measurement, translates the same measurement back to the original language. A comparison of the original and back-translated versions of the questionnaires is conducted to check linguistic equivalence. Linguistic equivalence can also be enhanced by having a group of bilingual people collectively involved in the translation process to ensure semantic equivalence across different languages. In addition, decentred translation aims to enhance naturalness and readability of the original and translated versions of an instrument in different languages by avoiding simple, verbatim reproduction of the original text in another language. Decentring translation methods entail comparing a set of sentences of one language to a similar set of sentences in another language in search of comparability between sentences in different languages.

Psychometric equivalence is another issue that should be addressed in cross-cultural research. Although a psychological construct is conceptually equivalent across cultural groups, reliability and validity of the measurement may be different across cultures. Advanced statistical analysis strategies, such as multi-group analyses, test psychometric equivalence of a measurement across different cultural groups. If results show invariance in factor structures, loadings, and error variances, this implies that psychometric non-equivalence of the measurement is lessened across cultural groups.

Testing conditions and contextual equivalence entails equivalence in research environments, settings, and procedures. When conducting a cross-cultural study, researchers need to ensure that all data collection procedures are similar in targeted cultural groups. Particularly, the researcher should be aware whether response choices are equitable across cultural groups. Often some cultural groups tend to choose moderate responses, avoiding extreme responses such as 'strongly agree or disagree'. This attitude could originate from culturally based value systems or social desirability concerns. When testing a task in different cultures in experimental studies, that task can be interpreted differently depending on test conditions, the experimental environment, participants' expectations, or importance of the task. Confronting such potential limitations to meet test conditions and contextual equivalence, researchers should design stringent research procedures so that the findings are meaningful and valid across cultures.

The last equivalence issue is sampling equivalence. Researchers need to make sure that samples in their study adequately represent the cultural groups. Often, cross-cultural researchers fail to see other possible demographic variables, such as ages, social economic status, regions, sport types, and competition standards, which could contaminate their findings.

In conclusion, cross-cultural researchers view 'culture' as a vital parameter to a cognitive, behavioural, and emotional understanding of human beings in physical activity. They challenge previously held beliefs and test the legitimacy of many psychological principles established by the mainstream cultures in other ethnic and cultural groups. In sport and exercise science, cross-cultural research is still in its infancy. Further efforts to test and refine theories of interest will improve our conceptual understanding of the influence of culture on cognition, behaviours, and emotions in sport and exercise science.

References

Betancourt, H. and Lopez, S.R. (1993) 'The Study of Culture, Ethnicity, and Race in American Psychology', *American Psychologist* 48: 629–37.

Helms, J.E. (1992) 'Why Is There no Study of Cultural Equivalence in Standardized Cognitive Ability Testing?', *American Psychologist* 47: 1083–101.

Triandis, H.C. (1996) 'The Psychological Measurement of Cultural Syndromes', *American Psychologist* 50: 407–15.

Further reading

Duda, J.L. and Hyashi, C.T. (1998) 'Measurement Issues in Cross-cultural Research within Sport and Exercise Psychology', in J.L. Duda (ed.) *Advances in Sport and Exercise Psychology Measurement*, 471–83, Morgantown WV: Fitness Information Technology.

MI-SOOK KIM

CROSS-TRAINING

Cross-training is a form of exercise whereby the exercise regimen is varied to include alternate body parts and/or exercise methods. According to *The American Heritage® Dictionary of the English Language, Fourth Edition*, the term cross-training means to alternate regimens while training in different sports. Cross-training incorporates at least two variations to the exercise program in order to challenge the body with alternate activity. This is accomplished by adding flexibility, weight training, and/or cardiovascular exercises, either alternately or in successive workouts, or by changing to exercise an alternate body part.

The overall benefits of cross-training have not been well documented in research, but some athletes find that performing regimens other than their own sport-specific program (see **sports specific injury**), facilitates achievement of peak performance. Peak performance requires optimal strength, endurance, cardiovascular fitness, and flexibility. These can all be achieved through cross-training. When variety is introduced in the exercise program, enhanced fitness can result from (1) improved strength and flexibility, (2) improved endurance, (3) improved muscle tone, and (4) effective weight loss. Training the entire body by exercising various parts will offer balanced fitness. One obvious benefit of cross-training is to prevent boredom. Adding variety to the workout improves motivation and can assist to keep the athlete interested.

Cardiovascular fitness improves with cross-training by utilizing the benefits of aerobic exercise. Aerobic exercise is sustained activity designed to enhance circulatory and respiratory effectiveness. Examples of aerobic exercise are jogging, cycling, or swimming.

One study presents evidence that sixty minutes of cross-training will assist in reducing state anxiety. It reports that one session of combined weight training for thirty minutes and aerobic exercise for thirty minutes reduced state anxiety in collegiate athletes. It also suggests that these exercises can be performed in either order and continue to gain benefit.

A very important benefit of cross-training is the ability to exercise while injured. For example if a lacrosse player should suffer a shoulder injury, rendering the athlete unable to play, he should continue to exercise by performing aerobic conditioning via a stationary bicycle, or if able, run on a treadmill, and perform lower body weight training in a gym, in order to keep fit.

Some sports scientists believe that cross-training can assist in injury prevention.

When a runner performs a sport specific training program, there is repetitive use of the same muscle groups over time, resulting in overuse. This may place the overused muscles in a position of potential injury. By exercising alternate muscle groups, injury may be avoided. Performing exercise involving the entire body may disperse the overall load placed on the joints, prevent injury, and provide for more balanced fitness.

An example of a cross-training program for a runner may include an upper extremity weight-training program alternating with core strengthening of the abdominals. To maintain or enhance their aerobic capacity, they may choose to swim, causing less strain on the muscles of the legs than an exercise such as cycling. For flexibility, the runner may choose yoga exercises to incorporate stretching with less strain on the lower body. An effective form of cross-training for a swimmer would be the addition of bicycling for aerobic fitness, combined with lower body weight training via free weights or machines, and yoga or Pilates for stretching. These activities could be implemented on alternating days to complement the sports-specific training.

In general cross-training may offer an athlete many benefits in the enhancement of peak performance but quality research on this subject is needed to further improve its effectiveness for elite athletes.

See also: sports specific injury

Further reading

Hale, B.S., Koch, K.R. and Raglin, J.S. (2002) 'State Anxiety Responses to 60 Minutes of Cross Training', British *Journal of Sports Medicine* 36, 2: 105.

Stamford, Bryant (1996) 'Cross-Training: Giving Yourself a Whole-Body Workout', *The Physician and Sports Medicine* 24, 9: September.

TERRY SUTHERLAND

CROWDING

Perceptions of crowding are subjective and personal. Crowding involves an individual's subjective evaluation of encounters with other users and uses at a site. People's reactions to the volume and density of users and their usage patterns and behaviour at a site will vary over time and space. Crowding has been widely considered a negative construct, but in some sports crowding is perceived as beneficial and a positive contribution to the experience of participants and spectators.

Crowding in sports studies has many dimensions. It arises in both participation in a sport (e.g. sailing, shooting, surfing) and in watching (spectator), in a variety of environments. For some sports(e.g. triathlons, ocean races), large numbers of participants may, to a point, be highly desirable for competitors who wish to test their skills against others. Similarly, for many people, the presence of a large spectator crowd may add greatly to the thrill of an event or sporting fixture, especially as people participate in crowd-based activities (e.g. singing national anthems and supporting national or regional teams). But crowding is about much more than numbers and density.

Any person's reaction to the presence of other individuals is influenced by psychological factors (e.g. personal values, goals, attitudes, motivations, expectations), social circumstances (the purpose of the site visit) and the nature of the landscape. The number or density of distribution of people, or differences in socioeconomic status, behaviour, or composition of other groups may be sources of perceptions of crowding and hence frustration and conflict.

The physical environment will significantly affect perceptions of crowding and satisfaction of participants or spectators. For sporting spectators, comfortable, well-spaced seating and good access to toilets and other services (e.g. food and drinks) are likely to induce less feelings of crowding than small, confined seating and large queues, and hence long delays, for services. That said, when queues are considered inevitable, entertainment may be provided or encouraged (e.g. street performances) to divert and capture people's attention. Other measures include careful organisation of people's movement through use of barricades, careful and plentiful directional signposting, separated entrance and exit points from sites and, if considered necessary, banning of the sale and consumption of alcohol. Internal environments can be manipulated and made comfortable by the provision of adequate ventilation and heating and cooling where appropriate.

It is necessary to anticipate the effects of crowding and crowd reactions in developing effective emergency evacuation plans. Thus a strong commitment to such measures for the Sydney Olympic Games in 2000 resulted in many exercises by police, volunteers, and army at games sites and important transit nodes (e.g. airport) prior to and during the games.

In sports which depend on the natural environment, such as surfing, site features (such as wave size, duration, and distribution) will significantly influence satisfaction levels and feelings of crowding. Thus, in the case of surfing, frequent good sets of waves widely distributed along a beach or series of beaches are likely to raise satisfaction levels and reduce feelings of crowding and likelihood of 'surf rage'. The capacity of the natural or designed landscape to 'absorb' users is certainly important.

Crowding can occur in local communities. Grand Prix, cycling tours and large-scale sporting events frequently bring crowds to a place for anything from a day to many weeks, on a one-off or annual basis. Problems such as traffic congestion and access to local resources and services and public parking often arise.

Where crowding occurs or is perceived to be likely to occur, it can have the effect of displacement and perhaps substitution. It may even discourage investment. Potential participants may be deterred from participating in a sport on particular days or times of day because of perceptions of possible crowding. So, for example, some golfers, preferring a quiet round, might substitute a time to play when there are likely to be less golfers on course, but this may not be their preferred time. Similarly, some surfers might prefer to organise time to surf very early in the morning or during weekdays when demand is likely to be lower.

'Crowding-out' arises when people are discouraged from participating or visiting a site when crowding is likely to be perceived to be too high. So, while many visitors are often attracted to large-scale events, many people eschew the crowding, congestion, delays, and other undesirable site characteristics that they have anticipated.

Measuring perceptions is difficult. Variables include people's number of previous visits, motivations and desired experiences, and the type of activity they are participating in; the adequacy of facilities; the characteristics and behaviours of others; and the site's geographic features. Observation research has been used to track the ways in which people use space, and surveys have been administered to sport participants and spectators. For example, rankings of perceived crowding as perceived by hunters of deer, pheasant, goose, and turkey, along with canoeists and other sporting recreationists have been reported by Shelby and Heberlein (1986).

Getz (1997: 85–6) suggests several measures in designing a site to enhance visitor experiences and minimise or prevent misbehaviour and other crowd-related problems. These include: providing ample space at access and egress points and through circular movement corridors; avoiding clutter and bottlenecks that lead to congestion or movement against the flow; one-way pedestrian systems; adequate directional signage; dispersing vital services; ensuring all staff are customer-oriented; separating vehicles and pedestrians; installing security devices; making good use of lighting; staff communication; and avoiding crowd stressors such as excessive sensory stimulation, overwhelming security and fencing.

Despite its frequent negative perceptions and interpretations, crowding can have positive effects. Ninomiya and Kikuchi (2004), for example, found social and competitive windsurfers preferred high levels of crowding in their sport because of the social interchange and conversations that take place in their activity spaces. The findings of this study reflect those found in some other water sports, such as kayaking and canoeing (e.g. Tarrant et al. 1997), and in festival and shopping or retail settings.

References

Getz, D.D. (1997) *Event Management and Event Tourism*, New York: Cognizant Communication Corporation.

Ninomiya, H. and Kikuchi, H. (2004) 'Recreation Specialization and Participation among Windsurfers: Aan Aapplication of Conjoint Analysis', *International Journal of Sport and Health Science* 2, 1: 1–7.

Shelby, B. and Heberlein, T.A. (1986) *Journal of Leisure Research*.

Tarrant, M., Cordell, H.K. and Kibler, T.L. (1997) 'Measuring Crowding for High-density River Recreation: The Effects of Situational Conditions and Personal Factors', *Leisure Sciences* 19, 1: 97–112.

JOHN M. JENKINS

CUE UTILIZATION

Athletes and researchers have commonly reported that attentional narrowing occurs with heightened arousal. Easterbrook's (1959) cue utilization theory has received extensive attention in the general and sport psychology literature with regards to the attentional narrowing phenomenon. Cue utilization refers to the total range of environmental cues in any given circumstances. Thus, the sport performer maintains an orientation toward the cue, associates a response to the cue, or directly responds to the cue. Easterbrook's theory predicts that under certain conditions, such as the presence of fear in the performance environment or attentional conflict, arousal will be heightened. As a direct result of the heightened arousal, attentional narrowing impacts perceptual sensitivity or the range of cue utilization. More specifically, this narrowing may be beneficial to performance; however, it may also eventually cause a loss of environmental sensitivity to cues necessary for best performance. Thus, with respect to performance, Easterbrook's theory predicts that performance varies under conditions of physiological arousal or cognitive anxiety, and varies with the number of task-relevant and irrelevant cues present.

Researchers most commonly discuss the relationship among attentional width, arousal, and task-relevant and irrelevant cues in three general arousal categories – low, moderate, and high. Under low arousal conditions, the attention width is broad. Performance under low arousal conditions is predicted to be low because the individual performer is uncritically accepting both task-irrelevant as well as task-relevant cues. This acceptance of the irrelevant cues is due to either lack of attention effort or low selectivity by the performer. Under moderate arousal, perceptual selectivity is theorized to be optimal; hence, performance is predicted to improve because the performer's perceptual selectivity has increased to a point at which task-irrelevant cues are eliminated. Thus, the performer is only attending to task-relevant cues. With increased arousal, beyond this optimal state of arousal and attentional width, further perceptual narrowing occurs. At high arousal, increased perceptual narrowing is predicted to impair performance owing to the attentional state that now has eliminated task-relevant and irrelevant cues. This state of perceptual narrowing is commonly referred to as tunnel vision.

Though Easterbrook's theory has been appealing for decades, some controversy has existed in the literature about the performer's attention under high arousal. As pointed out, Easterbrook argues that the range of usable cues has been severely restricted such that task-relevant cues have been eliminated, whereas others have suggested that high arousal is associated with distractibility. Perhaps it is also possible that high arousal with attentional focus on appropriate cues could enhance performance similar to moderate arousal. Regardless of this, research has supported Easterbrook's theory over many decades in a wide range of research task conditions. Lastly, while Easterbrook's theory is very appealing, it is important to realize that the attentional narrowing phenomenon is related to several other factors while conducting research or working with individual performers. These additional factors include the individual's skill and experience, the task complexity, and the performer's anxiety. These factors, as well as Easterbrook's theory, have been extensively discussed and related to other theories and models attempting to describe or predict the effects of arousal on individual performance such as Drive theory and the **Yerkes-Dodson law**.

See also: arousal and activation – effects of experience; catastrophe models

Reference

Easterbrook, J.A. (1959) 'The Effect of Emotion on Cue Utilization and the Organization of Behavior', *Psychological Review* 66: 183–201.

Further reading

Baddeley, A.D. (2000) 'Selective Attention and Performance in Dangerous Environments', *Human Performance in Extreme Environments* 5: 86–91.
Janelle, C.M., Singer, R.N. and Williams, A. (1999) 'External Distraction and Attentional Narrowing: Visual Search Evidence', *Journal of Sport and Exercise Psychology* 21: 70–91.

MARC LOCHBAUM
DEBBIE J. CREWS

CULTURAL GEOGRAPHY

Cultural geography is a sub-discipline of human geography and, reflecting the changing nature of the discipline of geography, has altered its course dramatically over the last two decades. From the 1920s the sub-discipline of cultural geography became strongly associated with the work of Carl Ortwin Sauer, who taught in the Department of Geography at the University of California at Berkeley from the 1920s until the 1970s. Sauer and the Berkeley School were interested in the ways in which culture shaped landscape to create 'cultural landscapes' as a result of the interventions of human agency. Thus, early cultural geographers were concerned with the ways in which humankind interacted with and transformed the natural environment through such activities as the domestication of animals, the diffusion of irrigation techniques and the evolution of folk societies. Such studies drew on both historical and anthropological traditions and provided a counter-balance to the school of environmental determinism that was dominant within geography during the early twentieth century.

Although sport did not feature in such early geographical research, many of the principles explored by Sauer and his colleagues are pertinent to studies of the ways in which participation in outdoor and extreme sports challenge the notion of environmental determinism. Moreover, leisure and tourism studies have engaged with Sauer's interest in the engagement between human agency and landscape form through research that has revealed the changing cultural significance and value of different types of leisure, tourism, and recreational landscapes over time.

In addition to being dominated by North American writing, early cultural geography research placed emphasis on material rather than symbolic culture, and on rural rather than urban societies. By the 1970s geographers in the UK, who had been influenced by the Chicago School of urban sociologists at the University of Chicago, were turning their attention to urban culture, everyday culture and sub-cultures in attempts to make sense of the spatial dimensions and impacts of human agency. Unlike the Berkeley School, those drawing on the work of the Chicago School, and the increasingly dominant Marxist and neo-Marxist sociology of the time, recognised the significance of power relations and cultural hegemony in their analyses of cultural politics. Drawing on this tradition, landscape is not simply the outcome of freely chosen human agency but is the product of power relations within society where 'human activity reshapes nature but, at the same time, this necessary activity shapes the human character and the social relations between people – there is a constant interaction of human subject and natural object in the historical process' (Peet 1989: 44).

By the late 1980s some geographers were proclaiming a 'new' cultural geography that engaged as much with the symbolism and consumption of cultural landscapes as with the material culture and production of landscapes (Jackson 1989). At this time of increasing cultural consumption both the materiality and symbolism or productive consumption of new forms of leisure-related culture began to be studied in much more depth (De Certeau 1984). Where human geography had previously been dominated by economic geography, social and cultural geographies began to play a more prominent role. A new type of research subject were studied by cultural geographers who were interested in the everyday cultures and sub-cultures of groups of people with distinct patterns of cultural consumption. This new geographical engagement with culture has become known as the 'cultural turn'.

The cultural turn represented a narrowing in the gap between social science disciplines such as sociology and geography in relation to humanities subjects such as literary criticism and cultural theory, such that cultural geography is now seen as belonging to both the social sciences and humanities. This closer relationship between the social and the cultural was informed by the increasing engagement with poststructural theory within the academy. Originating in literary criticism within the humanities, poststructural theory contested the 'grand theories' of both positivism and structuralism. Instead of claiming to know the totality of relationships between social and cultural phenomena, poststructuralism introduced uncertainty to our ways of knowing about the social and cultural world, including landscape. This uncertainty contested the post-Enlightenment view that knowledge could be produced in a rational, scientific manner to discover 'the truth' and that such truths could be represented in social models that could be replicated across time and space. In contrast, by placing stress on difference and diversity, poststructuralism emphasised the relative nature of knowledge and the existence of multiple truths that are not necessarily fixed in time and space. Thus landscapes, including those of sport and leisure, could take on meanings and symbolic values that were not fixed but in a state of perpetual flux dependent on the fashions, trends, and consumption patterns of the time.

Within sport studies engagements with poststructural theory resulted in a shift from critiques of ideology and sport participation to explorations of identity and sport behaviour. Examples of such research can be seen in the studies of sporting lifestyles and consumption patterns undertaken in relation to a range of sports that became popularised or re-popularised during the 1980s and 1990s, including surfing, skateboarding, snowboarding, mountain biking and extreme sports. These and other studies have shifted attention from landscapes used for sport to what Bale (2003) has defined as 'sportscapes'.

By the mid-1990s, however, critics were calling for a re-engagement with the material aspects of culture, or a linking of social geography with cultural geography so that the discipline did not experience what Bondi (1992: 166) warned of as 'the unharnessing of the symbolic and the sociological'. The last decade has seen a greater engagement between social and cultural geographies such that geographical studies of sporting landscapes have explored the inter-relationships between material and symbolic culture. Thus, recent poststructural analyses within cultural geography have also drawn attention to the ways in which knowledge of the social, cultural, and environmental world, including landscapes of sport, continue to be produced, legitimated, and reproduced by dominant groups, albeit often with the intention of developing sport within the landscape as a means of enhancing urban regeneration or social inclusion.

References and further reading

Aitchison, C., MacLeod, N. and Shaw, S. (2000) *Leisure and Tourism Landscapes: Social and Cultural Geographies*, London: Routledge.

Bale, J. (2003) *Sports Geography*, London: Routledge.

Bondi, L. (1992) 'Gender and Dichotomy', *Progress in Human Geography* 16, 1: 98–104.

Cosgrove, D. (1984) *Social Formation and Symbolic Landscape*, London: Croom Helm.

Crang, M. (1998) *Cultural Geographies*, London: Routledge.

de Certeau, M. (1984) *The Practice of Everyday Life*, Berkeley CA: University of California Press.

Jackson, P. (1989) *Maps of Meaning: An Introduction to Cultural Geography*, London: Allen and Unwin.

Peet, R. (1989) 'Introduction', in R. Peet and N. Thrift (eds) *New Models in Geography: The Political-Economy Perspective*, vol. 1, 43–7, London: Unwin Hyman.

CARA AITCHISON

CULTURAL HERITAGE

This term traditionally referred almost exclusively to the monumental remains of cultures, but has come to have a much wider use to incorporate new categories such as the industrial heritage or ethnographic heritage. These latter forms of intangible heritage incorporated for example by the United Nations Educational, Scientific and Cultural Organization (UNESCO) include the informational, spiritual, and philosophical systems upon which cultural production is based, as well as forms of culture such as the dramatic arts, languages, traditional music, and traditional sports and games.

The origins of sports and games in traditional societies, far from being separate from other forms of life (as to some extent is claimed for sport in modern societies), were bound up in religious ritual and magic. Roger Caillois in his classic text *Man, Play and Games*, describes games as falling into four: games of chance, games of competition, games of mimicry, and games of environmental experience, and argues that different game forms will predominate in different types of society. Whether one accepts such a functionalist account or not, it is nevertheless clear that traditional games and sports tell us much about social relations between genders, and generations in a given society, and of that society's conceptions of life and value systems.

In recent years sports infrastructure, stadia, competition locations, and sporting equipment have been increasingly recognised as important features of cultural heritage. Museums of sport such as the Olympic Museum in Lausanne have sprung up across the world and national governmental and non-governmental organisations have invested in the preservation and interpretation of sporting phenomena. English Heritage, for example, began an study in 2002 entitled *Sporting Chance*, which introduced the category of sporting heritage into its remit and sought to identify how elements of sporting heritage my be evaluated and preserved. Such initiatives reflect the trend of the breaking down of hierarchical distinction between high and low culture which has reinforced the significance of sport as a feature of cultural value.

References

Caillois, R. (1961) *Man, Play and Games*, New York: Free Press of Glencoe.

English Heritage (2002) *A Sporting Chance: Extra Time for England's Historic Sports Venues* (accessed 18/10/04) http://www.english-heritage.org.uk/Filestore/news/pdf/sportingchance.pdf

Peckham, R. (ed.) (2003) *Rethinking heritage: Cultures and Politics in Europe*, London: I.B. Tauris.

UNESCO (2003) *Cultural Heritage* (accessed 19/12/2003) http://www.unesco.org/culture/heritage

IAN P. HENRY

CULTURAL ISSUES FOR WOMEN

Historically, (a) perceptions relative to physiological differences between the sexes, (b) societal norms and attitudes, and (c) organizational rules and support (Lumpkin 1984) have generated an inequality of opportunities in sport for women. In the early 1900s, medical doctors and female physical educators thought that vigorous activity would endanger women's reproductive capacities and the development of 'unsightly' tissue.

During First World War, women had to participate in men's roles and began to fight for equal opportunities. However, they were remained in a disadvantageous position and granted as the 'weaker sex', particularly in competitive sports, even in Olympic Games.

Apparently, physical exertion and competition were not destined for women's nature; physical activity should be defined as exceptional. 'Anyone who has observed women of Africa on lengthy treks carrying heavy loads of firewood and water cannot help seeing how arbitrary our indicators of strength are' (Peterson and Runyan 1993). This observation should also be applicable to women in other ethics. In general perception, there is a distinctive role between the two sexes, and women have been perceived as both physically and mentally weaker.

The perception of women changes from time to time, especially in sport. Recently, researches indicate that the restriction on women/girls from participating and competing in sport has no scientific supporting ground. However, social and cultural issues are still under modification, due to the problem of social stigma. The number of events for men and women will still disproportionately favor men by a significant margin, and an ultimate division of male and female events still exists, such as in rhythmic gymnastics. The female triathalon is a new phenomenon in female athleticism which stems from pressures on female athletes to be unrealistically thin and not from the activity itself.

The development of women's participation at the Olympic Games reflects both the increasing integration of women in sport and its continuation as a field of male dominance. During the first three quarters of the twentieth century, women made up only a scarce proportion in the games. In fact, even in 1972, women were prohibited from participating in races of over 1,500 m, a holdover from the belief that females could not physically or mentally cope with the competitive demands of longer events. The number of events open to women has doubled between 1972 and 2004. In the 2004 Olympic Games, 46 per cent of the events were open to women. Women accounted for 40 per cent of the participants, and about half of these were Muslim women.

Nowadays, females in different age groups have acknowledged the benefits of exercise and the hazards of inactivity. They have the motive to exercise for health and beauty, especially females in developed countries. Meanwhile, a large proportion of women in developing countries would prefer to be inactive for social, cultural, or safety reasons. Increasing physical activity among girls and women is still a formidable public health challenge for many nations. Consequently, poverty also limits opportunities for women to take part in any kind of sports activity.

Women are still struggling for their rights in sports. In the World Conference on Women and Sports 2002, held in Canada, delegates from 100 countries conveyed the message that that all women should have the freedom to access to any kind of sport and physical activity, taking into consideration their needs and abilities. The goal of improving the systems of sports toward inclusion of safety and respect for women should be prioritized in future agendas.

References

DeFrantz, A.L. (2004) 'Olympic Women Enrich the Games', *Women's News*, 15 October.

Everhart, R.B. and Pemberton, Cynthia Lee A. (2001) *The Institutionalization of a Gender Biased Sport Value System*, Advancing Women Network. http://www.advancingwomen.com/awl/winter2001/everhart_pemberton.html

Goldstein, J.S. (2001) *War and Gender: How Gender Shapes the War System and Vice Versa*, ch. 3, Cambridge: Cambridge University Press.

Griffin, L.Y. (1997) 'Women in Sports', in Giles R. Scuderi, Peter D. McCann and Peter J. Bruno (eds) *Sports Medicine: Principle of Primary Care*, 86-7, St Louis MO: Mosby.

Pfister, G. (2000) 'Women and the Olympic Games', in Barbara L. Drinkwater (ed.) *Women in Sport: The Encyclopedia of Sports Medicine*, IOC medical commission/Blackwell Science.

President's Council on Physical Fitness and Sport (1997) *Physical Activity and Sport in the Lives of Girls: Physical and Mental Health Dimensions from an Interdisciplinary Approach*, Washington DC.

Report of International Working Group on Women and Sport, communiqué, Montreal, Canada, 19 May 2002

Smith, A.D. (1998) 'The Fit Woman of the 21st Century: Making Lifelong Exercise the Norm', *The Physician And Sportsmedicine* 26, 8: August.

ANGELA D. SMITH

CUSTOMER RELATIONSHIP MANAGEMENT

There is a paradigm shift taking place in the realm of marketing, from the conventional mass-marketing, with its primary goal of snaring as many customers as possible, to relationship and one-on-one marketing, which aim to deepen the relationship with the individual customer. Customer relationship management (CRM) is garnering attention as a means to that end. Specifically, CRM refers to a mechanism for initiating some kind of action toward the customer through analysis linking the customer and the product. In CRM, information is not simply sent out to a general customer database, but is customized for each individual customer. In the realm of sports, the NBA has adopted CRM to deepen their relationship with their fans and to aim for enhanced profits.

MUNEHIKO HARADA

D

DANCE

The diversity of dance

The substance of dance is the dynamics of movement in space. Characteristic of dance is that it can be practised as both a social activity and an art form. Different cultural and historical contexts have defined the practices of dance in different ways depending on the kind of techniques, paradigms, theories, and contexts that underlie it. Dance is sometimes defined as any patterned, rhythmic movement in space and time (Copeland and Cohen 1983). This very broad definition is based on the traditional theories of movement and art as imitation, expression, and form. A further, often mentioned aspect is that, in order to be defined as dance, the movements have to be non-utilitarian. This highlights a modern understanding of dance as abstract movement.

Dancing, a human practice embedded in all cultures and societies, has always had various meanings, from ritual to social gathering and from entertainment to art. Practised by different groups such as children, men, women, rich and poor, it is composed of an enormous variety of movement patterns, genres and styles according to the cultural context. In Western countries dance experienced a great upsurge of popularity in the twentieth century.

Dance since the 1920s

Since the 1920s the United States has seen waves of dance crazes, among them the lindy hop of the 1930s, the boogie-woogie and jitterbug of the 1940s, the cha-cha-cha and rock 'n' roll of the 1950s, the twist and various frenzied discothèque and go-go dances of the 1960s, the disco dances of the 1970s, and in the 1980s hip-hop evolving into an energetic style of street dancing called break dance. Tap dance and ballroom dancing have won wide popularity as entertainment and have been featured frequently in musical shows and movies.

Modern dance developed in the twentieth century as reaction to ballet. Its pioneers were, among others, Isadora Duncan, Loie Fuller and Ruth St Denis in the United States, as well as Rudolf Laban in Germany. Each rebelled against the rigid formalism of classical academic ballet and against the banality of show dancing. In America at the end of the 1920s the second generation of modern dance developed new techniques for expressing human passions and universal social themes. Martha Graham worked with principles of breathing as the primary source of dance and contraction and release as a basic principle of movement. Doris Humphrey worked with emphasis on gravity, with fall and recovery as the source of the dynamics of movement. Charles Weidman's gestural mime of movements abstracted from everyday situations provided a different kind of social commentary. By the end of World War II Merce Cunningham and other young choreographers had begun breaking the rules of the modern dance establishment, creating dances that had no theme, expressed no emotion, but were primarily about the investigation of movement freed from traditional aesthetic ideas. Alvin Ailey, another third-generation choreographer, combined elements of modern, jazz, and African dance in his work. In the 1960s and 1970s the use of improvisation based on ordinary, non-dance movements ranging from everyday movements to acrobatics and from military marching to sports and games played a significant part in modern and postmodern dance forms.

By the 1990s distinctions between modern dance, postmodern dance, ballet, show dance, social dance, and youth culture became less rigid than they once were. The dance styles of the twenty-first century combine elements from all sources of inspiration, creating a fusion of new genres and styles of dancing.

The concept of dance is as multifaceted as the concept of art and, as art, it can be used not only in the concrete practices of dance forms in all their varieties of historical, cultural, and situational contexts expressed through genres, techniques, and styles, but also as a metaphor for the experiential qualities of the varieties of human experience and existence. At a very basic level, not only dance and art but also human life is characterised by a wide spectrum of experiential and expressive dimensions as styles of experience and aesthetic communication.

Reference

Copeland, R. and Cohen, M. (1983) *What is dance? Readings in Theory and Criticism*, Oxford, New York, Toronto, Melbourne: Oxford University Press.

Further reading

Au, S. (1988) *Ballet and Modern Dance*. London: Thames and Hudson.
Cheney, G. (1989) *Basic Concepts in Modern Dance: A Creative Approach*, 3rd edn, rev. N.J. Pennington, Princeton NJ: Princeton Book Co.
Cohen, S.J., Dorris, G. *et al.* (eds) (1998) *International Encyclopaedia of Dance*, 6 vols, New York: Oxford University Press.
Craine, D. and Mackrell, D.J. (2000) *The Oxford Dictionary of Dance*, Oxford: Oxford University Press.
Dance, L.J. (2002) *Tough Fronts: The Impact of Street Culture on Schooling*, New York: RoutledgeFalmer.

LIZ ENGEL

DATABASE MARKETING

Database marketing, sometimes referred to as marketing information systems, involves the use of consumer information to tailor product offerings or marketing techniques on an individualised basis. Database marketing is one component of consumer relationship marketing, which is the use of different marketing techniques to forge personalised, long-term relationships between consumers and organisations. Sports organisations use database marketing in different ways, including direct mail, telemarketing, internet/website presence, and affinity cards. Research suggests that database marketing and consumer relationship marketing may be the key to increased profitability over the long run.

Database marketing has four primary functions: to segment and target potential customers; to retain and build relationships with current customers; to predict future purchases by customers based upon existing data; and to calculate the lifetime value of customers.

The direct mail marketing approach uses fan or sport consumer databases to send out flyers, catalogues, and other promotional materials through either traditional or electronic mail (email). The National Basketball Association (NBA) created a catalogue of team and league products in 1983 and discovered soon after that 70 per cent of catalogue sales resulted from direct mail-outs. The National Football League (NFL) has successfully used direct mail to stimulate season ticket sales. Sport sponsorships often include sharing of club database information with sponsors.

Telemarketing is another approach to database marketing. Professional teams often establish call centres to handle ticket or merchandise purchases. Season or special event tickets can also be sold via tele-marketing. Rice University, located in Houston, Texas, established a special event in 1998 entitled 'Operation Sellout', which used telemarketing to sell tickets (approximately 12,000 of 70,000 total) to a football game and literacy awareness special event featuring United States' First Lady Barbara Bush. Finally, many university and inter-scholastic athletics programmes use tele-marketing to conduct fundraising drives from alumni and supporters.

Perhaps no more important tool has been created for either database marketing or consumer relationship marketing than the internet and World Wide Web. Sport organisations are able to interact with con-sumers via websites, gathering information regarding preferences and tailoring product offerings and marketing approaches to individual concerns. Online shopping for merchandise and tickets makes consumer purchasing more comfortable and even inviting. Websites can track the most vis-ited pages or most purchased products and can adjust inventory online or in physical retail outlets, as well. Many web-based busi-nesses have also been established to either produce sports organisations websites for them or to sell sport licensed merchandise on their online websites.

Affinity cards are another means of track-ing consumer data and storing it in database management systems. Under this concept, already used extensively in the airlines, hospitality, retail, and grocery industries, sport consumers present a card (or other

device that can be scanned electronically) each time they attend a sporting event or make a purchase from a sport organisation-affiliated vendor. Consumers achieve bonu-ses or 'points' based upon how many events they attend or the amount of their pur-chases, eventually receiving special gifts, coupons, or reduced price offers as rewards. In return, the sport organisation is able to accumulate data, which can be used to tai-lor product and marketing offerings, as well as help build a more personal and loyal relationship with the consumer.

Many researchers have suggested that building more personalised and service-based relationships with consumers is the key to achieving real customer satisfaction and thus, a competitive advantage in the marketplace. As technology continues to develop, database marketing and consumer relationship marketing is likely to become more advanced and provide a growth area for sport organisations.

References

De Burca, S., Brannick, T. and Meenaghan, T. (1995) 'A Relationship Marketing Approach to Spectators as Consumers', *Irish Business and Administrative Research* 16: 86–100.
Jutkins, R. (1998) 'Direct Marketing: A New Strategy in the Sports Industry', *Direct Marketing* 60, 10 (February): 34–5.
'Scoring Big with the NBA' (1986, January). *Zip Target Marketing* 9, 1 (January): 25–7.

Further reading

Kotler, P. (1997) 'Managing Direct and Online Marketing', in P. Kotler (ed.) *Marketing Management: Analysis, Planning, Implementation, and Control*, 9th edn, Upper Saddle River NJ: Prentice Hall.

MICHAEL A. HUNT

DEEP HEAT

There are two techniques used to heat deep tissues: ultrasound and diathermy. Ultrasound uses acoustics or sound wave vibrations whereas diathermy uses electro-magnetic fields.

The clinical uses for ultrasound include heating connective tissues before stretch-ing and manual therapies, increasing the inflammatory response to promote healing, decreasing muscle spasms, and aiding in pain control. Most modern ultrasound units emit sound waves at frequencies between 1 and 3 MHz (audible sound is between 15 and 20 kHz) and generate heat by the vibration of a crystal in an alternating elec-trical current. This heat can than be absor-bed by tissue. Low-frequency vibrations penetrate deeper than high-frequency vibrations. To prevent sound wave disper-sion an ultrasound gel is used to transmit the ultrasound to the surface of the body. Tissues such as muscle, bone, and joint capsules with a higher protein concen-tration absorb more of the vibrations.

During the treatment, the ultrasound transducer must always be kept moving to prevent excessive heating of any one area. For deep tissue penetration (2–5 cm), 1 MHz frequency is used. In general, ultra-sound is not indicated for superficial tissues (depth of 0.5–2 cm), because heating pads are much easier to use and provide similar benefits at a significantly reduced cost.

Ultrasound can be delivered in a con-tinuous or a pulsed cycle. The continuous cycle provides maximal thermal effects. The thermal effects of heating tissues are multifold. Heat causes vasodilatation (widen-ing of the blood vessels) which increases blood flow and local metabolism. In addi-tion, heating alters the nerve conduction velocity and slows the pain signals sent to the brain. Finally, heat increases the elasti-city or flexibility of the tissues and decreases muscle spasm. Occasionally ultrasound is used to drive medications into tissues, a process known as phonophoresis, but its pharmacological effect is unknown.

Ultrasound treatment should never be used near the eyes, heart, genitalia, a preg-nant uterus, or pacemakers. In addition, ultrasound is absolutely contraindicated near a malignancy (cancer), over the spinal column or near an infection. In some indi-viduals with implants (joint replacements) that contain synthetic parts, the use of ultrasound may damage these materials.

Diathermy, the other method used to heat deep tissues, involves the application of elec-tromagnetic energy (similar to radio waves) to produce heat. Continuous short-wave diathermy is the most commonly used set-ting. An electrical current is set up in the tissues and the resultant electron movement generates frictional force and heat. Tissues with the greatest conductivity and least resistance, like muscles, tend to have the greatest increase in temperature. The advantage of diathermy over ultrasound is that it can heat a larger area of deep tissues.

During diathermy treatment the electro-magnetic energy is not localized to the treat-ment area, therefore a distance of 3 ft from the source should be maintained to prevent overexposure. In general, diathermy heats up to 5 cm below skin. Joint inflammation, large deep muscle injuries, subacute and chronic inflammatory conditions in deep-tissue layers, as well as treatment of non-healing fractures, are all indications for dia-thermy therapy. Contraindications, similar to those for ultrasound, include circulation pro-blems, bleeding tendencies (including men-struation), cancer, fever, inadequate sensation, pregnancy, pacemakers, and infections.

In general, deep heat should not be used acutely (the first 72 h) after injuries. Overall, deep heat is more effective than superficial heat for increasing joint range of motion and decreasing scar tissue formation. The effects of deep heat last 3–5 min after cessation of the treatment, therefore, stretching should be done immediately after application of heat, while the tissues are still warm and flexible.

Further reading

Kibler, W.B. and Duerler, K. (2003) 'Applica-tion of Heat', in J.C. DeLee, D. Drez Jr and

M.D. Miller (eds) *DeLee and Drez's Orthopedic Sports Medicine*, 2nd edn, 357–9, Philadelphia: W.B. Saunders.

Lehman, J.F. and De Lateur, B.J. (1990) 'Therapeutic Heat', in *Therapeutic Heat and Cold*, 4th edn, ch.9, 417–581, Baltimore: Williams and Wilkins.

JESSICA L. SCHUTZBANK

DEINDUSTRIALISATION

Deindustrialisation refers to the process whereby the proportion of national production and/or of the labour force engaged in the primary and secondary sectors of the economy is diminishing. Such a process is most apparent in the former leading industrial economies of the world. Such a process is not necessarily associated with a decline in production (in particular because of greater and more flexible use of automation) nor with decreased investment. Nevertheless, this was the case for Britain in the last quarter of the twentieth century, and thus was accompanied by concerns about the impact on social restructuring and social order.

Deindustrialisation, particularly in association with ideas of a post-industrial society, has also signalled a growing concern to promote the service or tertiary sector, and thus sporting services have been given greater emphasis by commercial and public sectors. Such services can be a source of profit *per se* (witness the growth of the growth of the health and fitness industries) or a vehicle for other profit centres (e.g. the use by media companies of sport as a vehicle for attracting advertising revenue), or can be used as an attractor of inward investment into cities and regions (e.g. in the isssue of sport in city marketing).

Deindustrialisation as a process is associated also with the loss of jobs in developed, high-wage economies (such as those in the United States and Western Europe) to developing economies, particularly in Asia. Jobs which are retained in the devel-

oped economies are those associated with either the service sector, or with high-value craft production. Sports equipment manufacture is a good example of how the service sector may design a product (e.g. a Nike shoe) and market it in the West with a high mark-up while industrial production is 'exported' to the developing economies of Southeast Asia with low production costs and low levels of labour power or trades union activity.

See also: post-industrialism

IAN P. HENRY

DELPHI METHOD

The term 'Delphi' relates to the Delphic Oracle of ancient Greece, a priestly entity who, in response to petitioning and in return for payment, would foretell people's future fortunes – often expressed in a cryptic manner. The Delphi method is therefore a forecasting technique based on the knowledge and expertise of modern 'oracles' or experts in a particular field.

Developed by the RAND Corporation in America, the technique involves asking a panel of experts to express their views separately on likely future developments in a particular field of interest. This information is then distilled into a forecast or forecasts. The number of experts involved can be as few as a dozen or so, or could number several hundred; they can be assembled in one place, as at a conference or, more commonly, they may be contacted by mail or email. In the first 'round' of the process the experts are asked a series of questions which can be in various forms, for example:

- What are the major changes you expect to see in X over the next 5/10/20/etc. years?
- When, if ever, do you expect event X to take place?

345

- What is the probability of each of events X, Y, Z happening in the next 5/10/20/etc. years?

The first of these question formats produces responses in the form of lists of events and the number of times they are mentioned by members of the panel. The second format produces a range of dates and a mean or median date from among the panel members. The third produces a range of probabilities and a mean or median score.

The technique involves a number of 'rounds' of questioning. The first question format could be used in the first round to establish a list of possible events. Alternatively, a list of events of interest may already be available, so the second or third question format might be used in the first round to establish the range of dates or probabilities from among the experts. In the first round the panel of experts tends to produce a wide range of differing opinions. The responses are then collated and fed back to the panel of experts in the second round, when they are invited to revise their opinions, if they wish, in the light of this information from their peers. The process is repeated for as many rounds as necessary to produce a stable situation – that is, where panel members are no longer changing their views. In practice the number of rounds may be limited by available time and resources and by a desire not to lose panel members through non-response. The collated views of the panel from the final round then provide the basis of the forecast.

One of the earliest uses of the technique in the recreation area was by Shafer *et al.* (1975), who asked a panel of 400 American recreation professionals and academics to indicate the most significant future events likely to take place in the area of outdoor sport and recreation. Among the predictions were:

- *by 1985:* Most people work a four-day, thirty-two hour week.

- *by 1990:* Year-round skiing on artificial surfaces.
- *by 2000:* Small recreational submarines common.
- Waste disposal bacteria incorporated into recreation equipment.
- *2050+:* First park established on the moon.
- Average worker has three month annual vacation.

With the wisdom of hindsight, it is clear that the technique is by no means always accurate. To a large extent it is dependent on the quality of the assembled panel. However, much of the value of the technique could be said to lie in its ability to open up debate and promote thought, rather than in the precise accuracy of its predictions.

References

Linstone, H.A. and Turoff, M. (eds) (1975) *The Delphi Method: Techniques and Applications*, Reading MA: Addison-Wesley.

Shafer, E.L., Moeller, G.H. and Russell, E.G. (1975) 'Future Leisure Environments', *Ekistics* 40, 236: 68–72.

Zalatan, A. (1994) *Forecasting Methods for Sport and Recreation*, Toronto: Thompson Educational Publishing.

A.J. VEAL

DEMAND

Demand in economic terms represents the desire and willingness of consumers to take part in sport. Demand analysis is the analysis of the sport participation decision. We are interested in analysing the factors that result in participation or non-participation in active sport. The neoclassical economics approach starts the analysis at the most micro level, the individual consumer's demand for a specific activity. All other aspects of demand can then be deduced once we have analysed this consumer choice situation. The approach models the balancing act of the consumer to match the pleasure he or she obtains from taking part in sport with the costs of doing so.

However, although sport generates immediate consumption benefits that fit the conventional consumer choice model in economics, there is an investment demand element to the demand for sport because of the health benefits generated through long-term participation in active recreation. This makes the modelling of the demand for sport more complicated than it is for most other commodities. In addition, there are serious reservations as to whether the neo-classical approach, however adjusted to take account of these complications, can ever completely explain the consumer's decision to take part in sport. This criticism is based on the assumptions on which the model is based.

The starting point for the analysis of consumer behaviour in sport is the theory of consumer demand. This has remained virtually unaltered for over a century. The consumer is regarded as having a given set of tastes and preferences and, facing a given set of prices of goods and services, allocates his income in such a way as to maximise utility, which results in a spending pattern where the relative marginal utilities of different goods are equated to relative prices. Economic theory concentrates on such 'rational' maximising behaviour. This approach often adopts a hierarchical approach to modelling the demand for sport, with the demand for the sporting activity playing the role of the parent demand function and the demand for sports facilities, sports equipment, sports clothing, and sports shoes are treated as derived demands from this logically prior parent demand to take part in the activity.

In this case, the quantity demanded for the parent demand function is a measure of sports participation. In the case of the separate derived demand functions the quantity demanded will be the consumer's expenditure on the sports goods or services

(e.g. on sports equipment). Thus instead of one demand function we have one parent demand function and several derived demand functions for each element of the derived demands.

As an example of this approach, we can look at the demand for badminton. The parent demand function is concerned with the consumer's decision to take part in badminton or not. If the consumer decides to participate then he or she will require a racquet, shuttlecocks, clothing, and foot-wear. In addition, he or she will have to rent a court at a sports centre or club, and travel to and from the facility. All these extra demands, including the demand for sports-related travel are treated as derived demands from the decision to participate in badminton.

However, although the approach may be suitable for most sports, there are others where the hierarchical approach is less appropriate. For some activities all the elements are demanded simultaneously and it is not possible to distinguish such a parent/derived demand relationship.

For instance, for many people the decision to participate in skiing involves the purchase of a package holiday. The very name 'package' means that what is being purchased is a composite commodity with several different elements included. In the case of a ski holiday the package may include air travel to and from the country with the ski resort, transport from the air-port to the accommodation and back, food and accommodation for the duration of the holiday, ski pass, ski school, and equipment hire. Some packages may include only some of these elements, others may include them all. When the consumer makes the decision to participate in skiing, a single price is paid for this composite commodity, the ski holiday. However, this single price is even then not the total cost of taking part in skiing. The consumer will still pay for travel to and from the airport, maybe parking at the airport, additional spending while on holiday, and maybe new clothes purchased for the holiday. Thus the composite commodity of taking part in skiing is larger than the package holiday.

In such circumstances, it is more appropriate to treat the quantity demanded as the total expenditure on the skiing trip. Even for other sports that are not packaged in this way it is possible to use such a 'composite commodity' model and treat the total expenditure on taking part in the sport as the relevant dependent variable in the model, even though it is the consumer that may do the packaging.

Other approaches to the demand for sport seem more appropriate than neo-classical consumer choice theory. Becker (1965) introduced a novel approach to consumer demand that is particularly relevant for the demand for sport. His approach uses a household production function, which demonstrates that an activity such as sport, undertaken by an individual or household, involves inputs of market goods and time. Becker terms these activities 'composite commodities'. Each composite commodity involves different inputs of market goods and time, so that when the price of time or market goods alters, the effect on consumption of different activities will be varied.

In the long run, as real wage rates increase, the price of time rises relative to the price of market goods. Time is a finite input to household production, whereas market goods can be continually expanded. The change in relative prices causes consumption patterns to alter. As the relative price of time and market goods changes, household production and consumption also alters to a different package of time-intensive and goods-intensive commodities. As wage rates rise the end result is falling consumption of time-intensive commodities. In practice the household and individual face not just the two-dimensional choice represented, but a multi-dimensional choice between composite commodities of varying degrees of time-intensity and goods-intensity.

Becker's household production approach provides an alternative model of consumer demand for sport and recreation activities. It is a more useful framework than the classical utility-maximising model since it not only gives us demand functions for the activities but the model also generates derived demand for facilities, travel, and recreation goods. It is a hierarchical demand model, with the demand for activity playing the role of the parent demand function, and the time input plays a crucial role in the analysis.

Reference

Becker, G.S. (1965) 'A Theory of the Allocation of Time', *Economic Journal* 75: 3.

CHRIS GRATTON

DEMARKETING

Marketing can be used as a means of discouraging as well as of encouraging people to attend sports events. This process has been termed demarketing to emphasize that marketing activities may be used to decrease the number of people desiring to attend an event. There are two contexts when such a strategy is likely to be particularly prominent: (i) when hooliganism by fans is perceived likely to cause problems; and (ii) when the demand for an event exceeds the capacity of a facility to accommodate it.

In these situations, organizations sometimes practice demarketing by using the marketing mix variables to dissuade people from attending the event. For example:

- *Promotion*: reduce promotional efforts; promote alternate opportunities to see the team in action; stress the large numbers of people likely to attend, the overcrowding in the arena and the possibility of hooliganism; stress difficulties associated with staying in the area e.g. traffic jams, difficulty in parking.

- *Distribution*: ban parking near the facility; require the use of public transportation.
- *Price*: raise the admission price; create a queuing situation to obtain tickets to increase the time and opportunity costs of the experience.

Demarketing is not a negative concept. It is a technique for matching customer demand with a sport organization's product supply. A proactive effort to decrease the demand can lead to an increase in customer satisfaction through preserving a higher quality experience for those who do attend. Demarketing has to be subtly and gradually implemented in order not to lose public support. The examples given previously under Promotion, Distribution, and Price generally would not be used in isolation, but rather would interact in some form of demarketing mix.

JOHN L. CROMPTON

DEMOCRACY

Definitions of democracy are numerous and highly contested. Some definitions emphasise the importance of particular institutions such as universal suffrage and independent judiciaries, others foreground particular values such as freedom of expression and a respect by government for the rule of law, while others stress the centrality of processes, such as regular elections and access to information. While democratic theory is concerned primarily with the particular arrangements for making decisions for a country, the same theory can be applied to all decision-making institutions including sports clubs and governing bodies.

One of the long-standing tensions within democratic theory is between the relative importance of representation and participa-

tion. An emphasis on representation suggests a role for the citizens that is limited to exercising the right to accept or refuse those who are to rule them. This elitist view of democracy assumes that the essence of democracy is defined by those conditions that would allow the competition between elites and would include the autonomy of political elite from the state, an independent civil service, and a political culture which stressed compromise and tolerance.

This narrow representational model of democracy has been criticised on a number of counts, particularly for the undue emphasis given to democracy as primarily a set of procedures for electing leaders. It has also been challenged for its uncritical acceptance of pluralist assumptions about the openness of democratic political systems, and for ignoring the possibility that power might be embedded in democratic institutions in such a way as to privilege certain groups, particularly business.

Many of the critics of the representative democratic model stress the importance of participation as the defining core of democracy. Increasingly athletes are arguing that it is insufficient that their interests are represented by others: athletes expect direct participation in the deliberations of bodies such as the IOC, the World Anti-Doping Agency and the international federations. Participatory democracy rejects as paternalistic the traditional notions of representative democracy.

A forceful variant on the critique of traditional representational democracy comes from feminists who argue that there is a gendered structural bias in liberal Western democracies and that concepts such as 'citizen' and 'the individual' reflect male definitions of needs and desires. In essence feminists challenge the dichotomy inherent within liberal democratic theory between the public and the private sphere and the implicit assumption that what is important for humanity takes place in the public sphere, thus ignoring the private sphere of the family and treating it as outside the compass of democratic concern.

Some recent attempts to capture the essence of democracy have tried to identify the primary indices for measuring democratisation. Common indicators include: basic freedoms (including freedom of speech and equal treatment under the law); citizenship and participation (including equal right to run for office and vote and regular elections); administrative codes (which would cover the behaviour of officials, procedures for redress of grievance, and transparency in decision-making); and social rights (to adequate education for example).

For both sports organisations and states, democracy, broadly defined, is a way of collective decision-making based on popular participation, and a form of governance in which people/members exercise control and where institutions are responsive to the interests of people/members while also respectful of the rights of minorities. However, around these core ideas debates will undoubtedly continue over the preferred balance between representation and participation, the institutions that best foster and support democracy, and the precise specification and interpretation of values.

Further reading

Carter, A. and Stokes, G. (2001) *Democratic Theory Today: Challenges for the 21st Century*, Cambridge: Polity Press.

Held, D. (1996) *Models of Democracy*, Cambridge: Polity Press.

BARRIE HOULIHAN

DIABETES MELLITUS

Diabetes mellitus is not one disease but a group of metabolic diseases characterised by hyperglycaemia resulting from defects in insulin secretion, insulin action, or both. Most cases of diabetes mellitus fall into two broad categories, namely (1) those where there is an absolute deficiency of insulin secretion (Type I – Insulin Dependent Diabetes Mellitus or IDDM); and (2) those where there is either resistance to insulin action (insulin resistance) or inadequate insulin secretion or both (Type II – Non Insulin Dependent Diabetes Mellitus or NIDDM). Type II NIDDM accounts for the majority (>90 per cent) of patients with diabetes mellitus. The criteria for the diagnosis of diabetes mellitus are as follows:

- Classic symptoms of polyuria, polydipsia, unexplained weight loss with a random blood glucose concentration >11.1 mmol l^{-1}
- Fasting (no caloric intake for at least 8 h) blood glucose concentration >7.0 mmol l^{-1}
- Blood glucose concentration >11.1 mmol l^{-1} at 2 h after a standard glucose load (75 g) – oral glucose tolerance test

The focus of this review will be the role that physical activity plays in the prevention and management of both Type I and Type II diabetes mellitus.

The role of physical activity in the prevention of Type I diabetes mellitus (IDDM)

In Type I diabetes mellitus, the primary disorder is lack of insulin following destruction of the pancreatic ß islet cells. This destruction is thought to occur as a result of an autoimmune process, but can also be secondary to pancreatic disease. Lack of physical activity is therefore not related to the cause of this disease.

The role of physical activity in the prevention of Type II diabetes mellitus (NIDDM)

It is well established that regular participation in physical exercise reduces the risk of developing Type II diabetes mellitus. Although the actual mechanisms have not been well identified, it appears that physical activity acts both directly by improving insulin sensitivity, and indirectly by inducing favourable changes in body mass and body composition. A number of important specific adaptations to exercise training have been shown to be of benefit in the prevention of Type II diabetes mellitus. These include:

- increased muscle mass and decreased body fat (central area);
- increased muscle glucose uptake during exercise;
- increased skeletal muscle blood flow;
- conversion of fast twitch glycolytic IIb muscle fibres to fast twitch oxidative IIa fibres (which are more insulin-sensitive and have greater capillary density);
- increased insulin-regulatable glucose transporters (GLUT4);
- improved control over hepatic glucose production.

The exact 'dose' of physical exercise for the prevention of Type II diabetes mellitus has not been well established. In one study, it has been shown that for every additional weekly energy expenditure or 500 kCal, the risk of Type II diabetes is reduced by 6 per cent. Data also indicate that the intensity of exercise is important, with greater reductions in risk if exercise training is conducted at a higher intensity. It has also been shown that the effects of exercise training are short-lived, and this implies that a long-term commitment to perform regular exercise training is necessary to reduce the risk of this disease.

Finally, it is important to emphasise that there are other general health benefits of regular exercise training, which can also reduce the risk of complications from Type II diabetes mellitus, in particular, the additional benefits on the cardiovascular system.

The role of physical activity in the management of Type I diabetes mellitus (IDDM)

Exercise training is an important component of the management of Type I diabetes mellitus. During an acute exercise bout, muscle contraction results in increased glucose uptake and an increased insulin sensitivity, which can continue for 4–6 h after exercise. This insulin-like effect of exercise has been shown to reduce the insulin requirements in these patients, but has not convincingly resulted in improved glucose control. Other beneficial effects of regular exercise training in patients with Type I diabetes mellitus are:

- increased functional capacity;
- improved blood lipid profile;
- reduced risk of cardiovascular complications;
- increased skeletal muscle capillary density;
- increased general well-being.

There are two important special considerations in Type I diabetes mellitus. An acute exercise bout can result in a further increase in blood glucose concentration and the development of ketosis if the blood glucose concentration before the onset of exercise is elevated above $16\,mmol\,l^{-1}$. Exercise training in these circumstances is contra-indicated. An acute exercise bout can also result in hypoglycaemia if the starting blood glucose is low. Exercise is therefore also contra-indicated if the blood glucose concentration is below $6\,mmol\,l^{-1}$.

The role of physical activity in the management of Type II diabetes mellitus (NIDDM)

Physical activity should be introduced as part of the management of all patients with Type II diabetes mellitus. The benefits of regular physical activity on glucose

351

metabolism and insulin sensitivity have already been mentioned. In addition, many abnormalities that are associated with Type II diabetes mellitus (hypertension, hyperlipidaemia, obesity) also respond very favourably to regular exercise training. Specific beneficial effects of regular exercise training in patients with Type II diabetes mellitus are as follows.

- increased blood glucose control;
- increased peripheral insulin sensitivity;
- increased physical work capacity;
- improved blood lipid profile;
- decreased hypertension;
- improved control of body weight;
- reduced risk of cardiovascular complications;
- increased general well-being.

Practical exercise prescription for patients with diabetes mellitus (Types I and II)

In general the exercise prescription is similar for patients with Type I and Type II diabetes mellitus. Prior to starting with regular exercise all patients should undergo a comprehensive medical assessment (history and physical examination). This examination should place emphasis on establishing that there is good blood glucose control, and to identify any complications of the disease (myocardial ischaemia, peripheral vascular disease, retinopathy, microalbuminuria, peripheral and/or autonomic neuropathy). All patients should also undergo an exercise stress electrocardiogram (ECG), consult with a nutritionist, and be informed of the potential risks of exercise training such as hypoglycaemia, hyperglycaemia, orthopaedic injuries related to peripheral neuropathy, increases in blood pressure during exercise, and the risk of cardiac complications.

The following are general guidelines for exercise prescription in patients with diabetes mellitus.

- Patients should ideally start the training programme in a supervised setting where medical staff are in attendance.
- Exercise training should be conducted three times or more per week.
- Exercise sessions should be at least 30–60 min and be preceded by an adequate warm-up and followed by a cool down.
- Activities can include brisk walking or jogging (unless complicated by injuries to feet), cycling, swimming, rowing, or aerobics.
- Exercise training at higher intensities is encouraged.

Practical recommendations to avoid metabolic complications (particularly in Type I IDDM) during exercise are listed.

- Patients with diabetes are encouraged to eat a carbohydrate meal 1–2 h before an exercise session.
- In Type I IDDM, the recommendation is not to inject any insulin less than 1 h before an exercise session, and to perhaps reduce the insulin dose just before exercise.
- Each session should ideally be preceded by determination of the blood glucose concentration.
- If the blood glucose concentration before exercise is lower than $6 \, \text{mmol} \, l^{-1}$, carbohydrates should be ingested before starting exercise training.
- If the blood glucose concentration before exercise is above $16 \, \text{mmol} \, l^{-1}$, the urinary ketones should be measured. Exercise training should be postponed if ketones are present, and blood glucose control must be established first.
- Carbohydrates should be available during an exercise session.

● Patients are encouraged to exercise with a partner who is familiar with the condition.

See also: cardiac rehabilitation

Further reading

Hamdy, O., Goodyear, L.J. and Horton, E.S. (2001) 'Diet and Exercise in Type 2 Diabetes Mellitus', *Endocrinol Metab Clin North Am* 30: 883–907.

MARTIN SCHWELLNUS

DIAGNOSTIC ULTRASOUND

The use of ultrasound to image soft tissue injury has increased greatly over the last five years, as a result of improvements in technology and the availability of cheaper dedicated musculoskeletal equipment.

Pulses of high-frequency sound are propagated into the tissues using a hand-held probe and a couplant jelly. Sound is attenuated, reflected, and refracted, producing a complex pattern of echoes that are detected by the probe. The delay and strength of the echo following the sound pulse allows a computer to construct a cross-sectional image. This process is repeated rapidly to give real-time moving images on a monitor as the probe position is altered to produce optimum image quality and to examine the tissues in different planes. Interpretation has to be performed by the operator at the time of the examination, making the technique operator-dependant. Since ultrasound is unable to penetrate bone, and the 10–20 MHz sound needed for high resolution is rapidly attenuated, good image quality is restricted to superficial soft tissues. The nature of the scanning technique, presence of many artefacts and the necessity of identifying anatomical structures in real time with a relatively restricted field of view result in a long learning curve. Diagnostic ultrasound has a number of advantages over **magnetic resonance imaging (MRI)**: it has high near field resolution, is rapid, has no contra-indications, is dynamic, can be used for guidance of injection/aspiration, and finally is less expensive. MRI allows visualisation of deeper tissues, including bone and articular cartilage and the images obtained are suitable for external review. Many of the indications for MRI are shared with diagnostic ultrasound, and the decision as to which modality to utilise often rests on the availability of skills and equipment.

The main indication for ultrasound is the study of superficial tendons for evidence of **tendinosis**, tears, calcific tendinitis, enthesitis, and to identify abnormalities in associated structures, particularly bursae. Muscle tears and haemaomas are well visualised and account for most of the remaining sports related examinations. In joint imaging, since many of the important structures are either deep or are obscured by bone, the main role is in guiding joint injection or aspiration. Ultrasound can, however, be useful to detect joint effusions, synovitis or erosions. Dynamic assessment has a role, despite limitations due to the necessity of keeping the probe parallel to, and near the structure studied, and the loss of image quality that occurs during movement. Superficial ligaments can be identified in larger joints such as the knee and ankle.

Indications in the hand and wrist include tenosynovitis, **tendon injury**, and thumb ulnacollateral ligament injuries. Elbow common extensor and flexor origin tendinosis is a frequently occurring sporting condition that is readily diagnosed. Collateral ligament injury may also be identified. In the shoulder, ultrasound is an accurate means of assessing the rotator cuff tendons for tendinosis, calcific tendinosis, and tears. Patellar tendinosis is the main sports indication in the knee, since collateral knee ligaments injury is associated with anterior cruciate and meniscal pathology, making MRI the imaging modality of choice. In the ankle Achilles tendinosis was one of the first and remains a very important indication, as are peroneal and tibialis posterior tendon pathology.

Although it has a more restricted set of indications than MRI, the inherent strengths of the technique and equipment developments make diagnostic ultrasound a developing area of sports medicine.

References

Gibbon, W.W. (1996) *Muslculoskeltal Ultrasound: The Essentials*, London: Greenwich Medical Media.

van Holsbeeck, M.T. and Introcaso, J.H. (eds) (2001) *Musculoskeletal Ultrasound*, St Louis MO: Mosby.

ROBERT COOPER

DIFFERENTIAL BOUNDARY LAYER SEPARATION

When an object – a sports object or a sports performer – travels through a stationary fluid, there is a thin layer of fluid particles close to the object in which viscous forces act. Far away from the object, the fluid is stationary while, at the object's surface, the fluid is flowing at the same rate as the object and there must be a velocity gradient linking the two zones. This region is called the **boundary layer**, and its characteristics have an important part to play in sport and, in particular, sports ball aerodynamics. Pressure gradients, caused by geometrical changes on the object, may cause the boundary layer to separate from the surface such that a low-pressure wake occurs behind the body (see also **boundary layer separation**). In general, the larger the wake, the greater is the drag force on the object (see **drag forces**).

Turbulence within the boundary layer can cause mixing between high-speed fluid particles close to the surface and low-speed fluid particles further away, which acts to stabilise the boundary layer and delay separation so that the wake behind the object is smaller. This turbulence can be caused by dimples, seams, and other roughness elements. Boundary layer separation may not be symmetrical on an object if it is spinning and this causes transverse forces to be applied, most noticeably on balls with roughness elements, such as golf balls with dimples and cricket balls with seams. To complicate matters, separation may occur differently on different sides of an object if the roughness varies. This may cause the reverse Magnus effect, in which a spinning sports ball moves laterally in the air in the opposite direction to the way the spin would normally suggest.

See also: ball swing and reverse swing; boundary layer; laminar and turbulent flow; lift forces – fundamentals; Magnus and negative Magnus effects

Further reading

Massey, B.S. (1992) *Mechanics of Fluids*, London: Chapman and Hall.

STEVE HAAKE

DIFFERENTIATION

Differentiation means distributing tasks over a number of units, i.e. over different social groups or positions. Systems theory in particular uses the term and the concept of differentiation.

Processes of differentiation are called functional when they are based on specialisation, as is the case in the division of labour, for example. Processes of differentiation can bring about vertical or horizontal divisions. They may be related to an imbalanced distribution of power and influence and consequently lead to the formation of different social classes and hierarchies. Characteristic of modern industrial societies is an increasingly horizontal differentiation; in these societies various sectors complement each other, such as industry, politics, the legal system and science, each with its own values, positions, and logic. According to the ideas of systems theory, the increasing compartmentalisation and division of labour in society guarantees the greatest possible efficiency in the execution of socially important tasks, but also requires considerable efforts with regard to integration.

Development of differentiation in sport

Sport is a social subsystem which, on the one hand, has uncoupled itself from other sectors as a result of differentiation processes and acquired a certain amount of autonomy. Even in countries in which sport is administered and controlled by the state, sport has its own values and rules. On the other hand, one can observe that the subsystem of sport is breaking up not only into numerous organisations and institutions, but also into its own subsystems, each with its own logic and scripts. From a systems theory perspective, the autonomy of sport can be attributed to the fact that its merits for a society as a whole, ranging from its capacity to represent a country internationally to its potential of promoting the health of its citizens, cannot be provided by any other of the social subsystems.

Intercultural comparisons show clearly that the degree of differentiation in a society is reflected in its physical culture. In Europe in the eighteenth and nineteenth centuries different forms of physical culture developed, such as gymnastics and German *Turnen*, through taking over functions belonging to the education, health, and military systems. However, the dominant physical culture of modern industrial nation-states was sport, which originated in England in the eighteenth and nineteenth centuries and spread all over the world. The development of modern sport was accompanied by numerous internal differentiation processes with regard not only to types of sport and their rules but also

to contests and the roles of the participants. In the nineteenth century a differentiation already began to take place of roles, tasks, and functions on the sports field, as well as in other areas: increasingly, referees, officials, coaches, sports doctors, sports journalists, and numerous other experts were needed, and there was also a growing specialisation among athletes themselves. This went hand-in-hand with an intensification with regard to both the time and effort expected of all those concerned. The processes of differentiation in sport were accompanied, and even driven forward, by a continuous increase in academic disciplines relating to sport, together with a specialisation of our knowledge of sport.

The globalisation of modern sport may, on the one hand, be interpreted as a process of standardisation, as a loss of the great diversity of traditional physical cultures. On the other hand, national and regional physical cultures have been integrated in sport, thus greatly increasing the spectrum of sporting activities. Further, extensive processes of differentiation are to be observed with regard to the meanings of sport as well as to sports facilities, apparatus, and providers.

Since the mid-twentieth century the 'sportification' of physical cultures (i.e. the enforcement of a one-dimensional code confined to winning and losing) has also been accompanied by an increasing tendency towards 'de-sportification'. This tendency, which has motivated new target groups – women and senior citizens, among others – to take up sport, has, moreover, changed the face of sport decisively. It has led to changes in expectations, motives, and practices; and the principles of modern sport, above all its orientation towards achievement and comparisons of performance, have lost some of their significance to a new orientation towards health and fun. The commercialisation of sport, the increasing significance of 'soft' sports such as walking or cycling, and also sport's potential to benefit society as a whole, are making the borders increasingly blurred between sport and other areas of society, e.g. politics, economics, or the health sector, thus putting sport's autonomy in jeopardy and possibly leading to converse processes of 'de-differentiation' and integration. Recreational sports, for example, might be uncoupled from the sport system and integrated into the health system.

Sport as a differentiated system today

At present there is a broad spectrum of different forms of sport, ranging from top-level competitive sport to health sport and fun sport, with differing aims, purposes, rules, rituals, and practices.

Today sport is provided by various organisations, institutions, and commercial providers. Even in those European countries in which sport clubs long had a monopoly in providing sports, such as Germany or the Scandinavian countries, private firms have established themselves alongside municipalities and even informal groups as providers of facilities from tennis courts to fitness studios.

Sports clubs, though, have also acted in order to meet the new demands put on them and have given themselves different kinds of profile. Some have developed into large clubs, professionally managed and providing a great variety of sporting activities, while others have specialised in particular sports. Moreover, in the clubs themselves strict boundaries are drawn not only between the different sections but also between top-level sports and competitive sport and 'sport for all'.

In spite of the growing demand for sport and the increasingly differentiated target groups, there is enormous competition in the 'sports market'. In club sports there was always a battle for members, power and influence, and these battles still break out repeatedly today. The divergent interests of associations and clubs are balanced by umbrella organisations, such as national sport federations, which represent their members in all issues of sport and also try to protect them against competition from other, especially commercial, providers of sport.

Differentiation has led to a huge diversity of the sports and sporting activities provided, to countless options and a wide variety of target groups, as well as to different sport models ranging from professional sports to informal sporting activities which have little or nothing in common with each other. It is impossible to foresee the implications of this for sport systems, especially as they are likely to differ from country to country.

Further reading

Bette, K.-H. (1992) *Theorie als Herausforderung. Beiträge zur systemtheoretischen Reflexion der Sportwissenschaft* [Theory as Challenge. Contributions to the System-theoretical Reflections in Sport Sciences], Aachen: Mayer und Mayer.

Dietrich, K. and Heinemann, K. (1989) *Der nicht-sportliche Sport.-Beiträge zum Wandel im Sport* [Sport which is not Sport – Contributions to the Changes in Sports], Schorndorf: Hofmann.

Digel, H. (1986) 'Über den Wandel der Werte in Gesellschaft, Freizeit und Sport' [About the Change of Values in Society, Leisure and Sport], in Deutscher Sportbund (ed.) *Die Zukunft des Sports* [The Future of Sport], 14–43, Schorndorf: Hofmann.

Lamprecht, M. and Stamm, H. (1995) 'Soziale Differenzierung und soziale Ungleichheit im Breitensport' [Social Differentiation and Social Inequality in Sport for All], *Sportwissenschaft* 25, 3: 265–84.

Schimank, U. (1996) *Theorien gesellschaftlicher Differenzierung*, Opladen: Leske und Budrich.

GERTRUD PFISTER

DIFFUSION

Diffusion is the dissemination of ideas or practices – either within a culture or across cultural borders – which lead to changes in society. Not only in the light of the current processes of (post)modernisation but also with regard to social change in general, the question arises of the extent to which these changes are attributable to influences from outside, and the extent to which are they due to developments from within, independent of external impulses.

Whether, and if so to what extent, and at what speed these processes of diffusion take place depends on numerous factors, such as the means of communication available, the appeal of the new ideas and their compatibility with prevailing social **values** and norms.

A brief look at traditional movement cultures clearly shows that a number of similar forms of movement like jumping and skipping with a rope developed independently of each other in different cultures and regions, while others such as horse-riding in North America were spread by traders, travellers, explorers, or conquerors. In the case of a great many movement cultures their paths and processes of diffusion can be reconstructed across regions, countries, and even continents.

The dominant movement culture of today's industrialised nation-states is modern sport, which, based on the principles of equal opportunity and oriented towards performance and contest, developed in Britain in the eighteenth and nineteenth centuries. Sport spread rapidly to Europe and the United States, as well as along the old colonial trade and control routes to countries in which the British Empire held sway. The cultural transfer of sport was so successful that today the word sport, along with its rules and its symbols, is understood the world over.

The spread of modern sport was brought about, on the one hand, by Britons, in particular traders, explorers, and sailors, as well as colonial officials who were loath to have to do without their leisure pursuits in their new, often temporary, homes. On the other hand, tourists to Britain or foreigners who had come there to study were 'infected' by the craze for sport and took the 'virus' home with them when they left. Opposition, for instance on the part of the gymnastics movement in Finland or the German *Turnen* movement (see **gymnastics, German**) could do nothing to hinder the victory of sport over other forms of physical activity.

Guttmann (1994) gives a detailed description of the development of sport in the countries of the Commonwealth as well as in countries which had trading links with the Empire. In all these countries similar patterns of adoption and diffusion can be documented which are attributable to the innate logic of sport: the 'import' of games from Britain by British citizens was followed by an (in most cases) short phase in which they were played informally, before schools integrated sport in their curriculum and/or clubs and associations were founded which then organised competitions and leagues, first of all at regional and national levels and later at international level.

In the scientific community, though, intense discussions focused on the question of whether the diffusion and 'universalisation' of modern sport could be explained solely with the imperialist strivings of industrial nations, above all those of Great Britain and the United States. Guttmann (1994) refuted the hypothesis that the 'universalisation' of sport was the result of 'cultural imperialism'. Frequently, he argued, typically English sports like football and hockey took hold in countries which did not belong to the Commonwealth. Nevertheless, like Maguire (1999) among others, he pointed out that the cultural hegemony of the Empire provided favourable conditions for the spread of sport, especially since the role model of the colonisers as well as real interference (for example in the school system) were taking effect in the British colonies. At the same time, however, the various cultures and ethnic groups also took an active part themselves in 'appropriating' and adapting sport games, i.e. changing sports to meet their own requirements and even using them as a weapon against the mother country of modern sport. Examples of this are cricket on the Trobriand Islands, which as *kirikiti* developed into a national recreational pastime, and hockey in India, which has at times been played at a higher level of skill than in Great Britain.

Although of British origin, sport has played a vital role ever since the nineteenth century in developing national identities and building nation-states. Both this and the international networking of sports organisations have driven forward the processes of diffusion and globalisation.

The diffusion of sport, especially of Olympic sports, was assisted by development aid, which was concentrated to a large degree on competitive sports in a small number of sport games, in particular football. At first, however, the orientation of modern sport towards contest and performance, as well as its logic based on victory and defeat, apparently clashed with the cultural codes and the social structures of traditional societies. But in the wake of industrialisation and modernisation sport then became the dominant movement culture in the 'third world', too. With the diffusion of sport, certain traditional movement cultures themselves became increasingly 'sportified' and, in turn, spread around the world – like dragon-boat racing and Asian martial arts – although it must be asked to what extent these forms of physical activity lose their cultural specificity and their regional roots by being integrated into the universal system of competitions and records.

Especially globalisation and the mass **media** then contributed towards making sport today not only one of the most important products of, but also one of the driving forces behind globalisation. Sport based on the Anglo-American model has developed into a global movement whose games, for example the **Olympic Games**,

bring people together in their billions, at least in front of the television screen.

Relatively new trends are to be seen in the world-wide **marketing** of top sportsmen and women who because of the globalisation of the market for sport may appear in events all over the world. The effects of these developments have yet to be seen.

Processes of diffusion are also increasingly observable in 'sport for all', as well as in the field of health, reflected in the upsurge of Asian forms of movement from t'ai chi to yoga. However, the import of foreign physical activities does not necessarily imply the adoption and espousal of the values and purpose originally associated with them.

References

Guttmann, A. (1994) *Games and Empires*, New York: Columbia University Press.
Maguire, J. (1999) *Global Sport*, Cambridge: Polity Press.

Further reading

Eisenberg, C. (1999) *English Sports und Deutsche Bürger*, Paderborn: Schoeningh Ferdinand GmbH.
Van Bottenburg, M. (2001) *Global Games*, Urbana and Chicago: University of Illinois Press.

GERTRUD PFISTER

DISABILITY

Although many people with impairments or disabilities actively take part in sports, they are faced with special situations. While often encountering barriers, they also have at their disposal both the potential and opportunities to overcome obstacles. Physical, psychological, or mental impairments and disabilities, however, are also social constructs since society decides upon the definition of disabilities as well as the norms, roles, and rules relating to them. Whether or not and to what extent a person with impairments is disabled always depends on the situation.

In large areas of sport for persons with a disability, a distinction must be made between rehabilitative sport, 'sport for all', and competitive sport. Especially in the areas of 'sport for all' one can observe an increasing tendency towards integration, where sports are played jointly by people with and without disabilities.

The development of sports for persons with a disability

As early as the nineteenth century, physical activity was integrated into the everyday lives of those in homes for the blind and facilities for the 'deaf and dumb' in various European countries. The large numbers of soldiers wounded in the First World War then led to the dedicated and systematic use of gymnastic and athletic exercises in military hospitals. This was an attempt by doctors to improve both the physical and mental well-being of the soldiers by offering them the chance to participate in **gymnastics** and sports.

Similarly, physical exercises were also used for rehabilitation purposes after the Second World War. The most famous example is the initiative of Ludwig Guttmann, an English doctor at Stoke Mandeville military hospital, who prescribed sport for soldiers with paraplegia. In the Federal Republic of Germany former soldiers with disabilities stemming from the war founded sport groups which amalgamated in 1951 to form an association which became the German Disabled War Veterans Sports Association in 1952. Similar organisations were established in many other countries.

Since the 1950s the medical orientation of sports for persons with a disability has increasingly been supplemented by goals and content taken from pedagogy and sport. At the same time, the range of target groups has extended, with a greater differentiation being made between the groups

themselves. Thus, more and more people with different congenital or acquired impairments and disabilities have been playing sports alongside former soldiers who have war-related disabilities. In addition, distinctions are made between physical disabilities, sensory impairments, mental and learning disabilities, and chronic diseases such as multiple sclerosis or asthma.

Provision and goals

Today people with disabilities take part in numerous kinds of sport, in a variety of contexts, one of these being general sport clubs which offer specific programmes for different target groups. Sport clubs for persons with disabilities are regulated by their corresponding national associations. In Germany, more than 300,000 people with disabilities belong to some 3,400 clubs, participating in sports under the guidance of specially qualified trainers and coaches.

As in sport generally, the aim of recreational sports and 'sport for all' is: to sustain and improve the body's physical functioning as well as personal well-being; to convey a positive self-image and attitude towards one's body; and to encourage the establishment of social relationships and networks.

The sports played by people with disabilities depend to a large extent on the kind of disability they have, although, in principle, no type of sport can be regarded as unsuitable. Nonetheless, the rules as well as the apparatus must be adapted to their needs. In addition, clubs may provide specific sports – often variations of well-known disciplines – that are almost exclusively played by people with disabilities, such as sitting volleyball and goalball.

Sport for persons with a disability also includes a great variety of measures for the rehabilitation of the chronically sick, with the aim of re-integrating them into social and working life. These measures are designed to help people with heart and

359

circulatory disorders, for example, or those with anatomic or neurological illnesses. In addition, physical therapy is carried out in health centres and clinics in the rehabilitation of numerous diseases, for instance after breast cancer operations. Here, besides the psycho-social objectives, the main aims are to compensate for motor skill deficits and restore the ability to 'function' in every day life.

Also belonging to sport for persons with a disability in a broader sense is the concept of 'moto-pedagogy', which attempts to influence personality through processes of psychomotor learning and to stabilise children with severe behavioural problems by means of game-like exercises.

Competitive sport

Sport can involve the holding of contests and the comparison of performances, and this also applies to sport for athletes with a disability. In competitive sports, disabilities play an important role according to the capacities demanded of the contestants by the different disciplines. As early as 1948, Ludwig Guttmann organised the first sporting contests for persons with a disability at Stoke Mandeville and proposed that international competitions for disabled athletes be held every four years. He succeeded in having his idea put into practice: in 1960, at the end of the Olympic Games in Rome, the first Paralympics took place, where the prefix 'para' stands for 'parallel'. Thus, the Paralympic Summer Games have been held since 1960 and, since 1976, Winter Games have also taken place for athletes with disabilities. The aim of these Games is to give athletes with disabilities the same opportunities and experiences as 'able bodied' athletes.

Since 1950, numerous international associations have been founded to look after the interests of various groups of people with disabilities, but it was not until 1989 that an umbrella organisation, the International Paralympic Committee, was set up to regulate international sports for the disabled.

The rapid rise of the Paralympic movement, which has also been reflected in increasing academic interest, has brought key issues of sport for the disabled into the focus of public attention. Serious difficulties for athletes with disabilities are posed in particular by the classification system, which should be designed to guarantee fair starting conditions for the contestants. A further problem area concerns the relatively low prestige of sports for persons with a disability, which finds expression in the lack of funding as well as the lack of media interest. Funding is essential, not the least due to the increasing use of technology in disability sports, such as in the development of sophisticated artificial limbs and wheelchairs, but it is leading to ever greater financial burdens for both athletes and associations, in particular, for athletes from developing countries.

While highly motivated athletes take part in the Paralympics after lots of hard training, the Special Olympics are aimed at persons with intellectual disabilities, some of whom have low performance levels and often only a limited understanding of sport contests and their rules. The first international Special Olympics were held in Chicago in 1968 at the suggestion of Eunice Kennedy-Shriver, and since that time have developed into a world-wide movement. Besides international Summer and Winter Games, which take place every two years, regional and national Special Olympics are held at which the coming together of people with and without disabilities is more important than athletic performance. But Special Olympics can also support segregation tendencies and may place too much emphasis on disablement.

References

Collins, M. and Kay, T. (2003) *Sport and Social Exclusion*, London: Routledge.

DePauw, K. and Gavron, S. (1995) *Disability and Sport*, Champaign IL: Human Kinetics.

Doll-Tepper, G. (1999) 'Disability Sport', in J. Riordan and A. Krüger (eds) *The International Politics of Sport in the 20th Century*, 177–90, London: E&FN Spon.

Nixon, H.L. II (2000) 'Sport and Disability', in J. Coakley and E. Dunning (eds) *Handbook of Sports Studies*, 422–39, London: Sage.

GERTRUD PFISTER

DISCOID LATERAL MENISCUS IN CHILDREN

The normal lateral meniscus resembles a crescent moon in shape, but during development some lateral menisci become thickened and shaped like a round saucer rather than a crescent. Abnormal shape development is generally attributed to lateral meniscus hypermobility. The discoid meniscus tears more readily than normal menisci. Symptomatic or torn menisci can be partially removed and the remaining tissue sculpted to function as much as possible like a normal meniscus. Complete excision leads to premature osteoarthritis.

Meniscal hypermobility may result from congenitally lax knee ligaments or deficient posterior attachment of the lateral meniscus to the knee capsule. Discoid lateral menisci have never been reported in fetuses or infants, but children as young as two years of age have required surgery for symptomatic discoid lateral menisci. Although discoid medial menisci have been reported, the discoid lateral meniscus is found far more frequently. The thick. discoid meniscus tears more readily than a normal meniscus, often in a horizontal cleavage pattern. A palpable, tender, lateral meniscal cyst may occur when joint fluid leaks through the torn meniscus into the cyst. The cyst may change in size depending on the patient's activity level.

Children under the age of five years generally have one of two presentations of discoid lateral meniscus. Some children sit in the 'W' position with their knees in front of them and their buttocks on the floor between their heels. In this position, the lateral femoral condyle subluxates or even dislocates from its corresponding tibial plateau. The knee may become stuck in this position, and the child will have pain until the tibia and its attached discoid lateral meniscus can be reduced back under the lateral femoral condyle. A palpable or audible 'clunk' accompanies reduction. Children with this presentation are typically very loose-jointed, and both the dislocation and the reduction occur with minimal force. The knee rarely swells following these episodes, but the child may limp for up to a few hours following an episode. Most children seem to outgrow this problem as joint laxity naturally decreases with age.

For some young children the presenting symptom of discoid lateral meniscus is incomplete extension of the knee compared with the opposite side. A parent may report that the knee appears to give way, causing the child to fall. A painful limp lasts just a few minutes or a few hours and the child then appears normal. The knee may not fill with fluid following these episodes, but it often becomes chronically mildly enlarged, in a fusiform shape compared with the normal knee. The older prepubertal child's presenting symptoms are also usually lack of full extension and mild knee swelling, but chronic mild pain that is made worse with the giving way episodes is more typical in the older child. The differential diagnosis also includes arthritis and infection.

Older children and adolescents are more likely to present with a symptomatic, torn, discoid meniscus following relatively trivial trauma such as rotation through a hyperflexed knee. Usually there are several traumatic episodes before the young person seeks medical attention. By then the knee often has a small effusion, lacks full extension, and perhaps even lacks full flexion. The lateral joint line is tender. Flexion-rotation testing such as McMurray's tests traps or compresses the injured meniscus between the femoral condyle and the tibial plateau. In the case of a horizontal cleavage tear, the femoral aspect of the meniscus may become prominent anteriorly as the flexion-rotation testing is performed and then suddenly flatten back down as the joint is reduced. The separated superior or inferior leaflet may tear through to the articular surface, causing further catching and pain.

Plain radiographs may show flattening of the lateral femoral condyle and the lateral tibial plateau, and loss of the normal peak of the lateral tibial spine. The lateral joint space may appear widened. Remember when evaluating comparison views of the opposite knee that the condition is often bilateral! Magnetic resonance imaging has high specificity for discoid lateral meniscus, with the meniscus crossing the entire lateral compartment for too many scan slices. However, sensitivity is poor, especially in children.

Most people with discoid lateral menisci never know they have them and never require surgical intervention. However, symptoms may limit sports and even normal walking. Non-operative measures have not proven effective in restoring lost knee extension or function. The recommended surgical approach is arthroscopic partial meniscectomy. The surgeon sculpts a meniscal rim with a width of approximately 3–5 mm. Even if a cleavage tear extends all the way to the menisco-capsular junction, healing over of the peripheral portion of these tears can be found on subsequent arthroscopy. Total lateral meniscectomy should be avoided, as it leads to premature and severe osteoarthritis of the lateral compartment. If the posterior meniscus is unstable, it should be secured to the adjacent posterior knee capsule. Drainage and repair of a lateral meniscal cyst may require a limited open approach.

See also: meniscus injury

ANGELA D. SMITH

DISCOURSE

In discourse, language is conceived not simply as a tool for description and communication – language as an abstract entity such as lexicon and set of grammatical rules (linguistics) – but as a social practice, therefore, it has to be understood in relation to social problems, e.g. racism, gender, and class, as well as other sets of rules derived from people's shared narratives, meaning systems, signs, and symbols, described in discourse analysis as the features of language use. Consequently, discourse analysis, which focuses in studying discourse as text and talk in social practices, aims at analysing discursive strategies that we employ in different social environments (e.g. media, family, political institutions) in order to establish multiple realities or remaking(s) of the world. Thus, the task of discourse analysis is not applying pre-existing categories to participants talk, but rather to identify the ways in which participants (themselves) produce, construct and employ concepts, arguments, and meanings. According to Wood and Kroger (2000) discourse analysts take nothing for granted and question everything, including their own categories and assumptions. The aim is to go beyond content to see how discourse is used purposefully or not to achieve particular functions and effects, that is, to see the way the world is socially constructed based on multiple and relative realities, rather than a singular reality. Moreover, discourse analysis seeks to unmask ideologically often obscured structures of power, political control, and dominance, given that the discourse we use usually serves to reinforce our interests, positions, and privileges.

Discourse analysis is usually used to analyse transcripts of talk from everyday institutional settings, transcripts of open-ended interviews or a document of some kind. Part of discourse analysis may involve coding a set of materials, but this is an analytic preliminary used to make the quantity of materials more manageable rather than a procedure that performs the analysis itself (Silverman 1998:158). Analytical concepts and categories related to contents, features, and structures might be used to help the researcher in finding what to look for during the analysis functions (Wood and Kroger 2000: 99).

Discourse on sport has proved fertile ground for discussion of the communication of interests relating to gender, 'race', and religious and political world-views. Discourse analysis is becoming widely used by social scientists who are taking post-modernist and postfeminist positions to analyse the concept of male-white dominance and the impact that this dominance can have on the general discourse about sport as a mode of practice and field of study. Discourse analysis is also used by linking sport, post-colonial and media studies to analyse how concepts such as the 'national identity' of elite athletes are depicted in the media discourse to describe 'our' nation's creativity and success in relation to 'their' (other nations) failure; or the impact that political discourse (e.g. opening ceremonies and speeches) can have in the construction of meanings around the staging of international sporting competitions. Discourse analysis is also used to investigate sport policies, particularly the manner in which policy-makers are constructing through their language use a rationale behind the application of sport policies (at local, regional, and national levels). For instance, the professionalisation of sport; the use of sport as a tool for social inclusion in deprived areas; the utilisation of sport to develop multiculturalism and intercultural understanding among youth in the society and across nations; the employment of sport for urban regeneration.

References

Flick, U. (1998). *An Introduction to Qualitative Research*, London: Sage.

Silverman, D. (ed.) (1998) *Qualitative Research: Theory, Method and Practice*, London: Sage.

Wood, L.A. and Kroger, R.O. (2000) *Doing Discourse Analysis: Method for Studying Action in Talk and Text*, London: Sage.

MAHFOUD AMARA

DISLOCATION

Joints have the important function of providing locomotion for the human skeleton. The joints are therefore flexible to allow a range of movement that is needed to perform various movements. Although the joints have some inherent stability, they can dislocate depending upon the force of trauma.

Dislocation means the displacement of the joint from its original position. The more flexible the joints are the less stability they have. The shoulder joint is the most flexible, with a wide range of movement in all directions. It is there fore the most common joint to be dislocated. In contrast, the knee joint has a range of movement in one direction. It is therefore a constrained joint with very low incidence of dislocation.

Joints are either ball and socket or hinged. The hip joint is a ball and socket, like the shoulder joint, but it is much more stable than the shoulder and therefore has a lower incidence of dislocation. The joints have static and dynamic stabilizers. The static stabilizers include include the bony anatomy of the joint, the attached ligaments, whereas the dynamic stabilizers are the surrounding muscles.

The dislocations occur mainly as a traumatic event. This could be the result of a high-energy force or any abnormal force that is applied to a joint in a vulnerable position. There are other conditions where there is generalized laxity and shoulder dislocations occur with minimal or no trauma at all.

Dislocation of the shoulder occurs in the abduction external rotation position when an anteriorly directed force can dislocate the shoulder anteriorly. Similarly, a posteriorly directed force on a flexed hip can dislocate the hip joint posteriorly. This is seen in road traffic accidents when the knees hit the dashboard of the car and an axial force is directed longitudinally to the hip joint, which pushes the joint out of the socket. This type of dislocation is usually associated with fracture of the ipsilateral femur. Other joints that are frequently dislocated are the small joints of the hand, mainly the interphalyngeal joints. The knee and the elbow dislocate less commonly. Knee dislocation is a very serious injury, with a very high incidence of neurovascular injury.

Patients present with pain and obvious deformity. There may be associated bone fracture. A clinical examination should carefully assess the soft tissue cover and the neurovascular status; for example, in the anterior dislocation there is a possibility of damage to the axillary nerve, which can cause dysaesthesia over the upper arm, and weakness of the deltoid function. Dislocation of the hip joint can result in sciatic nerve palsy. Radiographic assessment picks up the dislocation with ease, and different views of the joint are taken to ascertain the direction of dislocation and the associated fractures.

Dislocations should be reduced as early as possible to relieve pain, but also to lessen any risk of injury to the neurovascular structure. In the case of hip dislocation the femoral head is at risk of developing avascular necrosis as the blood supply to the femoral head is compromised; therefore the dislocation should be reduced within six hours of dislocation. Even if the femoral head is reduced, the risk of avascular necrosis remains and patients should be made aware of this.

Dislocations can be reduced either under local anesthesia or general anesthesia. In young, muscular individuals general anesthesia is frequently required for complete relaxation. Further radiographs are taken once the joint is relocated to make sure that the attempt has been successful. Patients then undergo a period of rehabilitation. In younger patients with shoulder dislocations there is high risk of recurrent dislocation, and operative treatment is quite often necessary.

IMRAN ILYAS

DISTANCE DECAY

In the context of sport, the term 'distance decay' is used to refer to the tendency for the level of use of a sporting facility, as a proportion of the resident population, to fall with distance from the facility. This has been observed in relation to a number of types of recreational facility. The phenomenon 'makes sense', since the cost of travelling to the facility, in terms of both time, money, and effort, generally increases with distance, so it is not surprising to find that a smaller and smaller proportion of the population is willing or able to expend the requisite time, money, and effort to visit a facility as travel distance and travel time increases. As the distance and associated time and money costs increase, the costs of the visit begin to outweigh the benefits for more and more people. For some, the constraint may not be costs as such, but the absolute amount of time available in a given period, so that it may not be possible to make the round trip to visit the facility in the time available. It should be noted that it is the *visit rate* which falls with distance, not necessarily the number of visits. The visit rate is the number of visits per 100 population for a given time-period, such as a week. If we imagine concentric rings around the facility, the area of the rings increases with distance and so the number of people living in each ring may increase with distance, depending on the population density. The relationship between the visit rate and the distance from the facility may display a systematic pattern – for example, the visit rate might be found to fall by half as the distance doubles. Such relationships have been used as the basis for development of the gravity model.

A.J. VEAL

DIURETICS

Diuretics are drugs that potentiate urinary excretion of fluids and electrolytes and have legitimate medical uses in the treatment of congestive heart failure and hypertension. There are more advantageous drugs and it would rarely, if ever, be necessary to use diuretics therapeutically in an athlete. In reality, athletes use diuretics for the following reasons: (1) in order to qualify for weight-class limits (e.g. boxing, wrestling, etc.); (2) to reduce weight in sports where thinness is rewarded (e.g. figure skating, gymnastics); (3) to alter urinary excretion rates and/or concentrations of banned substances to avoid a drug test; and (4) to attenuate fluid retention associated with other drugs (e.g. anabolic steroids). All of these reasons circumvent the rules of sport and account for the ban on diuretics by most sports organizations.

Although grouped as a class by its effects, the mechanism of action differs among various types of diuretics. There are osmotic diuretics, e.g. mannitol, which increases urination by delivering an osmotic load to the kidneys. Carbonic anhydrase inhibitors act at the proximal tubule and increase urination, as well as urinary acidification. Although drugs in this category, such as acetazolamide, are weak diuretics, they can be useful for the treatment and prevention of acute mountain sickness. The thiazides act primarily on the distal tubule of the nephron and reduce sodium reabsorption, leading to diuresis and natriuresis. Another class of diuretics that work at the distal tubule are those that spare potassium. The most powerful are the loop diuretics, e.g.

furosemide, which can dramatically reduce renal concentrating ability. Finally, there is the case of probenecid, an uricosoric agent for gout treatment, which delays excretion of many compounds. Although this latter property was previously used to extend the half-life of penicillin therapy, it has been used by athletes to delay excretion of (and thus mask) anabolic steroids.

Used improperly, diuretic use can have serious consequences. Even under careful supervision for true medical indications, diuretics have a high incidence of electrolyte imbalances, such as hypokalemia. In athletes, diuretics can cause significant hypovolemia, hypotension, muscle cramping and disturbances of magnesium, sodium, potassium, and calcium. Not only does dehydration impede performance, it is a well known risk factor for the development of heat illness. An athlete attempting to rapidly lose weight in order to qualify for a weight class may use diuretics, intense exercise, saunas or steam rooms, rubber suits, and stimulants in a potentially dangerous combination. Indeed, studies of wrestlers, lightweight football players and rowers have revealed a significant incidence of diuretic use in order to 'make weight'.

As stated previously, athletes usually use diuretics to either mask the presence of ergogenic drugs or circumvent the rules of a sport, despite their negative effects on performance. The athlete makes a conscious decision that the damaging effects of the diuretic will be outweighed by the advantage of using an anabolic steroid or competing at a lower weight class. Indeed, many studies have documented the disadvantages of volume depletion and performance is clearly reduced with diuretic use.

In addition to health concerns, diuretics are banned because they can be used to manipulate urine samples. Under drug testing codes, **manipulation of samples** is considered a positive test and using a diuretic to mask a banned drug falls under this provision. Effective drug testing can detect most diuretics by a combination of liquid chromatography-tandem mass spectrometry and should be able to detect their presence for up to four days after ingestion.

GARY GREEN

DOPING, HISTORY OF

When humans compete – either in war, business, or sport – the competitors seek to achieve an advantage over their opponent. Frequently they have used drugs to gain the upper hand. However, throughout much of history, drug use to improve athletic performance was not considered cheating. It was openly viewed as standard practice and it was not until after World War I that there was any widespread attempt to admonish doping in sport or consider it a formal rules violation.

Historically, use of performance-enhancing drugs has focused primarily on either increasing strength or overcoming fatigue. The ancients empirically derived the anabolic (muscle building) function of the testes by observing the effects of castration on domesticated animals. The use of stimulants also dates to ancient times. The Greeks drank brandy and wine concoctions and ate hallucinogenic mushrooms and sesame seeds to enhance performance; and likewise, Roman gladiators used stimulants to improve battle stamina.

The last half of the nineteenth century saw the beginnings of modern medicine and, not coincidentally, significant growth the use of drugs to improve performance. While the primary emphasis was on stimulants as ergogenic aids, this period also marked the birth of scientific experimentation with the anabolic effects of hormones. During this period stimulant use among athletes was commonplace, and there was no attempt to conceal drug use. Swimmers, distance runners, sprinters, and cyclists used a wide assortment of drugs including, ether,

alcohol, caffeine, cocaine, nitroglycerine, and even strychnine.

During the first three decades of the twentieth century athletes continued to use a variety of substances for their purported 'stimulant' effects. However, noticeably absent is any mention of the use of amphetamines, although they were first synthesized in 1887. It was not until the mid-1930s that amphetamines were identified as a central nervous system stimulant. At the time, amphetamines were publicized as 'a means of dissipating mental fog' and were thereafter adopted by college students and truck drivers 'to ward off sleep and clear their minds'.

The first systematic uses of amphetamines as an ergogenic aid were seen during World War II, when both Axis and Allied powers used these drugs to combat fatigue, improve endurance, or perhaps to create a sense of fearlessness.

The use of 'pep pills' by prewar college students, combined with the experiences of servicemen, appears to have introduced amphetamines to professional and amateur athletes at the end of World War II. By the late 1960s there was solid evidence of amphetamine use in a variety of sports, including auto racing, basketball, baseball, boxing, cycling, football, rugby, skating, skiing, soccer, squash, swimming, tennis, track and field, weightlifting, and wrestling.

World attention focused on amphetamine use during the 1960 Summer Olympics when Knud Jensen, a Danish cyclist, collapsed during competition and died. Autopsy results revealed the presence of amphetamines. Subsequently, during the 1967 Tour de France, the English cyclist Tom Simpson collapsed and died. His autopsy showed high levels of methamphetamine, a vial of which had been found in his pocket at the time of his death. The impact of Simpson's death was extensive, because this was the first doping death to be televised. His death substantially added to the mounting pressure on the International

Olympic Committee (IOC) and member federations to move beyond 'anti-doping codes' and actually establish drug testing programs, which they did at the end of 1967.

The age of anabolics began in 1889 when seventy-two-year-old Charles Edouard Brown-Sequard, a prominent physiologist and neurologist, self-administered injections containing 'first, blood of the testicular veins; secondly, semen; and thirdly, juice extracted from a testicle ... from a dog or guinea pig'. He enthusiastically described 'radical' changes in his health including significant improvements in physical and mental energy. While today most experts believe the 'rejuvenation' experienced by Brown-Sequard was a result of the placebo effect, he demonstrated a rudimentary understanding of testicular function and presaged the potential value of hormonal replacement or supplementation therapy.

The origins of systematic use of anabolic steroids in sport have been attributed to their successful use by Soviet weightlifting teams in the early 1950s. Thereafter, Dr John Ziegler, a US team physician, returned to the United States and experimented with testosterone, and later with an anabolic steroid, on himself and a few weightlifters in the York Barbell Club. Several of these weightlifters achieved championship status, and word-of-mouth stories of the efficacy of steroids spread by the early 1960s to other strength-intensive sports, such as field events and American football.

As is the case with other sports around the world, there have been numerous doping scandals in American professional sports over the past six decades, involving primarily the use of stimulants and anabolics. Amphetamine use appeared in the National Football League (NFL) immediately after World War II. The use of amphetamines became so extensive that the term 'Sunday Syndrome' was coined by a team doctor to describe the withdrawal symptoms following games.

Following their initiation of (anabolic) steroid use by weightlifters and throwers in the early 1960s, American football players began to incorporate these drugs into their training regimens. In 1963 the San Diego Chargers placed Dianabol (a popular anabolic steroid of the era) on the training table. It is fair to assume that trades, coaching changes and word-of-mouth interaction among football players and other strength athletes further facilitated the diffusion of steroid use throughout the NFL. Continued speculation of epidemic levels of drug use, including human growth hormone, has been fueled further by a dramatic increase in the size of NFL players, from quarterbacks to offensive linemen. In 1987 only twenty-seven NFL players weighed more than 300 pounds, while in 1997 there were approximately 240 players over 300 pounds.

Amphetamine use in baseball started in the early 1960s, if not earlier. In professional baseball, amphetamines are not used to increase endurance as in cycling or to heighten aggressiveness as in football, but often to deal with the monotony and strain of a long season and numerous road trips.

As with football, the size and strength of professional baseball players appears to have increased markedly during the past fifteen years. As a consequence, fears of steroid use dramatically escalated during the 1990s.

In recent years, several current and former MLB players publicly estimated anabolic steroid use at well over 50 per cent. Although these figures are unsubstantiated, they likely reflect significant anabolic steroid use in this sport.

Cycling plays a central role in the history of doping. In 1879, 'Six Day' bicycle races began, each race proceeding continuously, day and night, for 144 hours. It is not surprising that stimulants and a variety of doping strategies were employed in these grueling contests of prolonged athletic exertion, including sugar cubes dipped in ether, alcohol-containing cordials, and even nitroglycerine. Other cyclists of the day used coffee 'spiked' with caffeine; and as the race progressed, they would add increasing doses of cocaine and strychnine.

After World War II, cycling competitions of that era were described as 'special hotbeds of doping'. In 1967 Jacques Anquetil, a five-time winner of the Tour de France, stated:

> For 50 years bike racers have been taking stimulants. Obviously we can do without them in a race, but then we will pedal 15 miles an hour [instead of 25]. Since we are constantly asked to go faster and to make even greater efforts, we are obliged to take stimulants.

The past forty years of doping in cycling has been described as the three drug eras of the sport: amphetamines in the 1960s and 1970s, anabolic steroids and cortisone in the 1980s, and, thereafter, human growth hormone (hGH) and erythropoietin (EPO).

The breadth and depth of the level of doping in the cycling world was exposed to full public view in the 1998 Tour de France when French customs police arrested a cycling team trainer for transporting performance-enhancing drugs. A subsequent investigation by French and Italian authorities implicated many of the top teams and riders in the sport as part of a highly organized, sophisticated, and long-lived doping scheme.

While modern Olympic athletes were using stimulants such as strychnine as early as 1904, anabolic steroid use did not become a major problem until the 1960s when strength athletes in weightlifting and the throwing events began to use them extensively. By the late 1960s, athletes in a number of track events were using stimulants and steroids.

During the 1976 Summer Olympic Games, blood doping, for the purpose of enhancing endurance performance, first came to the attention of the lay public when it

was alleged that several distance runners had used blood doping to achieve victory.

In 1984, at the Los Angeles Olympic Games, the use of hGH to increase strength, beta-blockers to reduce anxiety and muscle tremor, and blood doping were popular among athletes. While two weightlifters tested positive for diuretic use to reduce weight during the 1988 Seoul Olympics, the big story of the those games was Ben Johnson, winner of the 100-meter dash, testing positive for anabolic steroid use.

During the 1990s, all types of performance-enhancing substances, including erythropoietin (EPO), were being used in numerous Olympic sports, from cycling to distance running. Today there is increasing concern of designer drugs (such as THG, used to circumvent drug testing) and growing fear that gene transfer therapy may soon become the performance-enhancing technique of the new millennium.

National doping programs transcend the all-too-common informal collusion of elite athletes with coaches, rogue physicians and sport scientists to use performance-enhancing drugs. Rather they are constituted under the direction or strong support of government and sport federation officials, as well as with the active collaboration of mainstream- physicians and scientists.

Such was the case in the German Democratic Republic (GDR), where files of the Ministry of State Security ('Stasi') provided significant detail of the activities of the sport doping system that began in 1966. According to published reports, physicians and top scientists performed doping research and they administered these drugs to thousands of athletes, including children of fourteen years of age or younger, often without the knowledge of the athlete or their parents. Special emphasis was placed on administering androgens to women and adolescent girls as this proved particularly effective for sport performance.

In addition, it is reasonable to conclude that similar organized sport doping programs existed in the Soviet Union and other Soviet bloc countries. There is evidence that as early as 1945 the Soviet government held formal discussions regarding the viability of doping in sport (stimulants) and that by 1954 the Soviets were systematically using testosterone in weightlifting and thereafter in other sports.

Following the fall of European Communism, many East German coaches relocated and a number of them began working in China's sport programs. The Chinese established the National Research Institute, a high-performance sport science laboratory that appears to parallel the GDR's Research Institute for Physical Culture and Sports in Leipzig. Shortly thereafter, Chinese female athletes moved from a position of relative obscurity to world dominance, especially in swimming, track and field, and weightlifting.

Looking at elite sport in the twentieth century through the eyes of historians and journalists as well as the athletes themselves, an unmistakable picture emerges of a sustained doping pandemic of huge proportions in elite sport. A number of sport federations for decades have covered up the doping problem, conveniently looked the other way, or instituted drug-testing programs that were doomed to fail. When the Dubin commission – formed in Canada after the sprinter Ben Johnson's positive steroid test in 1988 – investigated the extent of doping in Olympic sport, it referred to a 'conspiracy of silence' and a 'pact of ignorance' among those in sport organizations when it came to discussing drug use.

Further reading

Bahrke, M. and Yesalis, C. (eds) (2002) *Performance Enhancing Substances in Sport and Exercise*, Champaign IL: Human Kinetics.

Courson, S. (1991) *False Glory*, Stamford CT: Longmeadow Press.

Hoberman, J. (1992) *Mortal Engines*, New York: Free Press.

Francis, C. (1990) *Speed Trap*, New York: St Martin's Press.

Franke, W. and Berendonk, B. (1997) 'Hormonal Doping and Androgenization of Athletes: A Secret Program of the German Democratic Republic Government', *Clinical Chemistry* 43, 7: 1262–79.

Mandell, A. (1976) *The Nightmare Season*, New York: Random House.

Voy, R. (1991) *Drugs, Sport, and Politics*, Champaign IL: Leisure Press.

Wilson, W. and Derse, E. (eds) (2001) *Doping in Elite Sport*, Champaign IL: Human Kinetics.

CHARLES E. YESALIS
MICHAEL S. BAHRKE

DRAG FORCES – PRESSURE, SKIN FRICTION, AND WAVE DRAG

If an object is symmetrical with respect to the fluid flow past, such as a non-spinning soccer ball, the fluid dynamic force acts in the direction opposite from the motion of the object and is termed a drag force. Drag forces resist motion and, therefore, generally restrict sports performance. They can have beneficial propulsive effects, as in swimming and rowing. To maintain a runner in motion at a constant speed against a drag force requires an expenditure of energy equal to the product of the drag force and the speed. If no such energy is present, as for a projectile, the object will decelerate at a rate proportional to its frontal area A – the area presented to the fluid flow – and inversely proportional to its mass m. The ratio m/A is crucial in determining how much effect air resistance has on projectile motion. A shot, with a very high ratio of m/A, is hardly affected by air resistance whereas a cricket ball, with only 1/16th the value of m/A of the shot, is more affected. A table tennis ball, with 1/250th the value of m/A of the shot has a greatly altered trajectory.

Pressure drag

Pressure drag – or wake drag – contributes to the fluid resistance experienced by, for

369

example, projectiles and runners. This is the major drag force in most sports and is caused by **boundary layer separation** leaving a low-pressure wake behind the object. The object, tending to move from a low-to a high-pressure region, experiences a drag force. Minimising the disturbance that the object causes to the fluid flow, a process known as streamlining, can reduce the pressure drag. An oval shape, like a rugby ball, has only two-thirds of the drag of a spherical ball with the same frontal area. The drag is very small on a stream-lined aerofoil shape. Streamlining is impor-tant in motor car and motorcycle racing, and discus and javelin throwing. Swimmers and skiers can reduce the pressure drag forces acting on them by adopting stream-lined shapes. The adoption of a streamlined shape is of considerable advantage to downhill skiers.

To enable comparisons to be made between objects of similar geometry, it is conventional to plot graphs of drag coeffi-cient (C_D), that is the drag force (D) divi-ded by the product of the frontal area of the body (A) and the free stream dynamic pressure ($\rho v^2/2$), where ρ is the density of the fluid, against Reynolds number (see also **non-dimensional groups**), which is proportional to the speed (v) of the object through the fluid. Such graphs show a dra-matic change in the drag coefficient on a smooth ball as the **boundary layer** flow changes from laminar to turbulent. As this transition occurs, the drag coefficient decreases by about 65 per cent with no change of speed. This occurs at the critical Reynolds number. Promoting a turbulent boundary layer is an important mechanism in reducing pressure drag if the speed is close to that necessary to achieve the cri-tical Reynolds number. At such speeds, which are common in ball sports, rough-ening the surface promotes turbulence in the boundary layer. The decrease in drag coefficient then occurs over a wider speed range and starts at a lower speed. The nap

of tennis balls, the dimples on a golf ball, and the seam on a cricket ball are examples of roughness helping to induce boundary layer transition, thereby reducing drag. Within the Reynolds number range 110,000–175,000, which corresponds to ball speeds off the tee of 45–70 m s^{-1}, the dimples on a golf ball cause the drag coefficient to decrease proportionally to speed. The drag force then increases only proportionally to speed, rather than speed squared, benefiting the hard-hitting player. Many sport balls are not uniformly rough. Then, within a speed range somewhat below the critical Rey-nolds number, it is possible for roughness elements on one part of the ball to stimulate transition of the boundary layer to turbu-lent flow, while the boundary layer flow on the smoother portion of the ball remains laminar.

Skin friction drag

Skin friction drag is the force caused by friction between the molecules of fluid and a solid boundary. It is only important for streamlined bodies for which separation and, hence, pressure drag has been mini-mised. Unlike pressure drag, skin friction drag is reduced by having a laminar as opposed to a turbulent boundary layer. This occurs because the rate of shear at the solid boundary is greater for turbulent flow. Reduction of skin friction drag is an important consideration for racing cars, racing motor cycles, gliders, hulls of boats, skiers and ski-jumpers, and, perhaps, swimmers. It is minimised by reducing the roughness of the surfaces in contact with the fluid.

Wave drag

This occurs only in sports in which an object moves through both water and air. As the object moves through the water, the pressure differences at the boundary cause the water level to rise and fall and waves are generated. The energy of the waves is provided by the object, which experiences a resistance to its motion. The greater the speed of the body, the larger is the wave drag, which is important in most aquatic sports. Wave drag also depends on the wave patterns generated and the dimensions of the object, particularly its waterline length. The drag is often expressed as a function of the Froude number. Speedboats and racing yachts are designed to plane – to ride high in the water – at their highest speeds so that wave drag – and pressure drag – are very small. In swimming, the wave drag is small compared with the pressure drag, unless the swimmer's speed is above about $1.6\,\mathrm{m\,s}^{-1}$ when a bow wave is formed. The design of racing yacht hulls to optimise drag and lift forces has now become very sophisticated.

Other forms of drag

Spray-making drag occurs in some water sports because of the energy involved in generating spray. It is usually negligible, except perhaps during high-speed turns in surfing and windsurfing. Induced drag arises from a three-dimensional object that is generating lift. It can be minimised by having a large aspect ratio – the ratio of the dimension of the object perpendicular to the flow direction to the dimension along the flow direction. Long, thin wings on gliders minimise the induced drag, whereas a javelin has entirely the wrong shape for this purpose.

See also: aerodynamics of sails; hydrodynamics of boat hulls; hydrodynamics of oars; javelin and discus aerodynamics; laminar and turbulent flow

Further reading

Bartlett, R.M. (1997) *Introduction to Sports Biomechanics*, ch. 4, London: E&FN Spon.

ROGER BARTLETT

DRUG EDUCATION

Although **drug testing** is a high-profile topic, drug education is a necessity for any sports organization that promotes a drug-free environment. In order to be effective, drug education must account for the 3 categories of drug use by athletes, i.e. recreational, ergogenic and therapeutic. An educational component must reflect the fact that an athlete's decision to use marijuana (see **cannabinoids**) is very different from the decision to use anabolic steroids (see **anabolic-androgenic steroids**). Just as the athlete has distinctive goals in using various drugs, the educational program should be tailored to those needs.

Educational programs have mainly focused on deterrence of recreational drug use. This is often fostered by either a paternalistic notion or a goal of ensuring optimum performance by players. Education in this area should focus on the negative performance effects of most of these drugs. Although not tested in most programs, alcohol (see **alcohol – doping and nutrition**; **alcohol – social science**) is clearly the leading recreational drug of abuse and responsible for most of the adverse consequences. In addition to educating athletes about their ergolytic effects, it is important to teach decision-making skills. In most cases, the long-term damage from recreational drugs is not from their direct pharmacologic effects, it is from the collateral damage of impaired judgment, e.g. driving while intoxicated, unwanted sexual activity, physical violence, etc. Since it is impossible to educate athletes about every potential drug and situation, guidance in decision-making skills is imperative.

One effective method of recreational drug education is the team as a positive peer group. The author has found that teams can be trained to set normative behavior and acceptable standards that are agreed to by the team itself. Compliance is more likely if the rules come from the team, rather than the coach, and teams often erect more stringent regulations than coaches. One successful approach has been to train selected team members as mentors in the areas of decision-making and drug use. The mentors act as the first line of education and awareness and can be instrumental in affecting change.

Education for therapeutic drugs focuses on awareness of therapeutic alternatives and of which drugs are banned. Further, athletes need to keep their team physicians informed of all therapeutic drugs, both over-the-counter and prescription, in order to avoid running afoul of drug testing. In addition, many drugs in this class can have negative effects on performance and physicians need to be aware of alternatives. For example, a beta blocker (see **beta-blockers**) may be an accepted treatment for hypertension, but would significantly decrease performance and an angiotension converting enzyme inhibitor might be a better choice in an athlete. The consequences were demonstrated by the Romanian gymnast in the 2000 Summer Olympics who lost her medal as a result of ingesting pseudoephedrine. Although the pseudoephedrine was dispensed by her physician, it is ultimately the athlete's responsibility for their urine sample.

Perhaps the most difficult area to address in terms of education is ergogenic drugs. Most of these drugs have low abuse potential, i.e. they are unlikely to result in tolerance and addiction. They are also unlikely to have short-term adverse effects or result in negative social, financial, or legal problems. As opposed to recreational drugs like cocaine, ergogenic drug use will rarely produce the type of symptoms that would bring an individual to a physician for treatment. In fact, just the opposite usually occurs. For example, the use of anabolic steroids can cause a professional athlete to perform better, make more money and become more famous. How then can athletes be deterred from their use by education?

Surveys of why athletes don't use performance-enhancing drugs have yielded useful information for drug education. The most common response is that it is against one's beliefs, i.e. ergogenic drug use constitutes cheating. While it may sound naive, clearly stating the position that performance-enhancing drugs violate the spirit of fair competition can be effective. Even if it only serves to reinforce those who already hold that position, drug use may be curtailed. When a clean athlete is confronted with an uncontrolled culture of ergogenic drug use, he/she has three options: (1) compete at a competitive disadvantage; (2) decide to use drugs; or (3) quit the sport. None of these are attractive options, and the more athletes who believe it is unethical to use banned drugs, the more likely the culture will change.

In addition to clear messages on the use of banned substances, educational programs can provide alternatives. Goldberg *et al.* launched the ATLAS program that combined mentors with accurate drug information and alternatives to anabolic steroids in high-school students. Unfortunately, the large degree of positive reinforcement that results from ergogenic drug use ultimately requires drug testing and punitive sanctions to deter use. Indeed, some purely educational programs on anabolic steroids have demonstrated increases in drug use.

As an adjunct to drug testing, education at a minimum should inform athletes of a sport's banned drug list, organizational drug policies and the consequences of a positive test. It is unfair to expect an athlete to comply with a testing program and not be fully informed of the ramifications. Educational sessions should not only disseminate information, but should be treated with the same rigor as obtaining informed consent in research.

In addition to being drug specific, educational programs must begin at an early age. Most studies have revealed that patterns of drug use are established in high school, and primary prevention should commence before that. Programs that begin in college or later are unlikely to be effective methods of behavior change and can do little more than distribute information. Although standards do exist for drug testing programs, educational programs are haphazard and effective programs still need to be established.

Reference

Goldberg, L., MacKinnon, D.P., Elliot, D.L. *et al.* (2000) 'The Adolescents' Training and Learning to Avoid Steroids (ATLAS) Program: Preventing Drug Use and Promoting Health Behaviors', *Arch Pediatr Adolesc Medicine* 154: 332–8.

GARY GREEN

DRUG TESTING

Although drug use in organized athletics has been documented since the 1800s, formalized drug testing at the Olympic level did not begin until 1964, and it was not until 1983 that laboratories were accredited by the International Olympic Committee (IOC). The past twenty years have seen technological advancements in both the detection by laboratories and avoidance by athletes.

Although this entry focuses on the technical issues of a drug test, the most important aspects occur prior to the urine sample entering the laboratory. The collection of samples and chain of custody must be rigorous to ensure the integrity of the sample, both in terms of false-negative and false-positive results (see **collection issues**; **chain of custody issues**). For example, if a specimen has been manipulated in any way, the validity of the result is in question (see **manipulation of samples**). Similarly, if the chain of custody is not strictly followed before the sample reaches the laboratory, the results will be invalidated.

When an athlete's career and reputation are at risk, strict forensic standards are required and results are often appealed to the highest international courts (see **appeal process**). Once a sample is received at an IOC-accredited laboratory, the chain of custody regarding the collection procedure is verified and the sample is logged in. Samples are analyzed by code number so that the laboratory does not know the identity of the person. Olympic samples are collected in both 'A' and 'B' containers and they are checked to ensure that all seals are intact and have not been tampered with. Only the 'A' bottle is opened at this time and aliquoted for analysis, whereupon the laboratory begins its own chain of custody to account for the sample at every step of the analytic process. If the 'A' sample is suspect on screening, then a second portion is taken from the 'A' bottle for confirmation. If the result is confirmed, the laboratory reports the sample to the sports authority. The athlete then has the option of being present when the 'B' bottle is opened and analyzed for subsequent confirmation. Only if the 'A' and 'B' results match is the athlete considered to be positive for a substance.

Although different methods are used for screening for various substances, gas chromatography-mass spectrometry (GC-MS) is used to confirm most results. GC-MS offers a 'fingerprint' of organic substances and is legally admissible in court. GC-MS is the test that is used in **anabolic-androgenic steroid testing** and has reduced the use of exogenous **anabolic-androgenic steroids** by improving detection, in some cases up to a year after use.

In addition to the actual GC-MS analysis, sample preparation is extremely important in drug testing and improves sensitivity. For example, in order to detect most stimulants (and opiates) the urine sample is subjected to acidic deconjugation that results in free molecules. Following that, the sample is extracted and then derivatized. This is performed in the manner analogous to anabolic steroid testing, the resulting product further improving the GC-MS. In addition to these methods, some laboratories utilize the liquid chromatography-mass spectrometry (LC-MS) method to aid in the detection of **diuretics** that are used as masking agents.

While GC-MS has been the standard method for many years, athletes have turned to substances not easily detectable with this method, and this has resulted in the development of new techniques, such as **carbon-isotope ratio testing** and iso-electric focusing for drugs like **erythropoietin (EPO)/Darbepoietin**. Although GC-MS is effective for less sophisticated athletes, it is expected that newer methods will be required in order to continue to deter drug use at the elite level.

GARY GREEN

DRUGS

Ever since the nineteenth century drugs have been used in sport in order to alleviate injuries and damage sustained in sport and also to improve sporting performance. Further motives for administering medication of this kind were to regulate phases of sleeping and waking, as well as to improve moods and mental states. Sports in which so-called performance-enhancing drugs were made wider use of were endurance sports such as cycling, long-distance running, or professional football. Until the 1920s there was no controversy over drug usage. However, by the 1970s a new stage had been reached in which sport and with it drugs were increasingly used as weapons in the Cold War. It has now been proved that drugs were developed, produced, and administered in the German Democratic Republic with official approval.

Effects of drugs as performance enhancers

Stimulants were the first drugs to be used in sport. 'Pep pills' contain highly addictive amphetamine, especially Pervitin®, or methamphetamine, the possession of which is illegal. These drugs are used to increase performance, strengthen the ego and, above all, to suppress alarm signals in the body such as thirst, tiredness, exhaustion, or pain. Since the 1980s psychoactive drugs have also been used for this purpose.

Anabolic steroids, available since the 1960s in the form of tablets or injections (and today also as ointment or plasters) are misused, since they increase muscle size and strength more than is possible in training without such drugs. In addition, anabolic steroids shorten the period of recovery after great exertion and thus enable athletes to increase the scope and intensity of training.

Anabolic steroids, which are chemical compounds produced from the male sex hormone, testosterone, bring about changes in the sexual organs as well as in behaviour. Thus, in women they lead, among other things, to masculinisation and in men to increased aggression. Beta-2-adrenergic agonists such as Clenbuterol®, used in the fattening of calves as well as in the treatment of asthma, also have an effect on muscle growth although they are not classed as anabolic steroids.

Peptide hormones, artificial blood, and also the intake of the athlete's stored blood, lead to a 10 per cent increase in endurance capability. Growth hormones and insulin increase performance by accelerating the body's energy turnover.

A further procedure used in manipulating performance is the intake of biologically effective substances in unnaturally high concentrations (e.g. creatine). The border between doping and the permissible influencing of performance is blurred, especially in the case of so-called nutrition supplements.

Other drugs are used not to increase performance but to prevent the detection of doping in tests.

Drugs and doping

When athletes use drugs but do not take part in competitions governed by rules of fair play, this is their personal decision – a decision which, ethically and morally, is viewed in different ways. There are countries, for example, where people are punished who harm or mutilate themselves or who are guilty of drug abuse.

As soon as drugs are administered within the IOC's sport system, athletes must comply with the prohibition on doping. Since there are varying definitions of doping, the World Anti-Doping Agency (WADA) has drawn up a list of prohibited substances and methods in order to provide clarity. Accordingly, doping is the intake of substances or the use of methods named in this list.

In disputes about doping, three arguments have emerged against the misuse of drugs in sports.

1. Doping violates the principle of equal chances for all competitors. Doping is therefore unfair – in the same way as cheating or bribing the referee.
2. Doping is detrimental to health. Numerous dangerous side-effects have been scientifically proven.
3. Doping is especially dangerous for girls and women, comparable with criminal sexual abuse or bodily damage. Taking anabolic steroids, for example, leads, among other things, to changes in the structure of the body and often irreversible damage to the sexual organs.

Rules, controls, punishment

The growing abuse of drugs in sport at national and international levels has led to regulations on doping. For approximately the past thirty years drug testing has taken place during competitions and for some twelve years – as a reaction to new doping practices – there have been random doping controls during training. The latter seems to have been very effective, since in the past decade the average achievement in elite sports has decreased despite considerable improvements in training practices.

Whether or not self-administered misuse or mandatory doping against the will of or without the knowledge of the athlete are treated in the same way depends on the international sport federation and/or a country's legal system. Even the punishment of drug abuse differed before the WADA code was accepted by the Olympic sports federations. This code prescribes the testing of urine samples taken during training or after a competition by IOC accredited anti-doping laboratories. Even concealing the abused pharmaceuticals from detection in a doping control or refusing to give a urine sample to a controller ('no show') are deemed positive cases. The highest court of appeal is the Court of Arbitration in Switzerland (CAS), with more than 250 lawyers and judges.

In addition, there is a Therapeutic Use Exemption Committee which supervises the use of banned substances in cases of necessary medical treatment. Nowadays regulations allow transsexuals undergoing male hormone treatment to take part in competitions since, although testosterone is a powerful doping substance, it is used in this case in medication for either transformed biological women or male competitors who have undergone surgical removal of the testes (which produce testosterone) after cancer of the scrotum.

In many states special anti-doping laws exist. France and Italy even punish drug abuse with imprisonment.

Drug abuse in Sport for All

Investigations in the USA and other countries have shown that the abuse of drugs like anabolic steroids is a phenomenon which is not confined to Olympic sports. Indeed, it is widespread in fitness centres and in body-building (e.g. the Californian 'Muscle Beach'). Moreover, for two decades doping practices have also been increasing in American youth culture, where mostly male high-school students abuse drugs in order to improve their appearance.

A systematic investigation in Germany has produced clear results: dangerous anabolic steroids were used in all fifty-five commercial sports studios surveyed. The users consisted of 22 per cent of male and 8 per cent of female visitors, who were poorly, or not at all, informed about the effects of these drugs on their health. In 88 per cent of cases the products used were anabolic steroids, mainly bought illegally; only in 19 per cent of cases were the steroids prescribed by doctors. Drug abuse in fitness studios has a positive correlation with a low level of education and a low-status occupation (Boos and Wulff 2005). Similar results were obtained in research in other countries, e.g. Italy (Donati 2005).

Doping is part of a general social trend towards wanting to solve individual and social problems with the help of drugs. This is just as true of 'happiness pills' and anti-ageing preparations as it is of nutrition supplements which contain steroids. However, the effects on the health of adolescents and women are particularly problematic. Here is a link for fighting against doping in sport, social drugs, and the tendency of 'over-medication', by abusing pharmaceuticals in order to feel better or avoid ageing – which, after all, is a natural and necessary process in the development of human beings.

References

Boos, C. and Wulff, P. (2005) 'Medicament Abuse by Leisure Sportsmen and Women in the Field of Physical Fitness', in G. Spitzer (ed.) *Doping in European Sport*, London: Routledge, in press.

Dezelsky, T.L., Toohey, J.V. and Shaw, R.S. (1985) 'Non-medical Drug Use Behaviour at Five United States Universities: A 15-Year Study', *Bulletin Narcotics* 37, 2–3: 49–53.

Donati, A. (2005) 'Doping in Italian Sport (1974–2004)', in G. Spitzer (ed.) *Doping in European Sport*, London: Routledge, in press.

WADA code: www.WADA-AMA.org

Further reading

Houlihan, B. (1999) 'Dying to Win. Doping in Sport and the Development of Anti-Doping Policy', Strasbourg: Council of Europe.

Spitzer, G. (2004) *Doping in der DDR* [Doping in the GDR], 3rd edn, Cologne: Sport und Buch Strauss.

Waddington, I. (2000) *Sport Health and Drugs. A Critical Perspective*, London/New York: Taylor and Francis.

GISELHER SPITZER

DURATION OF REHABILITATION

Duration refers to the length of time needed to achieve the goals of the rehabilitation process, in other words, the restoration of normal form and function. In the case of athletes, it includes the time needed to return to optimal sports performance. The total duration of the rehabilitation process can vary from days to months, depending on the nature of the injury, the presence of associated injuries, the need for surgical intervention, the level of sports competition, age of the athlete, the availability of optimal rehabilitation professionals with sports medicine knowledge, and many other factors. A more conservative approach to rehabilitation prevalent 20–30 years ago has been substituted by more aggressive rehabilitation protocols that have shortened the time between injury or surgery and return to competition. This has resulted from a combination of several factors, including a better understanding of the physiological and biomechanical demands of various sports, enhanced knowledge of the physiology of injury and tissue healing, improved medical and surgical interventions, and the development of optimal rehabilitation protocols.

When recommending exercise (see **rehabilitation exercises**) for rehabilitation purposes, a detailed exercise prescription is needed. This prescription must define four basic elements, including type of exercise, frequency, intensity, and duration. The latter is defined differently depending on the type of exercise. For example, when an injury has resulted in a loss of range of motion or flexibility, stretching exercises must be included in the rehabilitation program (see **flexibility and stretching**). The duration of each stretch must be defined as well as the duration of the training. In general, when using static stretches, each stretch should last approximately 30–60 seconds. When using proprioceptive neuromuscular facilitation techniques, each stretch should last approximately ten seconds to be effective. Given that almost all sports need good flexibility, the duration of the flexibility training is equal to the duration of the sports training.

Many, if not all, sports injuries result in muscle weakness and atrophy directly or indirectly. Strengthening exercises are part of most rehabilitation routines. Like with flexibility training, duration must also be defined when recommending exercises to enhance muscle strength and mass. The duration of various elements of the exercise prescription must be addressed. When lifting weights to develop strength, each repetition (or lift) should last several seconds; many have recommended 2–3 seconds for each of the three phases of the exercise including lifting the weight (concentric action), holding it (static or isometric action), and lowering the weight (eccentric action). When performing power training exercises the lift is usually done at faster speeds. The duration of the rest period between repetitions is usually several seconds but this may depend on whether the lift was maximal or near-maximal, in which case it is several minutes. Likewise, the duration of the rest period between sets is also dependent on the purpose of the training. Shorter resting periods (thirty seconds to one minute) are typical of weight-training programs to develop local muscular endurance. Longer duration resting periods (2–3 min) between sets are used. Weight-training is designed to enhance strength. The duration of the

training sessions depends on the number of muscle groups to be trained, the number sets per muscle group, and the number of repetitions per set.

Finally, the exercise prescription for endurance training should specify the duration of the endurance component of the rehabilitation program. If we assume that all athletes should have a good level of cardiovascular endurance, the recommended duration of endurance exercises is approximately 30 min. Many sports, such as the marathon and road cycling, require a very high level of endurance. These athletes increase the duration of their endurance training as the rehabilitation process advances.

Further reading

Frontera, W.R. (ed.) (2002) *Rehabilitation of Sports Injuries: Scientific Basis*, Oxford: Blackwell Science.

WALTER R. FRONTERA

DYNAMICAL SYSTEMS THEORY

Dynamical systems theory is a discipline of mathematics that includes several overlapping sub-disciplines such as chaos theory, the sciences of complexity, non-linear thermodynamics, and synergetics. This theoretical approach was established by the great French mathematician Henri Poincaré in the early 1900s, but has only been related to the study of human movement behaviour since the 1980s (see also **ecological approach**). Dynamical systems are prevalent in nature and their behaviour can develop along different trajectories over time, primarily because they are open to energy flows within and external to the system.

The principle aim of dynamical systems theorists is to study the great diversity of natural complex phenomena from a systemic viewpoint. Analysis of the behaviour of any complex system microscopically – on a small scale – typically reveals most of the interaction between its parts. At first glance, the interactions between the small units of the system seem random and unconstrained. In fact, most complex systems are characterised by macroscopic pattern formation – large-scale. At this scale, individual components are capable of self-organising to form functional and coherent patterns, such as the movement patterns of humans. Therefore, a key issue for understanding the behaviour of complex systems concerns how large-scale coordination patterns occur between the many small-scale degrees of freedom, or component parts.

The **kinematics**, or displacement and velocity characteristics, of human movement patterns can be depicted within numerical graphs known as phase portraits. Phase portraits are used to depict the stable patterns, the attractors, which the movement system tends to settle into. Critical changes, transitions, in coordination often occur as a function of a key control variable altering the stability of the system. For example, studies using the dynamical systems approach have examined the effect of movement frequency upon coordination of rhythmical inter-limb tasks.

Further reading

Kelso, J.A.S. (1995) *Dynamic Patterns: The Self-organisation of Brain and Behaviour*, Cambridge MA: MIT Press.

CHRIS BUTTON

DYNAMICAL SYSTEMS THEORY – CONSTRAINTS

In dynamical systems theory, the concept of 'constraint' is very important as it explains how self-organising processes (see **self-organization**) are harnessed to produce goal-directed behaviour. Constraints are the range of factors that can both limit, and facilitate, the organisation of human movement coordination. Karl Newell broadly categorised constraints into three types,

namely, task, environmental, and organismic (Newell 1986). The constraints model forms a multidisciplinary and holistic foundation upon which an understanding of motor behaviour can be constructed.

Constraints surround the human movement system and their interaction influences the configurations that are possible. For example in soccer, a player's coordination patterns are dependent upon factors such as the rules of the game and relevant equipment – task – the weather and the crowd – environmental – as well as the player's own anthropometry and physical and mental status – organismic. Therefore, in sport, the constraints that act upon performers are highly varied and dynamic. Dynamical systems theory is based upon the premise that movement behaviour is the emergent product of the interaction among these factors.

Considering some examples within sport, it is obvious that each constraint evolves across its own distinctive time scale. Returning to soccer, certain task constraints, such as a defender approaching to make a tackle, change much more rapidly than others such as the offside law, which might be altered only once over several seasons. Likewise, fatigue changes over the course of a game are more readily apparent than developmental changes through a player's career. In a similar vein, certain constraints have a greater influence over behaviour than others. In sports such as gymnastics or ice-skating, in which movement form is very important, the task constraint of a set sequence of moves is critical. However, in sports in which environmental constraints are particularly demanding, such as climbing or windsurfing, coordination should fit closely alongside these factors. Nonetheless, it is important to recognise the role played by each constraint on movement behaviour. In this respect, the constraints model represents an excellent framework on which teachers or coaches can base an understanding of the learner.

Task constraints are particularly relevant in this context as practitioners can manipulate them relatively easily, to guide a learner's search without overburdening him or her with information.

As an individual develops and acquires more movement patterns over time, a range of functional coordination patterns is gradually formed to subserve performance of necessary skills. Theorists often use the metaphor of a perceptual-motor landscape to describe the influence of constraints upon evolving movement patterns. The landscape consists of an array of different movement configurations, or attractors, any of which could be used to solve a movement problem. Constraints help to shape the landscape, forming valleys of movement stability as well as rugged peaks where more inconsistent patterns lie. As a function of practice, the learner can form deeper, more stable attractors so that certain skills become reproducible over time. Further, progress through the landscape is strongly influenced by key constraints, termed 'rate-limiters'. For example, young children learning to catch may be unable to perform a one-handed catch because their hand is not big enough to grasp the ball; as their hand size increases, their capacity to perform one-handed catches dramatically improves. A common misunderstanding of the term constraint is that it tends to imply only a negative confining influence upon behaviour. Instead, constraints should be viewed positively, as they are also the ingredients that enable movement solutions.

Newell (1985) identified three stages through which learners proceed as they move across the perceptual-motor landscape. Early in learning, when trying to pick up a new movement skill such as the overarm serving action in volleyball, the initial process may be described as a search for a suitable 'coordination' pattern – an attractor in the landscape – to achieve the task goal. The learner, who desperately needs some consistency, often seizes upon a rather basic, but fixed, motor pattern. Once the relationships between body parts and the basic coordination of the serving action with respect to important environmental objects – the volleyball – and surfaces – the orientation of the upright on the court floor – have been established, the performer is faced with the challenge of gaining a tighter fit between the assembled movement pattern and the performance environment. Hence, this second phase requires learners to gain 'control' over their coordination within specific environments. Then, in the 'skill' phase, experimenting with the control of the action can optimise performance. For example, the force, duration, and amplitude of the movement pattern for tennis serving may be altered less consciously by servers as they seek an optimal solution to the challenge of serving under different task constraints. Depending on the existing layout of the landscape, which is continually being shaped by genetic factors and experience, learners will progress through the stages of coordination, control, and skill at different rates, as individual dynamics and task demands either compete or cooperate to support task performance.

Learners can benefit from subtle manipulations of constraints to direct the search for coordination patterns. For example, an informational constraint, such as augmented feedback provided by an instructor, is often used to provide guidance on appropriate techniques. Alternatively, changes in game-related factors, such as equipment properties, playing area, or the rules of a practice session, are common teaching strategies that demand an active problem-solving approach on behalf of the learner.

Constraints do not act independently: they interact with each other. This makes an explanation of human behaviour using the traditional scientific assumption of cause and effect relationships very difficult. Instead, dynamical systems theorists prefer to consider the simultaneous influence of multiple causes. Small changes in any constraints could combine to produce significant changes in behaviour, depending on the sensitivity of the landscape at the time. In this sense, movement variation is not necessarily 'noise' or 'error', but could signal successful adaptation to a unique set of constraints. The interaction of key constraints makes it difficult to isolate differences in athletic performance with mono-disciplinary explanations. In summary, movement performance is viewed from dynamical systems theory as a personal struggle to implement change. In other words, each individual learner has to seek and assemble a unique solution that will help him or her to satisfy particular constraints.

See also: dynamical systems theory – processes; self-organization; stability and adaptability in human movement patterns

References

Newell, K.M. (1985) 'Coordination, Control and Skill', in D. Goodman, R.B. Wilberg and I.M. Franks (eds) *Differing Perspectives in Motor Learning, Memory, and Control*, 295–317, Amsterdam: Elsevier.
—— (1986) 'Constraints on the Development of Coordination', in M.G. Wade and H.T.A. Whiting (eds) *Motor Development in Children: Aspects of Coordination and Control*, 341–60, Dordrecht: Martinus Nijhoff.

Further reading

Davids, K., Button, C. and Bennett, S.J. (2004) *Acquiring Movement Coordination: A Constraints-Led Approach*, Champaign IL: Human Kinetics.

CHRIS BUTTON

DYNAMICAL SYSTEMS THEORY – PROCESSES

Dynamical systems theory is one approach that has been related to the study of how humans control and learn movement. Several important concepts that are linked to dynamical systems theory will be described in this entry, including phase space, stability, scanning, transitions, and mapping behavioural demands onto intrinsic dynamics. The process of **self-organization**, which is fundamental to this approach, will also be outlined. The holistic and multidisciplinary nature of this approach has placed dynamical systems theory among the most popular theories of motor behaviour from the late 1980s onwards.

The application of dynamical systems theory has infiltrated many scientific disciplines because it is concerned with the behaviour of complex systems, such as the human movement system, and how they change over time. It is one of three distinct but related fields of study that fall under the general theoretical umbrella of ecological psychology; the others are perception-action theory and non-linear thermodynamics. Ecological approaches share a common aim of explaining movement behaviour without emphasising abstract cognitive processes of representation and information processing within the central nervous system. The roots of dynamical systems theory are grounded in mathematics, and include several overlapping sub-disciplines such as chaos theory and synergetics. Using this theory, scientists create non-linear dynamical equations to capture how a high-dimensional complex system – one with many independent degrees of freedom – tends to self-organise globally into stable patterns. These macroscopic patterns or 'attractor states' emerge as a result of energy exchange between the multiple levels of the dynamical system.

In human movement, coordination patterns can be conceived of as a product of the limbs and body parts harmonising together under constraint. The organisation of movement is plotted within a numerical phase space, which refers to all of the hypothetical motor solutions a human could adopt. A phase space can be constructed by measuring the relative position and velocity characteristics of the independent components within the system. Although a central controller is not necessary for self-organisation to occur, this does not imply that coordination is a completely random process in which any pattern can emerge. Instead, humans learn how to map specific behavioural requirements onto existing movement tendencies as they interact with their environment.

The principles of dynamical systems theory within **motor control** were first demonstrated in a series of classical experiments involving bimanual rhythmical finger movements (Kelso 1981). In Kelso's work it was demonstrated that the relative phasing between the index fingers was attracted to one of two stable patterns, in-phase, with synchronous abduction-adduction, or anti-phase, with alternating abduction-adduction. The relative phase of any two oscillating systems, such as the legs during walking, is the phase lag in one system's cycle of movement compared to the other. Relative phase is a particularly pertinent variable to monitor in such tasks, as it collectively describes the organisation of the system parts. When participants in Kelso's experiments began oscillating their fingers in the anti-phase pattern, they eventually switched to in-phase as the frequency of a pacing metronome was increased. The sudden phase transitions from one state of coordination to the other were not brought about by some intentional change prescribed by the individual, but by the self-organising properties of the motor system. These transitions were the result of a critical control parameter, movement frequency, leading the participants into a more stable movement solution. Further, when a transition occurred it was marked by critical fluctuations in relative phase before and after the event, suggesting that the movement system typically requires some time to move out of, and 'relax' back into, stable states of organisation.

The competition or cooperation that exists between stable patterns – called intrinsic dynamics – and behavioural requirements can be expressed in dynamical terms. In some tasks, for which there is a close match between the intrinsic dynamics and the behavioural demands, individuals can quickly settle into their own stable states. However, many tasks in sport require the performer to put together complex sequences of actions that do not readily map onto their intrinsic dynamics. For this reason, practitioners often see great differences in the rates at which individual learners pick up movement skills over time. The process of learning unfamiliar coordination patterns requires the performer to break the symmetry that naturally exists in the body. For these reasons, it is more likely that athletes perceive the properties of the environment in relation to their own body, action capabilities, and relative location, rather than in extrinsic units, such as metres.

Motor learning involves the formation of new attractors to support goal-directed movements and the passage from one organised state of the system to another. As an individual develops and acquires more movement patterns over time, a range of attractors or functional coordination patterns is gradually formed into a landscape to sub-serve performance of necessary skills. For example, in basketball a range of shooting skills may be developed such as freethrow, lay-up, jump-shot, and the slamdunk. When a new task is being learned, this process involves not just one feature changing, but the whole attractor layout changing. As the stability of one set of skills becomes enhanced through practice, it is possible that another pre-existing skill may be stabilised or destabilised depending on its relative spatio-temporal similarity.

One effective way of probing the whole perceptual-motor landscape during learning in research studies has been to use a 'scanning procedure'. This technique requires the participant to intentionally vary an order parameter, such as relative phase, in steps. As the behaviour of the order parameter is monitored, the observer is effectively scanning the coordination patterns for stable and unstable regions, differing in variability of selected measures. The technique of scanning at different times during learning can result in 'snapshots' of the individual's attractor layout as it is evolving, revealing the relative stability of regions over time.

The empirical features described here, and also in many other related experiments since Kelso's early work, were simulated using a few simple mathematical equations in what has become known as the HKB model (Haken *et al.* 1985). This model also had some interesting implications for other features of the dynamical movement system, such as the relationship between attractor stability and the speed at which the system would return to the attractor after an external perturbation. Known as relaxation time, this variable has been used to test the stability of attractors in a variety of tasks. Since this innovative work, similar coordination tendencies, such as transitions, multi-stability, and sensitivity to frequency and amplitude, have been found with many rhythmical movements. However, it seems that, although different rhythmical tasks may have different potential functions and, therefore, different attractor regimes, the same self-organisational principles hold. Questions have been asked about whether this approach is able to address fundamental issues in human movement, including the control of discrete movements, intentionality, and more complex skills. These concerns are likely to become strong influences in guiding future work.

See also: ecological approach; information processing approach; motor programs – problems; stability and adaptability in human movement patterns

References

Haken, H., Kelso, J.A.S. and Bunz, H. (1985) 'A Theoretical Model of Phase Transitions in Human Hand Movements', *Biological Cybernetics* 51: 347–56.

Kelso, J.A.S. (1981) 'On the Oscillatory Basis of Movement', *Bulletin of the Psychonomic Society* 18: 63.

Further reading

Kelso, J.A.S. (1995) *Dynamic Patterns: The Self-organisation of Brain and Behaviour*, Cambridge MA: MIT Press.

CHRIS BUTTON

DYSMENORRHEA

Dysmenorrhea is the medical term for painful or difficult menstrual flow. Half of all menstruating women suffer from this unpleasant condition, and about 10 per cent are incapacitated for two to three days during the menstrual cycle, because of pain. It is referred as primary dysmenorrhea, when an underlying causative pathology can not be found. Secondary dysmenorrhea differs from primary in that the pain is caused by a pelvic abnormality or disease. Pain is the paramount symptom caused by dysrhythmic contractions (cramps) of the uterus. In primary dysmenorrhea pain occurs in ovulatory cycles and usually appears within the first year after menarche. The pain is dull or throbbing and pinpointed at the suprapubic area, radiating to the lower back or the thighs. It begins from hours to a couple of days before menstruation, reaching its peak during the first day and resolving after two or three days. Nausea and vomiting, headache, diarrhoea, nervousness and premenstrual irritability, flushing, abdominal bloating, dizziness, and faintness are symptoms that women with dysmenorrhea may experience.

In primary dysmenorrhea, myometrial cramps are due to the production of prostaglandins (hormone-like substances) secreted by the endometrium, which is the lining of the uterus. Prostaglandins exhibit vasoconstrictive and muscle contractive action to the uterus. The result is insufficient blood supply, leading to stimulation of the pain receptors. Leukotrienes are another group of substances that can mediate pain by heightening the sensitivity of type C pain neurons of the uterus, whereas anaerobic metabolites may have the same effect. The posterior pituitary hormone vasopressin is involved in myometrial hypersensitivity and decreased blood flow. Psychological and behavioural factors have also been suggested as causes of primary dysmenorrhea.

The diagnostic approach is initiated with history-taking and thorough clinical examination in order to rule out coexisting or aetiologic pathology, especially life threatening conditions such as ectopic pregnancy or pelvic neoplasm. Positive family history, age at menarche, smoking, obesity, alcohol consumption during menses, and nulliparity are amongst the predisposing factors. The progression of age and pregnancy attribute in resolution of dysmenorrhea with a mechanism which is not very well known yet. Laboratory and imaging studies are helpful in setting the diagnosis, although there are none specifically for dysmenorrhea tests. Mandatory tests are complete blood count and erythrocyte sedimentation rate (ESR) so as to exclude inflammation, cervical culture to rule out sexually transmitted diseases, human chorionic gonadotropin (hCG) to diagnose pregnancy, and cancer antigen 125 (CA-125) assay to detect a neoplasm. Ultrasound investigation together with computed tomography (CT) and magnetic resonance imaging (MRI) are useful as they are non–invasive and provide a lot of information. In doubtful cases, inspection of the abdomen with the insertion of a thin tube with a lens and a light (laparoscopy) or the visual examination of the cervical canal and the internal of the uterus using a viewing instrument inserted through the vagina (hysteroscopy), may give the solution to the diagnostic dilemma.

The clinician must bear in mind the long list of diseases and abnormalities which can cause dysmenorrhea and rule them out before characterising it as primary. Some of the most commonly diagnosed causes of secondary dysmenorrhea are endometriosis (ectopic endometrial tissue), adenomyosis (endometrial tissue within uterine wall), pelvic infection (e.g. acute salpingitis), uterine myoma (fibroids) or polyps, adhesions, congenital uterine or vaginal abnormalities, ovarian cysts, cervical strictures or stenosis, and intrauterine contraceptive devices.

Pharmacological treatment includes pain killers (e.g. acetaminophen), non-steroidal anti-inflammatory drugs (e.g. naproxen, ibuprofen, diclofenac, mefenamic acid) and oral contraceptives if dysmenorrhea is recalcitrant to the previously mentioned medication. Treatment of any underlying pathology is of crucial importance and leads to the resolution of secondary dysmenorrhea.

Reference

Alzubaidi, N., Calis, K.A. and Nelson, L.M. (2003) 'Dysmenorrhea', *e-medicine*, March 2003.

STYLIANOS PAPALEXANDRIS
EMANUEL T. PAPACOSTAS
NIKOLAOS G. MALLIAROPOULOS

E

EATING DISORDERS

Definitions

Slimness is today the ideal and the norm, and slimming or staying slim has become an obsession in Western societies in spite of – or perhaps even because of – the growing number of people who are overweight. Indicators of this 'slimming terror' are the numerous diets on the market and the increase in eating disorders, which are mainly related to attempts to lose weight.

Physical activities and exercise are one way of achieving the bodily ideals which especially girls and young women strive for – reducing the intake of calories is the other. Common methods of reducing the intake of calories are eating less, but also vomiting, as well as taking laxatives and diuretics. When these practices become habits and even neuroses, one speaks of eating disorders, whereby a distinction is made between anorexia nervosa and bulimia. Obesity, which is of no significance in the context of sport, is not dealt with here.

Both of these eating disorders are serious illnesses and are attributable to a combination of various causes and the interaction of socio-cultural, biological, and psychological factors. Here, not only social ideals and norms may play a role but also family structures or psychical and physical dispositions. The majority of those affected are young women aged between the ages of 15 and 24; 1 per cent of this age group suffers from anorexia while up to 10 per cent have eating disorders generally. But even menopausal women and men are not immune: around 5 per cent of anorexia sufferers are male, and the figures are currently rising. Affected by these illnesses are frequently ambitious, capable girls. Common theories link eating disorders to the rejection of ideals of femininity and the striving for power over one's body. Eating disorders have serious medical side-effects; they affect both health and well-being and may even lead to death. Anorexia and bulimia are, moreover, mental disorders related to a distorted view of one's body, to anxiety and depression as well as to emotional dysfunction and conflicts in relationships.

Anorexia nervosa

Anorexics reduce their intake of food to a minimum for fear of putting on weight. In this case, the perception of their body, their weight, and their appearance is morbidly distorted. Even when their weight decreases to below 85 per cent of their standard weight, anorexics do not give up their rejection and their abhorrence of food. Not infrequently anorexia ends in death, either from starvation or by the sufferer committing suicide.

Bulimia nervosa

In the case of bulimia sufferers, too, everything revolves around body weight, through which self-image and self-assurance is determined. Unlike anorexics, they interrupt their periods of fasting in order to indulge in 'binge eating'; they eat great amounts of food in a short time without being able to control themselves. In order not to put on weight, they try to prevent their body's consumption of calories by purging the stomach either by vomiting or by taking laxatives and diuretics. Bulimia patients suffer above all from the consequences of vomiting, for example from electrolyte imbalances or inflammation of the mucous membrane.

Anorexia and bulimia are two sides of the same coin and, not infrequently, these two forms of eating disorder are alternating phases.

Sport and eating disorders

Between sport and eating disorders there are quite a number of complex interconnections.

On the one hand, numerous women with eating disorders play sports excessively, not least because athletic training is one of their strategies for losing weight. On the other hand, in many sports it is an advantage to be light and to have little body fat – and, thus, little ballast – in comparison to one's active body mass. Therefore, among sportswomen, especially top-level athletes, the risk of being affected by these disorders is considerably higher than on the general population of the same age cohort. This is true, first, of endurance sports such as cycling, cross-country skiing, or long distance running; second, of disciplines with weight categories like rowing or judo; and, finally, of aesthetically oriented sports, for example rhythmic sportive gymnastics or figure skating. That male athletes can also suffer from anorexia when less weight promises greater success in their sport is shown by the example of ski jumpers. Whereas sport federations have so far taken little notice of the risks female athletes expose themselves to through anorexia, the bodily changes of male ski jumpers quickly led to changes in the regulations of the sport. Now jumpers who are below a certain body mass index are required to use shorter skis.

Symptoms

Characteristic of patients with eating disorders is their refusal to acknowledge that they are ill. Thus, as a rule, they seek neither advice nor help. In sport there are good ways of recognising symptoms of eating disorders. Coaches and trainers should look for unusual weight losses and bodily signs such as failure to menstruate, unusual tiredness – but also hyperactivity – and stress fractures. The behaviour of anorexics is especially conspicuous: they are greatly preoccupied with their weight and believe they are fat; they avoid situations in which their not eating might be noticed; and they train more than necessary.

In the case of bulimia sufferers, vomiting and laxatives produce diagnosable effects: fluctuations in weight, dehydration, and failure to menstruate. Their behaviour, especially as far as eating is concerned, is unpredictable: they spend lots of time in the bathroom and are inclined to be moody. Since, as a rule, bulimia sufferers have 'normal' weight, this eating disorder is not so easy to detect.

Causes, effects, and treatment

Frequently it is trainers who urge top-level athletes to lose weight – or even coerce them into doing so. Yielding to the great pressures put on them, women athletes try to attain their supposedly 'ideal' weight, often using radical measures. This may lead to their weight going up and down, the so called yo-yo-effect, and thus to the danger of eating disorders. Fellow athletes, the mass media, as well as the whole social environment, can be involved in the concern and the control of an athlete's weight.

A great problem for some top-level girl athletes is posed by bodily changes during puberty, which force many girl gymnasts, for example, to give up gymnastics because their fully developed bodies do not have the proportions essential for gymnastics on apparatus. It is no wonder, then, that in this difficult phase girls try to achieve the desired (and required) figure by dieting.

A further cause of the relatively high incidence of eating disorders among top-level women athletes might be found in the additional stress they have to cope with. Injuries, for instance, which necessitate a reduction in the amount of training, may lead to attempts by the athletes to keep their energy balance stable and prevent a feared increase in weight by eating less.

Eating disorders have an adverse effect on sporting performance and may result in medical complications especially when playing sports, for example cardiac arrhythmia, but also psychological problems.

Sport and eating disorders form an unholy alliance, the so-called 'female triad', i.e. the combination of an insufficient intake of nutrition, great amounts of energy spent on training, and loss of weight. Especially the inadequate proportion of body fat causes hormonal disturbances, which can lead to secondary amenorrhea (cessation of menstruation either for a short time or for longer) and, related to this, to reduced bone mass (osteoporosis). Studies have shown that some female athletes have the bone mass normally found in older women, and this loss is apparently impossible to compensate for.

All those involved in top-level competitive sports, from the athletes themselves to officials, must be informed about the 'female triad'. Useful information material is now available, which contains advice and lists indicators of eating disorders.

The treatment of eating disorders should be left to experts. In the case of top-level sportswomen, specialists must be consulted who are familiar with the sport or type of sport which the patient plays. Specialists must gain the confidence of the athlete and be capable of putting themselves in their position with regard to their daily routines and their training in order to be able to recommend and carry out practicable measures and therapies. Together with their patients they must work towards the aim of good health and thus good performance. In doing so, specialists must take irrational fears of putting on weight seriously. As a rule, breaking off training is not a measure which is acceptable to their patients. A reduction in the amount of training, however, would seem appropriate.

More effective than curing the disorder is prevention. A particularly important role in prevention can be played by well informed trainers, since trainers are usually persons of trust for athletes and thus have a great influence on their behaviour. More than anyone else, they can make it clear to athletes that health is a prerequisite of lasting sporting success.

References

Bordo, S. (1993) *Unbearable Weight: Feminism, Western Culture, and the Body*, Berkeley CA: University of California Press.

Fallon, P., Katzman, M. and Wooley, S. (eds) (1993) *Feminist Perspectives on Eating Disorders*, New York: New Guilford Press.

Hobart, J. and Smucke, D. (2000) 'The Female Athlete Triad', *American Family Physician*, 1 June. http://www.aafp.org/afp/20000601/3357.html

Otis, C.L., Drinkwater, B., Johnson, M., Loucks, A. and Wilmore, J. (1997) 'American College of Sports Medicine Position Stand: The Female Athlete Triad', *Medicine and Science in Sports and Exercise* 29, 5: i–ix.

Smith, A.D. (1996) 'The Female Athlete Triad: Causes, Diagnosis and Treatment', *Phys Sportsmed* 24(7): July. http://www.physsportsmed.com/issues/jul_96/smith.htm

Yeager, K., Agostini, R., Nattiiv, A. and Drinkwater, B. (1993) 'The Female Athlete Triad: Disordered Eating, Amenorrhea, Osteoporosis', *Medicine and Science in Sports and Exercise* 25: 775–7.

GERTRUD PFISTER

ECCENTRIC EXERCISES

An eccentric muscle action occurs when a muscle produces force at the same time it is increasing in length. This is in contrast to a concentric action in which the muscle decreases in length, and an isometric action (see **isometric training**) in which the muscle length does not change.

Eccentric muscle action takes place in most athletic activities. A good example is the action of leg extension to stand up from a squatted position. It is an active movement requiring muscle energy, yet the lengths of several muscles in the hips, thighs, and lower legs are increasing. Other examples include lowering a load (eccentric) versus lifting it (concentric) and running down a slope (eccentric) versus running up a slope (concentric). Eccentric action is thought to be especially important in shock absorption during landing after a jump and rapid deceleration of a limb during quick changes in direction. Both movements are typical of sports such as basketball and volleyball.

It is important to incorporate eccentric training exercises into a complete strengthening program or rehabilitation program because eccentric actions enhance the benefits of resistance training exercises. It is easy to include eccentric contractions into weight training or lifting exercise routines. One needs to continue to contract the muscle group, and control the weight, during the relaxation or lowering phase of the exercise, instead of allowing the weight to fall passively back to the starting position.

The following is an example of how to incorporate eccentric strengthening into a typical biceps curl with a free weight in the hand. Bend the elbow and bring the weight slowly up to the top of the range of motion (concentric contraction). Pause at the top, keeping the muscle contracted (isometric contraction). Then slowly lower the weight, concentrating on controlling the descent of the weight as the biceps muscle lengthens and returns to the starting position (eccentric contraction). A good pace is to count to three slowly as the weight is lifted, pause at the top of the motion for a slow count of three, then lower the weight back down to a slow count of five. This pattern can be duplicated for any strengthening exercise using free weights or special weight-training devices.

Eccentric actions require less energy to generate the same amount of force compared to concentric actions. This is in part explained by the fact that eccentric actions activate fewer muscle fibers, resulting in less fatigue and perceived exertion. However, higher absolute muscle forces can be developed during eccentric exercise, and this may lead to slightly higher demands on a person's heart (increased venous blood return, mean arterial pressure, and stroke volume).

Work done on muscles during eccentric exercise is dissipated more readily through the muscles, and the muscle temperature is higher by about two degrees Celsius. Eccentric exercise is generally associated with a greater degree of post-exercise muscle soreness. This means that eccentric exercise should be incorporated slowly into a training routine, especially if the athlete is not accustomed to this type of exercise.

References

Frontera, W.R. and Silver, J.K. (eds) (2002) *Essentials of Physical Medicine and Rehabilitation*, Philadelphia PA: Hanley and Belfus Inc.

Grabiner, M.D. (2000) 'Neuromechanics of the Initial Phase of Eccentric Contraction-Induced Muscle Injury', in V. Zatsiorsky (ed.) *Biomechanics in Sport: Performance Enhancement and Injury Prevention. Volume IX of the Encyclopaedia of Sports Medicine*, 588–606, Oxford: Blackwell Science.

Kisner, C. and Colby, L.A. (2002) *Therapeutic Exercise: Foundations and Techniques*, Philadelphia PA: F.A. Davis Company.

Prilutsky, B.I. (2000) 'Eccentric Muscle Action in Sport and Exercise', in V. Zatsiorsky (ed.) *Biomechanics in Sport: Performance Enhancement and Injury Prevention. Volume IX of the Ency-clopaedia of Sports Medicine*, 56–86, Oxford: Blackwell Science.

CHARISE L. IVY

ECOLOGICAL APPROACH

The ecological approach comprises three distinct but related theories, each concerned with understanding the basis of human **motor control** and **motor learning**: **information-movement coupling**, stemming from ecological psychology; **dynamical systems theory**; and the non-linear thermodynamic theory of perception-action cycles. The stimulus for the emergence of the ecological approach in the 1980s and the 1990s grew out of dissatisfaction amongst many theorists with traditional cognitive-based explanations of movement behaviour. The essential problem is in understanding how humans, with many redundant degrees of freedom, develop control and coordination to perform goal-directed movements. Ecological approaches share a common goal of explaining movement behaviour without making indirect assumptions about the role of a central controller or executive within the central nervous system.

The critical issues and objectives of an ecological approach can be summarised as follows. A need is recognised to adopt a systems perspective in viewing the human being as a system composed of many interacting subsystems. The appropriate scale of analysis for the movement system is at the level of the performer-environment interaction. Further, there is a close and reciprocal link between a living system and its environment. From the ecological approach, a critical point is that living systems possess their own sources of energy and are 'open' to energy exchanges with the environment. In essence, these sources of energy act as perceptual information for supporting, guiding, and regulating movement. In analysing human coordination, the emphasis is

on studying functional goal-directed movement activity, such as those performed in the context of sport. Finally, the ecological approach recognises the need for a multi-disciplinary framework to examine processes of cognition, decision-making, intentional planning, and perception and action in human movement systems.

See also: information processing approach

References

Bernstein, N.A. (1967) *The Control and Regulation of Movements*, London: Pergamon Press.
Davids, K., Button, C. and Bennett, S.J. (2004) *Acquiring Movement Coordination: A Constraints-led Approach*, Champaign IL: Human Kinetics.

CHRIS BUTTON

ECOLOGICAL SPORTS

The increasing severity of environmental degradation and pollution is prompting a call for paradigm changes on many levels, in society as well as in individuals. A similar groundswell is occurring in the field of sports. The Centennial Olympic Congress, held in Paris on 23 June 1994, identified the environment as being a critical issue for the future development and prosperity of the Olympic Movement. In recent years, the Olympic Games have emphasized coexistence with the environment, placing a high priority on environmentally conscious development. The 1994 Olympic Games in Lillehammer, Norway, was a proposal for a Green Olympiad: with a high level of environmental awareness and a will to coexist with nature, an attempt was made to link the Olympic Movement itself to activities for environmental conservation. The 2000 Games in Sydney, Australia, was an all-out effort at an environmentally friendly Olympics, accompanied by the announcement that the environmental standards used for constructing facilities for the Games would be thereafter be applied to the construction of all public facilities in New South Wales. From now on, there is a need to take environmental friendliness into consideration in the construction of sporting facilities as well as in the promotion of sports.

MUNEHIKO HARADA

E-COMMERCE

E-commerce refers to the entire range of electronic commercial transactions carried out over the computer network. With the rapid spread of the internet, it has increasingly come to refer to transactions that use the internet. There are two categories to e-commerce: B to C, where companies deal with the consumer, and B to B, in which companies deal with other companies. Initially, personal computers, books, CDs, and local specialty products were dominant in B to C transactions, but with the establishment of virtual malls on the internet, coupled with a newly aggressive stance on the part of consumer goods manufacturers, for whom this mode presented a new marketing channel, a broad spectrum of products, including services, are now dealt with in B to C. Some sporting goods manufacturers are responding to customer demand by setting up websites where they can receive orders for customized products. Meanwhile, B to B transactions deal mainly with standardized products such as components and raw materials: a global network, far beyond the existing trading relationships, has evolved. In B to B, transactions are not limited to companies dealing with companies: electronic marketplaces now connect the procurement and sales operations of multiple companies.

MUNEHIKO HARADA

ECONOMIC IMPORTANCE OF SPORT

Sport is now recognised as an important sector of economic activity. Studies of the economic importance of sport in national economies carried out in the USA, Canada, Australia, New Zealand, and many countries in Europe, typically show that sport accounts for between 1.5 and 2 per cent of both national gross domestic product and employment, and up to 3 per cent of consumer expenditure.

The first UK study was carried out in 1985 and was then repeated every five years until 1995 and every three years since then. All these UK studies have used the same approach, the **national income accounting** framework, to the estimation of the economic importance of sport. Although UK studies have used the national income accounting framework, to estimate the economic importance of sport, most other studies have used **input-output analysis**.

In a simplistic model of the economy, households spend their money on the goods and services produced by firms. There is a flow of money (consumers' expenditure) from households to firms and a flow of goods and services (output) from firms to households. Households also sell their labour services to firms in return for the payment of income. Since all factor services are owned by households then the total amount paid out for these services by firms makes up national income. The total amount of income is spent on goods and services so that total expenditure equals total income, and both correspond to the total value of goods and services produced, total output.

If we wished to measure the economic importance of sport in such a model we have three choices: total expenditure on sports goods and services by households, which would be exactly matched by the value of sports goods and services produced by firms, which also would match the incomes of households supplying factor services to firms producing sports goods and services. The measurement of these totals would be a sub-set of the national income accounts, which measure all flows of expenditure

389

(total final expenditure), income (national income) and output (national product).

Obviously such a model is unrealistic since there is no government, no saving and investment, and no foreign countries. The model can easily be adapted to take account of flows to and from an overseas sector and a government sector, and a financial markets sector (saving and investment). Any flows from households out of total expenditure that does not go to purchase goods and services from firms (e.g. saving) is a 'leakage' from the circular flow of income. Any flow entering the circular flow from one of these other sectors (e.g. investment) is an injection into the system. Thus taxation, saving, and imports are leakages; whilst government expenditure, investment expenditure, and exports are injections. If leakages and injections are equal then the size of national income is constant. If injections are greater than leakages in total, then total expenditure increases as does output and income. Conversely, if leakages are greater than injections then total expenditure falls. The introduction of new sectors and the move to a more realistic model of the economy, allows national income to grow and decline, which of course is what happens in reality.

The circular flow of income model incorporating these other sectors is the conceptual model of the economy that lies behind the national income accounting approach to the estimation of the economic importance of sport. The estimation is now more complicated, since we must measure sport-related expenditure flows to and from the overseas sector and government, but essentially the principle is the same.

There is one other sector that must be added to the model, one which plays a crucial role in sport: the voluntary sector. Gershuny (1979) introduced the concepts of the formal and informal economy to incorporate the **voluntary sector** into the model. The formal economy is the one described above which is represented by market transactions. The informal economy refers to those activities where households contribute their own time together with market-purchased goods for the production of services they themselves consume. Unlike in the formal economy, the flow of labour services to the informal economy is not matched by an income flow in the opposite direction. In the informal economy, the household sector is part of the production sector: It is essentially the same as Becker's (1965) household production concept, except here several households combine together in the voluntary sector and 'produce' a product from which they can all derive benefit. The voluntary sector sports club is an example of such an informal economic activity. Members contribute their time and effort without payment for the 'production' of sporting opportunities. There is some formal sector economic activity, since members will pay subscriptions to the club, but the formal sector payments and receipts will be an underestimate of the true level of economic activity (ie. the true level of income, expenditure, and output).

References

Becker, G.S. (1965) 'A Theory of the Allocation of Time', *Economic Journal* 75, 3.

Gershuny, J.I. (1979) 'The Informal Economy: Its Role in Post-industrial Society', *Futures* 12, 1: 3–15.

CHRIS GRATTON

ECONOMIC REGENERATION

Over recent years there has been increasing emphasis on the role of sport in economic regeneration, and this has focused on economic impacts, and broader evaluations of economic costs and benefits of sport-led development. The role of sport in urban economies is one which has begun to be recognised, particularly in the context of deindustrialisation and the growing importance of the service sector in such circumstances. There is also a literature relating to the costs and benefits of stadium development, particularly in the US context, but with some more recent contributions relating to Britain. A particular sub-set of the literature on sport and economic regeneration relates to the benefits of hosting major sports **events**. A number of authors have addressed the role of the promotion of single large-scale events in economic development, while others have focused on the impact of programmes of significant sporting events in terms of economic impact or of social impact.

Over the last two decades many cities in the United States have invested vast amounts of money on sports stadia on the basis of arguments relating to economic benefits to the city from such investment. Most of these strategies have been based on professional team sports, in particular American football, baseball, ice-hockey, and basketball. Unlike the situation in Europe, professional teams in North America frequently move from city to city.

Since the late 1980s, cities have offered greater and greater incentives for these professional teams to move by offering to build new stadia to house them costing hundreds of millions of dollars. The teams just sit back and let cities bid up the price. They either move to the city offering the best deal or they accept the counter-offer invariably put to them by their existing hosts. This normally involves the host city building them a brand new stadium to replace their existing one which may only be ten or fifteen years old.

Baade (2003) indicates how, since the 1980s, escalating stadium construction costs have increased the size of stadium subsidies:

> the number of stadiums that have been built since 1987 to the present is unprecedented. Approximately 80 per cent of the professional sports facilities in the

United States will have been replaced or have undergone major renovation during this period of time. The new facilities have cost more than $19 billion in total, and the public has provided $13.6 billion, or 71 per cent, of that amount. In few, if any, instances have professional teams in the United States been required to open their books to justify the need for these subsidies. Rather, teams have convinced cities that to remain competitive on the field they have to be competitive financially, and this, teams claim, cannot be achieved without new playing venues.

This use of taxpayers' money to subsidise profit-making professional sports teams seems out of place in the North American context. The justification for such public expenditure is an economic one: the investment of public money is a worthwhile investment as long as the economic impact generated by having a major professional sports team resident in the city is sufficiently great. Economic impact refers to the total amount of additional expenditure generated within a host city (or area), which could be directly attributable to the staging of a particular event. Only visitors to the host economy as a direct result of an event being staged are eligible for inclusion in the economic impact calculations (i.e. the expenditure by people resident in the host area is not included on the basis that they would spend money locally irrespective of whether an event is taking place).

Baade (1996), Noll and Zimbalist (1997), and Coates and Humphreys (1999), however, showed no significant direct economic impact on the host cities from such stadium development. Crompton (1995; 2001) also argues that economic impact arguments in favour of such stadium construction using public subsidies have been substantially exaggerated. However, he goes on to suggest (2001; 2004) that there are other possible benefits to cities from such developments: increased community visibility, enhanced community image, stimulation of additional development related to the stadium, and psychic income to city residents from having a professional team in the city. The first three of these focus on the ability of such stadium developments to influence external audiences which may lead to inward investment into the host city and generate similar benefits to economic impact. Psychic income relates to the social and psychological benefit local residents may feel by identifying with the resident professional team. Although sports researchers are well aware of such benefits, they are notoriously difficult to measure effectively, and no evidence currently exists to suggest these broader benefits justify the high levels of public subsidies to professional sports teams in the USA.

The question that arises, therefore, is why such subsidies have grown to these massive levels in recent years. Quirk and Fort (1999) suggest an answer:

> As monopolies, sports leagues artificially restrict the number of teams below the number that would be in business if there was competition in the sport. By constantly keeping a supply of possible host cities – cities that could support a league team – on line, current host cities are in the unenviable position of being pressured to provide exorbitant subsidies to their teams or risk losing them.

Thus it is simply a problem of supply and demand, and the market power lies with the professional sport teams. Most economists are agreed that this phenomenon is not an example of sport contributing substantially to economic regeneration. However, some American cities have gone beyond the professional sport team stadium game, and taken a broader approach to using sport for economic regeneration. Indianapolis, Cleveland, Philadelphia, Kansas City, Baltimore, and Denver are examples of cities that have adopted broader sports-orientated economic regeneration

strategies, and Indianapolis is perhaps the best example out of these.

Schimmel (2001) and Davidson (1999) analyse how sport has been used in Indianapolis for economic regeneration of the city. Indianapolis is a Midwestern US city that in the mid-1970s was suffering from the decline of its heavy manufacturing base, in particular its car industry. Local politicians were keen to develop a new image of the city. As Schimmel indicates, the problem was not that the city had a bad image, but rather that the city had no image at all. The strategy was to target the expanding service sector economy in an attempt to redevelop the city's downtown area by using sport as a catalyst for economic regeneration and building. From 1974 to 1984, a total of $1.7 billion in public and private resources was invested in inner-city construction (Schimmel 2001), of which sporting infrastructure played a major role. The strategy included investment in facilities in professional team sports, but added to this a strategy of hosting major sports events in the city.

Between 1977 and 1991, 330 sports events were hosted by Indianapolis. Davidson (1999) attempted to measure the economic contribution of sport to the city in 1991. He found that in 1991, eighteen sport organisations and nine sport facilities in the city employed 526 employees. In addition, thirty-five sports events held in the city in 1991 generated additional spending of $97 million. He estimated the total economic contribution of sport organisations, facilities and events in Indianapolis in 1991 to be $133 million. In addition, other studies had shown that the sport strategy aimed at economic regeneration had resulted in other non-economic benefits, including increased sports participation by young people, increased pride in the city, and a enhanced image for the city resulting in more convention tourism. Although Indianapolis was an early example, the strategy of using sports events as a catalyst for urban regeneration became popular in both Europe and Australia in the 1980s and 1990s.

Several cities in the UK (Sheffield, Birmingham, and Glasgow) have used sport as a lead sector in promoting urban regeneration, in some cases using Indianapolis as a model, and these three cities were awarded National City of Sport status in 1995 partly because of this. They have all invested heavily in their sports infrastructure so that each has a portfolio of major sporting facilities capable of holding major sports events.

In addition to facilities, each city has a supporting structure of expertise in event bidding and management to ensure quality bids with a high probability of success and to guarantee high-quality event management. Events are a major vehicle for attracting visitors to the city, and hence contribute to urban regeneration. However, these cities are also involved with developing sport in the cities through performance and excellence programmes (e.g. training, squad preparation, coaching) and in community sports development, so that the local population benefits from the investment in sports infrastructure.

These and other cities have made a specific commitment to public investment in sport as a vehicle for urban regeneration. However, the quantity and distribution of returns to such public sector investment in sport, predominantly from local government, have been largely under-researched and remain uncertain. Often such investment attracts criticism because of media attention on a specific event, such as the World Student Games in Sheffield in 1991, and there has been little research on the medium- and long-term returns on such investment.

References

Baade, R.A. (1996) 'Professional Sports as Catalysts for Economic Development', *Journal of Urban Affairs*, 18, 1: 1–17.

—— (2003) 'Evaluating Subsidies for Professional Sports in the United States and Europe: A Public Sector Primer', *Oxford Review of Economic Policy* 19, 4: 585–97.

Coates, D. and Humphreys, B. (1999) 'The Growth of Sports Franchises, Stadiums and Arenas', *Journal of Policy Analysis* 18, 4: 601–24.

Crompton, J.L. (1995) 'Economic Impact Analysis of Sports Facilities and Events: Eleven Sources of Misapplication', *Journal of Sport Management* 9, 1:14–35.

—— (2001) 'Public Subsidies to Professional Team Sport Facilities in the USA', in C. Gratton and I.P. Henry (eds) *Sport in the City: The Role of Sport in Economic and Social Regeneration*, London: Routledge.

—— (2004) 'Beyond Economic Impact: An Alternative Rationale for the Public Subsidy of Major League Sports Facilities', *Journal of Sport Management* 18: 40–58.

Davidson, L. (1999) 'Choice of a Proper Methodology to Measure Quantitative and Qualitative Effects of the Impact of Sport', in C. Jeanreaud (ed.) *The Economic Impact of Sport Events*, Neuchatel: Centre International d'Etude du Sport (CIES).

Noll, R. and Zimbalist, A. (eds) (1997) *Sports, Jobs and Taxes*, Washington DC: Brookings Institution Press.

Quirk, J. and Fort, R. (1999) *Hard Ball: The Abuse of Power in Pro Team Sports*, Princeton NJ: Princeton University Press.

Schimmel, K.S. (2001) 'Sport Matters: Urban Regime Theory and Urban Regeneration in the Late Capitalist Era', in C. Gratton and I.P. Henry (eds) *Sport in the City: The Role of Sport in Economic and Social Regeneration*, London: Routledge.

CHRIS GRATTON

ECONOMICS

Sport economics is concerned with the economic analysis of the sports market, that is the demand for and supply of sporting opportunities. Sport is now recognised as an important sector of economic activity, but when the phrase 'economics of sport' is used, most people think of it as the analysis of the 'sports business', or the elite sector of the sports market that attracts massive amounts of money through sponsorship, payments for broadcasting rights, and paying spectators. For many, sports economics corresponds to the economics of **professional team sports**. Although money generated through professional sport, international sports competitions, and the televising of major sports events is both substantial and increasing, this is a fairly small part of the total sports market.

It is relatively easy to identify the amounts of money involved at the elite, increasingly professional, end of the sports market. It is less straightforward to identify the expenditure on sport in a country as a whole and the relative balance between the elite end of the sports market and the broad base of recreational sport. However, over recent years many countries have estimated the money value of the broad flow of resources into and out of sport, and such estimates indicate that the economic value of the recreational base of sport far exceeds that of the top of the sports hierarchy.

Figure 19 shows the hierarchical nature of the sports market, with a relatively small group of elite athletes at the top of the pyramid competing in national and international competitions. At this top level of

sport, money flows into sport from sponsorship, from paying spectators, and from television companies eager to broadcast this top level of competition.

Although this elite end of the sports market appears to be essentially commercial, it is also subsidised by government. Economics can help to both provide a rationale for and assess the cost effectiveness of such subsidy. Every country wishes to see their own sportsmen and sportswomen as international champions. There is a national demand in every country for international sporting success. Governments fund the top end of the sports market in order to 'produce' sporting excellence and international sporting success, both through their own direct expenditure and through their control of sports funds through government agencies.

At the bottom end of the pyramid we have recreational sport: people taking part in sport for fun, for enjoyment or maybe in order to get fitter and healthier. This part is also subsidised by government, but predominantly by local government through subsidies to sports facilities in the community and in schools. Again, economic analysis

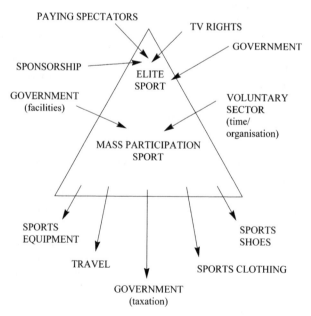

Figure 19. The Sports Market.

explores both the rationale and the efficiency of such government intervention. Government subsidies at this level are much higher than those directed at the elite end of the sports market. Figure 19 also identifies another important source of resources into sport, the voluntary sector. The resources the voluntary sector contributes to sport are massive, but the most important resource is the time that volunteers contribute to sport without payment and it is not an easy task putting a monetary valuation on this.

Although government and the voluntary sector support the recreational end of the sport market, there are substantial monetary flows from sports participants to the commercial sector through their expenditures on sports equipment, sports clothes, and sports shoes. These same participants also contribute to government revenue in the form of taxation on sport-related expenditures and incomes. In fact, in most developed countries the amount that sports participants give back to the government in taxation through expenditures on their sport participation is greater than the amount of government subsidies to sport. Sport gives more back to government than government gives to sport.

One final important area that is only just starting to be recognised and measured as a sport-related expenditure is sport-related travel. Leisure travel is an important part of travel expenditure, accounting for over 30 per cent of all travel expenditure. Sport-related travel has increased its share of all leisure travel consistently over the last twenty years so that it now accounts for about 10 per cent of leisure travel.

Figure 19 indicates the complex nature of the sports market. The supply-side of the sports market is a mixture of three types of provider: the public sector, the voluntary sector, and the commercial sector. Government supports sport both to promote mass participation and to generate excellence, but government also imposes taxation on sport. The commercial sector sponsors sport both at the elite level and at grass roots. Some of these sponsors (e.g. Nike, Adidas, Reebok) do so in order to promote their sports products and receive a return on this sponsorship through expenditure by sports participants on their products. Most of sports sponsorship is, however, from the non-sports commercial sector (e.g. Coca-Cola, McDonald's), where the motives for the sponsorship are less directly involved with selling a product to sports participants. Squeezed in between government and the commercial sector is the voluntary sector, putting resources into sport mainly through the contribution of free labour time, but needing also to raise enough revenue to cover costs, since the voluntary sector cannot raise revenue through taxation as government can.

If the supply side of the sport market is complicated, then so is the demand side. The demand for sport is a composite demand, involving the demand for free time; the demand to take part in sport; the demand for equipment, shoes, and clothing; the demand for facilities; and the demand for travel. Taking part in sport involves, therefore, the generation of demand for a range of goods and services which themselves will be provided by the mixture of public, commercial, and voluntary organisations discussed previously.

To this complexity of the demand to take part in sport, can be added the complication that the sports market is a mixture of both participant demand and spectator demands of different types. As we move up the hierarchy towards elite sport, there is an increasing demand to watch sporting competitions. Some of these spectators may also take part but many do not. The spectators may go to a specific sports event, or watch at a distance on television. Alternatively, they may not 'watch' at all, preferring to listen on the radio or read about it in newspapers. All of these activities are part of the demand side of the sports market.

In fact, market demand is even more complicated than this rather complex picture, since Figure 19 only represents the flows into and out of a national sports market. Increasingly it is more appropriate to talk about the global sports market. A small, but increasing, part of every country's sports market is international or global. There already exist sporting competitions that are of truly global dimensions: over two thirds of the world's population (over 3.5 billion people) watch some part of the global television coverage of the Olympic Games. The cumulative television audience for the football World Cup is normally over 40 billion. Equally there are commercial companies that produce, distribute, and market their product on a global basis. Nike designs its sports shoes in Oregon, USA, contracts out the production of these shoes to factories in Thailand, Indonesia, China, and Korea, and markets the shoes on a global basis using a symbol (the swoosh) and, in the past, three words that were understood throughout the world ('just do it'). Nike, in 1997, rose to 167th in the world's top 500 companies, with a market capitalisation of $17.5 billion.

The economic characteristics of sport: sport as a commodity

Sport can provide both psychic and physical benefits to participants. Psychic benefits can arise from the sense of well-being derived from being physically fit and healthy, the mental stimulation and satisfaction obtained from active recreation and the greater status achieved in peer groups. Physical benefits may relate directly to the health relationship with active recreation. Physical exercise, it is argued, is a direct, positive input into the health production function. There is some evidence to indicate that those who regularly engage in physical exercise are likely to live longer, have higher productivity over the course of their working lives, and have greater life satisfaction and an improved quality of life. It is useful to consider these potential benefits of sports participation within an economic discussion of what type of commodity sport is. The discussion follows similar approaches used by health economists (e.g. Cullis and West 1979).

It is possible to classify sport in three different ways. Firstly, sport is a *non-durable consumption good*: that is, the benefit that matters to the consumer is generated at the time of consumption. Most of sports spectating fits within this category of consumer demand (i.e. non-durable consumption good): the aesthetic appreciation and enjoyment of watching gymnastics or ice-skating; the tension and excitement of watching a Premier League football match. Each consumer will weigh up the potential satisfaction or 'utility' from consuming the product and make a judgment on whether this is worth more or less than the asking price. If more, then the consumer will be willing to pay for the admission ticket. Equally, most of participation of sport is of this non-durable consumption type: people taking part because they enjoy it and derive more satisfaction than it costs them to take part.

Participation in sport, however, can generate benefits that are not immediate. If taking part in sport results in the participant being physically in better shape, this is a *durable consumption good* since the benefits of sports consumption accrue over time: the activity (sport) gives utility (satisfaction) in the future as well as in the present. Further, like a durable good, the stock (of fitness) depreciates without regular participation.

In the case of both a non-durable and a durable consumption good, the analysis of consumer demand is similar in that we are looking at the motivation for consumption to be pleasure. In one case (non-durable) it is immediate, in the other (durable) there is a time dimension to the pleasure. However, there is another motivation to the consumption of sport that has nothing to do with pleasure. Sport can possess the characteristic of a *capital good*, one that yields a return as part of a *market production process*. If sport makes a person fitter and healthier then this improved health status may lead to a 'pay-off' in terms of increased productivity in the labour market and higher labour market income as a result. This is an extension of Becker's (1964) human capital theory. In the same way that machines can be of different qualities, so can people. A person can 'invest' in themself in order to increase this productivity. The obvious way to do this is through education, and it is in this area that human capital theory has been developed. However, health status is also a pecuniary investment in these terms, and since exercise contributes to health status, it becomes an investment good.

There is another aspect to sport as a pecuniary investment, yielding a rate of return in the market, that does not relate to the health connection referred to previously. This is the investment of time and effort in training that increases skill and performance to the point that a pecuniary return results from the sporting activity itself. The obvious examples of this are the elite sportsmen and sportswomen who earn their living through participation in sport. This is the classic case of human capital theory. The individual invests time and effort in training in order to become a capital good in the production process of producing a saleable market good. For example, the professional footballer is an integral part of the production process of producing a football match. Although the returns depend to a large extent on innate ability of the payer, the harder he (or she) trains and acquires new skills then the greater the reward. The increased reward is the return on the investment in training.

There is another sense in which sport can be regarded as a capital good. Becker (1965) adopted the term 'household production' to refer to the way consumers can combine their own time with market-purchased inputs of goods and services to 'produce' a leisure activity. In Becker's view, both non-work time and the goods and services purchased on the market should be regarded as necessary inputs for the production of the activity. For instance, to 'produce' a game of badminton requires the time input of the players, the purchase (or hire) or racquets and shuttlecock, and the hire charge for a court.

The relevance of Becker's household production concept for the classification of sport as a commodity is that some evidence exists that people who regularly take part in sport are also more active in a wide range of other leisure activities (e.g. socialising, going out for a drink, going out for a meal, etc.). If this is the case, the sport can be regarded as a *capital good* that yields a return in the *non-market production process*. Following this reasoning, sport is a 'non-pecuniary investment' in that it increases the 'productivity' of household production.

Different sports are likely to confer a different mix of benefits on participants. This mix of benefits is also likely to change with age and experience in the activity. Young participants are likely to be unaware of durable consumption good benefits or non-pecuniary and pecuniary investment benefits. They will be more interested in immediate pleasure and will not be keen to participate in an activity that does not give it. As they grow older, however, it is likely that awareness of the other three types of benefit increase, with a possible change in participation to take advantage of them.

Many of the benefits referred to in the classification above relate directly the relationship between participation in sport and health. Research indicates numerous potential physical and psychological benefits that follow from increased exercise. The benefits are wide-ranging and they indicate that exercise is particularly beneficial to the elderly and the chronically sick. On the other side of the coin we have health dis-benefits from sport. Sports injuries, and deaths from dangerous sports such as mountaineering and hang-gliding, are negative health aspects associated with sport. We need more quantitative research into the relative size of these positive and negative aspects of the sport-health connection. Evidence seems to indicate that whether the net effect is positive or negative depends on the choice of sport and the age of the participant. For participants over forty-five, the net effect seems to be clearly positive, but participants of this age are less likely to take part in dangerous sports or sports that produce high levels of sports injuries (such as football and rugby).

What this discussion reveals is the difficulty that the consumer faces in making a rational decision when it comes to sport. Economics assumes that consumers are perfectly knowledgeable and make rational choices. The rather complicated nature of the commodity that is sport makes rational decision-making difficult, since the consumer is unlikely to have sufficient knowledge about present and future benefits that will follow from taking part in sport.

Thus, the private demand curve of an individual is not a simple affair. The question is not simply: is the satisfaction I will get from taking part greater than the price I have to pay? Other factors complicate the issue. Some part of the satisfaction does not accrue immediately. The decision to participate depends to some extent on how we value today satisfaction that will be obtained in the future, that is the consumers' time discount rate. Also a person may participate now even though there is no present or future satisfaction from the activity itself. He or she participates purely as an investment that will yield a return. The decision depends again on their personal discount rate, i.e. the value of future financial returns compared with the benefits now of spending the time and money on something else. In general, for any one individual, participation will give aspects of all four benefits discussed above, but the relative weight of each category of benefits is likely to vary substantially from one individual to another.

References

Becker, G.S. (1964) *Human Capital*, New York: Columbia University Press.

Becker, G.S. (1965) A theory of the allocation of time, *Economic Journal*, 75, 3, 493–517.

Cullis, J.G. and West, P.A. (1979) *The Economics of Health: An Introduction*, London: Martin Robertson.

—— (1965) 'A theory of the Allocation of Time', *Economic Journal* 75, 3.

Gratton, C. and Taylor, P. (2000) *Economics of Sport and Recreation*, London: E&FN Spon.

Sandy, R., Sloane, P.J. and Rosentraub, M.S. (2004) *The Economics of Sport*, Basingstoke: Palgrave Macmillan.

CHRIS GRATTON

ECOSYSTEM MANAGEMENT

An ecosystem is a particular environment classified into general types (e.g. mountains, lakes, forests, deserts, grasslands, oceans) that operate according to interactions between living and non-living components. The major types of organism that make up the living (biotic) components of an ecosystem are classified into three areas: producers, consumers, and decomposers. All of these work together in flows of energy known as food chains and food webs. The defining characteristic of any ecosystem is its complex flow of relationships and interactions that are finely balanced to ensure sustainability. An ecosystem is able to achieve this because there is no waste – all organisms, dead or alive, are potential sources of food for other organisms. This recycling process also extends to gases and chemicals unseen by the human eye, for example the carbon cycle, which is necessary for the integrity of the earth's atmosphere and which protects humans from the harmful rays emitted by the sun.

Each of the various ecosystems contains characteristic plant and animal communities adapted to particular environmental condi-tions. One of the defining aspects of a par-ticular ecosystem is its climate – the general pattern of atmospheric or weather condi-tions and seasonal variations. The distribu-tion of the continents, oceans and their currents, and topographical features such as mountains, lakes, grasslands, and other landscape features determine average tem-peratures and rates of precipitation. Other more general factors affecting an ecosys-tem's climate include the amount of incoming solar energy, the earth's annual orbit around the sun and the chemical content in the atmosphere. The latter is often cited as a reason for higher levels of summer humidity in the world's largest car-using cities, such as New York and Los Angeles.

Human populations have managed eco-systems for thousands of years, certainly well before the beginning of civilization. For example the Australian Aboriginals, thought to have inhabited the continent for 40,000 years, were able to effectively man-age a range of ecosystems across the con-tinent, without exhausting their resources. In modern times ecosystem management has come to be more commonly thought of as the establishment and maintenance of reserves, parks, and other protected areas. The emphasis on this form of management is often species-centred. In contrast, an ecosystems approach to management would ensure the sustainability of an entire area's living and non-living systems, not just a narrow focus on certain plants and animals. The development of an ecosystems approach to the management of a full range of the earth's various landscapes would be diffi-cult, as it would require the protection of at least 10 per cent of the world's land area.

Ecosystems management and sport have generally had an uneasy relationship. Sporting organisations are often accused of putting their own interests before the pro-tection of ecosystems, for example the building of golf courses in sensitive and fragile environments and the large amount

of resources and pollution of the atmo-sphere that goes into the running of major international sporting competitions. This unease between environmentalists and sport-ing organisations softened somewhat with the adoption of environmental guidelines by the International Olympic Committee, first seen in practice during the Sydney 2000 Olympic Games, where efforts were made to reduce the impacts of the event and its infrastructure on the environment. Many of the games facilities used solar energy and the degraded industrial envir-onment in the main area where the games were held, was reclaimed. Mass transit transport links were built into the main stadium complex in order to reduce the reliance on cars; many of the materials used in the construction of facilities were from recycled sources; and there was an emphasis on the recycling of food and drink con-tainers used by the athletes and spectators.

Reference

Miller, T. (1990) *Living in the Environment*, 6th edn, Belmont CA: Wadsworth Publishing.

STEPHEN WEARING

EFFECTIVENESS AND EFFICIENCY

Sports organizations that receive govern-ment subsidies to at least partially fund delivery of services are evaluated against the following three criteria.

- *Effectiveness:* measuring the end results and the impacts of a service on a clientele;
- *Efficiency:* measuring the relationship between inputs and outputs and the amount of effort, expense, or waste involved in delivering a service;
- *Equity:* measuring fairness of delivery ('Who gets what?').

These three evaluative criteria have been integrated and subsumed into the con-temporary generic term, 'performance indicators'. However, they are discussed independently in this encyclopedia because they make distinctively different contributions to evaluation. The growing prominence of performance indicators on sport reflects pressure on managers to improve accountability for the investments made with tax funds by measuring the quality (effectiveness), impact (effectiveness and equity), and cost-effectiveness (efficiency) of sports programs.

The following benefits emanating from evaluating the performance of sports programs have been suggested.

* What gets measured gets done.
* If you don't measure results, you can't tell success from failure.
* If you can't see success, you can't reward it.
* If you can't reward success, you're probably rewarding failure.
* If you can't see success, you can't learn from it.
* If you can't recognize failure, you can't correct it.
* If you can demonstrate results, you can win public support.

This entry focuses on efficiency and effectiveness measures. The **equity** criterion is defined in a subsequent entry and its relevance is confined to publicly supported entities. The efficiency and effectiveness criteria are applicable to non-subsidized, profit-oriented sport organizations, but in these cases efficiency usually would be expressed in terms of profitability rather than in terms of effort, expense, or waste.

A primary concern in evaluation is defining what should be measured. Most evaluations tend to measure efficiency and ignore the other two criteria because they are not easily measured. However, citizens tend to be most concerned with output results, which suggests services should be primarily evaluated on their effectiveness. Efficiency asks the question 'Are we doing it right?' Effectiveness asks, 'Are we doing the right thing?' Both are relevant, but effectiveness is of greater importance because there is not much point in 'doing it right' if the organization is 'doing the wrong thing'. The validity of efficiency as an evaluation criterion can only be judged by its relationship to effectiveness. Counting amount of money received, cost per head, number of programs offered, number of participants attending, or other measures of efficiency reveals nothing about the impact of a sport organization's services on its clienteles.

Efficiency measures the relationship of inputs and outputs. It is concerned with the question, 'Is the sports supplier producing the output as inexpensively as possible?' A major challenge in efficiency measurement is to ensure that gains are not secured by reducing effectiveness. Thus, a sports organization may raise its efficiency by hiring less competent personnel at a lower cost, or by increasing the size of skills classes. In both cases, the cost per person serviced would fall, indicating a gain in efficiency, but the quality of the opportunity offered may deteriorate, leading to reductions in effectiveness. To avoid such spurious gains in efficiency, measures should relate to a given effectiveness standard. For example, the proportion of visitors/participants who report being satisfied at a given level with the service cost per head would be used, rather than only the service cost per head.

If the objectives of a service have been established in terms of the benefits it is intended to provide to a clientele, there should be a willingness and an ability to measure performance in terms of users' (and perhaps nonusers') evaluations of the extent to which they received specific benefits from the program. Hence, the first question to ask in evaluating the success of a program is 'Does the sports program offer the benefits that it was intended to deliver to clients?' Only when this question has been addressed is it appropriate to assess efficiency and ask, 'Is the program being delivered in the least costly way?'

Because efficiency and effectiveness are different criteria, programs may rate high on one criterion and low on the other. For example, large numbers of young people may be participating in a sports program, but they may receive minimal personal attention, coaching or playing time. Thus, while efficiency is high, effectiveness is low.

In the contemporary literature, three measures of effectiveness have emerged as being preeminent. They are: service quality, perceived value, and satisfaction. While each is a distinctive, separate construct, all three are interrelated. Most sports managers are likely to concur with the contention that their primary goal should be to provide high-quality, satisfying experiences which visitors/participants perceive to be good value so they will return. Each of these three output measures of effectiveness is described in the following paragraphs.

There is frequently confusion between the constructs of quality and satisfaction. The confusion stems from both of them emanating from the same conceptual root – the disconfirmation of expectations paradigm. This paradigm suggests that quality/satisfaction is determined by visitors comparing their perceptions of service performance/benefits received to their expectations. Expectations provide the baseline against which judgments of quality and satisfaction are made. An individual's expectations are confirmed when a service performs as expected (performance/experience equals expectations); positively disconfirmed when the service delivers more than expected (performance/experience exceeds expectations); and negatively disconfirmed when the service delivers less than expected (performance/experience is below expectations).

Although they share a common conceptual heritage, the two constructs are distinctly different. Service quality is defined as quality of the opportunity provided, i.e. quality of the attributes of a service that are under the control of a supplier. Evaluation is concerned with judgments about the performance of the sports opportunity supplier.

In contrast to quality of opportunity, satisfaction is defined as quality of experience. It is influenced not only by the attributes provided by the supplier, but also by the attributes brought to the opportunity by the sports visitor/participant. Sport experiences are defined as realizations of intrinsic outcomes from engagement in sport activities. Quality of experience is a psychological outcome or emotional response. Satisfaction is measured by how well sport activities are perceived to fulfill the basic needs and motives that stimulated the desire to participate in the activity.

Attributes of service quality can be controlled and manipulated by sport suppliers assuming the necessary resources are available. In contrast, level of satisfaction is dependent not only on quality of service attributes, but also on the status of a host of variables that may affect a service's recipients, such as the climate, their mood and disposition, or the group of people with whom they are participating. Such variables are outside the control of a sports supplier, but they are likely to be influential in determining level of satisfaction with an experience. Thus, a sports program may be perceived as being high quality, but an individual could report a low level of satisfaction after experiencing it because the weather was bad. Conversely, a high satisfaction outcome may result even when perceived quality of a sports offering is low because, for example, the social group interactions are sufficiently positive to offset the low quality service. Visitors/participants shape and create the sport experience, and sport suppliers have little influence how visitors/participants will react to opportunities that are provided. It has been observed that their experience is created through a transaction with the physical and social setting, including what the visitor/ participant brings to the process in terms of use, history, perceptions, comparisons, skills, equipment, identities, hopes, and dreams.

Using general questions such as 'Are you satisfied?' or 'How satisfied are you with ...?' is unlikely to produce useful responses, since almost all visitors/participants are likely to report they are satisfied. Such responses, however, do not necessarily reflect a high level of satisfaction even though that is what is reported. Rather, they reflect only a lack of dissatisfaction, which may translate to mediocrity rather than excellence. Only if the program is unusually bad are people likely to respond negatively to such generalized questions.

Given that a sport experience is substantially self-produced, it is illogical to evaluate an organization's performance as a sport supplier based on visitors'/participants' levels of satisfaction with their experience. Sports managers are unable to control what visitors bring to the setting, but they are able to control what is provided. Thus, it appears to be more useful and productive to focus evaluation efforts on the sport opportunities provided, rather than on the quality of sport experiences emerging from exposure to those opportunities.

More recent literature has introduced perceived service value as a third measure of effectiveness which complements quality and satisfaction. Perceived value is conceptualized as being a function of the interaction between service quality and the sacrifice investment necessary to participate in the sports program. Sacrifice is what is given up. It is comprised of both monetary and non-monetary dimensions. The monetary elements are likely to consist of the direct price and travel costs paid by visitors/ participants, while non-monetary elements of sacrifice include the opportunity cost of time, embarrassment costs, and effort costs.

A variety of instruments have been developed for measuring each of the three effectiveness constructs: service quality,

satisfaction, and perceived value. It is beyond the scope of this entry to describe them, but they are found primarily in the **marketing**, **leisure**, and tourism literatures, and can be adapted to the context of sport with relatively little effort.

JOHN L. CROMPTON

ELASTIC MODULUS AND RELATED PROPERTIES

The elastic modulus is a key parameter in the design of sports equipment subjected to high structural loads for which a specific elasticity, or stiffness, is required for performance, for example tennis racquets, snowboards, and vaulting poles. Elasticity is the ability of a material to deform under load and return to its original size and shape when the load is removed. The elasticity of a material can also be a measure of the strength of that material, in particular its resistance to bending – stiffness. Optimum elasticity is often balanced against the weight requirements for the equipment, a parameter known as specific stiffness. There are three elastic moduli: Young's modulus, the shear modulus, and the bulk modulus. When analysing a material's performance under realistic loads using finite element analysis software, a prerequisite for the model will be the specification of all three elastic moduli.

Young's modulus (E) is the most common and is often used as a measure of elasticity in relation to sports equipment design. It is found from the ratio of tensile, or compressive, stress to tensile, or compressive, strain, and is easily obtained by measuring the gradient of the linear-elastic part of the stress-strain curve in tension or compression (Table 9).

When conducting calculations that involve elastic moduli, there is likely to be a parameter called Poisson's ratio in the equation. This is the ratio of transverse contraction strain to longitudinal extension

Table 9. Young's modulus of various materials

Material	E (GPa)	Uses in sport
Steel	200	Ice skates, golf club shafts
Carbon-fibre reinforced polymers	70–200	Racquets, pole vaults, bicycles, fishing rods
Aluminium alloys	69–79	Bicycles, golf club heads, ski edges
Graphite-fibre reinforced polymers	7–45	Yacht hulls, windsurf boards (skin)
Human bone	17	Athletes
Wood	7–14	Cricket bats, baseball bats, hockey sticks
Nylon	2–4	Racquet strings
High-density polyethylene	0.7	Skis (base)
Leather	0.1–0.4	Footballs, sports shoes
Rigid polymer foams	0.1	Core filler for surf and windsurf boards
Ethylene vinyl acetate (EVA)	0.01–0.05	Sports shoe soles
Butyl rubber	0.001	Pressurised ball bladders

strain in the direction of the stretching force. Most common materials become narrower in cross section when they are stretched. Convention is that tensile deformation is considered positive and compressive deformation is considered negative. The reason is that most materials resist a change in volume more than they resist a change in shape. The value is always between 0.0 and 0.5 for materials having isotropic mechanical properties. For rubber, Poisson's ratio is close to the theoretical upper limit of 0.5. For most other common materials it is between 0.25 and 0.35. As all of these materials become thinner when stretched, Poisson's ratio is always positive (Table 10).

The shear modulus (G) is the ratio of shear stress to shear strain on the loading plane. It also applies to torsional load conditions. It can be found through the linear elastic slope of the stress-strain curve in shear. For isotropic materials it is related to Young's modulus and Poisson's ratio (v) by: $G = E / 2(1 + v)$. The shear modulus is actually a modulus of elasticity in shear, but

for ease of differentiation it is commonly referred to as the modulus of rigidity. The shear modulus is required to be non-negative for all materials, and $G > 0$. Shear modulus is important for equipment design where the main use results in shear or torsion loads; for example, the new standard of carbon-fibre track cycle frames used by Olympic champions have a very high torsional rigidity to counter the severe loads applied to the frame during the sprint events.

Bulk Modulus (K) measures the elastic volumetric response of a material to hydrostatic pressure. The concept of the bulk modulus is mainly applied to liquids, since for gases the compressibility is so great that the value of K is not a constant. For liquids the change in pressure occurring in many fluid mechanics problems are not significant to cause appreciable changes in density. It is, therefore, usual to ignore such changes and consider liquids as incompressible. Gases may also be treated as incompressible if the pressure changes are very small, but usually compressibility cannot be ignored.

See also: bone structure and properties; coefficient of restitution; materials selection for sport

Table 10. Poisson's ratio of four materials

Material	Poisson's ratio
Rubber	0.5
Polycarbonate	0.40
Titanium	0.33
Cork	~0

References

Ashby, M.F. and Jones, D.R.H. (1993) *Engineering Materials 1 – An Introduction to Their*

Properties and Applications, ch. 3, Oxford: Pergamon Press.

Easterling, R. (1993) *Advanced Materials for Sports Equipment*, ch. 1, London: Chapman and Hall.

DAVID CURTIS

ELBOW AND FOREARM

The elbow joint complex consists of a major hinge joint between the humerus of the upper arm and the ulna of the forearm plus a secondary hinge joint between the radius of the forearm and the humerus, both of which are constrained to uniaxial flexion-extension motion (see **cardinal plane movements**). A third joint occurs between the bones of the forearm; the proximal articulation of this, the radio-ulnar joint, is often considered to be part of the elbow joint because it is contained within the same articular capsule. The radio-ulnar joint allows pronation-supination of the forearm, which enables the hand to assume a pronated or supinated position at any elbow flexion angle.

In sports that have a large involvement of the upper extremity, the elbow is at risk of overuse injury. Large forces can be transmitted across the joint in hitting sports such as tennis and baseball. Overuse injuries can range from the severity of stress fractures of the humerus to tissue inflammation at tendon insertions caused by overuse of the muscle involved. These injuries are often related to incorrect technique. The many degrees of freedom of the upper extremity mean that a given movement of the hand can be achieved by many different positions and orientations of the proximal segments of the limb. Poor technique overstresses certain tissues and, as a result of the repetition of practice and competition, relatively minor deviations from the correct structural alignment of the limb can result in cumulative damage, leading to overuse injury.

See also: bones of the elbow and forearm; joints of the elbow and forearm; muscles of the elbow and forearm

Reference

Williams, P.L., Bannister, L.H., Berry, M.M., Collins, P., Dyson, M., Dussek, J.E. and Ferguson, M.W.J. (eds) (1995) *Gray's Anatomy: the Anatomical Basis of Medicine and Surgery*, Section 6, Edinburgh: Churchill Livingstone.

CLARE E. MILNER

ELBOW INJURY

The elbow joint is often injured after a fall, in sports as well as in road traffic accidents.

Distal humerus fracture has a bimodal age distribution. In the elderly it occurs after a minor fall while in the young it is the result of high-energy impact, such as a fall from heights or a road traffic accident.

Other associated injuries with this kind of fracture are fractures of the radius and ulna, in which case it is called a floating elbow. There may also be a fracture of the radial head. Displaced fractures of the distal humerus may have a concomitant neurovascular injury.

The initial examination needs careful assessment of the neurovascular status as well as the integrity of the skin, and also an examination of the entire upper limb. There may be fractures of the metacarpal or other small bones of the hand, which could otherwise be missed.

Lateral and AP radiographs may not be adequate because of shortening of the fracture. Traction radiographs are more helpful for preoperative planning.

The AO classification is widely used. This type of classification system defines the fracture pattern well, takes into consideration the articular involvement, and helps to plan surgery.

The nonarticular, nondisplaced fracture may be treated non-operatively with an above-elbow cast. However, if the fracture is displaced and there is intra-articular involvement then surgical reduction and fixation is the preferred option.

There are many factors that need consideration prior to surgical fixation: the age of the patient, the dominant hand, the profession, the type of fracture, and the quality of bone. In elderly patients the bone is fragile and quite often markedly osteopenic. This may make surgery difficult, and the quality of fixation may not be optimum, resulting in failure of fixation along with other surgical complications. In these cases non-operative treatment may be the best option and a sub-optimum result is acceptable.

The patient undergoing fracture surgery is placed on the table in a lateral decubitus position with the elbow resting on the support on the side and bent at 90°. A posterior approach is made. The ulnar nerve is first identified and protected. Many surgeons recommend an osteotomy of the olecranon. The fragment of the olecranon is lifted up with the triceps. The advantage of this approach is a clear view of the articular surface of the distal humerus. The articular fragments are then restored and fixed with screws. The epiphyseal fragment is then connected to the diaphysis with the help of two plates, preferably at right angles to each other. A reconstruction plate is stronger than semitubular plates. The olecranon is fixed back with a large screw or tension band wire. In some elderly patients with gross comminution of the distal fragment, the reconstruction is very difficult and this is either treated like bag of bones with early mobilization, or as a primary elbow arthroplasty.

There are a number of complications, which include infection; non-union; malunion; failure of fixation; damage to the neurovascular structures; and also olecranon osteotomy non-union. Prevention of these complications is important, and careful soft tissue dissection, as well as protection of neurovascular structures, is vital to avoid some of these complications. The non-union can be treated with revision fixation and bone grafting. Incidence of ulnar nerve

injury is reported at 15 per cent. Ulnar nerve transposition is preferred if there is impingement by the implant. Incidence of olecranon ostetomy non-union is around 30 per cent, but this can be reduced by the use of screw and chevron osteotomy.

Capitellum fractures result from shear force applied through the radial head. There may be concomitant fracture of the radial head, the medial collateral ligament, and the distal radioulnar joint. The capitellar fracture may be displaced or nondisplaced. Nondisplaced fractures are treated with cast immobilization. Displaced fractures do not have any ligament or muscle attachment and are therefore resistant to healing; they require operative fixation. A lateral approach is made and the fracture stabilized with a Herbert or mini-screw, usually from the back to the front. If the fracture is grossly comminuted then fixation may not be possible. A late instability of the elbow may develop, necessitating further treatment. Loss of elbow motion is also usual, with or without reconstruction.

Radial head fractures are common injuries, comprising 20–30 per cent of fractures around the elbow. These can occur as an isolated injury or in combination with other injuries like distal humerus fractures, capitellar fracture, medial collateral ligament injury, and distal radioulnar joint injury. The physical findings consist of tenderness and swelling around the radial head. Elbow movement is restricted and there may be a bony block. A radiograph may show the fracture clearly or it may not be easy to locate, but the clinical exam and the history should aid in making a diagnosis. There are numerous classification systems for this fracture, but the most commonly used one is Mason's classification. The fracture may be either nondisplaced or displaced. For most nondisplaced fractures nonoperative treatment is sufficient. Early mobilization is recommended and the patient regains motion as the pain and swelling subside. If the fracture is displaced to 2 mm, or a step-off of more than 20–30 per cent, or a bony block to the motion, then operative fixation is required. A lateral incision is made over the elbow. The posterior interosseous nerve requires protection. The radial fracture is reduced and fixed with Herbert or mini-screws. This restores the articular congruity and helps in early motion. If the radial head is grossly comminuted such that reconstruction is not possible, then the choices are either a radial head resection or prosthetic replacement. Total excision should be avoided, as the radial head is an elbow stabilizer in valgus stress; especially if the medial collateral ligament is also ruptured, it becomes the prime stabilizer of the elbow joint. A partial resection may be all that is required. Metal prosthetic replacement is superior to a silicone prosthesis, as the latter has caused synovitis and joint destruction, and has been largely abandoned.

Olecranon fractures result from a fall on the elbow. These fractures are usually displaced, but some only minimally. Surgical treatment for displaced fractures uses a posterior approach. The fracture is reduced and fixed with tension band wiring or with a screw. Early motion is then started. If the fracture is nondisplaced, i.e. less then 2 mm, with an intact extensor mechanism, then non-operative treatment with an above elbow cast is sufficient.

Ligaments and the capsule surround the elbow. The medial collateral ligament comprises the anterior, posterior, and oblique bands. This is an important ligament and can rupture in dislocations. There is also the lateral ligament and the annular ligament, which provides further stability to the joint. Dislocations are usually postereolateral and can result in neurovasular damage. The elbow should be reduced as soon as possible. Simple dislocations do well and may not need surgical intervention. Complex dislocations require fixation of fractures and reconstruction of ligaments. In some cases with very complex fracture dislocation, a hinged elbow arthroplasty may be indicated. A hinged external fixator may be required in other cases where fixation has been performed but the elbow remains unstable.

In children with displaced supracondylar fractures, closed reduction and k-wiring is the treatment of choice.

IMRAN ILYAS

ELBOW REHABILITATION

The elbow is a joint located midway down the arm, between the shoulder and wrist. It is a hinge joint and is comprised of the humerus bone proximally and the radius and ulna bones distally. The primary movement of the elbow is flexion and extension, which allows the arm to bend and straighten, as in performing a bicep curl. A secondary movement that originates at the elbow is pronation and supination of the forearm. This allows the palm of the hand to turn up and down. An example of this is the swimming stroke.

Fractures of the elbow, resulting from trauma in sports like judo, include that of the olecranon and medial epicondyle. Both fractures require immobilization, usually by a hard plaster cast. Rehabilitation that follows would include regaining any lost range of motion and strength.

Injuries resulting from overuse of the soft tissues such as muscles, tendons, and ligaments are common at the elbow. Lateral epicondylitis, also known as tennis elbow, occurs when the extensor muscles of the wrist and hand are overused. An example of such a movement would be repeatedly grasping a tennis racquet and practicing the backhand. Inappropriate racquet grip size and excessive cord tension contribute to this injury. The location of the pain may vary from at the outside of the elbow to along the top of the forearm. Treatment may include fitting the individual for a custom wrist splint to limit wrist movement, a forearm band to increase the pressure on the muscle mass and relief the forces transmitted to the tendon, the use of anti-inflammatory medications, and ultrasound to decrease inflammation. Iontophoresis, which uses an electrical current to drive a non-steroidal anti-inflammatory medication deep into the aggravated tissues, may also be used.

Medial epicondylitis, also known as golfer's elbow, occurs when the flexor muscles of the wrist and hand are overused. An example of such a movement would be repeatedly grasping the narrow shaft of a golf club and practicing a golf swing. Movements that cause pain may include repeated or sustained gripping, or a motion that requires a strong isometric contraction of the forearm such as pushing the hands together. Treatment is very similar to medial epicondylitis with a custom wrist splint prescribed, anti-inflammatory medication and/or ultrasound to decrease inflammation, and iontophoresis.

The rehabilitation of both, lateral and medial epicondylitis, includes initial gentle stretching of the forearm muscles using the other hand to apply the force. When pain and inflammation is controlled, strengthening of the respective muscle groups can be initiated with low weights. Eccentric muscle actions must be part of the strengthening program.

Cubital tunnel syndrome is compression of the ulnar nerve at the level of the elbow. The position of the ulnar nerve is superficial and thus is prone to entrapment and injury, for example in baseball pitchers. Symptoms include a weakened grasp and atrophy of the muscles of the web space or outside edge of the palm. Pain or numbness may be felt in the ring and small fingers or along the outside of the hand. Rehabilitation of cubital tunnel includes an orthotic device to limit flexion and activity modification to avoid prolonged resting on the elbow. In extreme cases, surgery may necessary to relieve the entrapment.

Reference

Frontera, W.R. and Silver, J.K. (eds) (2002) *Essentials of Physical Medicine and Rehabilitation*, 301–90, Philadelphia PA: Hanley and Belfus Inc.

LAURA RYAN

ELECTROMYOGRAPHY (EMG)

Electromyography is the technique for recording, as an electromyogram (EMG), changes in the electrical potential of a muscle when it is caused to contract by a motor nerve impulse. Each efferent alpha-motoneuron (or motor neuron) innervates from less than ten muscle fibres, for muscles used for fine control, to more than 1,000 for the weight-bearing muscles of the legs. The motor neuron forms a neuromuscular junction, or motor endplate, with each muscle fibre that it innervates. The term **motor unit** is used to refer to a motor neuron and all the muscle fibres it innervates, which can be spread over a wide area of the muscle. The motor unit can be considered the fundamental functional unit of neuromuscular control. Each nerve impulse causes all the muscle fibres of the motor unit to contract fully and almost simultaneously. The stimulation of the muscle fibre at the neuromuscular junction – or motor end-plate – results in a reduction of the electrical potential of the cell and a spread of the action potential through the muscle fibre. The motor action potential, or muscle fibre action potential, is the waveform resulting from this depolarisation wave. This propagates in both directions along each muscle fibre from the motor end-plate before being followed by a repolarisation wave.

The summation in space and time of motor action potentials from the fibres of a given motor unit is termed a motor unit action potential. A sequence of motor unit action potentials, resulting from repeated neural stimulation, is referred to as a motor unit action potential train. The physiological electromyogram is the sum, over space and time, of the motor unit action potential trains from the various motor units.

Electromyography offers the only method of objectively assessing when a muscle is active. It has been used to establish the roles that muscles fulfil, both individually and in muscle group actions (see **muscles – group action**), and provides information on the timing, or sequencing, of the activity of various muscles in sports movements. By studying the sequencing of muscle activation, the sports biomechanist can focus on several factors that relate to skill. These include the overlap of agonist and antagonist activity and the onset of antagonist activity at the end of a movement. Electromyography also allows the sports biomechanist to study changes in muscular activity during skill acquisition and as a result of training. Clarys and Cabri (1993) provided a comprehensive review of all aspects of the use of electromyography in the study of sports skills, and this paper is recommended to the interested reader. Electromyography can help to validate assumptions about muscle activity that are made when calculating the internal forces in the human musculoskeletal system.

Early researchers reported relatively simple, linear, or quadratic, relationships between the electromyogram and muscle tension in isometric and quasi-static muscle contractions. However, for the fast movements in sport, a similar relationship has proved elusive owing, at least in part, to the signal only providing information about the contractile component of the muscle. The electromyogram does not contain information about the contributions to the muscle force from the series and parallel elastic elements of the muscle (see **skeletal muscle – schematic models**).

See also: muscle contraction mechanics; muscle mechanics

References

Bartlett, R.M. (1997) *Introduction to Sports Biomechanics*, ch. 6, London: E&FN Spon.

Basmajian, J.V. and de Luca, C.J. (1985) *Muscles Alive: Their Functions Revealed by Electromyography*, Baltimore MD: Williams and Wilkins.

Clarys, J.P and Cabri, J.P. (1993) 'Electromyography and the Study of Sports Movements: A Review', *Journal of Sports Sciences* 11: 379–448.

ROGER BARTLETT

ELECTRONICS

Analysis of **kinematics** and **kinetics** is required for both optimisation of performance and **prevention of sports injury**. Historically, motion and force have been estimated by observation only. Visual observations are limited as motion leaves no record, very fast movements cannot be seen, it is hard for the human eye to simultaneously take in multiple components of a complex movement, and forces and moments can only be estimated indirectly, for example by observed accelerations. The advent of videos has facilitated qualitative analysis, but quantitative analysis requires the use of sensors.

A sensor is a device that measures a physical quantity. The word sensor is often used synonymously with the word transducer. However, this is not always correct: a transducer is specifically a device that converts one form of energy to another, an **electromyography** (EMG) sensor is not a transducer as the form of energy remains the same. Advances in electronics in the last few decades have led to a dramatic increase in the number of different sensors available, and just as dramatic a reduction in their cost. The process of **amplification and signal conditioning** modifies a sensor output to make it suitable for **computer interfacing** and subsequent **signal display and storage**.

Whenever measurements are to be made on humans, safety considerations must always be paramount. In particular, the risk of causing neural stimulation, particularly to the heart, and heat or electrolysis damage to tissues must be eliminated. Good electronics practice is to perform a risk analysis, use appropriate fusing, earth all exposed metal-work, and insulate any sensor that could contact the body. Where electrical contact is made to the body, the safety requirements for medical electrical equipment (International Electrotechnical Commission – IEC 60601) define best practice.

References

Horowitz, P. and Hill, W. (1989) *The Art of Electronics*, Cambridge: Cambridge University Press.

International Electrotechnical Commission (IEC) (1988) *IEC 60601–1, Medical Electrical Equipment – Part 1, General Requirements for Safety*, Geneva: IEC.

BEN HELLER

ELITE PERFORMERS – ANTECEDENTS OF STRESS AND ANXIETY

It is likely that elite performers experience the same personal and situational antecedents of state anxiety and antecedents of trait anxiety described in other entries (see **state anxiety – antecedents**; **trait anxiety – antecedents**). However, they are susceptible to additional sources of anxiety as well. These sources include dealing with the following:

- negative aspects of competition, such as experiencing competition worries and selection issues;
- negative significant-other relationships, for example, coach and team-mate problems, lack of social support, or parental pressure;
- demands and costs of sport, financial and otherwise;
- personal struggles, such as injury, and other traumatic experiences, for example having a significant other die.

All of these examples are likely to increase the elite performer's stress and anxiety. Information on the antecedents of stress and anxiety for elite performers is limited because most research into these topics has been conducted using convenience samples that include non-elite participants. What is known about elite performers generally comes from interview studies.

S.E. SHORT

ELITE SPORT

Elites are defined as: (1) people who occupy positions of power, with the ability to make decisions on matters that are important to the society as a whole; (2) people who are in the uppermost positions of a particular organisation in society, as measured by their power and/or prestige; or (3) people who are in the highest positions of a particular village, town, or city, as judged on the basis of power, prestige, and/or income. In other words, elite sports refer to sports that have nearly exclusive participation by a limited segment of the population, such as privileged social classes or groups of competitors. The antonymous concept to 'elite sports' is 'sports for the general public'.

MUNEHIKO HARADA

ENDORSEMENTS

The endorsement of products and services by athletes and sports figures is a marketing strategy used by companies to establish brand awareness and influence consumers' purchase intentions. Endorsements have become increasingly important to athletes as supplements to their salaries while playing and as additional income after their playing days are finished. Research upon endorsements has focused upon implications (positive and negative) for endorsers, implications (positive and negative) for companies, endorser selection criteria, and effects upon consumers.

Product endorsement by entertainment celebrities and even royalty can trace its history to the late 1800s. The practice of using sport figures as endorsers did not became popular until the late 1920s and 1930s, when Babe Ruth and Lou Gehrig (baseball); Chuck Taylor (basketball); and Bill Tilden and Fred Perry (tennis) began endorsing products. By 1995, however, United States companies were spending over one billion dollars per year to procure athlete endorsements.

Sports shoe and apparel companies have been one segment that has helped define the endorsement industry. Converse signed Chuck Taylor, a professional US basketball player and clinician, to be their first spokesperson in 1921 and later signed National Basketball Association (NBA) superstars Julius 'Dr J' Erving, Larry Bird, and Magic Johnson as endorsers during the 1970s and 1980s. Nike began using athlete endorsements in 1972, and just twelve years later signed an agreement with NBA rookie Michael Jordan that would redefine the endorsement industry. Jordan has earned over $500 million in career endorsements, not only from Nike but also from such companies as Quaker Oats (Gatorade), Sara Lee (Hanes underwear, Ball Park franks), General Mills (Wheaties cereal), Rayovac (batteries), Oakley (sunglasses), WorldCom (telephone cards), and McDonald's (hamburgers). In 1998, *Fortune* estimated Jordan's endorsement impact, dubbed the 'Jordan effect', upon Nike at $5.2 billion, and $408 million for all of his other endorsement companies.

In addition to current athletes, companies often choose other sports figures, such as former athletes, coaches, and broadcasters to represent their products. Such selections are often based either upon reaching different demographic segments (such as age groups) or because these sports figures are seen as more mature and less likely to have a negative impact upon the company in the event of controversy.

Endorsement research has focused on four main areas: implications for endorsers (sports figures); implications for companies; endorser selection criteria; and impact upon consumers.

Sports figures must be careful to associate with products/services that consumers will not find questionable ethically or in quality, such as alcohol or tobacco products. Likewise, companies must be careful to select endorsers who match their target image and are not likely to cause negative publicity for the company. There are many models and suggestions regarding the selection of an endorser, but most relate to source credibility and positive personal characteristics. Finally, the impact of endorsers upon consumers has been the target of many studies, spawning models such as the Source Credibility Model, the Source Attractiveness Model, the Meaning Transfer Model, and the Product Match-Up Hypothesis.

References

Johnson, R.S. (1998) The Jordan effect. *Fortune* 137, 12: 124–6, June.

Jowdy, E. and McDonald, M. (2002) 'Tara Nott Case Study: Celebrity Endorsements and Image Matching', *Sport Marketing Quarterly* 11, 3: 186–9.

Stone, G., Joseph, M. and Jones, M. (2003) 'An Exploratory Study on the Use of Sports Celebrities in Advertising: A Content Analysis', *Sport Marketing Quarterly* 12, 2: 94–102.

Till, B.D. (2001) 'Managing Athlete Endorser Image: The Effect of Endorsed Product', *Sport Marketing Quarterly* 10, 1: 35–42.

Further reading

Carter, D.M. (1996) *Keeping Score: An Inside Look at Sports Marketing*, Grants Pass OR: Oasis Press.

Pitts, B.G. and Stotlar, D.K. (1996) 'Marketing Through Endorsements and Sponsorships', in B.G. Pitts and D.K. Stotlar (eds) *Fundamentals of Sport Marketing*, Morgantown WV: Fitness Information Technology Inc.

MICHAEL A. HUNT

ENDURANCE – REHABILITATION ASPECTS

Endurance can be defined as the ability to sustain a given level of force or exercise intensity. From a clinical point of view, fatigue or the reduction in performance with time, is the opposite of endurance. Endurance that depends on local muscular factors is called local muscular endurance. Whole body endurance is more dependent on the function of the cardiovascular and respiratory systems. Endurance is measured in units of time. In sports events of long duration such as marathon running, the 1,500 m free style swimming event, and road cycling events, endurance is one of the most important determinants of performance.

There are many physiological determinants of endurance, including the oxidative capacity of muscle cells; the number of capillaries that transport blood and nutrients to the active muscles and dispose of metabolic by-products; the muscle's ability to utilize free fatty-acids as fuel and conserve glycogen stores; the capacity of the cardiovascular and respiratory systems to capture and transport oxygen in blood cells to the active muscles; and the psychological factors that influence tolerance to fatigue.

Sports injuries can result in significant losses of both local and cardiovascular endurance. This may be caused by direct injury to the muscle, or more commonly secondary to de-conditioning that accompanies rest and the cessation of the athlete's training program. The rehabilitation process must include exercises to increase endurance. Although, during the initial stages it may be more important to restore flexibility and muscle strength, once this objective is underway, it is important to incorporate endurance training into the program. The nature of the endurance exercise program is guided by the exercise prescription, which includes the type, frequency, duration, and intensity of the exercise. This prescription contains the basic instructions on how to use and combine exercises to achieve the goal of restoring normal endurance.

The hallmark of exercise training programs designed to increase local muscular endurance is the use of a high number of repetitions (more than twenty) with light loads (for example 20–40 per cent of the one repetition maximum) with some of the same equipment used to restore muscle strength (see **strengthening – rehabilitation aspects**). It is interesting to point out that strengthening exercises also increase local muscular endurance.

For the purpose of restoring cardiovascular endurance, sports activities such as walking, running, swimming, cycling, and rowing can be recommended. The selection of the type of equipment is usually determined by the nature of the injury. For example if the injury involves the ankle or knee, swimming may be chosen but if the injury involves the shoulder, cycling may be more appropriate. This is also known as cross-training (see **cross-training**). At the end of the second phase of rehabilitation and during the third phase, the selection is based on the similarities between the training method and the sport (see **rehabilitation – basic principles**); in other words, the principle of specificity of training. At that point in time, a road cyclist will benefit more from cycling than swimming.

In terms of frequency (number of sessions per week), endurance exercise is usually recommended 6–7 days per week. Endurance exercises can usually be combined with the other exercise components of the training program such as flexibility, strength, and balance. Initially, soon after the injury and in the presence of some symptoms and signs of inflammation, less intense and shorter sessions may be indicated. The intensity of the training is usually measured relative to the maximal aerobic power (VO_2 max) or to the athlete's maximal heart rate. Both can be measured and/or estimated in the laboratory or clinic.

The intensity range that is most frequently used in the rehabilitation clinic is 50–85 per cent of the maximal capacity of the athlete. Finally, each training session usually lasts for 20–40 min of continuous or intermittent endurance exercise.

References

Frontera, W.R. (ed.) (2002) *Rehabilitation of Sports Injuries: Scientific Basis*, Oxford: Blackwell Science.

Shephard, R.J. and Astrand, P.O. (eds) (2000) *Endurance in Sports*, Oxford: Blackwell Science.

WALTER R. FRONTERA

ENERGY STORAGE AND TRANSFER IN THE POLE VAULT

Pole vaulting originated as a method of clearing ditches, dykes, and other obstacles. This gradually evolved into a distance sport and then into a height discipline, which was subsequently accepted as one of the founding sports of the modern Olympic Games. The first Olympic winning height in the men's pole vault was 3.3 m by William Hoyt of the USA, while the current men's Olympic record is over 6 m. Clearly, improvements in performance seen over the century or so of the pole vault's Olympic existence have been dominated by improvements by the athletes themselves, through technique, coaching, nutrition, and training. The pole vault is rare, however, in that there are no restrictions on the dimensions or the materials that may be used for the pole; as we shall see later, technology has had a significance impact on the sport.

The essential physics of the pole vault is that of the conversion of the kinetic energy of the run-up to potential energy of the jump. The athlete runs towards the bar with the pole approximately horizontal with kinetic energy given by KE = $mv^2/2$, where m is the mass and v is the speed at

take-off. The pole is planted in a box and the forward momentum of the athlete bends the pole, storing some of the kinetic energy as **strain energy**. At the same time, as the pole bends, it acts as a pivot and rotates about its lowest point towards the vertical. During this rotation, the athlete swings his or her body upside down to one side of the pole so that, at the maximum bend and strain energy, the feet are pointing upwards.

The pole begins to return to its original shape, acting as a leaf spring, and converts strain energy to kinetic energy of the athlete, who by now is more or less vertically upside-down. The upward thrust from the pole and the athlete's momentum carries him or her up towards the bar, and the athlete twists to pass over it feet first and facing downwards. Thus, at the top of the vault, the athlete has converted the initial kinetic energy of the run-up into potential energy of the jump. There is some energy loss in the pole as it vibrates and as the athlete gives it a small push away to ensure that it doesn't knock the bar or supports.

If the athlete's speed at take-off is $10\,\mathrm{m\,s^{-1}}$ and the mass of the athlete and pole is 80 kg, then the input kinetic energy is about 4 kJ. If all this energy were converted to potential energy, then it would give the athlete a theoretical jump height of around 6.4 m (assuming that the athlete's centre of mass is about 1 m off the ground and that the pole weighs 5 kg). There is evidence, however, that the pole might be as little as 50 per cent efficient, so that half of its stored strain energy goes in to vibrations, sound, heat, and other losses rather than being returned to the athlete. This reduces the theoretical height and, therefore, energy must be introduced into the system in another way. This points to the athlete carrying out additional work during the vault, which is also stored in the pole, a portion of which is then returned to the athlete.

From a technological point of view, there are no limitations on the geometry or material of the pole, giving considerable latitude in design. The run-up is dominated by acceleration, so that the mass of the pole needs to be minimised if a high speed is to be attained by the athlete and the kinetic energy is to be maximised at take-off. Additionally, from a materials standpoint, the pole must store the maximum amount of energy it can while still being as light as possible. While the pole must be light and store energy, the bending stiffness of the pole must be just right for the athlete. If the pole is too stiff, then it will not bend and the athlete may have a shallow trajectory with little chance to carry out the gymnastic manoeuvre; if it is too flexible, the pole will bend too much and may not even supply enough upward thrust to get the athlete off the ground.

It is found that a merit index can be used to select appropriate materials for a pole vault and which satisfies the criteria suggested above. Merit indices are used in materials selection and allow the optimal choice of materials for specific applications. In the case of the pole vault, it is necessary to maximise the strain energy storage per unit mass, giving, Index $= \sigma_{max}^2/E\rho$, where σ_{max} is the maximum allowable stress in the pole, E is the Young's modulus and ρ the density. The constraints on the stiffness are given by $E = ML/(\theta \pi r^3 t)$, where M is the bending moment applied by the athlete, L is the length of the pole, θ is the angle to which the pole is bent, and r and t are the pole's average radius and thickness respectively.

Table 11 shows geometrical values and the applied bending moment for a typical

Table 11. Geometrical values and applied bending moment for a typical pole vault

Typical pole length	5m
Average pole radius	18–24 mm
Average pole thickness	2.5 mm
Bending moment applied by athlete	500–1,000 N

pole vault. Clearly, the bending moment applied depends upon the mass of the athlete and the speed of the run-up. This data shows that the Young's modulus for a pole should lie between about 10 and 100 GPa if the pole is to bend to a 90° arc.

Analysis of databases of material properties shows that the optimum materials for pole vaults are bamboo, glass-fibre reinforced composites, and carbon-fibre reinforced composites. Original poles, more than a hundred years ago, were made of solid wood such as hickory or ash. Quite quickly, the solid poles were replaced by hollow bamboo poles that were lighter to carry. These were relatively successful and used well into the 1960s, giving heights of over 4 m. These poles were still quite inflexible and would break if they bent too much, so that the technique was still to clear the bar with the head up and the feet down.

Glass-fibre poles were gradually introduced in the mid–1960s and heights rapidly increased because of the new technique the flexibility of the pole allowed. The introduction of carbon fibres in the 1980s further reduced weight and helped to raise the height of the bar, but the progression in the results were slowing by this point. Small improvements have continued to be made, such as a thickness variation along the pole, with the maximum thickness in the middle of the pole where the bending stresses are greatest. It has also been suggested that a pole might have a slight initial curvature to allow a smoother take-off and that the circular cross-section be changed to an ellipse to make the bending more efficient.

What is clear is that a change in material from wood to glass-fibre reinforced composite had a significant effect on performance, because of the adaptability of the athlete to the new techniques the material allowed. It is possible that the pole vault discipline is nearing its limit in performance, as it is difficult to see how more energy can be introduced into the system if the vaulter's speed of run-up has been maximised. However, the rules are extremely liberal and, if there is one sport in which the technology of the future might make a difference, then the pole vault is a strong candidate.

See also: materials selection for sport; strain energy

References

Burgess, S.C. (1996) 'The Design Optimisation of Poles for Pole Vaulting', in S.J. Haake (ed.) *The Engineering of Sport*, 83–90, Rotterdam: Balkema.

Wegst, U.G.K. and Ashby, M.F. (1996) 'Materials Selection for Sports Equipment', in S.J. Haake (ed.) *The Engineering of Sport*, 175–84, Rotterdam: Balkema.

STEVE HAAKE

ENGSO (EUROPEAN NON-GOVERNMENTAL SPORTS ORGANISATION)

The European Non-governmental Sports Organisation (ENGSO) is an organisation whose membership is made up of those European National Sports Confederations or National Olympic Committees, which are the national umbrella organisations for sports for their respective countries. The body, which was formally constituted in 1990, is a non-profit making organisation serving the interests of sport in the European context. Its constituent organisations represent national sport in its broadest sense – from children and youth, and 'sport for all' activities, to elite sports. ENGSO presently has forty national umbrella sports organisations as members, and in 2005 was the only European sports organisation granted consultative status by the Council of Europe.

The aims of the organisation include: promotion and defence of the independence and autonomy of sports in Europe; mediating the political and economic impacts of the European Union on sport in Europe; assisting in improving sports development; promoting development of East-West and North-South cooperation; raising the status and credibility of sports in the member countries, as well as actively combating the negative tendencies in sports; supporting voluntarism as an important factor for development in society; and promoting democracy in sports and equality between men and women in sports.

The organisation originally started life as an informal 'club' of NGOs from Western European states which began meeting in 1966 as a parallel to the meetings taking place among the sports committees of Eastern European states. It resisted taking on formal organisational status until 1990, when it adopted its current name and statutes. The break up of the communist bloc in Eastern Europe has seen the membership of the organisation grow to incorporate Eastern and Central as well as Western European membership. It has taken on a significant lobbying role in relation to the **European Union**, and in 2003 for example sought to persuade its members to encourage their national political representatives to press for the adoption of sport as a European Union competence to be incorporated into future treaties of the European Union.

IAN P. HENRY

ENHANCING SELF-CONFIDENCE

Self-confidence can be defined as the belief or certainty which individuals possess about their ability to be successful in a particular task. It is perceived as an attribute generally possessed by individuals who are self-reliant, self-assured, who believe in their own abilities and judgment, and are brave. Self-confidence has also been described as a multifaceted construct comprising three major interrelated components: competence, control, and commitment.

Evidence suggests that self-confident athletes have a greater sense of perceived competence, personal control, optimism, and more commitment. Self-confidence affects the incentive to undertake actions. It is often said to be the single best predictor of success, such that individuals who expect to succeed often do; those who expect to fail tend to have that prediction confirmed. The importance of high self-confidence to successful athletic performance has been reported in various sports and has attracted the interest of many researchers. More successful athletes have been found to exhibit higher efficacy expectations and the drive to persevere, even in the face of overwhelming adversity, than less successful athletes.

To develop effective strategies for enhancing self-confidence, it is important to delineate between self-confidence as a global construct and situation-specific self-confidence, referred to as self-efficacy. The two constructs have tended to be used interchangeably in sport psychology, signalling the debate on the conceptualisation and operational definition of sport confidence. Specifically, Vealey's (1986) conceptualisation of sport-confidence attracted much criticism from various scholars as being global, yet not adequately differentiating itself from self-efficacy, and for lack of clarity on how athletic success is measured. Overall, the study of self-confidence in sport has drawn heavily from Bandura's self-efficacy theory. Self-efficacy is a specific form of self-confidence. It entails the beliefs or convictions that individuals have about their abilities to execute a course of action or produce certain behaviour in specific circumstances. It is influenced by four sources: past performance accomplishments, vicarious experiences, verbal persuasion, and physiological arousal.

Scholars agree that strategies used to enhance self-efficacy should help cultivate feelings of sport confidence within the athlete. This suggests developing in an ath- lete a general awareness of how to use the various sources of self-efficacy. Given that past performance accomplishment is the most dependable source of efficacy, athletes could be trained to use positive imagery techniques that could help them visualise themselves performing successfully. Personal accounts from athletes suggest that role modelling and repeated successful performances could be very effective in enhancing self-confidence. Athletes could be exposed to role models with whom they can identify, as a way of enhancing their self-confidence. Similarly, instilling a greater sense of optimism in athletes, especially when faced with adversity, could enhance self-confidence.

Athletes could also be trained to develop an awareness of how their body feels when they are anxious or relaxed. Such awareness would help them manage arousal to attain ideal performance states. Positive **self-talk** and thought-stopping are among the most effective tools for enhancing self-confidence. Athletes could be trained to structure statements to emphasise the execution of a desired outcome or to stop negative statements and replace them with positive ones. Coaches could assist athletes to select or construct vivid and believable self-affirmation statements that could be used during training and competition. Athletes need to develop challenging, but realistic, performance goals, view failures as changeable, own their successes, and take control.

Reference

Vealey, R.S. (1986) 'Conceptualization of Sport-confidence and Competitive Orientation: Preliminary Investigation and Instrument Development', *Journal of Sport Psychology* 8: 221–46.

Further reading

Manzo, L. (2002) 'Enhancing Sport Performance: The Role of Confidence and Concentration', in J.M. Silva and D.E. Stevens (eds) *Psychological Foundations of Sport*, 247–71, Boston MA: Allyn and Bacon.

LEAPETSWE MALETE

ENTERTAINMENT AND SPORTS PROGRAMMING NETWORK (ESPN)

ESPN, Inc. is a multinational corporation consisting of television, radio, internet, and print media organisations focused upon sports and sports entertainment. It was founded in 1979 as a single cable channel (ESP-TV) by Bill and Scott Rasmussen in Bristol, Connecticut, United States, before reaching fame as the Entertainment and Sports Programming Network (ESPN). The full name was dropped in 1985 and is now simply known by the former acronym.

ESPN, Inc. is comprised of over forty international companies, including twenty-five television channels, a radio network (ESPN Radio), wireless networks, ESPN.com and other internet channels, *ESPN The Magazine*, restaurants (ESPN Club, ESPN Zone), and other organisations. ESPN is a subsidiary of the United States broadcast network ABC, Inc. and the Hearst Corporation also owns a 20 per cent interest.

More than any other single institution, ESPN helped facilitate the tremendous growth in professional and collegiate sports in the United States and in many other countries world-wide. By 2000, the three largest ESPN television channels (ESPN, ESPN2, ESPNews) were carried by more than 60,000 US cable providers and reached 76 million, 65 million, and 12 million US households, respectively. In 1998, profits by the original television channel alone (ESPN) reached $356 million on over $1.1 billion generated in revenue.

Although ESPN's daily news program, *SportsCenter*, remains the network's highest rated programme, ESPN has also helped popularise such programmes as the National Football League (NFL) and National Basketball Association (NBA) player drafts; National Collegiate Athletic Association (NCAA) men's and women's college basketball tournaments; the NCAA College World Series; the 'X Games', which include 'extreme' sports such as snowboarding, skateboarding, motocross, and surfing; 'outdoor sports' such as hunting and fishing; auto racing; rodeo; professional tennis and golf; and all of the North American professional sporting leagues, including the NFL, NBA, Major League Baseball (MLB), and National Hockey League (NHL).

ESPN's impressive list of sports broadcasters, reporters, and programme anchors over its history include such household names as Chris Berman, Dick Vitale, Greg Gumbel, Dan Patrick, Keith Olbermann, and Craig Kilborn. Although some, as Berman, have remained with the company since its inception, others, such as Olbermann and Kilborn, have been openly critical of ESPN, Inc. management after leaving.

ESPN has also seen its fair share of scandals. Tales of widespread gambling and drug use by employees date back to the early 1980s, while sexual harassment claims dogged the male-dominated network during the 1990s.

References

ESPN, Inc. website (2003) *ESPN.go.com* Retrieved 12 June 2003 from http://espn.go.com/sitetools/s/help/espn-faq.html#ESPN

Freeman, M. (2000) *ESPN: The Uncensored History*, Dallas TX: Taylor Publishing Company.

Olbermann, K. and Patrick, D. (1997) *The Big Show: Inside ESPN's SportsCenter*, New York: Pocket Books.

MICHAEL A. HUNT

ENVIRONMENT

The United Nations Environment Program (UNEP) defines environment as 'the area in which something exists or lives, the totality of the surrounding conditions'. The environment includes the built environment of cities as well as the more commonly referred to natural environment, which includes three main components: air, land, and water. The term environment is usually invoked to describe the external conditions that affect an organism or other specified system during its lifetime. Conversely, the term describes the manner in which organisms, such as human populations, affect the external environment in return. Often the term is used in a narrower context, such as economic environment, business environment or cultural environment, although for the purposes of this definition we shall focus on its wider, more general, meaning, as accessible sport and leisure opportunities rely on an optimal environment.

Humanity's relationship with the environment is critical to its well-being and survival, yet threats posed by human populations have only recently begun to enter the consciousness of Western societies. This curious ignorance of human/nature relations can be traced back to the philosophical shift in European thought known as the Enlightenment. The fifteenth-century philosophical works of René Descartes and Isaac Newton challenged the medieval notion of a natural environment imbued with spirit and mystery. Newton and Descartes believed the mysteries of nature could be reasoned and controlled through the language of mathematics. Descartes' famous dictum 'I think, therefore I am' placed a priority on the mind; the body and the environment were seen as secondary, a mere extension of human thought.

The Newtonian-Cartesian world view precipitated the birth of modern science and technology, and the notion of human progress. The industrial revolution, material wealth, urbanisation and, more recently, globalisation have generated environmental degradation on an unprecedented scale. The decline in environmental utility has focused the attention of theorists on the continued commitment to Enlightenment values, particularly the pursuit of 'progress'

and its concomitant economic growth. In contrast, members of traditional societies, such as Australian Aboriginals, South and North American Indians, and the tribal groups of Africa, have lived in greater harmony with their environments, ensuring the long-term sustainability of natural resources. In order to maximise sport and leisure opportunities for all citizens, governments need to maintain their country's physical, social, and cultural environments; this means having regard to mechanisms that will provide this, such as sustainable practices.

In the West, 'romantic' writers, who expressed the idea that nature was good and that wild nature was even better, first challenged the Enlightenment values of industrial progress in the eighteenth century. The ideas put forth by these authors (e.g. Wordsworth, Blake, and Coleridge) initiated a cultural shift. The fear and hatred of wild places was replaced with an appreciation and love for their beauty and mystery. The evolution of these ideas inspired the conservation and preservation movement of the late nineteenth century. More recently an expanded environmental consciousness in the West has led to the rise of a range of influential social and political movements. Environmentally sustainable development, or ESD, has now become enshrined in law in most countries in the West, and is subsequently reflected in government and corporate policy. Sport provides a catalyst to enhance these policies, and mechanisms to ensure citizens can use sport and leisure opportunities for self-fulfilment, developing communities, and cultural identity, as well as promoting international understanding and cooperation, and enhancing quality of life.

The principles of ESD are also now reflected in sport policy; for example, environmental sustainability is enshrined as a goal of the Olympic movement, and the Sydney 2000 and Athens 2004 Olympic Games consequently instituted a range of environmentally sustainable measures. Many

417

'green' political movements have arisen out of a desire to protect natural resources for recreational and sporting activities, for example surfing, horse riding, fishing, bush-walking, swimming, and rowing.

References

Chernushenko, D. (1994) 'Greening our Games: Running Sports Events and Facilities That Won't Cost the Earth', Ottawa: Centurion Publishing and Marketing.

Goldblatt, D. (1996) *Social Theory and the Environment*, Cambridge: Polity Press.

STEPHEN WEARING

ENVIRONMENTAL CONSTRAINTS

A constraint (see **constraints-led perspective**) is any factor that shapes or guides an action, thus influencing the self-organisation processes in a movement system. Environmental constraints can be physical or social. An important physical constraint is gravity, with which all biological systems on earth have to deal. General physical environmental constraints can be characterised by ambient temperature or energy flows, such as acoustic and optical information surrounding a performer. Children's motor development can be understood as an ongoing response to the constraint of gravity, and the appearance and disappearance of 'milestone' motor skills, particularly the stepping reflex, can be explained by changes in the muscle-to-fat ratio in growing movement systems that allow adaptation to gravitational forces on lower limb segments. Another important physical environmental constraint is altitude. The effects of altitude on the cardio-respiratory system affect movement solutions, and specific adaptive training is required for athletes performing at high altitude. Also, ambient temperature can affect muscle properties, which is why athletes perform rigorous warm-up routines in cold performance climates, such as when performing winter sports and physical activities. In very warm conditions athletes need to undergo heat acclimation training to help them respond appropriately.

Some environmental constraints are more specific. Biological systems, such as movement systems, are animate – as opposed to physical systems, which are inanimate – and generally non-conservative. That is to say, they are 'open' to energy flows and have energy flowing within the system. Openness refers to the ability of biological systems to adapt and attune to their environs. Energy surrounding such systems can act as an environmental constraint on emergent behaviour. Evolution of the sensory systems allows for the continual behavioural adaptation of biological movement systems to instantaneous internal and external changes. Functional coordination patterns – task-directed movements, and the transition from one to another, are guided by the information available to a biological system with sensory, for example visual, systems. Behaviours depicting successful task solutions surface under the instantaneous constraints of that behaviour, for example, saving a shot at goal in soccer, are successful only if they achieve their purpose while conforming to the constraints present at the time and place they are performed. All movements take place in an environment, thus movement coordination should be understood with reference to the environment in which it occurs, rather than separate from it. Trying to understand movement coordination in isolation from environmental constraints would result in the amplification of the degrees of freedom problem.

Since humans live in societies, some environmental constraints are of a social nature. Social constraints are found in socio-cultural contexts of behaviour, such as societal attitudes towards participation in sport, parental support, and peer group values. The physical activity patterns and sport choices of individuals can be constrained in subtle ways by social expectations and norms, including availability of facilities, media images and marketing influences on peer groups, national playing styles and cultural values, and expectations of performance.

See also: environmental stress – high altitude; environmental stress – temperature; optic variables

Reference

Williams, A.M., Davids, K. and Williams, J.G. (1999) *Visual Perception and Action in Sport*, London: E&FN Spon.

KEITH DAVIDS
STUART MOYLE

ENVIRONMENTAL STRESS

There are three predominant stresses to which athletes may be exposed in training, racing, or both – heat, cold, and reduced oxygen content in the inspired air as occurs at increasing altitude. To survive, humans require to regulate their body temperatures at between 35 and 41°C and to maintain the partial pressure of oxygen in their blood in excess of about 40 mm of mercury (Hg).

Low body temperatures of 35°C occur in swimmers exposed to cold water temperatures for many hours, for example, in English Channel swimmers. This occurs because the naked body exposed to a volume of water that is colder than the skin temperature is unable to produce heat as rapidly as it is lost by the process of conduction to the surrounding water. Wearing more appropriate clothing, in particular, dry or wet suits that maintain a layer of insulating water or air heated to body temperature, is the only way to prevent the ultimate development of a fatal hypothermia – low body temperature – when exposed to cold water for any prolonged period.

Elevated body temperatures of up to 41.5°C are frequently found in healthy winners of short distance, 5–15 km, running events contested in hot, humid, and windless environmental conditions. Such high body temperatures occur because the rate at which elite athletes produce heat when running at their maximum pace can exceed the capacity of the hot environment to absorb that heat. Fortunately, the brain also has protective mechanisms that reduce the allowable rate of energy production during **exercise in the heat**. As a result, incidences of severe heat injury – heat stroke – are remarkably uncommon in sport despite the frequency with which sport is played in severe environmental conditions.

As humans ascend to increasing altitude, they are exposed to a progressively lower partial pressure of oxygen in the inspired air. As a result the partial pressure of oxygen in the blood supplying their brains also falls. Although there are several physiological adaptations that increase this pressure, ultimately each human will reach an altitude at which they are no longer able to survive, since their blood oxygen pressure falls below that required for those crucial brain functions necessary for sustaining life. Exercise at altitude is also regulated by the brain to ensure that the exercise intensity that is allowed will not lower the blood oxygen partial pressure to the point at which consciousness is lost.

See also: environmental stress – high altitude; environmental stress – temperature; exercise in, and acclimatisation to, the cold

TIM NOAKES

ENVIRONMENTAL STRESS – HIGH ALTITUDE

Besides the obvious risks of falling with often fatal consequences, high altitude poses two distinct physiological challenges for the human body. The first is posed by the increasingly lower amount of oxygen in the air as one ascends to higher altitudes; the second is posed by the cold and wind. Fortunately, high altitude is usually dry, so that it is easier to keep clothes dry than in the cold and wet conditions that predominate at lower altitudes. However, the presence of high winds at altitude markedly increases the coldness of the environment by increasing the wind chill factor.

As the altitude above sea level increases, the barometric pressure falls. As a result of the decreasing pressure, the distance between oxygen molecules in the air is reduced. Consequently, the oxygen present in each litre of air decreases. Partially to compensate for this, humans need to breathe more often and more deeply at altitude. But despite this, as the altitude increases, the concentration, or partial pressure, of oxygen in the blood falls to values that are not compatible with sustained human life at altitudes much above about 7,000 m. That some humans are able to reach the summit of Mount Everest, at 8,840 m, attests to the phenomenal biology of some humans, to the value of oxygen inhalation for others, and to the quite remarkable ability of most humans to adapt to the stresses to which they are exposed for weeks to months.

Some of the original studies of exercise at altitude were undertaken by a United States research group led by David Dill and his colleagues from the Harvard University Fatigue Laboratory (see Dill 1938). Their research established two crucial findings. First, that peak blood lactate concentrations during maximum exercise fell with increasing altitude, a phenomenon since labelled the 'lactate paradox'. This finding is paradoxical since, according to the traditional cardiovascular-anaerobic model of exercise physiology, exercise at altitude should cause an increased skeletal muscle anaerobiosis, always terminating with very high blood lactate concentrations. The second paradoxical finding was that the maximum heart rate and output of the heart – cardiac output – likewise fell during exercise at increasing altitude. This is paradoxical, for the logic of the cardiovascular-anaerobic

model demands that if the principal responsibility of the cardiovascular system during exercise is the achievement of an – ultimately inadequate – oxygen supply to skeletal muscle, then the maximum cardiac output during exercise at increasing altitude must either stay the same or even increase at increasing altitude, to limit the effects of the progressive reduction in the concentration of oxygen in arterial blood.

Yet the evidence from many studies is now absolutely clear; the heart makes the exactly opposite adjustment, so that the maximum cardiac output falls with increasing altitude. Hence the conclusion must be that some unrecognised mechanism must exist to ensure that neither the heart nor the skeletal muscles ever become 'anaerobic' during maximal exercise at any altitude – from sea level to the summit of Mount Everest – in healthy humans.

Dill's colleague, H.T. Edwards (Edwards 1936) was the first to suggest a possible solution:

> The inability to accumulate large amounts of lactate at high altitudes suggests a protective mechanism preventing an already low arterial saturation from becoming markedly lower. ... It may be that the protective mechanism lies in an inadequate oxygen supply to essential muscles, e.g. the diaphragm or the muscles.

These studies invite two precise conclusions. First, that the oxygen demands of the skeletal muscles are not the cardinal priority and, hence, are not 'protected' during maximum exercise, at least at extreme altitude. Second, neither the skeletal muscles nor the heart becomes 'anaerobic' during maximal exercise under conditions of a severe reduction in the oxygen content of the inspired air – hypoxia. The sole conclusion must be that some type of regulator exists to limit maximum exercise at altitude. Further, this raises the possibility that the same control mechanism may also act similarly during maximum exercise at sea level. For if this is not the case, then the human design must have included a regulation specific to only one condition of exercise, namely that at extreme altitude. But if the opposite is the case, then the original design of the human must have anticipated that one day humans will wish to climb to the summit of Mount Everest so that a unique control active only under those conditions must be included.

Thus various studies have shown that under the precise conditions likely to induce anaerobiosis in either the heart or skeletal muscles – maximal exercise at altitude – neither the heart nor the active skeletal muscles show any evidence whatsoever for 'anaerobic' metabolism. This unexpected finding can be explained only if there is a 'governor', probably in the central nervous system (CNS), whose function is likely to prevent blood oxygen concentrations from dropping too low for the normal function of one or more organs, most probably the brain but also perhaps the heart as also proposed by Dill (1938): 'The capacity of the heart, as has already been suggested, is restricted at high altitude because of the deficiency in supply of oxygen to it'. The same governor could also serve a similar overall function at sea level, although the factor that needs protection at sea level is not the blood oxygen content, which remains high. Precisely what variable is 'protected' during maximal exercise at sea level remains uncertain. But the important point is that both at sea level and at altitude, exercise terminates before the development of an oxygen deficiency or with other evidence for any failure of its homeostatic regulation.

Accordingly, the conclusion would be that the proposed 'governor' acts to terminate exercise before any homeostatic failure. The proposed governor would work in the following manner: When the brain calculates that to continue at a particular exercise intensity will cause a failure of homeostasis in one or more organ systems, it reduces the number of muscle fibres that it allows to be active in the exercising muscles. As a result, the work output of the body falls, allowing homeostasis to be more easily sustained at this lower rate of energy turnover.

Confirmation for the presence of this theoretical governor comes from the work of Kayser et al. (1994). They showed that the amount of skeletal muscle that is recruited by the brain during exercise, and which is measured as skeletal muscle electromyographic activity (EMG) at peak exercise, falls with increasing altitude, but increases acutely with oxygen administration that immediately increases the partial pressure of oxygen in the arterial blood. They concluded: 'during chronic hypobaric hypoxia, the central nervous system may play a primary role in limiting exhaustive exercise and maximum accumulation of lactate in blood'. More recently Kayser has concluded that exercise 'begins and ends in the brain' (Kayser 2003).

Interestingly, had the human body been designed to function according to the modern physiologists' cardiovascular-anaerobic model, which requires that anaerobiosis first develops in skeletal muscle before maximal exercise is terminated, no climber would ever have reached the summit of Mount Everest or other high mountain, even with the use of supplemental oxygen. Rather, all would have succumbed to a combination of myocardial ischaemia and cerebral hypoxia while their skeletal muscles were exercising vigorously and unrestrainedly, in pursuit of anaerobiosis and fatigue.

In summary, studies of maximal exercise performance at extreme altitude confirm the hypothetical existence and action of a CNS 'governor', first proposed by A.V. Hill, the function of which is to ensure that no bodily system ever reaches its absolute maximal functional capacity, so that there is always some functional reserve. Thus, before the limits are reached, the brain reduces the number of skeletal muscle fibres that are active. As a consequence, skeletal muscle recruitment either fails to rise further or it falls, limiting the work output of the body. At the same time, the brain develops the sensations of fatigue to ensure that there is not conscious effort to override this sensible control mechanism. The resulting fall in work output insures that homeostasis can be more easily maintained. The presence of a 'governor' preventing the development of anaerobiosis in brain, heart, or skeletal muscle during exercise at altitude has interesting implications for theories of the value of exercise training at altitude. For its presence means that any beneficial effect of altitude training cannot result from repeated exposure of the brain, heart, or exercising skeletal muscle to greater extents of 'anaerobiosis' than can be achieved during maximal exercise at sea level. This might explain why there remains considerable controversy about the proven value of high-intensity training at altitude.

See also: central governor – evidence for; physiology of exercise

References

Dill, D.B. (1938) *Life, Heat and Altitude*, Cambridge MA: Harvard University Press.

Edwards, H.T. (1936) 'Lactic Acid in Rest and Work at High Altitude', *American Journal of Physiology* 116: 367–75.

Kayser, B. (2003) 'Exercise Begins and Ends in the Brain', *European Journal of Applied Physiology* 90: 411–19.

Kayser, B., Narici, M., Binzoni, T., Grassi, B. and Cerretelli, P. (1994) 'Fatigue and Exhaustion in Chronic Hypobaric Hypoxia: Influence of Exercising Muscle Mass', *Journal of Applied Physiology* 76: 634–40.

Noakes, T.D. (1997) 'Challenging Beliefs: Ex Africa Semper Aliquid Novi', *Medicine and Science in Sports and Exercise* 29: 571–90.

—— (1998) 'Maximal Oxygen Uptake: "Classical" Versus "Contemporary" Viewpoints. A Rebuttal', *Medicine and Science in Sports and Exercise* 30: 1381–98.

—— (2000) 'Physiological Models to Understand Exercise Fatigue and The Adaptations That Predict or Enhance Athletic Performance', *Scandinavian Journal of Medicine and Science in Sports* 10: 123–45.

Noakes, T.D., Peltonen, J.E. and Rusko, H.K. (2001) 'Evidence that a Central Governor Regulates Exercise Performance During Acute Hypoxia and Hyperoxia', *Journal of Experimental Biology* 204: 3325–34.

TIM NOAKES

ENVIRONMENTAL STRESS – TEMPERATURE

One of the physiological problems that athletes face during exercise is how to lose the excess body heat produced by muscle contraction. The converse challenge – maintaining a normal body temperature when exercising in cold and especially wet conditions in which heat loss is increased – becomes a problem only when exercising under extreme environmental conditions without adequate clothing to provide protection against cold, wet, and windy conditions.

The human body temperature, which is regulated in health between about 37 and 40°C depending on the time of day, the amount of exercise undertaken, and the environmental conditions, represents a balance between the rate of heat production by, and heat loss from, the body. Hence, changes in the rates of either heat production or heat loss or more commonly both, determine whether an abnormal rise in body temperature – heat stroke – or an excessive fall – hypothermia – is likely to develop and under what conditions.

During exercise, the chemical energy stored in the muscles in the form of adenosine triphosphate (ATP) is converted into the mechanical energy of motion. However, this process is inefficient, so that only 25 per cent of the chemical energy used by the muscles produces motion; the remaining 75 per cent is released as heat that must be lost from the body if the body temperature is to be safely regulated between 37 and 40°C.

This phenomenon inspired the Norwegian Roald Amundsen, leader of the first expedition to reach the South Pole in 1911, to remark that the human body is a furnace. And the furnace burns only more fiercely during exercise. Indeed, the rate at which the body produces heat is a linear function of speed, when running at any speed and when walking at speeds below 7 km h^{-1}. At higher walking speeds, energy production rises as an exponential function of walking speed, as is also the case in cycling. Thus in both cycling and very fast walking, it takes increasingly more energy to move just that little bit faster.

Thus, when ultra marathon runners run at an average pace of about 16 km h^{-1} during races of 90–100 km, they use about 56 kJ of energy every minute, or about 18,480 kJ in the 5.5 h that they require to complete these races. But, of the total amount of energy used, only about 4,000 kJ actually transport them from the start to the finish of their races. The remaining 14,480 kJ serve only to overheat the runners' bodies. To prevent their temperatures from rising to over 43°C, causing heat stroke, these athletes have to lose more than 90 per cent of the heat they produce.

Therefore, the challenge when exercising in warm conditions is to lose heat fast enough to ensure that the body temperature does not rise too far, causing heat stroke. Conversely, the test when exercising particularly in cold and wet environmental conditions is to retain that heat to prevent the development of hypothermia. Environmental conditions, in particular the environmental temperature, the wind speed, and the water content of the air, its humidity, determine the rate at which heat is lost from the body. Hence they determine the rate of body cooling at any given rate of heat production.

The normal average human skin temperature is 33°C. At any lower environmental temperature, heat will be lost from the skin to the environment as the body tries to heat up the air in direct contact with it. This process is known as conduction. The rate at which this heat will be lost by conduction from the body will, in turn, be determined by the magnitude of the temperature gradient – the steeper the gradient, the greater the heat loss – and the rapidity with which the air in contact with the skin, is replaced by colder air. Continual replacement of warmed air by cooler air causes loss of heat from the body, by means of convection. Convective heat loss rises as an exponential function of the speed at which air passes across the body, in effect the prevailing wind speed.

Therefore, wind of increasing speed dramatically increases the 'coldness' of any environmental temperature, in effect reducing the effective temperature to which the body is exposed and, thereby, increasing the rate of heat loss from the body. This is known as the wind chill factor.

The humidity of the air determines the extent to which heat can be lost to the environment in the form of sweat that evaporates from the skin surface and, to a lesser extent, from the respiratory membranes. This process is known as evaporation. This is the predominant source of heat loss in exercising humans, particularly in the heat, since each gram of water so evaporated removes 1.8 kJ of energy from the body. Only sweat that evaporates from the skin actively contributes to heat loss; sweat that drips from the skin fails to cool the body. As the humidity of the air rises, the efficiency of heat loss by evaporation falls, so that the ease of maintaining heat balance becomes increasingly difficult as the humidity rises above 60–70 per cent.

Whereas air is a poor conductor of heat and, hence, a good insulator, water conducts heat approximately twenty-five times faster than does air and is, hence, a very poor insulator. Thus, the thin layer of air trapped next to the skin by clothing is rapidly heated to the skin temperature, thereby producing a layer of insulation. But the saturation of clothing with water removes this insulating layer and essentially exposes the skin to whatever is the external temperature. This loss of insulation caused by water explains why saturated, wet clothing or swimming in cold water predisposes to the development of hypothermia. Under these conditions, the exposed human must either find dry, warm clothing and a warm shelter or die from hypothermia. There is no other realistic alternative. All deaths from hypothermia occur as an inevitable consequence of these fundamental laws of physics.

One final mechanism exists to ensure that humans are less likely to develop heat stroke when exercising in hot, warm, and humid conditions. Feedback from sensors throughout the body to a central regulator in the brain, the postulated central governor, monitor both the extent of the environmental stress to which the body is exposed, as well as the rate at which the body stores thermal energy during exercise in those environmental conditions. Since it is safe to exercise only to a body temperature of less than 42°C, on exposure to the prevailing environmental conditions at the onset of exercise, and on the basis of the rate at which thermal energy will be stored and the expected duration of the exercise, the brain calculates the rate at which work can be safely performed under those specific environmental conditions. The central governor, therefore, pre-sets the number of motor units in the active muscles that can be recruited to ensure that a safe rate of heat production is allowed for the expected duration of the exercise. At the same time, the brain pre-sets the rate at which the perception of effort increases during the exercise bout, so that the perceived effort of continuing to exercise becomes intolerable before the body is elevated to a dangerous temperature.

In this way, the brain ensures that heat stroke occurs uncommonly during exercise.

However, drugs that interfere with this central control mechanism and, in particular, with the perception of effort during exercise, make heat stroke more likely. So it is that some of the classic cases of heat stroke in famous athletes, including the tragic death of British cyclist Tom Simpson on the Mount Ventoux stage of the 1967 Tour de France, were clearly caused by the use of amphetamines or other centrally acting stimulants that override this usually effective safety mechanism.

See also: excessive heat stress effects; exercise in the heat; heat tolerance – affecting factors; thermal balance and thermoregulation

References

Marino, F.E., Lambert, M.I. and Noakes, T.D. (2004) 'Superior Performance of African Runners in Warm Humid but Not in Cool Environmental Conditions', *Journal of Applied Physiology* 96: 124–30.

Noakes, T.D. (2002) *Lore of Running, Third Edition*, ch. 4, Champaign IL: Human Kinetics.

TIM NOAKES

EPHEDRINE

Ephedrine, a sympathomimetic amine, has been implicated in the deaths of several athletes, and this has prompted a closer examination of ephedrine. Until 1994, ephedrine was mainly consumed in over-the-counter decongestants and prescription drugs, and the biggest concern was that it could be used to manufacture methamphetamine. The United States Dietary Supplement Health and Education Act (DSHEA) of 1994 ushered in a new era for **nutritional supplements**, and herbal ephedra has been advertised as both a weight-loss product and an energy booster. Despite its ban by most sports organizations, ephedrine's easy accessibility has created a large market for its stimulant properties as an ergogenic aid.

It is important to distinguish between pharmaceutical-grade ephedrine and herbal-extract ephedra sold as a dietary supplement. The latter has been available in China for thousands of years as Ma Huang, and although its active ingredient is ephedrine (one of many ephedra alkaloids), it also contains pseudoephedrine, methylphenedrine, methylpseudoephedrine and norpseduoephedrine (cathine). The presence of multiple compounds is further exacerbated by lack of governmental oversight due to DSHEA. Indeed, Gurley examined twenty ephedra-containing herbal supplements and found that half exhibited major discrepancies between content and the labels with significant lot-to-lot variations among products. This demonstrated that for ephedra, like many other dietary supplements, labels are not a reliable indicator of content.

Ephedrine is an adrenergic stimulant that causes vasoconstriction, bronchodilation, tachycardia, and is a weak inotrope. As such, it has been associated with cerebrovascular events, myocardial infarctions, major psychiatric symptoms, autonomic hyperactivity and death. At least 100 cases of death or severe reactions have been definitely or possibly related to ephedra in the United States. In about half of these cases, the individuals were less than thirty years old. Data from the 2001 United States Poison Control Centers revealed that ephedra products accounted for 64 per cent of all adverse reactions to herbs, yet only 4.3 per cent of herbal sales during that same time period.

Although athletes frequently consume ephedra products, there are no studies using ephedra-containing dietary supplements for performance-enhancement. The only related studies are a small number that used pharmaceutical ephedrine alone or in combination with caffeine. Most of these utilized military recruits as subjects and measured short-term use. Bell and colleagues demonstrated modest effects of ephedrine with increased power output and reduced ten-kilometer run times, although additive effects with caffeine were observed in some of the trials. It is essential to note that these tests do not reflect the typical usage patterns of athletes and results with ephedrine cannot be extrapolated to herbal ephedra-containing products.

Ephedra is also marketed as a thermogenic for weight loss, and this appeals to athletes who compete in sports where thinness is desirable. It is not surprising that the 2001 National Collegiate Athletic Association Drug Use survey found that wrestlers and gymnasts had very high rates of ephedrine use. Meta-analysis of research using ephedra and caffeine-containing herbal supplements or ephedrine plus caffeine revealed an additional two pounds of weight loss per month as compared to placebo in studies between 4 and 6 months duration.

Reports of adverse reactions have led supplement manufacturers to promote 'ephedrine-free' products, and many interpret this to mean 'stimulant-free'. In actuality, these products usually contain Citrus Aurantium, otherwise known at Bitter Orange of Zhi Shi. The main ingredient is likely synephrine, but it also contains octopamine and tyramine. Synephrine is a close relative of ephedrine and has similar effects, and will likely result in similar adverse reactions as the number of users increases.

Alarming reports of adverse reactions due to ephedra, including the deaths of several high-profile athletes, eventually led the United States Food and Drug Administration to ban the use of ephedra in dietary supplements in December 2003. However, it is apparent that athletes have a desire for **stimulants** and will likely continue to seek alternatives.

References

Bell, D.G., Jacobs, I., and Ellerington, K. (2001) 'Effects of Caffeine and Ephedrine on Anaerobic Exercise Performance', *Medicine and Science in Sports and Exercise* 33:1399–403.

Bent, S., Tiedt, T.N, Odden, M.C. and Shiplak, M.G. (2003) 'The Relative Safety of Ephedra Compared with Other Herbal Products', *Annals of Internal Medicine* 138: 468–71.

Gurley, B.J., Gardner, S.F. and Hubbard, M.A.. (2000) 'Content vs. Label Claims in Ephedra-containing Dietary Supplements', *American Journal of Health-Systems Pharmacology* 57:963–9.

GARY GREEN

EPILEPSY IN ATHLETES

Epilepsy can be defined as a convulsive disorder characterized by sudden, brief, repetitive and stereotyped alterations in behavior, which are presumed to be due to paroxysmal discharge of cortical and sub-cortical neurons. Epilepsy is a common neurological disorder, and about 10 per cent of the population will at some time in their life have a seizure. Epilepsy is therefore also common in children and young adults who are physically active and wish to participate in sport.

Does regular exercise increase the risk of seizures?

It is common for patients with epilepsy to enquire whether regular exercise increases the risk or perhaps decreases the risk of precipitating seizures. In a recently published study, the exercise habits in a sample of adult outpatients with epilepsy were compared with those in the general population of the same age and sex. The results of the study showed that in the majority of patients with epilepsy, physical exercise had no adverse effects, and a considerable proportion (36 per cent) claimed that regular exercise contributed to better seizure control. However, in approximately 10 per cent of the patients, exercise appeared to be a seizure precipitant, and this applied particularly to those with symptomatic partial epilepsy. The risk of sustaining serious seizure-related injuries by exercising seemed modest.

Participation in a structured program of fairly intensive leisure activity on seizure occurrence was also investigated in adults with medically intractable epilepsy. The relative risk of seizures did not differ significantly during activity days [0.71 (95 per cent CL: 0.38 to 1.33)] compared with days of relative rest. Cognitive exertion, including physical exercise, therefore had no adverse effect on seizure control.

Patients with chronic epilepsy (without visual sensitivity) were studied to determine if exposure to video-game material is a risk factor for seizures. The results of this study showed that seizures occurrence was similar during periods of video-game play and during alternative leisure activities, including physical exercise.

Physical activity alone or combined with other leisure activities, therefore, does not appear to increase the risk of seizure occurrence. The only exception may be in patients with an underlying structural brain lesion, where there may be an increased risk of seizures during physical exercise.

Are there special considerations for sports participation in patients with epilepsy?

Contact sports

It has been suggested that contact sports, in which there is an increased risk of head injury, may be contra-indicated in patients with epilepsy. However, there is no evidence to suggest that there is a greater risk for immediate or early seizures after a head injury in epileptic patients. Therefore, epileptic patients can safely engage in contact sports, provided normal precautions are taken to protect against head injury, such as wearing protective headgear.

Swimming and water sports

It has been well documented that recreational swimming by epileptic patients

426

compared to the general population, carries a fourfold increase in the risk of drowning. This risk is higher in children, and most drownings occurred when there was no supervision. Therefore, swimming for epileptic patients is not contra-indicated provided there is adequate (qualified lifeguard) supervision during swimming.

High-risk sports

There are sports where there may be a substantially increased risk of injury or even fatality if a seizure occurs during the activity. These would include sports such as rock climbing, parachuting, and hang gliding. Legal and ethical issues require careful consideration when participation in these sports is discussed with an athlete.

See also: head and neck injury-global scene of prevention; exercise-related headache

Reference

Millett, C.J., Johnson, A.L., Thompson, P.J. and Fish, D.R. (2001) 'A Study of the Relationship Between Participation in Common Leisure Activities and Seizure Occurrence', *Acta Neurol Scand* 103, 5: 300–3.

MARTIN SCHWELLNUS

EQUILIBRIUM AND STABILITY

More than one external force usually acts on the sports performer. The effect produced by this combination of forces – the force system – will depend on their magnitudes and relative directions. Figure 20 shows the biomechanical system of interest, here a runner, isolated from the surrounding world. The effects of those surroundings that, for the runner, ignoring air resistance, are weight and ground reaction force, are represented on the diagram as force vectors.

The effects of such force systems are often considered by using statics, a useful and mathematically simple and powerful branch of **mechanics**. Statics is used to

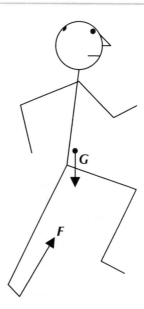

Figure 20. Free body diagram.

study force systems in which the forces are in equilibrium, such that they have no resultant effect on the object on which they act. This approach may seem somewhat limited in sport, in which the net, or resultant, effect of the forces acting is usually to cause the object to accelerate. If the resultant force passes through a runner's **centre of mass**, the runner can be represented as a point – the centre of mass – because only changes in **linear motion** will occur for such a force system. If, as is usually the case, as in the figure, the resultant force does not act through the centre of mass, a moment of force will tend to rotate the runner. It is possible to treat dynamic systems of forces, such as that in the figure, using the equations of static equilibrium. This involves introducing into the system an imaginary inertia force, which is equal in magnitude to the resultant force, but opposite in direction, to produce a quasi-static force system. The general equations of static equilibrium are: the sum of all the forces, including the imaginary inertia forces, is zero and the sum of all the moments of force, including inertia ones, is also zero. These equations of static equilibrium can be applied to all force systems that are static or have been made quasi-static through the use of inertia forces and moments.

Collinear systems consist of forces with the same line of action, such as the forces in a tug-of-war rope. Concurrent force systems also have the lines of action of the forces pass through a common point – the collinear system is a special case. Two-dimensional and three-dimensional concurrent force systems can be found in sport and exercise movements; as all forces pass through the centre of mass, no moment equilibrium equation is relevant. Parallel force systems have the lines of action of all the forces parallel. The tendency of the forces to rotate the object about some point means that the equation of moment equilibrium must be considered. The simple cases of first- and third-class levers in the human musculoskeletal system (see **muscle mechanics**) are examples of two-dimensional parallel force systems. General force systems may be two-dimensional, as for the runner in the figure, or three-dimensional, have none of the above simplifications, and are the ones normally found in sports biomechanics, such as the various soft tissue forces acting on a body segment.

When a force acting on a sports performer threatens the equilibrium of that person, for example, a wrestler being pulled or pushed over by another wrestler, causing him or her to topple about the base of support with the ground, then the stability of that position can be enhanced by one or more of the following actions. Lowering the **centre of mass** will reduce the moment arm of the toppling force. Increasing the base of support will provide scope for increasing the moment arm of the person's weight, which counters the toppling moment; moving the line of gravity – the vertical line through the centre of mass – towards the side of the base of support from which the threatening force

acts will then increase the stabilising moment.

Reference

Bartlett, R.M. (1997) *Introduction to Sports Biomechanics*, ch. 3, London: E&FN Spon.

ROGER BARTLETT

EQUIPMENT-PERFORMER INTERACTION

Engineering techniques are increasingly used to optimise the design of sports equipment. Consequently, materials with characteristics such as minimal weight, maximum strength, or optimal cushioning can be selected. However, it is important when applying engineering techniques to the design of sports equipment to ensure the end user is not neglected. For example, it may be tempting to design a golf club to allow maximal driving distance to be achieved off the tee, but this is approach is futile if the resulting golf club requires such effort from the golfer that injury results. Equipment-performer interaction is, therefore, an important aspect in the development of optimal equipment design.

The design of sports equipment ideally utilises the skills of a practitioner from the human sciences, typically a sports biomechanist. As well as wanting to use the most appropriate materials and structure for the specific equipment, the biomechanist is concerned with how the human reacts and adapts to their environment. A challenge to the sports biomechanist, therefore, is to improve understanding of how individuals typically respond to changes in their environment, such as a modification in playing surface, footwear, club, or racquet. This involves applying controlled, systematic changes in design and monitoring the human response.

An example of where equipment-performer interaction has been studied extensively is in sports shoe design. The isolated use of engineering techniques to shoe midsole design could focus on the selection of materials that optimally reduce and distribute loads. However, biomechanical studies have revealed that when humans run, wearing shoes of different material cushioning, similar forces occur. It appears that the human is able to adapt to the changes in cushioning provided by the shoe by manipulation of intrinsic cushioning mechanisms. Such knowledge has influenced the focus of resulting shoe designs. This example highlights the importance of considering the equipment-performer interaction and is, ideally, the approach that should be employed in design of all sports equipment.

See also: running shoes; sports equipment; sports footwear

References

Dabnichki, P. (1998) 'Biomechanical Testing and Sport Equipment Design', *Sports Engineering* 1: 93–106.

Frederick, E.C. (1986) 'Kinematically Mediated Effects of Sports Shoe Design: A Review', *Journal of Sports Sciences* 4: 169–84.

SHARON J. DIXON

EQUITY

Equity is concerned with fairness in the allocation of resources. It addresses the question, 'Who gets what?' Equity does not necessarily mean equality. Equality has to do with sameness in quantity and quality, while equity has to do with fairness and justice. An equity standard is implied whenever decisions are made in how public resources for sport are to be allocated.

In the context of sport, the equity debate flourishes at two levels. The first arises when one-off major construction projects use public money to develop stadia and arenas to stage mega events or to support major league professional sports franchises.

The second debate relates to the criteria to be used to allocate public resources for sport among competing constituencies.

The one-off, major facility issue has two dimensions. The first is relatively narrow and focused. It relates to who wins and who loses among the specific demographic groups located in the area where a major new facility is constructed. A city is not a unitary entity that is impacted uniformly by a major sport construction project. It has been noted that such projects have a tendency to displace groups of citizens located in the poorer sections of cities, either through mandatory relocation or more insidiously by substantial increases in housing and real estate values that may follow public improvements of the area. The people most affected by such displacement, typically are those who are least able to organize and finance community resistance to such proposals. For example, it has been reported that in the case of the Barcelona Olympic Games, the market price of old and new housing rose between 1986 and 1992 by 240 and 287 per cent, respectively, and 59,000 residents left Barcelona to live elsewhere between 1984 and 1992.

The second dimension is the financial nexus between who pays for, and who benefits from, major new facilities. The total investment in stadiums and arenas used by the 127 teams in the four major professional sports leagues in the US approaches $24 billion (in 2003 dollars), and the governments' share of this was over $15 billion (64 per cent). Labor strife in professional sports has been characterized as a battle between 'the haves and the have mores', but it has been observed that in the US much of the dispute between the owners and players is over the allocation of a revenue pool built by the tax dollars of citizens who can only dream of million-dollar salaries.

In essence, the public subsidies transfer income from ordinary people to highly paid owners, executives, and players. It is this perversion of fairness, obvious inequity, and irrationality which is galling to many. The Mayor of Houston opposed providing a publicly provided stadium for the NFL Houston Oilers because he had a hard time with the idea that average people are called on to pay for this out of the taxes on their house, and then can't afford to buy a ticket. (Ironically, his successor supported providing tax funds for a new stadium after the Oilers left the city.)

To the ordinary taxpayer, public subsidy seems unnecessary. There is a disconnect between the everyday lives of taxpayers and the economics of professional sports. They are out of kilter. Players are paid too much. Owners' franchise values and profits are too high. Tickets are unaffordable. Forty-five individuals from the *Forbes* magazine list of the wealthiest 400 Americans (all with net assets exceeding $500 million) owned a direct interest in a team in one of the four major leagues at the end of the millennium. Given these factors, the notion that public subsidy is needed seems ludicrous.

If public subsidy was not there, then the teams would have to compensate for its unavailability by using more of their revenues to repay the annual facility debt charges. This would leave less money available to remunerate players, owners, and executives whose salaries appear outrageously excessive to ordinary people. Without public subsidies, these individuals would still receive very large salaries, but the obviously inequitable transfer of resources from ordinary taxpayer to millionaire beneficiary would cease.

Governments at all levels – local, state, and national – expend substantial amounts of tax funds on sports. Thus, they are confronted with the core equity question of 'Who gets what?' There are four fundamentally different standards of equity that may be used to allocate these resources: compensatory, equality, market, and demand.

Compensatory equity involves allocating resources so that disadvantaged groups,

individuals or areas receive extra increments of resources. This criterion of equity perceives the primary role of sport allocations to be to create opportunities for the underprivileged. The definition of underprivileged frequently relates to those who are economically disadvantaged. Decisions to use this criterion often are based on a belief that those who are not underprivileged have more opportunities to access sport offerings.

The equality equity criterion entails allocating equal amounts of sports services to all citizens regardless of need or the amount of revenues contributed. The wide acceptance of this criterion is probably a reflection of traditional values, which recognize equal protection under the law. While equal opportunity ostensibly appears to adopt an egalitarian approach, it fails to accommodate the reality that residents do not have equal needs or wants for sporting opportunities, nor are they similarly equipped to take advantage of those opportunities.

Market equity entails allocating sport resources to groups or neighborhoods in proportion to the tax or fee revenues that they produce. This is consistent with the 'benefit principle' whereby resources are allocated as a 'deserved' reward in proportion to contribution of effort or abilities. This mechanism would lead to wealthier districts receiving additional service increments compared to their less wealthy counterparts. More commonly, it is operationalized by the 'user pay' principles, whereby sports programs are offered to those most willing and able to pay for them. This mechism is the standard used in the private sector where the central notion is that individuals are prepared to pay for what they really want and view as priorities. However, it ignores the social issues associated with equity.

A fourth criterion used for allocating sport resources is demand. This approach allocates resources on the basis of consumption, vociferous advocacy or complaints, or professional judgment. However, demand is more appropriately classified as a pseudo or surrogate standard of equity rather than as an independent, clearly defined criterion. This is the because it cannot guide the allocation of resources in a predetermined direction. It is a pragmatic, reactive approach to which sport organizations and agencies frequently resort because it is administratively convenient, but its use is likely to result in an unpredictable and inconsistent set of winners and losers. Demand may lead to adoption of a pattern of services reflecting any of the three equity alternates discussed previously, or it may deviate inconsistently among them.

Individual opinions as to what is fair and equitable are likely to be tempered by background and social position. In a heterogeneous, conflict-oriented society there is unlikely to be any prolonged consensus or even a majority opinion of what is equitable. Because subjective, normative judgments are involved, concepts of equity cannot be labeled right or wrong, only different.

Equity evaluates a different dimension of sports programs than effectiveness and efficiency. It complements them. Unfortunately, it is frequently ignored in evaluation with the result that a preferred equity criterion is often traded-off for gains in efficiency. For example, directing sports programs at the underprivileged is likely to be relatively expensive. Efficiency, in terms of cost per head served, would be substantially improved if such a compensatory equity standard was replaced by a market equity standard redirecting the sports program at those who can afford to pay. When the focus is only on efficiency, such shifts in the preferred equity criterion tend to take place, often stealthily and surreptitiously over time without any overt discussion or debate of the shift.

JOHN L. CROMPTON

ERYTHROPOIETIN (EPO)/ DARBEPOETIN

Erythropoietin (EPO), produced primarily in the kidney, is a hormone that regulates red blood cell mass in the human body. Severe anemia results from either a lack of EPO production, e.g. kidney failure, or EPO suppression, e.g. cancer. Recombinant human Erythropoietin (rHuEPO), named Epoetin alfa and beta, can treat these anemias and is produced through recombinant DNA technology. Since rHuEPO is able to increase the number of red blood cells and therefore increase endurance performance (see **maximal oxygen uptake**), it is being misused by athletes. rHuEPO misuse in otherwise healthy individuals has the potential for health risks, including death due to thrombotic events.

As early as 1906 there was some knowledge about the presence of a hormone that regulates the blood's red cell mass. Rabbits that received an injection of serum from anemic rabbits increased their red cell mass up to 40 per cent. The name 'Erythropoietin' (EPO) was introduced for this hormone in 1948. In 1957 the kidney was recognised as the main production site, and it was recognised that production was triggered by tissue hypoxia (see **exercise at altitude – medical aspects**). The new knowledge that patients with kidney failure suffered from severe anemia with very low levels of the hormone in the body led to intense research towards isolation and clean-up of EPO. This milestone was achieved in 1977 with the isolation of a few milligrams from urine of patients with aplastic anemia. This was enough material to successfully identify and clone the EPO gene. Using recombinant DNA technology, recombinant human EPO (rHuEPO) was created. EPO, and therefore also rHuEPO, is a so-called glycoprotein, i.e. it consists of an amino acid backbone (see **proteins and amino acids**) and attached sugar chains. These sugar chains are important for

431

its biological activity (Lappin and Rich 1996).

In 1987 rHuEPO was approved for marketing in two preparations: Epoetin alfa, manufactured by Amgen Inc., and Epoetin beta, from Boehringer-Mannheim (now Roche). Amgen Inc. later introduced a new erythropoietic drug named Darbepoetin alfa in 2001. Darbepoetin alfa was developed via changes in the genetic code of the EPO gene, and subsequently in the amino acid sequence, to yield a glycoprotein that carried two more sugar chains while maintaining the ability to bind to the EPO receptors on the red blood cell precursors. The additional sugar chains increased Darbepoetin alfa's half-life in the body. Thus, one weekly injection of Darbepoetin alfa has the same effect as three injections a week of rHuEPO. It is anticipated that other preparations of rHuEPO have been or will soon be released.

rHuEPO has improved the quality of life for kidney-failure patients considerably, and its therapeutic uses have been expanded to include inflammatory diseases, anemia caused by chemotherapy, autologous blood transfusions, and AIDS, among others. It is little wonder why rHuEPO is one of the best-selling drugs in the world.

Endurance performance is directly related to the availability of oxygen to the peripheral tissue. Blood transports oxygen, and oxygen-carrying capacity correlates with the number of red blood cells. After winning several medals at the 1984 Olympic Games in Los Angeles, members of the US Cycling federation team admitted using **blood doping** to boost their performances.

Blood doping through transfusion is a complicated procedure that requires considerable infrastructure and carries the risk of acquiring blood-borne diseases. Owing to that, it was not surprising that rumours of rHuEPO misuse in sport emerged soon after its release, since it can be given by a subcutaneous injection easily administered by the athlete. The ease of use, however,

does not equate to a lack of risk, and uncontrolled application can lead to thrombotic events and death. In the late 1980s several deaths among pro cyclists in the Netherlands and Belgium occurred, sparking the unconfirmed suspicion that recombinant EPO misuse played a role.

That led in part to the action of the **International Olympic Committee (IOC)** to add rHuEPO to its list of banned substances (see **peptide hormones**) in 1990. Since no effective measure to detect rHuEPO misuse existed, information about it use remained anecdotal until 1998. That year, during the multi-stage pro cycling race, the 'Tour de France', French police confiscated a car-load of banned drugs, amongst them rHuEPO. The car was driven by an employee of one of the participating teams. Interrogations led to the ban of the entire team from the Tour and of several riders from racing for several months.

These events shook both the public and the international federations, and efforts to develop a test to detect misuse were intensified. In 2000 such a test had its premier at the **Olympic Games** in Sydney. It consisted of an initial blood test that, when results were indicative for rHuEPO misuse, was followed by a urine test.

The blood test, developed by Australian scientists (Parisotto 2001), determined that an elevated red blood cell mass in conjunction with increased erythropoiesis and high EPO concentrations is not physiological and results from rHuEPO use. Such a test is considered 'indirect' since it measures changes caused by the banned drug. The urine test actually looks at the presence of rHuEPO and is therefore a 'direct' test. By means of separation in an electrical field and detection with a very sensitive and selective method, this test shows the so-called isoform patterns of hEPO in urine. (Lasne and De Ceaurriz 2000) The isoform pattern of rHuEPO is distinctively different from hEPO. The isoelectric focusing urine test also yields a pattern for darbepoetin alfa that is distinct from both hEPO and rHuEPO.

No cases of misuse were found during the 2000 Sydney Summer Olympics. In the following year two pro cyclists were found to be misusing rHuEPO, although one was acquitted due to procedural errors (see **legal issues**). The next advance occurred during the 2002 Salt Lake City Winter Olympics when the combined blood/urine test uncovered the misuse of the newly licensed Darbepoetin alfa by three athletes. Two of these athletes were stripped of their gold medals, and their use of Darbepoetin alfa (instead of rHuEPO) may have been because it was thought not to be detectable at the time of the Salt Lake City games.

Misuse of rHuEPO not only affects professional cycling and cross-country skiing, but also track and field, as evidenced by the case of a Moroccan long-distance runner. This athlete had a positive urine test for rHuEPO in a sample collected one day before he set a new world record in the 3,000 m steeplechase in August 2002. Since the performance-enhancing effects of both rHuEPO and Darbepoetin alfa exceeds its window of detectability in the urine and blood, effective deterrence necessarily involves no-advanced-notice, out-of-competition testing. As recombinant technology continues to provide therapeutic advances in medicine, challenges such as those posed by rHuEPO and Darbepoetin alfa will continue for sport.

See also: allosteric modifiers of haemoglobin; haemoglobin manipulation; haemoglobin substitutes; plasma expanders

References

Lappin, T.R.J. and Rich, I.N. (1996) 'Erythropoietin – The First 90 Years', *Clin Lab Haem* 18: 137–45.

Lasne, F. and De Ceaurriz J. (2000) 'Recombinant Erythropoietin in Urine', *Nature* 405: 635.

Parisotto, R., Wu, M. and Ashenden, M.J. (2001) 'Detection of Recombinant Human Erythropoietin Abuse in Athletes Utilizing Markers of Altered Erythropoiesis', *Haematologica* 86: 128–37.

Further reading

Molineux, G., Foote, M.A. and Elliott, S.G. (eds) (2003) *Erythropoietins and Erythropoiesis*, Berlin: Birkhäuser Verlag.

ANDREAS BREIDBACH

ETHICAL CONSIDERATIONS

Introduction

Athletes at all levels, from casual amateurs to the most elite professional and Olympic competitors, seek to enhance their performance. Among the many means of enhancing performance, drugs have attracted special attention. To understand the ethics of performance enhancing drug use in sport, we must address three questions. First, why do athletes use performance enhancing drugs? Second, how and why should drugs be distinguished from other methods for enhancing performance? Third, what do athletes want and what does justice demand?

Why do athletes use performance enhancing drugs?: individual liberty and level playing fields

From the point of view of ethics, why athletes use drugs to enhance performance is significant. Contemporary Western ethical thought places great importance on individuals' rights to make decisions regarding their own lives. Justifying any program of control, prohibition and sanction therefore requires good arguments as to why we should not simply leave it up to each individual athlete whether to use performance enhancing drugs. We can call this the *presumption in favor of liberty*.

Individual liberty has its limits. We are not free to punch someone in the nose because we don't like the way he or she walks. Harm to others, then, constrains the scope of individual liberty. Philosophers like to distinguish between *self-regarding* and *other-regarding* actions. Self-regarding actions affect exclusively the person undertaking the action. Other-regarding actions affect persons beyond the actor. The categories of self- and other-regarding oversimplify the underlying reality – as if the consequences of all actions fell either wholly on the actor or entirely on others. In reality, actions fall along a continuum. Choosing between reading the newspaper or a magazine is, barring very odd circumstances, not likely to have notable impact on persons other than the reader. But many actions affect others significantly, including the decision whether to use performance enhancing drugs.

Competitive sport involves the direct comparison of performances. Winners and also-rans may be separated by fractions of seconds or inches. Athletes are motivated to maximize their performance and to not give up any advantage to their competitors. Top athletes monitor improvements in equipment and training regimens, diet, and whatever else might provide a competitive edge. A drug that made a tiny incremental improvement in performance might nonetheless make a crucial difference in a close competition. Athletes are loath to surrender such an advantage.

When some athletes choose to use performance enhancing drugs their actions are profoundly other-regarding. They are in effect tilting the playing field in their favor and cheating their fellow athletes out of the victories they might otherwise enjoy. So a decision that may at first glance look like an exercise of individual liberty – should I take this drug? – is instead an offense against that athlete's competitors. When a drug makes a notable difference in performance, such as recombinant human erythropoietin (rHuEPO) (see **erythropoietin (EPO)/ Darbepoetin**) in sports requiring endurance, athletes may feel themselves under

enormous pressure to use the drug if they believe their competitors are also using it. Athletes can find themselves trapped in an escalation of drug use akin to the escalation of an arms race. The presumption in favor of liberty yields to the quest for fair competition – a level playing field.

Distinguishing drugs from other methods for enhancing performance: gray zones, 'arbitrary' rules, and the meaning and value of sport

Critics of drug testing frequently claim that drugs are indistinguishable from other means for enhancing performance. This can be understood as a conceptual claim – that there is no coherent way to distinguish drugs from other forms of performance enhancement – or as an ethical claim – that we have no better ethical reasons for banning performance enhancing drugs than we have for banning other technologies of enhancement.

As for the conceptual claim, consider the (hypothetical) case of the roller-skating marathoner. Imagine that someone shows up for the Boston Marathon having duly registered, wearing typical running garb – except for her shoes, which have wheels on the bottom. She is wearing roller blades. Imagine further that there was nothing in the rules governing the Marathon that expressly prohibited roller blades. This imaginary skater might well finish first. Could anyone deny that those wheels were a means of enhancing her performance – covering the marathon's twenty-six-plus miles more rapidly? Could anyone maintain – with a straight face – that we can make no meaningful distinctions among methods of enhancing performance? Conceptually, performance enhancing drugs are like roller blades in the Boston Marathon. We can tell the difference between better running shoes and shoes with wheels. The roller-blading marathoner also hints at a fundamental ethical issue: wheels may provide a competitive advantage, but they do so by undermining what gives the sport its value and meaning, namely the combination of natural talents and admirable qualities, such as training, dedication, and the willingness to suffer, that separates winners from also-rans.

Making distinctions in the gray zones that characterize life in general and sport in particular can be very difficult, and critics often deride them as 'arbitrary'. But this confuses two different senses of the word. 'Arbitrary' can mean something completely without foundation and therefore indefensible. But there is a second, more benign, use of the word as a line drawn or distinction made at some point along a continuum. There may be no absolutely decisive reasons for drawing the line at precisely this point rather than slightly to one side or the other; but there are (1) good reasons for drawing a line at some defensible place; and (2) clear and meaningful differences between the ends of the continuum. Most rules governing sport are arbitrary in this benign sense. Why should a football match consist of two forty-five minute halves rather than, say, two forty- or fifty-minute halves, or three periods of thirty minutes each – or twenty-four hours of nonstop play? Why should a basketball team consist of five players and not four or six – or two or forty? In part, these rules are the product of experience and convention. But they also reflect an understanding of what is valued in the game. Basketball can be played two-on-two but it is a different game than with five to a side, which allows for more intricate team play. With forty players on a side, the court would become so crowded that driving, passing and dribbling might become impossible. Most of the skills that basketball exhibits would be irrelevant, and what we value about the current game would be lost.

What do athletes want?

Procedural justice requires fair procedures for determining what the rules will be,

most of all by giving a voice to the individuals on whom the burdens and benefits will fall. It is notable, then, that athletes are often among the most ardent advocates of drug testing and of strict penalties for their fellow athletes caught using prohibited performance enhancing drugs.

That many (though not all) athletes are staunch supporters of drug control should not be surprising. Consider the quandary faced by athletes who do not want to use performance enhancing drugs although their competitors are doing so. In the absence of effective drug control these athletes face three unhappy choices. First, they could continue to compete, knowing that they are giving up a significant edge. When drugs make a competitive difference, such as biosynthetic erythropoietin in endurance events, the honest athlete is at a powerful, perhaps insurmountable, disadvantage. Second, honest athletes might be discouraged and cease competing rather than facing the frustration of losing to drug-enhanced competitors they could have defeated in a fair match. Third, athletes could 'level the playing field' by using the same drugs as their competitors. Drug control programs can be understood as efforts to create just such a level playing field, the fair competition desired by most athletes, without having to use prohibited performance enhancing drugs.

Conclusion

The strongest ethical case for a drug control in sport is where: (1) the drugs in question undermine the sport's meaning, value and significance; (2) athletes themselves support drug control; and (3) the program is reasonably effective at maintaining a 'level playing field'.

References

Hoberman, J.M. (1992) *Mortal Engines: Scientific Ambition and the Dehumanization of Sport*, New York: Free Press.

Houlihan, B. (1999) *Dying to Win: Doping in Sport and the Development of Anti-doping Policy*, Strasbourg: Council of Europe.

Juengst, E.T. (1998) 'What Does "enhancement" Mean?', in E. Parens (ed.) *Enhancing Human Traits: Ethical and Social Implications*, Washington DC: Georgetown University Press.

Murray, T.H., Gaylin, W. and Macklin, R. (1984) *Feeling Good and Doing Better: Ethics and Nontherapeutic Drug Use*, Clifton NJ: Humana Press.

THOMAS H. MURRAY

ETHNIC MINORITY

An ethnic group is a designated social group within a cultural and social system that achieves its distinction on the basis of complex and variable traits such as religion, language, country of birth, value and belief system, race, or physical characteristics. Everyone belongs to an ethnic group. 'Ethnic minority' is used in reference to people from a group that displays different national or cultural traditions from the majority of the population in the society in which they live.

There are several sub-groups within the broader grouping of ethnic minority; two commonly constituted groupings are 'people of culturally and linguistically diverse backgrounds', and 'visible minority'. 'Culturally and linguistically diverse' refers to people who are not born in their country of residence and/or those whose first language is different from the official language of the country in which they live. 'Visible minority' refers to persons who are visibly different from the mainstream. For example, in a country with a predominantly Anglo-Saxon population the latter term denotes people who are non-Caucasian in race or non-white in colour. The labelling process that classifies certain groups as 'ethnic minorities' or 'visible minorities' suggests that these people are somehow different from the mainstream. The 'otherness' label or stereotypes attributed to a person's ethnic background can reinforce this difference. Thus, such labels should be used with caution.

Discrimination, racism, cultural identity, assimilation, and acculturation have been found to have an impact on sport participation patterns. Minority ethnic communities have been subject to widespread systemic discriminatory practices often perpetrated under the banner of various government policies promoting cultural purity, assimilation, integration, and multiculturalism. Experiences of discrimination and racism at both personal and institutional levels can deny equality of opportunity, and sport can produce, reproduce, or challenge these tendencies. In sport practice and policy, mainstream ethnic group members often wield the power, control resources, define the rules of access and involvement, and reinforce their vision of sport.

Investigations into the relationship between ethnicity, race, and sport have shown that in many instances ethnic minority group members are disadvantaged in their access to sporting opportunity. For example, evidence suggests that the low socio-economic status of many ethnic minority group members influences the sports played and the positions assumed. Positional discrimination or difference, has been the subject of detailed study, along with the use of sports as a vehicle for social mobility or 'getting out of the ghetto'. This research has broadly shown that ethnic minority players are more likely to occupy the less central and non-decision-making positions within a sports team. Further, lower-cost sports, such as football, are more easily accessible to certain ethnic group members because of monetary considerations, and thus attain a greater level of involvement. Membership requirements of many sport clubs have had restricted access based on race, colour, and religious discrimination.

While a substantial body of research has discredited the association of race with natural sporting ability, racial stereotypes in sports continue to persist. Certain ethnic minority groups are stereotyped as preferring certain sports due to assumed physical strength, body shape, mental attitude, or cultural heritage.

Conversely, in some societies ethnic minority groups control or dominate in sport. This has occurred in countries where the minority groups are better resourced, or control decision-making and government policy. In particular, settler or colonial countries are examples of where the original inhabitants have been displaced or marginalised in their sport participation.

See also: ethnocentricity

References

Cronin, M. and Mayall, D. (eds) (1998) *Sporting Nationalisms: Identity, Ethnicity, Immigration, and Assimilation*, London: Frank Cass.

Kirsch, G., Nolte, C. and Harris, O. (eds) (2000) *The Encyclopedia of Ethnicity and Sports in the US*, Westport CT: Greenwood Press.

TRACY TAYLOR

ETHNOCENTRICITY

All perspectives imply political arrangements and invariably exclude some groups, some voices, and ethnocentrism does just that. According to Finkielkraut (1989: 79), we become ethnocentric when we start assuming for ourselves the right of the monopoly of legitimacy, by denying those modes of thinking, science, and arts which are produced by 'others'. Consequently, the construction of 'our' world views – identity, culture, and ideology – will be based on the negation of 'others' conception of realities, e.g. nationalism and sense of belonging. This transforms 'our' interpretations of realities into an account of absolute truth, so as to give 'us' the right to universalise and impose our 'valid' conception of truth upon 'others'.

Assuming that our modern way of life constitutes 'progress' and that other societies that have not achieved (and in some cases not aspired to) our levels of material productivity (or level of morality and civilisation) are 'backward' (or decadent, atheist, and imperialist) (Hall and Valentine 1991).

This assumption of universal truth may take different forms or ideologies, for instance Eurocentrism, pax-Americana, Orientalism, Arabocentrism, Africanism, globalism (the universalisation of Western neo-liberalism), and it comes into play in such claims as cultural (civilisational) superiority, nationalism, divine laws, racial purity, liberalism, secularism, enlightenment, and scientific objectivity.

To break free from this tendency to universalise one's cultural norms and practice – whether at an individual or institutional level – to evaluate the culture or behaviour of members of other societies, it is paramount, according to Scheurich, to employ 'some sort' of cultural relativism and self-critical analysis, or 'self-critical pluralism'. This can be gained by opening up to other 'cultures' and 'value systems' without any philosophical or historical, pre-determined prejudices, and by applying what Mills (1959) defines as 'comparative sensitivity', or the process of learning about and understanding others', including 'our' own, cultures and societies, and by giving others the opportunity to express their differences. This is applicable also to sport as a mode of practice and field of study where Eurocentrism or European historicism has exclusively linked the emergence of modern sport to the triumph of Western rationality, thus denying the right of non-Western cultures to claim some form of intellectual or historical rights, leaving no choice to non-Western countries but to assimilate the Western secular values of modern sport. This, according to the dominant Western discourse, represents the norm that other nations and cultures (the 'rest') have to follow in order to integrate within the world of sport. As a consequence, indigenous or traditional (pre-modern, thus 'irrational') games were abandoned in favour of modern sport, which was seen as more lucrative, more rational, and more useful for the dissemination of political and ideological propaganda.

There is a need today, in the age of late modernity (characterised by the decentralisation of the West) to have a more pluralistic view about the development and practices of sport in non-Western contexts. However, the opening of a local debate about modern sport should aim (as Edward Said has urged) neither at replacing one set of authorities and dogmas – 'Eurocentrism' – by another – 'Arabo-centric, Islamist, or Africanist', nor at substituting one centre for another. Hence the aim, in line with Said's approach: 'should neither be that of separatism nor that of reverse exclusivism'.

References

Finkielkraut, A. (1989) *La Défaite de la Pensée*, Paris: Gallimard.

Hall, M.A. and Valentine, J. (eds) (1991) *Sport in Canadian Society*, Toronto: McLelland and Stewart.

Mills, C. Wright (1959) *The Sociological Imagination*, New York: Oxford University Press.

Said, E. (2001) *Reflections on Exile: And Other Literary and Cultural Essays*, 380, London: Granta Books.

Scheurich, J. (1997) *Research Method in the Postmodern*, Brighton: Falmer Press.

MAHFOUD AMARA

EUROPEAN SPORTS CHARTER

The Charter is a thirteen-article agreement between the ministers of sport of the **Council of Europe** signed in 1992. The Charter is intended to provide a basis for the national policies for sport, and, when appropriate any relevant legislation, of the member states, as well as informing the work of the national sports organisations in the elaboration of their policies. The document replaced the former European Sport for All Charter, which had come into force in 1975.

The first two of the Charter's articles deal with the aims and definition and scope of the document.

1. To enable every individual to participate in sport and notably:
   a. to ensure that all young people should have the opportunity to receive physical education instruction and the opportunity to acquire basic sports skills,
   b. to ensure that everyone should have the opportunity to take part in sport and physical recreation in a safe and healthy environment,
   c. and, in cooperation with the appropriate sports organisations,
   d. to ensure that everyone with the interest and ability should have the opportunity to improve their standard of performance in sport and reach levels of personal achievement and/or publicly recognised levels of excellence.
2. To protect and develop the moral and ethical bases of sport and the human dignity and safety of those involved in sport, by safeguarding sport, sportsmen and women from exploitation for political, commercial and financial gain and from practices that are abusive or debasing including the abuse of drugs and the sexual harassment and abuse, particularly of children, young people and women.

Remaining articles deal with the nature of the sports movement (the need for a healthy voluntary, public, and commercial sector), access to facilities and activities (ensuring no discrimination, access for the disadvantaged, and an appropriate variety and range of facilities); 'building the foundation' (ensuring appropriate physical education provision during the formative years); developing participation, improving performance, and supporting top level and professional sport; fostering human resources (by the development of courses for coaches and administrators, and technical specialists); ensuring sustainable development (in particular taking account of the natural environment in the practice of, and provision for, sport); development of a information and research system on sport; provision of financial resources; and the fostering of domestic and international competition. The document is also accompanied by the provision of a code of ethics.

The European Sports Charter is one of three major policy documents in relation to sport of the Council of Europe, the other two being the Anti-doping Convention and the Convention on Spectator Violence and Misbehaviour. These documents in effect indicate a moral commitment on the part of the signatories rather than an enforceable set of actions.

IAN P. HENRY

EUROPEAN UNION

The European Union (EU) is a group of democratic European states committed by treaty to cooperation and/or joint action in a range of policy domains. It is distinct from the **Council of Europe**, an older, larger, and looser association of European states. In the first decades of the European Economic Community immediately after the signing of the Treaty of Rome in 1957 which established it, the EEC focused on cooperation between member countries in respect of trade and the economy, but the EU's role has grown so that it now also deals with a much wider set of policy areas, including citizens' rights; ensuring freedom, security and justice; job creation; regional development; and environmental protection. However, it has no specific legal competence (powers provided by treaty) to intervene in the domain of sport except insofar as such policy intervention relates to

other spheres of policy activity (e.g. the regulation of economic competition, or the freedom of movement of persons, capital, goods, and services) where the EU does have specific legal competence.

European integration is based on four founding treaties. The first is the treaty establishing the European Coal and Steel Community (ECSC), which came into force in July 1952 and expired on July 2002. The second is the treaty establishing the European Economic Community (EEC) signed in Rome in 1957. The third is the treaty establishing the European Atomic Energy Community (Euratom), also signed in Rome in 1957. (These two treaties are often referred to as the 'Treaties of Rome' – when the term 'Treaty of Rome' is used, this refers only to the EEC treaty.) Finally, the Treaty on European Union, which was signed in Maastricht in February 1992, entered into force in November 1993. The Maastricht Treaty simplified the name of the European Economic Community to 'the European Community'. It also introduced new forms of policy cooperation and action between the member state governments (e.g. on defence, and in the area of justice and home affairs). By adding this inter-governmental cooperation to the existing 'Community' system, the Maastricht Treaty created a new structure which is political as well economic. This is the European Union (EU).

The original member states of the EC were France, Germany, Luxembourg, Belgium, the Netherlands, and Italy. The founding treaties have been amended on a number of occasions, in particular when new member states acceded in 1973 (Denmark, Ireland, United Kingdom), 1981 (Greece), 1986 (Spain, Portugal), 1995 (Austria, Finland, Sweden), and 2004 (Cyprus, the Czech Republic, Estonia, Hungary, Latvia, Lithuania, Malta, Poland, Slovakia, Slovenia). There have also been major reforms introducing institutional changes and new areas of responsibility for the European institutions:

- The Merger Treaty, signed in Brussels in April 1965 and which came into force in July 1967, introduced a Single European Commission and a Single European Council of the then three European Communities (ECSC, Euratom, and EEC);
- The Single European Act (SEA), which came into force on 1 July 1987, introduced the measures required for the achievement of the Internal Market;
- The Treaty of Amsterdam, which came into force in May 1999, amended and renumbered the EU and EC treaties. Consolidated versions of the EU and EC treaties are attached to it.
- The Treaty of Nice came into force in February 2003. The Treaty of Nice, the former Treaty of the EU and the Treaty of the EC have been merged into one consolidated version.

Although the EU has no specific competence in sport, it has shown an increasing interest in the sporting area. After controversial discussions about the establishment of a competence, the Treaty of Amsterdam incorporated a 'Declaration' on sport as an annex:

> The Conference emphasises the social significance of sport, in particular its role in forging identity and bringing people together. The Conference therefore calls on the bodies of the European Union to listen to sports associations when important questions affecting sport are at issue. In this connection, special consideration should be given to the particular character of amateur sport.

This was added to by the Nice Declaration of 2000, which was adopted by the Council of Ministers as a joint declaration though it was not incorporated into the treaty. Although the text is not legally binding, it is nonetheless of special importance. Never before has the relevance of sport to the European Union been so fully discussed and elaborated at the highest political level. The themes addressed in the declaration are as follows:

- Declaration on the specific characteristics of sport and its social function in Europe, of which account should be taken in implementing common policies.
- The need for protection and fostering of amateur sport and sport for all.
- The role of sports federations.
- The preservation of sports training policies to ensure quality and availability of such training.
- Protection of young sportsmen and women.
- The economic context of sport and solidarity between all levels of sport in the disbursement, for example, of financial benefits from media rights deals.
- A review of transfer systems in professional sport.

Although the EU has no specific competence in sport, there are perhaps five areas of intervention in which the EU has impacted upon sport or employed sport for other purposes. These are:

1. Sport as trade – here for example the EU's guaranteeing of freedom of movement of individuals as evidenced in the Bosman ruling has had a profound effect on player rosters, since it did away with the quota system which limited the number of foreign players a club could play, and on football finances since players at the end of their contracts became free agents and could not be sold by their clubs.
2. Sport as a tool of economic regeneration – the Regional Development Fund has been used to fund sporting events and infrastructure associated with regeneration projects.

3. Sport and social integration – sport has been used as a tool to combat social exclusion among for example immigrant groups.
4. Sport as an ideological tool – sport has been used under the European Awareness budget for promoting a sense of European identity, as for example with the EU sponsorship of the European Ryder Cup golf team.
5. Sport as international aid – assistance in the form of sport aid has been offered by the EU in much the same way as individual states offer such aid as a means of promoting international relations.

References

Henry, I.P. (2003) 'Sport, the Role of the European Union and the Decline of the Nation State?', in B.M.J. Houlihan (ed.) *Sport and Society*, London: Sage.
Petry, K., Steinbach, D., Tokarski, W. and Jesse, B. (eds) (2004) *Two Players, One Goal: Sport in the European Union*, Aachen: Meyer & Meyer. http://www.sport-in-europe.com/SIU/HTML/FRMInh.htm

IAN P. HENRY

EVALUATION

Evaluation is a process applied in a wide range of settings. Here it is discussed in relation to the management of facilities or programmes for sport. It can also be used in relation to the exercise of individual athletic performance, but that context is not discussed here. Evaluation is the process of assessing the outcomes of an action and the costs and procedures involved in achieving those outcomes, and comparing them with the original intentions, and/or with internal or external reference criteria. The process of evaluation can be applied to small-scale, short-term activities – for example a single sports training session – or to large-scale, long-term activities – for example, a ten-year national plan to double the number of medals won at the Olympic Games. The aim of evaluation is to make a judgment as to the success or failure of an action, with a view to repeating successful actions, improving on moderately successful action, and, in the case of failures, improving significantly or possibly ignoring such activity altogether.

Evaluation might be seen as the process of addressing a series of questions, which can be divided into three groups.

Goals

(a) What outcomes were intended?

Evidence

(b) What outcomes were achieved?
(c) What procedures were followed to achieve the outcomes?
(d) What resources were used to achieve the outcomes?

Judgment

(e) How does (b) compare with (a)?
(f) How does (b) or (d) or the ratio of (b) to (d) compare with other examples of this type of facility/programme or with this facility/programme in earlier periods?
(g) How does (b) or (d) or the ratio of (b) to (d) compare with pre-determined benchmark values?

A number of prerequisites is therefore required for effective evaluation: the intentions/objectives must be clear and measurable; and data collection procedures must be in place to: measure and record the outcomes, the procedures followed to achieve the outcomes, and the resources used. This seems simple enough – indeed, it is often achieved intuitively without any formal procedures (we are all able to judge when a match, or training session has gone well or badly). In the commercial sector the process may also be relatively simple, where outcomes are measured in only in terms of sales and profits. But the procedure can pose considerable challenges for complex programmes of activity, where numerous inputs and outputs of a quantitative and qualitative nature are involved. The process hinges particularly on the clear statement of intentions or goals, which should ideally include reference to all relevant criteria. For example, a goal for a sport team's season might be: 'to improve on last year's league position by at least three places'. But if financial costs and injury to players are also relevant criteria, the goal should be expressed: 'to improve on last year's league position by at least three places with no more than a 10 per cent increase in costs and with no increase in player injuries'.

Evaluation can be achieved by:

* simply comparing outcomes with intentions: whether the programme/facility was successful in its own terms (item (e) previously);
* comparing the outcomes with earlier performance: whether the performance of programme/facility has improved, stayed the same or declined in terms of cost-effectiveness or benefit-cost ratio (item (f) previously); or
* comparing outcomes with 'benchmark' criteria: whether the programme/facility has met organisational, professional, or industry norms or standards in terms of cost-effectiveness or benefit-cost ratios (item (g)).

The third approach pre-supposes the existence of external norms or standards promulgated within the organisation itself or by a professional or industry body. We see such standards produced in other fields – for example fuel efficiency and safety assessments for passenger cars. They are not common in the sports area, but some efforts have recently been made by Sport England to produce such standards for the management of sports halls and swimming pools, covering such issues as access by various social groups, financial efficiency, and utilisation (see Sport England 2000).

See also: benchmarking; performance indicators

References

Henderson, K.M. and Bialeschki, D. (1995) *Evaluating Leisure Services: Making Enlightened Decisions*, State College PA: Venture.

Kestner, J.L. (1996) *Program Evaluation for Sport Directors*, Champaign IL: Human Kinetics.

Sport England (2000) *Performance Measurement for Local Authority Sports Halls and Swimming Pools*, London: Sport England.

A.J. VEAL

EVENTS

The study of hallmark events or mega-events became an important part of tourism literature in the 1980s. Since then the economics of sports tourism at major sports events has become an increasing part of this event tourism literature. Many governments around the world have adopted national sports policies that specify that hosting major sports event is a major objective. A broad range of benefits has been suggested for both the country and the host city from staging major sports events, including: urban regeneration legacy benefits, sporting legacy benefits, tourism and image benefits, social and cultural benefits, as well as the economic benefits, which will be the main focus here. It is well known that cities and countries compete fiercely to host the Olympic Games or the soccer World Cup. However, over recent years there has been increasing competition to host less globally recognised sports events in a wide range of other sports where spectator interest is less assured and where the economic benefits are not so clear-cut.

The literature on the economics of major sports events is relatively recent. One of the first major studies in this area was the study of the impact of the 1985 Adelaide Formula 1 Grand Prix (Burns *et al.* 1986). This was followed by Brent Ritchie's in-depth study of the 1988 Calgary Winter Olympics (Ritchie 1984; Ritchie and Aitken 1984; 1985; Ritchie and Lyons 1987; 1990; Ritchie and Smith 1991). In fact, immediately prior to these studies it was generally thought that hosting major sports events was a financial liability to host cities, following the large debts faced by Montreal after hosting the 1976 Olympics. There was a general change in attitude following the 1984 Los Angeles Olympics, which made a clear profit.

Mules and Faulkner (1996) point out that even with such mega-events as Formula 1 Grand Prix races and the Olympics, it is not always an unequivocal economic benefit to the cities that host the event. They emphasise that, in general, staging major sports events often results in the city authorities losing money even though the city itself benefits greatly in terms of additional spending in the city. Thus the 1994 Brisbane World Masters Games cost the city A\$2.8 million to organise but generated a massive A\$50.6 million of additional economic activity in the state economy. Mules and Faulkner's basic point is that it normally requires the public sector to finance the staging of the event and incurring these losses in order to generate the benefits to the local economy. They argue that governments host such events and lose taxpayers' money in the process in order to generate spillover effects or externalities.

It is not a straightforward job, however, to establish a profit and loss account for a specific event. Major sports events require investment in new sports facilities, and often this is paid for in part by central government or even international sports bodies. Thus some of this investment expenditure represents a net addition to the local economy, since the money comes in from outside. Also such facilities remain after the event has finished, acting as a platform for future activities that can generate additional tourist expenditure. (Mules and Faulkner 1996).

Sports events are increasingly seen as part of a broader tourism strategy aimed at raising the profile of a city, and therefore success cannot be judged on simply profit-and-loss basics. Often the attraction of events is linked to a re-imaging process, and in the case of many cities, is invariably linked to strategies of urban regeneration and tourism development. Major events if successful have the ability to project a new image and identity for a city. The hosting of major sports events is often justified by the host city in terms of long-term economic and social consequences, directly or indirectly resulting from the staging of the event (Mules and Faulkner 1996). These effects are primarily justified in economic terms, by estimating the additional expenditure generated in the local economy as the result of the event, in terms of the benefits injected from tourism-related activity and the subsequent re-imaging of the city following the success of the event.

Cities staging major sports events have a unique opportunity to market themselves to the world. Increasing competition between broadcasters to secure broadcasting rights to major sports events has led to a massive escalation in fees for such rights, which in turn means broadcasters give blanket coverage at peak times for such events, enhancing the marketing benefits to the cities that stage them.

Although much of the literature has been concerned with the estimation of economic impacts generated through **multiplier effects**, more recent studies have emphasised additional benefits. Such benefits might include a notional value of exposure achieved from media coverage and the associated place marketing effects related to hosting and broadcasting an event which might encourage visitors to return in future, or alternatively an investigation into any sports development impacts, which may encourage young people to get more involved in sport. Collectively these additional benefits could be monitored using a more holistic 'balanced scorecard' approach to event evaluation, as outlined in Figure 21.

The evidence suggests there is a wide diversity in the range of economic benefits that sports events can generate. Some events have little more than a local impact. Others contribute substantially to the economic activity in the local economy, as well as promoting the local area to an international audience. When building a strategy for economic regeneration through sports events, careful consideration should be given to which events to bid for and the overall balance of sports events over an event year.

Local government must not only take a lead role in strategic terms but also in underwriting the operating and staging costs of sporting events. Often the events themselves do not generate a surplus. Local government facilitates and supports such events in order to generate the real economic benefits to the local community. However, there is a distribution problem in that local taxpayers are in effect subsidising the economic benefits that accrue to hotels, restaurants, and other leisure and tourism operators, the main beneficiaries of increased visitor spending. The rationale for this is that the local community benefits from increased employment opportunities.

References

Burns, J.P.A., Hatch, J.H. and Mules, F.J. (eds) (1986) *The Adelaide Grand Prix: The Impact of a Special Event*, Adelaide: Centre for South Australian Economic Studies.

Mules, T. and Faulkner, B. (1996) 'An Economic Perspective on Major Events', *Tourism Economics* 12, 2.

Ritchie, J.R.B. (1984) 'Assessing the Impact of a Hallmark Event: Conceptual and Research Issues', *Journal of Travel Research* 23, 1: 2–11.

Ritchie, J.R.B. and Aitken, C.E. (1984) 'Assessing the Impacts of the 1988 Olympic Winter Games: The Research Program and Initial Results', *Journal of Travel Research* 22, 3: 17–25.

—— (1985) 'OLYMPULSE II – Evolving Resident Attitudes Towards the 1988 Olympics', *Journal of Travel Research* 23 (winter): 28–33.

Ritchie, J.R.B. and Lyons, M.M. (1987) 'OLYMPULSE III/IV: A Mid-term Report on Resident Attitudes Concerning the 1988 Olympic Winter Games', *Journal of Travel Research* 26 (summer): 18–26.

—— (1990) 'OLYMPULSE VI: A Post-event Assessment of Resident Reaction to the XV Olympic Winter Games', *Journal of Travel Research* 28, 3: 14–23.

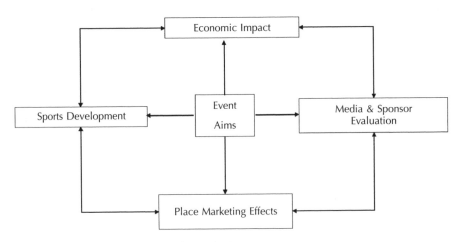

Figure 21. The 'Balanced Scorecard' approach to evaluating events.

Ritchie, J.R.B. and Smith, B.H. (1991) 'The Impact of a Mega Event on Host Region Awareness: A Longitudinal Study', *Journal of Travel Research* 30, 1: 3–10.

CHRIS GRATTON

EXCESSIVE HEAT STRESS EFFECTS

Three groups of people are especially at risk when exposed to excessive environmental heat stress. Elderly people with heart disease living in housing that does not have air conditioning are unable to maintain their body temperatures, since they are unable to increase the output of the heart – cardiac output. Without an increase in cardiac output, people with heart disease are unable to increase heat loss from the body by transporting the heat from the areas of heat production to the skin, from where it is lost to the environment either through convection or evaporation – sweating. Unable to lose heat appropriately, their body temperatures rise progressively until temperatures in excess of 42°C are reached, causing death from heatstroke. The only effective prevention is to ensure that the elderly with heart disease live in air-conditioned rooms during summer heat.

The second group comprises persons with a variety of genetic disorders of skeletal muscle metabolism, known collectively as the malignant hyperthermia disorders. When exposed to various different stressors, the muscles of affected persons undergo a rapid and apparently irreversible breakdown – rhabdomyolysis – associated with an uncontrolled metabolic activity that generates inordinate amounts of heat – malignant hyperthermia. Stressors that can cause this problem include exercise – whether or not it is in the heat, anaesthesia with specific drugs, fasting or eating a low-carbohydrate diet whilst continuing to exercise vigorously, and the use of certain recreational drugs including amphetamines or the ephedra compounds. Toxic substances released from dying muscle further complicate the disease, since they cause kidney and, ultimately, heart failure, leading to death. When this condition occurs in a predisposed person during exercise, it should be labelled exercise-induced malignant hyperthermia, to contrast it with the condition of environmentally- and exercise-induced heatstroke, which occurs in otherwise healthy athletes who exercise in environmental conditions that are too hot. The condition of exercise-induced malignant hyperthermia explains why some athletes can develop what appears to be typical heatstroke even when exercising in relatively cool environmental conditions.

The third group at risk are athletes who exercise at maximum effort in environmental conditions that are too extreme. Under these conditions, the athlete's rate of heat production exceeds the rate at which they are able to lose that heat into the environment. This is not the result of any physiological failure on the part of the athlete, but results purely from the physical limitations in heat transfer imposed by the excessively hot and humid environmental conditions. It follows that the athletes most at risk of this environmentally- and exercise-induced heatstroke are those elite athletes who generate the most heat during exercise of very high intensity but relatively short duration, of tens of minutes, because they are able to exercise at the limits of their very high capacity even in adverse environmental conditions. As the exercise duration is increased, for example, from tens of minutes to hours, the exercise intensity that can be sustained falls substantially, causing the rate of heat production to fall and, hence, also the risk of environmentally- and exercise-induced heatstroke. This explains why this type of heatstroke is more likely to occur in athletes competing in running races of 5–10 km than it is in 42 km marathon runners.

Fortunately, from the 1970s our understanding of the factors causing heatstroke in sport has increased, so that more effective preventive measures have been introduced.

The most important of these include the scheduling of sporting events requiring sustained high rates of energy expenditure, such as 10–42 km running events, for the cooler times of the day and year. In addition, athletes have become aware of the need to pre-acclimatise by training in the heat if they are to compete in the heat, and they are also aware that they must moderate their racing speeds when competing in hot environmental conditions. The final factor is the provision of frequent aid stations during competitive races, at which athletes have greater access to fluids for drinking and for sponging over their bodies. Although there is no evidence that this fluid provision directly reduces the risk of environmentally- and exercise-induced heatstroke, it does improve the athlete's comfort and forms part of a comprehensive programme for the prevention of heat injury during exercise.

Although it is popularly believed that the diagnostic category of exercise-induced heat illness should, in addition to environmentally- and exercise-induced heatstroke, include such conditions as (heat) muscle cramps and heat exhaustion, as examples of medical disorders caused by abnormalities in heat balance, there is no evidence that this is correct. Thus the body temperatures of persons diagnosed with these conditions are not abnormally elevated, nor does the treatment of these conditions require that those affected be cooled, as is the case in a person with environmentally- and exercise-induced heatstroke, who will die unless cooled rapidly and adequately. Nor are these conditions specific only to exercise in the heat; muscle cramps and 'exhaustion' are as likely to occur during equally demanding exercise in cold conditions.

See also: exercise in the heat; heat tolerance – affecting factors; thermal balance and thermoregulation; thermal regulation in hot environments

References

Noakes, T.D. (2000a) 'Exercise in the Heat', in P. Brukner and K. Khan (eds) *Clinical Sports Medicine, Second Edition*, 798–806, New York: McGraw-Hill.
—— (2000b) 'Medical Coverage of Endurance Events', in P. Brukner and K. Khan (eds) *Clinical Sports Medicine, Second Edition*, 865–71, New York: McGraw-Hill.
—— (2000c) 'Hyperthermia, Hypothermia and Problems of Hydration', in R.J. Shephard and P.-O. Åstrand (eds) *Endurance in Sport, Second Edition*, 591–613, Oxford: Blackwell Science.
—— (2002) *Lore of Running, Third Edition*, ch. 4, Champaign IL: Human Kinetics.

TIM NOAKES

EXCESSIVE TRAINING RISKS IN CHILDREN

Children involved in sports should be encouraged to participate in a variety of different activities and develop a wide range of skills. Young athletes who specialize in just one sport may be denied the benefits of varied activity while facing additional physical, physiologic, and psychological demands from intense training and competition.

Child athletes have superior cardiac functional capacity compared with nonathletes. Nonetheless, there is some cause for caution.

A limited number of studies have failed to identify an adverse effect of intense endurance training on the heart of the child athlete. In these investigations, no differences in resting echocardiograms or electrocardiograms have been observed between trained prepubertal runners and nonathletes.

Based on these limited data, currently there is no indication that intense training of the child athlete results in injury to the heart. However, closer study of the cardiac characteristics of children training at elite levels is necessary before this conclusion can be verified. Careful assessment of cardiovascular status (heart murmurs, abnormal rhythms) remains important in ongoing medical care of the child athlete.

Overuse injuries (tendinitis, apophysitis, stress fractures) can be consequences of excessive sports training in child and adult athletes. Certain aspects of the growing athlete may predispose the child and adolescent to repetitive stress injuries such as traction apophysitis (Osgood-Schlatter disease, Sever's disease, medial epicondylitis ['Little League elbow']), injuries to developing joint surfaces (osteochondritis dissecans), and/or injuries to the immature spine (spondylolysis, spondylolisthesis, vertebral apophysitis).

Because of the potential for long-term growth disturbances, injuries to epiphyseal growth centers are a particular concern for young athletes.

For child athletes, an adequate diet is critical because nutritional needs are increased by both training and the growth process. Young athletes and their parents are frequently unaware of the appropriate components of a training diet. Total caloric intake; balanced diet; and iron and calcium intake are areas of particular concern.

Athletic girls tends to experience menarche at a later age than non-athletic girls, leading to concern that intensive sports training might delay sexual maturation. Undernutrition, training stress and low levels of body fat have been hypothesized to account for this delay.

Secondary amenorrhea, or cessation of menstrual cycles after menarche, can occur as a result of intense athletic training. Prolonged amenorrhea may cause diminished bone mass from the associated decrease in estrogen secretion, augmenting the risk for stress fractures and the potential for osteoporosis in adulthood. Efforts to improve nutrition or diminish training volume in these girls may permit resumption of menses and diminish these risks.

Studies of males have indicated no evidence of an adverse effect on sexual maturation related to sports training. Progression of Tanner stages of pubertal development has not been observed to be retarded in athletic-compared with non-athletic adolescents.

Considerable research has addressed the anxiety and stress that can affect children who engage in competitive sports, but little data exists about the effects of more intense or sustained training on young athletes. Anecdotal reports suggest risks of 'burnout' from physical and emotional stress, missed social and educational opportunities, and disruptions of family life. Unrealistic parental expectations and/or exploitation of young athletes for extrinsic gain can contribute to negative psychological consequences for elite young athletes.

Child athletes differ from adults in their thermoregulatory responses to exercise in the heat. They sweat less, create more heat per body mass, and acclimatize slower to warm environments. As a result, child athletes may be more at risk from heat-related injuries in hot, humid conditions. They also should be aware that limiting sports play and training in hot, humid conditions, and ensuring adequate fluid intake, can prevent heat injury.

High-level sports are high-risk for young athletes in many ways. One of the most serious threats is doping. It is widely known that the use of drugs in sports is hazardous for the health of the athletes. The increasing number of young athletes competing in high-level sports is very likely to lead some of them to doping in order to win. Education about the hazardous effects of doping on health should be offered to all people involved at any level of sports, and this could be the only effective weapon against the threat of doping.

NIKOLAOS G. MALLIAROPOULOS

EXERCISE AND BACK PAIN – GLOBAL CONCERN

Back problems are common. Orthopedic literature has revealed the tendency of a 70–90 per cent lifetime incidence of low back pain (LBP) in the average population. LBP is the second commonest cause for consulting a physician, and accounts for the highest medical expenses relating to work-related injury. But back pain is most frequently a self-limiting problem that can be managed efficiently with conservative measures. Despite similar results obtained with analogous treatments, significant differences have been shown between the epidemiology of back pain in athletes and in non-athletes. However, the most common back ailments affecting athletes can be prevented by recognizing the epidemiological patterns that contribute to their development and by implementing programs to combat them.

Predisposing factors for back pain

Among the general public

- Poor conditioning, strength and flexibility of the back muscles and ligaments as well as postural deformities;
- Age over 40–50 years;
- Low level of formal education and social class;
- Physical and psychosocial workload;
- Smoking;
- Osteoarthritis.

Among athletes

In addition to the above factors, compared with nonathletes athletes usually subject their spines to larger, more prolonged forces which place them at greater risk of back injury. The normal extensor to flexor strength in lumbar stabilizing muscles is 1.3 to 1, which is reported to be substantially reduced in athletes with back pain. Sudden increases in the intensity or duration of workout, improper technique while performing athletic activities, poor equipment, and inappropriate footwear, can also contribute to back pain and must be taken into account.

It is important to recognise predisposing factors for the prevention of sports related

back pain. Further, a flexibility program for the pelvis, hamstrings, and hip extensors should be initiated in order to maintain the proper balance of elasticity in these structures.

Etiology

The differential diagnosis of back pain in both athletes and nonathletes is exhaustive and includes soft tissue injury, spondylolysis/spondylolisthesis, disk herniation and radiculopathy, Scheuermann's kyphosis, fractures, tumors, infections, primary inflammatory conditions, and non-spine-related referred pain from various other anatomical locations.

Acute back strain or sprain is the most common cause of back pain among the general population, especially athletes, and is commonly believed to be more prevalent in persons with poor flexibility, coordination, posture, and muscle strength, although a direct cause-and-effect relationship has not been proven.

Repetitive hyperextension maneuvers such as carried out in gymnastics, wrestling, or diving, appear to be associated with disproportionately higher rates of spondylolysis.

Recent studies have revealed that back pain is common in racquet-sport players because of the constant rotation of the torso required in these activities. Also in weight lifters over the age of forty, disk degeneration is believed to occur in 80 per cent of men and 65 per cent of women.

Sacral stress fractures occur almost exclusively in individuals participating in high-level running sports, such as track or marathon.

Role of exercise in controling back pain

Regular exercise is the most potent weapon against back problems. Many studies have shown a dramatic reductions in LBP in individuals who are physically fit. In addition, the person in good physical shape is much less likely to injure their back during work or daily activities.

The natural stimulus for the back to heal is active exercise, done in a controled, gradual, and progressive manner. Movement distributes nutrients into the disc space and soft tissue in the spine to keep the discs, muscles, ligaments, and joints healthy; conversely, lack of exercise can worsen back pain by leading to stiffness, weakness, and de-conditioning. Generally, a patient's exercise program for LBP should encompass a combination of stretching (such as hamstring stretching), strengthening exercises (such as dynamic lumbar stabilization exercise, Mckenzie exercise, or other back exercise programs), and low-impact aerobic exercising (such as walking, bicycling, water therapy, or swimming).

References

Bono, C.M. (2004) 'Low Back Pain in Athletes', *Journal of Bone and Joint Surgery – American* 86-A, 2: 382–96, February.

Dutton, M. (2004) *Orthopaedic Examination, Evaluation, and Intervention*, 1152–3, McGraw Hill.

Kolettis, G.J. (2004) *Can Exercise Control Back Pain?*, last updated 08/11/2004. www.spineuniverse.com/displayarticle.php/article605.html

Prahlow, N.D., Buschbacher, R.M. *et al.* (2002) 'Back', in Ralph M. Buschbacher (ed.) *Practical Guide to Musculoskeletal Disorders*, 2nd edn, 98–109, Boston MA: Butterworth-Heinemann.

Trainor, T.J. and Trainor, M.A. (2004) 'Etiology of Low Back Pain in Athletes', *Current Sports Medicine Reports* 3: 41–6.

KAI MING CHAN

EXERCISE AND CANCER

It has been well documented that the participation in regular physical activity is associated with a decrease in death from all causes. In the West, cancer is still one of the commonest causes of death in the adult population. It is therefore not surprising that the participation in regular physical activity may be linked to a decreased risk of developing cancer.

Cancer is not one disease, but many different cancers can occur in different organs, each with their own set of risk factors. It is therefore important to consider the link between physical exercise and specific cancers, and not just all cancers. The purpose of this section is to discuss (1) the relationship between the participation in regular physical activity and the development of different types of cancer; (2) whether regular exercise training has any role in the treatment of cancer; and (3) practical exercise guidelines for cancer sufferers.

Does regular exercise training prevent the development of cancers?

To date, more than sixty-eight published studies report on the association of regular physical activity and overall risk of developing cancer, whereas more than 160 studies have examined the relationship between exercise training and cancer of specific organs. The main findings of these studies will be discussed briefly (Friedenreich 2001; Thune and Furberg 2001).

Exercise and the risk of all types of cancer

In general, most studies show that participation in regular physical activity is associated with a decrease in the risk of developing cancer. This is stronger for males compared to females. There also appears to be a so-called 'dose-response' effect, indicating that the higher the 'dose' of regular exercise is, the lower the risk of developing cancer becomes.

Exercise and cancer of the large bowel (colon and rectum)

The link between regular exercise training and cancer of the large bowel is well investigated. Most studies show that there is a strong protective effect against the development of cancer of the colon by participating in regular physical activity. The following specific observations have been made:

- Participation in regular physical activity reduces the risk of developing colon cancer between 10 and 70 per cent.
- Three hours of high- or four hours of moderate-intensity exercise per week can reduce the risk of colon cancer by about 50 per cent.
- Continuous rather than short-term exercise training appears to be more protective.

The mechanism by which regular exercise training may protect against the development of bowel cancer is not clear. It may be related to a more rapid transit time of ingested material or through the positive effects of exercise on the immune system.

Exercise and cancer of the breast, ovaries, and endometrium

It has been shown that regular exercise training results in a reduction of about 30 per cent in the risk of developing breast cancer. This association has been observed in pre-, peri-, and post-menopausal women. It also appears that a higher 'dose' of regular exercise is associated with a greater reduction in risk of breast cancer. It has been estimated that about four hours of moderate intensity physical activity per week will result in a decreased risk of developing breast cancer in women. The mechanism for this is not well researched, but it may be related to the fact that exercise training favorably alters the sex hormones in females and so decreases the risk of breast cancer.

Fewer studies have related regular physical activity to the risk of developing endometrial cancer. Most of these studies indicate that exercise training protects against endo-

metrial cancer, and the risk appears to be reduced by between 20 and 80 per cent in different studies. More research studies are required to confirm this finding.

The relationship between exercise training and cancer of the ovaries has not been well investigated. A few preliminary observations indicate that even in this condition, exercise training may reduce the risk.

Exercise and prostate or testicular cancer

It has been suggested that the reduction in circulating testosterone observed in male athletes, may result in a decrease in the risk of prostate and testicular cancer in men. In twenty-eight published studies, fourteen show a reduction in the risk of prostate cancer. However, in only ten of nineteen studies is there a clear 'dose' response relationship. There is therefore at present insufficient evidence to suggest that regular exercise training decreases the risk of prostate cancer.

The relationship between increased exercise training and testicular cancer is also not well established. More scientific studies are needed before a reduction in risk of testicular cancer due to exercise training can be confirmed.

Exercise and lung cancer

Exercise training is associated with an increase in the ventilation and perfusion of the lung. This may decrease the contact time between lung tissue and potential carcinogens, and result in a reduction in lung cancer. However, not many studies have been conducted to test this hypothesis. Some studies have shown that exercise training can reduce the risk of lung cancer, and that the reduction is related to increased 'dose' of exercise. In one study, it has been found that four hours of vigorous physical activity per week is required to reduce the risk of developing lung cancer.

Does regular exercise training benefit the patient suffering from cancer?

Over 8 million people are diagnosed with cancer every year world-wide. The question whether regular physical exercise is beneficial to these patients has been investigated in about thirty-six published studies. The results of the majority of these studies (85 per cent) indicate that regular exercise training improves the quality of life of these patients. It is therefore becoming an important component in the treatment of these patients.

Practical guidelines for exercise prescription for patients with cancer

Exercise prescription for cancer patients should be designed for each individual dependent on the type, stage, and associated complication of the cancer. However, a few general guidelines are listed in Table 12.

Table 12. Practical guidelines for exercise prescription in cancer patients

Exercise prescription	Guidelines for cancer patients
Mode of exercise	Involve large muscle groups Walking and cycling are recommended
Frequency of exercise	3–5 times per week
Intensity of exercise	Depends on level of conditioning and side effects from treatment 60–80% of maximum heart rate (220 – age in years)
Duration of exercise	Total of 20–30 min Can be intermittent shorter bouts with rest intervals
Progression of exercise training	Initially increase frequency and duration Later, exercise intensity can be increased

Summary

There is fairly strong evidence that regular exercise training (3–4 hours of moderate to vigorous activity per week) can reduce the risk of developing any cancer, but more specifically colon and breast cancer. Regular exercise training also increases the quality of life in patients diagnosed with cancer, and should be encouraged. However, exercise prescription should be tailored to each individual under the guidance of health professionals trained in the field.

See also: exercise in the aged

References

Friedenreich, C.M. (2001) 'Physical Activity and Cancer Prevention: From Observational to Intervention Research', *Cancer Epidemiol Biomarkers Prev* 10: 287–301.
Thune, I. and Furberg, A.S. (2001) 'Physical Activity and Cancer Risk: Dose-response and Cancer, All Sites and Site-specific', *Med Sci Sports Exerc* 33: S530 – S550.

Further reading

Courney, K.S. and Mackey, J.R. (2000) 'Exercise in the Treatment of Cancer: Benefits, Guidelines and Precautions', *International SportMed Journal* 1, 5.

MARTIN SCHWELLNUS

EXERCISE AND DEGENERATIVE ARTHRITIS – RESEARCH

Degenerative arthritis is one of the common causes of chronic joint pain and disability and imposes enormous personal, social, and economic burdens. It is defined as the chronic breakdown of cartilage in the joints. The synonym for degenerative arthritis is osteoarthritis. It is characterized by increased joint pain, muscle weakness, and functional limitations in people over forty-five. These individuals require an extensive rehabilitative exercise program to alleviate pain.

Regular exercise helps control symptoms of osteoarthritis. Exercise-induced improvements in pain and disability have been shown to be associated with the physiological enhancements in muscle strength, endurance, stability in joints, and flexibility. Among the more than 100 different types of arthritis conditions, osteoarthritis is the most common. Studies have shown that almost half of all older adults have arthritis. The breakdown of cartilage in joints in osteoarthritis patients is the result of wear that occurs during sports activities. Commonly observed symptoms include lameness, swollen joints, and muscle atrophy. The prevalence of this disease world-wide can be demonstrated by statistical data which show that 20 million people in the United States have been affected by osteoarthritis, while the Japanese population has a higher rate of incidence, but the ultimate reason for this is still unclear. Other ethnic groups such as the South African blacks, East Indians, and Southern Chinese have a relatively lower rate (Hurley *et al.* 2002). Osteoarthritis causes major impacts on individuals and societies in all countries. Realization of the impact of bone and joint disorders in society world-wide in nowadays has emphasized the importance of research development to seek possible improvements for the older age group suffering from osteoarthritis.

Advancing age has been epidemiologically proven to be associated with the increase in the prevalence of osteoarthritis (Lawrence *et al.* 1989). However, osteoarthritis causes recurrent pain and stiffness, especially after long periods of rest such as sleep, and loss of joint function, which is the result of physical inactivity in older people. As people grow older, their flexibility and balance inevitably decrease, but with appropriate stretching exercises, the decline can be halted and the condition improved. To prevent the development of this disease, the best way is to keep oneself physically active. Exercise need not be intense at all; it can involve normal walking, jogging, swimming, hiking, etc. These exercises help prevent active wearing of the cartilage, keeping the bones stronger. With respect to osteoarthritis patients, they require a specialized exercise program, since they do not want their cartilages to wear down further. This program should include various home-based stretching exercises, stamina exercises, and probably moderate jogging. Patients should seek their physician's advice before participating in exercise. An accurate assessment of the disease severity must be made by the physician. Not every type of exercise is beneficial for patients, and this is vital to keep in mind. Meanwhile, physiotherapy may assist in reducing pain and stiffness of the joints.

The role of exercise in osteoarthritis is being increasingly evaluated. Research has been carried out extensively world-wide to study the pros and cons of physical activities for established osteoarthritis patients. Prevention measures are clear: adherence to routine physical activities and maintenance of a healthy, balanced, and nutritious diet are particularly helpful. With respect to the management of osteoarthritis patients, a specialized exercise program is essential; there must be no attempt to overload any joints with extra force. In order to minimize the prevalence of this disease, cooperation between the society and health professionals from various health organizations is required. Further extensive research may find a solution to this global concern, and thus allow the elderly to enjoy a pain-free life.

References

Hurley, M.V., Mitchell, H.L. and Walsh, N. (2002) 'In Osteoarthritis, the Psychological Benefits of Exercise Are as Important as Physiological Improvements', *Exercise and Sport Sciences Reviews* 31, 3: 138–43.

Lawrence, R., Hochberg, M., Kelsey, J., McDuffie, F.C., Medsger, T.A. Jr, Felts, W.R. and Shulman, L.E. (1989) 'Estimates of the Prevalence of Selected Arthritic and Musculoskeletal Diseases in the United States', *Journal of Rheumatology* 16, 4: 427–41.

VICTOR W.T. HO

EXERCISE AND FERTILITY (MALES)

The relationship between exercise training and fertility has been well studied in the female. However, in males this relationship is not clear. There are a number of environmental factors that can influence male fertility. These include: ambient temperature, exposure to pesticides, exposure to chemicals, altered hormonal milieu, drugs, and other therapeutic treatments (anti-cancer drugs) (Sharpe 2000).

In this entry, the role of physical activity and sports participation will be explored. There are three important questions. First, does a sedentary lifestyle increase the risk of developing male infertility; second, does high-intensity and prolonged training can negatively affect the hormonal balance in athletes; and finally, does substance abuse by athletes negatively affect male fertility?

Physical activity, sedentary lifestyle, and scrotal temperature

There is some evidence to suggest that a sedentary lifestyle is associated with reduced male fertility. The mechanism for this has been attributed to prolonged sitting, resulting in the inability of the scrotum to undergo effective thermoregulation. Elevated scrotal temperature has been identified as a very important negative effect on semen quality. Elevation of the scrotal temperature above 40°C for a short time period (30 min) has been shown to have major adverse consequences. Similarly, and more importantly, smaller elevations in scrotal temperature (0.7–2.5°C) also negatively affect semen quality. Therefore a combination of a sedentary lifestyle, tight fitting underwear and high ambient temp-

erature (summer) can result in increased risk of poor semen quality.

Endurance training, hormonal alterations, and male infertility

Most of the available scientific data focus mainly on the effects of endurance exercise training on the physiology of female reproduction. There is some controversy on whether endurance training alters the reproductive physiology of males. The two aspects that have to be considered are, first, the effects of endurance training on the hormonal profile (hypothalamic-pituitary-gonadal or H-P-G axis); and second, the effects of endurance training on the semen profile.

There have been some reports to indicate that high-intensity training or large volumes of training can, in some males, be associated with a decrease in the concentration of circulating testosterone. The mechanism may be peripheral (enhanced hepatic clearance or increased tissue utilization) or central (a disturbance of the H-P-G axis). To support the latter, there is some evidence that some endurance-trained men have decreases in luteinising hormone (LH) pulsatility, or a change in the pituitary response to hypothalamic stimulation by exogenous hormones such as gonadotrophin-releasing hormone (GnRH), thyrotropin-releasing hormone (TRH), or corticotrophin-releasing hormone (CRH). The findings of decreased levels of the circulating testosterone concentration in male athletes are, however, not consistent, and the clinical significance is not known. In one study, excessive training in males has been associated with a reduction in bone mineral density. It has been suggested, without firm scientific evidence, that this may be related to decreases in circulating testosterone.

Quantitative and qualitative analyses of the semen ejaculate in male athletes has been conducted in a number of studies. In one of the best studies on the semen of high-mileage runners ($>100\,km\,week^{-1}$) compared to matched sedentary controls, the following were reported in the runner group: (i) a reduced total sperm count but still within normal limits; (ii) reduced sperm motility; (iii) a slight reduction in spermatozoa with normal morphology; (iv) a higher proportion of immature spermatozoa; and (v) an increased leucocyte count in the semen.

There is only one study to date that has related hormonal changes and alterations in the semen ejaculate to reduced fertility capacity in highly trained male athletes. In this report on an artificial insemination program, it has been observed that donors with a high level of physical fitness have lower pregnancy rates compared to donors with normal physical activity levels. Although the interaction between male infertility and physical training requires further research, it appears that high-intensity training or excessive volumes of training may reduce male fertility. Practical advice to prospective fathers, who are also highly trained athletes, would be to reduce their training if there is a suggestion of male infertility.

Athletes, ergogenic drugs, and male fertility

It is well documented that athletes using androgenic anabolic steroids short-term have reduced sperm counts, and therefore reduced fertility. It is not known whether these acute effects have a more lasting permanent negative effect on fertility even when these drugs are not used any longer.

Practical advice to male athletes to improve fertility

- Avoid exercise which involves prolonged periods of sitting, e.g. cycling or rowing (to avoid high scrotal temperatures).
- Perform regular upright ambulatory type exercise (walking, jogging, running, soccer).
- Wear lightweight, cool clothing (improve scrotal thermoregulation).
- Avoid traumatic injury to the genital area (use protective devices).
- Avoid high-intensity prolonged exercise training.
- Do not use any ergogenic drugs, in particular, androgenic anabolic steroids.

Reference

Sharpe, R.M. (2000) 'Lifestyle and Environmental Contribution to Male Infertility', *Br Med Bull* 56: 630–42.

Further reading

Cumming, D.C., Wheeler, G.D. and Harber, V.J. (1994) 'Physical Activity, Nutrition, and Reproduction', *Ann NY Acad Sci* 709: 55–76.

MARTIN SCHWELLNUS

EXERCISE AND OSTEOPOROSIS – PUBLICATIONS

Osteoporosis has been a major public health concern among the higher-risk population, that is, the older age group. However, the fact is that knowledge of osteoporosis is crucial for people in any age group. Independent of gender, age, or ethnicity; from Asians to Americans, athletes to housewives, an understanding of osteoporosis would benefit all and contribute to an improved quality of life. Statistics have shown that this major public health threat affects approximately 44 million Americans, but it is a worldwide health-related problem. Osteoporosis is characterized by an excessively low bone mineral density, thus an increased risk of osteoporotic fractures. There is a linear relationship between bone mineral density (BMD) and risk of developing osteoporosis.

The degree of seriousness of this international public health concern has awakened a group of health care professionals who understand the significant, world-wide impact of osteoporosis and related musculoskeletal disorders. Publications and relevant information on every aspect of osteoporosis are widely available. These include scientific journals and books written by professionals from various organizations who are particularly concerned with the problem. Much of the literature focuses on the relationship between osteoporosis and exercise. Apart from the fact that a healthy, balanced, nutritious diet is required for preventing osteoporotic fractures, physical activities are an important risk factor in the development of osteoporosis and other related musculoskeletal disorders.

Many publications have shown that exercise plays an essential role in prevention of osteoporosis. The major cause of the disease is reduced BMD: a low bone mineral density causes bone to become fragile, and is the result of either reduced osteoblastic activity, or enhanced activity of the osteoclasts. Osteoblasts are defined as cells that are responsible for bone formation, while osteoclasts are responsible for bone resorption. Their combined activities give rise to the overall bone mineral density. Research has shown that a moderate level of physical activity keeps bones stronger and denser. It has been shown that weight-bearing and resistance exercises both contribute to a higher BMD. Another study has assessed the combined effects of exercise and hormone replacement therapy (HRT) on BMD in postmenopausal women. The major concern for postmenopausal women is that the rate of bone loss accelerates to 1–2 per cent per year, when compared to the time prior to menopause; where the rate of bone loss is less than 1 per cent per annum (WHO 1994). With respect to the latter study, scientists postulated that the combined effect of exercise and HRT is more beneficial than HRT treatment alone, and their results confirmed the hypothesis.

Among all osteoporotic fractures, hip fractures are statistically shown to be the most serious type. To address this international health concern, scientists have shown via extensive research that hip bone mineral density is improved by high-impact aerobic exercise in postmenopausal women and men over fifty years old. These so-called high-impact aerobic exercises include step and jumping exercises, specifically to load the proximal femur and spine (Welsh and Rutherford 1996).

In most cases, exercise has a positive effect on the the prevention of osteoporosis. However, in some cases, exercise shows a negative effect. Examples are ballet dancers and women with long-term exercise amenorrhoea. This group has a greater risk of having osteoporosis or osteopenia – a milder form of osteoporosis. In general, statistics indicate that the risk for women of developing osteoporosis is four times greater than that for men.

Thousands of scientific journals and papers are published world-wide, and these sources are incredibly helpful for information about every aspect of osteoporosis. More innovative discoveries from further extensive research will enable health professionals to improve people's quality of life. Cooperation among different organizations is necessary to produce meaningful research results. Their great work should continue in order to allow people around the world to acquire a meaningful life.

KAI MING CHAN

EXERCISE AND PREGNANCY

Regular exercise training is a well recognized as a positive health behavior, and more women wish to start or continue with a regular exercise program throughout their pregnancy. However, there are potential risks and benefits of regular exercise training during pregnancy and immediately after delivery for both the mother and the fetus.

What are the potential risks of maternal exercise to the pregnant mother?

There is a very low risk of medical complications that may be associated with exercise training in a woman with an uncomplicated pregnancy. However, some physiological changes can result in some risk to the exercising pregnant woman.

Maternal hypoglycemia

Carbohydrate utilization by skeletal muscle is increased during strenuous exercise, and hypoglycemia can occur during prolonged exercise, particularly if adequate amounts of carbohydrates are not consumed before and during exercise. There is also some evidence to suggest that blood glucose utilization is enhanced in the last trimester of pregnancy. There may be a risk that hypoglycemia can develop more easily during exercise in the last trimester compared to the normal risk during exercise in the non-pregnant state.

Chronic fatigue

Fatigue is one of the most common symptoms during pregnancy. There is a possibility that regular exercise may exacerbate fatigue. However, in one study, mothers who exercised regularly during pregnancy subjectively assessed that they were less fatigued than a sedentary control group.

Musculoskeletal injury risk

Pregnant women who exercise may have an increased risk of developing musculoskeletal injuries because of (i) increased ligamentous laxity; (ii) increased body weight; and (iii) altered distribution of mechanical forces such as an arched back. However, no studies have shown that the risk of injury is increased as a result of exercise training in pregnancy. Specific exercise training in the antenatal period may even reduce the risk of musculoskeletal injury.

What are the potential risks of maternal exercise to the fetus?

Spontaneous abortion in the first trimester

At present there is no good scientific evidence to suggest that the risk of spontaneous abortion in the first trimester is higher in the exercising mother.

Fetal hyperthermia and congenital malformations

It has been suggested, mainly from animal studies, that during maternal exercise an increase in core temperature may result in fetal abnormalities, but data from human studies are limited.

Fetal hypoxia

Although it has been suggested that the fetus may experience transient hypoxia during a bout of maternal exercise because of a decrease in uterine blood flow, recent evidence does not appear to substantiate this. Placental blood flow is spared during maternal exercise, and fetal bradycardia, which is an indication of fetal hypoxia, is rare during maternal exercise.

Premature labor

Acute exercise is associated with increased sympathetic activity, in particular noradrenaline, which could stimulate myometrial activity. The theoretical possibility exists that acute exercise can induce premature labor, but this has not been shown.

Altered obstetric outcome

A number of studies have been conducted to examine the relationship between maternal exercise and pregnancy outcome. A summary of the major findings of these studies is as follows.

- Women with higher scores on a fitness test (cycle ergometer test) tended to have heavier babies and shorter labors.
- Running during pregnancy was associated with normal foetal development and a lower incidence of obstetric complications.
- Continued exercise after twenty-eight weeks was associated with earlier delivery, less maternal weight gain and lighter babies.
- Mean hospital stay is lower in an exercise group compared to a control group.
- Regular exercise during pregnancy improved self-image, decreased pregnancy discomforts, and relieved tension.

The majority of studies in humans indicate that regular exercise during pregnancy is associated with either no change or definite positive obstetric outcomes.

What are the potential benefits of maternal exercise to the pregnant mother?

Maternal conditioning

Regular exercise training results in increased fitness, general health benefits, increased weight control and improved physical well-being in the pregnant woman.

Facilitation of labor

Exercise training results in enhanced maternal work capacity and improved muscle function. Therefore, regular exercise during pregnancy appears to reduce the duration of the active stage of labor in primigravid but not multigravid woman.

Prevention of gestational diabetes

Gestational diabetes is a state of carbohydrate intolerance, which can occur in late pregnancy due to the interference of the actions of insulin by placental hormones. Regular exercise training has been shown to reduce the risk of gestational diabetes by reducing insulin requirements and increasing fat oxidation.

Prevention of low back pain

Gestational low back pain is reported to occur in 50 per cent of all pregnancies. A number of factors have been postulated to cause this back pain. These include: (i) exaggeration of the lumbar lordosis; (ii) increased loading of the lumbar spine by the weight of the gravid uterus; (iii) loss of abdominal muscle strength and tone; and (iv) increased laxity of the pelvic and sacroiliac joints. Muscle conditioning in the antenatal period can prevent the onset of back pain.

Psychological benefits

Pregnancy is associated with a number of common emotional and cognitive reactions. Regular exercise has been shown to have positive effects on some of these pregnancy-associated psychological factors.

What are the potential benefits of maternal exercise to the fetus?

The potential benefit of regular maternal exercise training to the fetus has already been mentioned. Most studies indicate that exercise training results in a shorter active stage of labor, no significant alterations in the 1-min and 5-min Apgar scores, and potential short- and long-term positive neurodevelopmental effects on the fetus.

What are the guidelines for exercise prescription during pregnancy?

As a first step, it is recommended that all pregnant women undergo a complete health, obstetric, medical, and musculoskeletal assessment prior to starting an exercise program. This is to exclude the existence of potential absolute and relative contra-indications to exercise in pregnancy (Table 13).

457

The next step is to subject the mother to a graded exercise test during which maternal heart rate, blood pressure, and rating of perceived exertion are documented and fetal heart rate is monitored. This enables the clinician to prescribe a suitable exercise program.

Third, the pregnant woman is carefully educated to recognize the following warning signs indicating when exercise should be terminated:

- vaginal bleeding
- shortness of breath before starting an exercise session
- dizziness
- headache
- chest pain
- muscle weakness
- calf pain or swelling (need to rule out thrombophlebitis)
- preterm labor
- decreased fetal movement
- amniotic fluid leakage

Finally, an individual exercise program is based on the following principles of exercise prescription (Table 14).

Exercise should be conducted in a cool environment (early in the morning or late afternoon) to prevent hyperthermia. Light,

Table 13. Absolute and relative contra-indications to maternal exercise during pregnancy

Absolute contra-indications to exercise in pregnancy	Relative contra-indications to exercise in pregnancy
Hemodynamically significant heart disease	Severe anemia
Restrictive lung disease	Unevaluated maternal cardiac arrhythmia
Incompetent cervix/cerclage	Chronic bronchitis
Multiple gestation at risk for premature labor	Poorly controlled type 1 diabetes mellitus
Persistent 2nd or 3rd trimester vaginal bleeding	Extreme morbid obesity
Placenta previa after 26 weeks gestation	Extreme underweight (BMI < 12)
Premature labor during the current pregnancy	History of extremely sedentary lifestyle
Ruptured membranes	Intrauterine growth restriction in current pregnancy
Pregnancy induced hypertension	Poorly controlled maternal hypertension/pre-eclampsia
	Orthopedic limitations
	Poorly controlled seizure disorder
	Poorly controlled thyroid disease
	Heavy smoker

Table 14. Principles of exercise prescription during pregnancy

Type of exercise	Endurance activities (walking, cycling, swimming). Resistance exercise and flexibility training is recommended.
	Avoid contact sports and higher-risk activities (scuba diving, rock climbing).
	Core stabilizing exercises are highly recommended.
	Specific rehabilitative exercises are recommended based on the musculoskeletal assessment.
	Water-based exercise programs are particularly beneficial as immersion reduces the risk of pooling of blood in the lower limbs, decreasing the risk of hypotension.
Intensity of exercise	Rating of perceived exertion of 12–14 (on a scale of 6–20)
	Training heart rate of 60–80% of maximal heart rate
Duration of exercise	30–60min of sustained exercise training at the recommended intensity
Frequency of exercise	Most days of the week
Progression of exercise	Previously sedentary women should gradually increase the duration to up to 30min per session.
	Previously trained women could initially continue at the same exercise load but expect a gradual decrease as the pregnancy continues.

comfortable clothing and shock absorbing footwear should be worn. A light meal consisting of mainly carbohydrate should be consumed two hours before exercise to prevent hypoglycemia.

See also: pregnancy; lower back injury; diabetes mellitus

References

Artal, R. and O'Toole, M. (2003) 'Guidelines of the American College of Obstetricians and Gynecologists for Exercise During Pregnancy and the Postpartum period', *Br.J Sports Med* 37: 6–12.

Kramer, M.S. (2002) 'Aerobic Exercise for Women During Pregnancy', *Cochrane Database Syst Rev* CD000180.
http://www.cochrane.org

MARTIN SCHWELLNUS

EXERCISE AND THE HUMAN IMMUNODEFICIENCY VIRUS (HIV)

AIDS, or Acquired Immune Deficiency Syndrome, which is caused by the Human Immunodeficiency Virus (HIV) was first recognized in 1981. There is considerable debate on the precise impact of the HIV pandemic on the global population, including the sporting population. The association between sports participation, physical activity, and HIV infection can therefore not be ignored. Specific issues that are of importance are the possible risk of HIV transmission during sports participation, and the effect of regular exercise on HIV infection.

Can HIV transmission occur during sports participation?

The transmission of the virus from one individual to another has been linked directly to blood, semen, and cervical secretions with likely transmission occurring through breast-feeding. The primary routes of transmission are therefore by sexual contact with an infected person, particularly enteral exposure to infected blood or blood products, and perinatally from an infected mother to her child.

To date, no cases of HIV transmission have been recorded in either the sporting or the non-sporting population through contact with saliva, social contact, or sharing facilities such as living space, toilets, bathrooms, and eating and cooking facilities. The risk of HIV infection in athletes is the same as that in the general population if there is a history of engaging in well established high-risk behaviors for HIV transmission.

Although there is documentation of only a single possible case of HIV disease as a result of sports participation in contact sports, there is a need to establish clear guidelines for the prevention of HIV transmission during sports participation. As early as 1989 the International Sports Medicine Federation (FIMS), together with the World Health Organization (WHO), published guidelines for the prevention of HIV transmission during contact sport (WHO position statement 1989). Subsequently, others have published similar guidelines.

There are no epidemiological data available to calculate the risk of HIV transmission during sports participation. At best, a theoretical risk of transmission in a sport can be calculated by considering the following variables:

- the estimated carrier rate of HIV in athletes (percentage of participants that are HIV-positive)
- the estimated chance of an open bleeding wound in a sports participant (incidence of open bleeding wounds)
- the estimated chance of two players with open bleeding wounds making contact (incidence of physical contact between two participants)
- the estimated chance of transmission of the virus when infected blood makes contact with an open bleeding wound (estimated to be 0.3–0.5 per cent)

Using this approach, the risk of HIV transmission in a game has been calculated as 0.0000000104 in American football. This can be translated to approximately one player becoming infected per 100 million games. Clearly, this is a very low risk and is probably the reason why there is no widespread documentation of HIV infection in American football players.

These estimates will differ between different populations (higher seroprevalence) and sports (higher risks of bleeding and player contact). For instance, in a boxing fight of twelve rounds, the risk of an open bleeding wound has been documented as 47 per cent. The risk of seroconversion in professional boxers has been calculated as 0.00021 or 1 in 4,760 fights. The risk of seroconversion after contact between two boxers may also be higher than that of a needle stick injury because blood may be forced into the wound by the nature of the blow, and contact may be repetitive.

Despite the lack of accurate scientific data in other contact sports, the prevention of HIV disease in sportspeople has to be addressed by establishing clear guidelines for sports participants, administrators, and medical personnel involved in sport.

Practical guidelines: preventing HIV transmission during sports

General guidelines

In general the risk of HIV transmission during sports is higher in contact sports, where there is a risk of transmission through contamination of open lesions, wounds or mucous membranes of a non-infected individual with infected blood or blood products.

Specific guidelines for sportspeople

The following are specific guidelines for the individual athlete to reduce the risk of HIV transmission during sports:

- An athlete who engages in high-risk behavior is advised to seek medical attention regarding possible HIV infection.
- Athletes with known HIV infection should seek medical and legal counseling before considering further participation in sport.
- Athletes with known HIV infection should inform medical personnel of their condition if they sustain an open wound or skin lesions during sports participation so that these can be managed appropriately.

Specific guidelines for sports administrators

Sports administrators, including coaches and managers, have special opportunities for the meaningful education of athletes with respect to HIV and should encourage athletes to seek counseling. Finally, they also have an important role in ensuring that adequate medical care is available for their sportspeople.

Specific guidelines for medical personnel attending to athletes

Guidelines for medical personnel in preventing HIV disease in sportspeople are:

- All open skin lesions sustained during sports participation should be treated appropriately before allowing the athlete to return to the playing field.
- The following treatment of open skin lesions is recommended:
  - immediate cleaning of the wound with a suitable antiseptic such as hypochloride (bleach, Milton), 2 per cent gluteraldehyde (Cidex), organic iodines or 70 per cent alcohol (ethyl alcohol, isopropyl alcohol).
  - The open wound should be covered securely so that there is no risk of exposure to blood or blood

products prior to returning to the playing field.

- All first aiders and medical personnel attending to athletes with open wound lesions should wear protective gloves to decrease the risk of HIV transmission.

Is participation in regular exercise of benefit to patients with HIV disease?

Recently, the beneficial effects of exercise training for HIV positive patients (Stages I to III) were summarized as follows:

Stage I

- increased CD4 cells
- possible delay in onset of symptoms
- increase in muscle function and size

Stage II

- increase in CD4 cells (lesser magnitude of change)
- possible diminished severity and frequency of some symptoms

Stage III

- effects on CD4 cells are not known
- effects on symptoms are inconclusive

These findings indicate that exercise can play a beneficial role in the pre-HIV test counseling of potentially infected patients, and that regular moderate-intensity exercise can play a role in the management of early, asymptomatic individuals with HIV infection.

What are the practical guidelines for exercise prescription in patients with HIV disease?

General guidelines

Before initiating any type of exercise training, all HIV-infected individuals regardless of age or stage of disease should:

- have a complete physical examination
- discuss exercise plans with a physician or exercise specialist
- comply with normal exercise testing and prescription guidelines.

Specific guidelines based on stage of the disease

Healthy asymptomatic HIV seropositive

- unrestricted exercise activity
- continue competition
- avoid overtraining

AIDS-related complex

- continue exercise training on symptom-listed basis
- avoid strenuous exercise
- reduce or curtail exercise during acute illness

Diagnosed AIDS

- remain physically active
- continue exercise training on symptom-limited basis
- avoid strenuous exercise
- reduce or curtail exercise during acute illness

See also: exercise and the immune system

References

Nixon, S., O'Brien, K., Glazier, R.H. and Tynan, A.M. (2002) 'Aerobic Exercise Interventions for Adults Living with HIV/ AIDS', *Cochrane.Database Syst Rev.* CD001796. http:// www.cochrane.org

Stringer, W.W. (1999) 'HIV and Aerobic Exercise. Current Recommendations', *Sports Med* 28: 389–95.

MARTIN SCHWELLNUS

EXERCISE AND THE IMMUNE SYSTEM

The immune system is a complex system in the body that is composed of bone marrow, lymphoid tissue, circulating cells in the blood, and soluble mediators including antibodies, complement proteins, cytokines, and interferons. This complex system recognizes abnormal proteins:

1. on the surface of the body (such as mucosal surfaces in the respiratory and gastro-intestinal tracts);
2. that penetrate the surface and are in the tissues and in the blood and lymphatic circulations; and
3. that are on abnormal cells such as cancer cells. Once the abnormal proteins are recognized, the immune system can destroy the invading organisms or cells. Proteins that will recognize the characteristics of these abnormal proteins are also produced, and these play a role in future exposure to the foreign material and organisms.

Both an acute bout of physical exercise or regular exercise training can influence the immune system. Over the past 20–30 years, the effect of physical exercise on the immune system has been studied extensively. These responses are complex and are not yet understood fully. In this section, a summary of the effects of an acute exercise bout and the effects of regular exercise training on the immune system will be presented. The clinical implications of these effects will be discussed briefly, as well as practical guidelines for the exercising individual to maintain a healthy immune system.

Effects of an acute bout of exercise on elements of the immune system

The effects of an acute bout of exercise on the immune system have been studied extensively (Rowbottom and Green 2002). In general these effects can be summarized first as those related to changes in the number of cells in the blood, and second as those related to changes in the function of these cells. The effects are related to the intensity and the duration of the exercise bout. In general, it has been observed that the greater the intensity and the longer the duration of the exercise bout, the larger the effect that is observed. The changes in the immune system in response to an acute bout of exercise are summarized in Table 15.

An acute bout of high-intensity or prolonged exercise therefore appears to have some detrimental effects on the immune system. This has resulted in the hypothesis that there is an 'open window' period after an acute high intensity, prolonged exercise bout during which an individual may be more susceptible to an infection. It has been

Table 15. Immediate and delayed (few hours) effects of an acute bout of exercise on elements of the immune system

	Type of cell / protein	Immediate effect of an acute exercise bout	Delayed effect (few hours) after an acute exercise bout
Cell number	Leucocytes	Increase	Increase
	Neutrophils	Increase	Increase
	All lymphocytes	Increase	Decrease
	T helper lymphocytes	Decrease	Increase
	T suppressor lymphocytes	No change	No change
	B lymphocytes	No change	Increase
	Natural Killer (NK) cells	Increase	Decrease
Cellular function	T lymphocyte proliferative response	Decrease	Decrease
	In vitro immunoglobulin production	Decrease	Decrease
	Total Natural Killer cell activity (NKCA)	Increase	Decrease

suggested that the duration of this period is between 3 and 72 hours after exercise. However, it has also been shown that exercise of a more moderate intensity does not result in these changes, and may even 'enhance' elements of the immune function.

Effects of regular exercise training on elements of the immune system

The effects of regular exercise training have also been studied (Mackinnon 2000). Once again, the effects are related to the amount of training, and affect both cell number as well as function. The effects of moderate training (intensity and volume) and intense training on elements of the immune system are summarized in Table 16.

In summary, regular training at a moderate intensity and duration appears to have beneficial effects on the immune system, whereas prolonged and intense training results in some depression of immune function. These observations have resulted in the hypothesis that the relationship between regular training (training load) and the immune function is best represented by a J-shaped curve, where no exercise training represents a baseline in immune function, which is enhanced by moderate training intensity and duration. However, the immune system appears to be depressed by high-intensity, prolonged exercise training.

Clinical implications of exercise on the immune system

The main clinical implications of the effects of an acute exercise bout as well as regular exercise training on the immune system are as follows.

- An acute bout of high-intensity, prolonged exercise may depress the immune system and increase the risk of infections.
- An acute bout of moderate-intensity exercise appears to have some beneficial effects on the immune system, and is the preferred exercise prescription for patients where the immune system requires 'stimulation' (e.g. cancer patients and patients with HIV disease).
- Regular exercise training at a moderate intensity and duration enhances immune function, and may be a mechanism for the observed benefits of regular exercise training on risk of upper respiratory tract infections, cancer development, and other chronic diseases.

Table 16. The effects of regular moderate and intense training elements of the immune system

	Type of cell / protein	Effects of moderate training	Effects of intense training
Cell number	Leucocytes	No change	No change or decrease
	Neutrophils	No change	No change or slight increase
	All lymphocytes	No change	No change or decrease
	Natural Killer (NK) cells	No change	No change or decrease
Cellular function	T lymphocyte proliferative response	No change or decrease	Increase
	Total Natural Killer cell activity (NKCA)	Increase or no change	Decrease
	Serum immunoglobulin concentration	No change	No change
	Mucosal immunoglobulin concentration	No change	No change or decrease

- Prolonged exercise training at high intensities by endurance athletes is associated with a depression of the immune system, and may be responsible for some of the observed symptoms and signs in the 'overtraining syndrome'.
- Nutritional modifications of the immune system in order to 'stimulate' and 'protect' immune function during high-intensity prolonged exercise have been investigated.
- There is some evidence to suggest that carbohydrate supplements during exercise, which will prevent the development of hypoglycaemia, results in improved immune function during exercise.
- Recent evidence suggests that upper respiratory tract symptoms observed after prolonged endurance exercise are not caused by bacterial or viral infections, but by some other, as yet undetermined, cause.

Practical guidelines for exercising individuals to maintain a healthy immune system

Based on current evidence, the following general guidelines for exercising individuals to protect and enhance their immune systems can be given. It must be stated that this is an active area of research, and these guidelines may change as more information becomes available.

- Moderate-intensity (60–80 per cent of maximum age-predicted heart rate) and duration of exercise (<60 min) is advisable.
- Maintain a healthy balanced diet including vitamins and minerals.
- Avoid hypoglycaemia during exercise by supplementation with carbohydrates before and during exercise.
- Avoid other psychosocial stressors in association with periods of more intense exercise training.

- Avoid rapid weight loss and chronic fatigue.

See also: exercise and cancer; exercise and upper respiratory tract infections

References

Mackinnon, L.T. (2000) 'Chronic Exercise Training Effects on Immune Function', *Med Sci Sports Exerc* 32: S369–S376.
Rowbottom, D.G. and Green, K.J. (2002) 'Acute Exercise Effects on the Immune System', *Med Sci Sports Exerc* 32: S396–S405.

MARTIN SCHWELLNUS

EXERCISE AND TRAINING RESPONSE OF CELLULAR STRUCTURES

Skeletal muscle demonstrates remarkable plasticity in response to various stimuli, including chronic exercise training. The outcome of such adaptation is to improve the functional capacity of muscle and, by extension, exercise performance. It is a well established biological tenet that changes in cell function are coupled with changes in cell structure. These alterations, however, are specific to the mode of exercise, whether endurance – aerobic, or resistance – weight-training. Some of the fundamental morphological adaptations displayed by myofibres in response to endurance and resistance exercise will be addressed here.

Myosin

Human skeletal muscle exhibits an impressive range of capabilities. For example, the same quadriceps muscles used by an athlete to run more than 42 km during a marathon, may express potent explosive power during a brief power event such as the 100 m sprint. To a large extent, this versatility is explained by the various isoforms of the myosin heavy chain (MHC) that have been identified in muscle. Myosin, along with actin, serves as the contractile filament within the myofibres (see

muscle contraction mechanics). The myosin molecule comprises two heavy and four light chains, forming a hexamer structure. Regularly interspersed along the length of the myosin heavy chain are globular heads that express the adenosine triphosphatase (ATPase) that enables actin-myosin cross bridge formation and, thus, tension generation through the hydrolysis of adenosine triphosphate (ATP). In human muscle, three MHC isoforms have been identified: MHC I has the lowest ATPase activity and slowest contractile velocity, MHC IIA displays intermediate ATPase activity and rate of myofilament movement, while MHC IIX features high ATPase potential and contractile velocity. A fourth isoform, MHC IIB, has been identified in small quadruped mammals and evinces an even greater speed of myofilament movement than the IIX isoform. The predominant MHC isoform expressed by a myofibre determines the staining properties of that fibre during histochemical analysis and serves as the basis for the fibre-typing method most commonly used by sport and exercise scientists.

Both endurance and resistance training have been shown to alter MHC isoform expression in myofibres. Although the stimulus of exercise training does not appear to be sufficiently potent to induce conversions between type I and II fibres, it does alter the distribution of type II subtypes. Curiously, both endurance and resistance training elicit the same conversion among those subtypes, type IIX → IIA. During this transition in MHC isoform expression, fibres will contain more than one isoform. Such fibres are referred to as 'hybrids' and display intermediate contractile and histochemical staining properties. The presence of these hybrid fibres is not unique to trained muscle. Significant numbers of fibres in large untrained muscles have been found to co-express multiple MHC isoforms.

Unlike modifications in MHC isoform expression and, accordingly, fibre type composition, endurance and resistance training evoke contrasting adaptations in myofibre size. Typically, endurance exercise results in approximately a 10 per cent decrease in myofibre cross-sectional area. This is viewed as a beneficial adaptation, since it enhances the diffusion of gases – oxygen and carbon dioxide – as well as substrates such as glucose, across the fibre to be exchanged with the surrounding capillaries. Conversely, as contractile proteins and myofibrils are added, resistance training results in the hypertrophy of all three major types of myofibres.

Capillary supply

Because the walls of capillaries are thin, spanning no more than a single endothelial cell, they are the only blood vessels in which the exchange of gases with the surrounding tissue can occur. Skeletal muscle is considered to be some of the most metabolically active tissue in the body; accordingly, it is richly vascularised. Prolonged exercise training is accompanied by alterations in the capillarity of muscle. For many years it has been known that endurance training amplifies the capillary supply of myofibres. This has been confirmed whether capillarity is quantified as capillary contacts per fibre, capillary density – the number of capillaries within a microscopic field of view, or capillary-to-fibre ratio – the number of capillaries relative to the number of myofibres within a microscopic field of view. This capillary enrichment is due to endurance exercise causing a sustained increase in blood flow within the working muscle. The greater shear stress imparted on the inner capillary lining initiates a cascade of events that results in the formation of new capillaries, a process termed 'angiogenesis'.

Information about the effects of resistance training on capillarity is more equivocal than that for endurance training. Early research indicated that chronic weightlifting diminished the capillary density of trained

465

muscle. However, those findings were accounted for by the training-induced enlargement of myofibres. This hypertrophy of muscle cells in effect 'crowded out' the appearance of capillaries in any given microscopic field of view, reducing not only capillary density, but also the capillary-to-fibre ratio. Yet, when quantified as the number of capillary contacts per fibre, more recent investigations do not report diminutions in the capillary supply of resistance-trained muscle. Indeed, when quantifying capillarity in this way, there is evidence that resistance training does improve the capillarity of myofibres.

Mitochondria

Because of their prolific capacity to synthesise ATP, mitochondria have been dubbed the 'powerhouses' of the cell. Muscle fibres are amply endowed with mitochondria to provide adequate ATP to meet the high-energy demands of contracting muscle. Yet, mitochondrial content is not constant among the different fibre types. In human muscle mitochondrial density is greatest among type I fibres, which are those activated most frequently during daily activities, and are relied upon during endurance exercise. Indeed, it has been documented that a running training programme of several weeks can increase the oxidative enzyme activity of muscle tissue by 100 per cent. However, no increase in the energy-producing capacity of those enzymes is detected when enzyme activity is expressed relative to mitochondrial – rather than whole muscle – protein. These findings confirm that an increase in the enzyme content of pre-existing mitochondria is not a potential training-induced adaptation. Instead, to increase the mitochondrial protein content within muscle the biogenesis of new mitochondria must occur. Recent ultrastructural evidence has revealed that endurance training dramatically enhances the volume density of mitochondria within myofibres.

In contrast to endurance training, a programme of weight-training does not improve mitochondrial density, or oxidative enzyme activity, in skeletal muscle. In fact, as a consequence of training-induced cellular hypertrophy, resistance exercise typically results in reduced mitochondrial density and, when expressed relative to whole muscle protein content, diminished oxidative enzyme activity. Resistance training does not cause the elimination of mitochondria; rather, as cellular expansion occurs with the accretion of filamentous protein, the volume occupied by mitochondria within the myofibre is diluted.

Motor endplate

The motor endplate is a specialised region of the sarcolemma that receives synaptic input from the motor neuron innervating the myofibre. Although it occupies only one tenth of 1 per cent of the sarcolemmal surface, the endplate plays an essential role in the function of muscle, since this is where the excitation of the myofibre originates. As with other structural components of the muscle cell, the endplate undergoes remodelling as a result of prolonged exercise training. Endurance training of low intensity has been shown not only to increase the size of the endplate significantly, by 30 per cent, but also to render the structure more compact in its distribution of receptors for neurotransmitters. Resistance training also expands the endplate region, albeit to a smaller extent than is evident with endurance training. Moreover, the distribution of neurotransmitter receptors is more, rather than less, elaborate after resistance training.

MICHAEL R. DESCHENES

EXERCISE AND UPPER RESPIRATORY TRACT INFECTIONS

Upper respiratory tract infections (URTI) can be defined as an acute illness affecting the nasopharynx caused by microbial agents and which results in local and sometimes systemic symptoms. It is not a single illness and is caused by a number of different microbes, mostly viruses. URTI are the most common infections that affect the adult population including athletes. Adults acquire an average of 2–5 URTI per year. This article will briefly outline the current scientific facts regarding the most common questions that are of concern to athletes regarding URTI.

Does an acute exercise bout increase or decrease the risk of developing URTI?

There is some scientific evidence to support the hypothesis that an exercise bout that is prolonged (>60 min sessions) and performed at high intensity (>80 per cent of maximum ability) is associated with a depression in the immune system. This decrease in immunity can last from a few hours to a few days after an acute exercise bout. During this period, which has been termed the 'open window' period, there appears to be an increased risk of developing URTI.

It was found consistently that between 30 and 50 per cent of athletes participating in endurance events such as marathon and ultra-marathon running will develop symptoms of URTI. In these studies the runners at highest risk to developed symptoms were the faster runners (increased running speed), and the runners with an increased training load (>65 km per week).

Until recently it has been assumed that these symptoms are due to an infection resulting from a depressed immune system. However, in two recent scientific studies viral and bacterial cultures taken from the upper respiratory tracts of symptomatic athletes after an ultra-marathon have not shown any growth, indicating that there is no infection. These studies suggest that the symptoms that athletes experience are not the result of an infection, and other causes such as pollution and allergies are possibly responsible for these symptoms. The cause of these symptoms therefore requires further investigation.

Does regular exercise training increase or decrease the risk of developing URTI?

Epidemiological studies have shown that sedentary individuals have a higher incidence of URT symptoms compared with individuals that regularly perform exercise training at moderate 'dose' of exercise (50–70 per cent of maximum ability) and moderate weekly duration (3–5 sessions per week for 30–60 min per session). It has also been shown that athletes who engage in regular, intense, and prolonged training bouts have a chronic depression of the immune system, and this results in an increased incidence of URT symptoms. These findings have therefore shown that the risk of URT symptoms is (1) lowest when individuals are exposed to a moderate 'dose' of exercise; (2) slightly higher in sedentary individuals; and (3) highest in athletes performing intense and prolonged exercise. This has resulted in defining the relationship between the 'dose' of exercise and the risk of URT symptoms as a 'J-shaped' curve (see Figure 22).

Can the risk of developing symptoms of URTI after an acute exercise bout be reduced?

Recently there has been evidence to suggest that adequate nutrition may protect the

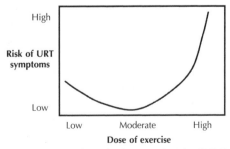

Figure 22. The relationship between the risk of URT symtoms and the 'dose' of exercise.

467

athlete from the immunosuppressive effects of high-intensity or prolonged exercise. Vitamin C (500 mg daily), glutamine and more recently carbohydrate supplementation may protect against the development of symptoms of URTI during sport. However, further scientific study is required to verify these early reports.

It can, however, be suggested that the following precautions be taken by athletes to reduce the risk of developing URTI symptoms.

- Space vigorous workouts and race events as far apart as possible.
- Avoid overtraining and chronic fatigue.
- Eat a well balanced diet.
- Get adequate sleep.
- Ensure adequate carbohydrate intake during exercise.
- Consider taking vitamin C, and glutamine supplements during periods of intense and prolonged training.

When can an athlete play sports again after URTI?

One of the most common clinical problems that medial staff attending to athletes face, is when a player can return to full activity after injury or illness. As mentioned previously, URTI are caused mainly by viruses. A number of these viruses can affect other organs, including skeletal muscle and cardiac muscle. Viral myocarditis following URTI can occur, and this has been associated with sudden death in athletes. The attending clinician must therefore make sure that an athlete does not return to full activity if there is a risk of myocarditis.

Viral myocarditis should be suspected in any athlete presenting with non-specific symptoms such as fatigue, dyspnea, palpitations or chest discomfort. In particular myocardial involvement should be ruled out in athletes who present with viral illness where there are prominent systemic symp-

toms such as headache, malaise, fever, myalgia, palpitations, and chest discomfort.

In an athlete where viral myocarditis is suspected, the findings on physical examination are usually non-specific. There may be general signs of a systemic viral infection. It is important to note that the presence of a tachycardia, which is out of proportion to the degree of pyrexia, is a useful pointer to myocardial involvement.

On cardiac auscultation the first heart sound may be muffled, and there may be a gallop. A transient apical systolic murmur may appear. In severe cases, clinical signs of congestive cardiac failure are present. A pericardial friction rub may be present if there is associated pericarditis.

In an athlete where there is any suspicion that there are systemic symptoms, or signs of viral myocarditis, sports participation must be avoided until symptoms have disappeared. Systemic symptoms include the following:

- fever;
- myalgia (muscle pains);
- tachycardia (increased resting pulse rate);
- excessive fatigue;
- swollen glands.

If the URTI is not associated with any of the above symptoms, mild exercise may in some cases (to be discussed with a physician) be permitted during the URTI. If the athlete does not develop any symptoms during this 'trial' of exercise, moderate-intensity exercise may be resumed.

Does a URT infection result in a decrease in exercise performance after clinical recovery?

Athletes who have recovered after URT infections, often complain of a residual decrease in performance. Although this may be due to the effects of a period of detraining during the recovery period, there is a possibility that there may be residual negative effects from the infection. This has never been investigated well in a scientific study. A pilot study has been undertaken during which athletes were followed during recovery from URTI and later during an equivalent period of detraining. The results of this study showed that there is a measurable decrease in exercise performance (treadmill running time) which lasts for 2–4 days after full clinical recovery from URTI. The practical suggestion resulting from this study is that athletes may experience a decline in performance for a few days following full clinical recovery from URTI. However, this is an area that requires further scientific study.

See also: exercise and the immune system

Reference

Nieman, D.C. (2002) 'Is Infection Risk Linked to Exercise Workload?', *Med Sci Sports Exerc* 32: S406–S411.

MARTIN SCHWELLNUS

EXERCISE-ASSOCIATED MUSCLE CRAMPS

About 30–50 per cent of all endurance athletes will experience cramping at some stage in their running careers. The causes, diagnosis, and treatment of cramping are still not well understood. Muscle cramps can be a manifestation of some underlying medical disease, but the majority of these medical diseases are rare and most athletes with cramping suffer from exercise-associated muscle cramping (EAMC). EAMC is defined as a 'painful spasmodic involuntary contraction of skeletal muscle that occurs during or immediately after muscular exercise'.

What causes cramps during exercise?

Early observations have led to the belief that cramps in athletes are caused by shortages of 'electrolytes' (sodium, chloride, magnesium), 'dehydration', or heat. However, there is a lack of scientific support for these theories and it appears that EAMC is caused by a disturbance in the normal control of the nerves that cause muscle contraction. The development of muscle fatigue appears to cause this lack of control.

Who is at risk of developing cramping during exercise?

Studies conducted among runners and cyclists have identified the following risk factors for EAMC:

- older age (years);
- longer history of running (running years);
- higher body mass index;
- shorter daily stretching time;
- irregular stretching habits;
- positive family history of cramping;
- high-intensity running (racing);
- long duration of running (most cramps occur after 30 km in a standard marathon);
- subjective muscle fatigue;
- hill running.

Important observations from these studies are that cramping is associated with premature muscle fatigue, and that poor stretching habits appear to increase the risk for EAMC. Muscles most prone to cramping are those that span across two joints (hamstring muscles, one of the front thigh muscles, some of the calf muscles and foot muscles). These are also the muscles that are often contracted in a shortened position during exercise.

Diagnosis of EAMC

The clinical features of EAMC are skeletal muscle fatigue followed by twitching of the muscle ('cramp prone state'). This progresses to spasmodic spontaneous contractions and eventual frank muscle cramping with pain.

Relief from the 'cramp prone state' occurs if the activity is stopped or if the muscle is stretched passively. Once activity is ceased, episodes of cramping are usually followed by periods of relief from cramping. Cramping can be precipitated by contraction of the muscle in a shortened position (inner range).

The clinical examination of an athlete with EAMC typically shows obvious distress, pain, a hard contracted muscle and visible fasciculation (twitching) over the muscle belly. In most instances the athlete is conscious, responds normally to stimuli, and is able to conduct a conversation. Vital signs and a general examination usually reveal no abnormalities. In particular, most runners with acute cramping are not dehydrated or hyperthermic.

An athlete who has generalized severe cramping or is confused, semi-comatosed or comatosed should be treated as an emergency and requires immediate hospitalization where full investigation is required.

Treatment of EAMC

The immediate treatment for acute cramping is passive stretching of the affected muscle groups and then holding the muscle in stretched position until fasciculation (twitching) ceases. Supportive treatment is by keeping the athlete at a comfortable temperature and by providing oral fluids if required. Athletes with recurrent acute EAMC should be investigated fully to exclude other medical conditions.

Prevention of EAMC

The key to the prevention of cramps is to protect the muscle from developing premature fatigue during exercise by being well trained, performing regular stretching, ensuring adequate nutritional intake (carbohydrate) and performing activity at a lower intensity and a shorter duration.

See also: muscle injury

470

Reference

Schwellnus, M.P. (1999) 'Skeletal Muscle Cramps During Exercise', *The Physician and Sports Medicine* 27, 12: 109–15.

MARTIN SCHWELLNUS

EXERCISE AT ALTITUDE – MEDICAL ASPECTS

Recreational, competitive, and professional athletes who are exposed to a rapid ascent to higher altitudes can develop medical complications that are broadly known as altitude sickness. Altitude sickness can range from less severe acute mountain sickness (AMS), to potentially life-threatening conditions such as high-altitude pulmonary edema (HAPE) or high-altitude cerebral edema (HACE). Other conditions such as chronic mountain sickness (CMS or Monge's disease), adult subacute mountain sickness, and subacute infantile mountain sickness will not be discussed in detail.

Acute mountain sickness (AMS)

Acute mountain sickness typically occurs when an unacclimatized, susceptible individual is exposed to a rapid ascent to altitudes above 2,500 or 3,000 m. Rapid ascent (2–3 days) to altitudes above 5,000 m will result in AMS in most individuals.

The symptoms of AMS can develop within 8–12 hours after rapid exposure to high altitude. The typical symptoms are headache, anorexia, nausea, vomiting, lethargy, ataxia (unsteady gait), breathlessness at moderate exertion, and poor sleep. Further complications such as retinal haemorrhages (High Altitude Retinal Haemorrhages – HARH) can occur and if this occurs near the optic disc, it may cause blurring of vision.

The main predisposing factors for the development of AMS are a rapid ascent, ascending to a high altitude (>500 m), and if the intensity of physical exertion is high.

Pre-ascent physical fitness, gender, and age are not related to the development of AMS.

The typical form of AMS is not associated with serious complications, and will improve rapidly if an individual stops ascending, and allows acclimatization to occur over a period of 2–3 days. Only a small percentage of individuals will develop more severe forms of altitude sickness.

The immediate treatment of AMS is to bring the patient to a lower altitude rapidly. In most instances this will resolve the symptoms over a time period. Other preventative measures and treatment options will be discussed in the section of high-altitude pulmonary edema.

Pathophysiology of acute mountain sickness (AMS)

As the air pressure falls during ascent, the reduced oxygen pressure in the alveoli of the lung results in a reduction in oxygen saturation in the arterial blood. This hypoxia results in a number of physiological effects in the cardiovascular, respiratory, renal endocrine and brain choroids plexus as shown in Table 17 (Coote 1995).

The initial shifts in fluid balance are probably the main cause of the clinical manifestations of acute mountain sickness. Hypoxia-induced vasodilatation increases hydrostatic pressure in the capillaries, and together with increased permeability results in fluid and some protein movement into the interstitium, resulting in edema. The cerebral manifestations of altitude sickness are probably due to vasodilatation of the cerebral arteries and some cerebral edema. Fluid accumulation in the alveoli will exacerbate hypoxia.

The immediate adaptation to exposure at altitude is a diuresis that results in a decrease of the plasma volume. This together with increased red cell production, which is induced by increased erythropoietin, increases the oxygen carrying capacity of the blood.

Table 17. Physiological responses to hypoxia in acute mountain sickness (AMS) (Coote 1995)

System	Response to hypoxia
Cardiovascular	Increased red cell number Increased permeability in the microcirculation Vasodilatation in the cerebral arteries Vasoconstriction in the pulmonary vascular bed
Respiratory	Increased ventilation Decreased pCO_2
Renal	Increased permeability in the microcirculation Diuresis with sodium loss
Endocrine	Decreased ADH (anti-diuretic hormone) Increased ACTH (adrenocorticotrophic hormone) Decreased plasma rennin activity Decreased angiotensin-converting enzyme, angiotensin II Decreased aldosterone Decreased atrial natriuretic peptide

High-altitude pulmonary edema (HAPE)

High-altitude pulmonary edema is a non-cardiogenic pulmonary edema that is life threatening and is usually preceded by acute mountain sickness. The prevalence of HAPE is <0.2 per cent in the general alpine mountaineering population when ascending to altitudes of about 4,500 m in 2–4 days. If the rate of ascent is more rapid (<24 hours) the incidence increases to 10 per cent, and is even higher if there is a previously documented history of HAPE (60 per cent of individuals). Therefore, higher altitudes (>500 m), rapid rate of ascent, and individual susceptibility are very important predisposing factors to the development of HAPE. There is also some evidence that children, and a history of recent respiratory tract infection, are also predisposing factors for HAPE.

The early symptoms of HAPE are exertional dyspnea, cough and reduced exercise performance. As the disease progresses, breathlessness becomes more severe, cough worsens and may become productive of pink frothy sputum. Eventually orthopnea, and dyspnea at rest occurs. Clinical examination shows cyanosis, tachypnea, tachycardia, and elevated body temperature (usually not >38.5°C). If concomitant cerebral edema occurs there is altered level of consciousness, and ataxia.

The immediate treatment of HAPE is to descend by at least 1,000 m of altitude, and provide supplemental oxygen (2–4 l min^{-1}). Additional medical treatment is to administer 20 mg nifedipine (slow release formulation) every six hours. If possible treatment in a portable hyperbaric chamber is indicated.

A number of other therapeutic agents have also been suggested as prevention and treatment options. These include acetazolamide, dexamethasone, spironolactone, progesterone, and diuretics.

Acetazolamide has been shown to reduce the severity and prevents AMS. The usual method of prophylactic administration is to commence with a daily dose of 500 mg in the twenty-four hours before ascent, and once altitude is reached, its use can be discontinued. It has also been used in the treatment of AMS in doses of 1.0–1.5 g daily.

Dexamethasone has been used in the management of AMS. The precise mechanism of its therapeutic benefit is not clear, but the main mechanisms for its therapeutic benefit are probably to reduce capillary wall permeability, reduce cerebral edema, and cause diuresis. Doses of 4 mg every six hours are required.

Spironolactone reduces the incidence of AMS symptoms probably as a result of competitive inhibition of aldosterone receptor sites, reducing sodium reabsorption in the distal tubules of the kidney and leading to a natruiresis. The disadvantage of spironolactone is that it is effective only in the presence of aldosterone, which is already reduced in AMS (Table 17).

The key to management of HAPE is prevention. The following preventative measures are indicated (Bärtsch 1999).

- Do not ascend if early symptoms of AMS are present.
- Descend if symptoms of AMS do not reduce after 24–48 hours.
- Avoid high-intensity physical exercise at altitude.
- Use a slow ascent to altitudes above 2,500 m (recommended as <350 m day^{-1} in susceptible individuals).
- Nifedipine (slow release form) can be used in susceptible individuals where a slow ascent is not possible (20 mg every eight hours).

High-altitude cerebral edema (HACE)

High altitude cerebral edema is the least common but the most dangerous form of altitude sickness. It is characterized by severe headache, hallucinations, ataxia, weakness, impaired mental function, stupor, and eventual death. The only effective treatment is immediate descent when the symptoms appear. Oxygen and hyperbaric treatment (in a pressure bag) can be used. Hyperosmolar infusions and corticosteroids have been suggested as treatment but their efficacy has not been well established.

See also: environmental stress – high altitude

References

Bärtsch, P. (1999) 'High Altitude Pulmonary Edema.' *Med Sci Sports Exerc* 31:S23–S27.

Coote, J. H. (1995) 'Medicine and Mechanisms in Altitude Sickness. Recommendations', *Sports Med* 20: 148–59.

MARTIN SCHWELLNUS

EXERCISE FOR HEALTH – GLOBAL SCENE OF HEALTH PROMOTION

What does exercise mean to you? What does exercise mean to every population around the world? The most interesting question is why do we need it to promote better health and a higher quality of life? Statistical data have shown that the life expectancy of humans is increasing gradually; what contributes to this global trend of evolution? Some major contributing factors involve additional health awareness in the human population; scientific innovations in the field of health advancing at a faster rate; and the availability of better health care facilities. The combined effects from the above factors would give rise to the gradual increase in life expectancy in the human population. In spite of this, other studies have also shown that a significant amount of people in the world do not acquire an adequate amount of physical activity and exercise. Population studies have confirmed a rise in physical inactivity with advancing age. With respect to young individuals and adults, the problem of physical inactivity is not a disastrous concern, but a significant amount of people do not carry out regular exercise to deal with the problem of a sedentary lifestyle. This sedentary lifestyle has become a major problem in most developed countries. Technological innovations, advanced modes of transportation, psychological pressure caused by excessive workloads, etc – all of these are major contributors towards the global concern of physical inactivity. There is a clear picture showing that exercise enhances the quality of life, prevents the development of age-related chronic diseases, maximizes the function of the body, and minimizes the adverse impact of ageing. Exercise is for everyone;

there is no difference between male and female, young and old; an individual from China or an individual from the UK; everyone is able to explore the benefits from exercise once adhered to. Many health organizations world-wide have been promoting the notion of 'sport for all', as has the International Olympic Committee (IOC), publicizing the meaning and the importance of exercise.

To understand the role of physical activity in a successful ageing process, the best way to illustrate the point is to look at the consequences of inactivity. What if we do not have a habit of regular exercise? What are the potential problems for inactive individuals? How can we maintain a healthy lifestyle? These questions will be addressed in depth. Every perspective of exercise for health will be discussed thoroughly, in order to provide some general but valuable information.

Studies have shown the extent of physical inactivity concern amongst the elderly. Based on the South Australian Physical Activity Survey in 1998, data showed that approximately 50 per cent of the population group aged between 60 and 64 years do not maintain a sufficient amount of physical activity (Hamdolf 2001). When normal chronological ageing is coupled with physical inactivity, the rate of onset of chronic diseases will be faster, while function of the body will also decelerate at a higher rate. This illustrates clearly that physical activity indeed decelerates the loss of bodily functions, whilst at the same time delaying the onset of chronic diseases. Generally, as people age they become more sedentary, they are not inclined to exercise as the majority are not sure what type of exercise program suits them best. Physical inactivity has been shown to be associated with increased cardiovascular disease, hypertension, type II diabetes mellitus, osteoporosis, osteoarthritis, colon cancer and altered cognition. Studies have shown that physical activity helps prevent the onset of disease while delaying the inevitable process of ageing.

Cardiovascular disease is a major cause of mortality in the United States. It often results from a lack of physical activity, obesity, smoking and drinking, etc. Regular aerobic exercises such as swimming, walking, and jogging were all shown to be beneficial treatments for cardiovascular disease. Aerobic exercise helps lower blood pressure, decrease levels of serum triglycerides, total cholesterol, lowering the low-density lipoprotein while raising the high-density lipoprotein – which are believed to be healthy lipids. Exercise also helps to burn off fat and thus decrease obesity (Straughan 2001).

With respect to osteoporosis, the process of bone loss accelerates from the third decade of life. Osteoporosis is a disease characterized by an excessively low bone mineral density, and thus causes an increased risk of fractures. There is a linear relationship between bone mineral density (BMD) and risk of developing osteoporosis. Normally, individuals will obtain their peak bone mass during their thirties; subsequently the rate of bone loss increases. This phenomenon is caused by hyperactive osteoclastic cells, while osteoblastic cells are not as active by comparison. The benefits of exercise in the prevention of osteoporosis are the strengthening of bone and muscles, and a delaying of the process of bone resorption, minimizing the risk of bone fractures. In addition, nutrition supplements may also help strengthen bones and increase the absorption of specific minerals. Suggested supplements are calcium and vitamin D. Calcium acts to strengthen bone while preventing fracture, whereas vitamin D helps to promote calcium absorption.

Studies have suggested the therapeutic effects of exercise, resistance training, and flexibility training on people with non-insulin dependent diabetes mellitus (type II diabetes). Type II diabetes is characterized by a deficiency in insulin. The ultimate treatment of this disease is to maintain a normal level of blood glucose and lipid. Therefore, in order to achieve and maintain the right level of serum glucose and lipid, the best way is to practice a physically active lifestyle. Further, maintaining a balanced, healthy diet that is low in sugar is crucial for treatment of the disease.

Unfortunately, the treatment of cancer is not so clearly defined, and an actual cure has yet to be found. When we bring cancer and sports medicine together, many will question if there is a direct relationship between the two, but recent research has shown that exercise may help during the cancer recovery processes, producing benefits such as gains in strength and improvements in endurance, as well as in the quality of life. Medical officers have been using exercise programs to assist cancer patients during their recovery (Durak 2001). Exercise does not solely provide physical health benefits for patients; it also provides psychological support. Cancer patients may be pessimistic; they often feel helpless, and tend to lose hope for the future. This is also an important issue for consideration, since such patients may need psychological treatment. Exercise helps them maintain a healthy and better quality life.

The basic recommended amount of physical activity an individual should engage in is approximately thirty minutes a day. Physical activity includes activities that require movement of different parts of the body, where intensity is not necessarily high. Exercise promotes good health, while preventing the development of various chronic diseases. Exercise is for people in any age group, and should be maintained in order to develop a more healthy lifestyle.

References

Durak, E. (2001) 'The Use of Exercise in the Cancer Recovery Process', *ACSM's Health and Fitness Journal* 5, 1: 6–10.

Hamdolf, P. (2001) 'Physical Inactivity: Our Primary Challenge', *Sport Health* 19, 3: 21.

Straughan, W. (2001) 'Active Ageing: Promoting and Maintaining Good Health', *Sport Health* 19, 3: 36–8.

VICTOR W.T. HO

EXERCISE IN CHILDREN – MEDICAL CONSIDERATIONS

In this entry, three areas related to the medical considerations in exercising children will be discussed. Initially, the importance and the basic outline of the pre-participation medical screening process will be discussed. This will be followed by a brief outline of the importance of regular physical activity for health benefits in children. Finally, the unique medical considerations to reduce the risk of sports injuries in children will be mentioned.

Pre-participation medical screening of children for sport

The purpose of a pre-participation medical screening is fourfold. First, it is to determine the general health of the child; second, it is to identify whether any disqualifying conditions exist that would affect sports participation; third, it is conducted to determine the maturation of the child so that guidance on appropriate sports participation can be given, and fourth it is to establish a doctor–patient relationship with the child so that future problems can be dealt with (Bratton 1997).

In surveys it has been shown that the pre-participation screening identifies that about 10 per cent of adolescents that are screened have a medical condition that influences advice on sports participation, with about 0.5–1 per cent of athletes being disqualified from sports participation due to a medical condition. The best timing to conduct pre-participation screening is at least 4–6 weeks prior to initiation of sports, so that time is allowed to introduce a suitable intervention. The frequency of this screening is variable, but in the normal healthy child it should be conducted every 1–3 years.

The pre-participation medical screening can be conducted as an individual consultation with a doctor (costly but very comprehensive), a station-based examination (cost-effective, good for large groups, but impersonal), or the 'locker room' type assessment (not private, superficial and not recommended).

The elements of a pre-participation medical screening are a medical history (most important as 60–80 per cent of medical conditions can be identified through the history), and an abbreviated physical examination (mostly cardio-pulmonary and musculoskeletal systems). In addition, special investigations may be requested. In general, the results of the pre-participation medical examination recommend any of the following to the child: sports participation with no restrictions; sports participation with some restrictions (specific guidelines must be given); or no participation in sports.

Pre-participation medical history

This is the most important part of the pre-participation medical screening. As most causes of sudden death in young (<30 years) athletes are the result of underlying cardiovascular disease, the important questions focus on this system. The following specific questions are important to exclude underlying cardiovascular disease.

- Have you ever been dizzy during or after exercise?
- Have you ever had chest pain during or after exercise?
- Do you tire more quickly than your friends during exercise?
- Have you ever had high blood pressure?
- Have you ever been told that you have a heart murmur?

- Have you ever had racing of your heart or skipped heartbeats?

Other information that is important in the medical history are:

- family history of myocardial infarction before the age of fifty years;
- the use of regular medication, social, and other drugs;
- a history of allergies (medication, bee stings, foods);
- past significant medical history (chronic diseases, hospitalizations, major trauma);
- past history of concussions or loss of consciousness;
- past history of heat stroke;
- previous disqualification from sports participation;
- past vaccinations;
- use of any medical appliances (glasses, contact lenses, hearing aids, braces);
- menstrual disturbances (female athletes).

Based on the outcome of the medical history, the physical examination and special investigations can be directed.

Pre-participation physical examination

The physical examination can take various formats, but the most cost effective is a stationed approach. Elements of the examination should include a general assessment of vital signs (temperature, pulse, blood pressure), a cardiorespiratory assessment, and an orthopedic screening assessment (such as the 90-second orthopedic examination by the American Academy of Pediatrics).

Pre-participation special investigations

Routine laboratory investigations are not required for most athletes. Urinalysis, visual acuity and hearing tests can be considered. Other investigations (electrocardiography, lung function testing, radiography, blood analyses) can be requested if indicated.

Once pre-participation medical screening is completed, an athlete is advised on the sports participation. Sports are categorized according to two criteria. First, a sport is classified as a contact/collision sport, a limited contact/impact sport, or a non-contact sport, and second, is classified as strenuous, moderately strenuous, or non-strenuous based on the level of intensity.

A discussion on the specific guidelines for sports participation for different medical conditions is beyond the scope of this entry but these are available (26th Bethesda Conference 1994; American Academy of Pediatrics 2001).

Childhood physical activity in the primary and secondary prevention of chronic disease

One of the greatest concerns in recent years has been the decrease in physical activity of children in developed countries. This is associated with an increase in the prevalence of childhood obesity and other chronic diseases of lifestyle that may only manifest later in life. In cross-sectional studies, it has been shown that higher levels of physical activity in children is associated with lower levels of body fat, increased bone mineral density, and lower levels of tobacco and alcohol use in children. Regular exercise training forms an important part of the intervention strategy for children suffering from a number of chronic conditions. Sothern et al. 1999 list the following chronic medical conditions for which exercise training in childhood is beneficial:

- obesity;
- type II diabetes mellitus;
- hypertension;
- low bone density and osteoporosis;
- HIV disease;
- cystic fibrosis;
- depression.

Physical activity should therefore be encouraged in children, and policy guidelines for physical activity and fitness in school-going children have been published (American Academy of Pediatrics 2000).

In general, the guidelines for physical activity participation in children to derive the health benefits of exercise are as follows.

- Recreational physical activity at school must be encouraged.
- Participation in school sports must be encouraged.
- Exercise frequency should be at least three times per week but preferably on most days of the week.
- Exercise duration should be at least thirty minutes of activity but preferably 30–60 min.
- Exercise intensity for health benefits must be of moderate intensity (based on 60–80 per cent of maximal heart rate calculated as 200-age in years).
- Sedentary behavior patterns must be discouraged and limited (television time, computer games).
- Excessive exercise training is discouraged as this can be associated with medical complications such as injuries, hormonal disturbances, and delayed menarche (female athletes).
- Children participating in intense sports activity require careful monitoring (nutritional assessments, body weight, sexual maturity, injuries, emotional stress).

Sports injuries in children

In the pre-pubertal and early pubertal years there is an exaggerated growth spurt. At this time, the child is more susceptible to musculoskeletal injury, in particular the growth plates. Specific injuries have been described in the growth areas, including the kneecap (Sinding-Larsson-Johanssen syndrome), proximal tibia (Osgood-Schlatters

syndrome), and the heel (Sever's disease). These injuries can be avoided by:

- careful monitoring of the growth spurt (regular measurements of the height or shoe size);
- avoiding excessive repetitive loading of the skeleton during phases of rapid growth;
- maintaining musculoskeletal flexibility;
- carefully structured exercise programme that includes some resistance training.

See also: exercise and cancer

References

26th Bethesda Conference (1994) 'Recommendations for Determining Eligibility for Competition in Athletes with Cardiovascular Abnormalities', 6–7 January, *Med Sci Sports Exerc* 26: S223 – S283.

American Academy of Pediatrics (2000) 'Physical Fitness and Activity in Schools (RE9907)', *Pediatrics* 105: 1156–7.

—— (2001) 'Medical Conditions Affecting Sports Participation (RE0046)', *Pediatrics* 107: 1205–9.

Bratton, R.L. (1997) 'Preparticipation Screening of Children for Sports. Current Recommendations', *Sports Med* 24: 300–7.

Sothern, M.S., Loftin, M., Suskind, R.M., Udall, J.N. and Blecker, U. (1999) 'The Health Benefits of Physical Activity in Children and Adolescents: Implications for Chronic Disease Prevention', *Eur J Pediat* 158: 271–4.

MARTIN SCHWELLNUS

EXERCISE IN COLD – MEDICAL ASPECTS

The human body functions in a very narrow core temperature range (of 3 to 4°C). The core temperature is very well regulated in the brain by the hypothalamus, which responds to the temperature of the blood as well as nervous system input from the periphery. When the body is exposed to a fall in ambient temperature, heat is lost by the following four mechanisms.

1. *Radiation:* heat loss by radiation, which is dependent only on the difference in the temperature of the body and that of the environment, and not on factors such as air movement, and wetness.
2. *Conduction:* heat loss by direct contact between the body and a colder object and is dependent on the conductivity of the object in contact with the body (water has a thermal conductivity 10–25 times greater than air, which explains why heat is lost more rapidly if the skin is in contact with water compared with air).
3. *Convection:* heat loss by the constant movement of the heated surface layer of air or water that is in contact with the body. Convection accounts for the rapid cooling that is associated with wind (wind-chill factor) or cold water (immersion).
4. *Evaporation:* heat loss by energy used in the conversion of liquid to gas, and this is dependent on the humidity of the ambient air.

Physiological responses to cold

Once signals to the brain indicate a reduction in ambient temperature, a number of involuntary and voluntary responses are implemented to increase heat production, and to reduce heat loss, so that core body temperature can be maintained.

Involuntary responses in response to exposure to cold include shivering, non-shivering thermogenesis, and vasoconstriction of the skin blood vessels. Cooling of the skin is an important signal to start shivering, which increases heat production by involuntary muscle contraction. Non-shivering thermogenesis occurs as a result of increased noradrenalin secretion, which generates heat through the metabolism of brown fat. Vasoconstriction increases skin temperature, but is limited in areas such as the scalp and face – hence the importance of covering these areas when exposed to cold.

The human's ability to survive in cold environments largely depends on the voluntary responses to exposure to cold. The most important voluntary response is to select appropriate covering in the form of insulating clothing. Important aspects of clothing are the ability to keep the skin surface dry (wetsuits of divers), provide insulation (low thermal conductivity), and color (black clothing absorbs heat, and white clothing radiates heat). Physical exercise is another voluntary response to exposure to cold. Exercise can increase heat production, but can also increase heat loss by vasodilatation, and facilitating convective heat loss (movement through air or water).

Hypothermia

Definition

Hypothermia is defined as a core body temperature below 35°C. Mild to moderate hypothermia is defined as a core temperature of 32–35°C, whereas severe hypothermia is defined as a core temperature of less than 32°C.

Causes of hypothermia

The main cause of hypothermia is exposure to a cold environment where heat loss exceeds heat production. Excessively cold environments, particularly if associated with a significant convective heat loss (high wind-chill factor or cold water immersion) can rapidly reduce core body temperature. Factors that can aggravate this reduction in core temperature are: underlying disease (hypothyroidism, diabetes mellitus, hypopituitarism, stroke), drugs (alcohol, sedatives), blood loss and shock, and altered consciousness (semi-coma, coma).

Clinical features of hypothermia

The symptoms of hypothermia are related to the core temperature. In Table 18, the

Table 18. Symptoms and signs of hypothermia related to core temperature

Core temperature (°C)	Symptom/sign
36	Shivering
35	Confusion
34.5	Disorientation
33	Amnesia
31	Respiratory depression
30.5	Loss of consciousness
30	Cardiac arrhythmias
28	Bradycardia
27	Ventricular fibrillation
25	Death

symptoms and clinical signs of hypothermia and the average core temperature at which they occur are listed.

The rate at which a patient moves from one clinical symptom or sign to the next is dependent on many factors, including the weather, wind, wet skin, clothing, fluid and food intake, drugs, and the presence of any underling disease or injury.

Severe hypothermia is associated with a very high mortality rate (>75 per cent) and urgent treatment to prevent progression form mild to severe hypothermia is important and can be life-saving.

Management of hypothermia

The most important immediate treatment of hypothermia is to prevent further heat loss, and to commence with rewarming.

Immediate steps to prevent further heat loss can include:

- removing the patient from cold air or water (if immersed)
- removing wet clothes and replacing them with a blanket or dry clothing
- insulating the patient from contact with other cold surfaces (e.g. a cold floor)

Immediate steps to commence with rewarming can include:

- increasing the ambient temperature through heating (fires, heaters, heating blankets)
- if the patient is conscious and can consume fluid and food safely, providing warm energy drinks and food

All patients should be monitored regularly (core temperature, state of consciousness, vital signs). Any patient with severe hypothermia (core temperature < 32°C) should be evacuated and admitted to hospital for further management and observation.

In hospital, monitoring can include the following: core temperature, vital signs, renal function (urine output, blood electrolytes, and creatinine), cardiac function (electrocardiogram, central venous pressure, cardiac output), metabolic state (acid base status, blood glucose). Besides external warming, other rewarming techniques may be used. These can include inhalation of warm air, cavity lavage with heated fluid (peritoneum, pleura, mediastinum, stomach), administering warm intravenous fluids, dialysis with heated fluid, and extracorporeal circulation.

Special problem: immersion hypothermia

Immersion in cold water can be associated with rapid reductions in core temperature over a very short time period, making this one of the moist serious forms of exposure to a cold environment. If a person dressed only in thin clothing is immersed in water at 5°C, the core temperature can drop to 30°C in 60–90 min. The variables that will increase heat loss in water include:

- cold water temperature
- person with decreased per cent body fat
- wearing a thin layer of clothing
- rough or fast flowing water
- swimming or moving in the water
- surface area of the body (adopting a fetal position will prevent heat loss)

Frostbite

Frostbite can occur in the absence of hypothermia, and is defined as tissue injury as a result of exposure to cold. It usually occurs if the tissue temperature is reduced to $-2°C$ or less, and is caused by direct damage due to tissue freezing, decreased blood flow due to ischaemia, and the release of toxic substances during rewarming.

'Frostnip' occurs on the nose, cheeks, or ears and appears as white patches, which disappear on rewarming. There may be minor swelling with blisters, but there is no residual injury. Frostbite can be superficial (only affecting the skin), or deep (affecting underlying tissue), which can result in limb loss.

The symptoms and signs of frostbite are loss of sensation and white appearance of the skin, followed by swelling of the area. If exposure to cold progresses, the skin darkens, and becomes black and mummified. Eventually a clear line of demarcation develops between healthy and necrotic (dead) tissue.

The mainstay of treatment is rapid rewarming of the area. In controlled situations this can be achieved by immersing the frozen part in water at $43°C$. Analgesia must be given while re-warming takes place. Care must be taken not to re-warm the area and then allow the tissue to freeze again.

Following re-warming the following treatment can be administered:

- drying the area
- exposing the area to a clean, light, airy, and dry environment
- removing the roof of blisters under sterile conditions

Preventative measures for frostbite are:

- wearing dry, loose, and well insulated footwear and clothing
- maintaining good nutrition and hydration

- avoiding contact with metal or moisture
- changing wet clothing for dry clothing as soon as possible

See also: exercise at altitude – medical aspects

Reference

Noakes, T.D. (2000) 'Exercise and the Cold', *Ergonomics* 43: 1461–79.

MARTIN SCHWELLNUS

EXERCISE IN HEAT – HEATSTROKE

Heatstroke is a life threatening medical condition that is characterized by an elevated body temperature above $40°C$, which is accompanied by hot dry skin, and central nervous system abnormalities such as delirium, convulsions, and coma. Heatstroke has classically been defined as either non-exertional (associated with exposure to a high environmental temperature and humidity but with non-exercise component) or exertional heatstroke (associated with exercise performed in hot, humid environmental conditions). This section will only focus on the clinical presentation, treatment, and prevention of exertional heatstroke.

Clinical presentation of heatstroke

The two principle clinical manifestations of heatstroke are a raised core body temperature above $40°C$, and evidence of central nervous system dysfunction. In exertional heatstroke, there is a history of strenuous physical activity that is performed in hot humid conditions. The central nervous system manifestations of heatstroke can vary from inappropriate behavior or impaired judgment to delirium, convulsions, semi-coma, or coma.

Other systemic manifestations are tachycardia, hyperventilation, and hypotension. Heatstroke must be suspected in any collapsed athlete, and the rectal temperature should be measured in all collapsed athletes. A delay in the diagnosis can result in the major complications of heatstroke, which are related to multi-organ failure. This can manifest as encepahlopathy, rhabdomyolysis, acute renal failure, acute respiratory distress syndrome, myocardial injury, hepatocellular injury, intestinal ischaemia or infarction, pancreatic injury, or haemorrhagic complications such as disseminated intravascular coagulopathy with thrombocytopaenia.

Management of heatstroke

The two main objectives of treatment are to cool the patient, and to support the organ-system function. These objectives have to be achieved in the immediate out-of-hospital setting and in the intensive care facility of the hospital.

Immediate out-of-hospital treatment will consist of the following measures:

Rapid cooling

Therapeutic cooling is aimed at accelerating the heat transfer from the skin surface to the environment, without compromising the flow of blood to the skin. This is accomplished by conductive cooling (increasing the temperature gradient from the skin to the environment), evaporative cooling (increasing the water-vapor pressure between the skin and the environment) and finally by convective cooling (moving the air layer adjacent to the skin). Practical methods of cooling will include the following.

- Remove clothing.
- Place the patient in an area where these is a lower environmental temperature, and where air movement can be facilitated.
- Apply cold packs to the following areas: neck, axillae, and groin (conductive cooling).

- Apply continuous fanning to facilitate convective cooling.
- Spray the skin with water (to facilitate evaporative cooling).

Other supportive measures

The following supportive measures must be considered.

- Arrange for immediate transfer to a hospital with intensive care facilities.
- Ensure that the unconscious patient is in the coma position (lie on side) with the airway clear to minimize the risk of aspiration.
- Administer oxygen at $4 \, l \, min^{-1}$.
- Give isotonic saline.

Supportive in-hospital treatment will consist of the following.

- Monitor the rectal and skin temperatures.
- Continue cooling until the core (rectal) temperature is below 39.4°C, and the skin temperature between 30 and 33°C.
- Internal cooling methods such as gastric lavage and peritoneal lavage have been used.
- Control seizures (benzodiazepines may be used).
- Protect and control the airway (elective intubation may be considered).
- Administer intravenous fluids based on central venous pressure measurements (consider monitoring).
- Prevent myoglobin-induced renal injury by promoting renal blood flow, diuresis, and alkalization of the urine.
- Monitor serum electrolytes (potassium and calcium) and treat hyperkalaemia.

Prevention of heatstroke

The principles of preventing exertional heatstroke are as follows.

- Avoid strenuous exercise in very hot, humid conditions.
- Be aware that increased exercise intensity is a major determinant of heat production.
- Wear light, cool clothing that allows evaporative heat loss.
- Schedule exercise activities for cooler periods of the day.
- Be aware of the increased risk in an un-acclimatized athlete.
- Ensure adequate hydration, but be aware that drinking excessive fluids will not prevent heatstroke and may itself cause other medical conditions (hyponatraemia).

See also: collapsed endurance athlete; exercise in the heat

Reference

Bouchama, A. and Knochel, J.P. (2002) 'Heat Stroke', *NEJM* 346: 1978–88.

MARTIN SCHWELLNUS

EXERCISE IN THE AGED

Until recently, it has been suggested that approaching old age is a time to slow down and take a well earned rest. However, there is now substantial evidence that the participation in regular physical activity has many beneficial effects and promotes a healthier and more successful ageing process. In this section, the current understanding of the role of regular physical activity in ageing will be reviewed. In particular, the following aspects will be reviewed:

(1) Definitions of the 'elderly'; (2) Physiological benefits of regular physical activity during the ageing process; (3) Medical benefits of regular physical activity during the ageing process; and (4) Guidelines to commence physical activity in the elderly.

Definitions of the elderly

The definition of what constitutes the 'elderly' remains controversial. However, most gerontologists recognize the following categories of the elderly (see Table 19).

Physiological benefits of regular physical activity in the elderly

It has been well documented that the participation in regular physical activity has both immediate (within days) and long-term (weeks to months) physiological benefits for the older individual. The immediate and long-term benefits are summarized in Table 20.

Impaired glucose tolerance can affect as many as 40 per cent of the general population over the age of sixty-five years. Similarly, low levels of mental stimulation and arousal, as well as symptoms such as decreased appetite and constipation, are common in the elderly. A single bout of exercise or regular exercise after only a few sessions has benefits in improving these symptoms.

Ageing is associated with decreased cardiovascular endurance, reduced muscle strength and poor flexibility that results in an inability to perform the activities of daily living. This results in a poor quality of life

Table 19. Categories of the elderly

Parameter	Young-old	Middle-old	Old-old
Typical age (years)	65–75	75–85	>85
General health	Good	Increasing prevalence of chronic diseases	>90% affected by one or more chronic disease
Level of function	Moderate	Some impairment	Impaired
Physical disability	Little	Present to some degree	Present

Table 20. Physiological benefits of regular physical activity in the elderly

Benefit	Effect of physical exercise
Immediate	Improved regulation of blood glucose concentration
	Improved mental performance and cerebral arousal
	Improved appetite
	Regular bowel movements
Long-term	Increased cardiovascular endurance
	Increased muscle strength
	Increased flexibility
	Improved balance and coordination
	Increased bone strength
	Decreased obesity
	Improved lipid profile

and an increasing dependence. A structured exercise program, even if introduced late in life, can improve the functional physical ability of the individual. Improvements in cardiovascular endurance (10–20 per cent), muscle strength gains (30–80 per cent), and flexibility (10–15 per cent) have been reported following regular exercise training even at ages above eighty years.

The general risk of falling in the elderly is increased. Although many factors play a role, the improved balance and coordination that can occur after exercise training has been shown to reduce the risk of falling. Coupled with an increased bone strength that has been observed with training, the risk of fractures in the elderly is reduced.

Nutritional intervention and exercise training can treat obesity, which is associated with a number of health risks. These interventions also have beneficial effects on the lipid profile by decreasing serum triglyceride concentration and increasing high-density lipoprotein (HDL) concentrations in the blood.

Medical benefits of regular physical activity in the elderly

The physiological benefits that have been observed following regular exercise training in the elderly can result in direct medical benefits.

Increased lifespan and quality of life

Exercise programs, particularly if commenced at a younger age, can increase life expectancy by 1–2 years. This effect is less pronounced when exercise training commences later in life. However, one of the significant benefits of regular training in the elderly (young-old, middle-old and old-old) is that the quality of life improves (a benefit of 1.25–2.9 quality-adjusted life years), because of increased functional capacity resulting in the ability to live independently for longer.

Improved immune function

Moderate-intensity exercise training can result in improved immune function in the elderly. In particular, there are positive effects of exercise training on the T-helper cells, and natural killer cell (NK cell) activity.

Decreased risk of cardiovascular disease

A sedentary lifestyle is associated with a 2–3-fold increased risk of developing cardiovascular disease compared with active individuals. Also, in patients with established cardiovascular disease, the risk of death from heart disease can be reduced by 25 per cent if an active lifestyle is adopted as part of a **cardiac rehabilitation** program.

Regular exercise is beneficial in the prevention and treatment of related cardiac and other vascular diseases such as chronic cardiac failure, **hypertension**, **cerebrovascular disease**, and peripheral vascular disease.

Decreased risk of metabolic disorders

Participation in regular physical activity has also been linked strongly to a reduced risk of developing other metabolic disorders. In particular regular exercise reduces the risk of developing adult-onset **diabetes mellitus**, **hyperlipidaemia** (together with healthy eating habits) and **osteoporosis**.

Other medical benefits of regular exercise in the elderly

Regular exercise training has also been associated with a decreased risk of developing colon cancer, and possibly reproductive cancers in the female population, prostate cancer in males, and recently, pulmonary tumors. Further, graded physical activity is helpful in preparing elderly patients for surgery, and early exercise rehabilitation following surgery reduces the risk of complications such as stroke and deep vein thromboses. Finally, there are substantial benefits in preventing and treating musculoskeletal disorders in the elderly such as low back pain, **osteoarthritis**, and **rheumatoid arthritis** through well structured exercise programs.

Increased psychological and psycho-social well-being

It is now well established that elderly individuals participating in physical activity have improved psychological well-being compared with sedentary individuals. In one study, positive mood changes were reported in the active elderly population (60–69 years, and the over-seventies male and female groups)

Guidelines to commence physical activity in the elderly

A comprehensive medical assessment is vital before any person over the age of fifty starts with an exercise program. The reason for this is the higher prevalence of underlying chronic disease in the elderly. A medical assessment should consist of at least a full medical history, comprehensive medical examination (including cardiovascular, respiratory, neurological, and musculoskeletal examination). The clinical assessment should be followed by assessment of cardiovascular risk factors, and a functional capacity test (including a stress electrocardiogram). The exercise prescription for each patient must be individualized, and be under the care of a qualified professional such as a biokineticist. Recently, guidelines for exercise prescription for the elderly have been published.

Summary

Globally the ageing population is increasing. Participation in regular physical activity can increase lifespan and more importantly, the quality of life in the elderly, because of the physiological and medical benefits that exercise training has on that population. Prior to starting an exercise program, a medical assessment is required. Exercise prescription for the elderly must be individualized, and under the care of a health professional.

See also: cardiac rehabilitation; cardiovascular issues for seniors; diabetes mellitus; exercise and cancer

Reference

Mazzeo, R.S. and Tanaka, H. (2001) 'Exercise Prescription for the Elderly: Current Recommendations', *Sports Med* 31: 809–18.

Further reading

Chan, K.M., Chodzko-Zajko, W., Frontera, W. and Parker, A. (2002) *Active Ageing*, 1st edn, Hong Kong: Lippincott Williams and Williams.

MARTIN SCHWELLNUS

EXERCISE IN THE HEAT

The history of the marathon race, more than any other sport, is etched with the tragedy of deaths from exercise- and environmentally

EXERCISE IN THE HEAT

induced heatstroke. The hero of the 1908 Olympics in London, the diminutive Italian Dorando Pietri, lay in a semi-coma desperately close to death for the two days after his collapse in the final metres of the marathon. In the 1912 Olympic Games in Stockholm, the Portuguese runner Francisco Lazaro collapsed from exercise- and environmentally induced heatstroke after running nineteen miles, and died the next day. Jim Peters, the first marathon runner to break the 2 hr 20 min barrier, entered the Vancouver Stadium fifteen minutes ahead of his nearest rival in the 1954 Empire Games marathon, only to collapse before reaching the finishing line. The race was run in early afternoon heat during an unseasonable heatwave. It appears that Peters was not treated according to the modern principles of rapid cooling in an ice-cold bath. Instead, he reportedly languished for some hours before making a full recovery. He never again raced a marathon because he feared that, unable to restrain himself, he would suffer the same fate.

But a better understanding of human physiology would have allowed Peters safely to run another marathon race, even in the heat. A slower running pace, appropriate to the environmental conditions, some fluid ingestion during the race, and rapid immersion in ice-cold water if he had again overheated would have ensured his safe participation. More importantly, holding the marathon in the cooler European environmental conditions to which he was accustomed would have ensured that no cases of exercise- and environmentally induced heatstroke could have occurred.

Fortunately, since these disasters, three major changes have reduced the risk that athletes will develop exercise- and environmentally induced heatstroke during exercise. The more important of these changes are the following:

- Sporting events, particularly running races longer than 3 km, are no longer routinely held in the heat of the day, as was the case in the 1954 Empire Games marathon. Rather, those events in which high rates of energy expenditure and hence heat production are required over prolonged periods, are now usually scheduled in the cooler conditions of the early morning or late evening.
- Athletes have become aware of the need to pre-acclimatize by training in the heat if they are to compete in the heat.
- Athletes are now more aware than was Jim Peters that it is not safe to run at a maximum effort when the environmental conditions are unfavourable.

The facilities for providing the athletes with fluid replacement during exercise have greatly improved. Presently, refreshment stations are provided every 2–3 km and often more frequently at the most popular marathon races. There is, however, no independent evidence that such fluid replacement has contributed to the prevention of exercise- and environmentally induced heatstroke, although when fluids are available in excess and many athletes take more than 5 h to run such marathon races, the probability is increased that water intoxication – hyponatraemia – will develop.

Indeed, one of the remarkable paradoxes is that the unusual is observed and described and then that event is assumed to be the commonplace. Thus, Jim Peters' collapse was originally described because it was so unusual; yet, its very description leads to the assumption that it is the usual. The remarkable observation is how few reports there are of exercise- and environmentally induced heatstroke in all sports, including marathon running, during the past century, despite the hazardous environmental conditions in which many sporting events have been held in the past. There are probably two reasons for this.

485

First, the brain continually receives information about the body's skin, brain, and core body temperatures. As the temperature approaches 39–40°C, the brain reduces its recruitment of the exercising muscles and subconsciously informs the athlete that he or she is 'tired'. As a result, the athlete either slows down or stops completely. This reduces the rate at which the body produces heat and, provided the athlete seeks a cool, shady, and, preferably, windy place, soon reduces the body temperature, thereby preventing exercise- and environmentally induced heatstroke.

Second, the most important cause of heatstroke, as so clearly shown in the case of Jim Peters, is the environmental conditions in which the race is held. Whereas Peters ran faster in cooler conditions in Europe, he collapsed only when forced to race in those severe environmental conditions for which he was not prepared. Thus the most effective technique to ensure that athletes can compete safely in the heat is to ensure that they do not have to compete in the heat in the first place.

See also: excessive heat stress effects; heat tolerance – affecting factors; hyponatremia; thermal regulation in hot environments

References

Noakes, T.D. (2002) *Lore of Running, Third Edition*, ch. 4, Champaign IL: Human Kinetics.
Noakes, T.D. and Martin, D.E. (2002) 'Advisory Statement on Guidelines for Fluid Replacement During Marathon Running', *New Studies in Athletics* 17: 15–24.

TIM NOAKES

EXERCISE IN THE POST-PARTUM PERIOD

Regular exercise training is well recognized as positive health behavior, and more women wish to resume with a regular exercise program soon after delivery. However, there are potential risks and benefits of regular exercise training during the post-partum period for both the mother and the newborn infant.

Potential risks for the mother

There is a very low risk of medical complications with exercise training in the post-partum period. Concern has, however, been raised about the potential increased risk of musculoskeletal injury in the mother recovering from the physiological changes in the musculoskeletal system during pregnancy. Further, the effects of an acute bout of exercise on breast milk production and composition has been investigated.

Musculoskeletal injury

The prevalence of musculoskeletal complaints (hip, knee, and foot pain) is higher in the post-partum period, compared with a control group. This indicates that musculoskeletal complaints are a concern in this period, and that exercises performed incorrectly may exacerbate these complaints. A careful assessment of the complaints, and a specific exercise program is advised which may even reduce the risk of these complaints.

Decreased breast milk production

An acute exercise bout may decrease breast milk production. However, in a number of studies, after an acute bout of maximal or sub-maximal exercise, there was no reduction in breast milk production. Regular exercise training similarly did not reduce, and may even increase, breast milk production.

Altered breast milk composition

An acute bout of intense exercise is associated with an increase in blood lactate concentration, which may result in an increase in breast milk lactate concentration. This may alter the taste of breast milk and negatively affect infant feeding.

Concerns that exercise training may affect breast milk composition, energy content, IgA concentrations and breast milk electrolyte concentrations have been raised. The effects of exercise training on breast milk composition has been studied and the following can be concluded:

- Moderate intensity maternal exercise (<75 per cent maximal effort) does not affect breast milk lactate concentrations.
- Moderate intensity exercise does not affect breast milk composition (pH, lipid, ammonium, urea).
- Maximal-intensity exercise does not affect breast milk electrolyte concentrations.
- A combination of dieting (35 per cent energy deficit) and exercise training did not alter breast milk composition.
- Moderate-intensity exercise does not negatively affect infant feeding.
- Although an acute exercise bout of maximal exercise intensity reduces breast milk IgA concentrations for 10–30 min after exercise, this recovers to normal concentrations by 60 min post-exercise.

Maternal exercise in the post-partum period appears to have no negative effects on breast milk composition or feeding patterns, provided the exercise bout is conducted more than one hour before feeding, and is of moderate intensity.

Potential risks to the infant

There is no good scientific evidence to suggest that maternal exercise in the post-partum period negatively affects infant feeding, provided that (1) maximal exercise is not conducted immediately before feeding; and (2) severe calorie restriction together with maternal exercise does not occur.

Potential benefits to the mother

Increased fitness

Maternal exercise training in the post-partum period results in increased endurance capacity and increased muscle strength.

Increased pelvic floor muscle strength

Following vaginal delivery, stress incontinence is increased. Specific exercise training to increase pelvic floor muscle strength reduces symptoms of stress incontinence and is recommended as part of the exercise prescription in the post-partum period.

Increased bone mineral density

Regular exercise training in the post-partum period may reduce the bone mineral loss that accompanies lactation, but this has not been confirmed.

Weight loss

Many women institute measures to reduce body weight in the post-partum period by dieting and exercise. Studies have shown that both calorie restricting diets and exercise are effective in reducing body weight, but the rate of weight loss in lactating females should not exceed 1–2 kg per month. This is to ensure that normal infant feeding is maintained.

Improved psychological well-being

Mothers participating in exercise programs in the post-partum period have improved psychological well-being, and are more likely to participate in fun activities.

Potential benefits to the infant

Although there are no direct benefits of maternal exercise in the post-partum period to the growing child, studies do show that maternal exercise is safe for the child, and improved maternal well-being is likely to have indirect beneficial effects on the growing child.

Guidelines for exercise prescription

All women in the post-partum period should undergo a normal post-partum obstetric, medical, and musculoskeletal assessment prior to starting an exercise program in the post-partum period to assess muscu-loskeletal complaints, and any complications following delivery. General guidelines for maternal exercise in the post-partum period are listed in Table 21.

The following practical guidelines for exercise prescription are recommended (Table 22).

Exercise should be conducted in a cool environment (early in the morning or late afternoon) to prevent hyperthermia. Light, comfortable clothing and shock absorbing

Table 21. General guidelines and their rationale for exercise prescription in the post-partum period

Guideline	Rationale
Moderate intensity exercise training in the lactating mother	Decreased lactic acid in breast milk which does not affect infant feeding
Maternal weight loss through exercise and diet of less than 1–2 kg per month	No negative effects on infant growth and weight gain
Exercise training 4–5 times per week	No negative effects on infant growth and weight gain
Careful assessment and diagnosis of musculoskeletal complaints post partum	Avoid incorrect exercise prescription which may exacerbate these complaints
Perform exercise training immediately after feeding to ensure that the next feed takes place at least 1 hour after exercise	Decrease the risk of reduced IgA concentrations in breast milk

Table 22. Principles of exercise prescription during the post-partum period

Type of exercise	Predominantly non-weight bearing activity is recommended in the initial post-partum period (up to 2 months) to reduce the risk of musculoskeletal injury
	Endurance activities (walking, cycling, swimming) to regain endurance capacity and for weight loss are recommended
	Resistance exercise and flexibility training is recommended only after 6 weeks post-partum and with care to reduce the risk of musculoskeletal injury
	Core stabilising exercises are highly recommended
	Pelvic floor exercises are highly recommended
	Specific rehabilitative exercises are recommended based on the musculoskeletal assessment
Intensity of exercise	Rating of perceived exertion of 12–14 (on a scale of 6–20)
	An initial training intensity of <75% maximum heart rate in the lactating mother is recommended
Duration of exercise	30–60 min of sustained exercise training at the recommended intensity
Frequency of exercise	Most days of the week
	In the lactating mother, exercise bouts should be performed immediately after feeds
Progression of exercise	Previously sedentary women should gradually increase the duration to up to 30 min per session

footwear should be worn. A supportive, firm brassiere is recommended for lactating women.

See also: exercise and pregnancy

References

Cary, G.B. and Quinn, T.J. (2001) 'Exercise and Lactation: Are They Compatible?', *Can J Appl Physiol* 26: 55–75.

Larson-Meyer, D.E. (2002) 'Effect of Postpartum Exercise on Mothers and Their Offspring: A Review of the Literature', *Obes Res* 10: 841–53.

MARTIN SCHWELLNUS

EXERCISE IN, AND ACCLIMATISATION TO, THE COLD

Optimum exercise performance in long-distance running events occurs at an environmental temperature of about 11–13°C. At higher environmental temperatures, athletes generate heat too rapidly for the achievement of an optimum heat balance. As a consequence, the regulatory centres in the brain ensure that only a pace that will permit safe heat balance will be allowed if the exercise is to be prolonged. In contrast, the reason why exercise performance is impaired at environmental temperatures below about 10°C is unknown, since logic suggests that higher rates of energy expenditure, that is, higher exercise intensities, could be sustained without the risk that heat injury would develop. Perhaps feedback from temperature sensors in the skin and the respiratory tract detect the coldness of the environment and the inspired air and regulate the speed of movement and the rate of breathing specifically to ensure that cold injury to either the skin or the respiratory tract does not occur during exercise in extremely cold conditions.

The key to safe exercise in the cold is to be properly clothed and to remain dry, since this ensures that the insulating layer of air next to the skin is equal to the skin temperature. However, if the clothing becomes saturated, the insulating layer is lost and the rate of heat loss to the environment is dramatically increased. It follows that the only adaptation most exercisers require to ensure that they can exercise safely in cold conditions, is not primarily a physiological adaptation in bodily function. Rather it is to ensure that they purchase and use the clothing that is appropriate to all possible environmental conditions that they might experience. When these include wet, very cold, and windy conditions, it is imperative that the outer layer of the clothing is totally water resistant, for example, an oilskin raincoat or jacket.

Long-distance, particularly English Channel, swimmers face the challenge that they are unable to wear appropriately insulating clothing to retard the rate of heat loss to the water that is always colder than their skin temperatures. Hence, the body temperatures of all swimmers must ultimately fall to the temperature of the water in which they are swimming. The swimmer's body build, particularly the body fat and body muscle content, then becomes the critical factor determining the rate at which he or she will cool during a long-distance swim. This is because both fat and inactive muscles receive a low blood flow and, therefore, act together as important insulators retarding heat loss from the body. However, once the muscles become active, their blood flow increases, turning this potential insulator into a very effective heat conductor.

Under these conditions, the size of the layer of subcutaneous fat overlying the active muscles becomes the only remaining insulator and the determinant of the rate of body cooling. It is probable that the same applies in out-of-water activities; individuals who are more muscular and fatter are likely to cool down more slowly when exposed to very cold environmental conditions.

Accordingly, one of the more important physiological adaptations to cold-water swimming is to increase the muscle and fat mass to improve insulation. It is also likely that other subtle adaptations occur in blood flow distribution patterns in those who train repeatedly in cold water, thereby increasing the insulating capacity and reducing the rate of heat loss from actively contracting muscles. There are also likely to be other subtle whole body changes that increase the capacity to exercise for longer before a critically low body temperature is reached.

More practically, when humans exercising on land in cold, wet, and windy conditions become too tired to continue exercising, either because they are already developing hypothermia or because of the onset of exhaustion, the further development of a fatal hypothermia will only be prevented if most of the following measures are taken. The hypothermic person is taken expeditiously to buildings or geographical features that provide shelter from the wind and rain and where there is an external source of heating as well as a change of dry, water-repellent clothes, and also a source of food. More clothing is required because the change from running or walking to the resting state has a marked effect on the rate of heat production and, thus, the amount of clothing needed to maintain body temperature, even at relatively mild temperatures. For this reason it is essential that extra clothes, including water-repellent outer clothing, both jacket and over-trousers, are always taken when exercising in cold and potentially wet and windy conditions.

See also: thermal regulation – effects of clothing; thermal regulation in cold environments

References

Noakes, T.D. (2000) 'Exercise and the Cold', *Ergonomics* 43: 1461–79.
—— (2002) *Lore of Running, Third Edition*, ch. 4, Champaign IL: Human Kinetics.

TIM NOAKES

EXERCISE PRESCRIPTION

Exercise as a preventive or treatment measure has been well known for thousands of years. Books from ancient Chinese, Greek, and Roman sources, among other cultural artefacts, talk about physical fitness as one of the most important factors for health. In fact, only the upper social classes throughout history have been victims of too little physical activity causing obesity and associated problems; the bodies of most people have, through excessive physical labour, suffered overuse rather than underuse problems. Correspondingly, the medical profession has been taught, through generations, to prescribe rest rather than increased activity for common medical conditions. The last century has totally changed this outlook, taking the conservative medical profession by surprise. With the industrial revolution, and generally improving living standards, more and more jobs have been less physically demanding; fast junk food has entered the scenario; and physical fitness has been something for professional athletes or highly motivated people to achieve in an artificial environment such as a a gym. If we look at early Olympic history, training was not even particularly suggested as a means of top performance until after the First World War. Preparations for the marathon suggested by the literature of the time involved drinking port wine or champagne and eating eggs; not to run a certain amount of miles. Early Olympic winners were no doubt persons with great talent and physical capacity deriving from their daily work or habits rather than from controlled training.

In contrast, physical activity has been prescribed for certain medical conditions by generations of medical professionals. This has included visits to places of high altitude and long walks in the fresh air for treatment of tuberculosis. Also after surgery, in the 1930s, early mobilisation and controlled highly active physiotherapy was prescribed after disc surgery. However, the magnitude of problems arising from obesity and bad health relating to low levels of physical activity is increasing exponentially by the day. The need for exercise to be prescribed for these patients has correspondingly increased. Unfortunately, the people who normally prescribe medications for diseases, the doctors, currently learn very little about these issues in medical school. Further, health spas and similar facilities, very popular and most likely very efficient fifty and more years ago, have unfortunately lost their attraction for the stressed of today.

The World Health Organization has declared that controlled physical activity is the primary 'drug of choice' in the treatment of osteoporosis, asthma, diabetes, obesity and a number of other extremely common diseases like high blood pressure and other cardiovascular problems. It is also well known how immobilisation and inactivity negatively affects performance and well-being; in this respect the impact of gravity is of great importance. It has been well documented how people returning from high altitude after climbing Mount Everest, or returning from a space mission in a non-gravity situation, or standing up from their beds after a long convalescence from injury, have lost their ability to stand or walk due to extensive loss of muscle. But the negative effect of immobilisation has finally been impressed on the medical profession, leading to revolutionary changes in treatment policies for disorders and injuries. This has further reduced the frontier from traditional long convalescence periods in hospitals to day-case surgery and early mobilisation.

How do we know what exercise to prescribe for what condition? There are two major aspects to consider. The first is to understand the reason for a particular prescription. This means that we have to understand the disorder and diagnosis for which we prescribe exercise. This is usually the job for a medical doctor. However, we also need to understand the advantages, limitations, and risks of various kinds of physical activity. This appears in the curriculum of very few, if any, medical schools. Thus if a doctor prescribed jogging to improve general fitness for a patient with knee osteoarthritis, he would not only miss the point, but indeed aggravate the knee symptoms. This would give physical activity a bad reputation, when in fact the outcome will have been caused by insufficient knowledge of the impact of running on the knee joint. Another example of misuse is swimming, which is a commonly prescribed physical activity for back problems. If this patient is not informed that it is important to lower the head position by looking downwards into the water whilst swimming, the hyperextension of the cervical spine and corresponding increased lordosis of the lower back can cause further problems. In contrast, doctors are sometimes prone to prescribe immobilisation and rest when in fact this would postpone healing and restoration of tissues during convalescence. A patient with an Achilles tendon rupture, despite treatment, is often told to rest until healing, which takes several months. This is not necessary, and in fact slows the return to normal activity and sports; cycling, for example, can be performed at any point in time for this condition. By simply putting the pedal under the heel and adjusting the saddle correspondingly, the condition of the Achilles tendon then has no relevance at all for pedalling. Physical activity is often prescribed for weight reduction. If the training is too focused on anaerobic activity the effect could be the opposite, leading to increased hunger and thus more fat deposition. By focusing on low-intensity, long-duration, non-impact activities, the metabolism can be directed towards burning off fat without triggering hunger, and thus improving the chance of long-term success. In some cases, prescription of physical activities can be detrimental if not carefully controlled.

Patients with some diseases may simply not cope with the metabolic demands or the impact. A patient suffering from anorexia will obviously be further harmed by more activity, and should be directed in the opposite direction by someone who understands the complexity of this disorder. Contrastingly, an overweight middle-aged woman with no background in sports or physical activities who is prescribed to join a work-out group in a gym is a typical example of predisposed failure. Without the requisite tensile strength in virtually all tissues involved, a few sessions of jumping and twisting will easily cause stress fractures, overuse conditions, or even fall accidents. This does not mean that we should fear the use of physical activity. In an asthmatic or diabetic patient, a carefully prescribed and monitored physical activity will no doubt decrease the need for medications and improve performance and quality of life. It has also been shown that a high physical activity level is closely linked to high bone density, good muscle control, less fall accidents, and a decreased incidence of fractures. So, there is no doubt about the value of a controlled level of physical activity for health. However, these examples clearly show that it is of vital importance that anyone who is involved in the prescription of exercise for health promotion has to understand the benefits and risks involved. In practical terms this often means that exercise prescription is a team job involving fitness instructors, PE teachers, physiotherapists, and doctors. It is also important to emphasise the importance of more and better education for doctors and other health professionals facing these problems in the future.

CHRISTER ROLF

EXERCISE-RELATED HEADACHE

Participation in physical activity can be associated with the development of headache. The etiology of exercise-related headache may be as a result of any of the normal causes of headache encountered in the non-exercising population, or it may be associated with physical activity itself. It is now recognized that there are specific causes of headaches that are related to participation in physical activity. These are known as exercise-related headaches.

Epidemiology of exercise-related headaches

There is very little information on the frequency of exercise-related headaches. In a single study, exercise-related headaches were reported in 36 per cent of respondents to a questionnaire. In this study, headaches were divided into those associated with head trauma, and those not related to head trauma. In each of these sub-categories, headaches were either of the migraine type or not (see Table 23).

From this single report it appears that most headaches in athletes are not related to previous trauma, and are not of the migraine type.

Table 23. Frequency of exercise-related headaches

History of trauma	Type	Cause	Frequency among athletes with headaches
No head trauma	Migraine	Effort related migraine	9%
	Non-migraine	Effort-exertion headache	60%
		Other	3%
Head trauma	Migraine	Trauma triggered migraine	6%
	Non-migraine	Post-traumatic headache	22%

Source: Williams and Nukuda 1994.

492

General clinical approach to the athlete with exercise-related headache

In all patients, including athletes, the first step is to obtain a good clinical history. Specific features in the clinical history to consider are: age of the athlete, onset of the headaches, past history of trauma, nature of the headache (onset, site, radiation, associated symptoms, type of pain, aggravating and relieving factors), other general medical history, and the use of any drugs or medication. In exercise-related headaches, it is important to obtain a clear history of how the headache relates to the exercise activity.

The medical history should be followed by a full clinical examination that should focus on the neurological system, and include a careful local head and neck examination. Specific features on examination to look out for would be: vital signs (blood pressure, pulse, and temperature), general mental status, speech, gait, balance, coordination, cranial nerve examination, ear, nose and throat examination, visual field and acuity, and fundus examination.

The following features on the history and examination should alert the physician to the possibility that there may be potentially serious intra-cranial pathology that will require special investigations (McCrory 2000):

- sudden onset of severe headache;
- progressively increasing pain over a few days;
- new or unaccustomed headache;
- persistent unilateral headache;
- chronic headache with localized pain
- stiff neck, fever, and other signs of meningism;
- focal neurological signs;
- nocturnal headaches or headaches that are present on waking up in the morning;
- local or systemic signs or symptoms.

Specific headache syndromes related to exercise: clinical features and management

The International Headache Society (IHS) has established criteria for the classification of exercise-related headache. Whilst there is some overlap between these syndromes, this is still a useful classification of the different syndromes that athletes may present with.

Athletes may suffer from syndromes that are common in the general population, such as migraine, tension-type headache, and cervicogenic headache. These will not be discussed in this section, and only the headache syndrome specifically related to exercise will be briefly reviewed.

Effort headache

Effort headache is the most common form of exercise-related headache and appears to be related more to endurance-type exercise. More specific clinical features of this headache are as follows:

- mild to severe headache;
- an association with endurance exercise, particularly in hot weather;
- throbbing in nature;
- short duration (4–6 h);
- not exercise-intensity dependent (occurs with sub-maximal and maximal-intensity exercise);
- prodromal 'migraine' type symptoms may occur;
- associated with a past history of headaches.

The management of effort headaches is to avoid the circumstances that are associated with the headache, such as type of activity or hot weather. Pharmacological treatment can be used and moderate success has been achieved with the use of prophylactic non-steroidal anti-inflammatory drugs. Care has to be taken with these drugs as they can have detrimental side effects during exercise,

493

notably renal side effects. Other anti-migraine preparations have also been used. It is also important to investigate athletes with effort headache, as cases of more serious intra-cranial pathology have been documented as causing this condition.

Benign exertional headache (BEH)

Benign exertional headache has been described over fifty years ago, and is characterized by an onset that is related to straining when performing a Valsalva-type maneuver. The specific clinical features of BEH are:

- headache precipitated by exercise (usually straining such as weightlifting, competitive swimming);
- bilateral, throbbing, with some features of a migraine in some patients;
- lasts from few minutes to twenty-four hours;
- related to high-intensity exercise;
- is usually not associated with other intracranial pathology.

The proposed mechanism of the headache is not clear but may be related to arterial spasm and dilatation of the pain-sensitive venous sinuses at the base of the brain as a result of increased arterial blood pressure during exercise. The implication is that this type of headache is of a vascular nature. The treatment of the condition is to avoid the precipitating type of activity, reducing exercise intensity and medication. Medical treatment includes the prophylactic use of non-steroidal anti-inflammatory drugs, notably indomethacin. However, care has to be taken as these drugs have other negative side effects during exercise, notably on the renal system. Other drugs such as ergotamine, methysergide, and propanolol have also been used with variable success.

Post-traumatic headache

Post-traumatic headache represents a number of different syndromes. The IHS criteria for acute post-traumatic headache include the following features:

- headache onset less than fourteen days after trauma;
- headache that disappears within eight weeks after trauma;
- significant head trauma (as documented by loss of consciousness, post-traumatic amnesia of more than ten minutes, other abnormalities documented on physical examination or special investigations).

Other types of post-traumatic headache that have been described are as follows:

- post-traumatic migraine – mild head trauma can induce migraine;
- extracranial vascular headache – periodic headaches which develop at the site of head of scalp trauma;
- dysautonomic cephalgia – an unusual type of headache resulting from local injury to the sympathetic trunk and adjacent ganglia in the neck triggering autonomic symptoms;
- tension-type headache – syndrome similar to cervicogenic headache.

External compression headache

This type of headache has been described most commonly in swimmers, and results from excessive pressure on the face by tight facemasks. The etiology is believed to be continuous stimulation of cutaneous nerves by the application of pressure.

High-altitude headache

High-altitude headache is part of the symptom complex of acute mountain sickness. It occurs within twenty-four hours after rapid ascents above 3,000 m. The headaches are vascular in nature and are more common in unacclimatized individuals. Treatment is to descend to a lower altitude. Medical treatment has been the use of acetazolamide, ibuprofen or sumatriptan.

Hypercapnia headache

Divers can develop headaches as a result of a number of causes, including cold exposure, temporo-mandibular pain from biting on the mouthpiece too tightly, sinus-related headaches, and the previously mentioned external compression headache. Increased CO_2 accumulation can also result in a hypercapnia headache in this group.

See also: exercise at altitude – medical aspects

References

McCrory, P. (2000) 'Headaches and Exercise', *Sports Med* 30: 221–9.

Williams, S.J. and Nukuda, H. (1994) 'Sports and Exercise Headache: Part 1. Prevalence Among University Students', *Br J Sports Med* 28: 90–5.

MARTIN SCHWELLNUS

EXERCISE-RELATED MENSTRUAL ABNORMALITIES

Competitive sports participation in female athletes has increased since the mid-1970s. There is thus an increasing need to understand the specific medical conditions related to sports participation in female athletes. One of these areas is related to exercise-related menstrual abnormalities that can occur in female athletes.

The normal female menstrual cycle varies greatly in length from 22 to 36 days in women between the ages of 20 and 40 years. Typically, the cycle is divided into the menstrual phase (coinciding with menstrual bleeding), followed by the follicular phase (dominated by estrogens), and the last phase, which is dominated by progesterone and is known as the luteal phase. The regulation of these phases is complex and involves the hypothalamus, pituitary gland, and ovaries. Positive and negative feedback from hormones regulate this cycle. Pulsatile release of gonadotropin-releasing hormone (GnRH) from the hypothalamus controls the release of follicle stimulating hormone (FSH) and luetinising hormone (LH) from the anterior pituitary gland. FSH stimulates growth and development of the primary follicles in the ovary leading to ovulation, while LH is responsible for estrogen production and secretion from the corpus luteum, which in turn releases progesterone for the maintenance of the endometrium. This is a highly complex and intricate control system, and intense or prolonged exercise training has been associated with disturbances of the normal menstrual cycle.

What types of menstrual cycle abnormalities can occur in athletes?

The following menstrual abnormalities have been observed in female athletes:

- athletic amenorrhoea (defined as 0–3 periods per year)
- oligomenorrhoea (defined as 4–9 periods per year)
- anovulation and shortened luteal phases (duration of less than fourteen days)
- delayed menarche (no occurrence of menses before sixteen years of age)
- dysmenorrhoea (pelvic pain or cramps at any time during the menstrual cycle)

How frequent are exercise-related menstrual abnormalities in athletes?

There are no precise data on the prevalence of menstrual abnormalities in female athletes. This is due to the wide variation of menstrual abnormalities in the general population, and the wide variation of the physical demands of different sports. Also very few well conducted studies have been done to document the epidemiology of these conditions. However, it has been shown that the prevalence of menstrual abnormalities is higher in athletes (ranging from 1 to 66 per cent) than in non–athletes (ranging from 2 to 5 per cent). It is also evident that menstrual abnormalities are more common in sports in which there is a high physical demand (high-intensity and increased duration of training) as well as sports where body weight control and esthetics are important (ballet, gymnastics).

What are the factors associated with exercise-related menstrual abnormalities in athletes?

Amenorrhoea, oligomenorrhoea, anovulation, short luteal phase, and delayed menarche

Amenorrhoea, oligomenorrhoea, anovulation, short luteal phase, and delayed menarche are common. The precise causes for these abnormalities are not clear. It appears that these conditions represent a continuum rather than separate entities (Burrows and Bird 2000). There appears to be consensus that the main abnormality in these conditions is that exercise alters, in some as yet unknown way, the pulsatile release of GnRH, which then has a concomitant effect on LH release, and consequently affects estrogen and progesterone concentrations. The mechanisms possibly responsible for the altered pulsatile release of GnRH are numerous (De Cree 1998) and relate to increased physical stress during exercise, nutritional deprivation, physical illness, and mental stress.

Dysmenorrhoea

Although there is anecdotal evidence that dysmenorrhoea is less common in highly trained female athletes, this has not been confirmed in well conducted scientific studies. Possible mechanisms for the decrease in dysmenorrhoea have been linked to increased circulating opioids during exercise as well as decreased levels of progesterone after ovulation.

What are the consequences of exercise-related menstrual abnormalities in athletes?

Effects of menstrual abnormalities on exercise performance

Fluctuations in female athletic performance have been attributed to alterations in the menstrual cycle. However, recent reviews of the literature show that there is no significant effect of the phases of the menstrual cycle on physiological determinants of endurance performance (Burrows and Bird 2000).

Effects of menstrual abnormalities on fertility

Female fertility can be affected by many factors that affect normal reproductive function. Broadly, these factors fall into four categories: (i) nutritional deprivation; (ii) physical illness; (iii) psychological stress; and (iv) rapidly increasing or excessive exercise. Exercise-related menstrual abnormalities that can negatively affect fertility are amenorrhoea, anovulatory cycles, and shortening of the luteal. It is however important to emphasize that other factors such as emotional stress, nutrition, and physical illness must be excluded. These factors are often present in high-level athletes.

Once all other causes of infertility have been excluded, the following practical advice for the female athlete with possible infertility can be given.

- Decrease the exercise intensity by 10–20 per cent.
- Gain 1–2 kg body weight.
- Monitor their basal body temperature for three months.
- Seek psychological counsel to deal with any excessive emotional stress.

Further investigations and the use of medication may be required if ovulation has not returned to normal within 3–4 months.

Osteopaenia and osteoporosis

High training loads and restricted energy intake are often seen in female athletes in an attempt to retain low body mass. This together with the development of exercise-related menstrual abnormalities, in particular amenorrhoea, have led to the description of a syndrome known as the 'female athletic triad'. The female athletic triad is composed of the following three conditions: amenorrhoea, disordered eating, and osteoporosis. The female athletic triad has significant negative health consequences for the female athlete and requires investigation and treatment.

Guidelines for the clinical assessment of the athlete with exercise-related menstrual abnormalities

Once an athlete consults the physician with a menstrual abnormality that is possibly related to exercise, a careful history and examination must be performed before the condition is ascribed to exercise training. Other systemic conditions must be ruled out, and include pregnancy, thyroid disease, reproductive system abnormalities, diabetes mellitus, and other endocrinopathies. Careful evaluation of the athlete's exercise program, psychological status, dietary and eating habits are required. If the clinical evaluation is normal, and the only suspected cause is an increased training load, then advice to reduce training intensity and duration for 2–3 months can be given. If menses resume following a reduction in training, generally no further evaluation is required. A full endocrine and gynecological evaluation is required if menses do not resume on reducing exercise training load and intensity.

A young athlete who presents to the physician with delayed menarche requires a full normal gynecological and endocrine evaluation to determine the cause, before ascribing it to increased exercise training.

See also: female athletic triad; osteoporosis

References

Burrows, M. and Bird, S. (2000) 'The Physiology of the Highly Trained Female Endurance Runner', *Sports Med* 30: 281–300.
De Cree, C. (1998) 'Sex Steroid Metabolism and Menstrual Irregularities in the Exercising Female. A Review', *Sports Med* 25: 369–406.

MARTIN SCHWELLNUS

EXERCISE TESTING AND PRESCRIPTION

Although exercise testing may be done for various reasons, the main reason for testing is to provide information for the prescription of exercise training. Testing can be summarised under the headings of screening, and testing to set goals and monitor performance.

Screening

A sedentary person about to start an exercise programme is advised to undergo screening to identify any risks that might be associated this. A Physical Activity Readiness Questionnaire (PAR-Q) has been developed to identify those for whom exercise might be inappropriate. A coronary artery disease risk appraisal test should also be administered. This test gathers information on age, any family history of coronary artery disease, current smoking habits, blood pressure, blood lipid profile, diabetes, and physical activity habits; it indicates whether the client should have a more detailed examination by a physician, including a stress electrocardiogram (ECG) before starting an exercise programme. An ECG is a tracing of the changes in electrical potential during the heartbeat, and can be used to diagnose heart disease.

Testing to set goals

Various characteristics associated with health and fitness can be evaluated at the start of a training programme or training

497

cycle and used to set goals for the exercise. The same fitness characteristics can also be measured regularly during a training cycle to measure the efficacy of the training programme. Examples of characteristics associated with health and fitness, along with examples of tests, are shown below.

Body composition can be assessed using anthropometric techniques, bioelectrical impedance or dual X-ray densitometry. Imaging techniques can also be used to measure local or whole body fat and muscle composition. Decisions about which technique to use should be made on the requirements, such as required precision of the measurement, frequency of the measurement, and cost.

Flexibility is defined as the maximum range of motion of a joint and is measured in degrees, usually with a goniometer or a Leighton's flexometer. Flexibility of a joint is specific to that joint. The sit-and-reach test, which is a common flexibility test used in health-oriented fitness testing, measures lower back and hip flexor flexibility, useful for health and fitness purposes.

Muscle strength is defined as the maximum strength generated by a specific muscle group. The simplest measure of dynamic muscle strength is the single repetition maximum (1-RM), which is the heaviest weight that can be lifted once. The 1-RM bench press is a valid measure of upper body strength, and the squat and leg press are measures of lower body strength. Strength can also be measured during a static or isometric contraction, for example, with a handgrip dynamometer or cable tensiometer. However, these forms of muscle function tests are poor predictors of overall muscle strength. Devices that control the speed of contraction through accommodating resistance can also be used to measure isokinetic strength. These isokinetic devices are useful for quantifying muscle strength after an orthopaedic injury.

Muscle endurance describes the characteristic of the muscle to resist fatigue while contracting repeatedly against a resistance. A common field test for measuring abdominal muscle endurance is the number of sit-ups completed in 60 s. This test needs to be well controlled by the person administering it, with particular emphasis on reducing the use of the hip flexors. Another field test for measuring upper body muscle endurance is the number of push-ups completed in 60 s. The endurance of an isolated muscle can also be measured using free weights, machine weights, or an isokinetic dynamometer. This test is useful for monitoring the effects of training.

Muscle power can be measured during a vertical jump. The vertical jump can be measured during a squat or a counter-movement jump. During a squat jump, the participant starts the jump from a stationary position where the knees are bent to 90°. During a counter-movement jump, the participant starts from a standing position, bends the knees to 90° and in one movement jumps upwards. Depending on the available equipment, either the actual jump height, time to peak height, or the ground reaction forces can be measured to calculate muscle power. Muscle power can also be measured during a Wingate test on a cycle ergometer. This is a 30 s maximal effort test. This measurement of muscle power is more relevant for sport performance than for assessing health.

Cardiorespiratory endurance is defined as the ability to resist fatigue during medium-to-high-intensity exercise while using a relatively large muscle mass, and is dependent on the combined function of the heart, lungs, circulatory system, and skeletal muscles. The **maximal oxygen uptake** (VO_2max) is the traditional measurement of cardiorespiratory endurance. The VO_2max test involves exercising at an increasing workload while the volume of the expired air is measured and the composition of the expired air is analysed for oxygen and carbon dioxide. The difference between the volume of the inspired oxygen and oxygen in the expired air is the oxygen consumed by the body. The oxygen consumption coinciding with exhaustion is defined as the VO_2 max. Various protocols on the treadmill, walking and running, or cycle ergometer can be used to elicit the VO_2 max. Field tests, such as the 20 m shuttle test or 2 km run test, can also be used to estimate VO_2max indirectly. The VO_2 max of a sedentary person can increase by about 15 to 20 per cent after training. Heart rate during submaximal exercise can also be used as an indirect marker of training status. As fitness improves the submaximal heart rate decreases.

Agility and motor coordination represent the functioning of the neuromuscular system and is particularly relevant for sports performance. There are various sports specific tests that measure agility and motor coordination relevant to the sport. These tests usually involve completing a controlled task, which mimics the event, as quickly as possible.

After a profile of the fitness characteristics of a client has been established, an exercise programme can be prescribed, taking into account their specific strengths and weaknesses.

Prescription

The exercise, or fitness, test provides a trainer with the information necessary to draw up a training plan or schedule of exercises that is based on the client's short- and long-term goals expressed in the Physical Activity Readiness Questionnaire. In general, the training plan for healthy individuals:

- reflects different needs for fitness, health or sport performance as expressed by an individual, as well as specific needs, such as weight loss, **stress management**, or dealing with chronic diseases of lifestyle;
- takes into consideration the client's likes, dislikes, and preferences, such as a preference for a gym or outdoor training environment;
- breaks down exercises into aerobic – usually the largest part – for cardiovascular fitness and endurance, strength or **resistance training** to increase muscle strength, and flexibility – stretching – to prevent injury and increase circulation;
- must provide variety to enable the individual to enjoy exercising as a way of life and stay motivated;
- incorporates the components of frequency, intensity, type of exercise, and time or duration – FITT. This must allow for progression as the individual's fitness improves, particularly if shown in the fitness reassessment, but there must also be an opportunity for recovery between exercises and rest between exercise sessions;
- must be dynamic in allowing for modification of the exercises prescribed on the spot, such as changes in intensity or number of repetitions.

This has provided a general overview of exercise prescription. It has not dealt with exercises for special groups of people, such as the elderly, children, high-risk clients, pregnant women, and clients with bad backs.

References

American College of Sports Medicine (1995) *ACSM's Guidelines for Exercise Testing and Prescription*, Philadelphia PA: Williams and Wilkins.

Bar-Or, O. (1987) 'The Wingate Anaerobic Test. An Update on Methodology, Reliability and Validity', *Sports Medicine* 4: 381–94.

Thomas, S., Reading, J. and Shephard, R.J. (1992) 'Revision of the Physical Activity Readiness Questionnaire (PAR-Q)', *Canadian Journal of Sports Science* 17: 338–45.

MIKE LAMBERT
YVONNE BLOMKAMP

EXPERIENTIAL MARKETING

Marketing, in the usual sense, refers to the marketing of products or services. However, that is not enough in modern business; what is important is the effort to transform such marketing into 'experiences' with economic value. That is, the recognition of 'experiences' as a unique, economically meaningful offering leads to new avenues of wealth – this is essential for economic growth. An example in the context of sports might be a customer, visiting Nike Town to buy a pair of basketball shoes, who is greeted by a 4.5-meter high photograph of Michael Jordan. Other approaches might include basketball courts, set up inside the sales area, where customers can try out their choices. In professional sports, enhancing the product value of 'experiences' might give the club more control over ticket prices.

MUNEHIKO HARADA

EXTERNAL-INTERNAL FOCUS OF ATTENTION

The verbal and visual delivery of augmented information to the learner has been a primary concern for motor learning theorists for many years. A **constraints-led perspective** implies that the role of augmented information is to direct the learners' continually evolving search for solutions that satisfy the **constraints** imposed on them. A critical question concerns the augmented instructional constraints that best direct learners' search for coordination solutions. The effects of many different types of verbal instruction have been investigated in the motor learning literature. Research has shown that the provision of augmented knowledge of performance benefits the learning of complex multi-degree of freedom coordination patterns. One important issue is whether improvements in task outcome performance occur when participants view movement dynamics in an effort to imitate a model's movement topology or form, or if a model provides adequate information about the movement effects. It seems that learners are concerned with information about the image of the act – the focus on movement dynamics or topological form – and the image of achievement – the focus on the movement effects to be achieved. An interesting question is, when during learning should information be provided from either of these perspectives? Such proposals have been supported by research showing beneficial effects of instructions and **feedback** as a function of an external focus of attention – with an emphasis on movement effects on the environment – compared to an internal focus on the movement of specific body parts.

Despite these theoretical arguments, it is as yet unclear how the amount of instruction provided interacts with task constraints and focus of attention for effective motor learning. Questions remain over the provision of augmented knowledge of performance for the acquisition of complex movement tasks involving many motor system degrees of freedom, and an adequate theoretical framework has not been provided to enhance our understanding of this topic. A constraints-led approach provides a potentially useful theoretical rationale for informing practical applications of augmented knowledge of results. If the aim of providing feedback during motor learning is to direct learners' search activities, then it is clear that 'less means more'. Theoretically, there is justification for providing infrequent augmented knowledge of results with an external focus of attention to allow the learner to exploit **self-organization** processes in the motor system during practice. Some evidence exists to show how reduced feedback leads to just as effective motor learning as high-frequency feedback. For example, studies on the acquisition of soccer skills have examined the effects of frequency of feedback as a function of directed search on learning to perform a lofted pass. Feedback statements were manipulated to direct the search of learners to either their movement dynamics or movement effects. The movement dynamic feedback comprised statements such as, 'Position your foot below the ball's midline to lift the ball' and 'Position your body weight and the non-kicking foot behind the ball', and pattern-effect feedback comprised statements such as 'Strike the ball below its midline to lift it; that is, kick underneath it', and 'To strike the ball, create a pendulum-like motion with as long a duration as possible'. The results (see Figure 23) showed clear evidence of an immediate effect on performance outcome and learning experienced by both of the external-focus – or movement-effect – feedback groups. Further, the interaction between feedback frequency and directed search resulted in more effective performance during both practice and retention in the group receiving reduced (one third of trials) external-focus, or movement-effect, feedback relative to the constant (all trials) external-focus feedback group.

Therefore, receiving external focus feedback once in every three trials is as functional for learning as receiving external focus feedback on every trial. These findings also highlight the detrimental effects that directing search to movement dynamics and body parts has on later learning and performance in complex skills, although early in learning an internal focus may help stabilise a functional coordination pattern. Instructions that direct a learner's search to

movement dynamics may deprive them of the opportunity to discover and satisfy the multiple task constraints unique to each individual. Instructions relating to the task goal early in practice should try to direct the search towards relevant feedback sources that take into account their movement effects on the environment. It appears that movement effects are an ideal interface between the performer and environment, and that directed search should aim to exploit the information sources it affords in support of action. In this way, performance consequences are realised and used in the development of an image of achievement to support further action. A less prescriptive and more self-regulated feedback mechanism, which complements discovery learning and encourages the player to explore the task environment, seems to be a more appropriate instructional technique. With practice, the development of the image of achievement acts as a guiding mechanism and is a key constraint in shaping movement dynamics to the task requirements. Feedback and instruction should be used to complement this process by directing the learner's search to relevant aspects of the image of achievement – the movement effect – to support movement behaviour. This will also enable the learner's self-organising processes to occur under constraint during goal-directed behaviour.

In summary, research findings suggest that the role of augmented information during practice should be to direct the learner's search towards movement dynamics, useful for developing an image of the act, early in learning to help learners to stabilise a functional coordination pattern. However, later learning instructions and feedback should emphasise movement effects to provide an external focus on the image of achievement. An emphasis on task outcomes in feedback and instructions provides better opportunities for learners' search of the task during practice, and constrains the emergence of movement behaviour. It has

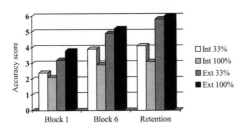

Figure 23. Effect of external (ext) and internal (int) feedback on performance.

been argued that an external focus of attention does not interfere with self-organisation processes of the movement dynamics as performers explore the task. Other research supports this argument of the constraints-led approach, showing that an external focus allows discovery learners to focus on an image of achievement alone, facilitating performance and learning in a slalom skiing task and when learning a tennis forehand drive. The effects of instructions towards an external focus of attention were not due to distracting performers from an explicit focus on their movement dynamics, but were influential in allowing self-organisation processes to regulate task performance and learning implicitly.

See also: knowledge of results – bandwidth; knowledge of results – summary; skill-acquisition stages – control; skill-acquisition stages – coordination; skill-acquisition stages – skill

KEITH DAVIDS